THE LEGAL ENVIRONMENT OF BUSINESS

Text and Cases

ETHICAL, REGULATORY, GLOBAL, AND E-COMMERCE ISSUES

SEVENTH EDITION

Frank B. Cross
Herbert D. Kelleher
Centennial Professor in Business Law
University of Texas at Austin

Roger LeRoy Miller
Institute for University Studies
Arlington, Texas

Australia • Brazil • Japan • Korea • Mexico • Singapore • Spain • United Kingdom • United States

THE LEGAL ENVIRONMENT OF BUSINESS, 7th Edition
TEXT & CASES
Ethical, Regulatory, Global, and E-Commerce Issues

Frank B. Cross

Roger LeRoy Miller

Vice President and Editorial Director: Jack Calhoun

Editor-in-Chief: Rob Dewey

Acquisitions Editor: Vicky True

Senior Developmental Editor: Jan Lamar

Executive Marketing Manager: Lisa L. Lysne

Marketing Manager: Jennifer Garamy

Marketing Coordinator: Gretchen Wildauer

Associate Marketing Communications Manager: Jill Schleibaum

Production Manager: Bill Stryker

Technology Project Manager: Kristen Meere

Manufacturing Buyer: Kevin Kluck

Compositor: Parkwood Composition New Richmond, WI

Senior Art Director: Michelle Kunkler

Internal Designer: Bill Stryker

Cover Designer: Jen2Design, Cincinnati, OH

Website Coordinator: Brian Courter

Library of Congress Control Number: 2008925366

Student's Edition:
ISBN-13: 978-0-324-59000-5
ISBN-10: 0-324-59000-8

Instructor's Edition:
ISBN-13: 978-0-324-66483-6
ISBN-10: 0-324-66483-4

South-Western Cengage Learning
5191 Natorp Blvd.
Mason, OH 45040
USA

Cengage Learning products are represented in Canada by Nelson Education, Ltd.

For your course and learning solutions, visit **academic.cengage.com**
Purchase any of our products at your local college store or at our preferred online store **www.ichapters.com**

Contents in Brief

APPENDICES

Contents

The Foundations 1

Unit 2 The Public and International Environment 105

The Commercial Environment 193

Chapter 22
Immigration and Labor Law 549

Unit 6 The Regulatory Environment 579

Chapter 23
Consumer Protection 580

Chapter 24
Environmental Law 598

Chapter 25
Land-Use Control and Real Property 617

Chapter 26
Antitrust and Monopoly 641

Chapter 27
Antitrust and Restraint of Trade 661

Chapter 28
Investor Protection and Corporate Governance 679

Appendices

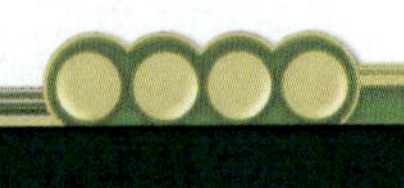

CONCEPT SUMMARIES

EXHIBITS

INSIGHT INTO THE GLOBAL ENVIRONMENT

INSIGHT INTO E-COMMERCE

INSIGHT INTO ETHICS

EMERGING TRENDS IN THE LEGAL ENVIRONMENT OF BUSINESS

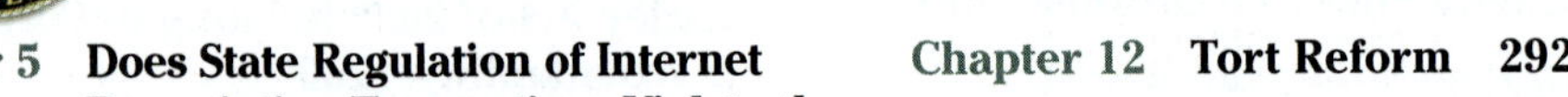

CONTEMPORARY LEGAL DEBATES

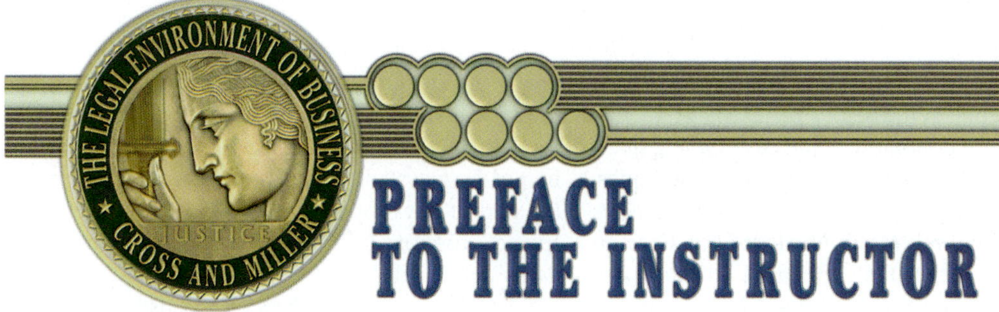

PREFACE TO THE INSTRUCTOR

The study of the legal environment of business has universal applicability. A student entering virtually any field of business must have at least a passing understanding of the legal environment in order to function in the real world. Additionally, students preparing for a career in accounting, government and political science, economics, and even medicine can use much of the information they learn in a business law and legal environment course. In fact, every individual throughout his or her lifetime can benefit from a knowledge of contracts, employment relationships, land-use control and real property, and other topics. Consequently, we have fashioned this text as a useful "tool for living" for all of your students.

For the Seventh Edition, we have spent a great deal of effort making this book more contemporary, exciting, and visually appealing than ever before to encourage your students to learn the law. We have also designed many new features and special pedagogical devices that focus on the legal, ethical, global, and e-commerce environments, while addressing core curriculum requirements.

What Is New in the Seventh Edition

Instructors have come to rely on the coverage, accuracy, and applicability of *The Legal Environment of Business.* To make sure that our text engages your students' interests, solidifies their understanding of the legal concepts presented, and provides the best teaching tools available, we now offer the following items either in the text or in conjunction with the text.

New *Insight* Features

For the Seventh Edition, we have created **three special new *Insight* features—*Insight into E-Commerce, Insight into Ethics,* and *Insight into the Global Environment.*** These features, which appear in selected chapters, provide valuable insights into how the courts and the law are dealing with specific contemporary issues. Each of these features ends with a critical-thinking question that explores some cultural, environmental, political, social, or technological aspect of the issue.

1. ***Insight into E-Commerce*—**When the topic involves some new technology or how the Internet is affecting a particular area of law, we include an *Insight into E-Commerce* feature. For example, Chapter 1 contains an *Insight into E-Commerce* feature on *How the Internet Is Expanding Precedent,* Chapter 14 has a feature on *Search Engines versus Copyrights,* and Chapter 28 includes a feature entitled *Moving Company Information to the Internet.*
2. ***Insight into Ethics*—**When the topic has ethical implications, we include an *Insight into Ethics* feature. For example, Chapter 3's *Insight into Ethics* feature is entitled *Implications of an Increasingly Private Justice System.*
3. ***Insight into the Global Environment*—**Because business transactions today are increasingly global, we have also included a feature that discusses global implications or explains how foreign nations deal with a particular topic. For example, there is an *Insight into the Global Environment* feature in Chapter 4 titled *Breach of Trust Issues Hit Major German Corporations,* and one in Chapter 11 on *International Use and Regulation of the Internet.*

Two Critical-Thinking Questions at the End of *Every* Case Presented in This Text

In every chapter of the Sixth Edition of *West's Legal Environment of Business,* we included one longer case excerpt followed by two case-ending questions designed to guide students' analysis of the case and help build their legal reasoning skills. For the Seventh Edition, we continue to offer one longer excerpt—now labeled as an ***Extended Case*—**with two critical-thinking questions in every chapter. These extended cases may be used for case-briefing assignments and are also tied to the *Special Case Analysis* questions found in every unit of the text.

Because of the popularity of the case-ending questions, for this edition, we've also included two questions for all cases. In addition to the *What If the Facts Were Different?* questions and *Impact of This Case on Today's Law* sections that appeared in the Sixth Edition, we've devised an entirely new set of questions. These new *Dimension* questions focus on meeting aspects of your curriculum requirements, including:

- *The Ethical Dimension*
- *The E-Commerce Dimension*
- *The Global Dimension*
- *The Legal Environment Dimension*

Suggested answers to all questions following cases can be found in both the *Instructor's Manual* and the *Answers Manual* that accompany this text. (The full title of this manual is *Answers to Questions and Case Problems and Alternate Problem Sets with Answers.*)

Greater Emphasis on Critical Thinking

Today's business leaders are often required to think "outside the box" when making business decisions. For this reason, **we have added a number of critical-thinking elements for the Seventh Edition** that are designed to challenge students' understanding of the materials beyond simple retention. Your students' critical-thinking and legal reasoning skills will be increased as they work through the numerous pedagogical devices within the book. Almost every feature and every case presented in the text conclude with some type of critical-thinking question. These questions include *For Critical Analysis, What If the Facts Were Different?* and the *Ethical, E-Commerce, Global,* and *Legal Environment Dimension* questions discussed previously. They also include the new *Special Case Analysis* questions and the questions in the *Reviewing* features, which are described next.

New *Special Case Analysis* Questions

Through the years, instructors have frequently requested that we teach their legal environment students how to analyze case law. We discuss the fundamental topic of how to read and understand case law in Chapter 1 and cover How to Brief Cases and Analyze Case Problems in Appendix A. For this edition, we have gone one step further: in selected chapters of the text, we provide a *Special Case Analysis* question that is based on the *Extended Case* excerpt in that chapter. The *Special Case Analysis* questions are part of the *Questions and Case Problems* that appear at the end of the chapter. We offer at least one of these special questions for every unit in the text to build students' analytical skills.

The *Special Case Analysis* questions test students' ability to perform IRAC (Issue, Rule, Application, and Conclusion) case analysis. Students must identify the legal issue presented in the chapter's *Extended Case,* determine the *rule* of law, *apply* the rule to the facts of the case, and describe the court's *conclusion.* Instructors can assign these questions as homework or can use them in class to elicit student participation and teach case analysis. (A variation of these questions is also available in the IRAC Case Analysis section of CengageNOW for *The Legal Environment of Business:* Interactive Assignment System, which will be discussed shortly.)

Reviewing Features in Every Chapter

For the Seventh Edition of *The Legal Environment of Business,* we have included a new and improved feature at the end of every chapter that helps solidify students' understanding of the chapter materials. The feature appears just before the *Terms and Concepts* and is entitled *Reviewing [chapter topic].* Each of these features presents a hypothetical scenario and then asks a series of questions that require students to identify the issues and apply the legal concepts discussed in the chapter. These features are designed to help students review the chapter topics in a simple and interesting way and see how the legal principles discussed in the chapter affect the world in which they live. An instructor can use these features as the basis for in-class discussion or encourage students to use them for self-study prior to completing homework assignments. **Suggested answers to the questions posed in the *Reviewing* features can be found in both the *Instructor's Manual* and the *Answers Manual* that accompany this text.**

The *Reviewing* features are also tied to a new set of questions for each chapter in the Web-based CengageNOW system, to be discussed next. Students can read through the scenario in the text and then answer the four Applications and Analysis questions online. **By using the CengageNOW system, students will receive instant feedback on their answers to these questions, and instructors will obtain automatically graded assignments that**

enable them to assess students' understanding of the materials.

Improved Content and Features on CengageNOW for *The Legal Environment of Business:* Interactive Assignment System

For those instructors who want their students to learn how to identify and apply the legal principles they study in this text, we have created new content and improved the features of our Web-based product for this edition. The system provides interactive, automatically graded assignments for every chapter and unit in this text. For each of the twenty-eight chapters, we have devised different categories of multiple-choice questions that stress different aspects of learning the chapter materials. By using the optional **CengageNOW** system, students can complete the assignments from any location via the Internet and can receive instant feedback on why their answers to questions were incorrect or correct (if the instructor wishes to allow feedback). Instructors can customize the system to meet their own specifications and can track students' progress.

1. **Chapter Review Questions**—The first set of ten to fifteen questions reviews the basic concepts and principles discussed in the chapter. These questions often include questions based on the cases presented in the text.
2. **Brief Hypotheticals**—The next group of seven to ten questions emphasizes spotting the issue and identifying the rule of law that applies in the context of a short factual scenario.
3. **Legal Reasoning**—The third category includes five questions that require students to analyze the factual situation provided and apply the rules of law discussed in the chapter to arrive at an answer.
4. **IRAC Case Analysis**—The next set of four questions for each chapter requires students to perform all the basic elements of legal reasoning (identify the *issue*, determine the *rule* of law, *apply* the rule to the facts presented, and arrive at a *conclusion*). These questions are based on the *Extended Case* excerpts that appear in each chapter and include the *Special Case Analysis* questions that appear in each unit of the text.
5. **Application and Analysis**—The final set of four questions for each chapter is new and is linked to the *Reviewing* features (discussed previously) that appear in every chapter of the text. The student is required to read through the hypothetical scenario, analyze the facts presented, identify the issues in dispute, and apply the rules discussed in the chapter to answer the questions.
6. **Essay Questions**—In addition to the multiple-choice questions available on CengageNOW, we now also provide essay questions that allow students to compose and submit essays online. Students' essays are automatically recorded to the gradebook, which permits instructors to quickly and easily evaluate the essays and record grades.
7. **Video Questions**—CengageNOW also now includes links to the Digital Video Library for *The Legal Environment of Business* so that students can access and view the video clips and answer questions related to the topics in the chapter.
8. **Cumulative Questions for Each Unit**—In addition to the questions relating to each chapter, the CengageNOW system provides a set of cumulative questions, entitled "Synthesizing Legal Concepts," for each of the six units in the text.
9. **Additional Advantages of CengageNOW**—Instructors can utilize the system to upload their course syllabi, create and customize homework assignments, keep track of their students' progress, communicate with their students about assignments and due dates, and create reports summarizing the data for an individual student or for the whole class.

Expanded Ethics Coverage and New Questions of Ethics in Every Chapter

For the Seventh Edition of *The Legal Environment of Business,* we have significantly revised and updated the chapter on ethics and business decision making (Chapter 4). The chapter now presents a more practical, realistic, case-study approach to business ethics and the dilemmas facing businesspersons today. The emphasis on ethics is reiterated in materials throughout the text, particularly the *Focus on Ethics* features that conclude every unit, the *Insight into Ethics* features, and the pedagogy that accompanies selected cases and features. We also discuss **corporate governance issues** as appropriate within the ethics chapter, the corporations chapter, and the *Focus on Ethics* feature that concludes Unit One.

For this edition, we have also added ***A Question of Ethics* to every chapter of the text, many of which are based on a case from 2007.** These problems provide modern-day examples of the kinds of ethical issues faced by businesspersons and the ways courts typically resolve them.

More on the Sarbanes-Oxley Act of 2002

In a number of places in this text, we discuss the Sarbanes-Oxley Act of 2002 and the corporate scandals that led to the passage of that legislation. For example, Chapter 4 contains a section examining the requirements of the Sarbanes-Oxley Act relating to confidential reporting systems. In Chapter 28, we discuss this act in the context of securities law and present an exhibit (Exhibit 28–5) containing some of the key provisions of the act relating to corporate accountability with respect to securities transactions.

Because the act is a topic of significant concern in today's business climate, we also include excerpts and explanatory comments on the Sarbanes-Oxley Act of 2002 as Appendix H. Students and instructors alike will find it useful to have the provisions of the act immediately available for reference.

The Legal Environment of Business on the Web

For the Seventh Edition of *The Legal Environment of Business,* we have redesigned and streamlined the text's Web site so that users can easily locate the resources they seek. When you visit our Web site at **academic.cengage.com/blaw/cross**, you will find a broad array of teaching/learning resources, including the following:

- ***Relevant Web sites*** for all of the *Emerging Trends* features that are presented in this text.
- ***Sample answers*** to the *Case Problem with Sample Answer,* which appears in the *Questions and Case Problems* at the end of every chapter. This problem/answer set is designed to help your students learn how to answer case problems by acquainting them with model answers to selected problems. In addition, we offer the answers to the hypothetical *Questions with Sample Answers* on the Web site, as well as in the text (Appendix I).
- ***Videos*** referenced in the *Video Questions* (discussed shortly) that appear in selected chapters of this edition of *The Legal Environment of Business.*
- ***Internet exercises*** for every chapter in the text (at least two per chapter). These exercises have been refocused to provide more practical information to business law students on topics covered in the chapters and to acquaint students with the legal resources that are available online.
- ***Interactive quizzes*** for every chapter in this text.
- ***Glossary terms*** for every chapter in the text.
- ***Flashcards*** that provide students with an optional study tool to review the key terms in every chapter.
- ***PowerPoint slides*** that have been revised for this edition.
- ***Legal reference materials*** including a "Statutes" page that offers links to the full text of selected statutes referenced in the text, a Spanish glossary, and links to other important legal resources that are available for free on the Web.
- ***Law on the Web features*** that provide links to the URLs that appear at the end of every chapter in the text.
- ***Link to CengageNOW for* The Legal Environment of Business: *Interactive Assignment System*** with different types of questions related to every chapter in the text and one set of cumulative questions for each unit in the text.
- ***Link to our Digital Video Library*** that offers a compendium of more than sixty-five video scenarios and explanations.
- ***Online Legal Research Guide*** that offers complete yet brief guidance to using the Internet and evaluating information obtained from the Internet. As an online resource, it now includes hyperlinks to the Web sites discussed for click-through convenience.
- ***Court case updates*** that present summaries of new cases from various West legal publications, are continually updated, and are specifically keyed to chapters in this text.

A Comprehensive Digital Video Library

For this edition of *The Legal Environment of Business,* we continue to include special *Video Questions* at the end of selected chapters. Each of these questions directs students to the text's Web site (at **academic.cengage.com/blaw/cross**) to view a video relevant to a topic covered in the chapter. This is followed by a series of questions based on the video. The questions are again repeated on the Web site, when the student accesses the video. An access code for the videos can be packaged with each new copy of this textbook for no additional charge. If Digital Video Library access did not come packaged with the textbook, students who would like to purchase it can do so online at **academic.cengage.com/blaw/dvl**.

These videos can be used for homework assignments, discussion starters, or classroom demonstrations and are useful for generating student interest. Some of the videos are clips from actual movies, such as *The Jerk* and *Bowfinger.* By watching a video and answering the questions, students will gain an understanding of how the legal concepts they have studied in the chapter apply to the real-life situation portrayed in the video. **Suggested answers for all of the *Video Questions* are given in both the *Instructor's Manual* and the *Answers Manual* that accompany this text.** The videos are part of our Digital Video Library, a compendium of more than sixty-five video scenarios and explanations.

Additional Special Features of This Text

We have included in *The Legal Environment of Business,* Seventh Edition, a number of pedagogical devices and special features, including those discussed here.

Emerging Trends

Presented throughout this text are a number of features titled *Emerging Trends.* These features examine new developments in business law and the legal environment and their potential effect on businesspersons. Here are some examples of these features:

- *E-Discovery and Cost-Shifting* (Chapter 2).
- *Stand-Your-Ground Laws* (Chapter 7).
- *New Issues in Online Privacy and Employment Discrimination* (Chapter 21).

Contemporary Legal Debates

Contemporary Legal Debates features are also interspersed throughout this edition of *The Legal Environment of Business.* These features introduce the student to a controversial issue that is now being debated within the legal community. A *Where Do You Stand?* section concluding each feature asks the student to identify her or his position on the issue. Some examples of these features are:

- *Are Online Fantasy Sports Gambling?* (Chapter 9).
- *Tort Reform* (Chapter 12).
- *Should the EPA Take the Threat of Global Warming into Account?* (Chapter 24).

Concept Summaries

Whenever key areas of the law need additional emphasis, we provide a *Concept Summary.* These summaries have always been a popular pedagogical tool in this text. There are now many of these summaries, a number of which have been modified to achieve greater clarity.

Exhibits

When appropriate, we also illustrate important aspects of the law in graphic form in exhibits. In all, more than fifty exhibits are featured in *The Legal Environment of Business,* Seventh Edition. For this edition, we have added six new exhibits, and we have modified existing exhibits to achieve better clarity. Some examples of the new exhibits are:

- Exhibit 3–1 Basic Differences in the Traditional Forms of ADR
- Exhibit 14–1 Existing Generic Top Level Domain Names
- Exhibit 18–1 Directors' Management Responsibilities
- Exhibit 28–1 Basic Functions of the SEC

An Effective Case Format

For this edition, we have carefully selected recent cases that not only provide on-point illustrations of the legal principles discussed in the chapter but also are of high interest to students. In all, more than 70 percent of the cases in the Seventh Edition are from 2007 or 2008.

As mentioned, for this edition we have included one *Extended Case* per chapter that is presented entirely in the court's language and does not include any paraphrased section on the case's background and facts or the decision and remedy. The remaining cases in each chapter appear in our usual format, which now includes two case-ending questions for every case in this edition of the text. We also provide bracketed definitions for any terms in the opinion that might be difficult for students to understand. Cases may include one or more of the following sections, a few of which have already been described:

- ***Company Profiles***—Certain cases include a profile describing the history of the company involved to give students an awareness of the context of the case before the court. Some profiles include the URL for the company's Web site.
- ***What If the Facts Were Different?***—One case in each chapter concludes with this special section. The student is asked to decide whether a specified change in the facts of the case would alter its outcome. **Suggested answers to these questions are included in both the *Instructor's Manual* and the *Answers Manual* that accompany this text.**
- ***The Ethical [E-Commerce, Global, or Legal Environment] Dimension***—As discussed previously, these special new questions ask students to explore different aspects of the issues of the case and help instructors meet core curriculum requirements for business law. **Suggested answers to these questions are included in both the *Instructor's Manual* and the *Answers Manual* that accompany this text.**
- ***International Considerations***—These sections let your students know how the particular issue before the court is treated in other countries.
- ***Impact of This Case on Today's Law***—Because many students are unclear about how some of the older cases presented in this text affect today's court rulings, we include a special section at the end of landmark and classic cases that clarifies the relevance of the particular case to modern law.

Two Test Banks Available

To provide instructors with even greater flexibility in teaching, we offer two separate test banks, each with a complete set of questions for every chapter of *The Legal Environment of Business,* Seventh Edition. These two test banks have been significantly revised and many new questions added. Those instructors who would like to alternate the tests they give their students each semester can now do so without having to create additional testing materials. In addition, instructors who would like to pick and choose from the questions offered have twice as many options for questions in each category (true/false, multiple choice, essay).

Questions and Case Problems with Sample Answers

In response to those instructors who would like students to have sample answers available for some of the questions and case problems, we have included two questions with sample answers in each chapter. The *Question with Sample Answer* is a hypothetical question for which students can access a sample answer in Appendix I at the end of the text. Every chapter also has one *Case Problem with Sample Answer* that is based on an actual case and answered on the text's Web site (located at **academic.cengage.com/blaw/cross**). Students can compare the answers provided to their own answers to determine whether they have done a good job of responding to the question and to learn what should be included when answering the end-of-chapter questions and case problems.

The Most Complete Supplements Package Available Today

This edition of *The Legal Environment of Business* is accompanied by a vast number of teaching and learning supplements. We have already mentioned the CengageNOW for *The Legal Environment of Business:* Interactive Assignment System and the supplemental resources available on the text's Web site at **academic.cengage.com/blaw/cross**. In addition, there are numerous other supplements, including those listed below, that make up the complete teaching/learning package for the Seventh Edition. For further information on the *The Legal Environment of Business* teaching/learning package, contact your local sales representative or visit the *The Legal Environment of Business* Web site.

Printed Supplements

- ***Instructor's Manual***—Includes case synopses, additional cases addressing the issue for selected cases, background information, teaching suggestions, and lecture enhancements, as well as suggested answers to all the case-ending and feature-ending questions, the questions in the *Reviewing* features at the end of each chapter, and additional materials on the *Focus on Ethics* sections at the end of each unit. (Also available on the *Instructor's Resource CD,* or IRCD.)
- ***Study Guide***—Includes essay questions and sample CPA exam questions.
- ***Two comprehensive Test Banks***—*Test Bank 1* and *Test Bank 2* each contain multiple-choice questions with answers, true/false questions with

answers, and two short essay questions per chapter. Additionally, there is one question for every *Emerging Trends* and *Contemporary Legal Debates* feature, and two multiple-choice questions for each *Focus on Ethics* section. (Also available on the IRCD.)

- ***Answers to Questions and Case Problems and Alternate Problem Sets with Answers***—Provides answers to all the questions and case problems presented in the text, including the new *Special Case Analysis* questions, *A Question of Ethics,* and *Video Questions,* as well as suggested answers to all of the case-ending questions, feature-ending questions, and the questions in the *Reviewing* features at the end of each chapter. (Also available on the IRCD.)

Software, Video, and Multimedia Supplements

- ***Instructor's Resource CD-ROM (IRCD)***—The IRCD includes the following supplements: *Instructor's Manual, Answers Manual, Test Bank 1* and *Test Bank 2,* Case-Problem Cases, Case Printouts, Lecture Outline System, PowerPoint slides, ExamView, *Instructor's Manual* for the *Drama of the Law* video series, *Handbook of Landmark Cases and Statutes in Business Law and the Legal Environment, Handbook on Critical Thinking and Writing in Business Law and the Legal Environment,* and *A Guide to Personal Law.*
- **ExamView Testing Software** (also available on the IRCD).
- **Lecture Outline System** (also available on the IRCD).
- **PowerPoint slides** (also available on the IRCD).
- **WebTutor**—Features chat, discussion groups, testing, student progress tracking, and business law course materials.
- **Case-Problem Cases** (available only on the IRCD).
- **Transparencies** (available only on the IRCD).
- **Westlaw®**—Ten free hours for qualified adopters.
- **Digital Video Library**—Provides access to more than sixty-five videos, including the *Drama of the Law* videos and video clips from actual Hollywood movies. Access to our Digital Video Library is available in an optional package with each new text at no additional cost. If the Digital Video Library access did not come packaged with the textbook, your students can purchase it online at **academic.cengage.com/blaw/dvl**.
- **Videos**—Qualified adopters using this text have access to the entire library of videos in VHS format, a vast selection covering most business law issues. For more information about these videotapes, visit **academic.cengage.com/blaw/vl**.

For Users of the Sixth Edition

First of all, we want to thank you for helping make *The Legal Environment of Business* the best-selling legal environment text in America today. Second, we want to make you aware of the numerous additions and changes that we have made in this edition—many in response to comments from reviewers. For example, we have added more examples and incorporated the latest United States Supreme Court decisions throughout the text as appropriate.

Every chapter of the Seventh Edition has been revised as necessary to incorporate new developments in the law or to streamline the presentations. A number of new trends in business law are also addressed in the cases and special features of the Seventh Edition. Other major changes and additions made for this edition include the following:

- Chapter 2 (The Court System)—To provide greater clarity on important foundational issues, many parts of this chapter were reworked, including the discussions of personal jurisdiction, Internet jurisdiction, standing to sue, and appellate review. The section on electronic evidence and discovery issues has been updated to include the federal rules that took effect in 2006.
- Chapter 3 (Alternative and Online Dispute Resolution)—A chart was added to illustrate the differences among various methods of alternative dispute resolution, and we present a 2006 United States Supreme Court decision on arbitration clauses. In addition, the discussion of electronic filing systems and online dispute resolution was updated. An *Insight into Ethics* feature was added to discuss how the use of private judges is affecting the justice system.
- Chapter 4 (Ethics and Business Decision Making)—This chapter has been significantly revised and now includes a new section that provides step-by-step guidance on making ethical business decisions. Several new cases were added, and an *Insight into*

the Global Environment feature addresses ethical issues faced by German corporations.

- Chapter 5 (Constitutional Law)—The chapter has been thoroughly revised and updated to incorporate recent United States Supreme Court decisions, such as the case restricting students' free speech rights at school events. New examples have been added throughout, and the materials reworked to focus on business context. The chapter includes discussions of the USA Patriot Act's effect on constitutional rights and recent decisions on preemption, unprotected speech, freedom of religion, and privacy rights. A *Contemporary Legal Debates* feature addresses whether *State Regulation of Internet Prescription Transactions Violates the Dormant Commerce Clause.*
- Chapter 6 (Administrative Law)—This chapter has been reworked to focus on the practical significance of administrative law for businesspersons. A new section was added on the Administrative Procedures Act, and another section addresses how the courts give *Chevron* deference to agency rules. Informal agency actions are covered, and a new subsection discusses the exhaustion doctrine.
- Chapter 7 (Criminal Law and Cyber Crime)—New materials on identity theft and criminal spamming laws were added, and the existing materials were streamlined to focus more on corporate criminal liability. An updated discussion of sentencing guidelines is included, and the discussion of defenses to criminal charges was revised. An *Emerging Trends* feature covers *Stand-Your-Ground Laws* (state laws allowing the use of deadly force in homes and vehicles to thwart violent crimes such as robbery, carjacking, and sexual assault).
- Chapter 9 (Contract Formation)—We have added more examples to clarify and enhance our contract law coverage. We have also included more up-to-date information and a new *Contemporary Legal Debates* feature entitled *Are Online Fantasy Sports Gambling?* We have chosen cases, problems, and examples for this chapter (and Chapter 10) that garner student interest and have revised the text to improve clarity and reduce legalese.
- Chapter 12 (Torts and Cyber Torts)—A discussion of the compensatory and punitive damages available in tort actions was added, and a *Contemporary Legal Debates* feature addresses *Tort Reform.* Three recent high-interest cases are included, one on the scope of an Internet service provider's immunity for online defamation, another on negligent misrepresentation, and the other on invasion of privacy. New subsections discuss trends in appropriation (right of publicity) claims and abusive or frivolous litigation.
- Chapter 14 (Intellectual Property and Internet Law)—The materials on intellectual property rights have been thoroughly revised and updated to reflect the most current laws and trends. Recent United States Supreme Court cases are incorporated. A subsection on counterfeit goods and a law addressing counterfeit goods has been added to the trademark section. The materials on domain names, cybersquatting, and licensing have been revamped. The section on patents was expanded and new examples were added. The discussion of file-sharing was updated, and a case is presented in which Sony Corporation brought a successful suit for copyright infringement against an individual who had downloaded eight songs. The chapter also includes updated information on international treaties protecting intellectual property and an *Insight into E-Commerce* feature on *Search Engines versus Copyright Owners.*
- Chapter 15 (Creditor-Debtor Relations and Bankruptcy)—This chapter has been revised to be more up to date and comprehensible. The bankruptcy law materials are based on law after the 2005 Reform Act and include updated dollar amounts of various provisions of the Bankruptcy Code.
- Chapters 16 through 18 (the Business Environment unit)—This unit has been substantially revised and updated to improve the flow and clarity, and provide more practical information and recent examples. In Chapter 16 (Sole Proprietorships, Franchises and Partnerships), we added a section on the Franchise Rule that includes the 2007 amendments to the rule. In our coverage of partnerships, we added several examples, reworked the section on fiduciary duties, and clarified the materials on dissociation. The most significant changes in the unit were made to the Corporations chapter (Chapter 18), which has been updated throughout. We added coverage of the landmark case *Guth v. Loft* (on the duty of loyalty), a new exhibit, and updated materials on Sarbanes-Oxley. We also added discussions of various committees of the board of directors, corporate sentencing guidelines, and proxies, including new e-proxy rules. The topic of shareholder voting concerning executive pay is discussed, and a *Contemporary Legal*

Debates feature explores the possibility of *A Shareholder Access Rule.*

- Chapter 20 (Employment Relationships) and Chapter 21 (Employment Discrimination)—These two chapters covering employment law have been thoroughly updated to include discussions of legal issues facing employers today. Chapter 20 includes updated minimum wage figures and Social Security and Medicare percentages. It also discusses overtime rules and provides the most current information on employment monitoring. Chapter 21 now includes the latest developments and United States Supreme Court decisions, such as a decision that set the standard of proof for retaliation claims. The text discussion of burden of proof in unintentional discrimination cases has been revised and clarified. A feature examines *New Issues in Online Privacy and Employment Discrimination.*
- Chapter 24 (Environmental Law)—The materials on air pollution and the subsection on wetlands have been updated. Several of the cases in the chapter are from the United States Supreme Court, and a *Contemporary Legal Debates* feature discusses the impact of the 2007 Supreme Court decision in *Massachusetts v. Environmental Protection Agency* relating to global warming.
- Chapter 25 (Land-Use Control and Real Property)—We have substantially revised this chapter, which now includes more information on real estate sales contracts, including listing agreements, escrow agreements, marketable title, title searches, and title insurance.
- Chapters 26 and 27 (Antitrust Law)—We added new examples and coverage of leading cases throughout these chapters, particularly in the discussions of price fixing, relevant product market, and relevant geographic market.
- Chapter 28 (Investor Protection and Corporate Governance)—Our coverage of securities law was revamped to make this difficult topic more understandable to students. The chapter now includes a new exhibit and overview of the functions of the Securities and Exchange Commission and a practical explanation of the *Howey* test. We also provide a simplified list of the contents of a registration statement and an updated discussion of the registration process that clarifies current rules on a free writing prospectus.

Acknowledgments for Previous Editions

Since we began this project many years ago, a sizable number of business law and the legal environment professors and others have helped us in various phases of the undertaking. The following reviewers offered numerous constructive criticisms, comments, and suggestions during the preparation of all previous editions.

Peter W. Allan
Victor Valley College

Wm. Dennis Ames
Indiana University of Pennsylvania

Thomas M. Apke
California State University, Fullerton

Linda Axelrod
Metropolitan State University

Jane Bennett
Orange Coast College

Sam Cassidy
University of Denver

Angela Cerino
Villanova University

David Cooper
Fullerton College

Steven R. Donley
Cypress College

Paul F. Dwyer
Siena College

Joan Gabel
Georgia State University

Gamewell Gant
Idaho State University

Arlene M. Hibschweiler
SUNY Fredonia

Barbara W. Kincaid
Southern Methodist University

Marty P. Ludlum
Oklahoma City Community College

Marty Salley McGee
South Carolina State University

Robert Mitchum
Arkansas State University, Beebe

Kathleen A. Phillips
University of Houston

David Redle
University of Akron

Larry A. Strate
University of Nevada, Las Vegas

Dawn Swink
Minnesota State University, Mankato

Brian Terry
Johnson and Wales University

John Theis
Mesa State College

Michael G. Walsh
Villanova University

Glynda White
Community College of Southern Nevada

LeVon E. Wilson
Western Carolina University

John A. Wrieden
Florida International University

Mary-Kathryn Zachary
State University of West Georgia

We would also like to give credit to the following reviewers for their useful input during development of CengageNOW for *The Legal Environment of Business:* Interactive Assignment System:

Nena Ellison
Florida Atlantic University

Jacqueline Hagerott
Franklin University

Melanie Morris
Raritan Valley Community College

William H. Volz
Wayne State University

As in all past editions, we owe a debt of extreme gratitude to the numerous individuals who worked directly with us or at Cengage Learning. In particular, we wish to thank Rob Dewey and Vicky True for their helpful advice and guidance during all of the stages of this new edition. We extend our thanks to Jan Lamar, our longtime developmental editor, for her many useful suggestions and for her efforts in coordinating reviews and ensuring the timely and accurate publication of all supplemental materials. We are also indebted to Lisa Lysne for her support and excellent marketing advice, and to Brian Courter and Kristen Meere for their skills in managing the Web site.

Our production manager and designer, Bill Stryker, made sure that we came out with an error-free, visually attractive Seventh Edition. We appreciate his efforts more than he can ever imagine. We are also indebted to the staff at Parkwood Composition, our compositor. Their ability to generate the pages for this text quickly and accurately made it possible for us to meet our ambitious printing schedule.

We especially wish to thank Katherine Marie Silsbee for her management of the entire project, as well as for the application of her superb research and editorial skills. We also wish to thank Lavina Leed Miller for her significant contributions to this project, and William Eric Hollowell, who co-authored the *Instructor's Manual,* the *Study Guide,* and the two Test Banks, for his excellent research efforts. We were fortunate enough to have the proofreading services of Lorretta Palagi and Judy Kiviat. We also thank Vickie Reierson and Roxanna Lee for their proofreading and other assistance, which helped to ensure an error-free text. Finally, we thank Suzanne Jasin of K & M Consulting for her many special efforts on this project.

In addition, we would like to give special thanks to all of the individuals who were instrumental in developing and implementing the new CengageNOW for *The Legal Environment of Business:* Interactive Assignment System. These include Rob Dewey, Jan Lamar, Lisa Lysne, and Kristen Meere at Cengage, and Katherine Marie Silsbee, Roger Meiners, Lavina Leed Miller, William Eric Hollowell, Lucien Dhooge, and Kristi Wiswell who helped develop the content for this unique Web-based product.

Through the years, we have enjoyed an ongoing correspondence with many of you who have found points on which you wish to comment. We continue to welcome all comments and promise to respond promptly. By incorporating your ideas, we can continue to write a legal environment text that is best for you and best for your students.

F.B.C.
R.L.M.

PREFACE TO THE STUDENT

Welcome to the legal environment of business. You are about to embark on the study of one of the most important topics you should master in today's changing world. A solid understanding of the legal environment of business can, of course, help you if you are going into the world of business. If you decide on a career in accounting, economics, finance, political science, or history, understanding how the legal environment works is crucial. Moreover, in your role as a consumer, you will be faced with some legal issues throughout your lifetime—renting an apartment, buying a house, obtaining a mortgage, and leasing a car, to mention only a few. In your role as an employee (if you don't go into business for yourself), you will need to know what rights you have and what rights you don't have. Even when you contemplate marriage, you will be faced with legal issues.

What You Will Find in This Text

As you will see as you thumb through the pages in this text, we have tried to make your study of the legal environment of business as efficient and enjoyable as possible. To this end, you will find the following aids:

1. **Mastering Terminology**—through ***key terms*** that are boldfaced, listed at the end of each chapter, and explained fully in the ***Glossary*** at the end of the book.
2. **Understanding Concepts**—through numerous ***Concept Summaries*** and ***Exhibits.***
3. **Observing the Law in the Context of the Real World**—through a ***Reviewing feature*** at the end of every chapter.
4. **Seeing How Legal Issues Can Arise**—through ***Video Questions*** based on Web-available short videos, many from actual Hollywood movies.
5. **Figuring Out How the Law Is Evolving**—through a feature called ***Emerging Trends.***
6. **Determining Today's Legal Controversies**—through a feature called ***Contemporary Legal Debates.***
7. **Gaining Insights into How the Law Affects or Is Affected by Other Issues**—through three new ***Insight*** features called ***Insight into E-Commerce, Insight into Ethics,*** and ***Insight into the Global Environment.***

The above list, of course, is representative only. You will understand much more of what the law is about as you read through the ***court cases*** presented in this book, including ***Extended Case excerpts,*** which will give you a feel for how the courts really decide cases, in the courts' language.

Improving Your Ability to Perform Legal Reasoning and Analysis

Although the legal environment of business may seem to be a mass of facts, your goal in taking this course should be an increased ability to use legal reasoning and analysis to figure out how legal situations will be resolved. To this end, you will find the following key learning features to assist you in mastering legal reasoning and analysis:

- **Finding and Analyzing Case Law**—In Chapter 1, you will find a section with this title that explains:
  1. Legal citations.
  2. The standard elements of a case.
  3. The different types of opinions a court can issue.
  4. How to read and understand cases.
- **Briefing a Case**—In Appendix A, you will see how to brief and analyze case problems. This explanation teaches you how to break down the elements of a case and will improve your ability to answer the ***Case Problems*** in each chapter.
- **Questions with Sample Answers**—At the end of each chapter, there is one hypothetical factual scenario that presents a legal question for which you can access a ***sample answer*** in Appendix I (and also on the text's Web site). This allows you to

practice and to see if you are answering the hypothetical problems correctly.

- **Case Problems with Sample Answers**—Each chapter has a series of chapter-ending ***Case Problems.*** You can find an answer to one problem in each chapter on this book's student companion Web site at **academic.cengage.com/blaw/cross**. You can easily compare your answer to the court's answer in the actual case.
- **Impact of This Case on Today's Law**—Each landmark classic case concludes with a short section that explains the relevance of older case law to the way courts reason today.
- **What If the Facts Were Different?**—This section, found at the end of selected cases, encourages you to think about how the outcome of a case might be different if the facts were altered.
- **The Ethical [E-Commerce, Global, or Legal Environment] Dimension**—Every case in this text concludes with two critical-thinking questions, which may include *What If the Facts Were Different?* questions, as discussed above. For this edition, we've included several new possibilities—*(The Ethical Dimension, The E-Commerce Dimension, The Global Dimension,* and *The Legal Environment Dimension.)* These questions ask you to explore the law in a variety of contexts to help you meet the specific curriculum requirements for business law students.

The Companion Student Web Site

As already mentioned, the companion student Web site at **academic.cengage.com/blaw/cross** provides you with short videos on various legal topics and with sample answers to one case problem per chapter. In addition, you will find the following:

- ***Interactive quizzes*** for every chapter.
- A ***glossary*** of terms for every chapter in the text.
- ***Flashcards*** that provide an optional study tool for reviewing the key terms in every chapter.
- ***Appendix A: How to Brief and Analyze Case Problems*** that will help you analyze cases. This useful appendix for the book is also provided on the Web site and can be downloaded.
- ***Legal reference materials*** including a "Statutes" page that offers links to the full text of selected statutes referenced in the text, a Spanish glossary, and links to other important legal resources available for free on the Web.
- ***Internet exercises*** for every chapter in the text (at least two per chapter) that introduce you to how to research the law online.
- ***Relevant Web sites*** for additional research for *Emerging Trends* features as well as links to the URLs listed in the *Law on the Web* section at the end of each chapter.
- ***Online Legal Research Guide*** that offers complete yet brief guidance to using the Internet and evaluating information obtained from the Internet. As an online resource, it now includes hyperlinks to the Web sites discussed for click-through convenience.
- ***Court case updates*** for follow-up research on topics covered in the text.
- ***Link to CengageNOW for* The Legal Environment of Business: *Interactive Assignment System*** with different types of questions related to every chapter in the text and one set of cumulative questions for each unit in the text. (Available on an instructor's request; see below.)

Interactive Assignments on the Web

Some of you may have instructors who provide assignments using our world-class interactive Web-based system, called **CengageNOW for *The Legal Environment of Business:* Interactive Assignment System.**

CengageNOW for *The Legal Environment of Business:* Interactive Assignment System allows you to improve your mastery of legal concepts and terminology, legal reasoning and analysis, and much more. Your instructor will give you further information if she or he decides to use this Web-based system.

Of course, whether or not you are using the CengageNOW system, you will wish to consider purchasing the *Study Guide,* which can help you get a better grade in your course (see the inside cover for details).

The law is all around you—and will be for the rest of your life. We hope that you begin your first course in business law and the legal environment with the same high degree of excitement that we, the authors, always have when we work on improving this text, now in its Seventh Edition. *The Legal Environment of Business* has withstood the test of time—thousands of students before you have already used and benefited by it.

Dedication

To Max,

You've come a long ways
in a few short years.
Your hard work, courage,
and mature sense of what is right
will serve you well.

R.L.M.

To my parents and sisters.

F.B.C.

UNIT ONE
The Foundations

CONTENTS

CHAPTER 1

Business and Its Legal Environment

One of the important functions of law in any society is to provide stability, predictability, and continuity so that people can be sure of how to order their affairs. If any society is to survive, its citizens must be able to determine what is legally right and legally wrong. They must know what sanctions will be imposed on them if they commit wrongful acts. If they suffer harm as a result of others' wrongful acts, they must know how they can seek redress. By setting forth the rights, obligations, and privileges of citizens, the law enables individuals to go about their business with confidence and a certain degree of predictability. The stability and predictability created by the law provide an essential framework for all civilized activities, including business activities.

What do we mean when we speak of "the law"? Although this term has had, and will continue to have, different definitions, they are all based on a general observation: at a minimum, **law** consists of *enforceable rules governing relationships among individuals and between individuals and their society*. These "enforceable rules" may consist of unwritten principles of behavior established by a nomadic tribe. They may be set forth in a law code, such as the Code of Hammurabi in ancient Babylon (c. 1780 B.C.E.) or the law code of one of today's European nations. They may consist of written laws and court decisions created by modern legislative and judicial bodies, as in the United States. Regardless of how such rules are created, they all have one thing in common: they establish rights, duties, and privileges that are consistent with the values and beliefs of their society or its ruling group.

Those who embark on a study of the legal environment will find that these broad statements leave unanswered some important questions concerning the nature of law. Part of the study of law, often referred to as **jurisprudence,** involves learning about different schools of jurisprudential thought and discovering how the approaches to law characteristic of each school can affect judicial decision making.

We open this introductory chapter with an examination of that topic. We then look at an important question for any student reading this text: How does the legal environment affect business decision making? We next describe the basic sources of American law, the common law tradition, and some general classifications of law. We conclude the chapter with sections offering practical guidance on several topics, including how to find the sources of law discussed in this chapter (and referred to throughout the text) and how to read and understand court opinions.

SECTION 1 Schools of Jurisprudential Thought

You may think that legal philosophy is far removed from the practical study of business law and the legal environment. In fact, it is not. As you will learn in the chapters of this text, how judges apply the law to specific disputes, including disputes relating to the business world, depends in part on their philosophical approaches to law.

Clearly, judges are not free to decide cases solely on the basis of their personal philosophical views or on their opinions about the issues before the court. A judge's function is not to *make* the laws—that is the function of the legislative branch of government—but to interpret and apply them. From a practical point of view, however, the courts play a significant role in defining what the law is. This is because laws enacted by legislative bodies tend to be expressed in general terms. Judges thus have some flexibility in interpreting and applying the law. It is because of this flexibility that different courts can, and often do, arrive at different conclusions in cases that involve nearly identical issues, facts, and applicable laws. This flexibility also means that each judge's unique personality, legal philosophy, set of values, and intellectual attributes necessarily frame the judicial decision-making process to some extent.

Over time several significant schools of legal, or jurisprudential, thought have evolved. We now look at some of them.

The Natural Law School

An age-old question about the nature of law has to do with the finality of a nation's laws, such as the laws of the United States at the present time. For example, what if a particular law is deemed to be a "bad" law by a substantial number of that nation's citizens? Must a citizen obey the law if it goes against his or her conscience to do so? Is there a higher or universal law to which individuals can appeal? One who adheres to the natural law tradition would answer these questions in the affirmative. **Natural law** denotes a system of moral and ethical principles that are inherent in human nature and that people can discover through the use of their natural intelligence, or reason.

The natural law tradition is one of the oldest and most significant schools of jurisprudence. It dates back to the days of the Greek philosopher Aristotle (384–322 B.C.E.), who distinguished between natural law and the laws governing a particular nation. According to Aristotle, natural law applies universally to all humankind.

The notion that people have "natural rights" stems from the natural law tradition. Those who claim that a specific foreign government is depriving certain citizens of their human rights implicitly are appealing to a higher law that has universal applicability. The question of the universality of basic human rights also comes into play in the context of international business operations. Should rights extended to workers in the United States, such as the right to be free of discrimination in the workplace, be extended to workers employed by a U.S. firm doing business in another country that does not provide for such rights? This question is rooted implicitly in a concept of universal rights that has its origins in the natural law tradition.

The Positivist School

In contrast, **positive law,** or national law (the written law of a given society at a particular point in time), applies only to the citizens of that nation or society. Those who adhere to the **positivist school** believe that there can be no higher law than a nation's positive law. According to the positivist school, there is no such thing as "natural rights." Rather, human rights exist solely because of laws. If the laws are not enforced, anarchy will result. Thus, whether a law is "bad" or "good" is irrelevant. The law is the law and must be obeyed until it is changed—in an orderly manner through a legitimate lawmaking process. A judge with positivist leanings probably would be more inclined to defer to an existing law than would a judge who adheres to the natural law tradition.

The Historical School

The **historical school** of legal thought emphasizes the evolutionary process of law by concentrating on the origin and history of the legal system. Thus, this school looks to the past to discover what the principles of contemporary law should be. The legal doctrines that have withstood the passage of time—those that have worked in the past—are deemed best suited for shaping present laws. Hence, law derives its legitimacy and authority from adhering to the standards that historical development has shown to be workable. Adherents of the historical school are more likely than those of other schools to strictly follow decisions made in past cases.

Legal Realism

In the 1920s and 1930s, a number of jurists and scholars, known as legal realists, rebelled against the historical approach to law. **Legal realism** is based on the idea that law is just one of many institutions in society and that it is shaped by social forces and needs. The law is a human enterprise, and judges should take social and economic realities into account when deciding cases. Legal realists also believe that the law can never be applied with total uniformity. Given that judges are human beings with unique personalities, value systems, and intellects, different judges will obviously bring different reasoning processes to the same case.

Legal realism strongly influenced the growth of what is sometimes called the **sociological school** of jurisprudence. This school views law as a tool for promoting justice in society. In the 1960s, for example, the justices of the United States Supreme Court played a leading role in the civil rights movement by upholding long-neglected laws calling for equal treatment for all Americans, including African Americans and other minorities. Generally, jurists who adhere to this philosophy of law are more likely to depart from past decisions than are those jurists who adhere to the other schools of legal thought. *Concept Summary 1.1* reviews the schools of jurisprudential thought.

SECTION 2 Business Activities and the Legal Environment

As those entering the world of business will learn, laws and government regulations affect virtually all business activities—from hiring and firing decisions to workplace safety, the manufacturing and marketing of products, business financing, and more. To make good business decisions, a basic knowledge of the laws and regulations governing these activities is beneficial—if not essential. Realize also that in today's world a knowledge of "black-letter" law is not enough. Businesspersons are also pressured to make ethical decisions. Thus, the study of business law necessarily involves an ethical dimension.

Many Different Laws May Affect a Single Business Transaction

As you will note, each chapter in this text covers a specific area of the law and shows how the legal rules in that area affect business activities. Though compartmentalizing the law in this fashion promotes conceptual clarity, it does not indicate the extent to which a number of different laws may apply to just one transaction.

Consider an example. Suppose that you are the president of NetSys, Inc., a company that creates and maintains computer network systems for its clients, including business firms. NetSys also markets software for customers who require an internal computer network. One day, Hernandez, an operations officer for Southwest Distribution Corporation (SDC), contacts you by e-mail about a possible contract concerning SDC's computer network. In deciding whether to enter

CONCEPT SUMMARY 1.1
Schools of Jurisprudential Thought

School of Thought	Description
THE NATURAL LAW SCHOOL	One of the oldest and most significant schools of legal thought. Those who believe in natural law hold that there is a universal law applicable to all human beings. This law is discoverable through reason and is of a higher order than positive (national) law.
THE POSITIVIST SCHOOL	A school of legal thought centered on the assumption that there is no law higher than the laws created by the government. Laws must be obeyed, even if they are unjust, to prevent anarchy.
THE HISTORICAL SCHOOL	A school of legal thought that stresses the evolutionary nature of law and that looks to doctrines that have withstood the passage of time for guidance in shaping present laws.
LEGAL REALISM	A school of legal thought, popular during the 1920s and 1930s, that left a lasting imprint on American jurisprudence. Legal realists generally advocated a less abstract and more realistic and pragmatic approach to the law, an approach that would take into account customary practices and the circumstances in which transactions take place. Legal realism strongly influenced the growth of the *sociological school* of jurisprudence, which views law as a tool for promoting social justice.

into a contract with SDC, you should consider, among other things, the legal requirements for an enforceable contract. Are there different requirements for a contract for services and a contract for products? What are your options if SDC **breaches** (breaks, or fails to perform) the contract? The answers to these questions are part of contract law and sales law.

Other questions might concern payment under the contract. How can you guarantee that NetSys will be paid? For example, if payment is made with a check that is returned for insufficient funds, what are your options? Answers to these questions can be found in the laws that relate to negotiable instruments (such as checks) and creditors' rights. Also, a dispute may occur over the rights to NetSys's software, or there may be a question of liability if the software is defective. Questions may even be raised as to whether you and Hernandez had the authority to make the deal in the first place. A disagreement may arise from other circumstances, such as an accountant's evaluation of the contract. Resolutions of these questions may be found in areas of the law that relate to intellectual property, e-commerce, torts, product liability, agency, business organizations, or professional liability.

Finally, if any dispute cannot be resolved amicably, then the laws and the rules concerning courts and court procedures spell out the steps of a lawsuit. Exhibit 1–1 illustrates the various areas of law that may influence business decision making.

Ethics and Business Decision Making

Merely knowing the areas of law that may affect a business decision is not sufficient in today's business world. Businesspersons must also take ethics into account. As you will learn in Chapter 4, *ethics* is generally defined as the study of what constitutes right or wrong behavior. Today, business decision makers need to consider not just whether a decision is legal, but also whether it is ethical.

Throughout this text, you will learn about the relationship between the law and ethics, as well as about some of the types of ethical questions that often arise in the business context. For example, the unit-ending *Focus on Ethics* features in this text are devoted solely to the exploration of ethical questions pertaining to selected topics treated within the unit. We have also added several new features for this edition that stress

EXHIBIT 1–1 • Areas of the Law That May Affect Business Decision Making

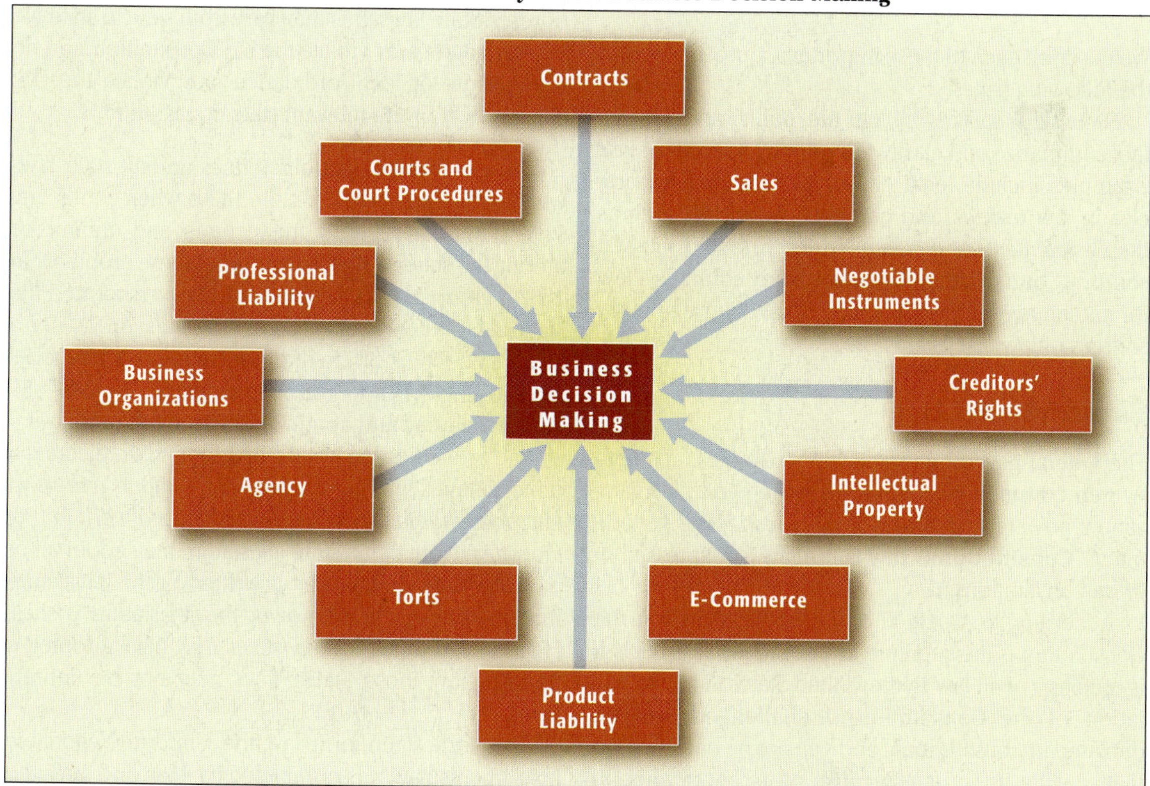

the importance of ethical considerations in today's business climate. These include the new *Ethical Dimension* questions that conclude many of the cases presented in this text and the *Insight into Ethics* features that appear in selected chapters. We have also included *A Question of Ethics* case problems at the ends of the chapters to introduce you to the ethical aspects of specific cases involving real-life situations. Additionally, Chapter 4 offers a detailed look at the importance of ethical considerations in business decision making.

Section 3 Sources of American Law

There are numerous sources of American law. *Primary sources of law,* or sources that establish the law, include the following:

1. The U.S. Constitution and the constitutions of the various states.
2. Statutory law—including laws passed by Congress, state legislatures, or local governing bodies.
3. Regulations created by administrative agencies, such as the Food and Drug Administration.
4. Case law and common law doctrines.

We describe each of these important sources of law in the following pages.

Secondary sources of law are books and articles that summarize and clarify the primary sources of law. Examples include legal encyclopedias, treatises, articles in law reviews, and compilations of law, such as the *Restatements of the Law* (which will be discussed shortly). Courts often refer to secondary sources of law for guidance in interpreting and applying the primary sources of law discussed here.

Constitutional Law

The federal government and the states have separate written constitutions that set forth the general organization, powers, and limits of their respective governments. **Constitutional law** is the law as expressed in these constitutions.

According to Article VI of the U.S. Constitution, the Constitution is the supreme law of the land. As such, it is the basis of all law in the United States. A law in violation of the Constitution, if challenged, will be declared unconstitutional and will not be enforced, no matter what its source. Because of its importance in the American legal system, we present the complete text of the U.S. Constitution in Appendix B.

The Tenth Amendment to the U.S. Constitution reserves to the states all powers not granted to the federal government. Each state in the union has its own constitution. Unless it conflicts with the U.S. Constitution or a federal law, a state constitution is supreme within the state's borders.

Statutory Law

Laws enacted by legislative bodies at any level of government, such as the statutes passed by Congress or by state legislatures, make up the body of law generally referred to as **statutory law.** When a legislature passes a statute, that statute ultimately is included in the federal code of laws or the relevant state code of laws (these codes are discussed later in this chapter).

Statutory law also includes local **ordinances**—statutes (laws, rules, or orders) passed by municipal or county governing units to govern matters not covered by federal or state law. Ordinances commonly have to do with city or county land use (zoning ordinances), building and safety codes, and other matters affecting the local community.

A federal statute, of course, applies to all states. A state statute, in contrast, applies only within the state's borders. State laws thus may vary from state to state. No federal statute may violate the U.S. Constitution, and no state statute or local ordinance may violate the U.S. Constitution or the relevant state constitution.

Uniform Laws The differences among state laws were particularly notable in the 1800s, when conflicting state statutes frequently made trade and commerce among the states difficult. To counter these problems, in 1892 a group of legal scholars and lawyers formed the National Conference of Commissioners on Uniform State Laws (NCCUSL) to draft **uniform laws,** or model laws, for the states to consider adopting. The NCCUSL still exists today and continues to issue uniform laws.

Each state has the option of adopting or rejecting a uniform law. *Only if a state legislature adopts a uniform law does that law become part of the statutory law of that state.* Note that a state legislature may adopt all or part of a uniform law as it is written, or the legislature may rewrite the law however the legislature wishes. Hence, even though many states may have adopted a uniform law, those states' laws may not be entirely "uniform."

The earliest uniform law, the Uniform Negotiable Instruments Law, was completed by 1896 and adopted in every state by the early 1920s (although not all states used exactly the same wording). Over the following decades, other acts were drawn up in a similar manner. In all, more than two hundred uniform acts have been issued by the NCCUSL since its inception. The most ambitious uniform act of all, however, was the Uniform Commercial Code.

The Uniform Commercial Code The Uniform Commercial Code (UCC), which was created through the joint efforts of the NCCUSL and the American Law Institute,[1] was first issued in 1952. All fifty states,[2] the District of Columbia, and the Virgin Islands have adopted the UCC. It facilitates commerce among the states by providing a uniform, yet flexible, set of rules governing commercial transactions. The UCC assures businesspersons that their contracts, if validly entered into, normally will be enforced.

As you will read in later chapters, from time to time the NCCUSL revises the articles contained in the UCC and submits the revised versions to the states for adoption. During the 1990s, for example, four articles (Articles 3, 4, 5, and 9) were revised, and two new articles (Articles 2A and 4A) were added. Amendments to Article 1 were approved in 2001 and have now been adopted by a majority of the states. Because of its importance in the area of commercial law, we cite the UCC frequently in this text. We also present excerpts of the UCC in Appendix C.

Administrative Law

Another important source of American law is **administrative law,** which consists of the rules, orders, and decisions of administrative agencies. An **administrative agency** is a federal, state, or local government agency established to perform a specific function. Administrative law and procedures, which will be examined in detail in Chapter 6, constitute a dominant element in the regulatory environment of business. Rules issued by various administrative agencies now affect virtually every aspect of a business's operations, including its capital structure and financing, its hiring and firing procedures, its relations with employees and unions, and the way it manufactures and markets its products.

1. This institute was formed in the 1920s and consists of practicing attorneys, legal scholars, and judges.
2. Louisiana has not adopted Articles 2 and 2A (covering contracts for the sale and lease of goods), however.

Federal Agencies At the national level, numerous **executive agencies** exist within the cabinet departments of the executive branch. The Food and Drug Administration, for example, is an agency within the Department of Health and Human Services. Executive agencies are subject to the authority of the president, who has the power to appoint and remove officers of federal agencies. There are also major **independent regulatory agencies** at the federal level, such as the Federal Trade Commission, the Securities and Exchange Commission, and the Federal Communications Commission. The president's power is less pronounced in regard to independent agencies, whose officers serve for fixed terms and cannot be removed without just cause.

State and Local Agencies There are administrative agencies at the state and local levels as well. Commonly, a state agency (such as a state pollution-control agency) is created as a parallel to a federal agency (such as the Environmental Protection Agency). Just as federal statutes take precedence over conflicting state statutes, so federal agency regulations take precedence over conflicting state regulations.

Case Law and Common Law Doctrines

The rules of law announced in court decisions constitute another basic source of American law. These rules of law include interpretations of constitutional provisions, of statutes enacted by legislatures, and of regulations created by administrative agencies. Today, this body of judge-made law is referred to as **case law.** Case law—the doctrines and principles announced in cases—governs all areas not covered by statutory law or administrative law and is part of our common law tradition. We look at the origins and characteristics of the common law tradition in some detail in the pages that follow. See *Concept Summary 1.2* on the following page for a review of the sources of American law.

The Common Law Tradition

Because of our colonial heritage, much of American law is based on the English legal system, which originated in medieval England and continued to evolve in the following centuries. Knowledge of this system is necessary to understanding the American legal system today.

CONCEPT SUMMARY 1.2
Sources of American Law

Source	Description
Constitutional Law	The law as expressed in the U.S. Constitution and the state constitutions. The U.S. Constitution is the supreme law of the land. State constitutions are supreme within state borders to the extent that they do not violate a clause of the U.S. Constitution or a federal law.
Statutory Law	Laws (statutes and ordinances) created by federal, state, and local legislatures and governing bodies. None of these laws may violate the U.S. Constitution or the relevant state constitution. Uniform statutes, when adopted by a state, become statutory law in that state.
Administrative Law	The rules, orders, and decisions of federal, state, or local government administrative agencies.
Case Law and Common Law Doctrines	Judge-made law, including interpretations of constitutional provisions, of statutes enacted by legislatures, and of regulations created by administrative agencies.

Early English Courts

The origins of the English legal system—and thus the U.S. legal system as well—date back to 1066, when the Normans conquered England. William the Conqueror and his successors began the process of unifying the country under their rule. One of the means they used to do this was the establishment of the king's courts, or *curiae regis.* Before the Norman Conquest, disputes had been settled according to the local legal customs and traditions in various regions of the country. The king's courts sought to establish a uniform set of customs for the country as a whole. What evolved in these courts was the beginning of the **common law**—a body of general rules that applied throughout the entire English realm. Eventually, the common law tradition became part of the heritage of all nations that were once British colonies, including the United States.

Courts of Law and Remedies at Law The early English king's courts could grant only very limited kinds of **remedies** (the legal means to enforce a right or redress a wrong). If one person wronged another in some way, the king's courts could award as compensation one or more of the following: (1) land, (2) items of value, or (3) money. The courts that awarded this compensation became known as **courts of law,** and the three remedies were called **remedies at law.** (Today, the remedy at law normally takes the form of monetary **damages**—an amount given to a party whose legal interests have been injured.) Even though the system introduced uniformity in the settling of disputes, when a complaining party wanted a remedy other than economic compensation, the courts of law could do nothing, so "no remedy, no right."

Courts of Equity and Remedies in Equity Equity is a branch of law, founded on what might be described as notions of justice and fair dealing, that seeks to supply a remedy when no adequate remedy at law is available. When individuals could not obtain an adequate remedy in a court of law, they petitioned the king for relief. Most of these petitions were decided by an adviser to the king, called a **chancellor,** who had the power to grant new and unique remedies. Eventually, formal chancery courts, or **courts of equity,** were established.

The remedies granted by the equity courts became known as **remedies in equity,** or equitable remedies. These remedies include *specific performance* (ordering a party to perform an agreement as promised), an *injunction* (ordering a party to cease engaging in a specific activity or to undo some wrong or injury), and *rescission* (the cancellation of a contractual obligation). We discuss these and other equitable remedies in more detail at appropriate points in the chapters that follow, particularly in Chapter 10.

As a general rule, today's courts, like the early English courts, will not grant equitable remedies unless the remedy at law—monetary damages—is inadequate. For example, suppose that you form a contract (a legally binding agreement—see Chapter 9) to purchase a parcel of land that you think will be just perfect for your future home. Further suppose that the seller breaches this agreement. You could sue the seller for the return of any deposits or down payment you might have made on the land, but this is not the remedy you really seek. What you want is to have the court order the seller to go through with the contract. In other words, you want the court to grant the equitable remedy of specific performance because monetary damages are inadequate in this situation.

Equitable Maxims In fashioning appropriate remedies, judges often were (and continue to be) guided by so-called **equitable maxims**—propositions or general statements of equitable rules. Exhibit 1–2 lists some important equitable maxims. The last maxim listed in that exhibit—"Equity aids the vigilant, not those who rest on their rights"—merits special attention. It has become known as the equitable doctrine of **laches** (a term derived from the Latin *laxus,* meaning "lax" or "negligent"), and it can be used as a defense. A **defense** is an argument raised by the **defendant** (the party being sued) indicating why the **plaintiff** (the suing party) should not obtain the remedy sought. (Note that in equity proceedings, the party bringing a lawsuit is called the **petitioner,** and the party being sued is referred to as the **respondent.**)

The doctrine of laches arose to encourage people to bring lawsuits while the evidence was fresh. What constitutes a reasonable time, of course, varies according to the circumstances of the case. Time periods for different types of cases are now usually fixed by **statutes of limitations.** After the time allowed under a statute of limitations has expired, no action (lawsuit) can be brought, no matter how strong the case was originally.

Legal and Equitable Remedies Today

The establishment of courts of equity in medieval England resulted in two distinct court systems: courts of law and courts of equity. The systems had different sets of judges and granted different types of remedies. During the nineteenth century, however, most states in the United States adopted rules of procedure that resulted in the combining of courts of law and equity. A party now may request both legal and equitable remedies in the same action, and the trial court judge may grant either or both forms of relief.

The distinction between legal and equitable remedies remains relevant to students of business law, however, because these remedies differ. To seek the proper remedy for a wrong, one must know what remedies are available. Additionally, certain vestiges of the procedures used when there were separate courts of law and equity still exist. For example, a party has the right to demand a jury trial in an action at law, but not in an action in equity. Exhibit 1–3 on the next page summarizes the procedural differences (applicable in most states) between an action at law and an action in equity.

The Doctrine of *Stare Decisis*

One of the unique features of the common law is that it is *judge-made* law. The body of principles and doctrines that form the common law emerged over time as judges decided legal controversies.

EXHIBIT 1–2 • Equitable Maxims

1. *Whoever seeks equity must do equity.* (Anyone who wishes to be treated fairly must treat others fairly.)
2. *Where there is equal equity, the law must prevail.* (The law will determine the outcome of a controversy in which the merits of both sides are equal.)
3. *One seeking the aid of an equity court must come to the court with clean hands.* (Plaintiffs must have acted fairly and honestly.)
4. *Equity will not suffer a wrong to be without a remedy.* (Equitable relief will be awarded when there is a right to relief and there is no adequate remedy at law.)
5. *Equity regards substance rather than form.* (Equity is more concerned with fairness and justice than with legal technicalities.)
6. *Equity aids the vigilant, not those who rest on their rights.* (Equity will not help those who neglect their rights for an unreasonable period of time.)

detail on intentional torts). Case precedents involving similar facts and issues thus would be relevant. Often, more than one rule of law will be applicable to a case.

3. *How do the rules of law apply to the particular facts and circumstances of this case?* This step is often the most difficult because each case presents a unique set of facts, circumstances, and parties. Although cases may be similar, no two cases are ever identical in all respects. Normally, judges (and lawyers and law students) try to find **cases on point**—previously decided cases that are as similar as possible to the one under consideration. (Because of the difficulty—and importance—of this step in the legal reasoning process, we discuss it in more detail in the next subsection.)
4. *What conclusion should be drawn?* This step normally presents few problems. Usually, the conclusion is evident if the previous three steps have been followed carefully.

Forms of Legal Reasoning Judges use many types of reasoning when following the third step of the legal reasoning process—applying the law to the facts of a particular case. Three common forms of reasoning are deductive reasoning, linear reasoning, and reasoning by analogy.

Deductive Reasoning. Deductive reasoning is sometimes called *syllogistic reasoning* because it employs a **syllogism**—a logical relationship involving a major premise, a minor premise, and a conclusion. Consider the hypothetical case presented earlier, in which the plaintiff alleged that the defendant committed assault by threatening her while she was sleeping. The judge might point out that "under the common law of torts, an individual must be *aware* of a threat of danger for the threat to constitute assault" (major premise); "the plaintiff in this case was unaware of the threat at the time it occurred" (minor premise); and "therefore, the circumstances do not amount to an assault" (conclusion).

Linear Reasoning. A second important form of legal reasoning that is commonly employed might be thought of as "linear" reasoning because it proceeds from one point to another, with the final point being the conclusion. A comparison will help make this form of reasoning clear. Imagine a knotted rope, with each knot tying together separate pieces of rope to form a tightly knotted length. As a whole, the rope represents a linear progression of thought logically connecting various points, with the last point, or knot, representing the conclusion. Suppose that a tenant in an apartment building sues the landlord for damages for an injury resulting from an allegedly inadequately lit stairway. The court may engage in a reasoning process involving the following "pieces of rope":

1. The landlord, who was on the premises the evening the injury occurred, testifies that none of the other nine tenants who used the stairway that night complained about the lights.
2. The fact that none of the tenants complained is the same as if they had said the lighting was sufficient.
3. That there were no complaints does not prove that the lighting was sufficient but does prove that the landlord had no reason to believe that it was not.
4. The landlord's belief was reasonable because no one complained.
5. Therefore, the landlord acted reasonably and was not negligent with respect to the lighting in the stairway.

From this reasoning, the court concludes that the tenant is not entitled to compensation on the basis of the stairway's allegedly insufficient lighting.

Reasoning by Analogy. Another important type of reasoning that judges use in deciding cases is reasoning by *analogy*. To reason by **analogy** is to compare the facts in the case at hand to the facts in other cases and, to the extent that the patterns are similar, to apply the same rule of law to the present case. To the extent that the facts are unique, or "distinguishable," different rules may apply. For example, in case A, the court held that a driver who crossed a highway's center line was negligent. Case B involves a driver who crosses the line to avoid hitting a child. In determining whether case A's rule applies in case B, a judge would consider what the reasons were for the decision in A and whether B is sufficiently similar for those reasons to apply. If the judge holds that B's driver is not liable, that judge must indicate why case A's rule is not relevant to the facts presented in case B.

There Is No One "Right" Answer

Many persons believe that there is one "right" answer to every legal question. In most situations involving a legal controversy, however, there is no single correct result. Good arguments can often be made to support either side of a legal controversy. Quite often, a case does not involve a "good" person suing a "bad" person. In many cases, both parties have acted in good faith in some measure or in bad faith to some degree.

Additionally, each judge has her or his own personal beliefs and philosophy, which shape, at least to some extent, the process of legal reasoning. This means that the outcome of a particular lawsuit before a court cannot be predicted with absolute certainty. In fact, in some cases, even though the weight of the law would seem to favor one party's position, judges, through creative legal reasoning, have found ways to rule in favor of the other party in the interests of preventing injustice. Legal reasoning and other aspects of the common law tradition are reviewed in *Concept Summary 1.3*.

The Common Law Today

Today, the common law derived from judicial decisions continues to be applied throughout the United States. Common law doctrines and principles govern all areas *not* covered by statutory or administrative law. In a dispute concerning a particular employment practice, for example, if a statute regulates that practice, the statute will apply rather than the common law doctrine that applied prior to the enactment of the statute.

The Continuing Importance of the Common Law

Because the body of statutory law has expanded greatly since the beginning of this nation, thus narrowing the applicability of common law doctrines, it might seem that the common law has dwindled in importance. This is not true, however. For one thing, even in areas governed by statutory law, there is a significant interplay between statutory law and the common law. For example, many statutes essentially codify existing common law rules, and regulations issued by various administrative agencies usually are based, at least in part, on common law principles. Additionally, the courts, in interpreting statutory law, often rely on the

CONCEPT SUMMARY 1.3
The Common Law Tradition

Aspect	Description
ORIGINS OF THE COMMON LAW	The American legal system is based on the common law tradition, which originated in medieval England. Following the conquest of England in 1066 by William the Conqueror, king's courts were established throughout England, and the common law was developed in these courts.
LEGAL AND EQUITABLE REMEDIES	The distinction between remedies at law (compensation with money or items of value, such as land) and remedies in equity (including specific performance, injunction, and rescission of a contractual obligation) originated in the early English courts of law and courts of equity, respectively.
CASE PRECEDENTS AND THE DOCTRINE OF *STARE DECISIS*	In the king's courts, judges attempted to make their decisions consistent with previous decisions, called precedents. This practice gave rise to the doctrine of *stare decisis*. This doctrine, which became a cornerstone of the common law tradition, obligates judges to abide by precedents established in their jurisdictions.
STARE DECISIS AND LEGAL REASONING	Legal reasoning refers to the reasoning process used by judges in applying the law to the facts and issues of specific cases. Legal reasoning involves becoming familiar with the key facts of a case, identifying the relevant legal rules, applying those rules to the facts, and drawing a conclusion. In applying the legal rules to the facts of a case, judges may use deductive reasoning, linear reasoning, or reasoning by analogy.

common law as a guide to what the legislators intended.

Furthermore, how the courts interpret a particular statute determines how that statute will be applied. If you wanted to learn about the coverage and applicability of a particular statute, for example, you would necessarily have to locate the statute and study it. You would also need to see how the courts in your jurisdiction have interpreted and applied the statute. In other words, you would have to learn what precedents have been established in your jurisdiction with respect to that statute. Often, the applicability of a newly enacted statute does not become clear until a body of case law develops to clarify how, when, and to whom the statute applies.

Restatements of the Law

The American Law Institute (ALI) has drafted and published compilations of the common law called *Restatements of the Law*, which generally summarize the common law rules followed by most states. There are *Restatements of the Law* in the areas of contracts, torts, agency, trusts, property, restitution, security, judgments, and conflict of laws. The *Restatements*, like other secondary sources of law, do not in themselves have the force of law, but they are an important source of legal analysis and opinion on which judges often rely in making their decisions.

Many of the *Restatements* are now in their second, third, or fourth editions. We refer to the *Restatements* frequently in subsequent chapters of this text, indicating in parentheses the edition to which we are referring. For example, we refer to the second edition of the *Restatement of the Law of Contracts* as simply the *Restatement (Second) of Contracts*.

Classifications of Law

The substantial body of the law may be broken down according to several classification systems. For example, one classification system divides law into substantive law and procedural law. **Substantive law** consists of all laws that define, describe, regulate, and create legal rights and obligations. **Procedural law** consists of all laws that delineate the methods of enforcing the rights established by substantive law. Other classification systems divide law into federal law and state law, private law (dealing with relationships between private entities) and public law (addressing the relationship between persons and their governments), and national law and international law. Here we look at still another classification system, which divides law into civil law and criminal law, as well as at what is meant by the term *cyberlaw*.

Civil Law and Criminal Law

Civil law spells out the rights and duties that exist between persons and between persons and their governments, as well as the relief available when a person's rights are violated. Typically, in a civil case, a private party sues another private party (although the government can also sue a party for a civil law violation) to make that other party comply with a duty or pay for the damage caused by failure to comply with a duty. Much of the law that we discuss in this text is civil law. Contract law, for example, covered in Chapters 9 and 10, is civil law. The whole body of tort law (see Chapters 12 and 13) is also civil law.

Criminal law, in contrast, is concerned with wrongs committed *against the public as a whole.* Criminal acts are defined and prohibited by local, state, or federal government statutes. Criminal defendants are thus prosecuted by public officials, such as a district attorney (D.A.), on behalf of the state, not by their victims or other private parties. (See Chapter 7 for a further discussion of the distinction between civil law and criminal law.)

Cyberlaw

As mentioned, the use of the Internet to conduct business transactions has led to new types of legal issues. In response, courts have had to adapt traditional laws to situations that are unique to our age. Additionally, legislatures have created laws to deal specifically with such issues. Frequently, people use the term **cyberlaw** to refer to the emerging body of law that governs transactions conducted via the Internet. Cyberlaw is not really a classification of law, nor is it a new *type* of law. Rather, it is an informal term used to describe traditional legal principles that have been modified and adapted to fit situations that are unique to the online world. Of course, in some areas new statutes have been enacted, at both the federal and the state levels, to cover specific types of problems stemming from online communications. Throughout this book, you will read how the law in a given area is evolving to govern specific legal issues that arise in the online context.

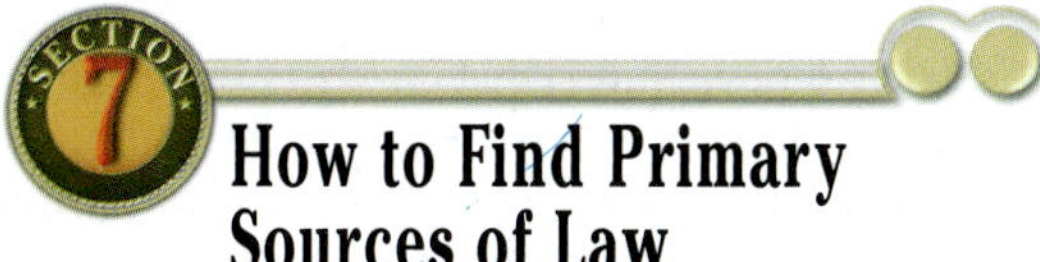

How to Find Primary Sources of Law

This text includes numerous citations to primary sources of law—federal and state statutes, the U.S. Constitution and state constitutions, regulations issued by administrative agencies, and court cases. (A **citation** is a reference to a publication in which a legal authority—such as a statute or a court decision or other source—can be found.) In this section, we explain how you can use citations to find primary sources of law. Note that in addition to the primary sources being published in sets of books as described next, most federal and state laws and case decisions are also available online.

Finding Statutory and Administrative Law

When Congress passes laws, they are collected in a publication titled *United States Statutes at Large*. When state legislatures pass laws, they are collected in similar state publications. Most frequently, however, laws are referred to in their codified form—that is, the form in which they appear in the federal and state codes. In these codes, laws are compiled by subject.

United States Code The *United States Code* (U.S.C.) arranges all existing federal laws by broad subject. Each of the fifty subjects is given a title and a title number. For example, laws relating to commerce and trade are collected in Title 15, "Commerce and Trade." Titles are subdivided by sections. A citation to the U.S.C. includes both title and section numbers. Thus, a reference to "15 U.S.C. Section 1" means that the statute can be found in Section 1 of Title 15. ("Section" may also be designated by the symbol §, and "Sections," by §§.) In addition to the print publication of the U.S.C., the federal government also provides a searchable online database of the *United States Code* at **www.gpoaccess.gov/uscode/index.html**.

Commercial publications of federal laws and regulations are also available. For example, West Group publishes the *United States Code Annotated* (U.S.C.A.). The U.S.C.A. contains the official text of the U.S.C., plus notes (annotations) on court decisions that interpret and apply specific sections of the statutes. The U.S.C.A. also includes additional research aids, such as cross-references to related statutes, historical notes, and library references. A citation to the U.S.C.A. is similar to a citation to the U.S.C.: "15 U.S.C.A. Section 1."

State Codes State codes follow the U.S.C. pattern of arranging law by subject. They may be called codes, revisions, compilations, consolidations, general statutes, or statutes, depending on the preferences of the states. In some codes, subjects are designated by number. In others, they are designated by name. For example, "13 Pennsylvania Consolidated Statutes Section 1101" means that the statute can be found in Title 13, Section 1101, of the Pennsylvania code. "California Commercial Code Section 1101" means that the statute can be found under the subject heading "Commercial Code" of the California code in Section 1101. Abbreviations are often used. For example, "13 Pennsylvania Consolidated Statutes Section 1101" is abbreviated "13 Pa. C.S. § 1101," and "California Commercial Code Section 1101" is abbreviated "Cal. Com. Code § 1101."

Administrative Rules Rules and regulations adopted by federal administrative agencies are initially published in the *Federal Register*, a daily publication of the U.S. government. Later, they are incorporated into the *Code of Federal Regulations* (C.F.R.). Like the U.S.C., the C.F.R. is divided into fifty titles. Rules within each title are assigned section numbers. A full citation to the C.F.R. includes title and section numbers. For example, a reference to "17 C.F.R. Section 230.504" means that the rule can be found in Section 230.504 of Title 17.

Finding Case Law

Before discussing the case reporting system, we need to look briefly at the court system (which will be discussed in detail in Chapter 2). There are two types of courts in the United States, federal courts and state courts. Both the federal and state court systems consist of several levels, or tiers, of courts. *Trial courts*, in which evidence is presented and testimony given, are on the bottom tier (which also includes lower courts that handle specialized issues). Decisions from a trial court can be appealed to a higher court, which commonly is an intermediate *court of appeals*, or an *appellate court*. Decisions from these intermediate courts of appeals may be appealed to an even higher court, such as a state supreme court or the United States Supreme Court.

State Court Decisions Most state trial court decisions are not published in books (except in New

York and a few other states, which publish selected trial court opinions). Decisions from state trial courts are typically filed in the office of the clerk of the court, where the decisions are available for public inspection. Written decisions of the appellate, or reviewing, courts, however, are published and distributed (both in print and via the Internet). As you will note, most of the state court cases presented in this book are from state appellate courts. The reported appellate decisions are published in volumes called *reports* or *reporters*, which are numbered consecutively. State appellate court decisions are found in the state reporters of that particular state. Official reports are volumes that are published by the state, whereas unofficial reports are privately published.

Regional Reporters. State court opinions appear in regional units of the National Reporter System, published by West Group. Most lawyers and libraries have the West reporters because they report cases more quickly, and are distributed more widely, than the state-published reporters. In fact, many states have eliminated their own reporters in favor of West's National Reporter System. The National Reporter System divides the states into the following geographic areas: *Atlantic* (A. or A.2d), *North Eastern* (N.E. or N.E.2d), *North Western* (N.W. or N.W.2d), *Pacific* (P., P.2d, or P.3d), *South Eastern* (S.E. or S.E.2d), *South Western* (S.W., S.W.2d, or S.W.3d), and *Southern* (So. or So.2d). (The *2d* and *3d* in the preceding abbreviations refer to *Second Series* and *Third Series*, respectively.) The states included in each of these regional divisions are indicated in Exhibit 1–4, which illustrates West's National Reporter System.

Case Citations. After appellate decisions have been published, they are normally referred to (cited) by the name of the case; the volume, name, and page number of the state's official reporter (if different from West's National Reporter System); the volume, name, and page number of the National Reporter; and the volume, name, and page number of any other selected reporter. (Citing a reporter by volume number, name, and page number, in that order, is common to all citations; often, as in this book, the year the decision was issued will be included in parentheses, just after the citations to reporters.) When more than one reporter is cited for the same case, each reference is called a *parallel citation*.

Note that some states have adopted a "public domain citation system" that uses a somewhat different format for the citation. For example, in Wisconsin, a Wisconsin Supreme Court decision might be designated "2008 WI 40," meaning that the case was decided in the year 2008 by the Wisconsin Supreme Court and was the fortieth decision issued by that court during that year. Parallel citations to the *Wisconsin Reports* and West's *North Western Reporter* are still included after the public domain citation.

Consider the following case citation: *Ramirez v. Health Net of Northeast, Inc.*, 285 Conn. 1, 938 A.2d 576 (2008). We see that the opinion in this case can be found in Volume 285 of the official *Connecticut Reports*, which reports only the decisions of the Supreme Court of Connecticut, on page 1. The parallel citation is to Volume 938 of the *Atlantic Reporter, Second Series*, page 576. In presenting opinions in this text, in addition to the reporter, we give the name of the court hearing the case and the year of the court's decision. Sample citations to state court decisions are explained in Exhibit 1–5 on pages 18–20.

Federal Court Decisions Federal district (trial) court decisions are published unofficially in West's *Federal Supplement* (F.Supp. or F.Supp.2d), and opinions from the circuit courts of appeals (reviewing courts) are reported unofficially in West's *Federal Reporter* (F., F.2d, or F.3d). Cases concerning federal bankruptcy law are published unofficially in West's *Bankruptcy Reporter* (Bankr. or B.R.).

The official edition of the United States Supreme Court decisions is the *United States Reports* (U.S.), which is published by the federal government. Unofficial editions of Supreme Court cases include West's *Supreme Court Reporter* (S.Ct.) and the *Lawyers' Edition of the Supreme Court Reports* (L.Ed. or L.Ed.2d). Sample citations for federal court decisions are also listed and explained in Exhibit 1–5.

Unpublished Opinions Many court opinions that are not yet published or that are not intended for publication can be accessed through Westlaw® (abbreviated in citations as "WL"), an online legal database maintained by West Group. When no citation to a published reporter is available for cases cited in this text, we give the WL citation (see Exhibit 1–5 for an example). Can a court consider unpublished decisions as persuasive precedent? See this chapter's *Insight into E-Commerce* feature on pages 22 and 23 for a discussion of this issue.

Old Case Law On a few occasions, this text cites opinions from old, classic cases dating to the nineteenth century or earlier; some of these are from the

EXHIBIT 1–4 • West's National Reporter System—Regional/Federal

Regional Reporters	Coverage Beginning	Coverage
Atlantic Reporter (A. or A.2d)	1885	Connecticut, Delaware, District of Columbia, Maine, Maryland, New Hampshire, New Jersey, Pennsylvania, Rhode Island, and Vermont.
North Eastern Reporter (N.E. or N.E.2d)	1885	Illinois, Indiana, Massachusetts, New York, and Ohio.
North Western Reporter (N.W. or N.W.2d)	1879	Iowa, Michigan, Minnesota, Nebraska, North Dakota, South Dakota, and Wisconsin.
Pacific Reporter (P., P.2d, or P.3d)	1883	Alaska, Arizona, California, Colorado, Hawaii, Idaho, Kansas, Montana, Nevada, New Mexico, Oklahoma, Oregon, Utah, Washington, and Wyoming.
South Eastern Reporter (S.E. or S.E.2d)	1887	Georgia, North Carolina, South Carolina, Virginia, and West Virginia.
South Western Reporter (S.W., S.W.2d, or S.W.3d)	1886	Arkansas, Kentucky, Missouri, Tennessee, and Texas.
Southern Reporter (So. or So.2d)	1887	Alabama, Florida, Louisiana, and Mississippi.
Federal Reporters		
Federal Reporter (F., F.2d, or F.3d)	1880	U.S. Circuit Courts from 1880 to 1912; U.S. Commerce Court from 1911 to 1913; U.S. District Courts from 1880 to 1932; U.S. Court of Claims (now called U.S. Court of Federal Claims) from 1929 to 1932 and since 1960; U.S. Courts of Appeals since 1891; U.S. Court of Customs and Patent Appeals since 1929; U.S. Emergency Court of Appeals since 1943.
Federal Supplement (F.Supp. or F.Supp.2d)	1932	U.S. Court of Claims from 1932 to 1960; U.S. District Courts since 1932; U.S. Customs Court since 1956.
Federal Rules Decisions (F.R.D.)	1939	U.S. District Courts involving the Federal Rules of Civil Procedure since 1939 and Federal Rules of Criminal Procedure since 1946.
Supreme Court Reporter (S.Ct.)	1882	United States Supreme Court since the October term of 1882.
Bankruptcy Reporter (Bankr.)	1980	Bankruptcy decisions of U.S. Bankruptcy Courts, U.S. District Courts, U.S. Courts of Appeals, and the United States Supreme Court.
Military Justice Reporter (M.J.)	1978	U.S. Court of Military Appeals and Courts of Military Review for the Army, Navy, Air Force, and Coast Guard.

NATIONAL REPORTER SYSTEM MAP

Pacific
North Western
South Western
North Eastern
Atlantic
South Eastern
Southern

EXHIBIT 1–5 • How to Read Citations

STATE COURTS

274 Neb. 796, 743 N.W.2d 632 (2008)[a]

N.W. is the abbreviation for West's publication of state court decisions rendered in the *North Western Reporter* of the National Reporter System. *2d* indicates that this case was included in the *Second Series* of that reporter. The number 743 refers to the volume number of the reporter; the number 632 refers to the page in that volume on which this case begins.

Neb. is an abbreviation for *Nebraska Reports,* Nebraska's official reports of the decisions of its highest court, the Nebraska Supreme Court.

159 Cal.App.4th 1114, 72 Cal.Rptr.3d 81 (2008)

Cal.Rptr. is the abbreviation for West's unofficial reports—titled *California Reporter*—of the decisions of California courts.

8 N.Y.3d 422, 867 N.E.2d 381, 835 N.Y.S.2d 530 (2007)

N.Y.S. is the abbreviation for West's unofficial reports—titled *New York Supplement*—of the decisions of New York courts.

N.Y. is the abbreviation for *New York Reports,* New York's official reports of the decisions of its court of appeals. The New York Court of Appeals is the state's highest court, analogous to other states' supreme courts. In New York, a supreme court is a trial court.

___ Ga.App. ___, 656 S.E.2d 222 (2008)

Ga.App. is the abbreviation for *Georgia Appeals Reports,* Georgia's official reports of the decisions of its court of appeals. The blank lines in this citation (or any other citation) will be filled in once the appropriate volume of the case reporter is printed and a page number becomes available.

FEDERAL COURTS

___ U.S. ___, 127 S.Ct. 1513, 167 L.Ed.2d 422 (2007)

L.Ed. is an abbreviation for *Lawyers' Edition of the Supreme Court Reports,* an unofficial edition of decisions of the United States Supreme Court.

S.Ct. is the abbreviation for West's unofficial reports—titled *Supreme Court Reporter*—of decisions of the United States Supreme Court.

U.S. is the abbreviation for *United States Reports,* the official edition of the decisions of the United States Supreme Court. The blank lines indicate that the volume has not yet been published and no page number is yet assigned.

a. The case names have been deleted from these citations to emphasize the publications. It should be kept in mind, however, that the name of a case is as important as the specific page numbers in the volumes in which it is found. If a citation is incorrect, the correct citation may be found in a publication's index of case names. In addition to providing a check on errors in citations, the date of a case is important because the value of a recent case as an authority is likely to be greater than that of older cases.

EXHIBIT 1–5 • How to Read Citations—Continued

FEDERAL COURTS (Continued)

512 F.3d 582 (9th Cir. 2008)

9th Cir. is an abbreviation denoting that this case was decided in the U.S. Court of Appeals for the Ninth Circuit.

478 F.Supp.2d 496 (S.D.N.Y. 2007)

S.D.N.Y. is an abbreviation indicating that the U.S. District Court for the Southern District of New York decided this case.

ENGLISH COURTS

9 Exch. 341, 156 Eng.Rep. 145 (1854)

Eng.Rep. is an abbreviation for *English Reports, Full Reprint,* a series of reports containing selected decisions made in English courts between 1378 and 1865.

Exch. is an abbreviation for *English Exchequer Reports*, which includes the original reports of cases decided in England's Court of Exchequer.

STATUTORY AND OTHER CITATIONS

18 U.S.C. Section 1961(1)(A)

U.S.C. denotes *United States Code*, the codification of *United States Statutes at Large.* The number 18 refers to the statute's U.S.C. title number and 1961 to its section number within that title. The number 1 in parentheses refers to a subsection within the section, and the letter A in parentheses to a subdivision within the subsection.

UCC 2–206(1)(b)

UCC is an abbreviation for *Uniform Commercial Code.* The first number 2 is a reference to an article of the UCC, and 206 to a section within that article. The number 1 in parentheses refers to a subsection within the section, and the letter b in parentheses to a subdivision within the subsection.

***Restatement (Second) of Torts,* Section 568**

Restatement (Second) of Torts refers to the second edition of the American Law Institute's *Restatement of the Law of Torts.* The number 568 refers to a specific section.

17 C.F.R. Section 230.505

C.F.R. is an abbreviation for *Code of Federal Regulations*, a compilation of federal administrative regulations. The number 17 designates the regulation's title number, and 230.505 designates a specific section within that title.

EXHIBIT CONTINUES

EXHIBIT 1–5 • How to Read Citations—Continued

Westlaw® Citations[b]

2008 WL 427478

WL is an abbreviation for Westlaw. The number 2008 is the year of the document that can be found with this citation in the Westlaw database. The number 427478 is a number assigned to a specific document. A higher number indicates that a document was added to the Westlaw database later in the year.

Uniform Resource Locators (URLs)

http://www.westlaw.com[c]

The suffix *com* is the top level domain (TLD) for this Web site. The TLD *com* is an abbreviation for "commercial," which usually means that a for-profit entity hosts (maintains or supports) this Web site.

westlaw is the host name—the part of the domain name selected by the organization that registered the name. In this case, West Group registered the name. This Internet site is the Westlaw database on the Web.

www is an abbreviation for "World Wide Web." The Web is a system of Internet servers that support documents formatted in *HTML* (hypertext markup language). HTML supports links to text, graphics, and audio and video files.

http://www.uscourts.gov

This is "The Federal Judiciary Home Page." The host is the Administrative Office of the U.S. Courts. The TLD *gov* is an abbreviation for "government." This Web site includes information and links from, and about, the federal courts.

http://www.law.cornell.edu/index.html

This part of a URL points to a Web page or file at a specific location within the host's domain. This page is a menu with links to documents within the domain and to other Internet resources.

This is the host name for a Web site that contains the Internet publications of the Legal Information Institute (LII), which is a part of Cornell Law School. The LII site includes a variety of legal materials and links to other legal resources on the Internet. The TLD *edu* is an abbreviation for "educational institution" (a school or a university).

http://www.ipl.org/div/news

This part of the Web site points to a static *news* page at this Web site, which provides links to online newspapers from around the world.

div is an abbreviation for "division," which is the way that the Internet Public Library tags the content on its Web site as relating to a specific topic.

ipl is an abbreviation for "Internet Public Library," which is an online service that provides reference resources and links to other information services on the Web. The IPL is supported chiefly by the School of Information at the University of Michigan. The TLD *org* is an abbreviation for "organization" (normally nonprofit).

b. Many court decisions that are not yet published or that are not intended for publication can be accessed through Westlaw®, an online legal database.

c. The basic form for a URL is "service://hostname/path." The Internet service for all of the URLs in this text is *http* (hypertext transfer protocol). Because most Web browsers add this prefix automatically when a user enters a host name or a hostname/path, we have omitted the http:// from the URLs listed in this text.

English courts. The citations to these cases may not conform to the descriptions given above because the reporters in which they were published were often known by the names of the persons who compiled the reporters and have since been replaced.

How to Read and Understand Case Law

The decisions made by the courts establish the boundaries of the law as it applies to virtually all business relationships. It thus is essential that businesspersons know how to read and understand case law. The cases that we present in this text have been condensed from the full text of the courts' opinions and are presented in a special format. In approximately two-thirds of the cases, we have summarized the background and facts, as well as the court's decision and remedy, in our own words and have included only selected portions of the court's opinion ("in the language of the court"). In the remaining one-third of the cases, we have provided a longer excerpt from the court's opinion without summarizing the background and facts or decision and remedy. For those who wish to review court cases as part of research projects or to gain additional legal information, the following sections will provide useful insights into how to read and understand case law.

Case Titles

The title of a case, such as *Adams v. Jones*, indicates the names of the parties to the lawsuit. The *v.* in the case title stands for *versus*, which means "against." In the trial court, Adams was the plaintiff—the person who filed the suit. Jones was the defendant. If the case is appealed, however, the appellate court will sometimes place the name of the party appealing the decision first, so the case may be called *Jones v. Adams* if Jones is appealing. Because some appellate courts retain the trial court order of names, it is often impossible to distinguish the plaintiff from the defendant in the title of a reported appellate court decision. You must carefully read the facts of each case to identify the parties. Otherwise, the discussion by the appellate court may be difficult to understand.

Terminology

The following terms, phrases, and abbreviations are frequently encountered in court opinions and legal publications. Because it is important to understand what is meant by these terms, phrases, and abbreviations, we define and discuss them here.

Parties to Lawsuits As mentioned previously, the party initiating a lawsuit is referred to as the *plaintiff* or *petitioner*, depending on the nature of the action, and the party against whom a lawsuit is brought is the *defendant* or *respondent*. Lawsuits frequently involve more than one plaintiff and/or defendant. When a case is appealed from the original court or jurisdiction to another court or jurisdiction, the party appealing the case is called the **appellant.** The **appellee** is the party against whom the appeal is taken. (In some appellate courts, the party appealing a case is referred to as the *petitioner*, and the party against whom the suit is brought or appealed is called the *respondent*.)

Judges and Justices The terms *judge* and *justice* are usually synonymous and represent two designations given to judges in various courts. All members of the United States Supreme Court, for example, are referred to as justices, and justice is the formal title often given to judges of appellate courts, although this is not always the case. In New York, a *justice* is a judge of the trial court (which is called the Supreme Court), and a member of the Court of Appeals (the state's highest court) is called a *judge*. The term *justice* is commonly abbreviated to J., and *justices* to JJ. A Supreme Court case might refer to Justice Alito as Alito, J., or to Chief Justice Roberts as Roberts, C.J.

Decisions and Opinions Most decisions reached by reviewing, or appellate, courts are explained in written **opinions.** The opinion contains the court's reasons for its decision, the rules of law that apply, and the judgment.

Unanimous, Concurring, and Dissenting Opinions. When all judges or justices unanimously agree on an opinion, the opinion is written for the entire court and can be deemed a *unanimous opinion*. When there is not a unanimous opinion, a *majority opinion* is written; the majority opinion outlines the

INSIGHT INTO E-COMMERCE
How the Internet Is Expanding Precedent

The notion that courts should rely on precedents to decide the outcome of similar cases has long been a cornerstone of U.S. law. Nevertheless, the availability of "unpublished opinions" over the Internet is changing what the law considers to be precedent. An *unpublished opinion* is a decision made by an appellate court that is not intended for publication in a reporter (the bound books that contain court opinions).[a] Courts traditionally have not considered unpublished opinions to be "precedent," binding or persuasive, and attorneys were often not allowed to refer to these decisions in their arguments.

An Increasing Number of Decisions Are Not Published in Case Reporters but Are Available Online

The number of court decisions not published in printed books has risen dramatically in recent years. By some estimates, nearly 80 percent of the decisions of the federal appellate courts are unpublished. The number is equally high in some state court systems. California's intermediate appellate courts, for example, publish only about 7 percent of their decisions.

Even though certain decisions are not intended for publication, they are posted ("published") almost immediately on online legal databases, such as Westlaw and Lexis. With the proliferation of free legal databases and court Web sites, the general public also has almost instant access to the unpublished decisions of most courts. This situation has caused a substantial amount of debate over whether unpublished opinions should be given the same precedential effect as published opinions.

Should Unpublished Decisions Establish Precedent?

Prior to the Internet, one might have been able to justify not considering unpublished decisions to be precedent on the grounds of fairness. How could courts and lawyers be expected to consider the reasoning in unpublished decisions if they were not printed in the case reporters? Now that opinions are so readily available on the Web, however, this justification is no longer valid. Moreover, it now seems unfair not to consider these decisions as

a. Recently decided cases that are not yet published are also sometimes called *unpublished opinions,* but because these decisions will eventually be printed in reporters, we do not include them here.

view supported by the majority of the judges or justices deciding the case. If a judge agrees, or concurs, with the majority's decision, but for different reasons, that judge may write a *concurring opinion.* A *dissenting opinion* presents the views of one or more judges who disagree with the majority's decision. The dissenting opinion is important because it may form the basis of the arguments used years later in overruling the precedential majority opinion.

Other Types of Opinions. Occasionally, a court issues a *per curiam* opinion. *Per curiam* is a Latin phrase meaning "of the court." In *per curiam* opinions, there is no indication as to which judge or justice authored the opinion. This term may also be used for an announcement of a court's disposition of a case that is not accompanied by a written opinion. Some of the cases presented in this text are *en banc* decisions. When an appellate court reviews a case *en banc,* which is a French term (derived from a Latin term) for "in the bench," generally all of the judges "sitting on the bench" of that court review the case.

A Sample Court Case

To illustrate the elements in a court opinion, we present an annotated opinion in Exhibit 1–6 on pages 24–26. The opinion is from an actual case that the United States Court of Appeals for the Ninth Circuit decided in 2008.

Background of the Case The Seattle Center is an entertainment "zone" near downtown Seattle, Washington, that attracts almost ten million tourists every year. The center encompasses theaters, arenas, museums, exhibition halls, conference rooms, outdoor stadiums, and restaurants. Street performers add to the festive atmosphere. Under the authority of the city, the center's director issued rules to address safety concerns and other matters. Staff at the Seattle Center

precedent to some extent because they are so publicly accessible.

Another argument against allowing unpublished decisions to be precedent concerns the quality of the legal reasoning set forth in these decisions. Staff attorneys and law clerks frequently write unpublished opinions so that judges can spend more time on the opinions intended for publication. Consequently, some claim that allowing unpublished decisions to establish precedent could result in bad precedents because the reasoning may not be up to par. If the decision is regarded merely as persuasive precedent, however, then judges who disagree with the reasoning are free to reject the conclusion.

The United States Supreme Court Changes Federal Rules on Unpublished Opinions after 2007

In spite of objections from several hundred judges and lawyers, the United States Supreme Court made history in 2006 when it announced that it would allow lawyers to refer to (cite) unpublished decisions in all federal courts. The new rule, Rule 32.1 of the Federal Rules of Appellate Procedure, states that federal courts may not prohibit or restrict the citation of federal judicial opinions that have been designated as "not for publication," "non-precedential," or "not precedent." The rule applies only to federal courts and only to unpublished opinions issued after January 1, 2007. It does not specify the effect that a court must give to one of its unpublished opinions or to an unpublished opinion from another court. Basically, the rule simply makes all the federal courts follow a uniform rule that allows attorneys to cite—and judges to consider as persuasive precedent—unpublished decisions beginning in 2007.

The impact of this new rule remains to be seen. At present, the majority of states do not allow their state courts to consider the rulings in unpublished cases as persuasive precedent, and this rule does not affect the states. The Supreme Court's decision, however, provides an example of how technology—the availability of unpublished opinions over the Internet—has affected the law.

CRITICAL THINKING

INSIGHT INTO THE SOCIAL ENVIRONMENT

Now that the Supreme Court is allowing unpublished decisions to form persuasive precedent in federal courts, should state courts follow? Why or why not?

cited one of the street performers, a balloon artist, for several rule violations. The artist filed a suit in a federal district court against the city and others, alleging that the rules violated his rights under the U.S. Constitution. The court issued a judgment in the plaintiff's favor. The city appealed to the United States Court of Appeals for the Ninth Circuit.

Editorial Practice You will note that triple asterisks (* * *) and quadruple asterisks (* * * *) frequently appear in the opinion. The triple asterisks indicate that we have deleted a few words or sentences from the opinion for the sake of readability or brevity. Quadruple asterisks mean that an entire paragraph (or more) has been omitted. Additionally, when the opinion cites another case or legal source, the citation to the case or other source has been omitted to save space and to improve the flow of the text. These editorial practices are continued in the other court opinions presented in this book. In addition, whenever we present a court opinion that includes a term or phrase that may not be readily understandable, a bracketed definition or paraphrase has been added.

Briefing Cases Knowing how to read and understand court opinions and the legal reasoning used by the courts is an essential step in undertaking accurate legal research. A further step is "briefing," or summarizing, the case. Legal researchers routinely brief cases by reducing the texts of the opinions to their essential elements. Generally, when you brief a case, you first summarize the background and facts of the case, as the authors have done for the cases presented within this text. You then indicate the issue (or issues) before the court. An important element in the case brief is, of course, the court's decision on the issue and the legal reasoning used by the court in reaching that decision. Detailed instructions on how to brief a case are given in Appendix A, which also includes a briefed version of the sample court case presented in Exhibit 1–6.

EXHIBIT 1–6 • A Sample Court Case—Continued

city's interests, and also contends that the rule does not match the city's asserted aims to reduce territorial disputes among performers, deter patron harassment, and facilitate the identification and apprehension of offending performers.

As a general matter, it is clear that a State's interest in protecting the safety and convenience of persons using a public forum is a valid governmental objective. Here, * * * the Seattle Center authorities enacted the permit requirement after encountering "chronic" territorial disputes between performers and threats to public citizens by street performers. [A city employee stated that]

> Before the performer rules went into effect * * * there were approximately 3 or 4 complaints by performers against other performers per week. If Magic Mike [Berger] was here, we could expect one or more from him. * * * The general complaints by performers against other performers would be 'that is my spot and he can't be there' and/or 'that performer is doing what I am doing and they won't move.'
>
> The general complaints by the tenants against performers usually concerned too much noise or blocking access.

These complaints show that street performances posed a threat to the city's interests in maintaining order in the Seattle Center and providing harassment-free facilities. We are satisfied that the city's permit scheme was designed to further valid governmental objectives.

* * * *

In the final major section of this excerpt of the opinion, the court states its decision and gives its order.

V

In sum, [the] Rules * * * satisfy the requirements for valid restrictions on expression under the First Amendment. Such content neutral and narrowly tailored rules * * * must be upheld.

The order granting summary judgment to Berger is REVERSED. The case is **REMANDED** to the district court for further proceedings consistent with this opinion.

Sent back.

REVIEWING Business and Its Legal Environment

Suppose the California legislature passes a law that severely restricts carbon dioxide emissions from automobiles in that state. A group of automobile manufacturers files suit against the state of California to prevent the enforcement of the law. The automakers claim that a federal law already sets fuel economy standards nationwide and that fuel economy standards are essentially the same as carbon dioxide emission standards. According to the automobile manufacturers, it is unfair to allow California to impose more stringent regulations than those set by the federal law. Using the information presented in the chapter, answer the following questions.

1. Who are the parties (the plaintiffs and the defendant) in this lawsuit?
2. Are the plaintiffs seeking a legal remedy or an equitable remedy? Why?
3. What is the primary source of the law that is at issue here?
4. Where would you look to find the relevant California and federal laws?

TERMS AND CONCEPTS

QUESTIONS AND CASE PROBLEMS

1–1. How does statutory law come into existence? How does it differ from the common law? If statutory law conflicts with the common law, which law will govern?

1–2. QUESTION WITH SAMPLE ANSWER

After World War II, which ended in 1945, an international tribunal of judges convened at Nuremberg, Germany. The judges convicted several Nazis of "crimes against humanity." Assuming that the Nazi war criminals who were convicted had not disobeyed any law of their country and had merely been following their government's (Hitler's) orders, what law had they violated? Explain.

- **For a sample answer to Question 1–2, go to Appendix I at the end of this text.**

1–3. Assume that you want to read the entire court opinion in the case of *Menashe v. V Secret Catalogue, Inc.*, 409 F.Supp.2d 412 (S.D.N.Y. 2006). The case focuses on whether "SEXY LITTLE THINGS" is a suggestive or descriptive trademark and on which of the parties to the suit used the mark first in commerce. (Note that this case is presented in Chapter 14 of this text as Case 14.2.) Refer to the subsection entitled "Finding Case Law" in this chapter, and then explain specifically where you would find the court's opinion.

1–4. This chapter discussed a number of sources of American law. Which source of law takes priority in the following situations, and why?

(a) A federal statute conflicts with the U.S. Constitution.
(b) A federal statute conflicts with a state constitutional provision.
(c) A state statute conflicts with the common law of that state.
(d) A state constitutional amendment conflicts with the U.S. Constitution.

1–5. In the text of this chapter, we stated that the doctrine of *stare decisis* "became a cornerstone of the English and American judicial systems." What does *stare decisis* mean, and why has this doctrine been so fundamental to the development of our legal tradition?

1–6. What is the difference between a concurring opinion and a majority opinion? Between a concurring opinion and a dissenting opinion? Why do judges and justices write concurring and dissenting opinions, given that these opinions will not affect the outcome of the case at hand, which has already been decided by majority vote?

1–7. Courts can overturn precedents and thus change the common law. Should judges have the same authority to overrule statutory law? Explain.

1–8. "The judge's role is not to make the law but to uphold and apply the law." Do you agree or disagree with this statement? Discuss fully the reasons for your answer.

1–9. Assume that Arthur Rabe is suing Xavier Sanchez for breaching a contract in which Sanchez promised to sell Rabe a Van Gogh painting for $3 million.

(a) In this lawsuit, who is the plaintiff and who is the defendant?
(b) Suppose that Rabe wants Sanchez to perform the contract as promised. What remedy would Rabe seek from the court?
(c) Now suppose that Rabe wants to cancel the contract because Sanchez fraudulently misrepresented the painting as an original Van Gogh when in fact it is a copy. What remedy would Rabe seek?
(d) Will the remedy Rabe seeks in either situation be a remedy at law or a remedy in equity? What is the difference between legal and equitable remedies?
(e) Suppose that the trial court finds in Rabe's favor and grants one of these remedies. Sanchez then appeals the decision to a higher court. On appeal, which party will be the appellant (or petitioner), and which party will be the appellee (or respondent)?

1–10. A QUESTION OF ETHICS

*On July 5, 1884, Dudley, Stephens, and Brooks—"all able-bodied English seamen"—and a teenage English boy were cast adrift in a lifeboat following a storm at sea. They had no water with them in the boat, and all they had for sustenance were two one-pound tins of turnips. On July 24, Dudley proposed that one of the four in the lifeboat be sacrificed to save the others. Stephens agreed with Dudley, but Brooks refused to consent—and the boy was never asked for his opinion. On July 25, Dudley killed the boy, and the three men then fed on the boy's body and blood. Four days later, a passing vessel rescued the men. They were taken to England and tried for the murder of the boy. If the men had not fed on the boy's body, they would probably have died of starvation within the four-day period. The boy, who was in a much weaker condition, would likely have died before the rest. [*Regina v. Dudley and Stephens, *14 Q.B.D. (Queen's Bench Division, England) 273 (1884)]*

(a) The basic question in this case is whether the survivors should be subject to penalties under English criminal law, given the men's unusual circumstances. Were the defendants' actions necessary but unethical? Explain your reasoning. What ethical issues might be involved here?
(b) Should judges ever have the power to look beyond the written "letter of the law" in making their decisions? Why or why not?

LAW ON THE WEB

Today, business law and legal environment professors and students can go online to access information on almost every topic covered in this text. A good point of departure for online legal research is the Web site for *The Legal Environment of Business*, Seventh Edition, which can be found at **academic.cengage.com/blaw/cross**. There you will find numerous materials relevant to this text and to business law generally, including links to various legal resources on the Web. Additionally, every chapter in this text ends with a *Law on the Web* feature that contains selected Web addresses.

You can access many of the sources of law discussed in Chapter 1 at the FindLaw Web site, which is probably the most comprehensive source of free legal information on the Internet. Go to

www.findlaw.com

The Legal Information Institute (LII) at Cornell Law School, which offers extensive information about U.S. law, is also a good starting point for legal research. The URL for this site is

www.law.cornell.edu

The Library of Congress offers extensive links to state and federal government resources at

www.loc.gov

The Virtual Law Library Index, created and maintained by the Indiana University School of Law, provides an index of legal sources categorized by subject at

www.law.indiana.edu/v-lib/index.html#libdoc

Legal Research Exercises on the Web

Go to **academic.cengage.com/blaw/cross**, the Web site that accompanies this text. Select "Chapter 1" and click on "Internet Exercises." There you will find the following Internet research exercises that you can perform to learn more about some of the important sources of law discussed in Chapter 1 and other useful legal sites on the Web.

Internet Exercise 1–1: Legal Perspective
Internet Sources of Law

Internet Exercise 1–2: Management Perspective
Online Assistance from Government Agencies

Internet Exercise 1–3: Social Perspective
The Case of the Speluncean Explorers

CHAPTER 2

The Court System

Today in the United States there are fifty-two court systems—one for each of the fifty states, one for the District of Columbia, and a federal system. Keep in mind that the federal courts are not superior to the state courts; they are simply an independent system of courts, which derives its authority from Article III, Section 2, of the U.S. Constitution. By the power given to it under Article I of the U.S. Constitution, Congress has extended the federal court system beyond the boundaries of the United States to U.S. territories such as Guam, Puerto Rico, and the Virgin Islands.[1] As we shall see, the United States Supreme Court is the final controlling voice over all of these fifty-two systems, at least when questions of federal law are involved.

Every businessperson will likely face a lawsuit at some time in his or her career. Thus, anyone involved in business needs to have an understanding of the American court systems, as well as the various methods of dispute resolution that can be pursued outside the courts. In this chapter, after examining the judiciary's role in the American governmental system, we discuss some basic requirements that must be met before a party may bring a lawsuit before a particular court. We then look at the court systems of the United States in some detail and follow a hypothetical civil case through a court. We will examine some alternative methods of settling disputes in Chapter 3.

1. In Guam and the Virgin Islands, territorial courts serve as both federal courts and state courts; in Puerto Rico, they serve only as federal courts.

The Judiciary's Role in American Government

As you learned in Chapter 1, the body of American law includes the federal and state constitutions, statutes passed by legislative bodies, administrative law, and the case decisions and legal principles that form the common law. These laws would be meaningless, however, without the courts to interpret and apply them. This is the essential role of the judiciary—the courts—in the American governmental system: to interpret the laws and apply them to specific situations.

As the branch of government entrusted with interpreting the laws, the judiciary can decide, among other things, whether the laws or actions of the other two branches are constitutional. The process for making such a determination is known as **judicial review.** The power of judicial review enables the judicial branch to act as a check on the other two branches of government, in line with the system of checks and balances established by the U.S. Constitution.[2]

The power of judicial review is not mentioned in the Constitution (although many constitutional scholars conclude that the founders intended the judiciary to have this power). Rather, this power was explicitly established by the United States Supreme Court in 1803 by its decision in *Marbury v. Madison*,[3] in which the Supreme Court stated, "It is emphatically the province and duty of the Judicial Department to say

2. In a broad sense, judicial review occurs whenever a court "reviews" a case or legal proceeding—as when an appellate court reviews a lower court's decision. When referring to the judiciary's role in American government, however, the term *judicial review* is used to indicate the power of the judiciary to decide whether the actions of the other two branches of government do or do not violate the U.S. Constitution.

3. 5 U.S. (1 Cranch) 137, 2 L.Ed. 60 (1803).

what the law is. . . . If two laws conflict with each other, the courts must decide on the operation of each. . . . So if the law be in opposition to the Constitution . . . [t]he Court must determine which of these conflicting rules governs the case. This is the very essence of judicial duty." Since the *Marbury v. Madison* decision, the power of judicial review has remained unchallenged. Today, this power is exercised by both federal and state courts.

Basic Judicial Requirements

Before a lawsuit can be brought before a court, certain requirements must be met. These requirements relate to jurisdiction, venue, and standing to sue. We examine each of these important concepts here.

Jurisdiction

In Latin, *juris* means "law," and *diction* means "to speak." Thus, "the power to speak the law" is the literal meaning of the term **jurisdiction.** Before any court can hear a case, it must have jurisdiction over the person (or company) against whom the suit is brought (the defendant) or over the property involved in the suit. The court must also have jurisdiction over the subject matter of the dispute.

Jurisdiction over Persons or Property

Generally, a particular court can exercise ***in personam* jurisdiction** (personal jurisdiction) over any person or business that resides in a certain geographic area. A state trial court, for example, normally has jurisdictional authority over residents (including businesses) of a particular area of the state, such as a county or district. A state's highest court (often called the state supreme court)[4] has jurisdictional authority over all residents within the state.

A court can also exercise jurisdiction over property that is located within its boundaries. This kind of jurisdiction is known as ***in rem* jurisdiction,** or "jurisdiction over the thing." For example, suppose that a dispute arises over the ownership of a boat in dry dock in Fort Lauderdale, Florida. The boat is owned by an Ohio resident, over whom a Florida court normally cannot exercise personal jurisdiction. The other party to the dispute is a resident of Nebraska. In this situation, a lawsuit concerning the boat could be brought in a Florida state court on the basis of the court's *in rem* jurisdiction.

Long Arm Statutes. Under the authority of a state **long arm statute,** a court can exercise personal jurisdiction over certain out-of-state defendants based on activities that took place within the state. Before a court can exercise jurisdiction over an out-of-state defendant under a long arm statute, though, it must be demonstrated that the defendant had sufficient contacts, or *minimum contacts,* with the state to justify the jurisdiction.[5] Generally, this means that the defendant must have enough of a connection to the state for the judge to conclude that it is fair for the state to exercise power over the defendant. For example, if an out-of-state defendant caused an automobile accident or sold defective goods within the state, a court will usually find that minimum contacts exist to exercise jurisdiction over that defendant. Similarly, a state may exercise personal jurisdiction over a nonresident defendant who is sued for breaching a contract that was formed within the state.

Corporate Contacts. Because corporations are considered legal persons, courts use the same principles to determine whether it is fair to exercise jurisdiction over a corporation.[6] A corporation normally is subject to personal jurisdiction in the state in which it is incorporated, has its principal office, and is doing business. Courts apply the minimum-contacts test to determine if they can exercise jurisdiction over out-of-state corporations.

The minimum-contacts requirement is usually met if the corporation advertises or sells its products within the state, or places its goods into the "stream of commerce" with the intent that the goods be sold in the state. For example, suppose that a business is incorporated under the laws of Maine but has a branch office and manufacturing plant in Georgia. The corporation also advertises and sells its products in Georgia. These activities would likely constitute sufficient contacts

4. As will be discussed shortly, a state's highest court is often referred to as the state supreme court, but there are exceptions. For example, in New York the supreme court is a trial court.

5. The minimum-contacts standard was first established in *International Shoe Co. v. State of Washington,* 326 U.S. 310, 66 S.Ct. 154, 90 L.Ed. 95 (1945).

6. In the eyes of the law, corporations are *legal persons*—entities that can sue and be sued. See Chapter 18.

with the state of Georgia to allow a Georgia court to exercise jurisdiction over the corporation.

Some corporations, however, do not sell or advertise products or place any goods in the stream of commerce. Determining what constitutes minimum contacts in these situations can be more difficult, as the following case—involving a resort hotel in Mexico and a hotel guest from New Jersey—illustrates.

CASE 2.1 Mastondrea v. Occidental Hotels Management S.A.

Superior Court of New Jersey, Appellate Division, 2007. 391 N.J.Super. 261, 918 A.2d 27.
lawlibrary.rutgers.edu/search.shtml[a]

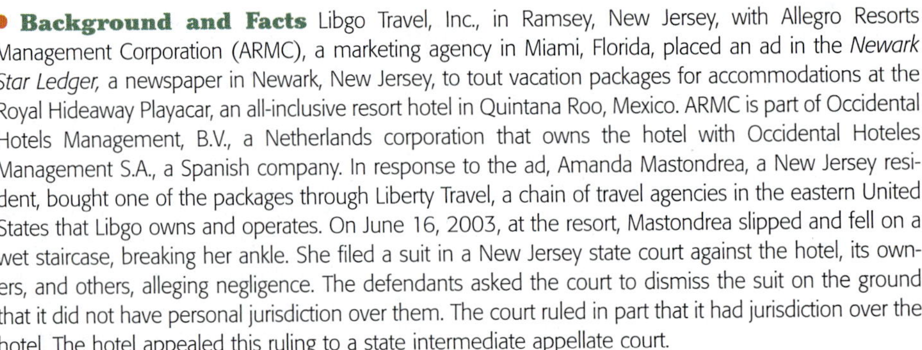

● **Background and Facts** Libgo Travel, Inc., in Ramsey, New Jersey, with Allegro Resorts Management Corporation (ARMC), a marketing agency in Miami, Florida, placed an ad in the *Newark Star Ledger,* a newspaper in Newark, New Jersey, to tout vacation packages for accommodations at the Royal Hideaway Playacar, an all-inclusive resort hotel in Quintana Roo, Mexico. ARMC is part of Occidental Hotels Management, B.V., a Netherlands corporation that owns the hotel with Occidental Hoteles Management S.A., a Spanish company. In response to the ad, Amanda Mastondrea, a New Jersey resident, bought one of the packages through Liberty Travel, a chain of travel agencies in the eastern United States that Libgo owns and operates. On June 16, 2003, at the resort, Mastondrea slipped and fell on a wet staircase, breaking her ankle. She filed a suit in a New Jersey state court against the hotel, its owners, and others, alleging negligence. The defendants asked the court to dismiss the suit on the ground that it did not have personal jurisdiction over them. The court ruled in part that it had jurisdiction over the hotel. The hotel appealed this ruling to a state intermediate appellate court.

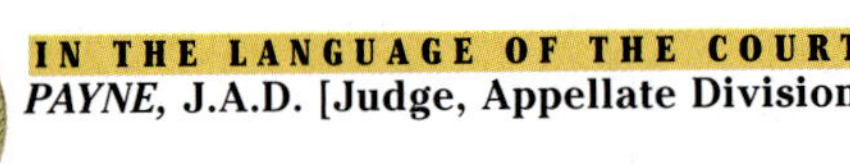

IN THE LANGUAGE OF THE COURT
***PAYNE,* J.A.D. [Judge, Appellate Division]**

* * * *

It is unquestionably true that the Hotel has no direct presence in New Jersey. * * * The Hotel's operations are located in Quintana Roo, Mexico. The Hotel is not registered, licensed or otherwise authorized to do business in New Jersey. It has no registered agent in this state for service of process, and it pays no state taxes. The Hotel maintains no business address here, it has never owned property or maintained any bank accounts in this state, and it has no employees in New Jersey.

However, * * * "Tour Operator Agreements" between the Hotel and Libgo * * * provide that the Hotel will allot a specific number of rooms at its resort to Libgo at agreed-upon rates. Libgo, as "tour operator," is then authorized by the Hotel to book those rooms on behalf of Libgo's customers. Pursuant to the contract, Libgo is required to provide the Hotel with weekly sales reports listing the number of rooms booked by Libgo and the rates at which those rooms were booked. It must also confirm all reservations in a writing sent to the Hotel.

Courts have generally sustained the exercise of personal jurisdiction over a defendant who, as a party to a contract, has had some connection with the forum state [the state in which the lawsuit is filed] or who should have anticipated that his conduct would have significant effects in that state. Here, the Hotel entered into a contract with a New Jersey entity, Libgo, which agreed to solicit business for the Hotel and derived a profit from that solicitation through sales of vacation packages. Although Libgo's business extends beyond New Jersey and throughout much of the East Coast, at least part of its customer base resides in this state. Likewise, as a result of this contract, the Hotel purposefully and successfully sought vacationers from New Jersey, and it derived a profit from them. Therefore, the Hotel should have reasonably anticipated that its conduct would have significant effects in New Jersey. [Emphasis added.]

* * * *

a. In the "SEARCH THE N.J. COURTS DECISIONS" section, type "Mastondrea" in the box, and click on "Search!" In the result, click on the case name to access the opinion. Rutgers University Law School in Camden, New Jersey, maintains this Web site.

CASE 2.1 CONTINUED

* * * Additional evidence of purposeful acts in New Jersey exists that fairly can be attributed to the Hotel and that are causally connected to plaintiff's decision to purchase the Hotel's vacation package * * * , [including] an ongoing, but undefined, relationship between the Hotel and * * * ARMC * * * . ARMC is a marketing organization that solicits business in the United States for the "Occidental Hotels & Resorts," a group of which the defendant Hotel is a part. ARMC does not have any direct contact with any of the potential customers of the various hotels that it promotes, and it does not itself sell travel or vacation packages. However, [ARMC] * * * works closely with Libgo in developing marketing strategies for the Occidental Hotels & Resorts in the New Jersey area pursuant to cooperative marketing agreements between ARMC and Libgo.

* * * *

* * * The defendant Hotel was featured, singly, [in 2003] in advertisements in the *Newark Star Ledger* on four occasions, including one in January * * * , prior to plaintiff's decision to book a vacation there.

We are satisfied * * * that * * * ARMC was operating [on behalf] of the Hotel when ARMC entered into cooperative marketing agreements with Libgo, and that ARMC's extensive contacts with Libgo in New Jersey regarding the marketing plan, together with the New Jersey fruits of that plan, can be attributed to the Hotel for jurisdictional purposes.

We are further persuaded that the *targeted advertising conducted pursuant to the cooperative marketing agreement on behalf of the Hotel provided the minimum contacts necessary to support * * * jurisdiction in this case.* [Emphasis added.]

- **Decision and Remedy** *The state intermediate appellate court affirmed the lower court's ruling. The appellate court concluded that the hotel had contacts with New Jersey, consisting of a tour operator contract and marketing activities through ARMC and Libgo, during the relevant time period and that, in response to the marketing, Mastondrea booked a vacation at the hotel. "[T]his evidence was sufficient to support the assertion of . . . personal jurisdiction over the Hotel in this State."*

- **What If the Facts Were Different?** *If Mastondrea had not seen Libgo and Allegro's ad, but had bought a Royal Hideaway vacation package on the recommendation of a Liberty Travel agent, is it likely that the result in this case would have been different? Why or why not?*

- **The Global Dimension** *What do the circumstances and the holding in this case suggest to a business firm that actively attempts to attract customers in a variety of jurisdictions?*

Jurisdiction over Subject Matter Subject-matter jurisdiction refers to the limitations on the types of cases a court can hear. Certain courts are empowered to hear certain kinds of disputes.

General and Limited Jurisdiction. In both the federal and the state court systems, there are courts of *general* (unlimited) *jurisdiction* and courts of *limited jurisdiction.* A court of general jurisdiction can decide cases involving a broad array of issues. An example of a court of general jurisdiction is a state trial court or a federal district court. An example of a state court of limited jurisdiction is a probate court. **Probate courts** are state courts that handle only matters relating to the transfer of a person's assets and obligations after that person's death, including issues relating to the custody and guardianship of children. An example of a federal court of limited subject-matter jurisdiction is a bankruptcy court. **Bankruptcy courts** handle only bankruptcy proceedings, which are governed by federal bankruptcy law (discussed in Chapter 15).

A court's jurisdiction over subject matter is usually defined in the statute or constitution creating the court. In both the federal and the state court systems, a court's subject-matter jurisdiction can be limited not only by the subject of the lawsuit but also by the sum in controversy, whether the case is a felony (a more serious type of crime) or a misdemeanor (a less serious type of crime), or whether the proceeding is a trial or an appeal.

Original and Appellate Jurisdiction. A court's subject-matter jurisdiction is also frequently limited to hearing cases at a particular stage of the dispute. Courts in which lawsuits begin, trials take place, and evidence is presented are referred to as *courts of* *original jurisdiction.* Courts having original jurisdiction are courts of the first instance, or trial courts. In the federal court system, the *district courts* are trial courts. In the various state court systems, the trial courts are known by different names, as will be discussed shortly.

Courts having appellate jurisdiction act as reviewing courts, or appellate courts. In general, cases can be brought before appellate courts only on appeal from an order or a judgment of a trial court or other lower court. In other words, the distinction between courts of original jurisdiction and courts of appellate jurisdiction normally lies in whether the case is being heard for the first time.

Jurisdiction of the Federal Courts Because the federal government is a government of limited powers, the jurisdiction of the federal courts is limited. Federal courts have subject-matter jurisdiction in two situations.

Federal Questions. Article III of the U.S. Constitution establishes the boundaries of federal judicial power. Section 2 of Article III states that "[t]he judicial Power shall extend to all Cases, in Law and Equity, arising under this Constitution, the Laws of the United States, and Treaties made, or which shall be made, under their Authority." In effect, this clause means that whenever a plaintiff's cause of action is based, at least in part, on the U.S. Constitution, a treaty, or a federal law, a **federal question** arises. Any lawsuit involving a federal question comes under the judicial authority of the federal courts and can originate in a federal court. People who claim that their constitutional rights have been violated, for example, can begin their suits in a federal court. Note that in a case based on a federal question, a federal court will apply federal law.

Diversity of Citizenship. Federal district courts can also exercise original jurisdiction over cases involving **diversity of citizenship.** This term applies whenever a federal court has jurisdiction over a case that does not involve a question of federal law. The most common type of diversity jurisdiction has two requirements:[7] (1) the plaintiff and defendant must be residents of different states, and (2) the dollar amount in controversy must exceed $75,000. For purposes of diversity jurisdiction, a corporation is a citizen of both the state in which it is incorporated and the state in which its principal place of business is located. A case involving diversity of citizenship can be filed in the appropriate federal district court. If the case starts in a state court, it can sometimes be transferred, or "removed," to a federal court. A large percentage of the cases filed in federal courts each year are based on diversity of citizenship.

As noted, a federal court will apply federal law in cases involving federal questions. In a case based on diversity of citizenship, in contrast, a federal court will apply the relevant state law (which is often the law of the state in which the court sits).

Exclusive versus Concurrent Jurisdiction When both federal and state courts have the power to hear a case, as is true in suits involving diversity of citizenship, **concurrent jurisdiction** exists. When cases can be tried only in federal courts or only in state courts, **exclusive jurisdiction** exists. Federal courts have exclusive jurisdiction in cases involving federal crimes, bankruptcy, and most patent and copyright claims; in suits against the United States; and in some areas of admiralty law (law governing transportation on ocean waters). State courts also have exclusive jurisdiction over certain subjects—for example, divorce and adoption. When concurrent jurisdiction exists, a party may choose to bring a suit in either a federal court or a state court.

Jurisdiction in Cyberspace

The Internet's capacity to bypass political and geographic boundaries undercuts the traditional basis on which courts assert personal jurisdiction. This basis includes a party's contacts with a court's geographic jurisdiction. As already discussed, for a court to compel a defendant to come before it, there must be at least minimum contacts—the presence of a salesperson within the state, for example. Are there sufficient minimum contacts if the only connection to a jurisdiction is an ad on a Web site originating from a remote location?

The "Sliding-Scale" Standard Gradually, the courts are developing a standard—called a "sliding-scale" standard—for determining when the exercise of personal jurisdiction over an out-of-state Internet-based defendant is proper. In developing this standard, the courts have identified three types of Internet

7. Diversity jurisdiction also exists in cases between (1) a foreign country and citizens of a state or of different states and (2) citizens of a state and citizens or subjects of a foreign country. These bases for diversity jurisdiction are less commonly used.

business contacts: (1) substantial business conducted over the Internet (with contracts and sales, for example); (2) some interactivity through a Web site; and (3) passive advertising. Jurisdiction is proper for the first category, is improper for the third, and may or may not be appropriate for the second.[8] An Internet communication is typically considered passive if people have to voluntarily access it to read the message and active if it is sent to specific individuals.

In certain situations, even a single contact can satisfy the minimum-contacts requirement. In one case, for example, a Texas resident, Connie Davis, sent an unsolicited e-mail message to numerous Mississippi residents advertising a pornographic Web site. Davis falsified the "from" header in the e-mail so that Internet Doorway appeared to be the sender. Internet Doorway filed a lawsuit against Davis in Mississippi, claiming that its reputation and goodwill in the community had been harmed. The federal court in Mississippi held that Davis's single e-mail to Mississippi residents satisfied the minimum-contacts requirement for jurisdiction. The court concluded that Davis, by sending the e-mail solicitation, should reasonably have expected that she could be "haled into court in a distant jurisdiction to answer for the ramifications."[9]

International Jurisdictional Issues

Because the Internet is international in scope, international jurisdictional issues have understandingly come to the fore. The world's courts seem to be developing a standard that echoes the requirement of "minimum contacts" applied by the U.S. courts. Most courts are indicating that minimum contacts—doing business within the jurisdiction, for example—are enough to exercise jurisdiction over a defendant. The effect of this standard is that a business firm may have to comply with the laws in any jurisdiction in which it actively targets customers for its products.

To understand some of the problems created by Internet commerce, consider a French court's judgment against the U.S.-based Internet company Yahoo!, Inc. Yahoo operates an online auction site on which Nazi memorabilia have been offered for sale. In France, the display of any objects depicting symbols of Nazi ideology is illegal and leads to both criminal and civil liability. The International League against Racism and Anti-Semitism filed a suit in Paris against Yahoo for displaying Nazi memorabilia and offering them for sale via its Web site.

The French court asserted jurisdiction over Yahoo on the ground that the materials on the company's U.S.-based servers could be viewed on a Web site accessible in France. The French court ordered Yahoo to eliminate all Internet access in France to the Nazi memorabilia offered for sale through its online auctions. Yahoo then took the case to a federal district court in the United States, claiming that the French court's order violated the First Amendment to the U.S. Constitution. Although the federal district court ruled in favor of Yahoo, the U.S. Court of Appeals for the Ninth Circuit reversed. According to the appellate court, U.S. courts lacked personal jurisdiction over the French groups involved.[10] The *Yahoo* case represents the first time a U.S. court was asked to decide whether to honor a foreign judgment involving business conducted over the Internet. The federal appeals court's ruling leaves open the possibility that Yahoo, and anyone else who posts anything on the Internet, could be held answerable to the laws of any country in which the message might be received. *Concept Summary 2.1* on the following page reviews the various types of jurisdiction, including jurisdiction in cyberspace.

Venue

Jurisdiction has to do with whether a court has authority to hear a case involving specific persons, property, or subject matter. **Venue**[11] is concerned with the most appropriate location for a trial. For example, two state courts (or two federal courts) may have the authority to exercise jurisdiction over a case, but it may be more appropriate or convenient to hear the case in one court than in the other.

Basically, the concept of venue reflects the policy that a court trying a suit should be in the geographic neighborhood (usually the county) where the incident leading to the lawsuit occurred or where the parties involved in the lawsuit reside. Venue in a civil case typically is where the defendant resides, whereas venue in a criminal case is normally where the crime occurred. Pretrial publicity or other factors, though, may require a change of venue to another community, especially in criminal cases in which the defendant's right to a fair and impartial jury has been impaired.

---

8. For a leading case on this issue, see *Zippo Manufacturing Co. v. Zippo Dot Com, Inc.*, 952 F.Supp. 1119 (W.D.Pa. 1997).

9. *Internet Doorway, Inc. v. Parks*, 138 F.Supp.2d 773 (S.D.Miss. 2001).

10. *Yahoo! Inc. v. La Ligue Contre le Racisme et l'Antisemitisme*, 379 F.3d 1120 (9th Cir. 2004), *cert.* denied, __ U.S. __, 126 S.Ct. 2332, 164 L.Ed.2d 841 (2006).

11. Pronounced *ven*-yoo.

CONCEPT SUMMARY 2.1 Jurisdiction

Type of Jurisdiction	Description
PERSONAL	Exists when a defendant is located within the territorial boundaries within which a court has the right and power to decide cases. Jurisdiction may be exercised over out-of-state defendants under state long arm statutes. Courts have jurisdiction over corporate defendants that do business within the state, as well as corporations that advertise, sell, or place goods into the stream of commerce in the state.
PROPERTY	Exists when the property that is subject to a lawsuit is located within the territorial boundaries within which a court has the right and power to decide cases.
SUBJECT MATTER	Limits the court's jurisdictional authority to particular types of cases. 1. *Limited jurisdiction*—Exists when a court is limited to a specific subject matter, such as probate or divorce. 2. *General jurisdiction*—Exists when a court can hear cases involving a broad array of issues.
ORIGINAL	Exists with courts that have the authority to hear a case for the first time (trial courts).
APPELLATE	Exists with courts of appeal and review. Generally, appellate courts do not have original jurisdiction.
FEDERAL	1. *Federal questions*—When the plaintiff's cause of action is based at least in part on the U.S. Constitution, a treaty, or a federal law, a federal court can exercise jurisdiction. 2. *Diversity of citizenship*—In cases between citizens of different states when the amount in controversy exceeds $75,000 (or in cases between a foreign country and citizens of a state or of different states and in cases between citizens of a state and citizens or subjects of a foreign country), a federal court can exercise jurisdiction.
CONCURRENT	Exists when both federal and state courts have authority to hear the same case.
EXCLUSIVE	Exists when only state courts or only federal courts have authority to hear a case.
JURISDICTION IN CYBERSPACE	Because the Internet does not have physical boundaries, traditional jurisdictional concepts have been difficult to apply in cases involving activities conducted via the Web. Gradually, the courts are developing standards to use in determining when jurisdiction over a Web site owner or operator in another state is proper. A significant legal challenge with respect to cyberspace transactions has to do with resolving jurisdictional disputes in the international context.

Standing to Sue

In order to bring a lawsuit before a court, a party must have **standing to sue,** or a sufficient "stake" in a matter to justify seeking relief through the court system. In other words, to have standing, a party must have a legally protected and tangible interest at stake in the litigation. The party bringing the lawsuit must have suffered a harm or been threatened with a harm by the action about which she or he has complained. At times, a person can have standing to sue on behalf of another person. For example, suppose that a child suffers serious injuries as a result of a defectively manufactured toy. Because the child is a minor, another person, such as a parent or a legal guardian, can bring a lawsuit on the child's behalf.

Standing to sue also requires that the controversy at issue be a **justiciable**[12] **controversy**—a controversy that is real and substantial, as opposed to hypothetical or academic. For example, to entice DaimlerChrysler Corporation to build a $1.2 billion Jeep assembly plant in the area, the city of Toledo, Ohio, gave the company a ten-year local property tax exemption as well as a state franchise tax credit. Toledo taxpayers filed a lawsuit in state court, claiming that the tax breaks violated the commerce clause in the U.S. Constitution. The taxpayers alleged that the tax exemption and credit injured them because they would have to pay higher taxes to cover the shortfall in tax revenues. In 2006, the United States Supreme Court ruled that the taxpayers lacked standing to sue over the incentive program because their alleged injury was "conjectural or hypothetical"—that is, there was no justiciable controversy.[13]

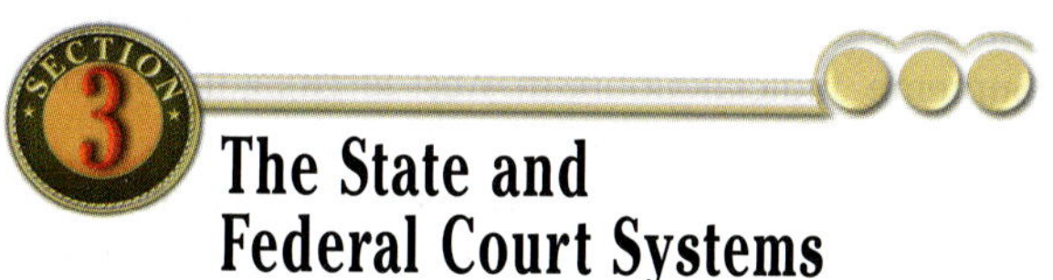

The State and Federal Court Systems

As mentioned earlier in this chapter, each state has its own court system. Additionally, there is a system of federal courts. Although no two state court systems are exactly the same, the right-hand side of Exhibit 2–1 illustrates the basic organizational framework characteristic of the court systems in many states. The exhibit also shows how the federal court system is structured. We turn now to an examination of these court systems, beginning with the state courts.

12. Pronounced jus-*tish*-a-bul.

13. *DaimlerChrysler v. Cuno*, 547 U.S. 332, 126 S.Ct.1854, 164 L.Ed.2d 589 (2006).

State Court Systems

Typically, a state court system includes several levels, or tiers, of courts. As indicated in Exhibit 2–1, state courts may include (1) local trial courts of limited jurisdiction, (2) state trial courts of general jurisdiction, (3) state courts of appeals (intermediate appellate courts), and (4) the state's highest court (often called the state supreme court). Generally, any person who is a party to a lawsuit has the opportunity to plead the case before a trial court and then, if he or she loses, before at least one level of appellate court. Finally, if the case involves a federal statute or federal constitutional issue, the decision of a state supreme court on that issue may be further appealed to the United States Supreme Court.

The states use various methods to select judges for their courts. Usually, voters elect judges, but in some states judges are appointed. For example, in Iowa, the governor appoints judges, and then the general population decides whether to confirm their appointment in the next general election. The states usually specify the number of years that judges will serve. In contrast, as you will read shortly, judges in the federal court system are appointed by the president of the United States

EXHIBIT 2–1 • The State and Federal Court Systems

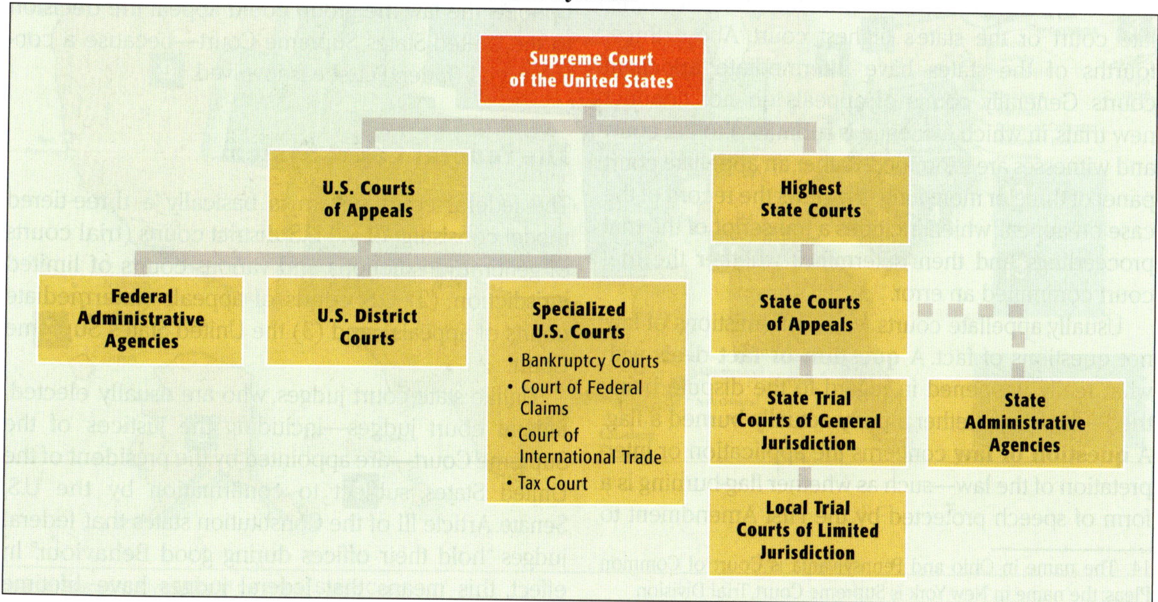

EMERGING TRENDS IN THE LEGAL ENVIRONMENT OF BUSINESS

E-Discovery and Cost-Shifting

Before the computer age, discovery involved searching through paper records—physical evidence. Today, less than 0.5 percent of new information is created on paper. Instead of sending letters and memos, for example, people send e-mails—almost 600 billion of them annually in the United States. The all-inclusive nature of electronic information means that electronic discovery (e-discovery) now plays an important role in almost every business lawsuit.

Changes in the Federal Rules of Civil Procedure

As e-discovery has become ubiquitous, the Federal Rules of Civil Procedure (FRCP) have changed to encompass it. Amended Section 26(f) of the FRCP, for example, requires that the parties confer about "preserving discoverable information" and discuss "any issues relating to . . . discovery of electronically stored information, including the electronic forms in which it should be produced."

The most recent amendment to Section 34(a) of the FRCP expressly permits one party to a lawsuit to request that the other produce "electronically stored information—including . . . data compilation stored in any medium from which information can be obtained." The new rule has put in place a two-tiered process for discovery of electronically stored information. Relevant and nonprivileged information that is reasonably accessible is discoverable as a matter of right. Discovery of less accessible—and therefore more costly to obtain—electronic data may or may not be allowed by the court. The problem of the costs of e-discovery is discussed further below.

The *Ameriwood* Three-Step Process

The new federal rules were applied in *Ameriwood Industries, Inc. v. Liberman,* a major case involving e-discovery in which the court developed a three-step procedure for obtaining electronic data.[a] In the first step, *imaging,* mirror images of a party's hard drives can be required. The second step involves *recovering* available word-processing documents, e-mails, PowerPoint presentations, spreadsheets, and other files. The final step is *full disclosure* in which a party sends the other party all responsive and nonprivileged documents and information obtained in the previous two steps.

a. 2007 WL 685623 (E.D.Mo. 2007).

Limitations on E-Discovery and Cost-Shifting

Complying with requests for electronically discoverable information can cost hundreds of thousands, if not millions, of dollars, especially if a party is a large corporation with thousands of employees creating millions of electronic documents. Consequently, there is a trend toward limiting e-discovery. Under the FRCP, a court can limit electronic discovery (1) when it would be unreasonably cumulative or duplicative, (2) when the requesting party has already had ample opportunity during discovery to obtain the information, or (3) when the burden or expense outweighs the likely benefit.

The Trial

Various rules and procedures govern the trial phase of the litigation process. There are rules governing what kind of evidence will or will not be admitted during the trial, as well as specific procedures that the participants in the lawsuit must follow.

Opening Statements At the beginning of the trial, both attorneys are allowed to make **opening statements** setting forth the facts that they expect to prove during the trial. The opening statement provides an opportunity for each lawyer to give a brief version of the facts and the supporting evidence that will be used during the trial. Then the plaintiff's case is presented. In our hypothetical case, Kirby's lawyer would introduce evidence (relevant documents, exhibits, and the testimony of witnesses) to support Kirby's position.

Rules of Evidence Whether evidence will be admitted in court is determined by the **rules of evidence**—a series of rules that have been created by the courts to ensure that any evidence presented during a trial is fair and reliable. The Federal Rules of Evidence govern the admissibility of evidence in federal courts.

Evidence Must Be Relevant to the Issues. Evidence will not be admitted in court unless it is relevant to the matter in question. **Relevant evidence** is evidence that tends to prove or disprove a fact in question or to establish the degree of probability of a fact or action. For example, evidence that a suspect's gun was in the home of another person when a victim was shot would be relevant—because it would tend to prove that the suspect did not shoot the victim.

Many courts are allowing responding parties to object to e-discovery requests on the ground that complying with the request would cause an undue financial burden. In a suit between E*Trade and Deutsche Bank, for example, the court denied E*Trade's request that the defendant produce its hard drives because doing so would create an undue burden.[b]

In addition, sometimes when a court finds that producing the requested information would create an undue financial burden, the court orders the party to comply but shifts the cost to the requesting party (usually the plaintiff). A major case in this area involved Rowe Entertainment and the William Morris Agency. When the e-discovery costs were estimated to be as high as $9 million, the court determined that cost-shifting was warranted.[c] In deciding whether to order cost-shifting, courts increasingly take into account the amount in controversy and each party's ability to pay. Sometimes, a court may require the responding party to restore and produce representative documents from a small sample of the requested medium to verify the relevance of the data before the party incurs significant expenses.[d]

b. *E*Trade Securities, LLC v. Deutsche Bank A.G.*, 230 F.R.D. 582 (D.Minn. 2005). This is a *Federal Rules Decision* not designated for publication in the *Federal Supplement*, citing *Zubulake v. UBS Warburg, LLC*, 2003 WL 21087884 (S.D.N.Y. 2003).

c. *Rowe Entertainment, Inc. v. William Morris Agency, Inc.*, 2002 WL 975713 (S.D.N.Y. 2002).

d. See, for example, *Quinby v. West LBAG*, 2006 WL 2597900 (S.D.N.Y. 2006).

IMPLICATIONS FOR THE BUSINESSPERSON

1. Whenever there is a "reasonable anticipation of litigation," all the relevant documents must be preserved. Preserving data can be a challenge, particularly for large corporations that have electronic data scattered across multiple networks, servers, desktops, laptops, handheld devices, and even home computers.
2. Even though an e-mail is deleted, it is not necessarily eliminated from one's hard drive, unless it is completely overwritten by new data. Thus, businesspersons should be aware that their hard drives can contain information they presumed no longer existed.

FOR CRITICAL ANALYSIS

1. How might a large corporation protect itself from allegations that it intentionally failed to preserve electronic data?
2. Given the significant and often burdensome costs associated with electronic discovery, should courts consider cost-shifting in every case involving electronic discovery? Why or why not?

RELEVANT WEB SITES

To locate information on the Web concerning the issues discussed in this feature, go to this text's Web site at **academic.cengage.com/blaw/cross**, select "Chapter 2," and click on "Emerging Trends."

Even relevant evidence may not be admitted in court if its reliability is questionable or if its probative (proving) value is substantially outweighed by other important considerations of the court. For example, a video or a photograph that shows in detail the severity of a victim's injuries would be relevant evidence, but the court might exclude this evidence on the ground that it would emotionally inflame the jurors.

Hearsay Evidence Not Admissible. Generally, hearsay is not admissible as evidence. **Hearsay** is defined as any testimony given in court about a statement made by someone else who was not under oath at the time of the statement. Literally, it is what someone heard someone else say. For example, if a witness in the Kirby-Carvello case testified in court concerning what he or she heard another observer say about the accident, that testimony would be hearsay, or secondhand knowledge. Admitting hearsay into evidence carries many risks because, even though it may be relevant, there is no way to test its reliability.

Examination of Witnesses Because Kirby is the plaintiff, she has the burden of proving that her allegations are true. Her attorney begins the presentation of Kirby's case by calling the first witness for the plaintiff and examining, or questioning, the witness. (For both attorneys, the types of questions and the manner of asking them are governed by the rules of evidence.) This questioning is called **direct examination.** After Kirby's attorney is finished, the witness is subject to **cross-examination** by Carvello's attorney. Then Kirby's attorney has another opportunity to question the witness in *redirect examination*, and Carvello's

example. At the federal level, members of Congress long have been concerned with bringing court costs and delay under control. These concerns led to legislation that required the federal courts to develop a plan to cut costs and reduce delay within the federal judicial system.

New Methods and Arrangements

The search for alternative means to resolve disputes has produced several distinct methods and arrangements. These range from neighbors sitting down over a cup of coffee to work out their differences to huge multinational corporations agreeing to resolve a dispute through a formal hearing before a panel of experts. All of these alternatives to traditional litigation make up what is broadly termed **alternative dispute resolution (ADR).**

ADR describes any procedure or device for resolving disputes outside the traditional judicial process. ADR is normally a less expensive and less time-consuming process than formal litigation. In some instances, it also has the advantage of being more private. Except in disputes involving court-annexed arbitration (discussed later in this chapter), no public record of ADR proceedings is created; only the parties directly involved are privy to the information presented during the process. This is a particularly important consideration in many business disputes, because such cases may involve sensitive commercial information. As you will read later in this chapter, today ADR also includes online methods of resolving disputes.

The great advantage of ADR is its flexibility. Normally, the parties themselves can control how the dispute will be settled, what procedures will be used, whether a neutral third party will be present or make a decision, and whether that decision will be legally binding or nonbinding. ADR also offers more privacy than court proceedings and allows disputes to be resolved relatively quickly.

Negotiation and Mediation

Alternative dispute resolution methods differ in the degree of formality involved and the extent to which third parties participate in the process. Generally, negotiation is the least formal method and involves no third parties. Mediation may be similarly informal but does involve the participation of a third party.

Negotiation

The simplest form of ADR is **negotiation.** In the process of negotiation, the parties come together informally, with or without attorneys to represent them. Within this informal setting, the parties air their differences and try to reach a settlement or resolution without the involvement of independent third parties. Because no third parties are involved and because of the informal setting, negotiation is the simplest form of ADR. Even if a lawsuit has been initiated, the parties may continue to negotiate their differences at any time during the litigation process and attempt to settle their dispute. Less than 10 percent of all corporate lawsuits, for example, end up in trial—the rest are settled beforehand.

Preparation for Negotiation In spite of the informality of negotiation, each party must carefully prepare his or her side of the case. The elements of the dispute should be considered, documents and other evidence should be collected, and witnesses should be prepared to testify. Negotiating from a well-prepared position improves the odds of obtaining a favorable result. Even if a dispute is not resolved through negotiation, preparation for negotiation will reduce the effort required to prepare for the next step in the dispute-resolution process.

Assisted Negotiation To facilitate negotiation, various forms of what might be called "assisted negotiation" have emerged in recent years. Assisted negotation, as the term implies, involves the assistance of a third party. Forms of ADR associated with the negotation process include mini-trials, early neutral case evaluation, and facilitation. Another form of assisted negotiation—the summary jury trial—will be discussed later in this chapter.

A **mini-trial** is a private proceeding in which each party's attorney briefly argues the party's case before the other party. Typically, a neutral third party, who acts as an adviser and an expert in the area being disputed, is also present. If the parties fail to reach an agreement, the adviser renders an opinion as to how a court would likely decide the issue. The proceeding assists the parties in determining whether they should negotiate a settlement of the dispute or take it to court.

In **early neutral case evaluation,** the parties select a neutral third party (generally an expert in the subject matter of the dispute) to evaluate their respective positions. The parties explain their positions to the case evaluator however they wish. The evaluator then assesses the strengths and weaknesses of the parties' positions, and this evaluation forms the basis for negotiating a settlement.

Disputes may also be resolved in a friendly, nonadversarial manner through **facilitation,** in which a third party assists parties to a dispute in reconciling their differences. The facilitator helps to schedule negotiating sessions and carries offers back and forth between the parties when they refuse to face each other in direct negotiations. Technically, facilitators are not to recommend solutions. In practice, however, they often do. In contrast, a mediator is expected to propose solutions.

Mediation

One of the oldest forms of ADR is mediation. In **mediation,** a neutral third party acts as a **mediator** and works with both sides in the dispute to facilitate a resolution. The mediator normally talks with the parties separately as well as jointly, emphasizes points of agreement, and helps the parties to evaluate their options. Although the mediator may propose a solution (called a mediator's proposal), he or she does not make a decision resolving the matter. The mediator, who need not be a lawyer, usually charges a fee for his or her services (which can be split between the parties). States that require parties to undergo ADR before trial often offer mediation as one of the ADR options or (as in Florida) the only option.

Mediation is essentially a form of assisted negotiation. We treat it separately here because traditionally it has been viewed as an alternative to negotiation. Additionally, a mediator usually plays a more active role than the neutral third parties in negotiation-associated forms of ADR.

Advantages of Mediation Few procedural rules are involved in the mediation process—far fewer than in a courtroom setting. The proceedings can be tailored to fit the needs of the parties—the mediator can be told to maintain a diplomatic role or be asked to express an opinion about the dispute, lawyers can be excluded from the proceedings, and the exchange of a few documents can replace the more expensive and time-consuming process of pretrial discovery. Disputes are often settled far more quickly in mediation than in formal litigation.

One of the biggest advantages of mediation is that it is not as adversarial in nature as litigation. In mediation, the mediator takes an active role and attempts to bring the parties together so that they can come to a mutually satisfactory resolution. The mediation process tends to reduce the antagonism between the disputants, allowing them to resume their former relationship while minimizing hostility. For this reason, mediation is often the preferred form of ADR for disputes involving business partners, employers and employees, or other parties involved in long-term relationships.

Today, characteristics of mediation are being combined with those of arbitration (to be discussed next). In *binding mediation,* for example, the parties agree that if they cannot resolve the dispute, the mediator can make a legally binding decision on the issue. In *mediation-arbitration,* or "med-arb," the parties first attempt to settle their dispute through mediation. If no settlement is reached, the dispute will be arbitrated.

Another important benefit of mediation is that the mediator is selected by the parties. In litigation, the parties have no control over the selection of a judge. In mediation, the parties may select a mediator on the basis of expertise in a particular field as well as for fairness and impartiality. To the degree that the mediator has these attributes, he or she will more effectively aid the parties in reaching an agreement over their dispute.

Disadvantages of Mediation Mediation is not without disadvantages. A mediator is likely to charge a fee. (This can be split between the parties, though, and thus may represent less expense than would both sides' hiring lawyers.)

Informality and the absence of a third party referee can also be disadvantageous. (Remember that a mediator can only help the parties reach a decision, not make a decision for them.) Without a deadline hanging over the parties' heads, and without the threat of sanctions if they fail to negotiate in good faith, they may be less willing to make concessions or otherwise strive honestly and diligently to reach a settlement. This can slow the process or even cause it to fail.

Arbitration

A more formal method of ADR is **arbitration,** in which an **arbitrator** (a neutral third party or a panel of experts) hears a dispute and imposes a resolution on the parties. Arbitration differs from other forms of ADR in that the third party hearing the dispute makes a decision for the parties. Exhibit 3–1 on page 66 outlines the basic differences among the three traditional forms of

EXHIBIT 3–1 • Basic Differences in the Traditional Forms of ADR

Type of ADR	Description	Neutral Third Party Present	Who Decides the Resolution
Negotiation	Parties meet informally with or without their attorneys and attempt to agree on a resolution.	No.	The parties themselves reach a resolution.
Mediation	A neutral third party meets with the parties and emphasizes points of agreement to bring them toward resolution of their dispute.	Yes.	The parties, but the mediator may suggest or propose a resolution.
Arbitration	The parties present their arguments and evidence before an arbitrator at a hearing, and the arbitrator renders a decision resolving the parties' dispute.	Yes.	The arbitrator imposes a resolution on the parties that may be either binding or nonbinding.

ADR. The key difference between arbitration and the forms of ADR just discussed is that in arbitration, the third party's decision may be legally binding on the parties. Usually the parties in arbitration agree that the third party's decision will be *legally binding*, although the parties can also agree to *nonbinding* arbitration.

When a dispute arises, the parties can agree to settle their differences informally through arbitration rather than formally through the court system. Alternatively, the parties may agree ahead of time that, if a dispute should arise, they will submit to arbitration rather than bring a lawsuit. If the parties agree that the arbitrator's decision will be legally binding, they are obligated to abide by the arbitrator's decision regardless of whether or not they agree with it. (See this chapter's *Insight into Ethics* feature on pages 70 and 71 for a discussion of some potential ethical implications of the use of arbitration.)

The federal government and many state governments favor arbitration over litigation. The federal policy favoring arbitration is embodied in the Federal Arbitration Act (FAA) of 1925.[1] The FAA requires that courts give deference to all voluntary arbitration agreements in cases governed by federal law. Virtually any dispute can be the subject of arbitration. A voluntary agreement to arbitrate a dispute normally will be enforced by the courts if the agreement does not compel an illegal act or contravene public policy.

The Federal Arbitration Act

The Federal Arbitration Act does not establish a set arbitration procedure. The parties themselves must agree on the manner of resolving their dispute. The FAA provides the means for enforcing the arbitration procedure that the parties have established for themselves.

Section 4 allows a party to petition a federal district court for an order compelling arbitration under an agreement to arbitrate a dispute. If the judge is "satisfied that the making of the agreement for arbitration or the failure to comply therewith is not in issue, the court shall make an order directing the parties to proceed with arbitration in accordance with the terms of the agreement."

Under Section 9 of the FAA, the parties to the arbitration may agree to have the arbitrator's decision confirmed in a federal district court. Through confirmation, one party obtains a court order directing another party to comply with the terms of the arbitrator's decision. Section 10 establishes the grounds by which the arbitrator's decision may be set aside (canceled). The grounds for setting aside a decision are limited to misconduct, fraud, corruption, or abuse of power in the arbitration process itself; a court will not review the merits of the dispute or the arbitrator's judgment.

The FAA covers any arbitration clause in a contract that involves interstate commerce. Business activities that have even remote connections or minimal effects on commerce between two or more states are considered to be included. Thus, arbitration agreements involving transactions only slightly connected to the flow of interstate commerce may fall under the FAA, even if the parties, at the time of contracting, did not expect their arbitration agreement to involve interstate commerce.

1. 9 U.S.C. Sections 1–15.

The question in the following case was whether a court or an arbitrator should consider a claim that an entire contract, including its arbitration clause, is rendered void by the alleged illegality of a separate provision in the contract.

CASE 3.1 Buckeye Check Cashing, Inc. v. Cardegna

Supreme Court of the United States, 2006. 546 U.S. 440, 126 S.Ct. 1204, 163 L.Ed.2d 1038.
www.law.cornell.edu/supct/index.html[a]

Background and Facts Buckeye Check Cashing, Inc., cashes personal checks for consumers in Florida. Buckeye agrees to delay submitting a check for payment in exchange for a consumer's payment of a "finance charge." For each transaction, the consumer signs a "Deferred Deposit and Disclosure Agreement," which states, "By signing this Agreement, you agree that i[f] a dispute of any kind arises out of this Agreement * * * th[e]n either you or we or third-parties involved can choose to have that dispute resolved by binding arbitration." John Cardegna and others filed a suit in a Florida state court against Buckeye, alleging that the "finance charge" represented an illegally high interest rate in violation of Florida state laws, rendering the agreement "criminal on its face." Buckeye filed a motion to compel arbitration. The court denied the motion. On Buckeye's appeal, a state intermediate appellate court reversed this denial, but on the plaintiffs' appeal, the Florida Supreme Court reversed the lower appellate court's decision. Buckeye appealed to the United States Supreme Court.

IN THE LANGUAGE OF THE COURT
Justice *SCALIA* delivered the opinion of the Court.

* * * *

* * * Section 2 [of the Federal Arbitration Act (FAA)] embodies the national policy favoring arbitration and places arbitration agreements on equal footing with all other contracts:

> A written provision in * * * a contract * * * to settle by arbitration a controversy thereafter arising out of such contract * * * shall be valid, irrevocable, and enforceable, save upon such grounds as exist at law or in equity for the revocation of any contract.

* * * The crux of the [respondents'] complaint is that the contract as a whole (including its arbitration provision) is rendered invalid by the * * * finance charge.

* * * *

* * * [Our holdings in previous cases] answer the question presented here by establishing three propositions. First, as a matter of substantive federal arbitration law, *an arbitration provision is severable [capable of being legally separated] from the remainder of the contract.* Second, unless the challenge is to the arbitration clause itself, *the issue of the contract's validity is considered by the arbitrator in the first instance.* Third, *this arbitration law applies in state as well as federal courts.* * * * Applying [those holdings] to this case, we conclude that because respondents [Cardegna and others] challenge the Agreement, but not specifically its arbitration provisions, those provisions are enforceable apart from the remainder of the contract. The challenge should therefore be considered by an arbitrator, not a court. [Emphasis added.]

* * * *

* * * Since, respondents argue, the only arbitration agreements to which [Section] 2 applies are those involving a "contract," and since an agreement void *ab initio* [from the beginning] under state law is not a "contract," there is no "written provision" in or "controversy arising out of" a "contract," to which [Section] 2 can apply. * * * We do not read "contract" so narrowly. The word appears four times in [Section] 2. Its last appearance is in the final clause, which allows a challenge to an arbitration provision "upon such grounds as exist at law or in equity for the revocation of any contract." There can be no doubt that "contract" as used this last time must include contracts that

a. In the "Supreme Court Collection" menu at the top of the page, click on "Search." When that page opens, in the "Search for:" box, type "Buckeye Check," choose "All decisions" in the accompanying list, and click on "Search." In the result, scroll to the name of the case and click on the appropriate link to access the opinion.

CASE CONTINUES

CASE 3.1 CONTINUED

later prove to be void. Otherwise, the grounds for revocation would be limited to those that rendered a contract voidable—which would mean (implausibly) that an arbitration agreement could be challenged as voidable but not as void. Because the sentence's final use of "contract" so obviously includes putative [alleged] contracts, we will not read the same word earlier in the same sentence to have a more narrow meaning.

- **Decision and Remedy** *The United States Supreme Court reversed the judgment of the Florida Supreme Court and remanded the case for further proceedings. The United States Supreme Court ruled that a challenge to the validity of a contract as a whole, and not specifically to an arbitration clause contained in the contract, must be resolved by an arbitrator.*

- **The Ethical Dimension** *Does the holding in this case permit a court to enforce an arbitration agreement in a contract that the arbitrator later finds to be void? Is this fair? Why or why not?*

- **The Legal Environment Dimension** *As indicated in the parties' arguments and the Court's reasoning in this case, into what categories can contracts be classified with respect to their enforceability?*

State Arbitration Statutes

Virtually all states follow the federal approach to voluntary arbitration. Most of the states and the District of Columbia have adopted the Uniform Arbitration Act, which was drafted by the National Conference of Commissioners on Uniform State Laws in 1955. Those states that have not adopted the uniform act nonetheless follow many of the practices specified in it.

Under the uniform act, the basic approach is to give full effect to voluntary agreements to arbitrate disputes between private parties. The act supplements private arbitration agreements by providing explicit procedures and remedies for enforcing arbitration agreements. The uniform act does not, however, dictate the terms of the agreement. Moreover, under both federal and state statutes, the parties are afforded considerable latitude in deciding the subject matter of the arbitration and the methods for conducting the arbitration process. In the absence of a controlling statute, the rights and duties of the parties are established and limited by their agreement.

The Arbitration Process

The arbitration process begins with a *submission.* **Submission** is the act of referring a dispute to an arbitrator. The next step is the *hearing,* in which evidence and arguments are presented to the arbitrator. The process culminates in an *award,* which is the decision of the arbitrator.

The right to appeal the award to a court of law is limited. If the award was made under a voluntary arbitration agreement, a court normally will not set it aside even if it was the result of an erroneous determination of fact or an incorrect interpretation of law by the arbitrator.

This limitation is based on at least two grounds. First, if an award is not treated as final, then rather than speeding up the dispute-resolution process, arbitration would merely add one more layer to the process of litigation. Second, the basis of arbitration—the freedom of parties to agree among themselves how to settle a controversy—supports treating an award as final. Having had the opportunity to frame the issues and to set out the manner for resolving the dispute, one party should not complain if the result was not what that party had hoped it would be.

Submission The parties may agree to submit questions of fact, questions of law, or both to the arbitrator. The parties may even agree to leave the interpretation of the arbitration agreement to the arbitrator. In the case of an existing agreement to arbitrate, the clause itself is the submission to arbitration.

The submission typically states the identities of the parties, the nature of the dispute to be resolved, the monetary amounts involved in the controversy, the location at which the arbitration is to take place, and the intention of the parties to be bound by the arbitrator's award. Exhibit 3–2 contains a sample submission form.

Most states require that an agreement to submit a dispute to arbitration be in writing. Moreover, because the goal of arbitration is speed and efficiency in

EXHIBIT 3–2 • Sample Submission Form

American Arbitration Association

Submission to Dispute Resolution

The named parties hereby submit the following dispute for resolution, under the rules of the American Arbitration Association:

Rules Selected: ☐ Commercial ☐ Construction
☐ Other ______________________ (describe)

Procedure Selected: ☐ Binding arbitration ☐ Mediation
☐ Other ______________________ (describe)

Nature of the Dispute (attach additional sheets if necessary):

Amount of Monetary Claim or Nature of Non-Monetary Claim:

Type of Business: Claimant ______________ Respondent ______________

Place of Hearing: ______________________

We agree that, if arbitration is selected, we will abide by and perform any award rendered hereunder and that a judgment may be entered on the award.

To be completed and signed by all parties
(attach additional sheets if necessary, please remember to obtain signatures)

Name of Party	Name of Party
Address	Address
City, State, and Zip Code	City, State, and Zip Code
(____) Telephone Fax	(____) Telephone Fax
Name of the Party's Attorney or Representative	Name of the Party's Attorney or Representative
Name of Firm (if applicable)	Name of Firm (if applicable)
Address	Address
City, State, and Zip Code	City, State, and Zip Code
(____) Telephone Fax	(____) Telephone Fax
Signed† (may be signed by a representative) Title	Signed† (may be signed by a representative) Title
Date: ____________	Date: ____________

Please file two signed copies and the non-refundable filing fee with the AAA.
For additional information, please visit our Web site at www.adr.org

† *Signatures of all parties are required.*

Form G1A-3/03

INSIGHT INTO ETHICS
Implications of an Increasingly Private Justice System

Downtown Houston boasts a relatively new courthouse with thirty-nine courtrooms, but more and more often, many of those courtrooms often stand empty. Has litigation in Texas slowed down? Indeed, it has not—the courtrooms are empty because fewer civil lawsuits are going to trial. A similar situation is occurring in the federal courts. In the northern district of Florida, for example, the four federal judges presided over only a dozen civil trials in 2007. In 1984, more than 12,000 civil trials were heard in our federal courts. Today, only about 3,500 federal civil trials take place annually. University of Wisconsin law professor Mark Galanter has labeled this trend the "vanishing trial." Two developments in particular are contributing to the disappearance of civil trials—arbitration and private judges.

Arbitration Is One Cause

Since the 1980s, corporations have been eschewing the public court system and taking cases to arbitration instead. Every day millions of Americans sign arbitration agreements, often unknowingly committing themselves to allow private arbitrators to solve their disputes with employers and the corporations with which they do business, such as cell phone service providers.

This trend raises some troublesome ethical issues, however. For one thing, arbitration agreements may force consumers to travel long distances to participate in these private forums. Perhaps more disturbing is that the supposedly neutral arbitrators may actually be captive to the industries they serve. Arbitrators are paid handsomely and typically would like to serve again. Thus, they may be reluctant to rule against a company that is involved in a dispute. After all, the company may well need arbitrators to resolve a subsequent dispute, whereas the other party—a consumer or employee—is unlikely to need the arbitrators again.

Private Judges Are Another Cause

Another reason for the decline in the number of civil trials in our public courts is the growing use of private judges. A private judge, who is usually a retired judge, has the power to conduct trials and grant legal resolutions of disputes. Private judges increasingly are being used to resolve commercial disputes, as well as divorces and custody battles, for two reasons. One reason is that a case can be heard by a private judge much sooner than it would be heard in a public court. The other reason is that proceedings before a private judge can be kept secret.

resolving controversies, most states require that matters be submitted within a definite period of time, generally six months from the date on which the dispute arises.

The Hearing Because the parties are free to construct the method by which they want their dispute resolved, they must state the issues that will be submitted and the powers that the arbitrator will exercise. The arbitrator may be given power at the outset of the process to establish rules that will govern the proceedings. Typically, these rules are much less restrictive than those governing formal litigation. Regardless of who establishes the rules, the arbitrator will apply them during the course of the hearing.

Restrictions on the kind of evidence and the manner in which it is presented may be less rigid in arbitration, partly because the arbitrator is likely to be an expert in the subject matter involved in the controversy. Restrictions may also be less stringent because there is less fear that the arbitrator will be swayed by improper evidence. In contrast, evidence in a jury trial must sometimes be presented twice: once to the judge, outside the presence of the jury, to determine if the evidence may be heard by the jury, and—depending on the judge's ruling—again, to the jury.

In the typical hearing format, the parties begin as they would at trial by presenting opening arguments to the arbitrator and stating what remedies should or should not be granted. After the opening statements have been made, evidence is presented. Witnesses may be called and examined by both sides. After all the evidence has been presented, the parties give their closing arguments. On completion of the closing arguments, the arbitrator closes the hearing.

The Award After each side has had an opportunity to present evidence and to argue its case, the arbitrator reaches a decision. The final decision of the arbitrator is referred to as an **award,** even if no money is conferred on a party as a result of the proceedings. Under most statutes, the arbitrator must render an award within thirty days of the close of the hearing.

In most states, the award need not state the arbitrator's findings regarding factual questions in the case. Nor must the award state the conclusions that the arbi-

In Ohio, for example, a state statute allows the parties to any civil action to have their dispute tried by a retired judge of their choosing who will make a decision in the matter.[a] Recently, though, private judging came under criticism in that state because private judges were conducting jury trials in county courtrooms at taxpayers' expense. A public judge, Nancy Margaret Russo, refused to give up jurisdiction over one case on the ground that private judges are not authorized to conduct jury trials. The Ohio Supreme Court agreed. As the state's highest court noted, private judging raises significant public-policy issues that the legislature needs to consider.[b]

One issue is that private judges charge relatively large fees. This means that litigants who are willing and able to pay the extra cost can have their case heard by a private judge long before they would be able to set a trial date in a regular court. Is it fair that those who cannot afford private judges should have to wait longer for justice? Similarly, is it ethical to allow parties to pay extra for secret proceedings before a private judge and thereby avoid the public scrutiny of a regular trial? Some even suggest that the use of private judges is leading to two different systems of justice.

a. See Ohio Revised Code Section 2701.10.

b. *State ex rel. Russo v. McDonnell,* 110 Ohio St.3d 144, 852 N.E.2d 145 (2006). (The term *ex rel.* is Latin for *ex relatione.* This phrase refers to an action brought on behalf of the state, by the attorney general, at the instigation of an individual who has a private interest in the matter.)

A Threat to the Common Law System?

The decline in the number of civil trials may also be leading to the erosion of this country's common law system. As discussed in Chapter 1, courts are obligated to consider precedents—the decisions rendered in previous cases with similar facts and issues—when deciding the outcome of a dispute. If fewer disputes go to trial because they are arbitrated or heard by a private judge, then they will never become part of the body of cases and appeals that form the case law on that subject. With fewer precedents on which to draw, individuals and businesses will have less information about what constitutes appropriate business behavior in today's world. Furthermore, private dispute resolution does not allow our case law to keep up with new issues related to areas such as biotechnology and the online world. Thus, the long-term effects of the decline of public justice could be a weakening of the common law itself.

CRITICAL THINKING

INSIGHT INTO THE SOCIAL ENVIRONMENT

If wealthier individuals increasingly use private judges, how will our justice system be affected in the long run?

trator reached on any questions of law that may have been presented. All that is required for the award to be valid is that it completely resolve the controversy.

Most states do, however, require that the award be in writing, regardless of whether any conclusions of law or findings of fact are included. If the arbitrator does state his or her legal conclusions and factual findings, then a letter or an opinion will be drafted containing the basis for the award. Even when there is no statutory requirement that the arbitrator state the factual and legal basis for the award, the parties may impose the requirement in their submission or in their predispute agreement to arbitrate.

Enforcement of Agreements to Submit to Arbitration

The role of the courts in the arbitration process is limited. One important role is played at the prearbitration stage. A court may be called on to order one party to an arbitration agreement to submit to arbitration under the terms of the agreement. The court in this role is essentially interpreting a contract. The court must determine what the parties have committed themselves to before ordering that they submit to arbitration.

The Issue of Arbitrability When a dispute arises as to whether or not the parties have agreed in an arbitration clause to submit a particular matter to arbitration, one party may file suit to compel arbitration. The court before which the suit is brought will not decide the basic controversy but must decide the issue of arbitrability—that is, whether the issue is one that must be resolved through arbitration. If the court finds that the subject matter in controversy is covered by the agreement to arbitrate, then a party may be compelled to arbitrate the dispute involuntarily.

Although the parties may agree to submit the issue of arbitrability to an arbitrator, the agreement must be explicit; a court will never *infer* an agreement to arbitrate. Unless a court finds an *explicit* agreement to have the arbitrator decide whether a dispute is arbitrable, the court will decide the issue. This is an important initial determination, because no party will be ordered to submit to arbitration unless the court is convinced that the party has consented to do so.

The terms of an arbitration agreement can limit the types of disputes that the parties agree to arbitrate. When the parties do not specify limits, however, disputes can arise as to whether the particular matter is covered by the arbitration agreement, and it is up to the court to resolve the issue of arbitrability. In the following case, the parties had previously agreed to arbitrate disputes involving their contract to develop software, but the dispute involved claims of copyright infringement (see Chapter 14). The question was whether the copyright infringement claims were beyond the scope of the arbitration clause.

CASE 3.2 NCR Corp. v. Korala Associates, Ltd.

United States Court of Appeals, Sixth Circuit, 2008. 512 F.3d 807.
www.ca6.uscourts.gov[a]

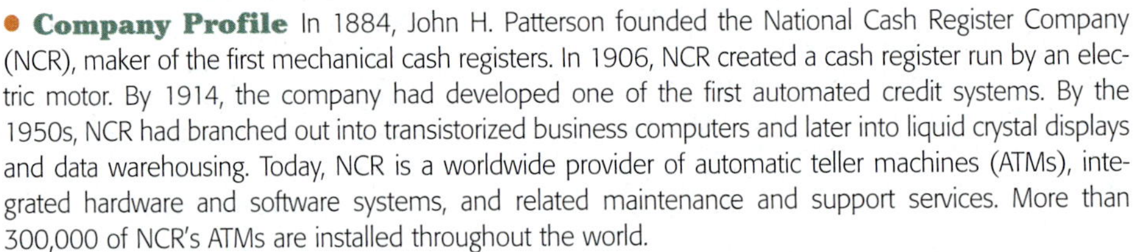

• **Company Profile** In 1884, John H. Patterson founded the National Cash Register Company (NCR), maker of the first mechanical cash registers. In 1906, NCR created a cash register run by an electric motor. By 1914, the company had developed one of the first automated credit systems. By the 1950s, NCR had branched out into transistorized business computers and later into liquid crystal displays and data warehousing. Today, NCR is a worldwide provider of automatic teller machines (ATMs), integrated hardware and software systems, and related maintenance and support services. More than 300,000 of NCR's ATMs are installed throughout the world.

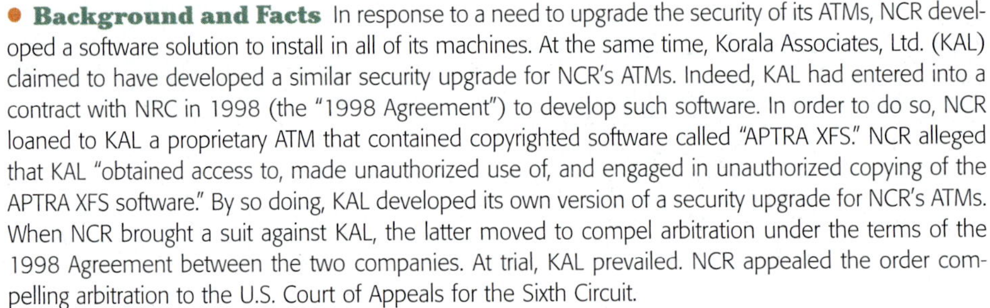

• **Background and Facts** In response to a need to upgrade the security of its ATMs, NCR developed a software solution to install in all of its machines. At the same time, Korala Associates, Ltd. (KAL) claimed to have developed a similar security upgrade for NCR's ATMs. Indeed, KAL had entered into a contract with NRC in 1998 (the "1998 Agreement") to develop such software. In order to do so, NCR loaned to KAL a proprietary ATM that contained copyrighted software called "APTRA XFS." NCR alleged that KAL "obtained access to, made unauthorized use of, and engaged in unauthorized copying of the APTRA XFS software." By so doing, KAL developed its own version of a security upgrade for NCR's ATMs. When NCR brought a suit against KAL, the latter moved to compel arbitration under the terms of the 1998 Agreement between the two companies. At trial, KAL prevailed. NCR appealed the order compelling arbitration to the U.S. Court of Appeals for the Sixth Circuit.

IN THE LANGUAGE OF THE COURT
Chief Justice *BATCHELDER* delivered the opinion of the Court.

* * * *

The arbitration clause contained within the 1998 Agreement provides that:

> Any controversy or claim arising out of or relating to this contract, or breach thereof, shall be settled by arbitration and judgment upon the award rendered by the arbitrator may be entered in any court having jurisdiction thereof. The arbitrator shall be appointed upon the mutual agreement of both parties failing which both parties will agree to be subject to any arbitrator that shall be chosen by the President of the Law Society.

The parties do not dispute that a valid agreement to arbitrate exists; rather the issue of contention is whether NCR's claims fall within the substantive scope of the agreement.

As a matter of federal law, any doubts concerning the scope of arbitrable issues should be resolved in favor of arbitration. Despite this strong presumption in favor of arbitration, "arbitration is a matter of contract between the parties, and one cannot be required to submit to arbitration a dispute which it has not agreed to submit to arbitration." *When faced with a broad arbitration clause, such as one covering any dispute arising out of an agreement, a court should follow the presumption of arbitration and resolve doubts in favor of arbitration. Indeed, in such a case, only an express provision excluding a specific dispute, or the most forceful evidence of a purpose to exclude the claim from arbitration, will remove the dispute from consideration by the arbitrators.* [Emphasis added.]

a. Click on "Opinions Search" and then on "Short Title;" and type "NCR." Next, click on the opinion link in the first column of the row corresponding to the name of this case.

CASE 3.2 CONTINUED

* * * *

* * * It is sufficient that a court would have to reference the 1998 Agreement for part of NCR's direct [copyright] infringement claim. Under these circumstances, we find that the copyright infringement claim as to APTRA XFS falls within the scope of the arbitration agreement.

• **Decision and Remedy** *The U.S. Court of Appeals for the Sixth Circuit affirmed part of the district court's decision. Specifically, it affirmed the judgment compelling arbitration as to NCR's claims relating to direct copyright infringement of the APTRA XFS software.*

• **The Ethical Dimension** *Could NCR have a claim that KAL engaged in unfair competition because KAL had engaged in unethical business practices? (Hint: Unfair competition may occur when one party deceives the public into believing that his or her goods are the goods of another.) Why or why not?*

• **The Legal Environment Dimension** *Why do you think that NCR did not want its alleged claims decided by arbitration?*

Mandatory Arbitration in the Employment Context A significant question in the last several years has concerned mandatory arbitration clauses in employment contracts. Many claim that employees' rights are not sufficiently protected when they are forced, as a condition of being hired, to agree to arbitrate all disputes and thus waive their rights under statutes specifically designed to protect employees. The United States Supreme Court, however, has held that mandatory arbitration clauses in employment contracts are generally enforceable.[2]

Compulsory arbitration agreements often spell out the rules for a mandatory proceeding. For example, an agreement may address in detail the amount and payment of filing fees and other expenses. Some courts have overturned provisions in employment-related agreements that require the parties to split the costs when an individual worker lacks the ability to pay. The court in the following case took this reasoning a step further.

2. For a landmark decision on this issue, see *Gilmer v. Interstate/Johnson Lane Corp.*, 500 U.S. 20, 111 S.Ct. 1647, 114 L.Ed.2d 26 (1991).

EXTENDED CASE 3.3

Morrison v. Circuit City Stores, Inc.

United States Court of Appeals, Sixth Circuit, 2003. 317 F.3d 646.
www.ca6.uscourts.gov/internet/index.htm[a]

***KAREN NELSON MOORE,* Circuit Judge.**

* * * *

* * * Plaintiff-Appellant Morrison, an African-American female with a bachelor's degree in engineering from the U.S. Air Force Academy and a master's degree in administration from Central Michigan University, submitted an application for a managerial position at a Circuit City store in Cincinnati, Ohio. As part of the application process, Morrison was required to sign a * * * "Dispute Resolution Agreement." This document contained an arbitration clause that required resolution of all disputes or controversies arising out of employment with Circuit City in an arbitral forum. * * * Circuit City would not consider any application for employment unless the arbitration agreement was signed * * *.

* * * *

a. This is a page within the Web site of the U.S. Court of Appeals for the Sixth Circuit. In the left-hand column, click on "Opinions Search." In the "Short Title contains" box, type "Morrison" and click "Submit Query." In the "Opinion" box corresponding to the name of the case, click on the number to access the opinion.

CASE CONTINUES

other exclusive career agents, Fraser prepared a letter to Nationwide's competitors asking whether they were interested in acquiring the represented agents' policyholders. Nationwide obtained a copy of the letter and searched its electronic file server for e-mail indicating that the letter had been sent. It found a stored e-mail that Fraser had sent to a co-worker indicating that the letter had been sent to at least one competitor. The e-mail was retrieved from the co-worker's file of already received and discarded messages stored on the server. When Nationwide canceled its contract with Fraser, he filed a suit in a federal district court against the firm, alleging, among other things, violations of various federal laws that prohibit the interception of electronic communications during transmission. In whose favor should the court rule, and why? Did Nationwide act ethically in retrieving the e-mail? Explain. [*Fraser v. Nationwide Mutual Insurance Co.*, 352 F.3d 107 (3d Cir. 2004)]

4–8. Ethical Conduct. Unable to pay more than $1.2 billion in debt, Big Rivers Electric Corp. filed a petition to declare bankruptcy in a federal bankruptcy court in September 1996. Big Rivers' creditors included Bank of New York (BONY), Chase Manhattan Bank, Mapco Equities, and others. The court appointed J. Baxter Schilling to work as a "disinterested" (neutral) party with Big Rivers and the creditors to resolve their disputes and set an hourly fee as Schilling's compensation. Schilling told Chase, BONY, and Mapco that he wanted them to pay him an additional percentage fee based on the "success" he attained in finding "new value" to pay Big Rivers' debts. Without such a deal, he told them, he would not perform his mediation duties. Chase agreed; the others disputed the deal, but no one told the court. In October 1998, Schilling asked the court for nearly $4.5 million in compensation, including the hourly fees, which totaled about $531,000, and the percentage fees. Big Rivers and others asked the court to deny Schilling any fees on the basis that he had improperly negotiated "secret side agreements." How did Schilling violate his duties as a "disinterested" party? Should he be denied compensation? Why or why not? [*In re Big Rivers Electric Corp.*, 355 F.3d 415 (6th Cir. 2004)]

4–9. Ethical Conduct. Ernest Price suffered from sickle-cell anemia. In 1997, Price asked Dr. Ann Houston, his physician, to prescribe OxyContin, a strong narcotic, for the pain. Over the next several years, Price saw at least ten different physicians at ten different clinics in two cities, and used seven pharmacies in three cities, to obtain and fill simultaneous prescriptions for OxyContin. In March 2001, when Houston learned of these activities, she refused to write more prescriptions for Price. As other physicians became aware of Price's actions, they also stopped writing his prescriptions. Price filed a suit in a Mississippi state court against Purdue Pharma Co. and other producers and distributors of OxyContin, as well as his physicians and the pharmacies that had filled the prescriptions. Price alleged negligence, among other things, claiming that OxyContin's addictive nature caused him injury and that this was the defendants' fault. The defendants argued that Price's claim should be dismissed because it arose from his own wrongdoing. Who should be held *legally* liable? Should any of the parties be considered *ethically* responsible? Why or why not? [*Price v. Purdue Pharma Co.*, 920 So.2d 479 (Miss. 2006)]

4–10. Ethical Leadership. In 1999, Andrew Fastow, chief financial officer of Enron Corp., asked Merrill Lynch, an investment firm, to participate in a bogus sale of three barges so that Enron could record earnings of $12.5 million from the sale. Through a third entity, Fastow bought the barges back within six months and paid Merrill for its participation. Five Merrill employees were convicted of conspiracy to commit wire fraud, in part, on an "honest services" theory. Under this theory, an employee deprives his or her employer of "honest services" when the employee promotes his or her own interests, rather than the interests of the employer. Four of the employees appealed to the U.S. Court of Appeals for the Fifth Circuit, arguing that this charge did not apply to the conduct in which they engaged. The court agreed, reasoning that the barge deal was conducted to benefit Enron, not to enrich the Merrill employees at Enron's expense. Meanwhile, Kevin Howard, chief financial officer of Enron Broadband Services (EBS), engaged in "Project Braveheart," which enabled EBS to show earnings of $111 million in 2000 and 2001. Braveheart involved the sale of an interest in the future revenue of a video-on-demand venture to nCube, a small technology firm, which was paid for its help when EBS bought the interest back. Howard was convicted of wire fraud, in part, on the "honest services" theory. He filed a motion to vacate his conviction on the same basis that the Merrill employees had argued. Did Howard act unethically? Explain. Should the court grant his motion? Discuss. [*United States v. Howard*, 471 F.Supp.2d 772 (S.D.Tex. 2007)]

4–11. A QUESTION OF ETHICS

Steven Soderbergh is the Academy Award–winning director of Erin Brockovich, Traffic, *and many other films. CleanFlicks, LLC, filed a suit in a federal district court against Soderbergh, fifteen other directors, and the Directors Guild of America. The plaintiff asked the court to rule that it had the right to sell DVDs of the defendants' films altered without the defendants' consent to delete scenes of "sex, nudity, profanity and gory violence." CleanFlicks sold or rented the edited DVDs under the slogan "It's About Choice" to consumers, sometimes indirectly through retailers. It would not sell to retailers that made unauthorized copies of the edited films. The defendants, with DreamWorks, LLC and seven other movie studios that own the copyrights to the films, filed a counterclaim against CleanFlicks and others engaged in the same business, alleging copyright infringement. Those filing the counterclaim asked the court to enjoin (prevent) CleanFlicks and the others from making and marketing altered versions of the films. [*CleanFlicks of Colorado, LLC v. Soderbergh, *433 F.Supp.2d 1236 (D.Colo. 2006)]*

(a) Movie studios often edit their films to conform to content and other standards and sell the edited versions to network television and other commercial buyers. In this case, however, the studios objected when CleanFlicks edited the films and sold the altered versions directly to consumers. Similarly, CleanFlicks made unauthorized copies of the studios' DVDs to edit the films, but objected to others' making unauthorized copies of the altered versions. Is there anything unethical about these apparently contradictory positions? Why or why not?

(b) CleanFlicks and its competitors asserted, among other things, that they were making "fair use" of the studios' copyrighted works. They argued that by their actions "they are criticizing the objectionable content commonly found in current movies and that they are providing more socially acceptable alternatives to enable families to view the films together, without exposing children to the presumed harmful effects emanating from the objectionable content." If you were the judge, how would you view this argument? Is a court the appropriate forum for making determinations of public or social policy? Explain.

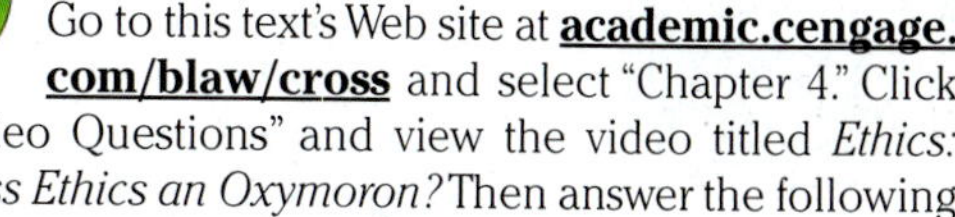

4-12. VIDEO QUESTION

Go to this text's Web site at **academic.cengage.com/blaw/cross** and select "Chapter 4." Click on "Video Questions" and view the video titled *Ethics: Business Ethics an Oxymoron?* Then answer the following questions.

(a) According to the instructor in the video, what is the primary reason that businesses act ethically?

(b) Which of the two approaches to ethical reasoning that were discussed in the chapter seems to have had more influence on the instructor in the discussion of how business activities are related to societies? Explain your answer.

(c) The instructor asserts that "[i]n the end, it is the unethical behavior that becomes costly, and conversely ethical behavior creates its own competitive advantage." Do you agree with this statement? Why or why not?

LAW ON THE WEB

For updated links to resources available on the Web, as well as a variety of other materials, visit this text's Web site at

academic.cengage.com/blaw/cross

South-Western Legal Studies in Business at Cengage Learning offers an in-depth "Inside Look" at the Enron debacle at

insidelook.westbuslaw.com

You can find articles on issues relating to shareholders and corporate accountability at the Corporate Governance Web site. Go to

www.corpgov.net

For an example of an online group that focuses on corporate activities from the perspective of corporate social responsibility, go to

www.corpwatch.org

Global Exchange offers information on global business activities, including some of the ethical issues stemming from those activities, at

www.globalexchange.org

Legal Research Exercises on the Web

Go to **academic.cengage.com/blaw/cross**, the Web site that accompanies this text. Select "Chapter 4" and click on "Internet Exercises." There you will find the following Internet research exercises that you can perform to learn more about the topics covered in this chapter.

Internet Exercise 4–1: Legal Perspective
Ethics in Business

Internet Exercise 4–2: Management Perspective
Environmental Self-Audits

UNIT ONE · FOCUS ON ETHICS

Ethics and the Foundations

In Chapter 4, we examined the importance of ethical standards in the business context. We also offered suggestions on how business decision makers can create an ethical workplace. Certainly, it is not wrong for a businessperson to try to increase his or her firm's profits. But there are limits, both ethical and legal, to how far businesspersons can go. In preparing for a career in business, you will find that a background in business ethics and a commitment to ethical behavior are just as important as a knowledge of the specific laws that are covered in this text. Of course, no textbook can give an answer to each and every ethical question that arises in the business environment. Nor can it anticipate the types of ethical questions that will arise in the future, as technology and globalization continue to transform the workplace and business relationships.

The most we can do is examine the types of ethical issues that businesspersons have faced in the past and that they are facing today. In the *Focus on Ethics* sections in this book, we provide examples of specific ethical issues that have arisen in various areas of business activity.

In this initial *Focus on Ethics* feature, we look first at the relationship between business ethics and the legal environment. We then examine various obstacles to ethical behavior in the business context. We conclude the feature by exploring the parameters of corporate social responsibility through a discussion of whether corporations have an ethical duty to the community or society at large.

Business Ethics and the Legal Environment

Business ethics and the legal environment are closely intertwined because ultimately the law rests on social beliefs about right and wrong behavior in the business world. Thus, businesspersons, by complying with the law, are acting ethically. Mere legal compliance (the "moral minimum" in terms of business ethics), however, is often not enough. This is because the law does not—and cannot—provide the answers for all ethical questions.

In the business world, numerous actions may be unethical but not necessarily illegal. Consider an example. Suppose that a pharmaceutical company is banned from marketing a particular drug in the United States because of the drug's possible adverse side effects. Yet no law prohibits the company from selling the drug in foreign markets—even though some consumers in those markets may suffer serious health problems as a result of using the drug. At issue here is not whether it would be legal to market the drug in other countries but whether it would be *ethical* to do so. In other words, the law has its limits—it cannot make all ethical decisions for us. Rather, the law assumes that those in business will behave ethically in their day-to-day dealings. If they do not, the courts will not come to their assistance.

Obstacles to Ethical Business Behavior

People sometimes behave unethically in the business context, just as they do in their private lives. Some businesspersons knowingly engage in unethical behavior because they think that they can "get away with it"—that no one will ever learn of their unethical actions. Examples of this kind of unethical behavior include padding expense accounts, casting doubts on the integrity of a rival co-worker to gain a job promotion, and stealing company supplies or equipment. Obviously, these acts are unethical, and some of them are illegal as well. In some situations, however, businesspersons who would choose to act ethically may be deterred from doing so because of situational circumstances or external pressures.

Ethics and the Corporate Environment Individuals in their personal lives normally are free to decide ethical issues as they wish and to follow through on those decisions. In the business world, and particularly in the corporate environment, rarely is such a decision made by *one* person. If you are an officer or a manager of a large company, for example, you will find that the decision as to what is right or wrong for the company is not totally yours to make. Your input may weigh in the decision, but ultimately a corporate decision is a collective undertaking.

Additionally, collective decision making, because it places emphasis on consensus and unity of opinion, tends to hinder individual ethical assertiveness. Suppose that a director has ethical concerns about a planned corporate venture that promises to be highly profitable. If the other directors have no such misgivings, the director who does may be swayed by the others' enthusiasm for the project and downplay her or his own criticisms.

Furthermore, just as no one person makes a collective decision, so no one person (normally) is held accountable for the decision. The corporate enterprise thus tends to shield corporate

personnel from both individual exposure to the consequences of their decisions (such as direct experience with someone who suffers harm from a corporate product) and personal accountability for those decisions.

FOCUS on ETHICS

Ethics and Management Much unethical business behavior occurs simply because management does not always make clear what ethical standards and behaviors are expected of the firm's employees. Although most firms now issue ethical policies or codes of conduct, these policies and codes are not always effective in creating an ethical workplace. At times, this is because the firm's ethical policies are not communicated clearly to employees or do not bear on the real ethical issues confronting decision makers. Additionally, particularly in a large corporation, unethical behavior in one corporate department may simply escape the attention of the officers in control of the corporation or those responsible for implementing and monitoring the company's ethics program.

Unethical behavior may also occur when corporate management, by its own conduct, indicates that ethical considerations take a back seat. If management makes no attempt to deter unethical behavior—through reprimands or employment terminations, for example—it will be obvious to employees that management is not all that serious about ethics. Likewise, if a company gives promotions or salary increases to those who clearly use unethical tactics to increase the firm's profits, then employees who do not resort to such tactics will be at a disadvantage. An employee in this situation may decide that because "everyone else does it," he or she might as well do it, too.

Of course, an even stronger encouragement to unethical behavior occurs when employers engage in blatantly unethical or illegal conduct and expect their employees to do so as well. An employee in this situation faces two options, neither of which is satisfactory: participate in the conduct or "blow the whistle" on (inform authorities of) the employer's actions—and, of course, risk being fired. (See Chapter 21 for a more detailed discussion of this ethical dilemma and its consequences for employees.)

Corporate Social Responsibility

As discussed in Chapter 4, just what constitutes corporate social responsibility has been debated for some time. In particular, questions arise concerning a corporation's ethical obligations to its community and to society as a whole.

A Corporation's Duty to the Community In some circumstances, the community in which a business enterprise is located is greatly affected by corporate decisions and therefore may be considered a stakeholder. Assume, for example, that a company employs two thousand workers at one of its plants. If the company decides that it would be profitable to close the plant, the employees—and the community—would suffer as a result. To be considered ethical in that situation (and, in some circumstances, to comply with laws governing plant shutdowns), a corporation must take both employees' needs and community needs into consideration when making such a decision.

Another ethical question sometimes arises when a firm moves into a community. Does the company have an obligation to evaluate first how its presence will affect that community (even though the community is not a stakeholder yet)? This question has surfaced in regard to the expansion of Wal-Mart Stores, Inc., into smaller communities. Generally, most people in such communities welcome the lower prices and wider array of goods that Wal-Mart offers relative to other, smaller stores in the area. A vocal minority of people in some communities, however, claim that smaller stores often find it impossible to compete with Wal-Mart's prices and thus are forced to go out of business. Many of these smaller stores have existed for years and, according to Wal-Mart's critics, enhance the quality of community life. These critics claim that it is unethical of Wal-Mart to disregard a town's interest in the quality and character of its community life.

In addition to expanding, Wal-Mart has been consolidating some of its smaller stores into large "superstores." As it consolidates, Wal-Mart is closing stores in some of the very towns in which it drove its smaller competitors out of business. This development raises yet another ethical question: Does a store such as Wal-Mart have an obligation to continue operations in a community once it has driven its competitors out of business?

A Corporation's Duty to Society Perhaps the most disputed area of corporate social responsibility is the nature of a corporation's duty to society at large. Those who contend that corporations should first and foremost attend to the goal of profit

(Continued)

measure is reasonable, it is generally held to be within the national taxing power. Moreover, the expansive interpretation of the commerce clause almost always provides a basis for sustaining a federal tax.

Article I, Section 8, also gives Congress its spending power—the power "to pay the Debts and provide for the common Defence and general Welfare of the United States." Congress can spend revenues not only to carry out its expressed powers but also to promote any objective it deems worthwhile, so long as it does not violate the Bill of Rights. The spending power necessarily involves policy choices, with which taxpayers may disagree.

Business and the Bill of Rights

The importance of a written declaration of the rights of individuals eventually caused the first Congress of the United States to submit twelve amendments to the U.S. Constitution to the states for approval. The first ten of these amendments, commonly known as the **Bill of Rights,** were adopted in 1791 and embody a series of protections for the individual against various types of interference by the federal government.[17] The protections guaranteed by these ten amendments are summarized in Exhibit 5–1.[18] Some of these constitutional protections apply to business entities as well. For example, corporations exist as separate legal entities, or *legal persons,* and enjoy many of the same rights and privileges as *natural persons* do.

Limits on Both Federal and State Governmental Actions

As originally intended, the Bill of Rights limited only the powers of the national government. Over time, however, the United States Supreme Court "incorporated" most of these rights into the protections against state actions afforded by the Fourteenth Amendment to the Constitution. That amendment, passed in 1868 after the Civil War, provides in part that "[n]o State shall . . . deprive any person of life, liberty, or property, without due process of law." Starting in 1925, the Supreme Court began to define various rights and liberties guaranteed in the U.S. Constitution as constituting "due process of law," which was required of state governments under the Fourteenth Amendment. Today, most of the rights and liberties set forth in the Bill of Rights apply to state governments as well as the national government. In other words, neither the federal government nor state governments can deprive persons of those rights and liberties.

The rights secured by the Bill of Rights are not absolute. As you can see in Exhibit 5–1, many of the rights guaranteed by the first ten amendments are described in very general terms. For example, the Fourth Amendment prohibits *unreasonable* searches and seizures, but it does not define what constitutes an unreasonable search or seizure. Similarly, the Eighth Amendment prohibits excessive bail or fines, but no definition of *excessive* is contained in that amendment. Ultimately, it is the United States Supreme Court, as the final interpreter of the Constitution, that defines our rights and determines their boundaries.

Freedom of Speech

A democratic form of government cannot survive unless people can freely voice their political opinions and criticize government actions or policies. Freedom of speech, particularly political speech, is thus a prized right, and traditionally the courts have protected this right to the fullest extent possible.

Symbolic speech—gestures, movements, articles of clothing, and other forms of expressive conduct—is also given substantial protection by the courts. For example, in 1989 the United States Supreme Court ruled that the burning of the American flag as part of a peaceful protest is a constitutionally protected form of expression.[19] Similarly, participating in a hunger strike, holding signs at an antiwar protest, or wearing a black armband would be protected as symbolic speech.

Reasonable Restrictions Expression—oral, written, or symbolized by conduct—is subject to reasonable restrictions. A balance must be struck between a government's obligation to protect its citizens and those citizens' exercise of their rights. Reasonableness is analyzed on a case-by-case basis. If a restriction imposed by the government is content neutral, then a court may allow it. To be content neutral, the restriction must be aimed at combating some

17. Another of these proposed amendments was ratified 203 years later (in 1992) and became the Twenty-seventh Amendment to the Constitution. See Appendix B.

18. See the Constitution in Appendix B for the complete text of each amendment.

19. *Texas v. Johnson,* 491 U.S. 397, 109 S.Ct. 2533, 105 L.Ed.2d 342 (1989).

EXHIBIT 5–1 • Protections Guaranteed by the Bill of Rights

First Amendment: Guarantees the freedoms of religion, speech, and the press and the rights to assemble peaceably and to petition the government.

Second Amendment: States that the right of the people to keep and bear arms shall not be infringed.

Third Amendment: Prohibits, in peacetime, the lodging of soldiers in any house without the owner's consent.

Fourth Amendment: Prohibits unreasonable searches and seizures of persons or property.

Fifth Amendment: Guarantees the rights to indictment by grand jury, to due process of law, and to fair payment when private property is taken for public use; prohibits compulsory self-incrimination and double jeopardy (being tried again for an alleged crime for which one has already stood trial).

Sixth Amendment: Guarantees the accused in a criminal case the right to a speedy and public trial by an impartial jury and with counsel. The accused has the right to cross-examine witnesses against him or her and to solicit testimony from witnesses in his or her favor.

Seventh Amendment: Guarantees the right to a trial by jury in a civil case involving at least twenty dollars.[a]

Eighth Amendment: Prohibits excessive bail and fines, as well as cruel and unusual punishment.

Ninth Amendment: Establishes that the people have rights in addition to those specified in the Constitution.

Tenth Amendment: Establishes that those powers neither delegated to the federal government nor denied to the states are reserved to the states and to the people.

a. Twenty dollars was forty days' pay for the average person when the Bill of Rights was written.

societal problem, such as crime, and not be aimed at suppressing the expressive conduct or its message. For example, courts have often protected nude dancing as a form of symbolic expression but have also allowed content-neutral laws that ban all public nudity, not just erotic dancing.[20]

The United States Supreme Court has also held that schools may restrict students' free speech rights at school events. In 2007, for example, the Court heard a case involving a high school student who had held up a banner saying "Bong Hits 4 Jesus" at an off-campus but school-sanctioned event. In a split decision, the majority of the Court ruled that school officials did not violate the student's free speech rights when they confiscated the banner and suspended the student for ten days. Because the banner could reasonably be interpreted as promoting the use of marijuana, and because the school had a written policy against illegal drugs, the majority concluded that the school's actions were justified. Several justices disagreed, however, noting that the majority's holding creates a special exception that will allow schools to censor any student speech that mentions drugs.[21]

20. See, for example, *Rameses, Inc. v. County of Orange,* 481 F.Supp.2d 1305 (M.D.Fla. 2007) and *City of Erie v. Pap's A.M.,* 529 U.S. 277, 120 S.Ct. 1382, 146 L.Ed.2d 265 (2000).

21. *Morse v. Frederick,* ___ U.S. ___, 127 S.Ct. 2618, 168 L.Ed.2d 290 (2007).

Corporate Political Speech Political speech by corporations also falls within the protection of the First Amendment. For example, many years ago the United States Supreme Court ruled that a Massachusetts statute, which prohibited corporations from making political contributions or expenditures that individuals were permitted to make, was unconstitutional.[22] Similarly, the Court has held that a law forbidding a corporation from placing inserts in its billing to express its views on controversial issues violates the First Amendment.[23] Although the Supreme Court has reversed this trend somewhat,[24] corporate political speech continues to be given significant protection under the First Amendment. For example, in 2003 and again in 2007 the Supreme Court struck down some portions of bipartisan campaign-finance reform laws as unconstitutional restraints on corporate political speech.[25]

22. *First National Bank of Boston v. Bellotti,* 435 U.S. 765, 98 S.Ct. 1407, 55 L.Ed.2d 707 (1978).

23. *Consolidated Edison Co. v. Public Service Commission,* 447 U.S. 530, 100 S.Ct. 2326, 65 L.Ed.2d 319 (1980).

24. See *Austin v. Michigan Chamber of Commerce,* 494 U.S. 652, 110 S.Ct. 1391, 108 L.Ed.2d 652 (1990), in which the Supreme Court upheld a state law prohibiting corporations from using general corporate funds for independent expenditures in state political campaigns.

25. *McConnell v. Federal Election Commission,* 540 U.S. 93, 124 S.Ct. 619, 157 L.Ed.2d 491 (2003); and *Federal Election Commission v. Wisconsin Right to Life, Inc.,* ___ U.S. ___, 127 S.Ct. 2652, 168 L.Ed.2d 329 (2007).

designed to prevent persons from viewing certain Web sites based on a site's Internet address or its **meta tags,** or key words. The CIPA was also challenged on constitutional grounds, but in 2003 the Supreme Court held that the act does not violate the First Amendment. The Court concluded that because libraries can disable the filters for any patrons who ask, the system is reasonably flexible and does not burden free speech to an unconstitutional extent.[34]

Because of the difficulties of policing the Internet as well as the constitutional complexities of prohibiting online obscenity through legislation, it remains a continuing problem in the United States (and worldwide).

Freedom of Religion

The First Amendment states that the government may neither establish any religion nor prohibit the free exercise of religious practices. The first part of this constitutional provision, which is referred to as the **establishment clause,** has to do with the separation of church and state. The second part of the provision is known as the **free exercise clause.**

The Establishment Clause The establishment clause prohibits the government from establishing a state-sponsored religion, as well as from passing laws that promote (aid or endorse) religion or that show a preference for one religion over another. Establishment clause issues often involve such matters as the legality of allowing or requiring school prayers, using state-issued school vouchers to pay for tuition at religious schools, teaching evolutionary versus creationist theory, and giving state and local government aid to religious organizations and schools.

Federal or state laws that do not promote or place a significant burden on religion are constitutional even if they have some impact on religion. "Sunday closing laws," for example, make the performance of some commercial activities on Sunday illegal. These statutes, also known as "blue laws" (from the color of the paper on which an early Sunday law was written), have been upheld on the ground that it is a legitimate function of government to provide a day of rest to promote the health and welfare of workers. Even though closing laws admittedly make it easier for Christians to attend religious services, the courts have viewed this effect as an incidental, not a primary, purpose of Sunday closing laws.

The Free Exercise Clause The free exercise clause guarantees that no person can be compelled to do something that is contrary to his or her religious beliefs. For this reason, if a law or policy is contrary to a person's religious beliefs, exemptions are often made to accommodate those beliefs.

When religious practices work against public policy and the public welfare, though, the government can act. For example, regardless of a child's or parent's religious beliefs, the government can require certain types of vaccinations in the interest of public welfare. The government's interest must be sufficiently compelling, however. The United States Supreme Court ruled in 2006 that the government had failed to demonstrate a sufficiently compelling interest in barring a church from the sacramental use of an illegal controlled substance. (The church members used hoasca tea, which is brewed from plants native to the Amazon rain forest and contains a hallucinogenic drug, in the practice of a sincerely held religious belief.)[35]

For business firms, an important issue involves the accommodation that businesses must make for the religious beliefs of their employees. Generally, if an employee's religion prohibits her or him from working on a certain day of the week or at a certain type of job, the employer must make a reasonable attempt to accommodate these religious requirements. The only requirement is that the belief be religious in nature and sincerely held by the employee.[36] (See Chapter 21 for a further discussion of religious freedom in the employment context.)

Searches and Seizures

The Fourth Amendment protects the "right of the people to be secure in their persons, houses, papers, and effects." Before searching or seizing private property, law enforcement officers must usually obtain a **search warrant**—an order from a judge or other public official authorizing the search or seizure.

Search Warrants and Probable Cause To obtain a search warrant, law enforcement officers must convince a judge that they have reasonable grounds, or probable cause, to believe a search will reveal evidence of a specific illegality. To establish **probable cause,** the officers must have trustworthy evidence that would convince a reasonable person

34. *United States v. American Library Association,* 539 U.S. 194, 123 S.Ct. 2297, 156 L.Ed.2d 221 (2003).

35. *Gonzales v. O Centro Espirita Beneficiente Uniao Do Vegtal,* 546 U.S. 418, 126 S.Ct. 1211, 163 L.Ed.2d 1017 (2006).

36. *Frazee v. Illinois Department of Employment Security,* 489 U.S. 829, 109 S.Ct. 1514, 103 L.Ed.2d 914 (1989).

that the proposed search or seizure is more likely justified than not. Furthermore, the Fourth Amendment prohibits *general* warrants. It requires a particular description of whatever is to be searched or seized. General searches through a person's belongings are impermissible. The search cannot extend beyond what is described in the warrant.

The requirement for a search warrant has several exceptions. One exception applies when the items sought are likely to be removed before a warrant can be obtained. For example, if a police officer has probable cause to believe that an automobile contains evidence of a crime and that the vehicle will likely be unavailable by the time a warrant is obtained, the officer can search the vehicle without a warrant.

Searches and Seizures in the Business Context Constitutional protection against unreasonable searches and seizures is important to businesses and professionals. Equally important is the government's interest in ensuring compliance with federal and state regulations, especially rules meant to protect the safety of employees and the public.

Because of the strong governmental interest in protecting the public, a warrant normally is not required for the seizure of spoiled or contaminated food. In addition, warrants are not required for searches of businesses in such highly regulated industries as liquor, guns, and strip mining. General manufacturing is not considered to be one of these highly regulated industries, however.

Generally, government inspectors do not have the right to search business premises without a warrant, although the standard of probable cause is not the same as that required in nonbusiness contexts. The existence of a general and neutral enforcement plan normally will justify issuance of the warrant. Lawyers and accountants frequently possess the business records of their clients, and inspecting these documents while they are out of the hands of their true owners also requires a warrant.

In the following case, after receiving a report of suspected health-care fraud, state officials entered and searched the office of a licensed physician without obtaining a warrant. The physician claimed that the search was unreasonable and improper.

CASE 5.3 U.S. v. Moon

United States Court of Appeals, Sixth Circuit, 2008. 513 F.3d 527.
www.ca6.uscourts.gov[a]

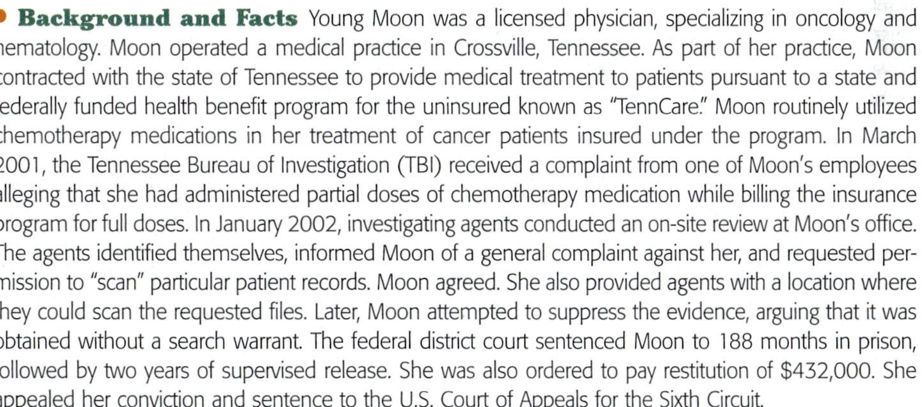

Background and Facts Young Moon was a licensed physician, specializing in oncology and hematology. Moon operated a medical practice in Crossville, Tennessee. As part of her practice, Moon contracted with the state of Tennessee to provide medical treatment to patients pursuant to a state and federally funded health benefit program for the uninsured known as "TennCare." Moon routinely utilized chemotherapy medications in her treatment of cancer patients insured under the program. In March 2001, the Tennessee Bureau of Investigation (TBI) received a complaint from one of Moon's employees alleging that she had administered partial doses of chemotherapy medication while billing the insurance program for full doses. In January 2002, investigating agents conducted an on-site review at Moon's office. The agents identified themselves, informed Moon of a general complaint against her, and requested permission to "scan" particular patient records. Moon agreed. She also provided agents with a location where they could scan the requested files. Later, Moon attempted to suppress the evidence, arguing that it was obtained without a search warrant. The federal district court sentenced Moon to 188 months in prison, followed by two years of supervised release. She was also ordered to pay restitution of $432,000. She appealed her conviction and sentence to the U.S. Court of Appeals for the Sixth Circuit.

IN THE LANGUAGE OF THE COURT
CLAY, **Circuit Judge.**

* * * *

The Fourth Amendment bars the government from conducting unreasonable searches and seizures. This prohibition extends to both private homes and commercial premises. Additionally, searches pursuant to criminal as well as administrative investigations must comport

a. Click on "Opinions Search" and in the "Short Title contains" box, type in "Moon." Click on Submit Query. Under "Published Opinions," select the link to "0820031p.06" to access the opinion.

CASE CONTINUES

CASE 5.3 CONTINUED to the strictures of the Fourth Amendment. Under the Fourth Amendment, searches "conducted without a warrant issued upon probable cause [are] per se unreasonable * * * subject only to a few specifically established and well-delineated exceptions."

*The well-delineated exception at issue here is consent. If an officer obtains consent to search, a warrantless search does not offend the Constitution. * * * Consent is voluntary when it is "unequivocal, specific and intelligently given, uncontaminated by any duress or coercion."* [Emphasis added.]

* * * *

We find that the district court's denial of the motion to suppress was not clearly erroneous inasmuch as Defendant voluntarily consented to the search of her office. The only evidence on the question of verbal consent was provided in the form of testimony by Agent Andy Corbitt of TBI at the suppression hearing. Agent Corbitt testified that three members of the TBI investigative team entered Defendant's office dressed in "business professional" attire, with weapons concealed. Agents identified themselves to Defendant, explained that there was an ongoing investigation and requested access to particular patient files. Defendant inquired about the nature of the investigation but was not informed of the specific nature of the allegations. Following this conversation, Defendant stated it would be "fine" for agents to access requested files and that they "could scan whatever [they] needed to." Further, Defendant provided agents with a space where they could scan the requested files.

Defendant, however, claims that the verbal consent was not voluntary as she merely acquiesced to a claim of lawful authority.

* * * Based on the totality of the circumstances, we find that Defendant voluntarily consented to the search of her office and therefore the motion to suppress was properly denied.

- **Decision and Remedy** *The U.S. Court of Appeals for the Sixth Circuit affirmed the district court's decision. Because Dr. Moon voluntarily allowed the agents to examine her files and to scan them, the resulting evidence did not need to be suppressed. A search warrant was not necessary.*

- **What If the Facts Were Different?** *Assume that Dr. Moon had proved that using partial doses of the chemotherapy drugs did not affect the "cure" rate for her cancer patients. Would the court have ruled differently? Why or why not?*

- **The Legal Environment Dimension** *Does the length of Dr. Moon's prison sentence seem appropriate here? Why or why not?*

Border Searches of Computers Warrantless border searches have long been upheld by the courts as means to prevent persons from physically bringing drugs, contraband, and illegal aliens into the United States. In recent years, the courts have also started allowing border guards to search through the temporary files stored on laptop computers and to use the history of Web pages viewed as criminal evidence.

Consider, for example, a 2006 case involving Stuart Romm, a suspended lawyer from Massachusetts who traveled to British Columbia on business. A border agent asked to see Romm's laptop computer and briefly examined the Internet cache, or temporary folder showing the history of Web sites that Romm had visited. The border guards discovered that Romm had looked at some child pornography Web sites and detained him while a forensic computer specialist analyzed the hard drive. Analysis confirmed that Romm had viewed ten images of child pornography and then deleted (or at least attempted to delete) the images from his computer. Romm was convicted and sentenced to serve ten to fifteen years in prison. A federal appellate court upheld his conviction.[37] The holding in this case could be applied to any type of illegal material found on a laptop computer during a border search, including unauthorized images of copyrighted materials or confidential business data (see Chapter 14).

Self-Incrimination

The Fifth Amendment guarantees that no person "shall be compelled in any criminal case to be a witness against himself." Thus, in any federal or state (because the due process clause extends the protection to state courts) proceeding, an accused person cannot be forced to give testimony that might subject him or her to any criminal prosecution.

37. *United States v. Romm*, 455 F.3d 990 (9th Cir. 2006).

The Fifth Amendment's guarantee against self-incrimination extends only to natural persons. Therefore, neither corporations nor partnerships receive Fifth Amendment protection. When a partnership is required to produce business records, it must do so even if the information provided incriminates the individual partners of the firm. In contrast, sole proprietors and sole practitioners (those who fully own their businesses) cannot be compelled to produce their business records. These individuals have full protection against self-incrimination because they function in only one capacity; there is no separate business entity.

Due Process and Equal Protection

Other constitutional guarantees of great significance to Americans are mandated by the *due process clauses* of the Fifth and Fourteenth Amendments and the *equal protection clause* of the Fourteenth Amendment.

Due Process

Both the Fifth and Fourteenth Amendments provide that no person shall be deprived "of life, liberty, or property, without due process of law." The **due process clause** of these constitutional amendments has two aspects—procedural and substantive. Note that the due process clause applies to "legal persons" (that is, corporations), as well as to individuals.

Procedural Due Process *Procedural* due process requires that any government decision to take life, liberty, or property must be made equitably; that is, the government must give a person proper notice and an opportunity to be heard. Fair procedures must be used in determining whether a person will be subjected to punishment or have some burden imposed on her or him. Fair procedure has been interpreted as requiring that the person have at least an opportunity to object to a proposed action before an impartial, neutral decision maker (which need not be a judge). Thus, for example, if a driver's license is construed as a property interest, the state must provide some sort of opportunity for the driver to object before suspending or terminating the license.

Substantive Due Process Substantive due process protects an individual's life, liberty, or property against certain government actions regardless of the fairness of the procedures used to implement them. Substantive due process limits what the government may do in its legislative and executive capacities.[38] Legislation must be fair and reasonable in content and must further a legitimate governmental objective. Only when state conduct is arbitrary, or shocks the conscience, however, will it rise to the level of violating substantive due process.[39]

If a law or other governmental action limits a fundamental right, the state must have a legitimate and compelling interest to justify its action. Fundamental rights include interstate travel, privacy, voting, marriage and family, and all First Amendment rights. Thus, a state must have substantial reason for taking any action that infringes on a person's free speech rights. In situations not involving fundamental rights, a law or action does not violate substantive due process if it rationally relates to any legitimate government purpose. Under this test, virtually any business regulation will be upheld as reasonable.

Equal Protection

Under the Fourteenth Amendment, a state may not "deny to any person within its jurisdiction the equal protection of the laws." The United States Supreme Court has interpreted the due process clause of the Fifth Amendment to make the **equal protection clause** applicable to the federal government as well. Equal protection means that the government cannot enact laws that treat similarly situated individuals differently.

Both substantive due process and equal protection require review of the substance of the law or other governmental action rather than review of the procedures used. When a law or action limits the liberty of all persons to do something, it may violate substantive due process; when a law or action limits the liberty of some persons but not others, it may violate the equal protection clause. Thus, for example, if a law prohibits all advertising on the sides of trucks, it raises a substantive due process question; if it makes an exception to allow truck owners to advertise their own businesses, it raises an equal protection issue.

In an equal protection inquiry, when a law or action distinguishes between or among individuals, the basis for the distinction, or classification, is examined.

38. *County of Sacramento v. Lewis,* 523 U.S. 833, 118 S.Ct. 1708, 140 L.Ed.2d 1043 (1998).

39. See, for example, *Breen v. Texas A&M University,* 485 F.3d 325 (5th Cir. 2007); *Hart v. City of Little Rock,* 432 F.3d 801 (8th Cir. 2005); *County of Sacramento v. Lewis,* 523 U.S. 833, 118 S.Ct. 1708, 140 L.Ed.2d 1043 (1998); and *United States v. Salerno,* 481 U.S. 739, 107 S.Ct. 2095, 95 L.Ed.2d 697 (1987).

Depending on the classification, the courts apply different levels of scrutiny, or "tests," to determine whether the law or action violates the equal protection clause. The courts use one of three standards: strict scrutiny, intermediate scrutiny, or the "rational basis" test.

Strict Scrutiny The most difficult standard to meet is that of *strict scrutiny.* Under strict scrutiny, the classification must be necessary to promote a *compelling state interest.* Generally, few laws or actions survive strict-scrutiny analysis by the courts.

Strict scrutiny is applied when a law or action prohibits some persons from exercising a fundamental right or classifies individuals based on a *suspect trait*—such as race, national origin, or citizenship status. For example, to prevent violence caused by racial gangs in prisons, corrections officials in California segregated prisoners by race for up to sixty days after they entered (or transferred to) a correctional facility. A prisoner challenged that policy. Ultimately, the United States Supreme Court held that all racial classifications, because they are based on a suspect trait, must be analyzed under strict scrutiny.[40]

Intermediate Scrutiny Another standard, that of *intermediate scrutiny,* is applied in cases involving discrimination based on gender or legitimacy. Laws using these classifications must be *substantially related to important government objectives.* For example, an important government objective is preventing illegitimate teenage pregnancies. Therefore, because males and females are not similarly situated in this regard—only females can become pregnant—a law that punishes men but not women for statutory rape will be upheld, even though it treats men and women unequally.

The state also has an important objective in establishing time limits (called *statutes of limitation*) for how long after an event a particular type of action can be brought. Such limits prevent persons from bringing fraudulent and stale (outdated) claims. Nevertheless, the limitation period must be substantially related to the important objective. Suppose that a state law requires illegitimate children to file a paternity action within six years of their birth in order to seek support from their biological fathers. This law will fail if legitimate children can seek support from their fathers at any time because distinguishing between support claims on the basis of legitimacy has no relation to the objective of preventing fraudulent or stale claims.

40. *Johnson v. California,* 543 U.S. 499, 125 S.Ct. 1141, 160 L.Ed.2d 949 (2005).

The "Rational Basis" Test In matters of economic or social welfare, a classification will be considered valid if there is any conceivable *rational basis* on which the classification might relate to a legitimate government interest. It is almost impossible for a law or action to fail the rational basis test. Thus, for example, a city ordinance that in effect prohibits all pushcart vendors, except a specific few, from operating in a particular area of the city will be upheld if the city provides a rational basis—such as reducing the traffic in the particular area—for the ordinance. In contrast, a law that provides unemployment benefits only to people over six feet tall would clearly fail the rational basis test because it could not further any legitimate government objective.

Privacy Rights

The U.S. Constitution does not explicitly mention a general right to privacy. In a 1928 Supreme Court case, *Olmstead v. United States,*[41] Justice Louis Brandeis stated in his dissent that the right to privacy is "the most comprehensive of rights and the right most valued by civilized men." The majority of the justices at that time did not agree, and it was not until the 1960s that a majority on the Supreme Court endorsed the view that the Constitution protects individual privacy rights. In a landmark 1965 case, *Griswold v. Connecticut,*[42] the Supreme Court held that a constitutional right to privacy was implied by the First, Third, Fourth, Fifth, and Ninth Amendments.

Federal Statutes Affecting Privacy Rights

In the last several decades, Congress has enacted a number of statutes that protect the privacy of individuals in various areas of concern. In the 1960s, Americans were sufficiently alarmed by the accumulation of personal information in government files that they pressured Congress to pass laws permitting individuals to access their files. Congress responded in 1966 with the Freedom of Information Act, which allows any person to request copies of any information on her or him contained in federal government files. In 1974, Congress passed the Privacy Act, which also gives persons the right to access such information. Since then, Congress has passed numerous other

41. 277 U.S. 438, 48 S.Ct. 564, 72 L.Ed. 944 (1928).
42. 381 U.S. 479, 85 S.Ct. 1678, 14 L.Ed.2d 510 (1965).

laws protecting individuals' privacy rights with respect to financial transactions, electronic communications, and other activities in which personal information may be gathered and stored by organizations.

Medical Information Responding to the growing need to protect the privacy of individuals' health records—particularly computerized records—Congress passed the Health Insurance Portability and Accountability Act (HIPAA) of 1996.[43] This act, which took effect on April 14, 2003, defines and limits the circumstances in which an individual's "protected health information" may be used or disclosed.

The HIPAA requires health-care providers and health-care plans, including certain employers who sponsor health plans, to inform patients of their privacy rights and of how their personal medical information may be used. The act also states that a person's medical records generally may not be used for purposes unrelated to health care—such as marketing, for example—or disclosed to others without the individual's permission. Covered entities must formulate written privacy policies, designate privacy officials, limit access to computerized health data, physically secure medical records with lock and key, train employees and volunteers on their privacy policies, and sanction those who violate the policies. These protections are intended to assure individuals that their health information, including genetic information, will be properly protected and not used for purposes that the patient did not know about or authorize.

The Patriot Act In the wake of the terrorist attacks of September 11, 2001, Congress passed legislation often referred to as the USA Patriot Act.[44] The Patriot Act has given government officials increased authority to monitor Internet activities (such as e-mail and Web site visits) and to gain access to personal financial information and student information. Law enforcement officials can now track a person's telephone and e-mail communications to find out the identity of the other party or parties. The government must certify that the information likely to be obtained by such monitoring is relevant to an ongoing criminal investigation but does not need to provide proof of any wrongdoing to gain access to this information.[45] Privacy advocates argue that this law adversely affects the constitutional rights of all Americans, and it has been widely criticized in the media, fueling a public debate over how to secure privacy rights in an electronic age.

Other Laws Affecting Privacy

State constitutions and statutes also protect individuals' privacy rights, often to a significant degree. Privacy rights are also protected under tort law (see Chapter 12). Additionally, the Federal Trade Commission has played an active role in protecting the privacy rights of online consumers (see Chapter 23). The protection of employees' privacy rights, particularly with respect to electronic monitoring practices, is an area of growing concern (see Chapter 20).

43. The HIPAA was enacted as Pub. L. No. 104-191 (1996) and is codified in 29 U.S.C.A. Sections 1181 *et seq.*

44. The Uniting and Strengthening America by Providing Appropriate Tools Required to Intercept and Obstruct Terrorism Act of 2001, also known as the USA Patriot Act, was enacted as Pub. L. No. 107-56 (2001) and extended in early 2006 by Pub. L. No. 109-173 (2006).

45. See, for example, a case in which a federal appeals court upheld the government's warrantless monitoring of electronic communications. *American Civil Liberties Union v. National Security Agency*, 493 F.3d 644 (6th Cir. 2007).

REVIEWING Constitutional Law

A state legislature enacted a statute that required any motorcycle operator or passenger on the state's highways to wear a protective helmet. Jim Alderman, a licensed motorcycle operator, sued the state to block enforcement of the law. Alderman asserted that the statute violated the equal protection clause because it placed requirements on motorcyclists that were not imposed on other motorists. Using the information presented in the chapter, answer the following questions.

1. Why does this statute raise equal protection issues instead of substantive due process concerns?
2. What are the three levels of scrutiny that the courts use in determining whether a law violates the equal protection clause?
3. Which standard of scrutiny, or test, would apply to this situation? Why?
4. Applying this standard, or test, is the helmet statute constitutional? Why or why not?

TERMS AND CONCEPTS

Bill of Rights 112
checks and balances 108
commerce clause 108
due process clause 121
equal protection clause 121
establishment clause 118
federal form of government 106
filtering software 117
free exercise clause 118
full faith and credit clause 107
meta tags 118
police powers 106
preemption 109
privileges and immunities clause 107
probable cause 118
search warrant 118
supremacy clause 109
symbolic speech 112

QUESTIONS AND CASE PROBLEMS

5–1. A Georgia state law requires the use of contoured rear-fender mudguards on trucks and trailers operating within Georgia state lines. The statute further makes it illegal for trucks and trailers to use straight mudguards. In approximately thirty-five other states, straight mudguards are legal. Moreover, in Florida, straight mudguards are explicitly required by law. There is some evidence suggesting that contoured mudguards might be a little safer than straight mudguards. Discuss whether this Georgia statute violates any constitutional provisions.

5–2. QUESTION WITH SAMPLE ANSWER

Thomas worked in the nonmilitary operations of a large firm that produced both military and nonmilitary goods. When the company discontinued the production of nonmilitary goods, Thomas was transferred to a plant producing military equipment. Thomas left his job, claiming that it violated his religious principles to participate in the manufacture of goods to be used in destroying life. In effect, he argued, the transfer to the military equipment plant forced him to quit his job. He was denied unemployment compensation by the state because he had not been effectively "discharged" by the employer but had voluntarily terminated his employment. Did the state's denial of unemployment benefits to Thomas violate the free exercise clause of the First Amendment? Explain.

- **For a sample answer to Question 5–2, go to Appendix I at the end of this text.**

5–3. A business has a backlog of orders, and to meet its deadlines, management decides to run the firm seven days a week, eight hours a day. One of the employees, Abe Placer, refuses to work on Saturday on religious grounds. His refusal to work means that the firm may not meet its production deadlines and may therefore suffer a loss of future business. The firm fires Placer and replaces him with an employee who is willing to work seven days a week. Placer claims that by terminating his employment, his employer has violated his constitutional right to the free exercise of his religion. Do you agree? Why or why not?

5–4. The framers of the U.S. Constitution feared the twin evils of tyranny and anarchy. Discuss how specific provisions of the Constitution and the Bill of Rights reflect these fears and protect against both of these extremes.

5–5. Freedom of Speech. Henry Mishkoff is a Web designer whose firm does business as "Webfeats." When Taubman Co. began building a mall called "The Shops at Willow Bend" near Mishkoff's home, Mishkoff registered the domain name "shopsatwillowbend.com" and created a Web site with that address. The site featured information about the mall, a disclaimer indicating that Mishkoff's site was unofficial, and a link to the mall's official site. Taubman discovered Mishkoff's site and filed a suit in a federal district court against him. Mishkoff then registered other various names, including "taubmansucks.com," with links to a site documenting his battle with Taubman. (A Web name with a "sucks.com" moniker attached to it is known as a *complaint name,* and the process of registering and using such names is known as *cybergriping.*) Taubman asked the court to order Mishkoff to stop using all of these names. Should the court grant Taubman's request? On what basis might the court protect Mishkoff's use of the names? [*Taubman Co. v. Webfeats,* 319 F.3d 770 (6th Cir. 2003)]

5–6. CASE PROBLEM WITH SAMPLE ANSWER

To protect the privacy of individuals identified in information systems maintained by federal agencies, the Privacy Act of 1974 regulates the use of the information. The statute provides for a minimum award of $1,000 for "actual damages sustained" caused by "intentional or willful actions" to the "person entitled to recovery." Buck Doe filed for certain disability benefits with an office of the U.S. Department of Labor (DOL). The application form asked for Doe's Social Security number, which the DOL used to identify his claim on documents sent to groups of claimants, their employers, and the lawyers involved in their cases. This disclosed Doe's Social Security number beyond the limits set by the Privacy Act. Doe filed a suit in a federal district court against the DOL, alleging that he was "torn . . . all to pieces" and "greatly concerned and worried" because of the disclosure of his Social Security number and its potentially "devastating" consequences. He did not offer any proof of actual injury, however. Should damages be awarded in such circumstances solely on the basis of the agency's conduct, or should proof of some actual injury be required? Why? [*Doe v. Chao,* 540 U.S. 614, 124 S.Ct. 1204, 157 L.Ed.2d 1122 (2004)]

- **To view a sample answer for Problem 5–6, go to this book's Web site at academic.cengage.com/blaw/cross, select "Chapter 5," and click on "Case Problem with Sample Answer."**

5–7. Due Process. In 1994, the Board of County Commissioners of Yellowstone County, Montana, created Zoning District 17 in a rural area of the county and a planning and zoning commission for the district. The commission adopted zoning regulations, which provided, among other things, that "dwelling units" could be built only through "on-site construction." Later, county officials were unable to identify any health or safety concerns that were addressed by requiring on-site construction. There was no evidence that homes built off-site would negatively affect property values or cause harm to any other general welfare interest of the community. In December 1999, Francis and Anita Yurczyk bought two forty-acre tracts in District 17. The Yurczyks also bought a modular home and moved it onto the property the following spring. Within days, the county advised the Yurczyks that the home violated the on-site construction regulation and would have to be removed. The Yurczyks filed a suit in a Montana state court against the county, alleging, among other things, that the zoning regulation violated their due process rights. Does the Yurczyks' claim relate to procedural or substantive due process rights? What standard would the court apply to determine whether the regulation is constitutional? How should the court rule? Explain. [*Yurczyk v. Yellowstone County,* 2004 MT 3, 319 Mont. 169, 83 P.3d 266 (2004)]

5–8. Supremacy Clause. The Federal Communications Act of 1934 grants the right to govern all *interstate* telecommunications to the Federal Communications Commission (FCC) and the right to regulate all *intrastate* telecommunications to the states. The federal Telephone Consumer Protection Act of 1991, the Junk Fax Protection Act of 2005, and FCC rules permit a party to send unsolicited fax ads to recipients with whom the party has an "established business relationship" if those ads include an "opt-out" alternative. Section 17538.43 of California's Business and Professions Code (known as "SB 833") was enacted in 2005 to provide the citizens of California with greater protection than that afforded under federal law. SB 833 omits the "established business relationship" exception and requires a sender to obtain a recipient's express consent (an "opt-in" provision) before faxing an ad to that party into or out of California. The Chamber of Commerce of the United States filed a suit against Bill Lockyer, California's state attorney general, seeking to block the enforcement of SB 833. What principles support the plaintiff's position? How should the court resolve the issue? Explain. [*Chamber of Commerce of the United States v. Lockyer,* 463 F.3d 1076 (E.D.Cal. 2006)]

5–9. Freedom of Speech. For decades, New York City has had to deal with the vandalism and defacement of public property caused by unauthorized graffiti. Among other attempts to stop the damage, in December 2005 the city banned the sale of aerosol spray-paint cans and broad-tipped indelible markers to persons under twenty-one years of age and prohibited them from possessing such items on property other than their own. By May 1, 2006, five people—all under age twenty-one—had been cited for violations of these regulations, while 871 individuals had been arrested for actually making graffiti. Artists who wished to create graffiti on legal surfaces, such as canvas, wood, and clothing, included college student Lindsey Vincenty, who was studying visual arts. Unable to buy her supplies in the city or to carry them in the city if she bought them elsewhere, Vincenty and others filed a suit in a federal district court on behalf of themselves and other young artists against Michael Bloomberg, the city's mayor, and others. The plaintiffs claimed that, among other things, the new rules violated their right to freedom of speech. They asked the court to enjoin the enforcement of the rules. Should the court grant this request? Why or why not? [*Vincenty v. Bloomberg,* 476 F.3d 74 (2d Cir. 2007)]

5–10. A QUESTION OF ETHICS

Aric Toll owns and manages the Balboa Island Village Inn, a restaurant and bar in Newport Beach, California. Anne Lemen owns the "Island Cottage," a residence across an alley from the Inn. Lemen often complained to the authorities about excessive noise and the behavior of the Inn's customers, whom she called "drunks" and "whores." Lemen referred to Theresa Toll, Aric's wife, as "Madam Whore." Lemen told the Inn's bartender Ewa Cook that Cook "worked for Satan," was "Satan's wife," and was "going to have Satan's children." She told the Inn's neighbors that it was "a whorehouse" with "prostitution going on inside" and that it sold illegal drugs, sold alcohol to minors, made "sex videos," was involved in child pornography, had "Mafia connections," encouraged "lesbian activity," and stayed open until 6:00 A.M. Lemen also voiced her complaints to potential customers, and the Inn's sales dropped more than

EXHIBIT 6–1 • Costs of Regulation to Businesses

Type of Regulation	Cost per Employee (<20 Employees)	Cost per Employee (500+ Employees)
All federal regulations	$7,647	$5,282
Environmental	$3,296	$ 710
Economic	$2,127	$2,952
Workplace	$ 920	$ 841
Tax compliance	$1,304	$ 780

they cannot take advantage of the economies of scale available to larger operations. Clearly, the costs of regulation to business are considerable—and are significantly higher today than they were in 2005.

Given the costs that regulation entails, business has a strong incentive to try to influence the regulatory environment. Whenever new regulations are proposed, as happens constantly, companies may lobby the agency to try to persuade it not to adopt a particular regulation or to adopt one that is more cost-effective. These lobbying efforts consist mainly of providing information to regulators about the costs and problems that the rule may pose for business. At the same time, public-interest groups may be lobbying in favor of more stringent regulation. The rulemaking process, including these lobbying efforts, is governed by administrative law. If persuasion fails, administrative law also provides a tool by which businesses or other groups may challenge the legality of the new regulation.

SECTION 2 Agency Creation and Powers

To create an administrative agency, Congress passes **enabling legislation,** which specifies the name, purposes, functions, and powers of the agency being created. Federal administrative agencies may exercise only those powers that Congress has delegated to them in enabling legislation. Through similar enabling acts, state legislatures create state administrative agencies, which commonly parallel federal agencies.

An agency's enabling statute defines its legal authority. An agency cannot regulate beyond the powers granted by the statute, and it may be required to take some regulatory action by the terms of that statute.

Enabling Legislation—An Example

Consider the enabling legislation for the Federal Trade Commission (FTC). The enabling statute for this agency is the Federal Trade Commission Act of 1914.[2] The act prohibits unfair methods of competition and deceptive trade practices. It also describes the procedures that the FTC must follow to charge persons or organizations with violations of the act, and it provides for judicial review of agency orders. The act grants the FTC the power to do the following:

1. Create "rules and regulations for the purpose of carrying out the Act."
2. Conduct investigations of business practices.
3. Obtain reports from interstate corporations concerning their business practices.
4. Investigate possible violations of federal antitrust statutes.[3]
5. Publish findings of its investigations.
6. Recommend new legislation.
7. Hold trial-like hearings to resolve certain kinds of trade disputes that involve FTC regulations or federal antitrust laws.

The authorizing statute for the FTC allows it to prevent the use of "unfair methods of competition," but does not define *unfairness.* Congress delegated that authority to the commission, thereby providing it with considerable discretion in regulating competition.

When regulated groups oppose a rule adopted by an agency, they often bring a lawsuit arguing that the rule was not authorized by the enabling statute and is therefore void. Conversely, a group may file a suit claiming that an agency has illegally *failed* to pursue regulation required by the enabling statute.

2. 15 U.S.C. Sections 41–58.
3. The FTC shares enforcement of the Clayton Act with the Antitrust Division of the U.S. Department of Justice.

Types of Agencies

As discussed in Chapter 1, there are two basic types of administrative agencies: executive agencies and independent regulatory agencies. Federal *executive agencies* include the cabinet departments of the executive branch, which were formed to assist the president in carrying out executive functions, and the subagencies within the cabinet departments. The Occupational Safety and Health Administration, for example, is a subagency within the U.S. Department of Labor. Exhibit 6–2 on page 132 lists the cabinet departments and some of their most important subagencies.

All administrative agencies are part of the executive branch of government, but *independent regulatory agencies* are outside the major executive departments. The Federal Trade Commission and the Securities and Exchange Commission are examples of independent regulatory agencies. These and other selected independent regulatory agencies, as well as their principal functions, are listed in Exhibit 6–3 on page 133.

The accountability of the regulators is the most significant difference between the two types of agencies. Agencies that are considered part of the executive branch are subject to the authority of the president, who has the power to appoint and remove federal officers. The president could give orders to the head of an executive agency and fire him or her for failing to carry them out. This power is less pronounced in regard to independent agencies, whose officers serve for fixed terms and cannot be removed without just cause. In practice, however, the president's ability to exert influence over independent regulatory agencies is often considerable because the president has the authority to appoint the members of the agencies.

All three branches of government exercise certain controls over agency powers and functions, as will be discussed later in this chapter, but in many ways administrative agencies function independently. None of the other branches, including the presidency, has the time and resources necessary to monitor the multitude of administrative actions constantly under way. For this reason, administrative agencies, which constitute the **bureaucracy,** are sometimes referred to as the "fourth branch" of the U.S. government.

Section 3 The Administrative Procedure Act

All federal agencies must follow specific procedural requirements in their rulemaking, adjudication, and other functions. Sometimes, Congress specifies certain procedural requirements in an agency's enabling legislation. In the absence of any directives from Congress concerning a particular agency procedure, the Administrative Procedure Act (APA) of 1946[4] applies.

The Arbitrary and Capricious Test

One of Congress's goals in enacting the APA was to provide for more judicial control over administrative agencies, which had assumed greater powers during the expansion of government that had taken place as a result of the Great Depression of the 1930s and World War II (1939–1945). To that end, the APA provides that courts should "hold unlawful and set aside" agency actions found to be "arbitrary, capricious, an abuse of discretion, or otherwise not in accordance with law."[5] Under this standard, parties can challenge regulations as contrary to law or so irrational as to be arbitrary and capricious.

The definition of what makes a rule arbitrary and capricious is a vague one, but it includes factors such as whether the agency has done any of the following:

1. Failed to provide a rational explanation for its decision.
2. Changed its prior policy without justification.
3. Considered legally inappropriate factors.
4. Entirely failed to consider a relevant factor.
5. Rendered a decision plainly contrary to the evidence.

The following case considers the application of the arbitrary and capricious standard.

4. 5 U.S.C. Sections 551–706.
5. 5 U.S.C. Section 706(2)(A).

EXTENDED CASE 6.1 **Fox Television Stations, Inc. v. Federal Communications Commission**

United States Court of Appeals, Second Circuit, 2007. 489 F.3d 444.

***POOLER,* Circuit Judge.**

* * * *

CASE CONTINUES

CASE 6.1 CONTINUED

The [Federal Communications Commission's (FCC's)] policing of "indecent" speech stems from 18 U.S.C. [Section] 1464, which provides that "[w]hoever utters any obscene, indecent, or profane language by means of radio communication shall be fined * * * or imprisoned not more than two years, or both." * * * The FCC first exercised its statutory authority to sanction indecent (but non-obscene) speech in 1975, when it found Pacifica Foundation's radio broadcast of comedian George Carlin's "Filthy Words" monologue indecent * * * .

* * * *

* * * Under the Commission's definition, "indecent speech is language that describes, in terms patently offensive as measured by contemporary community standards for the broadcast medium, sexual or excretory activities and organs.

* * * *

* * * During [a] January 19, 2003, live broadcast of the Golden Globe Awards, musician Bono stated in his acceptance speech "this is really, really, f***ing brilliant. Really, really, great."

* * * [On a complaint about the broadcast by individuals associated with the Parents Television Council, the] FCC held that any use of any variant of "the F-Word" inherently has sexual connotation and therefore falls within the scope of the indecency definition. * * * The Commission found the fleeting and isolated use of the word irrelevant and overruled all prior decisions in which fleeting use of an expletive was held not indecent.

* * * *

On February 21, 2006, * * * the Commission found * * * [Fox Television Stations, Inc.'s] broadcast of the 2002 Billboard Music Awards [and] Fox's broadcast of the 2003 Billboard Music Awards * * * indecent and profane. * * * [On the 2002 broadcast] Cher stated: "People have been telling me I'm on the way out every year, right? So f*** 'em." * * * [On the 2003 broadcast] Nicole Richie * * * stated: "Have you ever tried to get cow shit out of a Prada purse? It's not so f***ing simple."

Fox * * * filed a petition for review of the [FCC's] Order in [the U.S. Court of Appeals for the Second Circuit].

* * * *

Agencies are of course free to revise their rules and policies. Such a change, however, must provide a reasoned analysis for departing from prior precedent. *When an agency reverses its course, a court must satisfy itself that the agency knows it is changing course, has given sound reasons for the change, and has shown that the rule is consistent with the law that gives the agency its authority to act.* In addition, the agency must consider reasonably obvious alternatives and, if it rejects those alternatives, it must give reasons for the rejection * * * . *The agency must explain why the original reasons for adopting the rule or policy are no longer dispositive* [a deciding factor]. * * * [Emphasis added.]

* * * The primary reason for the crackdown on fleeting expletives advanced by the FCC is the so-called "first blow" theory * * * . Indecent material on the airwaves enters into the privacy of the home uninvited and without warning. * * * To say that one may avoid further offense by turning off the [television or] radio when he hears indecent language is like saying that the remedy for an assault is to run away after the first blow.

We cannot accept this argument as a reasoned basis justifying the Commission's new rule. First, the Commission provides no reasonable explanation for why it has changed its perception that a fleeting expletive was not a harmful "first blow" for the nearly thirty years between [the decisions in Pacifica's case] and Golden Globes. More problematic, however, is that the "first blow" theory bears no rational connection to the Commission's actual policy regarding fleeting expletives. * * * A re-broadcast of precisely the same offending clips from the two Billboard Music Award programs for the purpose of providing background information on this case would not result in any action by the FCC * * * .

The * * * Order makes passing reference to other reasons that purportedly support its change in policy, none of which we find sufficient. For instance, the Commission states that even non-literal uses of expletives fall within its indecency definition because it is "difficult (if not impossible) to distinguish whether a word is being used as an expletive or as a literal description of sexual or excretory functions." This defies any commonsense understanding of these words, which, as the general public well knows, are often used in everyday conversation without any "sexual or excretory" meaning. * * * Even the top leaders of our government have used variants of

CASE 6.1 CONTINUED

these expletives in a manner that no reasonable person would believe referenced "sexual or excretory organs or activities." [The court proceeded to recount examples of when President Bush and Vice President Cheney had used the questionable words in public.]

* * * *

Accordingly, we find that the FCC's new policy regarding "fleeting expletives" fails to provide a reasoned analysis justifying its departure from the agency's established practice. For this reason, Fox's petition for review is granted, the * * * Order is vacated, and the matter is remanded to the FCC for further proceedings consistent with this opinion.

QUESTIONS

1. According to the court's opinion in this case, is an administrative agency locked into its first interpretation of a statute? Why or why not?
2. Were the agency's reasons for its actions rejected in this case because the court disagreed with those reasons? Explain.

Rulemaking Procedures

Today, the major function of an administrative agency is **rulemaking**—the formulation of new regulations, or rules, as they are often called. The APA defines a *rule* as "an agency statement of general or particular applicability and future effect designed to implement, interpret, or prescribe law and policy."[6] Regulations are sometimes said to be *quasi-legislative* because, like statutes, they have a binding effect. Like those who violate statutes, violators of agency rules may be punished. Because agency rules have such great legal force, the APA established procedures for agencies to follow in creating rules. Many rules must be adopted using the APA's *notice-and-comment rulemaking* procedure.

Notice-and-comment rulemaking involves three basic steps: notice of the proposed rulemaking, a comment period, and the final rule. The APA recognizes some limited exceptions to these procedural requirements, but they are seldom invoked. If the required procedures are violated, the resulting rule may be invalid. The impetus for rulemaking may come from various sources, including Congress, the agency itself, or private parties who may petition an agency to begin a rulemaking (or repeal a rule). For example, environmental groups have petitioned for stricter pollution controls to combat global warming.

Notice of the Proposed Rulemaking When a federal agency decides to create a new rule, the agency publishes a notice of the proposed rulemaking proceedings in the *Federal Register*, a daily publication of the executive branch that prints government orders, rules, and regulations. The notice states where and when the proceedings will be held, the agency's legal authority for making the rule (usually its enabling legislation), and the terms or subject matter of the proposed rule. Courts have ruled that the APA requires an agency to make available to the public certain information, such as the key scientific data underlying the proposal.

Comment Period Following the publication of the notice of the proposed rulemaking proceedings, the agency must allow ample time for persons to comment in writing on the proposed rule. The purpose of this comment period is to give interested parties the opportunity to express their views on the proposed rule in an effort to influence agency policy. The comments may be in writing or, if a hearing is held, may be given orally.

The agency need not respond to all comments, but it must respond to any significant comments that bear directly on the proposed rule. The agency responds by either modifying its final rule or explaining, in a statement accompanying the final rule, why it did not make any changes. In some circumstances, particularly when the procedure being used in a specific instance is less formal, an agency may accept comments after the comment period is closed. The agency should summarize these *ex parte*[7] (private, "off-the-record") comments in the record for possible review.

6. 5 U.S.C. Section 551(4).

7. In Latin, *ex parte* means "from the part." In the law, it refers to one of the parties taking some action on his or her own, such as communicating with a judge or bringing a motion, without notifying the other party or giving the other party a chance to respond.

EXHIBIT 6–2 • Executive Departments and Important Subagencies

Department and Date Formed	Selected Subagencies
State (1789)	Passport Office; Bureau of Diplomatic Security; Foreign Service; Bureau of Human Rights and Humanitarian Affairs; Bureau of Consular Affairs; Bureau of Intelligence and Research
Treasury (1789)	Internal Revenue Service; U.S. Mint
Interior (1849)	U.S. Fish and Wildlife Service; National Park Service; Bureau of Indian Affairs; Bureau of Land Management
Justice (1870)[a]	Federal Bureau of Investigation; Drug Enforcement Administration; Bureau of Prisons; U.S. Marshals Service
Agriculture (1889)	Soil Conservation Service; Agricultural Research Service; Food Safety and Inspection Service; Forest Service
Commerce (1913)[b]	Bureau of the Census; Bureau of Economic Analysis; Minority Business Development Agency; U.S. Patent and Trademark Office; National Oceanic and Atmospheric Administration
Labor (1913)[b]	Occupational Safety and Health Administration; Bureau of Labor Statistics; Employment Standards Administration; Office of Labor-Management Standards; Employment and Training Administration
Defense (1949)[c]	National Security Agency; Joint Chiefs of Staff; Departments of the Air Force, Navy, Army; service academies
Housing and Urban Development (1965)	Office of Community Planning and Development; Government National Mortgage Association; Office of Fair Housing and Equal Opportunity
Transportation (1967)	Federal Aviation Administration; Federal Highway Administration; National Highway Traffic Safety Administration; Federal Transit Administration
Energy (1977)	Office of Civilian Radioactive Waste Management; Office of Nuclear Energy; Energy Information Administration
Health and Human Services (1980)[d]	Food and Drug Administration; Centers for Medicare and Medicaid Services; Centers for Disease Control and Prevention; National Institutes of Health
Education (1980)[d]	Office of Special Education and Rehabilitation Services; Office of Elementary and Secondary Education; Office of Postsecondary Education; Office of Vocational and Adult Education
Veterans Affairs (1989)	Veterans Health Administration; Veterans Benefits Administration; National Cemetery System
Homeland Security (2002)	U.S. Citizenship and Immigration Services; U.S. Customs and Border Protection; Transportation Security Administration; U.S. Coast Guard; Federal Emergency Management Agency

a. Formed from the Office of the Attorney General (created in 1789).
b. Formed from the Department of Commerce and Labor (created in 1903).
c. Formed from the Department of War (created in 1789) and the Department of the Navy (created in 1798).
d. Formed from the Department of Health, Education, and Welfare (created in 1953).

EXHIBIT 6–3 • Selected Independent Regulatory Agencies

Name and Date Formed	Principal Duties
Federal Reserve System Board of Governors (Fed) (1913)	Determines policy with respect to interest rates, credit availability, and the money supply.
Federal Trade Commission (FTC) (1914)	Prevents businesses from engaging in unfair trade practices; stops the formation of monopolies in the business sector; protects consumer rights.
Securities and Exchange Commission (SEC) (1934)	Regulates the nation's stock exchanges, in which shares of stock are bought and sold; enforces the securities laws, which require full disclosure of the financial profiles of companies that wish to sell stock and bonds to the public.
Federal Communications Commission (FCC) (1934)	Regulates all communications by telegraph, cable, telephone, radio, satellite, and television.
National Labor Relations Board (NLRB) (1935)	Protects employees' rights to join unions and bargain collectively with employers; attempts to prevent unfair labor practices by both employers and unions.
Equal Employment Opportunity Commission (EEOC) (1964)	Works to eliminate discrimination in employment based on religion, gender, race, color, disability, national origin, or age; investigates claims of discrimination.
Environmental Protection Agency (EPA) (1970)	Undertakes programs aimed at reducing air and water pollution; works with state and local agencies to help fight environmental hazards.
Nuclear Regulatory Commission (NRC) (1975)	Ensures that electricity-generating nuclear reactors in the United States are built and operated safely; regularly inspects operations of such reactors.

The Final Rule After the agency reviews the comments, it drafts the final rule and publishes it in the *Federal Register*. Such a final rule must contain a "concise general statement of . . . basis and purpose" that describes the reasoning behind the rule.[8] The final rule may change the terms of the proposed rule, in light of the public comments, but cannot change the proposal too radically, or a new proposal and a new opportunity for comment are required. The final rule is later compiled along with the rules and regulations of other federal administrative agencies in the *Code of Federal Regulations* (C.F.R.). Final rules have binding legal effect unless the courts later overturn them. For this reason, they are often referred to as legislative rules. *Legislative rules* are substantive in that they affect legal rights, whereas *interpretive rules* issued by agencies simply declare policy and do not affect legal rights or obligations (see the discussion of informal agency actions later in this chapter).

The court in the following case considered whether to enforce rules that were issued outside the rulemaking procedure.

8. 5 U.S.C. Section 555(c).

CASE 6.2 Hemp Industries Association v. Drug Enforcement Administration

United States Court of Appeals, Ninth Circuit, 2004. 357 F.3d 1012.

• **Background and Facts** The members of the Hemp Industries Association (HIA) import and distribute sterilized hemp seed and oil and cake derived from hemp seed. They also make and sell food and cosmetic products made from hemp seed and oil. These products contain only nonpsychoactive

CASE CONTINUES

QUESTIONS AND CASE PROBLEMS

6–1. For decades, the Federal Trade Commission (FTC) resolved fair trade and advertising disputes through individual adjudications. In the 1960s, the FTC began promulgating rules that defined fair and unfair trade practices. In cases involving violations of these rules, the due process rights of participants were more limited and did not include cross-examination. Although anyone found violating a rule would receive a full adjudication, the legitimacy of the rule itself could not be challenged in the adjudication. Any party charged with violating a rule was almost certain to lose the adjudication. Affected parties complained to a court, arguing that their rights before the FTC were unduly limited by the new rules. What will the court examine to determine whether to uphold the new rules?

6–2. QUESTION WITH SAMPLE ANSWER

Assume that the Food and Drug Administration (FDA), using proper procedures, adopts a rule describing its future investigations. This new rule covers all future circumstances in which the FDA wants to regulate food additives. Under the new rule, the FDA is not to regulate food additives without giving food companies an opportunity to cross-examine witnesses. At a subsequent time, the FDA wants to regulate methylisocyanate, a food additive. The FDA undertakes an informal rulemaking procedure, without cross-examination, and regulates methylisocyanate. Producers protest, saying that the FDA promised them the opportunity for cross-examination. The FDA responds that the Administrative Procedure Act does not require such cross-examination and that it is free to withdraw the promise made in its new rule. If the producers challenge the FDA in court, on what basis would the court rule in their favor?

- **For a sample answer to Question 6–2, go to Appendix I at the end of this text.**

6–3. Rulemaking. The Occupational Safety and Health Administration (OSHA) is part of the U.S. Department of Labor. OSHA issued a "Directive" under which each employer in selected industries was to be inspected unless it adopted a "Comprehensive Compliance Program (CCP)"—a safety and health program designed to meet standards that in some respects exceeded those otherwise required by law. The Chamber of Commerce of the United States objected to the Directive and filed a petition for review with the U.S. Court of Appeals for the District of Columbia Circuit. The Chamber claimed, in part, that OSHA did not use proper rulemaking procedures in issuing the Directive. OSHA argued that it was not required to follow those procedures because the Directive itself was a "rule of procedure." OSHA claimed that the rule did not "alter the rights or interests of parties, although it may alter the manner in which the parties present themselves or their viewpoints to the agency." What are the steps of the most commonly used rulemaking procedure? Which steps are missing in this case? In whose favor should the court rule and why? [*Chamber of Commerce of the United States v. U.S. Department of Labor,* 174 F.3d 206 (D.C.Cir. 1999)]

6–4. Arbitrary and Capricious Test. Lion Raisins, Inc., is a family-owned, family-operated business that grows raisins and markets them to private enterprises. In the 1990s, Lion also successfully bid on more than fifteen contracts awarded by the U.S. Department of Agriculture (USDA). In May 1999, a USDA investigation reported that Lion appeared to have falsified inspectors' signatures, given false moisture content, and changed the grade of raisins on three USDA raisin certificates issued between 1996 and 1998. Lion was subsequently awarded five more USDA contracts. Then, in November 2000, the company was the low bidder on two new USDA contracts for school lunch programs. In January 2001, however, the USDA awarded these contracts to other bidders and, on the basis of the May 1999 report, suspended Lion from participating in government contracts for one year. Lion filed a suit in the U.S. Court of Federal Claims against the USDA, seeking, in part, lost profits on the school lunch contracts on the ground that the USDA's suspension was arbitrary and capricious. What reasoning might the court employ to grant a summary judgment in Lion's favor? [*Lion Raisins, Inc. v. United States,* 51 Fed.Cl. 238 (2001)]

6–5. Investigation. Maureen Droge began working for United Air Lines, Inc. (UAL), as a flight attendant in 1990. In 1995, she was assigned to Paris, France, where she became pregnant. Because UAL does not allow its flight attendants to fly during their third trimester of pregnancy, Droge was placed on involuntary leave. She applied for temporary disability benefits through the French social security system, but her request was denied because UAL does not contribute to the French system on behalf of its U.S.-based flight attendants. Droge filed a charge of discrimination with the U.S. Equal Employment Opportunity Commission (EEOC), alleging that UAL had discriminated against her and other Americans. The EEOC issued a subpoena, asking UAL to detail all benefits received by all UAL employees living outside the United States. UAL refused to provide the information, in part, on the grounds that it was irrelevant and compliance would be unduly burdensome. The EEOC filed a suit in a federal district court against UAL. Should the court enforce the subpoena? Why or why not? [*Equal Employment Opportunity Commission v. United Air Lines, Inc.,* 287 F.3d 643 (7th Cir. 2002)]

6–6. Judicial Controls. Under federal law, when accepting bids on a contract, an agency must hold "discussions" with all offerors. An agency may ask a single offeror for "clarification" of its proposal, however, without holding "discussions" with the others.

Regulations define *clarifications* as "limited exchanges." In March 2001, the U.S. Air Force asked for bids on a contract. The winning contractor would examine, assess, and develop means of integrating national intelligence assets with the U.S. Department of Defense space systems, to enhance the capabilities of the Air Force's Space Warfare Center. Among the bidders were Information Technology and Applications Corp. (ITAC) and RS Information Systems, Inc. (RSIS). The Air Force asked the parties for more information on their subcontractors but did not allow them to change their proposals. Determining that there were weaknesses in ITAC's bid, the Air Force awarded the contract to RSIS. ITAC filed a suit in the U.S. Court of Federal Claims against the government, contending that the postproposal requests to RSIS, and its responses, were improper "discussions." Should the court rule in ITAC's favor? Why or why not? [*Information Technology & Applications Corp. v. United States,* 316 F.3d 1312 (Fed.Cir. 2003)].

6-7. CASE PROBLEM WITH SAMPLE ANSWER

Riverdale Mills Corp. makes plastic-coated steel wire products in Northbridge, Massachusetts. Riverdale uses a water-based cleaning process that generates acidic and alkaline wastewater. To meet federal clean-water requirements, Riverdale has a system within its plant to treat the water. It then flows through a pipe that opens into a manhole-covered test pit outside the plant in full view of Riverdale's employees. Three hundred feet away, the pipe merges into the public sewer system. In October 1997, the U.S. Environmental Protection Agency (EPA) sent Justin Pimpare and Daniel Granz to inspect the plant. Without a search warrant and without Riverdale's express consent, the agents took samples from the test pit. Based on the samples, Riverdale and James Knott, the company's owner, were charged with criminal violations of the federal Clean Water Act. The defendants filed a suit in a federal district court against the EPA agents and others, alleging violations of the Fourth Amendment. What right does the Fourth Amendment provide in this context? This right is based on a "reasonable expectation of privacy." Should the agents be held liable? Why or why not? [*Riverdale Mills Corp. v. Pimpare,* 392 F.3d 55 (1st Cir. 2004)]

- **To view a sample answer for Problem 6–7, go to this book's Web site at academic.cengage.com/blaw/cross, select "Chapter 6," and click on "Case Problem with Sample Answer."**

6-8. Rulemaking. The Investment Company Act of 1940 prohibits a mutual fund from engaging in certain transactions in which there may be a conflict of interest between the manager of the fund and its shareholders. Under rules issued by the Securities and Exchange Commission (SEC), however, a fund that meets certain conditions may engage in an otherwise prohibited transaction. In June 2004, the SEC added two new conditions. A year later, the SEC reconsidered the new conditions in terms of the costs that they would impose on the funds. Within eight days, and without asking for public input, the SEC readopted the conditions. The Chamber of Commerce of the United States—which is both a mutual fund shareholder and an association with mutual fund managers among its members—asked the U.S. Court of Appeals for the Second Circuit to review the new rules. The Chamber charged, in part, that in readopting the rules, the SEC relied on materials not in the "rulemaking record" without providing an opportunity for public comment. The SEC countered that the information was otherwise "publicly available." In adopting a rule, should an agency consider information that is not part of the rulemaking record? Why or why not? [*Chamber of Commerce of the United States v. Securities and Exchange Commission,* 443 F.3d 890 (D.C.Cir. 2006)]

6-9. Agency Powers. A well-documented rise in global temperatures has coincided with a significant increase in the concentration of carbon dioxide in the atmosphere. Some scientists believe that the two trends are related, because when carbon dioxide is released into the atmosphere, it produces a greenhouse effect, trapping solar heat. Under the Clean Air Act (CAA) of 1963, the Environmental Protection Agency (EPA) is authorized to regulate "any" air pollutants "emitted into . . . the ambient air" that in its "judgment cause, or contribute to, air pollution." Calling global warming "the most pressing environmental challenge of our time," a group of private organizations asked the EPA to regulate carbon dioxide and other "greenhouse gas" emissions from new motor vehicles. The EPA refused, stating, among other things, that Congress last amended the CAA in 1990 without authorizing new, binding auto emissions limits. The petitioners—nineteen states, including Massachusetts, and others—asked the U.S. Court of Appeals for the District of Columbia Circuit to review the EPA's denial. Did the EPA have the authority to regulate greenhouse gas emissions from new motor vehicles? If so, was its stated reason for refusing to do so consistent with that authority? Discuss. [*Massachusetts v. Environmental Protection Agency,* __ U.S. __, 127 S.Ct. 1438, 167 L.Ed.2d 248 (2007)]

6-10. A QUESTION OF ETHICS

To ensure highway safety and protect driver health, Congress charged federal agencies with regulating the hours of service of commercial motor vehicle operators. Between 1940 and 2003, the regulations that applied to long-haul truck drivers were mostly unchanged. (Long-haul drivers are those who operate beyond a 150-mile radius of their base.) In 2003, the Federal Motor Carrier Safety Administration (FMSCA) revised the regulations significantly, increasing the number of daily and weekly hours that drivers could work. The agency had not considered the impact of the changes on the health of the drivers, however, and the revisions were overturned. The FMSCA then issued a notice that it would reconsider

time period in a statute of limitations may be tolled—that is, suspended or stopped temporarily—if the defendant is a minor or is not in the jurisdiction. When the defendant reaches the age of majority or returns to the jurisdiction, the statute revives—that is, its time period begins to run or to run again.

Immunity

At times, the state may wish to obtain information from a person accused of a crime. Accused persons are understandably reluctant to give information if it will be used to prosecute them, and they cannot be forced to do so. The privilege against self-incrimination is guaranteed by the Fifth Amendment to the U.S. Constitution, which reads, in part, "nor shall [any person] be compelled in any criminal case to be a witness against himself." In cases in which the state wishes to obtain information from a person accused of a crime, the state can grant *immunity* from prosecution or agree to prosecute for a less serious offense in exchange for the information. Once immunity is given, the person now has an absolute privilege against self-incrimination and therefore can no longer refuse to testify on Fifth Amendment grounds.

Often, a grant of immunity from prosecution for a serious crime is part of the **plea bargaining** between the defending and prosecuting attorneys. The defendant may be convicted of a lesser offense, while the state uses the defendant's testimony to prosecute accomplices for serious crimes carrying heavy penalties.

Criminal Procedures

Criminal law brings the force of the state, with all of its resources, to bear against the individual. Criminal procedures are designed to protect the constitutional rights of individuals and to prevent the arbitrary use of power on the part of the government.

The U.S. Constitution provides specific safeguards for those accused of crimes. The United States Supreme Court has ruled that most of these safeguards apply not only in federal court but also in state courts by virtue of the due process clause of the Fourteenth Amendment. These protections include the following:

1. The Fourth Amendment protection from unreasonable searches and seizures.
2. The Fourth Amendment requirement that no warrant for a search or an arrest be issued without probable cause.
3. The Fifth Amendment requirement that no one be deprived of "life, liberty, or property without due process of law."
4. The Fifth Amendment prohibition against **double jeopardy** (trying someone twice for the same criminal offense).[17]
5. The Fifth Amendment requirement that no person be required to be a witness against (incriminate) himself or herself.
6. The Sixth Amendment guarantees of a speedy trial, a trial by jury, a public trial, the right to confront witnesses, and the right to a lawyer at various stages in some proceedings.
7. The Eighth Amendment prohibitions against excessive bail and fines and cruel and unusual punishment.

The Exclusionary Rule

Under what is known as the **exclusionary rule,** all evidence obtained in violation of the constitutional rights spelled out in the Fourth, Fifth, and Sixth Amendments generally is not admissible at trial. All evidence derived from the illegally obtained evidence is known as the "fruit of the poisonous tree," and such evidence normally must also be excluded from the trial proceedings. For example, if a confession is obtained after an illegal arrest, the arrest is the "poisonous tree," and the confession, if "tainted" by the arrest, is the "fruit."

As you will read shortly, under the *Miranda* rule, suspects must be advised of certain constitutional rights when they are arrested. For example, the Sixth Amendment right to counsel is one of the rights of which a suspect must be advised when she or he is arrested. In many cases, a statement that a criminal suspect makes in the absence of counsel is not admissible at trial unless the suspect has knowingly and voluntarily waived this right. In the following case, the United States Supreme Court considered at what point a suspect's right to counsel is triggered during criminal proceedings.

17. The prohibition against double jeopardy means that once a criminal defendant is found not guilty of a particular crime, the government may not reindict the person and retry him or her for the same crime. The prohibition does not preclude a *civil* lawsuit against the same person by the crime victim to recover damages. For example, a person found not guilty of assault and battery in a criminal case may be sued by the victim in a civil tort case for damages. Additionally, a state's prosecution of a crime will not prevent a separate federal prosecution of the same crime, and vice versa. For example, a defendant found not guilty of violating a state law can be tried in federal court for the same act, if the act is also defined as a crime under federal law.

EXTENDED CASE 7.3 Fellers v. United States

Supreme Court of the United States, 2004. 540 U.S. 519, 124 S.Ct. 1019, 157 L.Ed.2d 1016.

Justice *O'CONNOR* delivered the opinion of the Court.

* * * *

On February 24, 2000, after a grand jury indicted petitioner [John J. Fellers] for conspiracy to distribute methamphetamine, Lincoln Police Sergeant Michael Garnett and Lancaster County Deputy Sheriff Jeff Bliemeister went to petitioner's home in Lincoln, Nebraska, to arrest him. The officers knocked on petitioner's door and, when petitioner answered, identified themselves and asked if they could come in. Petitioner invited the officers into his living room.

The officers advised petitioner they had come to discuss his involvement in methamphetamine distribution. They informed petitioner that they had a federal warrant for his arrest and that a grand jury had indicted him for conspiracy to distribute methamphetamine. The officers told petitioner that the indictment referred to his involvement with certain individuals, four of whom they named. Petitioner then told the officers that he knew the four people and had used methamphetamine during his association with them.

After spending about 15 minutes in petitioner's home, the officers transported petitioner to the Lancaster County jail. There, the officers advised petitioner for the first time of his [right to counsel under the Sixth Amendment]. Petitioner and the two officers signed a * * * waiver form, and petitioner then reiterated the inculpatory [incriminating] statements he had made earlier, admitted to having associated with other individuals implicated in the charged conspiracy, and admitted to having loaned money to one of them even though he suspected that she was involved in drug transactions.

Before trial, petitioner moved to suppress the inculpatory statements he made at his home and at the county jail.

The District Court suppressed the "unwarned" statements petitioner made at his house but admitted petitioner's jailhouse statements * * * , concluding petitioner had knowingly and voluntarily waived his * * * rights before making the statements.

Following a jury trial at which petitioner's jailhouse statements were admitted into evidence, petitioner was convicted of conspiring to possess with intent to distribute methamphetamine. Petitioner appealed, arguing that his jailhouse statements should have been suppressed as fruits of the statements obtained at his home in violation of the Sixth Amendment. The [U.S.] Court of Appeals [for the Eighth Circuit] affirmed. * * * The Court of Appeals stated: " * * * The officers did not interrogate [the petitioner] at his home." * * * [Fellers appealed to the United States Supreme Court.]

* * * *

*The Sixth Amendment right to counsel is triggered at or after the time that judicial proceedings have been initiated * * * whether by way of formal charge, preliminary hearing, indictment, information, or arraignment.* We have held that an accused is denied the basic protections of the Sixth Amendment when there is used against him at his trial evidence of his own incriminating words, which federal agents * * * deliberately elicited from him after he had been indicted and in the absence of his counsel. [Emphasis added.]

We have consistently applied the *deliberate-elicitation standard* in * * * Sixth Amendment cases * * * . [Emphasis added.]

The Court of Appeals erred in holding that the absence of an "interrogation" foreclosed petitioner's claim that the jailhouse statements should have been suppressed as fruits of the statements taken from petitioner [Fellers] at his home. First, there is no question that the officers in this case deliberately elicited information from petitioner. Indeed, the officers, upon arriving at petitioner's house, informed him that their purpose in coming was to discuss his involvement in the distribution of methamphetamine and his association with certain charged co-conspirators. Because the ensuing discussion took place after petitioner had been indicted, outside the presence of counsel, and in the absence of any waiver of petitioner's Sixth Amendment rights, the Court of Appeals erred in holding that the officers' actions did not violate the Sixth Amendment standards * * * .

CASE CONTINUES

CASE 7.3 CONTINUED

Second, because of its erroneous determination that petitioner was not questioned in violation of Sixth Amendment standards, the Court of Appeals improperly conducted its "fruits" analysis * * * . Specifically, it * * * [held] that the admissibility of the jailhouse statements turns solely on whether the statements were knowingly and voluntarily made. The Court of Appeals did not reach the question whether the Sixth Amendment requires suppression of petitioner's jailhouse statements on the ground that they were the fruits of previous questioning conducted in violation of the Sixth Amendment deliberate-elicitation standard. We have not had occasion to decide whether [such statements should be excluded from trial] when a suspect makes incriminating statements after a knowing and voluntary waiver of his right to counsel notwithstanding earlier police questioning in violation of Sixth Amendment standards. We therefore remand to the Court of Appeals to address this issue in the first instance.

Accordingly, the judgment of the Court of Appeals is reversed, and the case is remanded for further proceedings consistent with this opinion.

It is so ordered.

QUESTIONS

1. Why did Fellers argue on appeal that his "jailhouse statements" should have been excluded from his trial?
2. Should Fellers's "jailhouse statements" have been excluded from his trial? Why or why not?

Purpose of the Exclusionary Rule The purpose of the exclusionary rule is to deter police from conducting warrantless searches and from engaging in other misconduct. The rule is sometimes criticized because it can lead to injustice. Many a defendant has "gotten off on a technicality" because law enforcement personnel failed to observe procedural requirements based on the above-mentioned constitutional amendments. Even though a defendant may be obviously guilty, if the evidence of that guilt was obtained improperly (without a valid search warrant, for example), it cannot be used against the defendant in court.

Exceptions to the Exclusionary Rule Over the last several decades, the United States Supreme Court has diminished the scope of the exclusionary rule by creating some exceptions to its applicability. For example, if illegally obtained evidence would have been discovered "inevitably" and obtained by the police using lawful means, the evidence will be admissible at trial.[18] The Court has also created a "good faith" exception to the exclusionary rule.[19] Under this exception, if the police officer who used a technically incorrect search warrant form to obtain evidence was acting in good faith, the evidence will be admissible. Additionally, the courts can exercise a certain amount of discretion in determining whether evidence has been obtained improperly—a possibility that somewhat balances the scales.

The *Miranda* Rule

In regard to criminal procedure, one of the questions many courts faced in the 1950s and 1960s was not whether suspects had constitutional rights—that was not in doubt—but how and when those rights could be exercised. Could the right to be silent (under the Fifth Amendment's prohibition against self-incrimination) be exercised during pretrial interrogation proceedings or only during the trial? Were confessions obtained from suspects admissible in court if the suspects had not been advised of their right to remain silent and other constitutional rights?

To clarify these issues, the United States Supreme Court issued a landmark decision in 1966 in *Miranda v. Arizona,* which we present here. Today, the procedural rights required by the Court in this case are familiar to virtually every American.

18. *Nix v. Williams,* 467 U.S. 431, 104 S.Ct. 2501, 81 L.Ed.2d 377 (1984).

19. *Massachusetts v. Sheppard,* 468 U.S. 981, 104 S.Ct. 3424, 82 L.Ed.2d 737 (1984).

CASE 7.4 Miranda v. Arizona

Supreme Court of the United States, 1966. 384 U.S. 436, 86 S.Ct. 1602, 16 L.Ed.2d 694.

• **Background and Facts** On March 13, 1963, Ernesto Miranda was arrested at his home for the kidnapping and rape of an eighteen-year-old woman. Miranda was taken to a Phoenix, Arizona, police station and questioned by two officers. Two hours later, the officers emerged from the interrogation room with a written confession signed by Miranda. A paragraph at the top of the confession stated that the confession had been made voluntarily, without threats or promises of immunity, and "with full knowledge of my legal rights, understanding any statement I make may be used against me." Miranda was at no time advised that he had a right to remain silent and a right to have a lawyer present. The confession was admitted into evidence at the trial, and Miranda was convicted and sentenced to prison for twenty to thirty years. Miranda appealed the decision, claiming that he had not been informed of his constitutional rights. The Supreme Court of Arizona held that Miranda's constitutional rights had not been violated and affirmed his conviction. The *Miranda* case was subsequently reviewed by the United States Supreme Court.

IN THE LANGUAGE OF THE COURT
Mr. Chief Justice *WARREN* delivered the opinion of the Court.

The cases before us raise questions which go to the roots of our concepts of American criminal jurisprudence; the restraints society must observe consistent with the Federal Constitution in prosecuting individuals for crime.

* * * *

At the outset, if a person in custody is to be subjected to interrogation, he must first be informed in clear and unequivocal terms that he has the right to remain silent.

* * * *

The warning of the right to remain silent must be accompanied by the explanation that anything said can and will be used against the individual in court. This warning is needed in order to make him aware not only of the privilege, *but also of the consequences of forgoing it.* [Emphasis added.]

The circumstances surrounding in-custody interrogation can operate very quickly to overbear the will of one merely made aware of his privilege by his interrogators. Therefore the right to have counsel present at the interrogation is indispensable to the protection of the Fifth Amendment privilege under the system we delineate today.

* * * *

In order fully to apprise a person interrogated of the extent of his rights under this system then, it is necessary to warn him not only that he has the right to consult with an attorney, but also that if he is indigent [without funds] a lawyer will be appointed to represent him. * * * The warning of a right to counsel would be hollow if not couched in terms that would convey to the indigent—the person most often subjected to interrogation—the knowledge that he too has a right to have counsel present.

• **Decision and Remedy** *The United States Supreme Court held that Miranda could not be convicted of the crime on the basis of his confession because his confession was inadmissible as evidence. For any statement made by a defendant to be admissible, the defendant must be informed of certain constitutional rights prior to police interrogation. If the accused waives his or her rights to remain silent and to have counsel present, the government must demonstrate that the waiver was made knowingly, voluntarily, and intelligently.*

• **Impact of This Case on Today's Law** *Police officers routinely advise suspects of their "*Miranda *rights" on arrest. When Ernesto Miranda himself was later murdered, the suspected murderer was "read his* Miranda *rights." Despite significant criticisms and later attempts to overrule the* Miranda *decision through legislation, the requirements stated in this case continue to provide the benchmark by which criminal procedures are judged today.*

CASE CONTINUES

CASE 7.4 CONTINUED

• **International Considerations** **The Right to Remain Silent in Great Britain** *The right to remain silent has long been a legal hallmark in Great Britain as well as in the United States. In 1994, however, the British Parliament passed an act that provides that a criminal defendant's silence may be interpreted as evidence of the defendant's guilt. British police officers are now required, when making an arrest, to inform the suspect, "You do not have to say anything. But if you do not mention now something which you later use in your defense, the court may decide that your failure to mention it now strengthens the case against you. A record will be made of everything you say, and it may be given in evidence if you are brought to trial."*

Congress's Response to the *Miranda* Ruling The Supreme Court's *Miranda* decision was controversial, and two years later Congress attempted to overrule it by enacting Section 3501 of the Omnibus Crime Control and Safe Streets Act of 1968.[20] Essentially, Section 3501 reinstated the rule that had been in effect for 180 years before the *Miranda* ruling—namely, that statements by defendants can be used against them as long as the statements are made voluntarily. The U.S. Department of Justice immediately refused to enforce Section 3501, however. Although the U.S. Court of Appeals for the Fourth Circuit attempted to enforce the provision in 1999, the United States Supreme Court reversed its decision in 2000. The Supreme Court held that the *Miranda* rights enunciated by the Court in the 1966 case were constitutionally based and thus could not be overruled by a legislative act.[21]

Exceptions to the *Miranda* Rule As part of a continuing attempt to balance the rights of accused persons against the rights of society, the Supreme Court has made a number of exceptions to the *Miranda* ruling. For example, the Court has recognized a "public safety" exception, holding that certain statements—such as statements concerning the location of a weapon—are admissible even if the defendant was not given *Miranda* warnings.[22] The Court has also clarified that, in certain circumstances, a defendant's confession need not be excluded as evidence even if the police failed to inform the defendant of his or her *Miranda* rights.[23] If other, legally obtained evidence admitted at trial is strong enough to justify the conviction without the confession, then the fact that the confession was obtained illegally can, in effect, be ignored.[24]

The Supreme Court has also ruled that a suspect must unequivocally and assertively request to exercise her or his right to counsel in order to stop police questioning. Saying, "Maybe I should talk to a lawyer" during an interrogation after being taken into custody is not enough. The Court held that police officers are not required to decipher the suspect's intentions in such situations.[25]

Criminal Process

As mentioned earlier in this chapter, a criminal prosecution differs significantly from a civil case in several respects. These differences reflect the desire to safeguard the rights of the individual against the state. Exhibit 7–3 summarizes the major steps in processing a criminal case. We now discuss three phases of the criminal process—arrest, indictment or information, and trial—in more detail.

Arrest Before a warrant for arrest can be issued, there must be probable cause for believing that the individual in question has committed a crime. As discussed in Chapter 5, *probable cause* can be defined as a substantial likelihood that the person has committed or is about to commit a crime. Note that probable cause involves a likelihood, not just a possibility. Arrests can be made without a warrant if there is no time to get one, but the action of the arresting officer is still judged by the standard of probable cause.

Indictment or Information Individuals must be formally charged with having committed specific crimes before they can be brought to trial. If issued by

20. 42 U.S.C. Section 3789d.
21. *Dickerson v. United States,* 530 U.S. 428, 120 S.Ct. 2326, 147 L.Ed.2d 405 (2000).
22. *New York v. Quarles,* 467 U.S. 649, 104 S.Ct. 2626, 81 L.Ed.2d 550 (1984).
23. *Moran v. Burbine,* 475 U.S. 412, 106 S.Ct. 1135, 89 L.Ed.2d 410 (1986).
24. *Arizona v. Fulminante,* 499 U.S. 279, 111 S.Ct. 1246, 113 L.Ed.2d 302 (1991).
25. *Davis v. United States,* 512 U.S. 452, 114 S.Ct. 2350, 129 L.Ed.2d 362 (1994).

EXHIBIT 7–3 • Major Procedural Steps in a Criminal Case

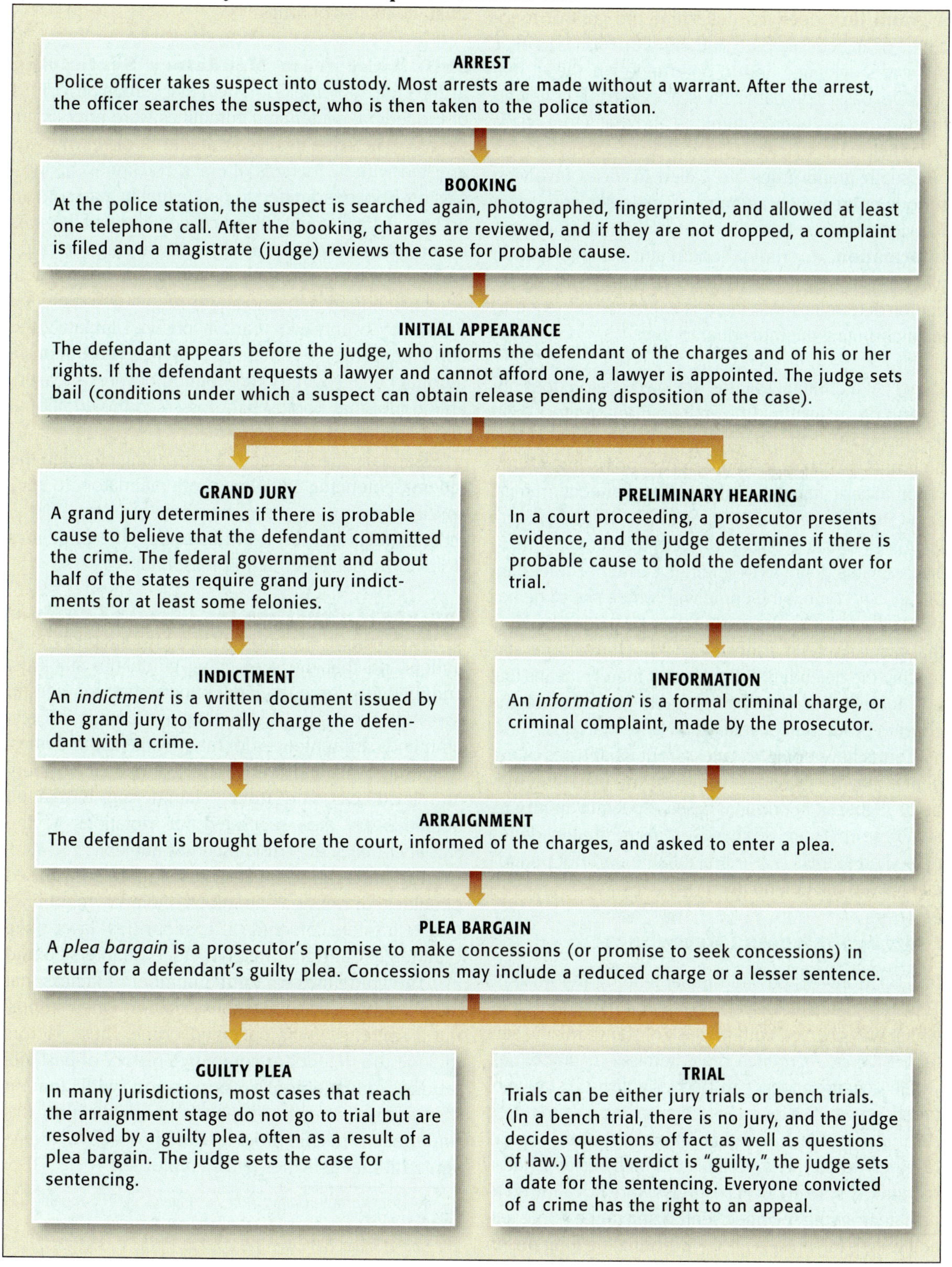

ARREST

Police officer takes suspect into custody. Most arrests are made without a warrant. After the arrest, the officer searches the suspect, who is then taken to the police station.

BOOKING

At the police station, the suspect is searched again, photographed, fingerprinted, and allowed at least one telephone call. After the booking, charges are reviewed, and if they are not dropped, a complaint is filed and a magistrate (judge) reviews the case for probable cause.

INITIAL APPEARANCE

The defendant appears before the judge, who informs the defendant of the charges and of his or her rights. If the defendant requests a lawyer and cannot afford one, a lawyer is appointed. The judge sets bail (conditions under which a suspect can obtain release pending disposition of the case).

GRAND JURY

A grand jury determines if there is probable cause to believe that the defendant committed the crime. The federal government and about half of the states require grand jury indictments for at least some felonies.

INDICTMENT

An *indictment* is a written document issued by the grand jury to formally charge the defendant with a crime.

PRELIMINARY HEARING

In a court proceeding, a prosecutor presents evidence, and the judge determines if there is probable cause to hold the defendant over for trial.

INFORMATION

An *information* is a formal criminal charge, or criminal complaint, made by the prosecutor.

ARRAIGNMENT

The defendant is brought before the court, informed of the charges, and asked to enter a plea.

PLEA BARGAIN

A *plea bargain* is a prosecutor's promise to make concessions (or promise to seek concessions) in return for a defendant's guilty plea. Concessions may include a reduced charge or a lesser sentence.

GUILTY PLEA

In many jurisdictions, most cases that reach the arraignment stage do not go to trial but are resolved by a guilty plea, often as a result of a plea bargain. The judge sets the case for sentencing.

TRIAL

Trials can be either jury trials or bench trials. (In a bench trial, there is no jury, and the judge decides questions of fact as well as questions of law.) If the verdict is "guilty," the judge sets a date for the sentencing. Everyone convicted of a crime has the right to an appeal.

a grand jury, such a charge is called an **indictment.**[26] A **grand jury** does not determine the guilt or innocence of an accused party; rather, its function is to hear the state's evidence and to determine whether a reasonable basis (probable cause) exists for believing that a crime has been committed and that a trial ought to be held.

Usually, grand juries are called in cases involving serious crimes, such as murder. For lesser crimes, an individual may be formally charged with a crime by an **information,** or criminal complaint. An information will be issued by a government prosecutor if the prosecutor determines that there is sufficient evidence to justify bringing the individual to trial.

Trial At a criminal trial, the accused person does not have to prove anything; the entire burden of proof is on the prosecutor (the state). As discussed at the beginning of this chapter, the burden of proof is higher in a criminal case than in a civil case. The prosecution must show that, based on all the evidence, the defendant's guilt is established *beyond a reasonable doubt.* If there is reasonable doubt as to whether a criminal defendant did, in fact, commit the crime with which she or he has been charged, then the verdict must be "not guilty." Note that giving a verdict of "not guilty" is not the same as stating that the defendant is innocent; it merely means that not enough evidence was properly presented to the court to prove guilt beyond a reasonable doubt.

Courts have complex rules about what types of evidence may be presented and how the evidence may be brought out in criminal cases, especially in jury trials. These rules are designed to ensure that evidence presented at trials is relevant, reliable, and not prejudicial toward the defendant.

Federal Sentencing Guidelines

In 1984, Congress passed the Sentencing Reform Act. This act created the U.S. Sentencing Commission, which was charged with the task of standardizing sentences for *federal* crimes. The commission's guidelines, which became effective in 1987, established a range of possible penalties for each federal crime and required the judge to select a sentence from within that range. In other words, the guidelines originally established a mandatory system because judges were not allowed to deviate from the specified sentencing range. Some federal judges felt uneasy about imposing the long prison sentences required by the guidelines on certain criminal defendants, particularly first-time offenders and those convicted in illegal substances cases involving small quantities of drugs.[27]

Shift Away from Mandatory Sentencing In 2005, the Supreme Court held that certain provisions of the federal sentencing guidelines were unconstitutional.[28] The case involved Freddie Booker, who was arrested with 92.5 grams of crack cocaine in his possession. Booker admitted to police that he had sold an additional 566 grams of crack cocaine, but he was never charged with, or tried for, possessing this additional quantity. Nevertheless, under the federal sentencing guidelines the judge was required to sentence Booker to twenty-two years in prison. Ultimately, the Supreme Court ruled that this sentence was unconstitutional because a jury did not find beyond a reasonable doubt that Booker had possessed the additional 566 grams of crack.

Essentially, the Supreme Court's ruling changed the federal sentencing guidelines from mandatory to advisory. Depending on the circumstances of the case, a federal trial judge may now depart from the guidelines if she or he believes that it is reasonable to do so.

Increased Penalties for Certain Criminal Violations It is important for businesspersons to understand that the sentencing guidelines still exist and provide for enhanced punishment for certain types of crimes. The U.S. Sentencing Commission recommends stiff sentences for many white-collar crimes, including mail and wire fraud, commercial bribery and kickbacks, and money laundering. Enhanced penalties are also suggested for violations of the Sarbanes-Oxley Act (discussed in Chapter 4).[29]

In addition, the commission recommends increased penalties for criminal violations of employment laws (see Chapters 21 and 22), securities laws (see Chapter 28), and antitrust laws (see Chapters 26 and 27). The guidelines set forth a number of factors that judges should take into consideration when imposing a sentence for a specified crime. These factors include the defendant company's history of past violations, management's cooperation with federal investigators, and the extent to which the firm has undertaken specific programs and procedures to prevent criminal activities by its employees.

26. Pronounced in-*dyte*-ment.

27. See, for example, *United States v. Angelos,* 347 F.Supp.2d 1227 (D.Utah 2004).

28. *United States v. Booker,* 543 U.S. 220, 125 S.Ct. 738, 160 L.Ed.2d 621 (2005).

29. As required by the Sarbanes-Oxley Act of 2002, the U.S. Sentencing Commission revised its guidelines in 2003 to impose stiffer penalties for corporate securities fraud—see Chapter 28.

Cyber Crime

Some years ago, the American Bar Association defined **computer crime** as any act that is directed against computers and computer parts, that uses computers as instruments of crime, or that involves computers and constitutes abuse. Today, because much of the crime committed with the use of computers occurs in cyberspace, many computer crimes fall under the broad label of **cyber crime.** Here we look at several types of activity that constitute cyber crimes against persons or property. Other cyber crimes will be discussed in later chapters as they relate to particular topics, such as banking or consumer law.

Cyber Theft

In cyberspace, thieves are not subject to the physical limitations of the "real" world. A thief can steal data stored in a networked computer with Internet access from anywhere on the globe. Only the speed of the connection and the thief's computer equipment limit the quantity of data that can be stolen.

Financial Crimes Computer networks also provide opportunities for employees to commit crimes that can involve serious economic losses. For example, employees of a company's accounting department can transfer funds among accounts with little effort and often with less risk than would be involved in transactions evidenced by paperwork.

Generally, the dependence of businesses on computer operations has left firms vulnerable to sabotage, fraud, embezzlement, and the theft of proprietary data, such as trade secrets or other intellectual property. As will be mentioned in Chapter 14, the piracy of intellectual property via the Internet is one of the most serious legal challenges facing lawmakers and the courts today.

Identity Theft A form of cyber theft that has become particularly troublesome in recent years is **identity theft.** Identity theft occurs when the wrongdoer steals a form of identification—such as a name, date of birth, or Social Security number—and uses the information to access the victim's financial resources. This crime existed to a certain extent before the widespread use of the Internet. Thieves would "steal" calling-card numbers by watching people using public telephones, or they would rifle through garbage to find bank account or credit-card numbers. The identity thieves would then use the calling-card or credit-card numbers or would withdraw funds from the victims' accounts. The Internet, however, has turned identity theft into perhaps the fastest-growing financial crime in the United States. The Internet provides those who steal information offline with an easy medium for using items such as stolen credit-card numbers while remaining protected by anonymity.

Three federal statutes deal specifically with identity theft. The Identity Theft and Assumption Deterrence Act of 1998[30] made identity theft a federal crime and directed the U.S. Sentencing Commission to incorporate the crime into its sentencing guidelines. The Fair and Accurate Credit Transactions Act of 2003[31] gives victims of identity theft certain rights in working with creditors and credit bureaus to remove negative information from their credit reports. This act will be discussed in detail in Chapter 23 in the context of consumer law. The Identity Theft Penalty Enhancement Act of 2004[32] authorized more severe penalties in aggravated cases in which the identity theft was committed in connection with the thief's employment or with other serious crimes (such as terrorism or firearms or immigration offenses).

Hacking

Persons who use one computer to break into another are sometimes referred to as **hackers.** Hackers who break into computers without authorization often commit cyber theft. Sometimes, however, their principal aim is to prove how smart they are by gaining access to others' password-protected computers and causing random data errors or making toll telephone calls for free.[33]

Cyberterrorism Hackers who, rather than trying to gain attention, strive to remain undetected so that they can exploit computers for a serious impact are called **cyberterrorists.** Just as "real" terrorists destroyed the World Trade Center towers and a portion of the Pentagon on September 11, 2001, cyberterrorists might explode "logic bombs" to shut down central computers. Such activities obviously can pose a danger to national security.

30. 18 U.S.C. Section 1028.
31. 15 U.S.C. Sections 1681 *et seq.*
32. 18 U.S.C. Section 1028A.
33. The total cost of crime on the Internet is estimated to be several billion dollars annually, but two-thirds of that total is said to consist of unpaid-for long-distance calls.

The Threat to Business Activities Any business may be targeted by cyberterrorists as well as hackers. The goals of a hacking operation might include a wholesale theft of data, such as a merchant's customer files, or the monitoring of a computer to discover a business firm's plans and transactions. A cyberterrorist might also want to insert false codes or data. For example, the processing control system of a food manufacturer could be changed to alter the levels of ingredients so that consumers of the food would become ill.

A cyberterrorist attack on a major financial institution, such as the New York Stock Exchange or a large bank, could leave securities or money markets in flux and seriously affect the daily lives of millions of citizens. Similarly, any prolonged disruption of computer, cable, satellite, or telecommunications systems due to the actions of expert hackers would have serious repercussions on business operations—and national security—on a global level. Computer viruses are another tool that can be used by cyberterrorists to cripple communications networks.

Spam

As we will discuss in Chapter 12, *spamming* (sending bulk unsolicited e-mail) has become a major problem for businesses. A few states, such as Maryland and Virginia, have passed laws that make spamming a crime.[34] Under the Virginia statute, it is a crime against property to use a computer or computer network "with the intent to falsify or forge electronic mail transmission information or other routing information in any manner." Attempting to send spam to more than 2,500 recipients in a twenty-four-hour period is a felony. The Virginia law also includes provisions authorizing the forfeiture of assets obtained through an illegal spamming operation. The Maryland law is similar in that it prohibits spamming that falsely identifies the sender, the routing information, or the subject. Under the Maryland law, however, the number of spam messages required to convict a person of the offense is much lower. Sending only ten illegal messages in twenty-four hours violates the statute, and the more spam sent, the more severe the punishment will be, up to a maximum of ten years in prison and a $25,000 fine.

In 2006, a Virginia appellate court upheld the first felony conviction for criminal spamming in the United States against Jeremy Jaynes, who until his arrest was the eighth most prolific spammer in the world. Jaynes, a resident of North Carolina, had sent more than ten thousand junk messages a day using sixteen Internet connections and a number of aliases (such as Gaven Stubberfield). Because he had sent some of the messages through servers in Virginia, the court found that Virginia had jurisdiction over Jaynes. He was convicted of three counts of felony spamming and sentenced to nine years in prison.

Prosecuting Cyber Crime

The "location" of cyber crime (cyberspace) has raised new issues in the investigation of crimes and the prosecution of offenders. A threshold issue is, of course, jurisdiction. A person who commits an act against a business in California, where the act is a cyber crime, might never have set foot in California but might instead reside in New York, or even in Canada, where the act may not be a crime. If the crime was committed via e-mail, the question arises as to whether the e-mail would constitute sufficient "minimum contacts" (see Chapter 2) for the victim's state to exercise jurisdiction over the perpetrator.

Identifying the wrongdoer can also be difficult. Cyber criminals do not leave physical traces, such as fingerprints or DNA samples, as evidence of their crimes. Even electronic "footprints" can be hard to find and follow. For example, e-mail may be sent through a remailer, an online service that guarantees that a message cannot be traced to its source.

For these reasons, laws written to protect physical property often are difficult to apply in cyberspace. Nonetheless, governments at both the state and the federal level have taken significant steps toward controlling cyber crime, both by applying existing criminal statutes and by enacting new laws that specifically address wrongs committed in cyberspace.

The Computer Fraud and Abuse Act

Perhaps the most significant federal statute specifically addressing cyber crime is the Counterfeit Access Device and Computer Fraud and Abuse Act of 1984 (commonly known as the Computer Fraud and Abuse Act, or CFAA).[35] Among other things, this act provides that a person who accesses a computer online, without authority, to obtain classified, restricted, or protected data (or attempts to do so) is subject to criminal prosecution. Such data could include financial and

34. See, for example, Maryland Code, Criminal Law, Section 3-805.1, and Virginia Code Ann. Sections 18.2–152.3:1.

35. 18 U.S.C. Section 1030.

credit records, medical records, legal files, military and national security files, and other confidential information in government or private computers. The crime has two elements: accessing a computer without authority and taking the data.

This theft is a felony if it is committed for a commercial purpose or for private financial gain, or if the value of the stolen data (or computer time) exceeds $5,000. Penalties include fines and imprisonment for up to twenty years. A victim of computer theft can also bring a civil suit against the violator to obtain damages, an injunction, and other relief.

REVIEWING Criminal Law and Cyber Crime

Edward Hanousek worked for Pacific & Arctic Railway and Navigation Company (P&A) as a roadmaster of the White Pass & Yukon Railroad in Alaska. Hanousek was responsible "for every detail of the safe and efficient maintenance and construction of track, structures and marine facilities of the entire railroad," including special projects. One project was a rock quarry, known as "6-mile," above the Skagway River. Next to the quarry, and just beneath the surface, ran a high-pressure oil pipeline owned by Pacific & Arctic Pipeline, Inc., P&A's sister company. When the quarry's backhoe operator punctured the pipeline, an estimated 1,000 to 5,000 gallons of oil were discharged into the river. Hanousek was charged with negligently discharging a harmful quantity of oil into a navigable water of the United States in violation of the criminal provisions of the Clean Water Act (CWA). Using the information presented in the chapter, answer the following questions.

1. Did Hanousek have the required mental state (*mens rea*) to be convicted of a crime? Why or why not?
2. Which theory discussed in the chapter would enable a court to hold Hanousek criminally liable for violating the statute regardless of whether he participated in, directed, or even knew about the specific violation?
3. Could the quarry's backhoe operator who punctured the pipeline also be charged with a crime in this situation? Explain.
4. Suppose that at trial, Hanousek argued that he could not be convicted because he was not aware of the requirements of the CWA. Would this defense be successful? Why or why not?

TERMS AND CONCEPTS

actus reus 150
arson 151
beyond a reasonable doubt 147
burglary 151
computer crime 169
consent 159
crime 147
cyber crime 169
cyberterrorist 169
double jeopardy 162
duress 159
embezzlement 152
entrapment 161
exclusionary rule 162
felony 148
forgery 152
grand jury 168
hacker 169
identity theft 169
indictment 168
information 168
larceny 151
mens rea 150
misdemeanor 149
money laundering 157
necessity 161
petty offense 149
plea bargaining 162
robbery 151
self-defense 160
white-collar crime 152

QUESTIONS AND CASE PROBLEMS

7-1. The following situations are similar (in all of them, Juanita's laptop computer is stolen), yet three different crimes are described. Identify the three crimes, noting the differences among them.

(a) While passing Juanita's house one night, Sarah sees a laptop computer left unattended on Juanita's lawn. Sarah takes the laptop, carries it home, and tells everyone she owns it.
(b) While passing Juanita's house one night, Sarah sees Juanita outside with a laptop computer. Holding Juanita at gunpoint, Sarah forces her to give up the computer. Then Sarah runs away with it.
(c) While passing Juanita's house one night, Sarah sees a laptop computer on a desk inside. Sarah breaks the front-door lock, enters, and leaves with the computer.

7-2. Which, if any, of the following crimes necessarily involves illegal activity on the part of more than one person?

(a) Bribery.
(b) Forgery.
(c) Embezzlement.
(d) Larceny.
(e) Receiving stolen property.

7-3. QUESTION WITH SAMPLE ANSWER

Armington, while robbing a drugstore, shot and seriously injured a drugstore clerk, Jennings. Subsequently, in a criminal trial, Armington was convicted of armed robbery and assault and battery. Jennings later brought a civil tort suit against Armington for damages. Armington contended that he could not be tried again for the same crime, as that would constitute double jeopardy, which is prohibited by the Fifth Amendment to the Constitution. Is Armington correct? Explain.

- **For a sample answer to Question 7-3, go to Appendix I at the end of this text.**

7-4. Rafael stops Laura on a busy street and offers to sell her an expensive wristwatch for a fraction of its value. After some questioning by Laura, Rafael admits that the watch is stolen property, although he says he was not the thief. Laura pays for and receives the wristwatch. Has Laura committed any crime? Has Rafael? Explain.

7-5. Theft of Trade Secrets. Four Pillars Enterprise Co. is a Taiwanese company owned by Pin Yen Yang. Avery Dennison, Inc., a U.S. corporation, is one of Four Pillars' chief competitors in the manufacture of adhesives. In 1989, Victor Lee, an Avery employee, met Yang and Yang's daughter Hwei Chen. They agreed to pay Lee $25,000 a year to serve as a consultant to Four Pillars. Over the next eight years, Lee supplied the Yangs with confidential Avery reports, including information that Four Pillars used to make a new adhesive that had been developed by Avery. The Federal Bureau of Investigation (FBI) confronted Lee, and he agreed to cooperate in an operation to catch the Yangs. When Lee next met the Yangs, he showed them documents provided by the FBI. The documents bore "confidential" stamps, and Lee said that they were Avery's confidential property. The FBI arrested the Yangs with the documents in their possession. The Yangs and Four Pillars were charged with, among other crimes, the attempted theft of trade secrets. The defendants argued in part that it was impossible for them to have committed this crime because the documents were not actually trade secrets. Should the court acquit them? Why or why not? [*United States v. Yang,* 281 F.3d 534 (6th Cir. 2002)]

7-6. CASE PROBLEM WITH SAMPLE ANSWER

The Sixth Amendment secures to a defendant who faces possible imprisonment the right to counsel at all critical stages of the criminal process, including the arraignment and the trial. In 1996, Felipe Tovar, a twenty-one-year-old college student, was arrested in Ames, Iowa, for operating a motor vehicle while under the influence of alcohol (OWI). Tovar was informed of his right to apply for court-appointed counsel and waived it. At his arraignment, he pleaded guilty. Six weeks later, he appeared for sentencing, again waived his right to counsel, and was sentenced to two days' imprisonment. In 1998, Tovar was convicted of OWI again, and in 2000, he was charged with OWI for a third time. In Iowa, a third OWI offense is a felony. Tovar asked the court not to use his first OWI conviction to enhance the third OWI charge. He argued that his 1996 waiver of counsel was not "intelligent" because the court did not make him aware of "the dangers and disadvantages of self-representation." What determines whether a person's choice in any situation is "intelligent"? What should determine whether a defendant's waiver of counsel is "intelligent" at critical stages of a criminal proceeding? [*Iowa v. Tovar,* 541 U.S. 77, 124 S.Ct. 1379, 158 L.Ed.2d 209 (2004)]

- **To view a sample answer for Problem 7-6, go to this book's Web site at academic.cengage.com/blaw/cross, select "Chapter 7," and click on "Case Problem with Sample Answer."**

7-7. Larceny. In February 2001, a homeowner hired Jimmy Smith, a contractor claiming to employ a crew of thirty workers, to build a garage. The homeowner paid Smith $7,950 and agreed to make additional payments as needed to complete the project, up to $15,900. Smith promised to start the next day and finish within eight weeks. Nearly a month passed with no work, while Smith lied to the homeowner that materials were on "back order." During a second month, footings were created for the foundation, and a subcontractor poured the concrete slab, but Smith did not return the homeowner's phone calls. After eight weeks, the homeowner confronted Smith, who promised to complete the job, worked on the site that day until lunch, and never returned. Three months later, the homeowner again confronted Smith, who promised to "pay [him] off" later that day but did not do so. In March 2002, the state of Georgia filed criminal charges against Smith. While his trial was pending, he promised to pay the homeowner "next week" but again failed to refund any of the funds paid. The value of the labor performed before Smith abandoned the project was between $800 and $1,000, the value of the materials was $367, and the subcontractor was paid $2,270. Did Smith commit larceny? Explain. [*Smith v. State of Georgia,* 592 S.E.2d 871 (Ga.App. 2004)]

7–8. Trial. Robert Michels met Allison Formal through an online dating Web site in 2002. Michels represented himself as the retired chief executive officer of a large company that he had sold for millions of dollars. In January 2003, Michels proposed that he and Formal create a *limited liability company* (a special form of business organization discussed in Chapter 17)—Formal Properties Trust, LLC—to "channel their investments in real estate." Formal agreed to contribute $100,000 to the company and wrote two $50,000 checks to "Michels and Associates, LLC." Six months later, Michels told Formal that their LLC had been formed in Delaware. Later, Formal asked Michels about her investments. He responded evasively, and she demanded that an independent accountant review the firm's records. Michels refused. Formal contacted the police. Michels was charged in a Virginia state court with obtaining funds by false pretenses. The Delaware secretary of state verified, in two certified documents, that "Formal Properties Trust, L.L.C." and "Michels and Associates, L.L.C." did not exist in Delaware. Did the admission of the Delaware secretary of state's certified documents at Michels's trial violate his rights under the Sixth Amendment? Why or why not? [*Michels v. Commonwealth of Virginia,* 47 Va.App. 461, 624 S.E.2d 675 (2006)]

7–9. White-Collar Crime. Helm Instruction Co. in Maumee, Ohio, makes custom electrical control systems. Helm hired Patrick Walsh in September 1998 to work as comptroller. Walsh soon developed a close relationship with Richard Wilhelm, Helm's president, who granted Walsh's request to hire Shari Price as Walsh's assistant. Wilhelm was not aware that Walsh and Price were engaged in an extramarital affair. Over the next five years, Walsh and Price spent more than $200,000 of Helm's money on themselves. Among other things, Walsh drew unauthorized checks on Helm's accounts to pay his personal credit cards and issued to Price and himself unauthorized salary increases, overtime payments, and tuition reimbursement payments, altering Helm's records to hide the payments. After an investigation, Helm officials confronted Walsh. He denied the affair with Price, claimed that his unauthorized use of Helm's funds was an "interest-free loan," and argued that it was less of a burden on the company to pay his credit cards than to give him the salary increases to which he felt he was entitled. Did Walsh commit a crime? If so, what crime did he commit? Discuss. [*State v. Walsh,* 113 Ohio App.3d 1515, 866 N.E.2d 513 (6 Dist. 2007)]

7–10. A QUESTION OF ETHICS

*A troublesome issue concerning the constitutional privilege against self-incrimination is the extent to which law enforcement officers may use trickery during an interrogation to induce a suspect to incriminate himself or herself. For example, in one case two officers questioned Charles McFarland, who was incarcerated in a state prison, about his connection to a handgun that had been used to shoot two other officers. McFarland was advised of his rights but was not asked whether he was willing to waive those rights. Instead, to induce McFarland to speak, the officers deceived him into believing that "[n]obody is going to give you charges." McFarland made incriminating admissions and was indicted for possessing a handgun as a convicted felon. [*United States v. McFarland, *424 F.Supp.2d 427 (N.D.N.Y. 2006)]*

(a) Review Case 7.4, *Miranda v. Arizona,* on pages 165–166 in this chapter. Should McFarland's statements be suppressed—that is, not be treated as admissible evidence at trial—because he was not asked whether he was willing to waive his rights prior to making his self-incriminating statements? Does the *Miranda* rule apply to McFarland's situation?
(b) Do you think that it is fair for the police to resort to trickery and deception to bring those who have committed crimes to justice? Why or why not? What rights or public policies must be balanced in deciding this issue?

7–11. VIDEO QUESTION

DIGITAL video

Go to this text's Web site at **academic.cengage.com/blaw/cross** and select "Chapter 7." Click on "Video Questions" and view the video titled *Casino.* Then answer the following questions.

(a) In the video, a casino manager, Ace (Robert DeNiro), discusses how politicians "won their 'comp life' when they got elected." "Comps" are the free gifts that casinos give to high-stakes gamblers to keep their business. If an elected official accepts comps, is he or she committing a crime? If so, what type of crime? Explain your answers.
(b) Assume that Ace committed a crime by giving politicians comps. Can the casino, Tangiers Corp., be held liable for that crime? Why or why not? How could a court punish the corporation?

(c) Suppose that the Federal Bureau of Investigation wants to search the premises of Tangiers for evidence of criminal activity. If casino management refuses to consent to the search, what constitutional safeguards and criminal procedures, if any, protect Tangiers?

LAW ON THE WEB

For updated links to resources available on the Web, as well as a variety of other materials, visit this text's Web site at

academic.cengage.com/blaw/cross

The Bureau of Justice Statistics in the U.S. Department of Justice offers an impressive collection of statistics on crime at the following Web site:

ojp.usdoj.gov/bjs

For summaries of famous criminal cases and documents relating to these trials, go to Court TV's Web site at

www.courttv.com/sitemap/index.html

Many state criminal codes are now online. To find your state's code, go to the following home page and select "States" under the link to "Cases & Codes":

www.findlaw.com

You can learn about some of the constitutional questions raised by various criminal laws and procedures by going to the Web site of the American Civil Liberties Union at

www.aclu.org

The following Web site, which is maintained by the U.S. Department of Justice, offers information ranging from the various types of cyber crime to a description of how computers and the Internet are being used to prosecute cyber crime:

www.cybercrime.gov

Legal Research Exercises on the Web

Go to **academic.cengage.com/blaw/cross**, the Web site that accompanies this text. Select "Chapter 7" and click on "Internet Exercises." There you will find the following Internet research exercises that you can perform to learn more about the topics covered in this chapter.

Internet Exercise 7–1: Legal Perspective
Revisiting *Miranda*

Internet Exercise 7–2: Management Perspective
Hackers

Internet Exercise 7–3: International Perspective
Fighting Cyber Crime Worldwide

CHAPTER 8

International Law in a Global Economy

International business transactions are not unique to the modern world. What is new in our day is the dramatic growth in world trade and the emergence of a global business community. Because the exchange of goods, services, and ideas (intellectual property) on a worldwide level is now routine, students of business law and the legal environment should be familiar with the laws pertaining to international business transactions.

Laws affecting the international legal environment of business include both international law and national law. **International law** can be defined as a body of law—formed as a result of international customs, treaties, and organizations—that governs relations among or between nations. International law may be public, creating standards for the nations themselves; or it may be private, establishing international standards for private transactions that cross national borders. **National law** is the law of a particular nation, such as Brazil, Germany, Japan, or the United States. In this chapter, we examine how both international law and national law frame business operations in the international context.

International Law

The major difference between international law and national law is that government authorities can enforce national law. What government, however, can enforce international law? By definition, a *nation* is a sovereign entity—which means that there is no higher authority to which that nation must submit. If a nation violates an international law and persuasive tactics fail, other countries or international organizations have no recourse except to take coercive actions—from severance of diplomatic relations and boycotts to, as a last resort, war—against the violating nation.

In essence, international law is the result of centuries-old attempts to reconcile the traditional need of each country to be the final authority over its own affairs with the desire of nations to benefit economically from trade and harmonious relations with one another. Sovereign nations can, and do, voluntarily agree to be governed in certain respects by international law for the purpose of facilitating international trade and commerce, as well as civilized discourse. As a result, a body of international law has evolved. In this section, we examine the primary sources and characteristics of that body of law, as well as some important legal principles and doctrines that have been developed over time to facilitate dealings among nations.

Sources of International Law

Basically, there are three sources of international law: international customs, treaties and international agreements, and international organizations and conferences. We look at each of these sources here.

International Customs One important source of international law consists of the international customs that have evolved among nations in their relations with one another. Article 38(1) of the Statute of the International Court of Justice refers to an international custom as "evidence of a general practice accepted as law." The legal principles and doctrines that you will read about shortly are rooted in international customs and traditions that have evolved over time in the international arena.

Treaties and International Agreements Treaties and other explicit agreements between or among foreign nations provide another important source of international law. A **treaty** is an agreement or contract between two or more nations that must be authorized and ratified by the supreme power of each nation. Under Article II, Section 2, of the U.S. Constitution, the president has the power "by and with the Advice and Consent of the Senate, to make Treaties, provided two-thirds of the Senators present concur."

A *bilateral* agreement, as the term implies, is an agreement formed by two nations to govern their commercial exchanges or other relations with one another. A *multilateral* agreement is formed by several nations. For example, regional trade associations such as the European Union (EU, which is discussed later in this chapter) are the result of multilateral trade agreements. Other regional trade associations that have been created through multilateral agreements include the Association of Southeast Asian Nations (ASEAN) and the Andean Common Market (ANCOM).

International Organizations In international law, the term **international organization** generally refers to an organization composed mainly of officials of member nations and usually established by treaty. The United States is a member of more than one hundred multilateral and bilateral organizations, including at least twenty through the United Nations. These organizations adopt resolutions, declarations, and other types of standards that often require nations to behave in a particular manner. The General Assembly of the United Nations, for example, has adopted numerous nonbinding resolutions and declarations that embody principles of international law. Disputes with respect to these resolutions and declarations may be brought before the International Court of Justice. That court, however, normally has authority to settle legal disputes only when nations voluntarily submit to its jurisdiction.

The United Nations Commission on International Trade Law has made considerable progress in establishing uniformity in international law as it relates to trade and commerce. One of the commission's most significant creations to date is the 1980 Convention on Contracts for the International Sale of Goods (CISG). The CISG is similar to Article 2 of the Uniform Commercial Code in that it is designed to settle disputes between parties to sales contracts (see Chapter 11). It spells out the duties of international buyers and sellers that will apply if the parties have not agreed otherwise in their contracts. The CISG governs only sales contracts between trading partners in nations that have ratified the CISG, however.

Common Law and Civil Law Systems

Companies operating in foreign nations are subject to the laws of those nations. In addition, international disputes often are resolved through the court systems of foreign nations. Therefore, businesspersons should understand that legal systems around the globe generally are divided into *common law* and *civil law* systems. As discussed in Chapter 1, in a common law system, the courts independently develop the rules governing certain areas of law, such as torts and contracts. These common law rules apply to all areas not covered by statutory law. Although the common law doctrine of *stare decisis* obligates judges to follow precedential decisions in their jurisdictions, courts may modify or even overturn precedents when deemed necessary.

In contrast to common law countries, most of the European nations, as well as nations in Latin America, Africa, and Asia, base their legal systems on Roman civil law, or "code law." The term *civil law,* as used here, refers not to civil as opposed to criminal law but to *codified* law—an ordered grouping of legal principles enacted into law by a legislature or other governing body. In a **civil law system,** the only official source of law is a statutory code. Courts interpret the code and apply the rules to individual cases, but courts may not depart from the code and develop their own laws. In theory, the law code sets forth all of the principles needed for the legal system. Trial procedures also differ in civil law systems. Unlike judges in common law systems, judges in civil systems often actively question witnesses. Exhibit 8–1 lists examples of the nations that use civil law systems and examples that use common law systems.

International Principles and Doctrines

Over time, a number of legal principles and doctrines have evolved and have been employed—to a greater or lesser extent—by the courts of various nations to resolve or reduce conflicts that involve a foreign element. The three important legal principles discussed next are based primarily on courtesy and respect, and

EXHIBIT 8–1 • The Legal Systems of Selected Nations

Civil Law		Common Law	
Argentina	Indonesia	Australia	Nigeria
Austria	Iran	Bangladesh	Singapore
Brazil	Italy	Canada	United Kingdom
Chile	Japan	Ghana	United States
China	Mexico	India	Zambia
Egypt	Poland	Israel	
Finland	South Korea	Jamaica	
France	Sweden	Kenya	
Germany	Tunisia	Malaysia	
Greece	Venezuela	New Zealand	

are applied in the interests of maintaining harmonious relations among nations.

The Principle of Comity Under what is known as the principle of **comity,** one nation will defer and give effect to the laws and judicial decrees of another country, as long as they are consistent with the law and public policy of the accommodating nation. For example, a Swedish seller and a U.S. buyer have formed a contract, which the buyer breaches. The seller sues the buyer in a Swedish court, which awards damages. The buyer's assets, however, are in the United States and cannot be reached unless the judgment is enforced by a U.S. court. In this situation, if a U.S. court determines that the procedures and laws applied in the Swedish court are consistent with U.S. national law and policy, the U.S. court will likely defer to, and enforce, the foreign court's judgment.

One way to understand the principle of comity (and the *act of state doctrine,* which will be discussed shortly) is to consider the relationships among the states in our federal form of government. Each state honors (gives "full faith and credit" to) the contracts, property deeds, wills, and other legal obligations formed in other states, as well as judicial decisions with respect to such obligations. On a worldwide basis, nations similarly attempt to honor judgments rendered in other countries when it is feasible to do so. Of course, in the United States the states are constitutionally required to honor other states' actions, whereas, internationally, nations are not *required* to honor the actions of other nations.

The Act of State Doctrine The **act of state doctrine** is a judicially created doctrine that provides that the judicial branch of one country will not examine the validity of public acts committed by a recognized foreign government within the latter's own territory. This doctrine is premised on the theory that the judicial branch should not pass judgment on the validity of foreign acts when to do so would upset the harmony of our international relations with that foreign nation.

When a Foreign Government Takes Private Property. The act of state doctrine can have important consequences for individuals and firms doing business with, and investing in, other countries. This doctrine is frequently employed in cases involving **expropriation,** which occurs when a government seizes a privately owned business or privately owned goods for a proper public purpose and awards just compensation. When a government seizes private property for an illegal purpose and without just compensation, the taking is referred to as a **confiscation.** The line between these two forms of taking is sometimes blurred because of differing interpretations of what is illegal and what constitutes just compensation.

For example, Flaherty, Inc., a U.S. company, owns a mine in Brazil. The government of Brazil seizes the mine for public use and claims that the profits Flaherty has already realized from the mine constitute just compensation. Flaherty disagrees, but the act of state doctrine may prevent that company's recovery in a U.S. court. Note that in a case alleging that a foreign government has wrongfully taken the plaintiff's property, the defendant government has the burden of proving that the taking was an expropriation, not a confiscation.

Doctrine May Immunize a Foreign Government's Actions. When applicable, both the act of state doctrine and the doctrine of *sovereign immunity,* which we

While restricting certain exports, the United States (and other nations) also use incentives and subsidies to stimulate other exports and thereby aid domestic businesses. The Revenue Act of 1971,[4] for instance, promoted exports by exempting from taxes the income earned by firms marketing their products overseas through certain foreign sales corporations. Under the Export Trading Company Act of 1982,[5] U.S. banks are encouraged to invest in export trading companies, which are formed when exporting firms join together to export a line of goods.

Import Controls

All nations have restrictions on imports, and the United States is no exception. Restrictions include strict prohibitions, quotas, and tariffs. Under the Trading with the Enemy Act of 1917,[6] for example, no goods may be imported from nations that have been designated enemies of the United States. Other laws prohibit the importation of illegal drugs, books that urge insurrection against the United States, and agricultural products that pose dangers to domestic crops or animals.

Importing goods that infringe U.S. patents is also prohibited. The International Trade Commission is an independent agency of the U.S. government that, among other duties, investigates allegations that imported goods infringe U.S. patents and imposes penalties if necessary. In the following case, the court considered an appeal from a party fined more than $13.5 million for importing certain disposable cameras.

4. 26 U.S.C. Sections 991–994.
5. 15 U.S.C. Sections 4001, 4003.
6. 12 U.S.C. Section 95a.

CASE 8.1 Fuji Photo Film Co. v. International Trade Commission

United States Court of Appeals, Federal Circuit, 2007. 474 F.3d 1281.

Background and Facts Fuji Photo Film Company owns fifteen patents for "lens-fitted film packages" (LFFPs), popularly known as disposable cameras. An LFFP consists of a plastic shell preloaded with film. To develop the film, a consumer gives the LFFP to a film processor and receives back the negatives and prints, but not the shell. Fuji makes and sells LFFPs. Jazz Photo Corporation collected used LFFP shells in the United States, shipped them abroad to insert new film, and imported refurbished shells back into the United States for sale. The International Trade Commission (ITC) determined that Jazz's resale of shells originally sold outside the United States infringed Fuji's patents. In 1999, the ITC issued a cease-and-desist order to stop the imports. While the order was being disputed at the ITC and in the courts, between August 2001 and December 2003 Jazz imported and sold 27 million refurbished LFFPs. Fuji complained to the ITC, which fined Jazz more than $13.5 million. Jack Benun, Jazz's chief operating officer, appealed to the U.S. Court of Appeals for the Federal Circuit.

IN THE LANGUAGE OF THE COURT
***DYK*, Circuit Judge.**

* * * *

* * * The Commission concluded that 40% of the LFFPs in issue were first sold abroad * * * . This conclusion was supported by substantial evidence. It was based on * * * the identifying numbers printed on the LFFPs and Fuji's production and shipping databases to determine where samples of Fuji-type LFFPs with Jazz packaging (i.e., ones that were refurbished by Jazz) were first sold.

Benun urges that the Commission's decision in this respect was not supported by substantial evidence, primarily arguing that Jazz's so-called informed compliance program required a finding in Jazz's favor. Benun asserts that this program tracked shells from collection through the refurbishment process to sale and insured that only shells collected from the United States were refurbished for sale here. The Commission rejected this argument for two reasons. First, it concluded that the program was too disorganized and incomplete to provide credible evidence that Jazz only refurbished shells collected from the United States. Second, the Commission concluded that at most the program could insure that Jazz only refurbished LFFPs collected from the United States, not LFFPs that were first sold here.

CASE 8.1 CONTINUED

Responding to the second ground, Benun urges that proof that Jazz limited its activities to shells collected in the United States was sufficient * * * because Fuji "infected the pool" of camera shells collected in the United States by taking actions that made it difficult for Jazz and Benun to insure that these shells were from LFFPs first sold here. These actions allegedly included allowing [one company] to import cameras with Japanese writing on them for sale in the United States; allowing [that company] to import spent shells into the United States for recycling; and allowing tourists to bring cameras first sold abroad into the United States for personal use. Under these circumstances, Benun argues that a presumption should arise that shells collected in the United States were first sold here. However, the Commission found that the number of shells falling into these categories was insignificant, and that finding was supported by substantial evidence. Moreover, there was evidence that Jazz treated substantial numbers of its own shells collected in the United States * * * as having been sold in the United States even though it knew that 90% of these shells were first sold abroad * * * .

In any event, the Commission's first ground—that the program was too incomplete and disorganized to be credible—was supported by substantial evidence. Since there was no suggestion that the incomplete and disorganized nature of the program was due to Fuji's actions, this ground alone was sufficient to justify a conclusion that Benun had not carried his burden to prove [the refurbished LFFPs had been sold first in the United States].

• **Decision and Remedy** *The U.S. Court of Appeals for the Federal Circuit held that Jazz had violated the cease-and-desist order, affirming this part of the ITC's decision. The court concluded, among other things, that "substantial evidence supports the finding that the majority of the cameras were first sold abroad."*

• **What If the Facts Were Different?** *Suppose that, after this decision, Jazz fully compensated Fuji for the infringing sales of LFFPs. Would Jazz have acquired the right to refurbish those LFFPs in the future? Explain.*

• **The Global Dimension** *How does prohibiting the importing of goods that infringe U.S. patents protect those patents outside the United States?*

Quotas and Tariffs Limits on the amounts of goods that can be imported are known as **quotas.** At one time, the United States had legal quotas on the number of automobiles that could be imported from Japan. Today, Japan "voluntarily" restricts the number of automobiles exported to the United States. **Tariffs** are taxes on imports. A tariff is usually a percentage of the value of the import, but it can be a flat rate per unit (such as per barrel of oil). Tariffs raise the prices of imported goods, causing some consumers to purchase more domestically manufactured goods.

Antidumping Duties The United States has specific laws directed at what it sees as unfair international trade practices. **Dumping,** for example, is the sale of imported goods at "less than fair value." *Fair value* is usually determined by the price of those goods in the exporting country. Foreign firms that engage in dumping in the United States hope to undersell U.S. businesses to obtain a larger share of the U.S. market. To prevent this, an extra tariff—known as an *antidumping duty*—may be assessed on the imports.

The procedure for imposing antidumping duties involves two U.S. government agencies: the International Trade Commission (ITC) and the International Trade Administration (ITA). The ITC assesses the effects of dumping on domestic businesses and then makes recommendations to the president concerning temporary import restrictions. The ITA, which is part of the Department of Commerce, decides whether imports were sold at less than fair value. The ITA's determination establishes the amount of antidumping duties, which are set to equal the difference between the price charged in the United States and the price charged in the exporting country. A duty may be retroactive to cover past dumping.

Minimizing Trade Barriers through Trade Agreements

Restrictions on imports are also known as *trade barriers*. The elimination of trade barriers is sometimes seen as essential to the world's economic well-being.

CASE 8.2 CONTINUED

as to any intent to apply it abroad, the statute's legislative history indicates that Congress gave no consideration to either the possibility or the problems of overseas application. In sharp contrast with this silence, Congress has provided expressly elsewhere in the Sarbanes-Oxley Act for extraterritorial enforcement of a different, criminal, whistleblower statute. By so providing, Congress demonstrated that it was well able to call for extraterritorial application when it so desired. Also in the Act, Congress has provided expressly for the extraterritorial application of certain other unrelated statutes, tailoring these so as to cope with problems of sovereignty and the like—again demonstrating Congress's ability to provide for foreign application when it wished. Here, however, while placing the whistleblower provision's enforcement in the hands of the DOL, a domestic agency, Congress has made no provision for possible problems arising when that agency seeks to regulate employment relationships in foreign nations, nor has Congress provided the DOL with special powers and resources to conduct investigations abroad. Furthermore, judicial venue provisions written into the whistleblower protection statute were made expressly applicable only to whistleblower violations within the United States and to complainants residing here on the date of violation, with no corresponding basis being provided for venue as to foreign complainants claiming violations in foreign countries.

These factors * * * not only fail to imply a clear congressional intent for extraterritorial application, but indicate that Congress never expected such application.

• **Decision and Remedy** *The U.S. Court of Appeals for the First Circuit affirmed the lower court's dismissal of Carnero's complaint under 18 U.S.C. Section 1514A. Congress "made no reference to [the statute's] application abroad and tailored the * * * statute to purely domestic application." This section of the act "does not reflect the necessary clear expression of congressional intent to extend its reach beyond our nation's borders."*

• **What If the Facts Were Different?** *Suppose that Carnero had been an American working for BSA and BSB. Would the result in this case have been the same? Discuss.*

• **The Legal Environment Dimension** *How might the court's decision in this case frustrate the basic purpose of the Sarbanes-Oxley Act, which is to protect investors in U.S. securities markets and the integrity of those markets?*

Antidiscrimination Laws

As will be explained in Chapter 21, federal laws in the United States prohibit discrimination on the basis of race, color, national origin, religion, gender, age, and disability. These laws, as they affect employment relationships, generally apply extraterritorially. Since 1984, for example, the Age Discrimination in Employment Act of 1967 has covered U.S. employees working abroad for U.S. employers. The Americans with Disabilities Act of 1990, which requires employers to accommodate the needs of workers with disabilities, also applies to U.S. nationals working abroad for U.S. firms.

For some time, it was uncertain whether the major U.S. law regulating discriminatory practices in the workplace, Title VII of the Civil Rights Act of 1964, applied extraterritorially. The Civil Rights Act of 1991 addressed this issue. The act provides that Title VII applies extraterritorially to all U.S. employees working for U.S. employers abroad. Generally, U.S. employers must abide by U.S. discrimination laws unless to do so would violate the laws of the country where their workplaces are located. This "foreign laws exception" allows employers to avoid being subjected to conflicting laws.

International Tort Claims

The international application of tort liability is growing in significance and controversy. An increasing number of U.S. plaintiffs are suing foreign (or U.S.) entities for torts that these entities have allegedly committed overseas. Often, these cases involve human rights violations by foreign governments. The Alien Tort Claims Act (ATCA),[7] adopted in 1789, allows even foreign citizens to bring civil suits in U.S. courts for injuries caused by violations of the law of nations or a treaty of the United States.

Since 1980, plaintiffs have increasingly used the ATCA to bring actions against companies operating in other countries. ATCA actions have been brought against companies doing business in nations such as

7. 28 U.S.C. Section 1350.

Colombia, Ecuador, Egypt, Guatemala, India, Indonesia, Nigeria, and Saudi Arabia. Some of these cases have involved alleged environmental destruction. In addition, mineral companies in Southeast Asia have been sued for collaborating with oppressive government regimes.

The following case involved claims against "hundreds" of corporations that allegedly "aided and abetted" the government of South Africa in maintaining its apartheid (racially discriminatory) regime.

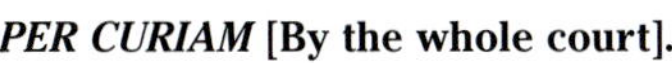

EXTENDED CASE 8.3

Khulumani v. Barclay National Bank, Ltd.

United States Court of Appeals, Second Circuit, 2007. 504 F.3d 254.

***PER CURIAM* [By the whole court].**

* * * *

The plaintiffs in this action bring claims under the Alien Tort Claims Act ("ATCA") against approximately fifty corporate defendants and hundreds of "corporate Does" [including Bank of America, N.A.; Barclay National Bank, Ltd.; Citigroup, Inc.; Credit Suisse Group; Deutsche Bank A.G.; General Electric Company; IBM Corporation; and Shell Oil Company]. The plaintiffs argue that these defendants actively and willingly collaborated with the government of South Africa in maintaining a repressive, racially based system known as "apartheid," which restricted the majority black African population in all areas of life while providing benefits for the minority white population.

Three groups of plaintiffs filed ten separate actions in multiple federal district courts asserting these apartheid-related claims. One group, the Khulumani Plaintiffs, filed a complaint against twenty-three domestic and foreign corporations, charging them with various violations of international law. The other two groups, the Ntsebeza and Digwamaje Plaintiffs, brought class action claims on behalf of the "victims of the apartheid related atrocities, human rights' violations, crimes against humanity and unfair [and] discriminatory forced labor practices."

* * * All of the actions [were transferred to a federal district court in] the Southern District of New York * * * . Thirty-one of the fifty-five defendants in the Ntsebeza and Digwamaje actions * * * [and] eighteen of the twenty-three defendants in [the Khulumani] action * * * filed * * * motion[s] to dismiss.

* * * *

Ruling on the defendants' motions to dismiss, the district court held that the plaintiffs failed to establish subject matter jurisdiction under the ATCA. * * * The district court therefore dismissed the plaintiffs' complaints in their entirety. * * * The plaintiffs filed timely notices of appeal [with the U.S. Court of Appeals for the Second Circuit].

* * * *

* * * [This court] vacate[s] the district court's dismissal of the plaintiffs' ATCA claims because the district court erred in holding that aiding and abetting violations of customary international law cannot provide a basis for ATCA jurisdiction. *We hold that * * * a plaintiff may plead a theory of aiding and abetting liability under the ATCA.* * * * [The majority of the judges on the panel that heard this case agreed on the result but differed on the reasons, which were presented in two concurring opinions. One judge believed that liability on these facts is "well established in international law," citing such examples as the Rome Statute of the International Criminal Court. Another judge stated that grounds existed in such resources of U.S. law as Section 876(b) of the *Restatement (Second) of Torts,* under which liability could be assessed in part for "facilitating the commission of human rights violations by providing the principal tortfeasor with the tools, instrumentalities, or services to commit those violations."] [Emphasis added.]

* * * *

* * * We decline to affirm the dismissal of plaintiffs' ATCA claims on the basis of the prudential concerns[a] raised by the defendants. * * * [T]he Supreme Court [has] identified two

a. The term *prudential concerns* refers to the defendants' arguments that the plaintiffs do not have standing to pursue their case in a U.S. court. Here, *prudential* means that the arguments are based on judicially (or legislatively) created principles rather than on the constitutionally based requirements set forth in Article III of the U.S. Constitution (the case or controversy clause).

CASE CONTINUES

"commercial activity" exception? Explain. [*Tonoga, Ltd. v. Ministry of Public Works and Housing of Kingdom of Saudi Arabia,* 135 F.Supp.2d 350 (N.D.N.Y. 2001)]

8–4. Import Controls. DaimlerChrysler Corp. made and marketed motor vehicles. DaimlerChrysler assembled the 1993 and 1994 model years of its trucks at plants in Mexico. Assembly involved sheet metal components sent from the United States. DaimlerChrysler subjected some of the parts to a complicated treatment process, which included the application of coats of paint to prevent corrosion, impart color, and protect the finish. Under federal law, goods that are assembled abroad using U.S.-made parts can be imported tariff free. A federal statute provides that painting is "incidental" to assembly and does not affect the status of the goods. A federal regulation states that "painting primarily intended to enhance the appearance of an article or to impart distinctive features or characteristics" is not incidental. The U.S. Customs Service levied a tariff on the trucks. DaimlerChrysler filed a suit in the U.S. Court of International Trade, challenging the levy. Should the court rule in DaimlerChrysler's favor? Why or why not? [*DaimlerChrysler Corp. v. United States,* 361 F.3d 1378 (Fed.Cir. 2004)]

8–5. Comity. E&L Consulting, Ltd., is a U.S. corporation that sells lumber products in New Jersey, New York, and Pennsylvania. Doman Industries, Ltd., is a Canadian corporation that also sells lumber products, including green hem-fir, a durable product used for home building. Doman supplies more than 95 percent of the green hem-fir for sale in the northeastern United States. In 1990, Doman contracted to sell green hem-fir through E&L, which received monthly payments plus commissions. In 1998, Sherwood Lumber Corp., a New York firm and an E&L competitor, approached E&L about a merger. The negotiations were unsuccessful. According to E&L, Sherwood and Doman then conspired to monopolize the green hem-fir market in the United States. When Doman terminated its contract with E&L, the latter filed a suit in a federal district court against Doman, alleging violations of U.S. antitrust law. Doman filed for bankruptcy in a Canadian court and asked the U.S. court to dismiss E&L's suit, in part, under the principle of comity. What is the "principle of comity"? On what basis would it apply in this case? What would be the likely result? Discuss. [*E&L Consulting, Ltd. v. Doman Industries, Ltd.,* 360 F.Supp.2d 465 (E.D.N.Y. 2005)]

8–6. Dumping. A newspaper printing press system is more than a hundred feet long, stands four or five stories tall, and weighs 2 million pounds. Only about ten of the systems are sold each year in the United States. Because of the size and cost, a newspaper may update its system, rather than replace it, by buying "additions." By the 1990s, Goss International Corp. was the only domestic maker of the equipment in the United States and represented the entire U.S. market. Tokyo Kikai Seisakusho (TKSC), a Japanese corporation, makes the systems in Japan. In the 1990s, TKSC began to compete in the U.S. market, forcing Goss to cut its prices below cost. TKSC's tactics included offering its customers "secret" rebates on prices that were ultimately substantially less than the products' actual market value in Japan. According to TKSC office memos, the goal was to "win completely this survival game" against Goss, the "enemy." Goss filed a suit in a federal district court against TKSC and others, alleging illegal dumping. At what point does a foreign firm's attempt to compete with a domestic manufacturer in the United States become illegal dumping? Was that point reached in this case? Discuss. [*Goss International Corp. v. Man Roland Druckmaschinen Aktiengesellschaft,* 434 F.3d 1081 (8th Cir. 2006)]

8–7. CASE PROBLEM WITH SAMPLE ANSWER

Jan Voda, M.D., a resident of Oklahoma City, Oklahoma, owns three U.S. patents related to guiding catheters for use in interventional cardiology, as well as corresponding foreign patents issued by the European Patent Office, Canada, France, Germany, and Great Britain. Voda filed a suit in a federal district court against Cordis Corp., a U.S. firm, alleging infringement of the U.S. patents under U.S. patent law and of the corresponding foreign patents under the patent law of the various foreign countries. Cordis admitted, "[T]he XB catheters have been sold domestically and internationally since 1994. The XB catheters were manufactured in Miami Lakes, from 1993 to 2001 and have been manufactured in Juarez, Mexico, since 2001." Cordis argued, however, that Voda could not assert infringement claims under foreign patent law because the court did not have jurisdiction over such claims. Which of the important international legal principles discussed in this chapter would be most likely to apply in this case? How should the court apply it? Explain. [*Voda v. Cordis Corp.,* 476 F.3d 887 (Fed.Cir. 2007)]

- **To view a sample answer for Problem 8–7, go to this book's Web site at academic.cengage.com/blaw/cross, select "Chapter 8," and click on "Case Problem with Sample Answer."**

8–8. SPECIAL CASE ANALYSIS

Go to Case 8.3, *Khulumani v. Barclay National Bank, Ltd.,* 504 F.3d 254 (2d Cir. 2007), on pages 185–186. Read the excerpt and answer the following questions.

(a) **Issue:** What was the main issue in this case?
(b) **Rule of Law:** What rule of law did the court apply?
(c) **Applying the Rule of Law:** Describe how the court applied the rule of law to the facts of this case.
(d) **Conclusion:** What was the court's conclusion in this case?

8-9. A QUESTION OF ETHICS

On December 21, 1988, Pan Am Flight 103 exploded 31,000 feet in the air over Lockerbie, Scotland, killing all 259 passengers and crew on board and 11 people on the ground. Among those killed was Roger Hurst, a U.S. citizen. An investigation determined that a portable radio-cassette player packed in a brown Samsonite suitcase smuggled onto the plane was the source of the explosion. The explosive device was constructed with a digital timer specially made for, and bought by, Libya. Abdel Basset Ali Al-Megrahi, a Libyan government official and an employee of the Libyan Arab Airline (LAA), was convicted by the Scottish High Court of Justiciary on criminal charges that he planned and executed the bombing in association with members of the Jamahiriya Security Organization (JSO) (an agency of the Libyan government that performs security and intelligence functions) or the Libyan military. Members of the victims' families filed a suit in a U.S. federal district court against the JSO, the LAA, Al-Megrahi, and others. The plaintiffs claimed violations of U.S. federal law, including the Anti-Terrorism Act, and state law, including the intentional infliction of emotional distress. [Hurst v. Socialist People's Libyan Arab Jamahiriya, *474 F.Supp.2d 19 (D.D.C. 2007)]*

(a) Under what doctrine, codified in which federal statute, might the defendants claim to be immune from the jurisdiction of a U.S. court? Should this law include an exception for "state-sponsored terrorism"? Why or why not?

(b) The defendants agreed to pay $2.7 billion, or $10 million per victim, to settle all claims for "compensatory death damages." The families of eleven victims, including Hurst, were excluded from the settlement because they were "not wrongful death beneficiaries under applicable state law." These plaintiffs continued the suit. The defendants filed a motion to dismiss. Should the motion be granted on the ground that the settlement bars the plaintiffs' claims? Explain.

LAW ON THE WEB

For updated links to resources available on the Web, as well as a variety of other materials, visit this text's Web site at

academic.cengage.com/blaw/cross

FindLaw, which is now a part of West Group, includes an extensive array of links to international doctrines and treaties, as well as to the laws of other nations, on its Web site. Go to

www.findlaw.com/12international

For information on the legal requirements of doing business internationally, a good source is the Internet Law Library's collection of laws of other countries. You can access this source at

www.lawguru.com/ilawlib/?id=52

Legal Research Exercises on the Web

Go to **academic.cengage.com/blaw/cross**, the Web site that accompanies this text. Select "Chapter 8" and click on "Internet Exercises." There you will find the following Internet research exercises that you can perform to learn more about the topics covered in this chapter.

Internet Exercise 8–1: Legal Perspective
The World Trade Organization

Internet Exercise 8–2: Management Perspective
Overseas Business Opportunities

UNIT TWO FOCUS ON ETHICS

The Ethics of Legal Avoidance

In the face of an agency investigation, a business may prevent or delay agency efforts by asserting legal challenges to the nature or manner of the investigation.

There remains, however, the question of whether—in an ethical rather than legal sense—a business should challenge any such investigation. We would be expected to challenge an unreasonable search of our homes. Regulatory investigations may be somehow different, though.

Most regulatory investigations have as their objective ensuring compliance with existing regulatory schemes or gathering information for future ones. Such schemes are designed to promote the public welfare. Though individuals may disagree about the effectiveness of the scheme or the individual motives of the regulators, society generally accepts the underlying purpose of the regulation—the promotion of public welfare. In such instances, businesses may have an ethical duty not to use legal means to avoid agency action. Indeed, they may have an ethical duty to aid in regulation by compliance, even though they may have a legal right to delay or avoid it.

Ethics and International Transactions

Conducting business internationally involves unique challenges, including, at times, ethical challenges. This is understandable, given that laws and cultures vary from one country to another. Consider the role of women. In the United States, equal employment opportunity is a fundamental public policy. This policy is clearly expressed in Title VII of the Civil Rights Act of 1964 (discussed in Chapter 21), which prohibits discrimination against women in the employment context. Some other countries, however, largely reject any professional role for women, which may cause difficulties for American women conducting business transactions in those countries. For example, when the World Bank sent a delegation that included women to negotiate with the Central Bank of Korea, the Koreans were surprised and offended. They thought that the presence of women meant that the Koreans were not being taken seriously.

There are also some important ethical differences among nations. In Islamic countries, for example, the consumption of alcohol and certain foods is forbidden by the Islamic religion. Thus, it would be thoughtless and imprudent to invite a Saudi Arabian business contact out for a drink. Additionally, in many foreign nations, gift giving is a common practice between contracting companies or between companies and government officials. To Americans, such gift giving may look suspiciously like an unethical (and possibly illegal) bribe. This has been an important source of friction in international business, particularly after the U.S. Congress passed the Foreign Corrupt Practices Act in 1977 (discussed in Chapters 4 and 7). This act prohibits U.S. business firms from offering certain side payments to foreign officials to secure favorable contracts.

DISCUSSION QUESTIONS

1. Do companies, such as Google, that do business on a global level have an ethical duty to foreign citizens not to suppress free speech, or is it acceptable to censor the information that they provide in other nations at the request of a foreign government?
2. The United States banned the pesticide DDT, primarily because of its adverse effects on wildlife. In Asia, however, DDT has been a critical component of the mosquito control necessary to combat malaria. Should the ban in the United States prevent U.S. firms from manufacturing DDT and shipping it to an Asian country, where it could be used to save lives? Why or why not?
3. What are some of the ethical implications for businesspersons doing business internationally? Should a company refuse to send its women employees to represent the company in nations that reject professional roles for women? Should businesspersons traveling abroad always observe the cultural and religious customs of that location? Why or why not?

UNIT THREE

The Commercial Environment

CONTENTS

Types of Contracts

There are many types of contracts. In this section, you will learn that contracts can be categorized based on legal distinctions as to formation, performance, and enforceability.

Contract Formation

As you can see in Exhibit 9–1, three classifications, or categories, of contracts are based on how and when a contract is formed. We explain each of these types of contracts in the following subsections.

Bilateral versus Unilateral Contracts

Every contract involves at least two parties. The *offeror* is the party making the offer. The *offeree* is the party to whom the offer is made. Whether the contract is classified as *unilateral* or *bilateral* depends on what the offeree must do to accept the offer and to bind the offeror to a contract.

Bilateral Contracts. If to accept the offer the offeree must only promise to perform, the contract is a *bilateral contract.* Hence, a bilateral contract is a "promise for a promise." No performance, such as payment of money or delivery of goods, need take place for a bilateral contract to be formed. The contract comes into existence at the moment the promises are exchanged.

For example, Javier offers to buy Ann's digital camcorder for $200. Javier tells Ann that he will give her the funds for the camera next Friday when he gets paid. Ann accepts Javier's offer and promises to give him the camcorder when he pays her on Friday. Javier and Ann have formed a bilateral contract.

Unilateral Contracts. If the offer is phrased so that the offeree can accept the offer only by completing the contract performance, the contract is a *unilateral contract.* Hence, a unilateral contract is a "promise for an act."[4] In other words, the time of contract formation in a unilateral contract is not at the moment when promises are exchanged but when the contract is *performed.* A classic example of a unilateral contract is as follows: O'Malley says to Parker, "If you carry this package across the Brooklyn Bridge, I'll give you $20." Only on Parker's complete crossing with the package does she fully accept O'Malley's offer to pay $20. If she chooses not to undertake the walk, there are no legal consequences.

Contests, lotteries, and other competitions involving prizes are examples of offers to form unilateral contracts. If a person complies with the rules of the contest—such as by submitting the right lottery number at the right place and time—a unilateral contract is formed, binding the organization offering the prize to a contract to perform as promised in the offer.

A Problem with Unilateral Contracts. A problem arises in unilateral contracts when the *promisor* (the one making the promise) attempts to *revoke* (cancel) the offer after the *promisee* (the one to whom the promise was made) has begun performance but before the act has been completed. The promisee can accept the offer only on full performance, and under

4. Clearly, a contract cannot be "one sided," because by definition, an agreement implies the existence of two or more parties. Therefore, the phrase *unilateral contract,* if read literally, is a contradiction in terms. As traditionally used in contract law, however, the phrase refers to the kind of contract that results when only one promise is being made (the promise made by the offeror in return for the offeree's performance).

EXHIBIT 9–1 • Classifications Based on Contract Formation

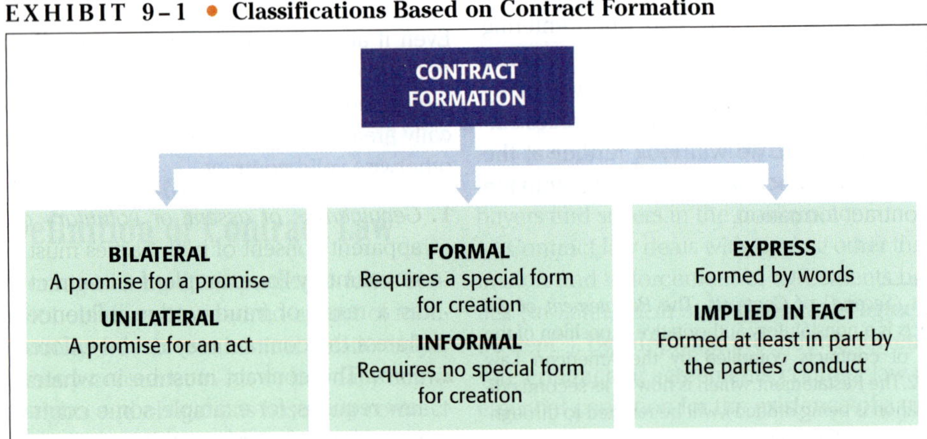

traditional contract principles, an offer may be revoked at any time before the offer is accepted. The present-day view, however, is that an offer to form a unilateral contract becomes irrevocable—cannot be revoked—once performance has begun. Thus, even though the offer has not yet been accepted, the offeror is prohibited from revoking it for a reasonable time period.

For instance, in the earlier example involving the Brooklyn Bridge, suppose that Parker is walking across the bridge and has only three yards to go when O'Malley calls out to her, "I revoke my offer." Under traditional contract law, O'Malley's revocation would terminate the offer. Under the modern view of unilateral contracts, however, O'Malley will not be able to revoke his offer because Parker has undertaken performance and walked all but three yards of the bridge. In these circumstances, Parker can finish crossing the bridge and bind O'Malley to the contract.

Formal versus Informal Contracts Another classification system divides contracts into formal contracts and informal contracts. *Formal contracts* are contracts that require a special form or method of creation (formation) to be enforceable. *Contracts under seal* are a type of formal contract that involves a formalized writing with a special seal attached.[5] In the past, the seals were often made of wax and impressed on the paper document. Today, the significance of the seal in contract law has lessened, though standard-form contracts still sometimes include a place for a seal next to the signature lines. *Letters of credit,* which are frequently used in international sales contracts, are another type of formal contract. As will be discussed in Chapter 11, letters of credit are agreements to pay contingent on the purchaser's receipt of invoices and bills of lading (documents evidencing receipt of, and title to, goods shipped).

Informal contracts (also called *simple contracts*) include all other contracts. No special form is required (except for certain types of contracts that must be in writing), as the contracts are usually based on their substance rather than their form. Typically, businesspersons put their contracts in writing to ensure that there is some proof of a contract's existence should problems arise.

5. The contract under seal has been almost entirely abolished under such provisions as UCC 2–203 (Section 2–203 of the UCC). In sales of real estate, however, it is still common to use a seal (or an acceptable substitute).

Express versus Implied-in-Fact Contracts Contracts may also be categorized as *express* or *implied* by the conduct of the parties. We look here at the differences between these two types of contracts.

Express Contracts. In an **express contract,** the terms of the agreement are fully and explicitly stated in words, oral or written. A signed lease for an apartment or a house is an express written contract. If a classmate calls you on the phone and agrees to buy your textbook from last semester for $45, an express oral contract has been made.

Implied-in-Fact Contracts. A contract that is implied from the conduct of the parties is called an **implied-in-fact contract** or an *implied contract.* This type of contract differs from an express contract in that the conduct of the parties, rather than their words, creates and defines the terms of the contract. (Note that a contract may be a mixture of an express contract and an implied-in-fact contract. In other words, a contract may contain some express terms, while others are implied.)

Requirements for Implied-in-Fact Contracts. For an implied-in-fact contract to arise, certain requirements must be met. Normally, if the following conditions exist, a court will hold that an implied contract was formed:

1. The plaintiff furnished some service or property.
2. The plaintiff expected to be paid for that service or property, and the defendant knew or should have known that payment was expected.
3. The defendant had a chance to reject the services or property and did not.

For example, suppose that you need an accountant to complete your tax return this year. You look through the Yellow Pages and find an accountant at an office in your neighborhood, so you drop by to see her. You go into the accountant's office and explain your problem, and she tells you what her fees are. The next day you return and give her administrative assistant all the necessary information and documents—canceled checks, W-2 forms, and so on. You then walk out the door without saying anything expressly to the assistant. In this situation, you have entered into an implied-in-fact contract to pay the accountant the usual and reasonable fees for her services. The contract is implied by your conduct and by hers. She expects to be paid for completing your tax return, and by bringing in the

Advertisements. In general, advertisements—including representations made in mail-order catalogues, price lists, and circulars—are treated not as offers to contract but as invitations to negotiate. Suppose that Loeser advertises a used paving machine. The ad is mailed to hundreds of firms and reads, "Used Loeser Construction Co. paving machine. Builds curbs and finishes cement work all in one process. Price: $42,350." If Star Paving calls Loeser and says, "We accept your offer," no contract is formed. Any reasonable person would conclude that Loeser was not promising to sell the paving machine but rather was soliciting offers to buy it. If such an ad were held to constitute a legal offer, and fifty people accepted the offer, there would be no way for Loeser to perform all fifty of the resulting contracts. He would have to breach forty-nine contracts. Obviously, the law seeks to avoid such unfairness.

Price lists are another form of invitation to negotiate or trade. A seller's price list is not an offer to sell at that price; it merely invites the buyer to offer to buy at that price. In fact, the seller usually puts "prices subject to change" on the price list. Only in rare circumstances will a price quotation be construed as an offer.

Although most advertisements and the like are treated as invitations to negotiate, this does not mean that an advertisement can never be an offer. On some occasions, courts have construed advertisements to be offers because the ads contained definite terms that invited acceptance (such as an ad offering a reward for the return of a lost dog).

Definiteness of Terms The second requirement for an effective offer involves the definiteness of its terms. An offer must have terms that are reasonably definite so that, if it is accepted and a contract formed, a court can determine if a breach has occurred and can provide an appropriate remedy. The specific terms required depend, of course, on the type of contract. Generally, a contract must include the following terms, either expressed in the contract or capable of being reasonably inferred from it:

1. The identification of the parties.
2. The identification of the object or subject matter of the contract (also the quantity, when appropriate), including the work to be performed, with specific identification of such items as goods, services, and land.
3. The consideration to be paid.
4. The time of payment, delivery, or performance.

An offer may invite an acceptance to be worded in such specific terms that the contract is made definite. Suppose that Marcus Business Machines contacts your corporation and offers to sell "from one to ten MacCool copying machines for $1,600 each; state number desired in acceptance." Your corporation agrees to buy two copiers. Because the quantity is specified in the acceptance, the terms are definite, and the contract is enforceable.

Courts sometimes are willing to supply a missing term in a contract when the parties have clearly manifested an intent to form a contract. If, in contrast, the parties have attempted to deal with a particular term of the contract but their expression of intent is too vague or uncertain to be given any precise meaning, the court will not supply a "reasonable" term because to do so might conflict with the intent of the parties. In other words, the court will not rewrite the contract.[10] The following case illustrates this point.

10. See Chapter 11 and UCC 2–204. Article 2 of the UCC specifies different rules relating to the definiteness of terms used in a contract for the sale of goods. In essence, Article 2 modifies general contract law by requiring less specificity.

EXTENDED CASE 9.3

Baer v. Chase

United States Court of Appeals, Third Circuit, 2004. 392 F.3d 609.

GREENBERG, **Circuit Judge.**

* * * *

[David] Chase, who originally was from New Jersey, but relocated to Los Angeles in 1971, is the creator, producer, writer and director of *The Sopranos.* Chase has numerous credits for other television productions as well. * * * Chase had worked on a number of projects involving organized crime activities based in New Jersey, including a script for "a mob boss in therapy," a concept that, in part, would become the basis for *The Sopranos.*

In 1995, Chase was producing and directing a *Rockford Files* "movie-of-the-week" when he met Joseph Urbancyk who was working on the set as a camera operator and temporary director of photography.

CASE 9.3 CONTINUED

[Through Urbancyk, Chase met Robert] Baer, * * * a New Jersey attorney [who] recently had left his employment in the Union County Prosecutor's Office in Elizabeth, New Jersey, where he had worked for the previous six years.

* * * *

Chase, Urbancyk, and Baer met for lunch on June 20, 1995 * * * , with Baer describing his experience as a prosecutor. Baer also pitched the idea to shoot "a film or television shows about the New Jersey Mafia." At that time Baer was unaware of Chase's previous work involving mob activity premised in New Jersey. At the lunch there was no reference to any payment that Chase might make to Baer for the latter's services * * * .

In October 1995, Chase visited New Jersey for three days. During this "research visit" Baer arranged meetings for Chase with Detective Thomas Koczur, Detective Robert A. Jones, and Tony Spirito who provided Chase with information, material, and personal stories about their experiences with organized crime. * * * Baer does not dispute that virtually all of the ideas and locations that he "contributed" to Chase existed in the public record.

After returning to Los Angeles, Chase sent Baer a copy of a draft of a *Sopranos* screenplay that he had written, which was dated December 20, 1995. Baer asserts that after he read it he called Chase and made various comments with regard to it. Baer claims that the two spoke at least four times during the following year and that he sent a letter to Chase dated February 10, 1997, discussing *The Sopranos* script.

* * * *

Baer asserts that he and Chase orally agreed on three separate occasions that if the show became a success, Chase would "take care of" Baer, and "remunerate Baer in a manner commensurate to the true value of his services."

Baer claims that on each of these occasions the parties had the same conversation in which Chase offered to pay Baer, stating "you help me; I pay you." Baer always rejected Chase's offer, reasoning that Chase would be unable to pay him "for the true value of the services Baer was rendering." Each time Baer rejected Chase's offer he did so with a counteroffer, "that I would perform the services while assuming the risk that if the show failed Chase would owe me nothing. If, however, the show succeeded he would remunerate me in a manner commensurate to the true value of my services." Baer acknowledges that this counteroffer * * * always was oral and did not include any fixed term of duration or price. * * * In fact, Chase has not paid Baer for his services.

On or about May 15, 2002, Baer filed a * * * complaint against Chase in [a federal] district court * * * [claiming among other things] * * * breach of implied contract. Eventually Chase brought a motion for summary judgment * * * . Chase claimed that the alleged contract * * * [was] too vague, ambiguous and lacking in essential terms to be enforced * * * .

The district court granted Chase's motion * * * .

* * * *

Baer predicates [bases] his contract claim on this appeal on an implied-in-fact contract * * * . The issue with respect to the implied-in-fact contract claim concerns whether Chase and Baer entered into an enforceable contract for services Baer rendered that aided in the creation and production of *The Sopranos.*

* * * *

* * * A contract arises from offer and acceptance, and must be sufficiently definite so that the performance to be rendered by each party can be ascertained with reasonable certainty. Therefore parties create an enforceable contract when they agree on its essential terms and manifest an intent that the terms bind them. *If parties to an agreement do not agree on one or more essential terms of the purported agreement, courts generally hold it to be unenforceable.* [Emphasis added.]

* * * *

* * * [The] law deems the price term, i.e., the amount of compensation, an essential term of any contract. An agreement lacking definiteness of price, however, is not unenforceable if the parties specify a practicable method by which they can determine the amount. However, *in the absence of an agreement as to the manner or method of determining compensation the purported agreement is invalid.* Additionally, *the duration of the contract is deemed an essential term and*

CASE CONTINUES

Problems may arise, though, when the parties involved are not dealing face to face. In such situations, the offeree should use an authorized mode of communication.

Acceptance takes effect, thus completing formation of the contract, at the time the offeree sends or delivers the communication via the mode expressly or impliedly authorized by the offeror. This is the so-called **mailbox rule,** which the majority of courts follow. Under this rule, if the authorized mode of communication is the mail, then an acceptance becomes valid when it is dispatched (placed in the control of the U.S. Postal Service)—*not* when it is received by the offeror.

The mailbox rule was created to prevent the confusion that arises when an offeror sends a letter of revocation but, before it arrives, the offeree sends a letter of acceptance. Thus, whereas a revocation becomes effective only when it is *received* by the offeree, an acceptance becomes effective on *dispatch* (when sent, even if it is never received), provided that an *authorized* means of communication is used.

The mailbox rule does not apply to instantaneous forms of communication, such as when the parties are dealing face to face, by telephone, or by fax. There is still some uncertainty in the courts as to whether e-mail should be considered an instantaneous form of communication to which the mailbox rule does not apply. If the parties have agreed to conduct transactions electronically and if the Uniform Electronic Transactions Act (to be discussed in Chapter 11) applies, then e-mail is considered sent when it either leaves control of the sender or is received by the recipient. This rule takes the place of the mailbox rule when the Uniform Electronic Transactions Act applies but essentially allows an e-mail acceptance to become effective when sent (as it would if sent by U.S. mail).

Authorized Means of Acceptance A means of communicating acceptance can be expressly authorized—that is, expressly stipulated in the offer—or impliedly authorized by the facts and circumstances surrounding the situation or by law.[14] An acceptance sent by means not expressly or impliedly authorized normally is not effective until it is received by the offeror.

When an offeror specifies how acceptance should be made (for example, by overnight delivery), *express authorization* is said to exist, and the contract is not formed unless the offeree uses that specified mode of acceptance. Moreover, both offeror and offeree are bound in contract the moment this means of acceptance is employed. For example, Shaylee & Perkins, a Massachusetts firm, offers to sell a container of antique furniture to Leaham's Antiques in Colorado. The offer states that Leaham's must accept the offer via FedEx overnight delivery. The acceptance is effective (and a binding contract is formed) the moment that Leaham's gives the overnight envelope containing the acceptance to the FedEx driver.

When the Preferred Means of Acceptance Is Not Indicated. Most offerors do not expressly specify the means by which the offeree is to accept. When the offeror does not specify expressly that the offeree is to accept by a certain means, or that the acceptance will be effective only when received, acceptance of an offer may be made by any medium that is *reasonable under the circumstances.*[15]

Whether a mode of acceptance is reasonable depends on what would reasonably be expected by parties in the position of the contracting parties. Courts look at prevailing business usages and other surrounding circumstances such as the method of communication the parties have used in the past and the means that were used to convey the offer. The offeror's choice of a particular means in making the offer implies that the offeree is authorized to use the same *or a faster* means for acceptance. Suppose that two parties have been negotiating a deal via fax and then the offeror sends a formal contract offer by priority mail without specifying the means of acceptance. In that situation, the offeree's acceptance by priority mail or by fax is impliedly authorized.

When the Authorized Means of Acceptance Is Not Used. An acceptance sent by means not expressly or impliedly authorized normally is not effective *until it is received by the offeror.* For example, suppose that Frank Cochran is interested in buying a house from Ray Nunez. Cochran faxes an offer to Nunez that clearly specifies acceptance by fax. Nunez has to be out of town for a few days, however, and doesn't

14. *Restatement (Second) of Contracts,* Section 30, provides that an offer invites acceptance "by any medium reasonable in the circumstances," unless the offer is specific about the means of acceptance. Under Section 65, a medium is reasonable if it is one used by the offeror or one customary in similar transactions, unless the offeree knows of circumstances that would argue against the reasonableness of a particular medium (the need for speed because of rapid price changes, for example).

15. *Restatement (Second) of Contracts,* Section 30. This is also the rule under UCC 2–206(1)(a).

have access to a fax machine. Therefore, Nunez sends his acceptance to Cochran via FedEx instead of by fax. In this situation, the acceptance is not effective (and no contract is formed) until Cochran receives the FedEx delivery. The use of an alternative method does not render the acceptance ineffective if the substituted method performs the same function or serves the same purpose as the authorized method.[16]

Exceptions The following are three basic exceptions to the rule that a contract is formed when an acceptance is sent by authorized means:

1. If the offeree's acceptance is not properly dispatched, in most states it will not be effective until it is received by the offeror. For example, if an offeree types in the recipient's e-mail address incorrectly when accepting an offer via e-mail, or if the offeree faxes an acceptance to the wrong telephone number, it will not be effective until received by the offeror. If U.S. mail is the authorized means for acceptance, the offeree's letter must be properly addressed and have the correct postage. Nonetheless, if the acceptance is timely sent and timely received, despite the offeree's carelessness in sending it, it may still be considered to have been effective on dispatch.[17]
2. If the offer stipulates when acceptance will be effective, then the offer will not be effective until the time specified. The offeror has the power to control the offer and can stipulate both the means by which the offer is accepted and the precise time that an acceptance will be effective. For example, an offer might state that acceptance will not be effective until it is received by the offeror, or it might make acceptance effective twenty-four hours after being shipped via DHL delivery.
3. Sometimes, an offeree sends a rejection first, then later changes his or her mind and sends an acceptance. Obviously, this chain of events could cause confusion and even detriment to the offeror, depending on whether the rejection or the acceptance arrived first. In such situations, the law cancels the rule of acceptance on dispatch, and the first communication received by the offeror determines whether a contract is formed. If the rejection arrives first, there is no contract.[18]

For a review of the effective time of acceptance, see *Concept Summary 9.3.*

Consideration

The fact that a promise has been made does not mean the promise can or will be enforced. Under Roman law, a promise was not enforceable without

16. See, for example, *Osprey, L.L.C. v. Kelly Moore Paint Co.*, 984 P.2d 194 (Okla. 1999).
17. *Restatement (Second) of Contracts*, Section 67.
18. *Restatement (Second) of Contracts*, Section 40.

CONCEPT SUMMARY 9.3
Effective Time of Acceptance

Acceptance	Time Effective
By Authorized Means of Communication	Effective at the time communication is sent (deposited in a mailbox or delivered to a courier service) via the mode expressly or impliedly authorized by the offeror (mailbox rule). *Exceptions:* 1. If the acceptance is not properly dispatched, it will not be effective until received by the offeror. 2. If the offeror specifically conditioned the offer on receipt of acceptance, it will not be effective until received by the offeror. 3. If acceptance is sent after rejection, whichever is received first is given effect.
By Unauthorized Means of Communication	Effective on receipt of acceptance by the offeror (if timely received, it is considered to have been effective on dispatch).

some sort of *causa*—that is, a reason for making the promise that was also deemed to be a sufficient reason for enforcing it. Under the common law, a primary basis for the enforcement of promises is consideration. **Consideration** is usually defined as the value (such as cash) given in return for a promise (such as the promise to sell a stamp collection on receipt of payment) or in return for a performance.

Often, consideration is broken down into two parts: (1) something of *legally sufficient value* must be given in exchange for the promise; and (2) usually, there must be a *bargained-for* exchange.

Legal Value

The "something of legally sufficient value" may consist of (1) a promise to do something that one has no prior legal duty to do, (2) the performance of an action that one is otherwise not obligated to undertake, or (3) the refraining from an action that one has a legal right to undertake (called a *forbearance*). Consideration in bilateral contracts normally consists of a promise in return for a promise, as explained earlier. For example, suppose that in a contract for the sale of goods, the seller promises to ship specific goods to the buyer, and the buyer promises to pay for those goods when they are received. Each of these promises constitutes consideration for the contract.

In contrast, unilateral contracts involve a promise in return for a performance. Suppose that Anita says to her neighbor, "When you finish painting the garage, I will pay you $100." Anita's neighbor paints the garage. The act of painting the garage is the consideration that creates Anita's contractual obligation to pay her neighbor $100.

What if, in return for a promise to pay, a person refrains from pursuing harmful habits (a forbearance), such as the use of tobacco and alcohol? Does such forbearance constitute legally sufficient consideration? In most situations, the answer is yes. Generally, a waiver of any legal right at the request of another party is a sufficient consideration for a promise.[19]

Bargained-For Exchange

The second element of consideration is that it must provide the basis for the bargain struck between the contracting parties. The promise given by the promisor (offeror) must induce the promisee (offeree) to offer a return promise, a performance, or a forbearance, and the promisee's promise, performance, or forbearance must induce the promisor to make the promise.

This element of bargained-for exchange distinguishes contracts from gifts. Suppose that Arlene says to her son, "In consideration of the fact that you are not as wealthy as your brothers, I will pay you $5,000." The fact that the word *consideration* is used does not, by itself, mean that consideration has been given. Indeed, this is not an enforceable promise because the son need not do anything in order to receive the promised $5,000.[20] The son need not give Arlene something of legal value in return for her promise, and the promised $5,000 does not involve a bargained-for exchange. Rather, Arlene has simply stated her motive for giving her son a gift.

Adequacy of Consideration

Legal sufficiency of consideration involves the requirement that consideration be something of legally sufficient value in the eyes of the law. Adequacy of consideration involves "how much" consideration is given. Essentially, adequacy of consideration concerns the fairness of the bargain. On the surface, fairness would appear to be an issue when the items exchanged are of unequal value. In general, however, a court will not question the adequacy of consideration if the consideration is legally sufficient. Under the doctrine of freedom of contract, parties are normally free to bargain as they wish. If people could sue merely because they had entered into an unwise contract, the courts would be overloaded with frivolous suits.

In extreme cases, a court may consider the adequacy of consideration in terms of its amount or worth because inadequate consideration may indicate that fraud, duress, or undue influence was involved or that the element of bargained-for exchange was lacking. It may also reflect a party's incompetence (for example, an individual might have been too intoxicated or simply too young to make a contract). Suppose that Dylan has a house worth $180,000 and sells it for $90,000. A $90,000 sale could indicate that the buyer unduly pressured Dylan into selling the house at that price or that Dylan was defrauded into selling the house at far below market value. (Of course, it might also indicate that Dylan was in a hurry to sell and that the amount was legally sufficient.)

19. For a classic case in which the court held that refraining from smoking, drinking, swearing, and playing cards or billiards for cash constituted legally sufficient consideration, see *Hamer v. Sidway*, 124 N.Y. 538, 27 N.E. 256 (1891).

20. See *Fink v. Cox*, 18 Johns. 145, 9 Am.Dec. 191 (N.Y. 1820).

Agreements That Lack Consideration

Sometimes, one of the parties (or both parties) to an agreement may think that consideration has been exchanged when in fact it has not. Here, we look at some situations in which the parties' promises or actions do not qualify as contractual consideration.

Preexisting Duty Under most circumstances, a promise to do what one already has a legal duty to do does not constitute legally sufficient consideration. The preexisting legal duty may be imposed by law or may arise out of a previous contract. A sheriff, for example, cannot collect a reward for providing information leading to the capture of a criminal if the sheriff already has a legal duty to capture the criminal.

Likewise, if a party is already bound by contract to perform a certain duty, that duty cannot serve as consideration for a second contract. For example, suppose that Bauman-Bache, Inc., begins construction on a seven-story office building and after three months demands an extra $75,000 on its contract. If the extra $75,000 is not paid, Bauman-Bache will stop working. The owner of the land, finding no one else to complete the construction, agrees to pay the extra $75,000. The agreement is unenforceable because it is not supported by legally sufficient consideration; Bauman-Bache was under a preexisting contract to complete the building.

Unforeseen Difficulties The rule regarding preexisting duty is meant to prevent extortion and the so-called holdup game. What happens, though, when an honest contractor who has contracted with a landowner to construct a building runs into extraordinary difficulties that were totally unforeseen at the time the contract was formed? In the interests of fairness and equity, the courts sometimes allow exceptions to the preexisting duty rule. In the example just mentioned, if the landowner agrees to pay extra compensation to the contractor for overcoming unforeseen difficulties, the court may refrain from applying the preexisting duty rule and enforce the agreement. When the "unforeseen difficulties" that give rise to a contract modification involve the types of risks ordinarily assumed in business, however, the courts will usually assert the preexisting duty rule.

Rescission and New Contract The law recognizes that two parties can mutually agree to rescind, or cancel, their contract, at least to the extent that it is executory (still to be carried out). *Rescission* is the unmaking of a contract so as to return the parties to the positions they occupied before the contract was made. When rescission and the making of a new contract take place at the same time, but the duties of both parties remain the same as in their rescinded contract, the courts frequently are given a choice of applying the preexisting duty rule or allowing rescission and letting the new contract stand.

Past Consideration Promises made in return for actions or events that have already taken place are unenforceable. These promises lack consideration in that the element of bargained-for exchange is missing. In short, you can bargain for something to take place now or in the future but not for something that has already taken place. **Past consideration** is no consideration.

Suppose that Blackmon became friends with Iverson when Iverson was a high school student who showed tremendous promise as an athlete. One evening, Blackmon suggested that Iverson use "The Answer" as a nickname in the summer league basketball tournaments. Blackmon said that Iverson would be "The Answer" to all of the National Basketball Association's woes. Later that night, Iverson said that he would give Blackmon 25 percent of any proceeds from the merchandising of products that used "The Answer" as a logo or a slogan. Because Iverson's promise was made in return for past consideration, it is unenforceable; in effect, Iverson stated his intention to give Blackmon a gift.[21] *Concept Summary 9.4* on page 214 provides a summary of the main aspects of consideration.

Promissory Estoppel

Under the doctrine of *promissory estoppel* (also called *detrimental reliance*), a person who has reasonably and substantially relied on the promise of another may be able to obtain some measure of recovery. This doctrine is applied in a wide variety of contexts in which a promise is otherwise unenforceable, such as when a promise is not supported by consideration. Under this doctrine, a court may enforce an otherwise unenforceable promise to avoid the injustice that would otherwise result. For the doctrine to be applied, the following elements are required:

1. There must be a clear and definite promise.
2. The promisee must justifiably rely on the promise.

21. *Blackmon v. Iverson*, 324 F.Supp.2d 602 (E.D.Pa. 2003).

delegatee fails to perform, the delegator is still liable to the obligee.

Third Party Beneficiaries

Another exception to the doctrine of privity of contract exists when the original parties to the contract intend at the time of contracting that the contract performance directly benefit a third person. In this situation, the third person becomes a **third party beneficiary** of the contract. As an **intended beneficiary** of the contract, the third party has legal rights and can sue the promisor directly for breach of the contract.

The benefit that an **incidental beneficiary** receives from a contract between two parties is unintentional. Because the benefit is *unintentional,* an incidental beneficiary cannot sue to enforce the contract. For example, suppose that Bollow contracts with Coolidge to build a recreational facility on Coolidge's land. Once the facility is constructed, it will greatly enhance the property values in the neighborhood. If Bollow subsequently refuses to build the facility, Tran, Coolidge's neighbor, cannot enforce the contract against Bollow, because Tran is an incidental beneficiary.

REVIEWING Contract Formation

Grant Borman, who was engaged in a construction project, leased a crane from Allied Equipment and hired Crosstown Trucking Co. to deliver the crane to the construction site. Crosstown, while the crane was in its possession and without permission from either Borman or Allied Equipment, used the crane to install a transformer for a utility company, which paid Crosstown for the job. Crosstown then delivered the crane to Borman's construction site at the appointed time of delivery. When Allied Equipment learned of the unauthorized use of the crane by Crosstown, it sued Crosstown for damages, seeking to recover the rental value of Crosstown's use of the crane. Using the information presented in the chapter, answer the following questions.

1. What are the four requirements of a valid contract?
2. Did Crosstown have a valid contract with Borman concerning the use of the crane? If so, was it a bilateral or a unilateral contract? Explain.
3. What are the requirements of an implied-in-fact contract? Can Allied Equipment obtain damages from Crosstown based on an implied-in-fact contract? Explain.
4. Does the Statute of Frauds apply to this contractual situation? Why or why not?

TERMS AND CONCEPTS

acceptance 208
adhesion contract 220
agreement 199
assignment 225
consideration 212
contract 195
counteroffer 208
covenant not to compete 218
delegation 225
estop 207
exculpatory clause 221
express contract 197
implied-in-fact contract 197
incidental beneficiary 226
intended beneficiary 226
mailbox rule 210
mirror image rule 208
mutual assent 199
offer 199
past consideration 213
promise 194
promissory estoppel 207
revocation 206
Statute of Frauds 224
third party beneficiary 226
unconscionable 220
voluntary consent (genuineness of assent) 221

QUESTIONS AND CASE PROBLEMS

9–1. Suppose that Everett McCleskey, a local businessperson, is a good friend of Al Miller, the owner of a local candy store. Every day on his lunch hour, McCleskey goes into Miller's candy store and spends about five minutes looking at the candy. After examining Miller's candy and talking with Miller, McCleskey usually buys one or two candy bars. One afternoon, McCleskey goes into Miller's candy shop, looks at the candy, and picks up a $1 candy bar. Seeing that Miller is very busy, he catches Miller's eye, waves the candy bar at Miller without saying a word, and walks out. Is there a contract? If so, classify it within the categories presented in this chapter.

9–2. QUESTION WITH SAMPLE ANSWER

Janine was hospitalized with severe abdominal pain and placed in an intensive care unit. Her doctor told the hospital personnel to order around-the-clock nursing care for Janine. At the hospital's request, a nursing services firm, Nursing Services Unlimited, provided two weeks of in-hospital care and, after Janine was sent home, an additional two weeks of at-home care. During the at-home period of care, Janine was fully aware that she was receiving the benefit of the nursing services. Nursing Services later billed Janine $4,000 for the nursing care, but Janine refused to pay on the ground that she had never contracted for the services, either orally or in writing. In view of the fact that no express contract was ever formed, can Nursing Services recover the $4,000 from Janine? If so, under what legal theory? Discuss.

- **For a sample answer to Question 9–2, go to Appendix I at the end of this text.**

9–3. Ball writes Sullivan and inquires how much Sullivan is asking for a specific forty-acre tract of land Sullivan owns. In a letter received by Ball, Sullivan states, "I will not take less than $60,000 for the forty-acre tract as specified." Ball immediately sends Sullivan a telegram stating, "I accept your offer for $60,000 for the forty-acre tract as specified." Discuss whether Ball can hold Sullivan to a contract for the sale of the land.

9–4. After Kira had had several drinks one night, she sold Charlotte a diamond necklace worth thousands of dollars for just $100. The next day, Kira offered the $100 to Charlotte and requested the return of her necklace. Charlotte refused to accept the $100 or return the necklace, claiming that there was a valid contract of sale. Kira explained that she had been intoxicated at the time the bargain was made and thus the contract was voidable at her option. Was Kira correct? Explain.

9–5. Intention. Music that is distributed on compact discs and similar media generates income in the form of "mechanical" royalties. Music that is publicly performed, such as when a song is played on a radio, used in a movie or commercial, or sampled in another song, produces "performance" royalties. Each of these types of royalties is divided between the songwriter and the song's publisher. Vincent Cusano is a musician and songwriter who performed under the name "Vinnie Vincent" as a guitarist with the group KISS in the early 1980s. Cusano co-wrote three songs—entitled "Killer," "I Love It Loud," and "I Still Love You"—that KISS recorded and released in 1982 on an album titled *Creatures of the Night.* Cusano left KISS in 1984. Eight years later, Cusano sold to Horipro Entertainment Group "one hundred (100%) percent undivided interest" of his rights in the songs "other than Songwriter's share of performance income." Later, Cusano filed a suit in a federal district court against Horipro, claiming in part that he never intended to sell the writer's share of the mechanical royalties. Horipro filed a motion for summary judgment. Should the court grant the motion? Explain. [*Cusano v. Horipro Entertainment Group,* 301 F.Supp.2d 272 (S.D.N.Y. 2004)]

9–6. CASE PROBLEM WITH SAMPLE ANSWER

As a child, Martha Carr once visited her mother's 108-acre tract of unimproved land in Richland County, South Carolina. In 1968, Betty and Raymond Campbell leased the land. Carr, a resident of New York, was diagnosed as having schizophrenia and depression in 1986, was hospitalized five or six times, and subsequently took prescription drugs for the illnesses. In 1996, Carr inherited the Richland property and, two years later, contacted the Campbells about selling the land to them. Carr asked Betty about the value of the land, and Betty said that the county tax assessor had determined that the land's *agricultural value* was $54,000. The Campbells knew at the time that the county had assessed the total property value at $103,700 for tax purposes. A real estate appraiser found that the *real market value* of the property was $162,000. On August 6, Carr signed a contract to sell the land to the Campbells for $54,000. Believing the price to be unfair, however, Carr did not deliver the deed. The Campbells filed a suit in a South Carolina state court against Carr, seeking specific performance of the contract. At trial, an expert real estate appraiser testified that the real market value of the property was $162,000 at the time of the contract. Under what circumstances will a court examine the adequacy of consideration? Are those circumstances present in this case? Should the court enforce the contract between Carr and the Campbells? Explain. [*Campbell v. Carr,* 361 S.C. 258, 603 S.E.2d 625 (App. 2004)]

- **To view a sample answer for Problem 9–6, go to this book's Web site at academic.cengage.com/blaw/cross, select "Chapter 9," and click on "Case Problem with Sample Answer."**

9–7. Requirements of the Offer. The Pittsburgh Board of Public Education in Pittsburgh, Pennsylvania, as required by state law, keeps lists of eligible teachers in order of their rank or standing. According to an "Eligibility List" form made available to applicants, no one may be hired to teach whose name is not within the top 10 percent of the names on the list. In 1996, Anna Reed was in the top 10 percent. She was not hired that year, although four other applicants who placed lower on the list—and not within the top 10 percent—were hired. In 1997 and 1998, Reed was again in the top 10 percent, but she was not hired until 1999. Reed filed a suit in a federal district court against the board and others. She argued in part that the state's requirement that the board keep a list constituted an offer, which she accepted by participating in the process to be placed on that list. She claimed that the board breached this contract by hiring applicants who ranked lower than she did. The case was transferred to a Pennsylvania state court. What are the requirements of an offer? Do the circumstances in this case meet those requirements? Why or why not? [*Reed v. Pittsburgh Board of Public Education,* 862 A.2d 131 (Pa.Cmwlth. 2004)]

9–8. Agreement. In 2000, David and Sandra Harless leased 2.3 acres of real property at 2801 River Road S.E. in Winnabow, North Carolina, to their son-in-law and daughter, Tony and Jeanie Connor. The Connors planned to operate a "general store/variety store" on the premises. They agreed to lease the property for sixty months with an option to renew for an additional sixty months. The lease included an option to buy the property for "fair market value at the time of such purchase (based on at least two appraisals)." In March 2003, Tony told David that the Connors wanted to buy the property. In May, Tony gave David an appraisal that estimated the property's value at $140,000. In July, the Connors presented a second appraisal that determined the value to be $160,000. The Connors offered $150,000. The Harlesses replied that "under no circumstances would they ever agree to sell their old store building and approximately 2.5 acres to their daughter . . . and their son-in-law." The Connors filed a suit in a North Carolina state court against the Harlesses, alleging breach of contract. Did these parties have a contract to sell the property? If so, what were its terms? If not, why not? [*Connor v. Harless,* 176 N.C.App. 402, 626 S.E.2d 755 (2006)]

9–9. Offer. In August 2000, in California, Terry Reigelsperger sought treatment for pain in his lower back from chiropractor James Siller. Reigelsperger felt better after the treatment and did not intend to return for more, although he did not mention this to Siller. Before leaving the office, Reigelsperger signed an "informed consent" form that read, in part, "I intend this consent form to cover the entire course of treatment for my present condition and for any future condition(s) for which I seek treatment." He also signed an agreement that required the parties to submit to arbitration "any dispute as to medical malpractice. . . . This agreement is intended to bind the patient and the health care provider . . . who now or in the future treat[s] the patient." Two years later, Reigelsperger sought treatment from Siller for a different condition relating to his cervical spine and shoulder. Claiming malpractice with respect to the second treatment, Reigelsperger filed a suit in a California state court against Siller. Siller asked the court to order the dispute to be submitted to arbitration. Did Reigelsperger's lack of intent to return to Siller after his first treatment affect the enforceability of the arbitration agreement and consent form? Why or why not? [*Reigelsperger v. Siller,* 40 Cal.4th 574, 150 P.3d 764, 53 Cal.Rptr.3d 887 (2007)]

9–10. Fraudulent Misrepresentation. According to the student handbook at Cleveland Chiropractic College (CCC) in Missouri, *academic misconduct* includes "selling . . . any copy of any material intended to be used as an instrument of academic evaluation in advance of its initial administration." Leonard Verni was enrolled at CCC in Dr. Aleksandr Makarov's dermatology class. Before the first examination, Verni was reported to be selling copies of the test. CCC investigated and concluded that Verni had committed academic misconduct. He was dismissed from CCC, which informed him of his right to an appeal. According to the handbook, at the hearing on appeal a student could have an attorney or other adviser, present witnesses' testimony and other evidence, and "question any testimony . . . against him/her." At his hearing, however, Verni did not bring his attorney, present evidence on his behalf, or question any adverse witnesses. When the dismissal was upheld, Verni filed a suit in a Missouri state court against CCC and others, claiming, in part, fraudulent misrepresentation. Verni argued that because he "relied" on the handbook's "representation" that CCC would follow its appeal procedure, he was unable to properly refute the charges against him. Can Verni succeed with this argument? Explain. [*Verni v. Cleveland Chiropractic College,* 212 S.W.3d 150 (Mo. 2007)]

9–11. A QUESTION OF ETHICS

Dow AgroSciences, LLC (DAS), makes and sells agricultural seed products. In 2000, Timothy Glenn, a DAS sales manager, signed a covenant not to compete. He agreed that for two years from the date of his termination, he would not "engage in or contribute my knowledge to any work or activity involving an area of technology or business that is then competitive with a technology or business with respect to which I had access to Confidential Information during the five years immediately prior to such termination." Working with DAS business, operations, and research and development personnel, and being a member of high-level teams, Glenn had access to confidential DAS information, including agreements with DAS's business partners, marketing plans, litigation details, product secrets, new product development, future plans, and pricing strategies. In 2006, Glenn resigned to work for Pioneer Hi-Bred International, Inc., a DAS competitor. DAS filed a suit in an Indiana state court against Glenn, asking that he be enjoined from accepting any "position that would call on him to use confidential DAS information." [Glenn v. Dow AgroSciences, LLC, *861 N.E.2d 1 (Ind.App. 2007)]*

(a) Generally, what interests are served by enforcing covenants not to compete? What interests are served by refusing to enforce them?
(b) What argument could be made in support of reforming (and then enforcing) illegal covenants not to compete? What argument could be made against this practice?
(c) How should the court rule in this case? Why?

9-12. VIDEO QUESTION

Go to this text's Web site at **academic.cengage.com/blaw/cross** and select "Chapter 9." Click on "Video Questions" and view the video titled *Mistake*. Then answer the following questions.

(a) What kind of mistake is involved in the dispute shown in the video (mutual or unilateral, mistake of fact or mistake of value)?
(b) According to the chapter, in what two situations would the supermarket be able to rescind a contract to sell peppers to Melnick at the incorrectly advertised price?
(c) Does it matter if the price that was advertised was a reasonable price for the peppers? Why or why not?

LAW ON THE WEB

For updated links to resources available on the Web, as well as a variety of other materials, visit this text's Web site at

academic.cengage.com/blaw/cross

The 'Lectric Law Library provides information on contract law, including a definition of a contract, the elements required for a contract, and so on. Go to

www.lectlaw.com/lay.html

A good way to learn more about how the courts decide such issues as whether consideration was lacking for a particular contract is to look at relevant case law. To find recent cases on contract law decided by the United States Supreme Court and the federal appellate courts, access Cornell University's School of Law site at

www.law.cornell.edu/topics/contracts.html

The *New Hampshire Consumer's Sourcebook* provides information on contract law, including consideration, from a consumer's perspective. You can access this site at

www.doj.nh.gov/consumer/sourcebook

Legal Research Exercises on the Web

Go to **academic.cengage.com/blaw/cross**, the Web site that accompanies this text. Select "Chapter 9" and click on "Internet Exercises." There you will find the following Internet research exercises that you can perform to learn more about the topics covered in this chapter.

Internet Exercise 9–1: Historical Perspective
Contracts in Ancient Mesopotamia

Internet Exercise 9–2: Ethical Perspective
Offers and Advertisements

Internet Exercise 9–3: Social Perspective
Online Gambling

CHAPTER 10

Contract Performance, Breach, and Remedies

Just as rules are necessary to determine when a legally enforceable contract exists, so also are they required to determine when one of the parties can justifiably say, "I have fully performed, so I am now discharged from my obligations under this contract." The legal environment of business requires the identification of some point at which the parties can reasonably know that their duties are at an end. Additionally, the parties to a contract need to know what remedies are available to them if the contract is breached.

Performance and Discharge

The most common way to **discharge,** or terminate, one's contractual duties is by the **performance** of those duties. For example, a buyer and seller have a contract for the sale of a 2009 Lexus for $39,000. This contract will be discharged on the performance by the parties of their obligations under the contract—the buyer's payment of $39,000 to the seller and the seller's transfer of possession of the Lexus to the buyer.

The duty to perform under a contract may be *conditioned* on the occurrence or nonoccurrence of a certain event, or the duty may be *absolute*. In the first part of this section, we look at conditions of performance and the degree of performance required. We then examine some other ways in which a contract can be discharged, including discharge by agreement of the parties and discharge by operation of law.

Conditions

In most contracts, promises of performance are not expressly conditioned or qualified. Instead, they are *absolute promises*. They must be performed, or the parties promising the acts will be in breach of contract. For example, Jerome contracts to sell Alfonso a painting for $10,000. The parties' promises—Jerome's transfer of the painting to Alfonso and Alfonso's payment of $10,000 to Jerome—are unconditional. The payment does not have to be made if the painting is not transferred.

In some situations, however, performance is contingent on the occurrence or nonoccurrence of a certain event. A **condition** is a possible future event, the occurrence or nonoccurrence of which will trigger the performance of a legal obligation or terminate an existing obligation under a contract.[1] If this condition is not satisfied, the obligations of the parties are discharged. Suppose that Alfonso, in the previous example, offers to purchase Jerome's painting only if an independent appraisal indicates that it is worth at least $10,000. Jerome accepts Alfonso's offer. Their obligations (promises) are conditioned on the outcome of the appraisal. Should the condition not be satisfied (for example, if the appraiser deems the value of the painting to be only $5,000), the parties' obligations to each other are discharged and cannot be enforced.

Discharge by Performance

The great majority of contracts are discharged by performance. The contract comes to an end when both parties fulfill their respective duties by performing the acts they have promised. Performance can also be

1. The *Restatement (Second) of Contracts,* Section 224, defines a *condition* as "an event, not certain to occur, which must occur, unless its nonoccurrence is excused, before performance under a contract becomes due."

accomplished by *tender*. **Tender** is an unconditional offer to perform by a person who is ready, willing, and able to do so. Therefore, a seller who places goods at the disposal of a buyer has tendered delivery and can demand payment. A buyer who offers to pay for goods has tendered payment and can demand delivery of the goods. Once performance has been tendered, the party making the tender has done everything possible to carry out the terms of the contract. If the other party then refuses to perform, the party making the tender can sue for breach of contract.

There are two basic types of performance—*complete performance* and *substantial performance*. A contract may stipulate that performance must meet the personal satisfaction of either the contracting party or a third party. Such a provision must be considered in determining whether the performance rendered satisfies the contract.

Complete Performance When a party performs exactly as agreed, there is no question as to whether the contract has been performed. When a party's performance is perfect, it is said to be complete.

Normally, conditions expressly stated in a contract must be fully satisfied for complete performance to take place. For example, most construction contracts require the builder to meet certain specifications. If the specifications are conditions, complete performance is required to avoid material breach (*material breach* will be discussed shortly). If the conditions are met, the other party to the contract must then fulfill her or his obligation to pay the builder. If the specifications are not conditions and if the builder, without the other party's permission, fails to comply with the specifications, performance is not complete. What effect does such a failure have on the other party's obligation to pay? The answer is part of the doctrine of *substantial performance*.

Substantial Performance A party who in good faith performs substantially all of the terms of a contract can enforce the contract against the other party under the doctrine of substantial performance. Note that good faith is required. Intentionally failing to comply with the terms is a breach of the contract.

Confers Most Benefits Promised in the Contract. Generally, to qualify as substantial, the performance must not vary greatly from the performance promised in the contract, and it must create substantially the same benefits as those promised in the contract. If the omission, variance, or defect in performance is unimportant and can easily be compensated for by awarding damages, a court is likely to hold that the contract has been substantially performed.

Courts decide whether the performance was substantial on a case-by-case basis, examining all of the facts of the particular situation. For example, in a construction contract, a court would look at the intended purpose of the structure and the expense required to bring the structure into complete compliance with the contract. Thus, the exact point at which performance is considered substantial varies.

Entitles Other Party to Damages. Because substantial performance is not perfect, the other party is entitled to damages to compensate for the failure to comply with the contract. The measure of the damages is the cost to bring the object of the contract into compliance with its terms, if that cost is reasonable under the circumstances. If the cost is unreasonable, the measure of damages is the difference in value between the performance that was rendered and the performance that would have been rendered if the contract had been performed completely. The following classic case emphasizes that there is no exact formula for deciding when a contract has been substantially performed.

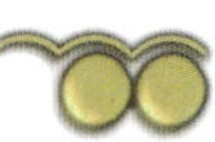

EXTENDED CASE 10.1 Jacob & Youngs v. Kent

Court of Appeals of New York, 1921. 230 N.Y. 239, 129 N.E. 889.

***CARDOZO*, J. [Judge]**

The plaintiff built a country residence for the defendant at a cost of upwards of $77,000, and now sues to recover a balance of $3,483.46, remaining unpaid. The work of construction ceased in June, 1914, and the defendant then began to occupy the dwelling. There was no complaint of defective performance until March, 1915. One of the specifications for the plumbing work provides that—

> All wrought-iron pipe must be well galvanized, lap welded pipe of the grade known as "standard pipe" of Reading manufacture.

CASE CONTINUES

CASE 10.1 CONTINUED

The defendant learned in March, 1915, that some of the pipe, instead of being made in Reading, was the product of other factories. The plaintiff was accordingly directed by the architect to do the work anew. The plumbing was then encased within the walls except in a few places where it had to be exposed. Obedience to the order meant more than the substitution of other pipe. It meant the demolition at great expense of substantial parts of the completed structure. The plaintiff left the work untouched, and asked for a certificate that the final payment was due. Refusal of the certificate was followed by this suit [in a New York state court].

The evidence sustains a finding that the omission of the prescribed brand of pipe was neither fraudulent nor willful. It was the result of the oversight and inattention of the plaintiff's subcontractor. Reading pipe is distinguished from Cohoes pipe and other brands only by the name of the manufacturer stamped upon it at intervals of between six and seven feet. Even the defendant's architect, though he inspected the pipe upon arrival, failed to notice the discrepancy. The plaintiff tried to show that the brands installed, though made by other manufacturers, were the same in quality, in appearance, in market value, and in cost as the brand stated in the contract—that they were, indeed, the same thing, though manufactured in another place. The evidence was excluded, and a verdict directed for the defendant. The [state intermediate appellate court] reversed, and granted a new trial.

We think the evidence, if admitted, would have supplied some basis for the inference that the defect was insignificant in its relation to the project. The courts never say that one who makes a contract fills the measure of his duty by less than full performance. They do say, however, that *an omission, both trivial and innocent, will sometimes be atoned for by allowance of the resulting damage, and will not always be the breach of a condition* * * * . [Emphasis added.]

* * * Where the line is to be drawn between the important and the trivial cannot be settled by a formula. In the nature of the case precise boundaries are impossible. The same omission may take on one aspect or another according to its setting. Substitution of equivalents may not have the same significance in fields of art on the one side and in those of mere utility on the other. Nowhere will change be tolerated, however, if it is so dominant or pervasive as in any real or substantial measure to frustrate the purpose of the contract. There is no general license to install whatever, in the builder's judgment, may be regarded as "just as good." The question is one of degree, to be answered, if there is doubt, by the triers of the facts, and, if the inferences are certain, by the judges of the law. *We must weigh the purpose to be served, the desire to be gratified, the excuse for deviation from the letter, the cruelty of enforced adherence. Then only can we tell whether literal fulfillment is to be implied by law as a condition.* [Emphasis added.]

In the circumstances of this case, we think the measure of the allowance is not the cost of replacement, which would be great, but the difference in value, which would be either nominal or nothing. Some of the exposed sections might perhaps have been replaced at moderate expense. The defendant did not limit his demand to them, but treated the plumbing as a unit to be corrected from cellar to roof. In point of fact, the plaintiff never reached the stage at which evidence of the extent of the allowance became necessary. The trial court had excluded evidence that the defect was unsubstantial, and in view of that ruling there was no occasion for the plaintiff to go farther with an offer of proof. We think, however, that the offer, if it had been made, would not of necessity have been defective because directed to difference in value. It is true that in most cases the cost of replacement is the measure. The owner is entitled to the money which will permit him to complete, unless the cost of completion is grossly and unfairly out of proportion to the good to be attained. When that is true, the measure is the difference in value. * * * The rule that gives a remedy in cases of substantial performance with compensation for defects of trivial or inappreciable importance has been developed by the courts as an instrument of justice. The measure of the allowance must be shaped to the same end.

The order should be affirmed, and judgment absolute directed in favor of the plaintiff upon the stipulation, with costs in all courts.

QUESTIONS

1. The New York Court of Appeals found that Jacob & Youngs had substantially performed the contract. To what, if any, remedy is Kent entitled?

CASE 10.1 CONTINUED

2. A requirement of substantial performance is good faith. Do you think that Jacob & Youngs substantially performed all of the terms of the contract in good faith? Why or why not?

• **Impact of This Case on Today's Law** *At the time of the* Jacob & Youngs *case, some courts did not apply the doctrine of substantial performance to disputes involving breaches of contract. This landmark decision contributed to a developing trend toward equity and fairness in those circumstances. Today, an unintentional and trivial omission or deviation from the terms of a contract will not prevent its enforcement but will permit an adjustment in the value of its performance.*

Performance to the Satisfaction of Another Contracts often state that completed work must personally satisfy one of the parties or a third person. The question then is whether this satisfaction becomes a condition precedent, requiring actual personal satisfaction or approval for discharge, or whether the test of satisfaction is an absolute promise requiring such performance as would satisfy a *reasonable person* (substantial performance).

When the subject matter of the contract is *personal,* a contract to be performed to the satisfaction of one of the parties is conditioned, and performance must actually satisfy that party. For example, contracts for portraits, works of art, and tailoring are considered personal. Therefore, only the personal satisfaction of the party fulfills the condition—unless a court finds the party is expressing dissatisfaction only to avoid payment or otherwise is not acting in good faith.

Most other contracts need to be performed only to the satisfaction of a reasonable person unless they *expressly state otherwise.* When such contracts require performance to the satisfaction of a third party (for example, "to the satisfaction of Robert Ames, the supervising engineer"), the courts are divided. A majority of courts require the work to be satisfactory to a reasonable person, but some courts hold that the personal satisfaction of the third party designated in the contract (Robert Ames, in this example) must be met. Again, the personal judgment must be made honestly, or the condition will be excused.

Material Breach of Contract

A **breach of contract** is the nonperformance of a contractual duty. The breach is *material* when performance is not at least substantial.[2] If there is a material breach, then the nonbreaching party is excused from the performance of contractual duties and can sue for damages resulting from the breach. If the breach is *minor* (not material), the nonbreaching party's duty to perform can sometimes be suspended until the breach has been remedied, but the duty to perform is not entirely excused. Once the minor breach has been cured, the nonbreaching party must resume performance of the contractual obligations undertaken.

Any breach entitles the nonbreaching party to sue for damages, but only a material breach discharges the nonbreaching party from the contract. The policy underlying these rules allows contracts to go forward when only minor problems occur but allows them to be terminated if major difficulties arise.

Anticipatory Repudiation

Before either party to a contract has a duty to perform, one of the parties may refuse to carry out his or her contractual obligations. This is called **anticipatory repudiation**[3] of the contract. When anticipatory repudiation occurs, it is treated as a material breach of contract, and the nonbreaching party is permitted to bring an action for damages immediately, even though the scheduled time for performance under the contract may still be in the future. Until the nonbreaching party treats an early repudiation as a breach, however, the repudiating party can retract her or his anticipatory repudiation by proper notice and restore the parties to their original obligations.[4]

An anticipatory repudiation is treated as a present, material breach for two reasons. First, the nonbreaching party should not be required to remain ready and willing to perform when the other party has already repudiated the contract. Second, the nonbreaching party should have the opportunity to seek a similar

2. *Restatement (Second) of Contracts,* Section 241.

3. *Restatement (Second) of Contracts,* Section 253; Section 2–610 of the Uniform Commercial Code (UCC).

4. See UCC 2–611.

contract elsewhere and may have a duty to do so to minimize his or her loss.[5]

Time for Performance If no time for performance is stated in the contract, a *reasonable time* is implied.[6] If a specific time is stated, the parties must usually perform by that time. Unless time is expressly stated to be vital, however, a delay in performance will not destroy the performing party's right to payment.[7] When time is expressly stated to be "of the essence" or vital, the parties normally must perform within the stated time period because the time element becomes a condition.

Discharge by Agreement

Any contract can be discharged by agreement of the parties. The agreement can be contained in the original contract, or the parties can form a new contract for the express purpose of discharging the original contract.

Discharge by Rescission As mentioned in previous chapters, *rescission* is the process by which a contract is canceled or terminated and the parties are returned to the positions they occupied prior to forming it. For **mutual rescission** to take place, the parties must make another agreement that also satisfies the legal requirements for a contract. There must be an *offer,* an *acceptance,* and *consideration.* Ordinarily, if the parties agree to rescind the original contract, their promises not to perform the acts stipulated in the original contract will be legal consideration for the second contract (the rescission).

Agreements to rescind executory contracts (in which neither party has performed) are generally enforceable, even if the agreement is made orally and even if the original agreement was in writing. An exception applies under the Uniform Commercial Code (UCC) to agreements rescinding a contract for the sale of goods, regardless of price, when the contract requires a written rescission. Also, agreements to rescind contracts involving transfers of realty must be evidenced by a writing.

When one party has fully performed, an agreement to cancel the original contract normally will not be enforceable. Because the performing party has received no consideration for the promise to call off the original bargain, additional consideration is necessary.

Discharge by Novation A contractual obligation may also be discharged through novation. A **novation** occurs when both of the parties to a contract agree to substitute a third party for one of the original parties. The requirements of a novation are as follows:

1. A previous valid obligation.
2. An agreement by all the parties to a new contract.
3. The extinguishing of the old obligation (discharge of the prior party).
4. A new contract that is valid.

For example, suppose that Union Corporation contracts to sell its pharmaceutical division to British Pharmaceuticals, Ltd. Before the transfer is completed, Union, British Pharmaceuticals, and a third company, Otis Chemicals, execute a new agreement to transfer all of British Pharmaceuticals' rights and duties in the transaction to Otis Chemicals. As long as the new contract is supported by consideration, the novation will discharge the original contract (between Union and British Pharmaceuticals) and replace it with the new contract (between Union and Otis Chemicals).

A novation expressly or impliedly revokes and discharges a prior contract. The parties involved may expressly state in the new contract that the old contract is now discharged. If the parties do not expressly discharge the old contract, it will be impliedly discharged if the new contract's terms are inconsistent with the old contract's terms.

Discharge by Substituted Agreement A *compromise,* or settlement agreement, that arises out of a genuine dispute over the obligations under an existing contract will be recognized at law. Such an agreement will be substituted as a new contract, and it will either expressly or impliedly revoke and discharge the obligations under any prior contract. In contrast to a novation, a substituted agreement does not involve a third party. Rather, the two original parties to the contract form a different agreement to substitute for the original one.

Discharge by Accord and Satisfaction For a contract to be discharged by accord and satis-

5. The doctrine of anticipatory repudiation first arose in the landmark case of *Hochster v. De La Tour,* 2 Ellis and Blackburn Reports 678 (1853), when an English court recognized the delay and expense inherent in a rule requiring a nonbreaching party to wait until the time of performance before suing on an anticipatory repudiation.

6. See UCC 2–204.

7. See, for example, *Manganaro Corp. v. Hitt Contracting, Inc.,* 193 F.Supp.2d 88 (D.D.C. 2002).

faction, the parties must agree to accept performance that is different from the performance originally promised. An *accord* is a contract to perform some act to satisfy an existing contractual duty. The duty has not yet been discharged. A *satisfaction* is the performance of the accord agreement. An accord and its satisfaction discharge the original contractual obligation.

Once the accord has been made, the original obligation is merely suspended. The obligor (the one owing the obligation) can discharge the obligation by performing either the obligation agreed to in the accord or the original obligation. If the obligor refuses to perform the accord, the obligee (the one to whom performance is owed) can bring action on the original obligation or seek a decree compelling specific performance on the accord.

Suppose that Frazer has a judgment against Ling for $8,000. Later, both parties agree that the judgment can be satisfied by Ling's transfer of his automobile to Frazer. This agreement to accept the auto in lieu of $8,000 in cash is the accord. If Ling transfers the car to Frazer, the accord is fully performed, and the debt is discharged. If Ling refuses to transfer the car, the accord is breached. Because the original obligation is merely suspended, Frazer can sue Ling to enforce the original judgment for $8,000 in cash or bring an action for breach of the accord.

Discharge by Operation of Law

Under certain circumstances, contractual duties may be discharged by operation of law. These circumstances include material alteration of the contract, the running of the statute of limitations, bankruptcy, and the impossibility or impracticability of performance.

Alteration of the Contract To discourage parties from altering written contracts, the law operates to allow an innocent party to be discharged when the other party has materially altered a written contract without consent. For example, contract terms such as quantity or price might be changed without the knowledge or consent of all parties. If so, the party who was not involved in the alteration can treat the contract as discharged or terminated.[8]

8. The contract is voidable, and the innocent party can also treat the contract as in effect, either on the original terms or on the terms as altered. For example, a buyer who discovers that a seller altered the quantity of goods in a sales contract from 100 to 1,000 by secretly inserting a zero can purchase either 100 or 1,000 of the items.

Statutes of Limitations As mentioned earlier in this text, statutes of limitations restrict the period during which a party can sue on a particular cause of action. After the applicable limitations period has passed, a suit can no longer be brought. For example, the limitations period for bringing suits for breach of oral contracts is usually two to three years; for written contracts, four to five years; and for recovery of amounts awarded in judgments, ten to twenty years, depending on state law. Lawsuits for breach of a contract for the sale of goods generally must be brought within four years after the breach occurs. By their original agreement, the parties can reduce this four-year period to not less than one year, but they cannot agree to extend it.

Bankruptcy A proceeding in bankruptcy attempts to allocate the assets the debtor owns to the creditors in a fair and equitable fashion. Once the assets have been allocated, the debtor receives a *discharge in bankruptcy.* A discharge in bankruptcy will ordinarily bar enforcement of most of the debtor's contracts by the creditors. Partial payment of a debt after discharge in bankruptcy will not revive the debt. (Bankruptcy will be discussed in detail in Chapter 15.)

Impossibility or Impracticability of Performance

After a contract has been made, supervening events (such as a fire) may make performance impossible in an objective sense. This is known as **impossibility of performance** and can discharge a contract.[9] Performance may also become so difficult or costly due to some unforeseen event that a court will consider it commercially unfeasible, or impracticable.

Objective Impossibility of Performance *Objective impossibility* ("It can't be done") must be distinguished from *subjective impossibility* ("I'm sorry, I simply can't do it"). For example, subjective impossibility occurs when a party cannot deliver goods on time because of freight car shortages or cannot make payment on time because the bank is closed. In effect, in each of these situations the party is saying, "It is impossible for *me* to perform," not "It is impossible for *anyone* to perform." Accordingly, such excuses do not discharge a contract, and the nonperforming party is normally held in breach of contract.

9. *Restatement (Second) of Contracts,* Section 261.

Note that to justify not performing the contract, the supervening event must have been unforeseeable at the time of the contract. Parties are supposed to consider foreseeable events, such as floods in a flood zone, at the time of contracting and allocate those risks accordingly through insurance and other means. Three basic types of situations, however, may qualify as grounds for the discharge of contractual obligations based on impossibility of performance:[10]

1. *When one of the parties to a personal contract dies or becomes incapacitated prior to performance.* For example, Fred, a famous dancer, contracts with Ethereal Dancing Guild to play a leading role in its new ballet. Before the ballet can be performed, Fred becomes ill and dies. His personal performance was essential to the completion of the contract. Thus, his death discharges the contract and his estate's liability for his nonperformance.
2. *When the specific subject matter of the contract is destroyed.* For example, A-1 Farm Equipment agrees to sell Gudgel the green tractor on its lot and promises to have it ready for Gudgel to pick up on Saturday. On Friday night, however, a truck veers off the nearby highway and smashes into the tractor, destroying it beyond repair. Because the contract was for this specific tractor, A-1's performance is rendered impossible owing to the accident.
3. *When a change in law renders performance illegal.* For example, a contract to build an apartment building becomes impossible to perform when the zoning laws are changed to prohibit the construction of residential rental property at the planned location. A contract to paint a bridge using lead paint becomes impossible when the government passes new regulations forbidding the use of lead paint on bridges.[11]

Temporary Impossibility An occurrence or event that makes performance temporarily impossible operates to suspend performance until the impossibility ceases. Then, ordinarily, the parties must perform the contract as originally planned. If, however, the lapse of time and the change in circumstances surrounding the contract make it substantially more burdensome for the parties to perform the promised acts, the contract is discharged.

The leading case on the subject, *Autry v. Republic Productions,*[12] involved an actor (Gene Autry) who was drafted into the army in 1942. Being drafted rendered the actor's contract temporarily impossible to perform, and it was suspended until the end of the war. When the actor got out of the army, the purchasing power of the dollar had so diminished that performance of the contract would have been substantially burdensome to him. Therefore, the contract was discharged.

A more recent example involves a contract entered into shortly before Hurricane Katrina hit Louisiana. On August 22, 2005, Keefe Hurwitz contracted to sell his home in Madisonville, Louisiana, to Wesley and Gwendolyn Payne for a price of $241,500. On August 26—just four days after the parties signed the contract—Hurricane Katrina made landfall and caused extensive property damage to the house. The cost of repairs was estimated at $60,000 and Hurwitz would have to make the repairs before the *closing date* (see Chapter 25). Hurwitz did not have the funds and refused to pay $60,000 for the repairs only to sell the property to the Paynes for the previously agreed-on price of $241,500. The Paynes filed a lawsuit to enforce the contract. Hurwitz claimed that Hurricane Katrina had made it impossible for him to perform and had discharged his duties under the contract. The court, however, ruled that Hurricane Katrina had only caused a temporary impossibility. Hurwitz was required to pay for the necessary repairs and to perform the contract as written. In other words, he could not obtain a higher purchase price to offset the cost of the repairs.[13]

Commercial Impracticability When a supervening event does not render performance objectively impossible, but does make it much more difficult or expensive to perform, the courts may excuse the parties' obligations under the contract. For someone to invoke the doctrine of **commercial impracticability** successfully, however, the anticipated performance must become significantly more difficult or costly than originally contemplated at the time the contract was formed.[14]

The added burden of performing not only must be extreme but also *must not have been known by the parties when the contract was made.* In one case, for example, the court allowed a party to rescind a con-

10. *Restatement (Second) of Contracts,* Sections 262–266; UCC 2–615.

11. *M. J. Paquet, Inc. v. New Jersey Department of Transportation,* 171 N.J. 378, 794 A.2d 141 (2002).

12. 30 Cal.2d 144, 180 P.2d 888 (1947).

13. *Payne v. Hurwitz,* ___ So.2d ___ (La.App. 2008).

14. *Restatement (Second) of Contracts,* Section 264.

tract for the sale of land because of a potential problem with contaminated groundwater under the land. The court found that "the potential for substantial and unbargained-for" liability made contract performance economically impracticable. Interestingly, the court in that case also noted that the possibility of "environmental degradation with consequences extending well beyond the parties' land sale" was just as important to its decision as the economic considerations.[15]

The contract dispute in the following case arose out of the cancellation of a wedding reception due to a power failure. Is a power failure sufficient to invoke the doctrine of commercial impracticability?

15. *Cape-France Enterprises v. Estate of Peed,* 305 Mont. 513, 29 P.3d 1011 (2001).

CASE 10.2 Facto v. Pantagis

Superior Court of New Jersey, Appellate Division, 2007. 390 N.J.Super. 227, 915 A.2d 59.
lawlibrary.rutgers.edu/search.shtml[a]

• **Background and Facts** Leo and Elizabeth Facto contracted with Snuffy Pantagis Enterprises, Inc., for the use of Pantagis Renaissance, a banquet hall in Scotch Plains, New Jersey, for a wedding reception in August 2002. The Factos paid the $10,578 price in advance. The contract excused Pantagis from performance "if it is prevented from doing so by an act of God (for example, flood, power failure, etc.), or other unforeseen events or circumstances." Soon after the reception began, there was a power failure. The lights and the air-conditioning shut off. The band hired for the reception refused to play without electricity to power their instruments, and the lack of lighting prevented the photographer and videographer from taking pictures. The temperature was in the 90s, the humidity was high, and the guests quickly became uncomfortable. Three hours later, after a fight between a guest and a Pantagis employee, the emergency lights began to fade, and the police evacuated the hall. The Factos filed a suit in a New Jersey state court against Pantagis, alleging breach of contract, among other things. The Factos sought to recover their prepayment, plus amounts paid to the band, the photographer, and the videographer. The court concluded that Pantagis did not breach the contract and dismissed the complaint. The Factos appealed to a state intermediate appellate court.

IN THE LANGUAGE OF THE COURT

SKILLMAN, **P. J.A.D. [Presiding Judge, Appellate Division]**

* * * *

Even if a contract does not expressly provide that a party will be relieved of the duty to perform if an unforeseen condition arises that makes performance impracticable, a court may relieve him of that duty if performance has unexpectedly become impracticable as a result of a supervening event. *In deciding whether a party should be relieved of the duty to perform a contract, a court must determine whether the existence of a specific thing is necessary for the performance of a duty and its * * * destruction or * * * deterioration * * * makes performance impracticable.* * * * A power failure is the kind of unexpected occurrence that may relieve a party of the duty to perform if the availability of electricity is essential for satisfactory performance. [Emphasis added.]

* * * *

The * * * Pantagis Renaissance contract provided: "Snuffy's will be excused from performance under this contract if it is prevented from doing so by an act of God (e.g., flood, power failure, etc.), or other unforeseen events or circumstances." Thus, the contract specifically identified a "power failure" as one of the circumstances that would excuse the Pantagis Renaissance's performance. We do not attribute any significance to the fact the * * * clause refers to a power failure as an example of an "act of God." *This term has been construed to refer not just to natural events such as storms but to comprehend all misfortunes and accidents arising from inevitable necessity which human prudence could not foresee or prevent.* Furthermore, the * * * clause in the

a. In the "Search by party name" section, select the "Appellate Division," type "Pantagis" in the "First Name:" box, and click on "Submit Form." In the result, click on the "click here to get this case" link to access the opinion. The Rutgers University School of Law in Camden, New Jersey, maintains this Web site.

CASE CONTINUES

CASE 10.2 CONTINUED

Pantagis Renaissance contract excuses performance not only for "acts of God" but also "other unforeseen events or circumstances." Consequently, even if a power failure caused by circumstances other than a natural event were not considered to be an "act of God," it still would constitute an unforeseen event or circumstance that would excuse performance. [Emphasis added.]

The fact that a power failure is not absolutely unforeseeable during the hot summer months does not preclude relief from the obligation to perform. * * * *Absolute unforeseeability of a condition is not a prerequisite to the defense of impracticability.* The party seeking to be relieved of the duty to perform only needs to show that the destruction, or * * * deterioration of a specific thing necessary for the performance of the contract makes performance impracticable. In this case, the Pantagis Renaissance sought to eliminate any possible doubt that the availability of electricity was a specific thing necessary for the wedding reception by specifically referring to a "power failure" as an example of an "act of God" that would excuse performance. [Emphasis added.]

It is also clear that the Pantagis Renaissance was "prevented from" substantial performance of the contract. The power failure began less than forty-five minutes after the start of the reception and continued until after it was scheduled to end. The lack of electricity prevented the band from playing, impeded the taking of pictures by the photographer and videographer and made it difficult for guests to see inside the banquet hall. Most significantly, the shutdown of the air conditioning system made it unbearably hot shortly after the power failure began. It is also undisputed that the power failure was an area-wide event that was beyond the Pantagis Renaissance's control. These are precisely the kind of circumstances under which the parties agreed * * * [in their contract] that the Pantagis Renaissance would be excused from performance.

* * * Where one party to a contract is excused from performance as a result of an unforeseen event that makes performance impracticable, the other party is also generally excused from performance.

* * * Therefore, the power failure that relieved the Pantagis Renaissance of the obligation to furnish plaintiffs with a wedding reception also relieved plaintiffs of the obligation to pay the contract price for the reception.

Nevertheless, since the Pantagis Renaissance partially performed the contract by starting the reception before the power failure, it is entitled * * * to recover the value of the services it provided to plaintiffs.

• **Decision and Remedy** *The state intermediate appellate court agreed that the power failure relieved Pantagis of its contractual obligation, but held that Pantagis's inability to perform also relieved the Factos of their obligation. The court reversed the dismissal and remanded the case for an award to the Factos of the amount of their prepayment less the value of the services they received.*

• **The Ethical Dimension** *Should Pantagis have offered to reschedule the reception? Would this have absolved Pantagis of the obligation to refund the Factos' prepayment? Explain.*

• **The Legal Environment Dimension** *Does a power failure always constitute the kind of unexpected occurrence that relieves a party of the duty to perform a contract? In what circumstances might a power failure have no effect on a contract? (Hint: Is electricity always necessary for the performance of a contract?)*

Frustration of Purpose A theory closely allied with the doctrine of commercial impracticability is the doctrine of **frustration of purpose.** In principle, a contract will be discharged if supervening circumstances make it impossible to attain the purpose both parties had in mind when making the contract. As with commercial impracticability and impossibility, the supervening event must not have been reasonably foreseeable at the time of the contracting. In contrast to impracticability, which usually involves an event that increases the cost or difficulty of performance, frustration of purpose typically involves an event that decreases the value of what a party receives under the contract.

Because many problems are foreseeable by contracting parties and value is subjective, courts rarely excuse contract performance on this basis. For example, in one case, New Beginnings was searching for a new location for its drug rehabilitation center. After receiving preliminary approval for the use of a particular building from the city zoning official, New Beginnings signed a three-year lease on the property. Then opposition from the community developed, and the city denied New Beginnings a permit to use the property for a rehab center. New Beginnings appealed the decision and eventually received a permit from the city, but by then the state was threatening to rescind all state contracts with New Beginnings if it moved into that location. Because New Beginnings would lose its funding if it actually moved onto the property, the value of the leased building was practically worthless. Nevertheless, the court refused to excuse New Beginnings from the lease contract on the ground of frustration of purpose because the situation was reasonably foreseeable.[16]

See Exhibit 10–1 for an illustration of the ways in which a contract may be discharged.

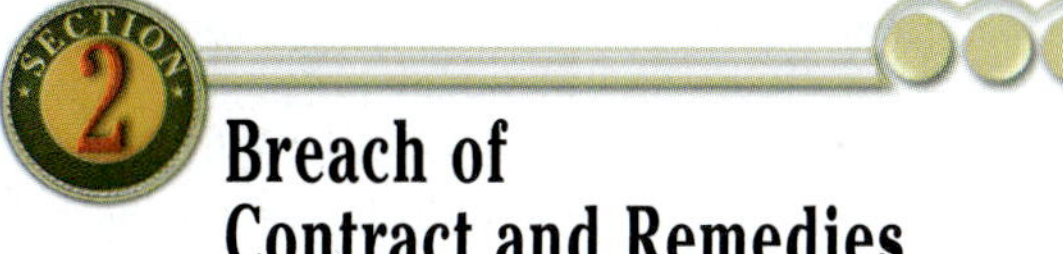

Section 2 Breach of Contract and Remedies

When one party breaches a contract, the other party—the nonbreaching party—can choose one or more of several remedies. A *remedy* is the relief provided for an innocent party when the other party has breached the contract. It is the means employed to enforce a right or to redress an injury.

16. *Adbar, L.C. v. New Beginnings C-Star,* 103 S.W.3d 799 (Mo.App. 2003).

The most common remedies available to a nonbreaching party include damages, rescission and restitution, specific performance, and reformation. As discussed in Chapter 1, a distinction is made between *remedies at law* and *remedies in equity*. Today, the remedy at law is normally monetary damages, which are discussed in the first part of this section. Equitable remedies include rescission and restitution, specific performance, and reformation, all of which will be examined later in this section. Usually, a court will not award an equitable remedy unless the remedy at law is inadequate. Special legal doctrines and concepts relating to remedies will be discussed in the final pages of this chapter.

Damages

A breach of contract entitles the nonbreaching party to sue for monetary damages. Damages are designed to compensate a party for harm suffered as a result of another's wrongful act. In the context of contract law, damages compensate the nonbreaching party for the loss of the bargain. Often, courts say that innocent parties are to be placed in the position they would have occupied had the contract been fully performed.[17]

17. *Restatement (Second) of Contracts,* Section 347; Section 1–106(1) of the Uniform Commercial Code (UCC).

EXHIBIT 10–1 • Contract Discharge

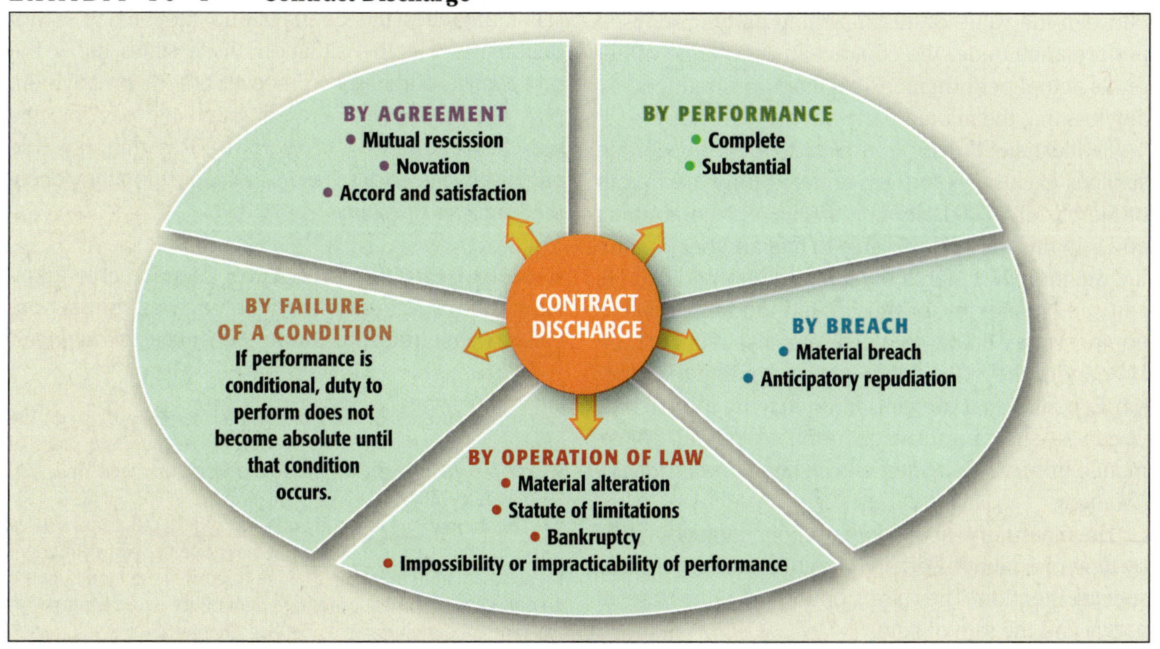

Realize at the outset, though, that to collect damages through a court judgment means litigation, which can be expensive and time consuming. Also keep in mind that court judgments are often difficult to enforce, particularly if the breaching party does not have sufficient assets to pay the damages awarded (as discussed in Chapter 2). For these reasons, the majority of actions for damages (or other remedies) are settled by the parties before trial.

Types of Damages There are basically four broad categories of damages:

1. Compensatory (to cover direct losses and costs).
2. Consequential (to cover indirect and foreseeable losses).
3. Punitive (to punish and deter wrongdoing).
4. Nominal (to recognize wrongdoing when no monetary loss is shown).

We look here at compensatory and consequential damages.

Compensatory Damages Damages compensating the nonbreaching party for the *loss of the bargain* are known as *compensatory damages.* These damages compensate the injured party only for damages actually sustained and proved to have arisen directly from the loss of the bargain caused by the breach of contract. They simply replace what was lost because of the wrong or damage. The standard measure of compensatory damages is the difference between the value of the breaching party's promised performance under the contract and the value of her or his actual performance. This amount is reduced by any loss that the injured party has avoided, however.

To illustrate: Wilcox contracts to perform certain services exclusively for Hernandez during the month of March for $4,000. Hernandez cancels the contract and is in breach. Wilcox is able to find another job during the month of March but can earn only $3,000. He can sue Hernandez for breach and recover $1,000 as compensatory damages. Wilcox can also recover from Hernandez the amount that he spent to find the other job. Expenses that are caused directly by a breach of contract—such as those incurred to obtain performance from another source—are known as *incidental damages.*

The measurement of compensatory damages varies by type of contract. Certain types of contracts deserve special mention. They are contracts for the sale of goods and the sale of land.

Sale of Goods. In a contract for the sale of goods, the usual measure of compensatory damages is an amount equal to the difference between the contract price and the market price.[18] Suppose that Chrylon Corporation contracts to buy ten model UTS network servers from an XEXO Corporation dealer for $8,000 each. The dealer, however, fails to deliver the ten servers to Chrylon. The market price of the servers at the time the buyer learns of the breach is $8,150. Chrylon's measure of damages is therefore $1,500 (10 × $150) plus any incidental damages (expenses) caused by the breach. In a situation in which the buyer breaches and the seller has not yet produced the goods, compensatory damages normally equal lost profits on the sale, not the difference between the contract price and the market price.

Sale of Land. Ordinarily, because each parcel of land is unique, the remedy for a seller's breach of a contract for a sale of real estate is specific performance—that is, the buyer is awarded the parcel of property for which she or he bargained (specific performance will be discussed more fully later in this chapter). When this remedy is unavailable (for example, when the seller has sold the property to someone else), or when the breach is on the part of the buyer, the measure of damages is ordinarily the same as in contracts for the sale of goods—that is, the difference between the contract price and the market price of the land. The majority of states follow this rule.

A minority of states follow a different rule when the seller breaches the contract and the breach is not deliberate.[19] In this situation, these states allow the prospective purchaser to recover any down payment plus any expenses incurred (such as fees for title searches, attorneys, and escrows). This minority rule effectively places purchasers in the position they occupied prior to the sale.

Consequential Damages Foreseeable damages that result from a party's breach of contract are called **consequential damages,** or *special damages.*

---

18. In other words, the amount is the difference between the contract price and the market price at the time and place at which the goods were to be delivered or tendered. See UCC 2–708 and 2–713.

19. "Deliberate" breaches include the seller's failure to convey the land because the market price has gone up. "Nondeliberate" breaches include the seller's failure to convey the land because an unknown easement (another's right of use over the property) has rendered title unmarketable. See Chapter 25.

They differ from compensatory damages in that they are caused by special circumstances beyond the contract itself. They flow from the consequences, or results, of a breach.

For example, if a seller fails to deliver goods, and the seller knows that a buyer is planning to resell these goods immediately, consequential damages will be awarded for the loss of profit from the planned resale. The buyer will also recover compensatory damages for the difference between the contract price and the market price of the goods.

To recover consequential damages, the breaching party must know (or have reason to know) that special circumstances will cause the nonbreaching party to suffer an additional loss. This rule was enunciated in the classic case of *Hadley v. Baxendale,* which is presented next. In reading this decision, it is helpful to understand that it was customary in the mid-1800s in England for large flour mills to have more than one crankshaft in the event that the main crankshaft broke and had to be repaired. Also, in those days it was common knowledge that flour mills did indeed have spare crankshafts. It is against this background that the parties in the case presented here argued their respective positions on whether the damages resulting from the loss of profits while the crankshaft was repaired were reasonably foreseeable.

CASE 10.3 Hadley v. Baxendale

Court of Exchequer, 1854. 156 Eng.Rep. 145.

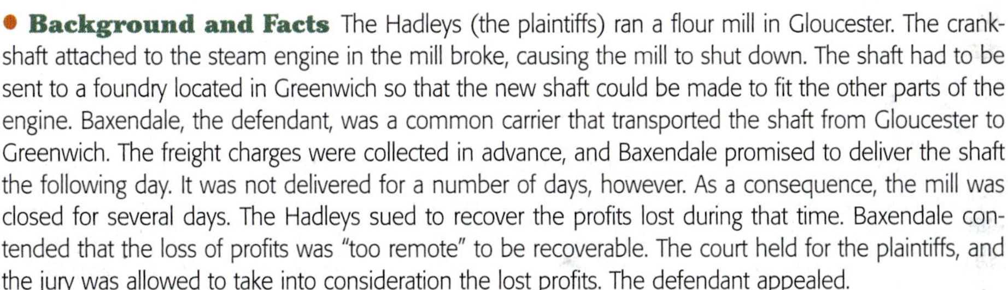

Background and Facts The Hadleys (the plaintiffs) ran a flour mill in Gloucester. The crankshaft attached to the steam engine in the mill broke, causing the mill to shut down. The shaft had to be sent to a foundry located in Greenwich so that the new shaft could be made to fit the other parts of the engine. Baxendale, the defendant, was a common carrier that transported the shaft from Gloucester to Greenwich. The freight charges were collected in advance, and Baxendale promised to deliver the shaft the following day. It was not delivered for a number of days, however. As a consequence, the mill was closed for several days. The Hadleys sued to recover the profits lost during that time. Baxendale contended that the loss of profits was "too remote" to be recoverable. The court held for the plaintiffs, and the jury was allowed to take into consideration the lost profits. The defendant appealed.

IN THE LANGUAGE OF THE COURT

***ALDERSON,* B. [Baron]**

* * * *

* * * Where two parties have made a contract which one of them has broken, the damages which the other party ought to receive in respect of such breach of contract should be such as may fairly and reasonably be considered either arising naturally, *i.e.,* according to the usual course of things, from such breach of contract itself, or such as may reasonably be supposed to have been in the contemplation of both parties, at the time they made the contract, as the probable result of the breach of it. Now, if the special circumstances under which the contract was actually made were communicated by the plaintiffs to the defendants, and thus known to both parties, the damages resulting from the breach of such a contract, *which they would reasonably contemplate,* would be the amount of injury which would ordinarily follow from a breach of contract under these special circumstances so known and communicated. * * * Now, in the present case, if we are to apply the principles above laid down, we find that the only circumstances here communicated by the plaintiffs to the defendants at the time the contract was made, were, that the article to be carried was the broken shaft of a mill, and that the plaintiffs were the millers of that mill. * * * Special circumstances were here never communicated by the plaintiffs to the defendants. It follows, therefore, that the loss of profits here cannot reasonably be considered such a consequence of the breach of contract as could have been fairly and reasonably contemplated by both the parties when they made this contract. [Emphasis added.]

CASE CONTINUES

CASE 10.3 CONTINUED

• **Decision and Remedy** *The Court of Exchequer ordered a new trial. According to the court, to collect consequential damages, the plaintiffs would have to have given express notice of the special circumstances that caused the loss of profits.*

• **Impact of This Case on Today's Law** *This case established the rule that when damages are awarded, compensation is given only for those injuries that the defendant could reasonably have foreseen as a probable result of the usual course of events following a breach. Today, the rule enunciated by the court in this case still applies. To recover consequential damages, the plaintiff must show that the defendant had reason to know or foresee that a particular loss or injury would occur.*

• **The E-Commerce Dimension** *If a Web merchant loses business due to a computer system's failure that can be attributed to malfunctioning software, can the merchant recover the lost profits from the software maker? Explain.*

Mitigation of Damages In most situations, when a breach of contract occurs, the innocent injured party is held to a duty to mitigate, or reduce, the damages that he or she suffers. Under this doctrine of **mitigation of damages,** the duty owed depends on the nature of the contract.

For example, some states require a landlord to use reasonable means to find a new tenant if a tenant abandons the premises and fails to pay rent. If an acceptable tenant is found, the landlord is required to lease the premises to this tenant to mitigate the damages recoverable from the former tenant. The former tenant is still liable for the difference between the amount of the rent under the original lease and the rent received from the new tenant. If the landlord has not used the reasonable means necessary to find a new tenant, presumably a court can reduce the award made by the amount of rent the landlord could have received had such reasonable means been used.

In the majority of states, persons whose employment has been wrongfully terminated owe a duty to mitigate damages suffered because of their employers' breach of the employment contract. In other words, wrongfully terminated employees have a duty to take similar jobs if they are available. If the employees fail to do this, the damages they are awarded will be equivalent to their salaries less the incomes they would have received in similar jobs obtained by reasonable means. The employer has the burden of proving that such a job existed and that the employee could have been hired. Normally, the employee is under no duty to take a job of a different type and rank, however.

Liquidated Damages Provisions

A **liquidated damages** provision in a contract specifies that a certain dollar amount is to be paid in the event of a *future* default or breach of contract. (*Liquidated* means determined, settled, or fixed.) For example, a provision requiring a construction contractor to pay $300 for every day he or she is late in completing the project is a liquidated damages provision. Liquidated damages provisions are frequently used in construction contracts because it is difficult to estimate the amount of damages that would be caused by a delay in completion. They are also common in contracts for the sale of goods.[20]

Liquidated damages differ from penalties. A **penalty** specifies a certain amount to be paid in the event of a default or breach of contract and is designed to penalize the breaching party. Liquidated damages provisions normally are enforceable. In contrast, if a court finds that a provision calls for a penalty, the agreement as to the amount will not be enforced, and recovery will be limited to actual damages. To determine if a particular provision is for liquidated damages or for a penalty, the court asks two questions:

1. When the contract was entered into, was it apparent that damages would be difficult to estimate in the event of a breach?
2. Was the amount set as damages a reasonable estimate and not excessive?[21]

If the answers to both questions are yes, the provision normally will be enforced. If either answer is no, the provision normally will not be enforced. For example, in a case involving a sophisticated business contract to lease computer equipment, the court held that a liquidated damages provision that valued computer equipment at more than four times its market value was a

20. Section 2–718(1) of the UCC specifically authorizes the use of liquidated damages provisions.

21. *Restatement (Second) of Contracts,* Section 356(1).

reasonable estimate. According to the court, the amount of actual damages was difficult to ascertain at the time the contract was formed because of the "speculative nature of the value of computers at termination of lease schedules."[22]

Rescission and Restitution

As discussed earlier in this chapter, rescission is essentially an action to undo, or terminate, a contract—to return the contracting parties to the positions they occupied prior to the transaction.[23] When fraud, a mistake, duress, undue influence, misrepresentation, or lack of capacity to contract is present, unilateral rescission is available. Rescission may also be available by statute.[24] The failure of one party to perform entitles the other party to rescind the contract. The rescinding party must give prompt notice to the breaching party.

Restitution Generally, to rescind a contract, both parties must make **restitution** to each other by returning goods, property, or funds previously conveyed.[25] If the physical property or goods can be returned, they must be. If the goods or property have been consumed, restitution must be made in an equivalent amount of cash.

Essentially, restitution refers to the plaintiff's recapture of a benefit conferred on the defendant through which the defendant has been unjustly enriched. For example, Katie pays $10,000 to Bob in return for Bob's promise to design a house for her. The next day Bob calls Katie and tells her that he has taken a position with a large architectural firm in another state and cannot design the house. Katie decides to hire another architect that afternoon. Katie can obtain restitution of the $10,000.

Restitution Is Not Limited to Rescission Cases Restitution may be appropriate when a contract is rescinded, but the right to restitution is not limited to rescission cases. Restitution may be sought in actions for breach of contract, tort actions, and other actions at law or in equity. Usually, restitution can be obtained when funds or property has been transferred by mistake or because of fraud. An award in a case may include restitution of funds or property obtained through embezzlement, conversion, theft, copyright infringement, or misconduct by a party in a confidential or other special relationship.

Specific Performance

The equitable remedy of **specific performance** calls for the performance of the act promised in the contract. This remedy is quite attractive to the nonbreaching party for three reasons:

1. The nonbreaching party need not worry about collecting the monetary damages awarded by a court (see the discussion in Chapter 2 of some of the difficulties that may arise when trying to enforce court judgments).
2. The nonbreaching party need not spend time seeking an alternative contract.
3. The performance is more valuable than the monetary damages.

Normally, however, specific performance will not be granted unless the party's legal remedy (monetary damages) is inadequate.[26] For this reason, contracts for the sale of goods rarely qualify for specific performance. The legal remedy—monetary damages—is ordinarily adequate in such situations because substantially identical goods can be bought or sold in the market. Only if the goods are unique will a court grant specific performance. For example, paintings, sculptures, or rare books or coins are so unique that monetary damages will not enable a buyer to obtain substantially identical substitutes in the market.

Sale of Land Specific performance is granted to a buyer in a contract for the sale of land. The legal remedy for breach of a land sales contract is inadequate because every parcel of land is considered to be unique. Monetary damages will not compensate a buyer adequately because the same land in the same location obviously cannot be obtained elsewhere. Only when specific performance is unavailable (for example, when the seller has sold the property to someone else) will monetary damages be awarded instead.

22. *Winthrop Resources Corp. v. Eaton Hydraulics, Inc.*, 361 F.3d 465 (8th Cir. 2004).

23. The rescission discussed here is *unilateral* rescission, in which only one party wants to undo the contract. In mutual rescission, both parties agree to undo the contract. Mutual rescission discharges the contract; unilateral rescission is generally available as a remedy for breach of contract.

24. The Federal Trade Commission and many states have rules or statutes allowing consumers to unilaterally rescind contracts made at home with door-to-door salespersons. Rescission is allowed within three days for any reason or for no reason at all. See, for example, California Civil Code Section 1689.5.

25. *Restatement (Second) of Contracts*, Section 370.

26. *Restatement (Second) of Contracts*, Section 359.

reformed. Other courts, however, will throw out the entire restrictive covenant as illegal.

Exhibit 10–2 graphically summarizes the remedies, including reformation, that are available to the nonbreaching party. *Concept Summary 10.1* reviews all the equitable remedies.

Election of Remedies

In many cases, a nonbreaching party has several remedies available. When the remedies are inconsistent with one another, the common law of contracts requires the party to choose which remedy to pursue. This is called *election of remedies.*

The Purpose of the Doctrine The purpose of the doctrine of election of remedies is to prevent double recovery. Suppose, for example, that McCarthy agrees in writing to sell his land to Tally. Then McCarthy changes his mind and repudiates the contract. Tally can sue for compensatory damages or for specific performance. If Tally could seek compensatory damages in addition to specific performance, she would recover twice for the same breach of contract. The doctrine of election of remedies requires Tally to choose the remedy she wants, and it eliminates any possibility of double recovery. In other words, the election doctrine represents the legal embodiment of the adage "You can't have your cake and eat it, too."

The doctrine has often been applied in a rigid and technical manner, leading to some harsh results. Suppose that Beacham is fraudulently induced to buy a parcel of land for $150,000. He spends an additional $10,000 moving onto the land and then discovers the fraud. Instead of suing for damages, Beacham sues to rescind the contract. The court allows Beacham to recover only the purchase price of $150,000 in restitution, but not the additional $10,000 in moving expenses (because the seller did not receive these funds, he or she will not be required to return them). So Beacham suffers a net loss of $10,000 on the transaction. If Beacham had elected to sue for damages instead of seeking the remedy of rescission and restitution, he could have recovered the $10,000 as well as the $150,000.

The UCC's Rejection of the Doctrine Because of the many problems associated with the doctrine of election of remedies, the UCC expressly rejects it.[29] As will be discussed in Chapter 11, remedies under the UCC are not exclusive but cumulative in nature and include all the available remedies for breach of contract.

Pleading in the Alternative Although the parties must ultimately elect which remedy to pursue, modern court procedures do allow plaintiffs to plead their cases "in the alternative" (pleadings were discussed in Chapter 2). In other words, when the plaintiff originally files a lawsuit, he or she can ask the court to order either rescission (and restitution) or damages, for example. Then, as the case progresses to trial, the parties can elect which remedy is most beneficial or appropriate, or the judge can order one remedy and not another. This process still prevents double recovery because the party can only be awarded one of the remedies that was requested.

Waiver of Breach

Under certain circumstances, a nonbreaching party may be willing to accept a defective performance of the contract. This knowing relinquishment of a legal right (that is, the right to require satisfactory and full performance) is called a **waiver.**

29. See UCC 2–703 and 2–711.

EXHIBIT 10–2 • Remedies for Breach of Contract

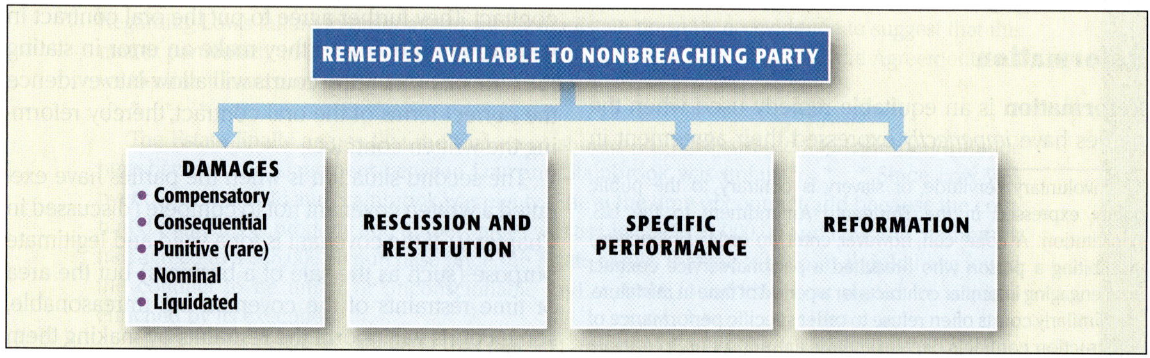

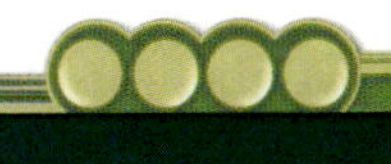

CONCEPT SUMMARY 10.1
Equitable Remedies

Remedy	Description
RESCISSION AND RESTITUTION	1. *Rescission*—A remedy whereby a contract is canceled and the parties are restored to the original positions that they occupied prior to the transaction. 2. *Restitution*—When a contract is rescinded, both parties must make restitution to each other by returning the goods, property, or funds previously conveyed.
SPECIFIC PERFORMANCE	An equitable remedy calling for the performance of the act promised in the contract. Only available when monetary damages would be inadequate—such as in contracts for the sale of land or unique goods—and never available in personal-service contracts.
REFORMATION	An equitable remedy allowing a contract to be "reformed," or rewritten, to reflect the parties' true intentions. Available when an agreement is imperfectly expressed in writing, such as when a mutual mistake has occurred.

Consequences of a Waiver of Breach When a waiver of a breach of contract occurs, the party waiving the breach cannot take any later action on it. In effect, the waiver erases the past breach; the contract continues as if the breach had never occurred. Of course, the waiver of breach of contract extends only to the matter waived and not to the whole contract.

Reasons for Waiving a Breach Businesspersons often waive breaches of contract to get whatever benefit is still possible out of the contract. For example, a seller contracts with a buyer to deliver to the buyer ten thousand tons of coal on or before November 1. The contract calls for the buyer to pay by November 10 for coal delivered. Because of a coal miners' strike, coal is hard to find. The seller breaches the contract by not tendering delivery until November 5. The buyer may be well advised to waive the seller's breach, accept delivery of the coal, and pay as contracted.

Waiver of Breach and Subsequent Breaches Ordinarily, the waiver by a contracting party will not operate to waive subsequent, additional, or future breaches of contract. This is always true when the subsequent breaches are unrelated to the first breach. For example, an owner who waives the right to sue for late completion of a stage of construction does not waive the right to sue for failure to comply with engineering specifications on the same job. A waiver will be extended to subsequent defective performance, however, if a reasonable person would conclude that similar defective performance in the future will be acceptable. Therefore, a *pattern of conduct* that waives a number of successive breaches will operate as a continued waiver. To change this result, the nonbreaching party should give notice to the breaching party that full performance will be required in the future.

The party who has rendered defective or less-than-full performance remains liable for the damages caused by the breach of contract. In effect, the waiver operates to keep the contract going. The waiver prevents the nonbreaching party from calling the contract to an end or rescinding the contract. The contract continues, but the nonbreaching party can recover damages caused by defective or less-than-full performance.

Contract Provisions Limiting Remedies

A contract may include provisions stating that no damages can be recovered for certain types of breaches or that damages must be limited to a maximum amount. The contract may also provide that the only remedy for breach is replacement, repair, or refund of the purchase price. Provisions stating that no damages can be recovered are called *exculpatory clauses*. Provisions that affect the availability of certain remedies are called *limitation-of-liability clauses*.

Whether these contract provisions and clauses will be enforced depends on the type of breach that is

Remember that parties to sales contracts are free to establish whatever terms they wish. The UCC comes into play when the parties have not, in their contract, provided for a contingency that later gives rise to a dispute. The UCC makes this very clear time and again by its use of such phrases as "unless the parties otherwise agree" and "absent a contrary agreement by the parties."

Offer

In general contract law, the moment a definite offer is met by an unqualified acceptance, a binding contract is formed. In commercial sales transactions, the verbal exchanges, the correspondence, and the actions of the parties may not reveal exactly when a binding contractual obligation arises. The UCC states that an agreement sufficient to constitute a contract can exist even if the moment of its making is undetermined [UCC 2–204(2), 2A–204(2)].

Open Terms According to contract law, an offer must be definite enough for the parties (and the courts) to ascertain its essential terms when it is accepted. The UCC states that a sales or lease contract will not fail for indefiniteness even if one or more terms are left open as long as (1) the parties intended to make a contract and (2) there is a reasonably certain basis for the court to grant an appropriate remedy [UCC 2–204(3), 2A–204(3)].

Although the UCC has radically lessened the requirement of definiteness of terms, keep in mind that if too many terms are left open, a court may find that the parties did not intend to form a contract.

The appendix that follows this chapter shows an actual sales contract used by Starbucks Coffee Company. The contract illustrates many of the terms and clauses that are typically contained in contracts for the sale of goods.

Open Price Term. If the parties have not agreed on a price, the court will determine a "reasonable price at the time for delivery" [UCC 2–305(1)]. If either the buyer or the seller is to determine the price, the price is to be fixed in good faith [UCC 2–305(2)]. Under the UCC, *good faith* means honesty in fact and the observance of reasonable commercial standards of fair dealing in the trade [UCC 2–103(1)(b)]. The concepts of *good faith* and *commercial reasonableness* permeate the UCC.

Sometimes the price fails to be fixed through the fault of one of the parties. In that case, the other party can treat the contract as canceled or fix a reasonable price. For example, Perez and Merrick enter into a contract for the sale of goods and agree that Perez will fix the price. Perez refuses to fix the price. Merrick can either treat the contract as canceled or set a reasonable price [UCC 2–305(3)].

Open Payment Term. When parties do not specify payment terms, payment is due at the time and place at which the buyer is to receive the goods [UCC 2–310(a)]. The buyer can tender payment using any commercially normal or acceptable means, such as a check or credit card. If the seller demands payment in cash, however, the buyer must be given a reasonable time to obtain it [UCC 2–511(2)]. This is especially important when the contract states a definite and final time for performance.

Open Delivery Term. When no delivery terms are specified, the buyer normally takes delivery at the seller's place of business [UCC 2–308(a)]. If the seller has no place of business, the seller's residence is used. When goods are located in some other place and both parties know it, delivery is made there. If the time for shipment or delivery is not clearly specified in the sales contract, then the court will infer a "reasonable" time for performance [UCC 2–309(1)].

Open Quantity Term. Normally, if the parties do not specify a quantity, a court will have no basis for determining a remedy. The UCC recognizes two exceptions in requirements and output contracts [UCC 2–306(1)].

In a **requirements contract,** the buyer agrees to purchase—and the seller agrees to sell—all or up to a stated amount of what the buyer *needs* or *requires*. There is implicit consideration in a requirements contract, for the buyer gives up the right to buy from any other seller, and this forfeited right creates a legal detriment. Requirements contracts are common in the business world and are normally enforceable. If, however, the buyer promises to purchase only if the buyer *wishes* to do so, or if the buyer reserves the right to buy the goods from someone other than the seller, the promise is illusory (without consideration) and unenforceable by either party.

In an **output contract,** the seller agrees to sell and the buyer agrees to buy all or up to a stated amount of what the seller *produces*. Again, because the seller essentially forfeits the right to sell goods to another buyer, there is implicit consideration in an output contract.

The UCC imposes a *good faith limitation* on requirements and output contracts. The quantity under such contracts is the amount of requirements or the amount of output that occurs during a *normal* production year. The actual quantity purchased or sold cannot be unreasonably disproportionate to normal or comparable prior requirements or output [UCC 2–306].

Merchant's Firm Offer Under regular contract principles (discussed in Chapter 9), an offer can be revoked at any time before acceptance. The major common law exception is an *option contract,* in which the offeree pays consideration for the offeror's irrevocable promise to keep the offer open for a stated period. The UCC creates a second exception, which applies only to firm offers for the sale or lease of goods made by a merchant (regardless of whether or not the offeree is a merchant). A **firm offer** arises when a merchant-offeror gives assurances *in a signed writing* that the offer will remain open. The merchant's firm offer is irrevocable without the necessity of consideration[3] for the stated period or, if no definite period is stated, a reasonable period (neither to exceed three months) [UCC 2–205, 2A–205].

Acceptance

Acceptance of an offer to buy, sell, or lease goods generally may be made in any reasonable manner and by any reasonable means. The UCC generally takes the position that if the offeree's response indicates a *definite* acceptance of the offer, a contract is formed, even if the acceptance includes terms additional to, or different from, those contained in the offer [UCC 2–207(1)].

Promise to Ship or Prompt Shipment The UCC permits acceptance of an offer to buy goods "either by a prompt promise to ship or by the prompt or current shipment of conforming or nonconforming goods" [UCC 2–206(1)(b)]. Conforming goods accord with the contract's terms; nonconforming goods do not. The prompt shipment of *nonconforming goods* constitutes both an *acceptance,* which creates a contract, and a *breach* of that contract. This rule does not apply if the seller **seasonably** (within a reasonable amount of time) notifies the buyer that the nonconforming shipment is offered only as an *accommodation,* or as a favor. The notice of accommodation must clearly indicate to the buyer that the shipment does not constitute an acceptance and that, therefore, no contract has been formed.

Communication of Acceptance Under the common law, because a unilateral offer invites acceptance by a performance, the offeree need not notify the offeror of performance unless the offeror would not otherwise know about it. The UCC is more stringent than the common law in this regard. Under the UCC, if the offeror is not notified that the offeree has accepted the contract by beginning performance, then the offeror can treat the offer as having lapsed before acceptance [UCC 2–206(2), 2A–206(2)].

Additional Terms If the acceptance includes terms additional to, or different from, those contained in the offer and one (or both) of the parties is a *nonmerchant,* the contract is formed according to the terms of the original offer submitted by the original offeror and not according to the additional terms of the acceptance [UCC 2–207(2)]. The drafters of the UCC created a special rule for merchants that is designed to avoid the "battle of the forms," which occurs when two merchants exchange standard forms containing different contract terms. Under UCC 2–207(2), in contracts *between merchants,* the additional terms *automatically* become part of the contract *unless:*

1. The original offer expressly limited acceptance to its terms,
2. The new or changed terms materially alter the contract, or
3. The offeror objects to the new or changed terms within a reasonable period of time.

What constitutes a material alteration of the contract is usually a question of fact that only a court (or a jury, in a jury trial) can decide. Generally, if the modification involves no unreasonable element of surprise or hardship for the offeror, a court is likely to hold that the modification did not materially alter the contract.

In the following case, the court explains the "revolutionary change in contract law" caused by the UCC's principles on additional terms.

3. If the offeree pays consideration, then an option contract (not a merchant's firm offer) is formed.

CASE 11.1 Sun Coast Merchandise Corp. v. Myron Corp.

Superior Court of New Jersey, Appellate Division, 2007. 393 N.J.Super. 55, 922 A.2d 782.
lawlibrary.rutgers.edu/search.shtml[a]

• **Background and Facts** Sun Coast Merchandise Corporation, a California firm, designs and sells products that businesses distribute as promotional items. Myron Corporation, a New Jersey firm, asked Sun about a flip-top calculator on which Myron could engrave the names of its customers. In December 2000, Myron began to submit purchase orders for about 400,000 of what the parties referred to as "Version I" calculators. In April 2001, Sun redesigned the flip-top. Over the next few weeks, the parties discussed terms for the making and shipping of 4 million of the "Version II" calculators before the Christmas season. By May 27, Myron had faxed four orders with specific delivery dates. Two days later, Sun announced a delayed schedule and asked Myron to submit revised orders. Unwilling to agree to the new dates, Myron did not honor this request. The parties attempted to negotiate the issue but were unsuccessful. Finally, Sun filed a suit in a New Jersey state court against Myron, claiming, among other things, breach of contract. The court entered a judgment in Sun's favor. On appeal to a state intermediate appellate court, Myron argued, among other things, that the judge's instruction to the jury regarding Sun's claim was inadequate.

IN THE LANGUAGE OF THE COURT
FISHER, **J.A.D. [Judge, Appellate Division]**

* * * *

The era when a valid, binding contract could only come into existence when a party's acceptance mirrored the other party's offer ended with the adoption of the Uniform Commercial Code (UCC). The UCC altered the common law approach, finding it to be inconsistent with the modern realities of commerce. * * * Article 2 of the UCC radically altered sales law and expanded our conception of a contract. The heart of this revolutionary change in contract law can be found in [New Jersey Statutes Annotated (N.J.S.A.)] 12A:2-207(1) [New Jersey's version of UCC 2–207(1)], which declares that "[a] definite and seasonable expression of acceptance or a written confirmation which is sent within a reasonable time operates as an acceptance even though it states terms additional to or different from those offered or agreed upon, unless acceptance is expressly made conditional on assent to the additional or different terms." *No longer are communicating parties left to debate whether an acceptance perfectly meets the terms of an offer, but instead the existence of a binding contract may be based on words or conduct, which need not mirror an offer, so long as they reveal the parties' intention to be bound.* [Emphasis added.]

Considering that the UCC permits the formation of a contract by way of conduct that reveals the parties' understanding that a contract exists, and notwithstanding the suggestion of additional or even non-conforming terms, the complex of communications between [Sun and Myron] demonstrates that neither can the formation of a contract be confirmed or foreclosed without a resolution of the existing factual disputes and the weighing of the significance of the parties' convoluted communications.

* * * *

In short, it is conceivable—and the jury could find—that the parties' inability to agree on certain terms reveals the lack of an intent to be bound; in other words, that their communications constituted mere negotiations that never ripened into a contract. By the same token, the jury could find that a contract was formed despite a failure or an inability to agree on all terms. N.J.S.A. 12A:2-207(2) provides that an acceptance coupled with the proposal of new or different terms does not necessarily preclude the formation of a contract. *In such a circumstance,* * * * *the new or different terms proposed by the offeree [could] become part of the contract* * * *. [Emphasis added.]

All these questions required that the factfinder analyze the meaning and significance of the parties' communications based upon the legal framework provided by the UCC.

* * * *

a. In the "SEARCH THE N.J. COURTS DECISIONS" section, type "Sun Coast" in the box, and click on "Search!" In the result, click on the case name to access the opinion.

CASE 11.1 CONTINUED

* * * The trial judge correctly determined that the [contentions about] contract formation * * * raised fact questions to be decided by the jury * * * .

* * * *

In describing for the jury what it takes for the parties to form a binding contract, the judge stated:

> A proposal to accept an offer on any different terms is not an acceptance of the original offer. If any new or different terms are proposed in response to the offer, the response is not an acceptance, but rather a counteroffer. A counteroffer is a new offer by the party making that proposal. The new offer must in turn be agreed to by the party who made the original offer for there to be an acceptance.

As we have already explained, the UCC does not require that a party's response mirror an offer to result in a binding contract. The offeree may propose additional or different terms without necessarily having the response viewed as a non-binding counteroffer. Instead, an offeree's proposal of additional or conflicting terms may be found to constitute an acceptance, and the other or different terms viewed as mere proposals to modify the contract thus formed.

The judge's misstatement in this regard was hardly harmless * * * . In describing when the law recognizes that a contract was formed, the judge provided the jury with erroneous instructions that struck directly at the heart of the case.

- **Decision and Remedy** *The state intermediate appellate court concluded that the judge's instruction to the jury with respect to the question of whether Sun and Myron had formed a contract was "fundamentally flawed" and "provided insufficient guidance for the jury's resolution of the issues." On this basis, the court reversed the lower court's judgment and remanded the case for a new trial.*

- **The Ethical Dimension** *How does the UCC's obligation of good faith relate to the application of the principles concerning additional terms?*

- **The Legal Environment Dimension** *Applying the correct principles to the facts in this case, how would you have decided the issue? Explain.*

Additional Terms May Be Stricken. The UCC provides yet another option for dealing with conflicting terms in the parties' writings. Section 2–207(3) states that conduct by both parties that recognizes the existence of a contract is sufficient to establish a contract for sale even though the writings of the parties do not otherwise establish a contract. In this situation, "the terms of the particular contract will consist of those terms on which the writings of the parties agree, together with any supplementary terms incorporated under any other provisions of this Act." In a dispute over contract terms, this provision allows a court simply to strike from the contract those terms on which the parties do not agree.

Suppose that SMT Marketing orders goods over the phone from Brigg Sales, Inc., which ships the goods with an acknowledgment form (confirming the order) to SMT. SMT accepts and pays for the goods. The parties' writings do not establish a contract, but there is no question that a contract exists. If a dispute arises over the terms, such as the extent of any warranties, UCC 2–207(3) provides the governing rule.

As noted previously, the fact that a merchant's acceptance frequently contains additional terms or even terms that conflict with those of the offer is often referred to as the "battle of the forms." Although the UCC tries to eliminate this battle, the problem of differing contract terms still arises in commercial settings, particularly when contracts are based on the merchants' standard forms, such as order forms and confirmation forms.

Consideration

The common law rule that a contract requires consideration also applies to sales and lease contracts. Unlike the common law, however, the UCC does not require a contract modification to be supported by new consideration. The UCC states that an agreement modifying a contract for the sale or lease of goods "needs no consideration to be binding" [UCC 2–209(1), 2A–208(1)].

Of course, any contract modification must be made in good faith [UCC 1–304]. For example, Jim agrees to lease certain goods to Louise for a stated price.

Subsequently, a sudden shift in the market makes it difficult for Jim to lease the items to Louise at the given price without suffering a loss. Jim tells Louise of the situation, and Louise agrees to pay an additional sum for leasing the goods. Later, Louise reconsiders and refuses to pay more than the original lease price. Under the UCC, Louise's promise to modify the contract needs no consideration to be binding. Hence, Louise is bound by the modified contract.

In this example, a shift in the market is a *good faith* reason for contract modification. What if there really was no shift in the market, however, and Jim knew that Louise needed the goods immediately but refused to deliver them unless Louise agreed to pay an additional sum? This sort of extortion of a modification without a legitimate commercial reason would be ineffective, because it would violate the duty of good faith. Jim would not be permitted to enforce the higher price.

The Statute of Frauds

As discussed in Chapter 9, the Statute of Frauds requires that certain types of contracts, to be enforceable, must be in writing or evidenced by a writing. The UCC contains Statute of Frauds provisions covering sales and lease contracts. Under these provisions, sales contracts for goods priced at $500 or more and lease contracts requiring total payments of $1,000 or more must be in writing to be enforceable [UCC 2–201(1), 2A–201(1)]. (Note that these low threshold amounts may eventually be raised.)

Sufficiency of the Writing

The UCC has greatly relaxed the requirements for the sufficiency of a writing to satisfy the Statute of Frauds. A writing or a memorandum will be sufficient as long as it indicates that the parties intended to form a contract and as long as it is signed by the party (or agent of the party) against whom enforcement is sought. The contract normally will not be enforceable beyond the quantity of goods shown in the writing, however. All other terms can be proved in court by oral testimony. For leases, the writing must reasonably identify and describe the goods leased and the lease term.

Special Rules for Contracts between Merchants

Once again, the UCC provides a special rule for merchants. The rule, however, applies only to sales (under Article 2); there is no corresponding rule that applies to leases (under Article 2A).[4] Merchants can satisfy the requirements of a writing for the Statute of Frauds if, after the parties have agreed orally, one of the merchants sends a signed written confirmation to the other merchant. The communication must indicate the terms of the agreement, and the merchant receiving the confirmation must have reason to know of its contents. Unless the merchant who receives the confirmation gives written notice of objection to its contents within ten days after receipt, the writing is sufficient against the receiving merchant, even though he or she has not signed anything [UCC 2–201(2)].

Exceptions

The UCC defines three exceptions to the writing requirements of the Statute of Frauds. An oral contract for the sale of goods priced at $500 or more or the lease of goods involving total payments of $1,000 or more will be enforceable despite the absence of a writing in the circumstances described in the following subsections [UCC 2–201(3), 2A–201(4)]. These exceptions and other ways in which sales law differs from general contract law are summarized in Exhibit 11–1.

Specially Manufactured Goods An oral contract is enforceable if (1) it is for goods that are specially manufactured for a particular buyer or specially manufactured or obtained for a particular lessee, (2) these goods are not suitable for resale or lease to others in the ordinary course of the seller's or lessor's business, and (3) the seller or lessor has substantially started to manufacture the goods or has made commitments for the manufacture or procurement of the goods. In these situations, once the seller or lessor has taken action, the buyer or lessee cannot repudiate the agreement claiming the Statute of Frauds as a defense.

Admissions An oral contract for the sale or lease of goods is enforceable if the party against whom enforcement is sought admits in pleadings, testimony, or other court proceedings that a sales or lease contract was made. In this situation, the contract will be enforceable even though it was oral, but enforceability will be limited to the quantity of goods admitted.

4. According to the comments accompanying UCC 2A–201 (Article 2A's Statute of Frauds), the "between merchants" provision was not included because "the number of such transactions involving leases, as opposed to sales, was thought to be modest."

EXHIBIT 11–1 • Major Differences between Contract Law and Sales Law

	Contract Law	Sales Law
Contract Terms	Contract must contain all material terms.	Open terms are acceptable if parties intended to form a contract, but contract is not enforceable beyond quantity term.
Acceptance	Mirror image rule applies. If additional terms are added in acceptance, counteroffer is created.	Additional terms will not negate acceptance unless acceptance is expressly conditioned on assent to the additional terms.
Contract Modification	Modification requires consideration.	Modification does not require consideration.
Irrevocable Offers	Option contracts (with consideration).	Merchants' firm offers (without consideration).
Statute of Frauds Requirements	All material terms must be included in the writing.	Writing is required only for sale of goods of $500 or more, but contract is not enforceable beyond quantity specified. Merchants can satisfy the writing requirement by a confirmatory memorandum evidencing their agreement. *Exceptions:* 1. Specially manufactured goods. 2. Admissions by party against whom enforcement is sought. 3. Partial performance.

Partial Performance An oral contract for the sale or lease of goods is enforceable if payment has been made and accepted or goods have been received and accepted. This is the "partial performance" exception. The oral contract will be enforced at least to the extent that performance *actually* took place.

Title, Risk, and Insurable Interest

Before the creation of the UCC, *title*—the right of ownership—was the central concept in sales law, controlling all issues of rights and remedies of the parties to a sales contract. There were numerous problems with this concept. For example, frequently it was difficult to determine when title actually passed from seller to buyer, and therefore it was also difficult to predict which party a court would decide had title at the time of a loss. Because of such problems, the UCC divorced the question of title as completely as possible from the question of the rights and obligations of buyers, sellers, and third parties (such as subsequent purchasers, creditors, or the tax collector).

In some situations, title is still relevant under the UCC, and the UCC has special rules for locating title. In most situations, however, the UCC has replaced the concept of title with three other concepts: (1) identification, (2) risk of loss, and (3) insurable interest.

In lease contracts, of course, title to the goods is retained by the lessor-owner of the goods. Hence, the UCC's provisions relating to passage of title do not apply to leased goods. Other concepts discussed in this chapter, though, including *identification, risk of loss,* and *insurable interest,* relate to lease contracts as well as to sales contracts.

Identification

Before any interest in specific goods can pass from the seller or lessor to the buyer or lessee, two conditions must prevail:

1. The goods must be in existence.
2. They must be identified as the specific goods designated in the contract.

Identification takes place when the goods are designated as the subject matter of a sales or lease contract. Title and risk of loss cannot pass to the buyer from the seller unless the goods are identified to the contract [UCC 2–105(2)]. (As mentioned, title to leased goods remains with the lessor—or, if the owner is a third party, with that party. The lessee does not acquire title to leased goods.) Identification is significant because it gives the buyer or lessee the right to insure (or obtain an insurable interest in) the goods and the right to recover from third parties who damage the goods.

Once the goods are in existence, the parties can agree in their contract on when identification will take place. If they do not so specify, however, and if the contract calls for the sale or lease of specific and ascertained goods that are already in existence, identification takes place at the time the contract is made [UCC 2–501(1), 2A–217].

Existing Goods If the contract calls for the sale or lease of specific and ascertained goods that are already in existence, identification takes place at the time the contract is made. For example, you contract to purchase or lease a fleet of five cars by the vehicle identification numbers of the cars.

Goods that are part of a larger mass are identified when the goods are marked, shipped, or somehow designated by the seller or lessor as the particular goods to pass under the contract. Suppose that a buyer orders one thousand cases of beans from a lot of ten thousand cases. Until the seller separates the one thousand cases of beans from the ten-thousand-case lot, title and risk of loss remain with the seller.

Future Goods If a sale or lease involves unborn animals to be born within twelve months after contracting, identification takes place when the animals are conceived. If a sale involves crops that are to be harvested within twelve months (or the next harvest season occurring after contracting, whichever is longer), identification takes place when the crops are planted; otherwise, identification takes place when the crops begin to grow. In a sale or lease of any other future goods, identification occurs when the goods are shipped, marked, or otherwise designated by the seller or lessor as the goods to which the contract refers.

When Title Passes

Once goods exist and are identified, the provisions of UCC 2–401 apply to the passage of title. Unless an agreement is explicitly made,[5] title passes to the buyer at the time and the place the seller performs the *physical delivery* of the goods [UCC 2–401(2)].

Shipment and Destination Contracts In the absence of agreement, delivery arrangements can determine when title passes from the seller to the buyer. In a **shipment contract,** the seller is required or authorized to ship goods by carrier, such as a trucking company. Under a shipment contract, the seller is required only to deliver the goods into the hands of a carrier, and title passes to the buyer at the time and place of shipment [UCC 2–401(2)(a)]. *Generally, all contracts are assumed to be shipment contracts if nothing to the contrary is stated in the contract.*

In a **destination contract,** the seller is required to deliver the goods to a particular destination, usually directly to the buyer, although sometimes the buyer designates that the goods should be delivered to another party. Title passes to the buyer when the goods are *tendered* at that destination [UCC 2–401(2)(b)]. A *tender of delivery* is the seller's placing or holding of conforming goods at the buyer's disposition (with any necessary notice), enabling the buyer to take delivery [UCC 2–503(1)].

Delivery without Movement of the Goods When the contract of sale does not call for the seller's shipment or delivery of the goods (when the buyer is to pick up the goods), the passage of title depends on whether the seller must deliver a *document of title,* such as a bill of lading or a warehouse receipt, to the buyer. A *bill of lading* is a receipt for goods that is signed by a carrier and that serves as a contract for the transportation of the goods. A *warehouse receipt* is a receipt issued by a warehouser for goods stored in a warehouse.

When a document of title is required, title passes to the buyer *when and where the document is delivered.* Thus, if the goods are stored in a warehouse, title passes to the buyer when the appropriate documents are delivered to the buyer. The goods never move. In fact, the buyer can choose to leave the goods at the same warehouse for a period of time, and the buyer's title to those goods will be unaffected.

When no documents of title are required, and delivery is made without moving the goods, title passes at

5. In many sections of the UCC, the words "unless otherwise explicitly agreed" appear, meaning that any explicit agreement between the buyer and the seller determines the rights, duties, and liabilities of the parties, including when title passes.

the time and place the sales contract is made, if the goods have already been identified. If the goods have not been identified, title does not pass until identification occurs. Consider an example. Rogers sells lumber to Bodan. It is agreed that Bodan will pick up the lumber at the yard. If the lumber has been identified (segregated, marked, or in any other way distinguished from all other lumber), title passes to Bodan when the contract is signed. If the lumber is still in general storage bins at the mill, title does not pass to Bodan until the particular pieces of lumber to be sold under this contract are identified [UCC 2–401(3)].

The Entrustment Rule According to UCC 2–403(2), entrusting goods to a merchant *who deals in goods of that kind* gives the merchant the power to transfer all rights to *a buyer in the ordinary course of business.* This is known as the *entrustment rule.* A buyer in the ordinary course of business is a person who—in good faith and without knowledge that the sale violates the rights of another party—buys goods in the ordinary course from a merchant (other than a pawnbroker) in the business of selling goods of that kind [UCC 1–201(9)].

In Sales Contracts. The entrustment rule basically allows innocent buyers to obtain title to goods purchased from merchants even if the merchants do not have good title. Consider an example. Jan leaves her watch with a jeweler to be repaired. The jeweler sells both new and used watches. The jeweler sells Jan's watch to Kim, a customer who does not know that the jeweler has no right to sell it. Kim, as a good faith buyer, gets good title against Jan's claim of ownership.[6]

Note, however, that Kim obtains only those rights held by the person entrusting the goods (here, Jan). Suppose instead that in this example, Jan had stolen the watch from Greg and then left it with the jeweler to be repaired. The jeweler then sold it to Kim. Kim would obtain good title against Jan, who entrusted the watch to the jeweler, but not against Greg (the real owner), who neither entrusted the watch to Jan nor authorized Jan to entrust it.

Red Elvis, an artwork by Andy Warhol, was at the center of the dispute over title in the following case.

6. Jan, of course, can sue the jeweler for the tort of conversion (or trespass to personal property) to obtain damages equivalent to the cash value of the watch (see Chapter 12).

CASE 11.2 Lindholm v. Brant

Supreme Court of Connecticut, 2007. 283 Conn. 65, 925 A.2d 1048.

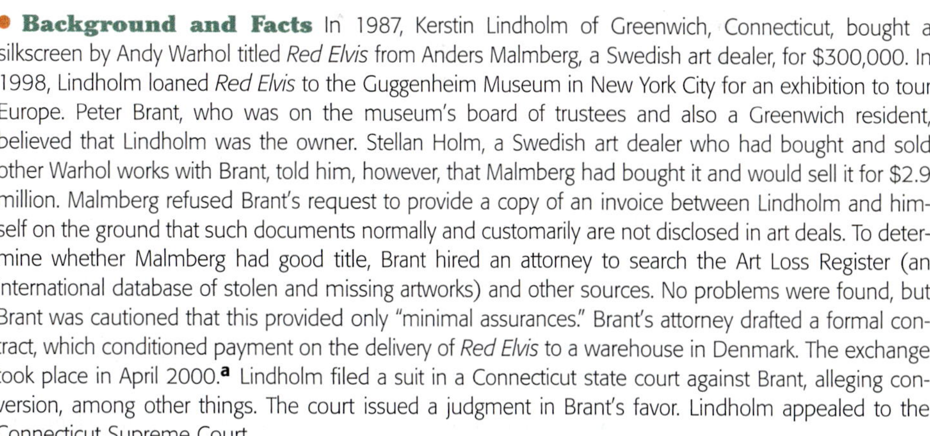

Background and Facts In 1987, Kerstin Lindholm of Greenwich, Connecticut, bought a silkscreen by Andy Warhol titled *Red Elvis* from Anders Malmberg, a Swedish art dealer, for $300,000. In 1998, Lindholm loaned *Red Elvis* to the Guggenheim Museum in New York City for an exhibition to tour Europe. Peter Brant, who was on the museum's board of trustees and also a Greenwich resident, believed that Lindholm was the owner. Stellan Holm, a Swedish art dealer who had bought and sold other Warhol works with Brant, told him, however, that Malmberg had bought it and would sell it for $2.9 million. Malmberg refused Brant's request to provide a copy of an invoice between Lindholm and himself on the ground that such documents normally and customarily are not disclosed in art deals. To determine whether Malmberg had good title, Brant hired an attorney to search the Art Loss Register (an international database of stolen and missing artworks) and other sources. No problems were found, but Brant was cautioned that this provided only "minimal assurances." Brant's attorney drafted a formal contract, which conditioned payment on the delivery of *Red Elvis* to a warehouse in Denmark. The exchange took place in April 2000.[a] Lindholm filed a suit in a Connecticut state court against Brant, alleging conversion, among other things. The court issued a judgment in Brant's favor. Lindholm appealed to the Connecticut Supreme Court.

IN THE LANGUAGE OF THE COURT

***SULLIVAN,* J. [Justice]**

* * * *

* * * "A person buys goods in the ordinary course if the sale to the person comports with the usual or customary practices in the kind of business in which the seller is engaged

a. Unaware of this deal, Lindholm accepted a Japanese buyer's offer of $4.6 million for *Red Elvis.* The funds were wired to Malmberg, who kept them. Lindholm filed a criminal complaint against Malmberg in Sweden. In 2003, a Swedish court convicted Malmberg of "gross fraud embezzlement." The court awarded Lindholm $4.6 million and other relief.

CASE CONTINUES

REVIEWING Sales, Leases, and E-Contracts, Continued

and GFI accepts the offer. Two months later, Egan has neither received the shipment nor heard anything further from GFI. Using the information presented in the chapter, answer the following questions.

1. Suppose that Egan refused to pay for the first shipment and sued GFI for breach of contract. Had GFI breached the contract? What would be GFI's best defense against this claim?
2. Assume that the second shipment of chips had not been destroyed in transit. In this situation, would GFI be in breach of contract because it only shipped 1,000 chips, not the contracted-for quantity (2,000 chips)?
3. With respect to the 1,000 chips that were destroyed in transit, which party must bear the loss? Why?
4. Regarding the final contract, does Egan have a right to ask GFI about its intentions to perform the contract? If so, does GFI have an obligation to respond? Explain.

TERMS AND CONCEPTS

browse-wrap term 280
click-on agreement 280
conforming goods 266
consignment 264
cover 269
cure 267
destination contract 260
e-contract 277
e-signature 280
express warranty 273
firm offer 255
forum-selection clause 279
identification 260
implied warranty 274
implied warranty of fitness for a particular purpose 276
implied warranty of merchantability 274
insurable interest 265
lease agreement 253
lessee 253
lessor 253
merchant 253
output contract 254
perfect tender rule 266
puffery 274
requirements contract 254
sale 253
sale on approval 265
sale or return 264
sales contract 252
seasonably 255
shipment contract 260
tangible property 253
tender of delivery 266

QUESTIONS AND CASE PROBLEMS

11-1. A. B. Zook, Inc., is a manufacturer of washing machines. Over the telephone, Zook offers to sell Radar Appliances one hundred model Z washers at a price of $150 per unit. Zook agrees to keep this offer open for ninety days. Radar tells Zook that the offer appears to be a good one and that it will let Zook know of its acceptance within the next two to three weeks. One week later, Zook sends, and Radar receives, notice that Zook has withdrawn its offer. Radar immediately thereafter telephones Zook and accepts the $150-per-unit offer. Zook claims, first, that no sales contract was ever formed between it and Radar and, second, that if there is a contract, the contract is unenforceable. Discuss Zook's contentions.

11-2. QUESTION WITH SAMPLE ANSWER

Anne is a reporter for *Daily Business Journal,* a print publication consulted by investors and other businesspersons. She often uses the Internet to conduct research for the articles that she writes for the publication. While visiting the Web site of Cyberspace Investments Corp., Anne reads a pop-up window that states, "Our business newsletter, *E-Commerce Weekly,* is available at a one-year subscription rate of $5 per issue. To subscribe, enter your e-mail address below and click 'SUBSCRIBE.' By subscribing, you agree to the terms of the subscriber's agreement. To read this agreement, click 'AGREEMENT.' " Anne enters her e-mail address, but does not click on "AGREEMENT" to read the terms. Has Anne entered into an enforceable contract to pay for *E-Commerce Weekly?* Explain.

- **For a sample answer to Question 11–2, go to Appendix I at the end of this text.**

11–3. On May 1, Sikora goes into Carson's retail clothing store to purchase a suit. Sikora finds a suit he likes for $190 and buys it. The suit needs alteration. Sikora is to pick up the altered suit at Carson's store on May 10. Consider the following separate sets of circumstances:

(a) One of Carson's major creditors obtains a judgment on the debt Carson owes and has the court issue a *writ of execution* (a court order to seize a debtor's property to satisfy a debt) to collect on that judgment all clothing in Carson's possession. Discuss Sikora's rights in the suit under these circumstances.

(b) On May 9, through no fault of Carson's, the store burns down, and all contents are a total loss. Between Carson and Sikora, who suffers the loss of the suit destroyed by fire? Explain.

11–4. McDonald has contracted to purchase five hundred pairs of shoes from Vetter. Vetter manufactures the shoes and tenders delivery to McDonald. McDonald accepts the shipment. Later, on inspection, McDonald discovers that ten pairs of the shoes are poorly made and will have to be sold to customers as seconds. If McDonald decides to keep all five hundred pairs of shoes, what remedies are available to her? Discuss.

11–5. Kirk has contracted to deliver to Doolittle one thousand cases of Wonder brand beans on or before October 1. Doolittle is to specify the means of transportation twenty days prior to the date of shipment. Payment for the beans is to be made by Doolittle on tender of delivery. On September 10, Kirk prepares the one thousand cases for shipment. Kirk asks Doolittle how he would like the goods to be shipped, but Doolittle does not respond. On September 21, Kirk, in writing, demands assurance that Doolittle will be able to pay on tender of the beans. Kirk asks that the money be placed in escrow prior to October 1 in a bank in Doolittle's city named by Kirk. Doolittle does not respond to any of Kirk's requests, but on October 5 he wants to file suit against Kirk for breach of contract for failure to deliver the beans as agreed. Discuss Kirk's liability for failure to tender delivery on October 1.

11–6. CASE PROBLEM WITH SAMPLE ANSWER

In 1998, Johnson Controls, Inc. (JCI), began buying auto parts from Q.C. Onics Ventures, LP. For each part, JCI would inform Onics of its need and ask the price. Onics would analyze the specifications, contact its suppliers, and respond with a formal quotation. A quote listed a part's number and description, the price per unit, and an estimate of units available for a given year. A quote did not state payment terms, an acceptance date, timing of performance, warranties, or quantities. JCI would select a supplier and issue a purchase order for a part. The purchase order required the seller to supply all of JCI's requirements for the part but gave the buyer the right to end the deal at any time. Using this procedure, JCI issued hundreds of purchase orders. In July 2001, JCI terminated its relationship with Onics and began buying parts through another supplier. Onics filed a suit in a federal district court against Johnson, alleging breach of contract. Which documents—the price quotations or the purchase orders—constituted offers? Which were acceptances? What effect would the answers to these questions have on the result in this case? Explain. [*Q.C. Onics Ventures, LP v. Johnson Controls, Inc.*, __ F.Supp.2d __ (N.D.Ind. 2006)]

- **To view a sample answer for Problem 11–6, go to this book's Web site at academic.cengage.com/blaw/cross, select "Chapter 11," and click on "Case Problem with Sample Answer."**

11–7. Shipment and Destination Contracts. In 2003, Karen Pearson and Steve and Tara Carlson agreed to buy a 2004 Dynasty recreational vehicle (RV) from DeMartini's RV Sales in Grass Valley, California. On September 29, Pearson, the Carlsons, and DeMartini's signed a contract providing that "seller agrees to deliver the vehicle to you on the date this contract is signed." The buyers made a payment of $145,000 on the total price of $356,416 the next day, when they also signed a form acknowledging that the RV had been inspected and accepted. They agreed to return later to have the RV transported out of state for delivery (to avoid paying state sales tax on the purchase). On October 7, Steve Carlson returned to DeMartini's to ride with the seller's driver to Nevada to consummate the out-of-state delivery. When the RV developed problems, Pearson and the Carlsons filed a suit in a federal district court against the RV's manufacturer, Monaco Coach Corp., alleging, in part, breach of warranty under state law. The applicable statute is expressly limited to goods sold in California. Monaco argued that this RV had been sold in Nevada. How does the Uniform Commercial Code (UCC) define a sale? What does the UCC provide with respect to the passage of title? How do these provisions apply here? Discuss. [*Carlson v. Monaco Coach Corp.*, 486 F.Supp.2d 1127 (E.D.Cal. 2007)]

11–8. Online Acceptances. Internet Archive (IA) is devoted to preserving a record of resources on the Internet for future generations. IA uses the "Wayback Machine" to automatically browse Web sites and reproduce their contents in an archive. IA does not ask the owners' permission before copying their material but will remove it on request. Suzanne Shell, a resident of Colorado, owns **www.profane-justice.org**, which is dedicated to providing information to individuals accused of child abuse or neglect. The site warns, "IF YOU COPY OR DISTRIBUTE ANYTHING ON THIS SITE YOU ARE ENTERING INTO A

CONTRACT." The terms, which can be accessed only by clicking on a link, include, among other charges, a fee of $5,000 for each page copied "in advance of printing." Neither the warning nor the terms require a user to indicate assent. When Shell discovered that the Wayback Machine had copied the contents of her site—approximately eighty-seven times between May 1999 and October 2004—she asked IA to remove the copies from its archive and pay her $100,000. IA removed the copies and filed a suit in a federal district court against Shell, who responded, in part, with a counterclaim for breach of contract. IA filed a motion to dismiss this claim. Did IA contract with Shell? Explain. [*Internet Archive v. Shell,* 505 F.Supp.2d 755 (D.Colo. 2007)]

11-9. Additional Provisions Affecting Remedies. Nomo Agroindustrial Sa De CV is a farm company based in Mexico that grows tomatoes, cucumbers, and other vegetables to sell in the United States. In the early 2000s, Nomo had problems when its tomato plants contracted a disease: tomato spotted wilt virus (TSWV). To obtain a crop that was resistant to TSWV, Nomo contacted Enza Zaden North America, Inc., an international corporation that manufactures seeds. Enza's brochures advertised—and Enza told Nomo—that its Caiman variety was resistant to TSWV. Based on these assurances, Nomo bought Caiman seeds. The invoice, which Nomo's representative signed, limited any damages to the purchase price of the seeds. The plants germinated from the Caiman seeds contracted TSWV, destroying Nomo's entire tomato crop. Nomo filed a suit in a federal district court against Enza, seeking to recover for the loss. Enza argued, in part, that any damages were limited to the price of the seeds. Can parties agree to limit their remedies under the UCC? If so, what are Nomo's best arguments against the enforcement of the limitations clause in Enza's invoice? What should the court rule on this issue? Why? [*Nomo Agroindustrial Sa De CV v. Enza Zaden North America, Inc.,* 492 F.Supp.2d 1175 (D.Ariz. 2007)]

11-10. SPECIAL CASE ANALYSIS

Go to Case 11.3, *Fitl v. Strek,* 269 Neb. 51, 690 N.W.2d 605 (2005), on pages 271 and 272. Read the excerpt and answer the following questions.

(a) **Issue:** What was the main issue in this case?
(b) **Rule of Law:** What rule of law did the court apply?
(c) **Applying the Rule of Law:** Describe how the court applied the rule of law to the facts of this case.
(d) **Conclusion:** What was the court's conclusion in this case?

11-11. A QUESTION OF ETHICS

*Scotwood Industries, Inc., sells calcium chloride flake for use in ice melt products. Between July and September 2004, Scotwood delivered thirty-seven shipments of flake to Frank Miller & Sons, Inc. After each delivery, Scotwood billed Miller, which paid thirty-five of the invoices and processed 30 to 50 percent of the flake. In August, Miller began complaining about the quality. Scotwood assured Miller that it would remedy the situation. Finally, in October, Miller told Scotwood, "[T]his is totally unacceptable. We are willing to discuss Scotwood picking up the material." Miller claimed that the flake was substantially defective because it was chunked. Calcium chloride maintains its purity for up to five years but chunks if it is exposed to and absorbs moisture, making it unusable. In response to Scotwood's suit to collect payment on the unpaid invoices, Miller filed a counterclaim in a federal district court for breach of contract, seeking to recover based on revocation of acceptance, among other things. [*Scotwood Industries, Inc. v. Frank Miller & Sons, Inc.,* *435 F.Supp.2d 1160 (D.Kan. 2006)]*

(a) What is revocation of acceptance? How does a buyer effectively exercise this option? Do the facts in this case support this theory as a ground for Miller to recover damages? Why or why not?
(b) Is there an ethical basis for allowing a buyer to revoke acceptance of goods and recover damages? If so, is there an ethical limit to this right? Discuss.

11-12. VIDEO QUESTION

Go to this text's Web site at **academic.cengage.com/blaw/cross** and select "Chapter 11." Click on "Video Questions" and view the video titled *E-Contracts: Agreeing Online.* Then answer the following questions.

(a) According to the instructor in the video, what is the key factor in determining whether a particular term in an online agreement is enforceable?
(b) Suppose that you click on "I accept" in order to download software from the Internet. You do not read the terms of the agreement before accepting it, even though you know that such agreements often contain forum-selection and arbitration clauses. The software later causes irreparable harm to your computer system, and you want to sue. When you go to the Web site and view the agreement, however, you discover that a choice-of-law clause in the contract specifies that the law of Nigeria controls. Is this term enforceable? Is it a term that should be reasonably expected in an online contract?
(c) Does it matter what the term actually says if it is a type of term that one could reasonably expect to be in the contract? What arguments can be made for and against enforcing a choice-of-law clause in an online contract?

LAW ON THE WEB

For updated links to resources available on the Web, as well as a variety of other materials, visit this text's Web site at

academic.cengage.com/blaw/cross

For information about the National Conference of Commissioners on Uniform State Laws (NCCUSL) and links to online uniform acts, go to

www.nccusl.org

For more information on shipment and destination contracts and a list of related commercial law Web links, go to

www.legalmatch.com/law-library/article/merchandise-risk-of-loss.html

Cornell University's Legal Information Institute offers online access to the UCC, as well as to UCC articles as enacted by particular states and proposed revisions to articles, at

www.law.cornell.edu/ucc/index.html

Legal Research Exercises on the Web

Go to **academic.cengage.com/blaw/cross**, the Web site that accompanies this text. Select "Chapter 11" and click on "Internet Exercises." There you will find the following Internet research exercises that you can perform to learn more about the topics covered in this chapter.

Internet Exercise 11–1: Legal Perspective
E-Contract Formation

Internet Exercise 11–2: Management Perspective
A Checklist for Sales Contracts

An Example of a Contract for the International Sale of Coffee

1 OVERLAND COFFEE IMPORT CONTRACT
OF THE
GREEN COFFEE ASSOCIATION
OF
NEW YORK CITY, INC.*

Contract Seller's No.: **504617**
Buyer's No.: **P9264**
Date: **10/11/09**

SOLD BY: **XYZ Co.**

TO: **Starbucks**

2 3 QUANTITY: **Five Hundred** (**500**) (Bags) Tons of **Mexican** coffee weighing about **152.117 lbs.** per bag.

4 PACKAGING: Coffee must be packed in clean sound bags of uniform size made of sisal, henequen, jute, burlap, or similar woven material, without inner lining or outer covering of any material properly sewn by hand and/or machine.
Bulk shipments are allowed if agreed by mutual consent of Buyer and Seller.

5 DESCRIPTION: **High grown Mexican Altura**

PRICE: At **Ten/$10.00 dollars** U.S. Currency, per **lb.** net, (U.S. Funds)
Upon delivery in Bonded Public Warehouse at **Laredo, TX** (City and State)

6 PAYMENT: **Cash against warehouse receipts**

Bill and tender to DATE when all import requirements and governmental regulations have been satisfied, and coffee delivered or discharged (as per contract terms). Seller is obliged to give the Buyer two (2) calendar days free time in Bonded Public Warehouse following but not including date of tender.

7 ARRIVAL: During **December** (Period) via **truck** (Method of Transportation)
from **Mexico** (Country of Exportation) for arrival at **Laredo, TX, USA** (Country of Importation)
Partial shipments permitted.

8 ADVICE OF ARRIVAL: Advice of arrival with warehouse name and location, together with the quantity, description, marks and place of entry, must be transmitted directly, or through Seller's Agent/Broker, to the Buyer or his Agent/Broker. Advice will be given as soon as known but not later than the fifth business day following arrival at the named warehouse. Such advice may be given verbally with written confirmation to be sent the same day.

9 WEIGHTS: (1) DELIVERED WEIGHTS: Coffee covered by this contract is to be weighed at location named in tender. Actual tare to be allowed.
(2) SHIPPING WEIGHTS: Coffee covered by this contract is sold on shipping weights. Any loss in weight exceeding **1/2** percent at location named in tender is for account of Seller at contract price.
(3) Coffee is to be weighed within fifteen (15) calendar days after tender. Weighing expenses, if any, for account of **Seller** (Seller or Buyer)

10 MARKINGS: Bags to be branded in English with the name of Country of Origin and otherwise to comply with laws and regulations of the Country of Importation, in effect at the time of entry, governing marking of import merchandise. Any expense incurred by failure to comply with these regulations to be borne by Exporter/Seller.

11 RULINGS: The "Rulings on Coffee Contracts" of the Green Coffee Association of New York City, Inc., in effect on the date this contract is made, is incorporated for all purposes as a part of this agreement, and together herewith, constitute the entire contract. No variation or addition hereto shall be valid unless signed by the parties to the contract.
Seller guarantees that the terms printed on the reverse hereof, which by reference are made a part hereof, are identical with the terms as printed in By-Laws and Rules of the Green Coffee Association of New York City, Inc., heretofore adopted.
Exceptions to this guarantee are:

12 ACCEPTED: **XYZ Co.** Seller
BY DM Agent

COMMISSION TO BE PAID BY: **Seller**

Starbucks Buyer
BY ________ Agent

ABC Brokerage Broker(s)

13 When this contract is executed by a person acting for another, such person hereby represents that he is fully authorized to commit his principal.

* Reprinted with permission of The Green Coffee Association of New York City, Inc.

1 This is a contract for a sale of coffee to be *imported* internationally. If the parties have their principal places of business located in different countries, the contract may be subject to the United Nations Convention on Contracts for the International Sale of Goods (CISG). If the parties' principal places of business are located in the United States, the contract may be subject to the Uniform Commercial Code (UCC).

2 Quantity is one of the most important terms to include in a contract. Without it, a court may not be able to enforce the contract. See Chapter 11.

3 Weight per unit (bag) can be exactly stated or approximately stated. If it is not so stated, usage of trade in international contracts determines standards of weight.

4 Packaging requirements can be conditions for acceptance and payment. See Chapter 10. Bulk shipments are not permitted without the consent of the buyer.

5 A description of the coffee and the "Markings" constitute express warranties. Warranties in contracts for domestic sales of goods are discussed generally in Chapter 11. International contracts rely more heavily on descriptions and models or samples.

6 Under the UCC, parties may enter into a valid contract even though the price is not set. See Chapter 11. Under the CISG, a contract must provide for an exact determination of the price.

7 The terms of payment may take one of two forms: credit or cash. Credit terms can be complicated. A cash term can be simple, and payment can be made by any means acceptable in the ordinary course of business (for example, a personal check or a letter of credit). If the seller insists on actual cash, the buyer must be given a reasonable time to get it. See Chapter 11.

8 *Tender* means the seller has placed goods that conform to the contract at the buyer's disposition. What constitutes a valid tender is explained in Chapter 11. This contract requires that the coffee meet all import regulations and that it be ready for pickup by the buyer at a "Bonded Public Warehouse." (A *bonded warehouse* is a place in which goods can be stored without paying taxes until the goods are removed.)

9 The delivery date is significant because, if it is not met, the buyer may hold the seller in breach of the contract. Under this contract, the seller can be given a "period" within which to deliver the goods, instead of a specific day, which could otherwise present problems. The seller is also given some time to rectify goods that do not pass inspection (see the "Guarantee" clause on page two of the contract). For a discussion of the remedies of the buyer and seller, see Chapter 11.

10 As part of a proper tender, the seller (or its agent) must inform the buyer (or its agent) when the goods have arrived at their destination. The responsibilities of agents are set out in Chapter 19.

11 In some contracts, delivered and shipped weights can be important. During shipping, some loss can be attributed to the type of goods (spoilage of fresh produce, for example) or to the transportation itself. A seller and buyer can agree on the extent to which either of them will bear such losses. See Chapter 11 for a discussion of the liability of common carriers for loss during shipment.

12 Documents are often incorporated in a contract by reference, because including them word for word can make a contract difficult to read. If the document is later revised, the entire contract might have to be reworked. Documents that are typically incorporated by reference include detailed payment and delivery terms; special provisions; and sets of rules, codes, and standards.

13 In international sales transactions, and for domestic deals involving certain products, brokers are used to form the contracts. When so used, the brokers are entitled to a commission. See Chapter 19.

(Continued)

TERMS AND CONDITIONS

14 **ARBITRATION:** All controversies relating to, in connection with, or arising out of this contract, its modification, making or the authority or obligations of the signatories hereto, and whether involving the principals, agents, brokers, or others who actually subscribe hereto, shall be settled by arbitration in accordance with the "Rules of Arbitration" of the Green Coffee Association of New York City, Inc., as they exist at the time of the arbitration (including provisions as to payment of fees and expenses). Arbitration is the sole remedy hereunder, and it shall be held in accordance with the law of New York State, and judgment of any award may be entered in the courts of that State, or in any other court of competent jurisdiction. All notices or judicial service in reference to arbitration or enforcement shall be deemed given if transmitted as required by the aforesaid rules.

15 **GUARANTEE:** (a) If all or any of the coffee is refused admission into the country of importation by reason of any violation of governmental laws or acts, which violation existed at the time the coffee arrived at Bonded-Public Warehouse, seller is required, as to the amount not admitted and as soon as possible, to deliver replacement coffee in conformity to all terms and conditions of this contract, excepting only the Arrival terms, but not later than thirty (30) days after the date of the violation notice. Any payment made and expenses incurred for any coffee denied entry shall be refunded within ten (10) calendar days of denial of entry, and payment shall be made for the replacement delivery in accordance with the terms of this contract. Consequently, if Buyer removes the coffee from the Bonded Public Warehouse, Seller's responsibility as to such portion hereunder ceases.

(b) Contracts containing the overstamp "No Pass-No Sale" on the face of the contract shall be interpreted to mean: If any or all of the coffee is not admitted into the country of Importation in its original condition by reason of failure to meet requirements of the government's laws or Acts, the contract shall be deemed null and void as to that portion of the coffee which is not admitted in its original condition. Any payment made and expenses incurred for any coffee denied entry shall be refunded within ten (10) calendar days of denial of entry.

16

CONTINGENCY: This contract is not contingent upon any other contract.

CLAIMS: Coffee shall be considered accepted as to quality unless within *fifteen* (15) calendar days after delivery at Bonded Public Warehouse or within *fifteen* (15) calendar days after all Government clearances have been received, whichever is later, either:

(a) Claims are settled by the parties hereto, or,

(b) Arbitration proceedings have been filed by one of the parties in accordance with the provisions hereof.

17 (c) If neither (a) nor (b) has been done in the stated period or if any portion of the coffee has been removed from the Bonded Public Warehouse before representative sealed samples have been drawn by the Green Coffee Association of New York City, Inc., in accordance with its rules, Seller's responsibility for quality claims ceases for that portion so removed.

(d) Any question of quality submitted to arbitration shall be a matter of allowance only, unless otherwise provided in the contract.

18

DELIVERY: (a) No more than three (3) chops may be tendered for each lot of 250 bags.

(b) Each chop of coffee tendered is to be uniform in grade and appearance. All expense necessary to make coffee uniform shall be for account of seller.

(c) Notice of arrival and/or sampling order constitutes a tender, and must be given not later than the fifth business day following arrival at Bonded Public Warehouse stated on the contract.

INSURANCE: Seller is responsible for any loss or damage, or both, until Delivery and Discharge of coffee at the Bonded Public Warehouse in the Country of Importation.

All Insurance Risks, costs and responsibility are for Seller's Account until Delivery and Discharge of coffee at the Bonded Public Warehouse in the Country of Importation.

19

Buyer's insurance responsibility begins from the day of importation or from the day of tender, whichever is later.

20

FREIGHT: Seller to provide and pay for all transportation and related expenses to the Bonded Public Warehouse in the Country of Importation.

EXPORT DUTIES/TAXES: Exporter is to pay all Export taxes, duties or other fees or charges, if any, levied because of exportation.

21

IMPORT DUTIES/TAXES: Any Duty or Tax whatsoever, imposed by the government or any authority of the Country of Importation, shall be borne by the Importer/Buyer.

INSOLVENCY OR FINANCIAL FAILURE OF BUYER OR SELLER: If, at any time before the contract is fully executed, either party hereto shall meet with creditors because of inability generally to make payment of obligations when due, or shall suspend such payments, fail to meet his general trade obligations in the regular course of business, shall file a petition in bankruptcy or, for an arrangement, shall become insolvent, or commit an act of bankruptcy, then the other party may at his option, expressed in writing, declare the aforesaid to constitute a breach and default of this contract, and may, in addition to other remedies, decline to deliver further or make payment or may sell or purchase for the defaulter's account, and may collect damage for any injury or loss, or shall account for the profit, if any, occasioned by such sale or purchase.

22

This clause is subject to the provisions of (11 USC 365 (e) 1) if invoked.

BREACH OR DEFAULT OF CONTRACT: In the event either party hereto fails to perform, or breaches or repudiates this agreement, the other party shall subject to the specific provisions of this contract be entitled to the remedies and relief provided for by the Uniform Commercial Code of the State of New York. The computation and ascertainment of damages, or the determination of any other dispute as to relief, shall be made by the arbitrators in accordance with the Arbitration Clause herein.

23

Consequential damages shall not, however, be allowed.

14 Arbitration is the settling of a dispute by submitting it to a disinterested party (other than a court) that renders a decision. The procedures and costs can be provided for in an arbitration clause or incorporated through other documents. To enforce an award rendered in an arbitration, the winning party can "enter" (submit) the award in a court "of competent jurisdiction." For a general discussion of arbitration and other forms of dispute resolution (other than courts), see Chapter 3.

15 When goods are imported internationally, they must meet certain import requirements before being released to the buyer. Because of this, buyers frequently want a guaranty clause that covers the goods not admitted into the country and that either requires the seller to replace the goods within a stated time or allows the contract for those goods not admitted to be void. See Chapter 10.

16 In the "Claims" clause, the parties agree that the buyer has a certain time within which to reject the goods. The right to reject is a right by law and does not need to be stated in a contract. If the buyer does not exercise the right within the time specified in the contract, the goods will be considered accepted. See Chapter 11.

17 Many international contracts include definitions of terms so that the parties understand what they mean. Some terms are used in a particular industry in a specific way. Here, the word *chop* refers to a unit of like-grade coffee bean. The buyer has a right to inspect ("sample") the coffee. If the coffee does not conform to the contract, the seller must correct the nonconformity. See Chapter 11.

18 The "Delivery," "Insurance," and "Freight" clauses, with the "Arrival" clause on page one of the contract, indicate that this is a destination contract. The seller has the obligation to deliver the goods to the destination, not simply deliver them into the hands of a carrier. Under this contract, the destination is a "Bonded Public Warehouse" in a specific location. The seller bears the risk of loss until the goods are delivered at their destination. Typically, the seller will have bought insurance to cover the risk. See Chapter 11 for a discussion of delivery terms and the risk of loss.

19 Delivery terms are commonly placed in all sales contracts. Such terms determine who pays freight and other costs and, in the absence of an agreement specifying otherwise, who bears the risk of loss. International contracts may use these delivery terms or they may use INCOTERMS, which are published by the International Chamber of Commerce. For example, the INCOTERM DDP (delivered duty paid) requires the seller to arrange shipment, obtain and pay for import or export permits, and get the goods through customs to a named destination.

20 Exported and imported goods are subject to duties, taxes, and other charges imposed by the governments of the countries involved. International contracts spell out who is responsible for these charges.

21 This clause protects a party if the other party should become financially unable to fulfill the obligations under the contract. Thus, if the seller cannot afford to deliver, or the buyer cannot afford to pay, for the stated reasons, the other party can consider the contract breached. This right is subject to "11 USC 365(e)(1)," which refers to a specific provision of the U.S. Bankruptcy Code dealing with executory contracts. Bankruptcy provisions are covered in Chapter 15.

22 In the "Breach or Default of Contract" clause, the parties agreed that the remedies under this contract are the remedies (except for consequential damages) provided by the UCC, as in effect in the state of New York. The amount and "ascertainment" of damages, as well as other disputes about relief, are to be determined by arbitration. Breach of contract and contractual remedies in general are explained in Chapter 11. Arbitration is discussed in Chapter 3.

23 Three clauses frequently included in international contracts are omitted here. There is no choice-of-language clause designating the official language to be used in interpreting the contract terms. There is no choice-of-forum clause designating the place in which disputes will be litigated, except for arbitration (law of New York State). Finally, there is no *force majeure* clause relieving the sellers or buyers from nonperformance due to events beyond their control.

CONTEMPORARY LEGAL DEBATES

Tort Reform

The question of whether our tort law system is in need of reform has aroused heated debate. While some argue that the current system imposes excessive costs on society, others contend that the system protects consumers from unsafe products and practices.

"End the Tort Tax and Frivolous Lawsuits," Say the Critics

Critics of the current tort law system contend that it encourages too many frivolous lawsuits, which clog the courts, and is unnecessarily costly. In particular, they say, damages awards are often excessive and bear little relationship to the actual damage suffered. Such large awards encourage plaintiffs to bring frivolous suits, hoping that they will "hit the jackpot." Trial lawyers, in turn, are eager to bring the suits because they are paid on a contingency-fee basis, meaning that they receive a percentage of the damages awarded.

The result, in the critics' view, is a system that disproportionately rewards a few lucky plaintiffs while imposing enormous costs on business and society as a whole. They refer to the economic burden that the tort system imposes on society as the "tort tax." According to one recent study, more than $300 billion per year is expended on tort litigation, including plaintiffs' and defendants' attorneys' fees, damages awards, and other costs. Most of the costs are from class-action lawsuits involving product liability or medical malpractice.[a] (A *class action* is a lawsuit in which a single person or a small group of people represents the interests of a larger group.) Although even the critics would not contend that the tort tax encompasses the entire $300 billion, they believe that it includes a sizable portion of that amount. Furthermore, they say, the tax appears in other ways. Because physicians, hospitals, and pharmaceutical companies are worried about medical malpractice suits, they have changed their behavior. Physicians, for example, engage in defensive medicine by ordering more tests than necessary. PricewaterhouseCoopers has calculated that the practice of defensive medicine increases health-care costs by more than $100 billion per year.

To solve the problems they perceive, critics want to reduce both the number of tort cases brought each year and the amount of damages awards. They advocate the following tort reform measures: (1) limit the amount of punitive damages that can be awarded; (2) limit the amount of general noneconomic damages that can be awarded (for example, for pain and suffering); (3) limit the amount that attorneys can collect in contingency fees; and (4) to discourage the filing of meritless suits, require the losing party to pay both the plaintiff's and the defendant's expenses.

"The Current System Promotes Fairness and Safefy," Say Their Opponents

Others are not so sure that the current system needs such drastic reform. They say that the prospect of tort lawsuits encourages companies to produce safer products and deters them from putting dangerous products on the market. In the health-care industry,

a. Lawrence J. McQuillan, Hovannes Abramyan, and Anthony P. Archie, *Jackpot Justice: The True Cost of America's Tort System* (San Francisco: Pacific Research Institute, 2007).

determined by the *reasonable person standard.*[2] The contact can be made by the defendant or by some force the defendant sets in motion—for example, a rock thrown, food poisoned, or a stick swung.

Compensation If the plaintiff shows that there was contact, and the jury (or judge, if there is no jury) agrees that the contact was offensive, then the plaintiff has a right to compensation. There is no need to establish that the defendant acted out of malice. The underlying motive does not matter, only the intent to bring about the harmful or offensive contact to the plaintiff. In fact, proving a motive is never necessary. A plaintiff may be compensated for the emotional harm or loss of reputation resulting from a battery, as well as for physical harm.

Defenses to Assault and Battery A defendant who is sued for assault, battery, or both can raise any of the following legally recognized defenses:

2. The *reasonable person standard* is an "objective" test of how a reasonable person would have acted under the same circumstances. See the subsection entitled "The Duty of Care and Its Breach" later in this chapter on page 305.

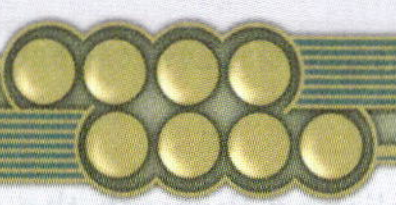

the potential for medical malpractice suits has led to safer and more effective medical practices.

Imposing limits on the amount of punitive and general noneconomic damages would be unfair, say the system's defenders, and would reduce efficiency in our legal and economic system. After all, corporations conduct cost-benefit analyses when they decide how much safety to build into their products. Any limitation on potential damages would mean that corporations would have less incentive to build safer products. Indeed, Professor Stephen Teret of the Johns Hopkins University School of Public Health says that tort litigation is an important tool for preventing injuries because it forces manufacturers to opt for more safety in their products rather than less.[b] Limiting contingency fees would also be unfair, say those in favor of the current system, because low-income consumers who have been injured could not afford to pay an attorney to take a case on an hourly fee basis—and an attorney would not expend the time needed to pursue a case without the prospect of a large reward in the form of a contingency fee.

Tort Reform in Reality

While the debate continues, the federal government and a number of states have begun to take some steps toward tort reform. At the federal level, the Class Action Fairness Act (CAFA) of 2005[c] shifted jurisdiction over large interstate tort and product liability class-action lawsuits from the state courts to the federal courts. The intent was to prevent plaintiffs' attorneys from shopping around for a state court that might be predisposed to be sympathetic to their clients' cause and to award large damages in class-action suits.

At the state level, more than twenty states have placed caps ranging from $250,000 to $750,000 on noneconomic damages, especially in medical malpractice suits. More than thirty states have limited punitive damages, with some imposing outright bans.

WHERE DO YOU STAND?

Large damages awards in tort litigation have to be paid by someone. If the defendant is insured, then insurance companies foot the bill. Ultimately, though, high insurance rates are passed on to consumers of goods and services in the United States. Consequently, tort reform that reduces the size and number of damages awards ultimately will mean lower costs of goods and services to consumers. The downside of these lower costs, though, might be higher risks of medical malpractice and dangerous products. Do you believe that this trade-off is real? Why or why not?

b. "Litigation Is an Important Tool for Injury and Gun Violence Prevention," Johns Hopkins University Center for Gun Policy and Research, July 15, 2006.

c. 28 U.S.C.A. Sections 1711–1715, 1453.

1. *Consent.* When a person consents to the act that is allegedly tortious, there may be a complete or partial defense to liability.
2. *Self-defense.* An individual who is defending her or his life or physical well-being can claim self-defense. In a situation of either *real* or *apparent* danger, a person may normally use whatever force is *reasonably* necessary to prevent harmful contact (see Chapter 7 for a more detailed discussion of self-defense).
3. *Defense of others.* An individual can act in a reasonable manner to protect others who are in real or apparent danger.
4. *Defense of property.* Reasonable force may be used in attempting to remove intruders from one's home, although force that is likely to cause death or great bodily injury normally cannot be used just to protect property.

False Imprisonment

False imprisonment is defined as the intentional confinement or restraint of another person's activities without justification. It involves interference with the freedom to move without restriction. The confinement

CASE 12.2 CONTINUED *defraud, i.e., to induce reliance; (d) justifiable reliance; and (e) resulting damage.*" Claims for negligent misrepresentation deviate from this set of elements. "*The tort of negligent misrepresentation does not require* scienter *or intent to defraud.* It encompasses '[t]he assertion, as a fact, of that which is not true, by one who has no reasonable ground for believing it to be true', and '[t]he positive assertion, in a manner not warranted by the information of the person making it, of that which is not true, though he believes it to be true.'" [Emphasis added.]

* * * *

It is well established that the kind of disclaimer in Paragraph 2.4 [of the commercial lease], which asserts that McClain had an adequate opportunity to examine the leased unit, does not insulate Octagon from liability for fraud or prevent McClain from demonstrating justified reliance on the Charanians' representations.

* * * *

Here, McClain alleges that the Charanians exaggerated the size of her unit by 186 square feet, or 7.6 percent of its actual size, and increased her share of the common expenses by 4 percent through a calculation that understated the size of the shopping center by 965 square feet, or 8.1 percent of its actual size. [These discrepancies] operated to increase the rental payments incurred by McClain's retail business by more than $90,000 over the term of the lease.

• **Decision and Remedy** *The Court of Appeal of the State of California, Second Appellate District, reversed the trial court's judgment with respect to McClain's claim for misrepresentation.*

• **The Ethical Dimension** *At what point do the misrepresentations about the size of the leased space become unethical—at 1 percent, 2 percent, or more?*

• **The Legal Environment Dimension** *What defense could the shopping center owners raise to counter McClain's claim?*

Abusive or Frivolous Litigation

Persons or businesses generally have a right to sue when they have been injured. In recent years, however, an increasing number of meritless lawsuits have been filed—sometimes simply to harass the defendant. Defending oneself in any legal proceeding can be costly, time consuming, and emotionally draining. Tort law recognizes that people have a right not to be sued without a legally just and proper reason. It therefore protects individuals from the misuse of litigation. Torts related to abusive litigation include malicious prosecution and abuse of process.

If the party that initiated a lawsuit did so out of malice and without probable cause (a legitimate legal reason), and ended up losing that suit, the party can be sued for *malicious prosecution*. In some states, the plaintiff (who was the defendant in the first proceeding) must also prove injury other than the normal costs of litigation, such as lost profits. *Abuse of process* can apply to any person using a legal process against another in an improper manner or to accomplish a purpose for which the process was not designed. The key difference between the torts of abuse of process and malicious prosecution is the level of proof. Abuse of process does not require the plaintiff to prove malice or show that the defendant (who was previously the plaintiff) lost in a prior legal proceeding.[12] Abuse of process is also not limited to prior litigation. It can be based on the wrongful use of subpoenas, court orders to attach or seize real property, or other types of formal legal process. *Concept Summary 12.1* reviews intentional torts against persons.

Business Torts

Most torts can occur in any context, but a few torts, referred to as **business torts,** apply only to wrongful interferences with the business rights of others. Business torts generally fall into two categories—interference with a contractual relationship and interference with a business relationship.

12. *Bernhard-Thomas Building Systems, LLC v. Duncan*, 918 A.2d 889 (Conn.App. 2007); and *Hewitt v. Rice*, 154 P.3d 408 (Colo. 2007).

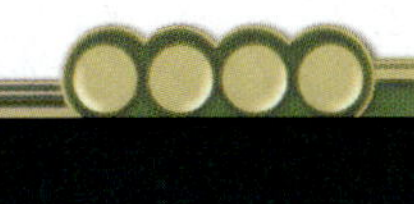

CONCEPT SUMMARY 12.1
Intentional Torts against Persons

Name of Tort	Description
ASSAULT AND BATTERY	Any unexcused and intentional act that causes another person to be apprehensive of immediate harm is an assault. An assault resulting in physical contact is battery.
FALSE IMPRISONMENT	An intentional confinement or restraint of another person's movement without justification.
INTENTIONAL INFLICTION OF EMOTIONAL DISTRESS	An intentional act that amounts to extreme and outrageous conduct resulting in severe emotional distress to another.
DEFAMATION (LIBEL OR SLANDER)	A false statement of fact, not made under privilege, that is communicated to a third person and that causes damage to a person's reputation. For public figures, the plaintiff must also prove that the statement was made with actual malice.
INVASION OF PRIVACY	Publishing or otherwise making known or using information relating to a person's private life and affairs, with which the public has no legitimate concern, without that person's permission or approval.
APPROPRIATION	The use of another person's name, likeness, or other identifying characteristic without permission and for the benefit of the user.
FRAUDULENT MISREPRESENTATION (FRAUD)	A false representation made by one party, through misstatement of facts or through conduct, with the intention of deceiving another and on which the other reasonably relies to his or her detriment.
ABUSIVE LITIGATION	The filing of a lawsuit without legitimate grounds and with malice or the use of a legal process in an improper manner.

Wrongful Interference with a Contractual Relationship

The body of tort law relating to *wrongful interference with a contractual relationship* has increased greatly in recent years. A landmark case in this area involved an opera singer, Joanna Wagner, who was under contract to sing for a man named Lumley for a specified period of years. A man named Gye, who knew of this contract, nonetheless "enticed" Wagner to refuse to carry out the agreement, and Wagner began to sing for Gye. Gye's action constituted a tort because it interfered with the contractual relationship between Wagner and Lumley. (Of course, Wagner's refusal to carry out the agreement also entitled Lumley to sue Wagner for breach of contract.)[13]

Three elements are necessary for wrongful interference with a contractual relationship to occur:

1. A valid, enforceable contract must exist between two parties.
2. A third party must know that this contract exists.
3. This third party must *intentionally induce* a party to the contract to breach the contract.

In principle, any lawful contract can be the basis for an action of this type. The contract could be between a firm and its employees or a firm and its customers. Sometimes, a competitor of a firm draws away one of the firm's key employees. Only if the original employer can show that the competitor knew of the contract's existence, and intentionally induced the breach, can damages be recovered from the competitor.

Wrongful Interference with a Business Relationship

Businesspersons devise countless schemes to attract customers, but they are prohibited from unreasonably interfering with another's business in their attempts to gain a greater share of the market. There is a difference between *competitive practices* and *predatory behavior*—actions undertaken with the intention of unlawfully driving competitors completely out of the market.

13. *Lumley v. Gye,* 118 Eng.Rep. 749 (1853).

Attempting to attract customers in general is a legitimate business practice, whereas specifically targeting the customers of a competitor is more likely to be predatory. For example, the mall contains two athletic shoe stores: Joe's and Sprint. Joe's cannot station an employee at the entrance of Sprint to divert customers to Joe's and tell them that Joe's will beat Sprint's prices. Doing this would constitute the tort of wrongful interference with a business relationship because it would interfere with a prospective (economic) advantage; such behavior is commonly considered to be an unfair trade practice. If this type of activity were permitted, Joe's would reap the benefits of Sprint's advertising.

Although state laws vary on wrongful interference with a business relationship, generally a plaintiff must prove that the defendant used predatory methods to intentionally harm an established business relationship or prospective economic advantage. The plaintiff must also prove that the defendant's interference caused the plaintiff to suffer economic harm.

Defenses to Wrongful Interference

A person will not be liable for the tort of wrongful interference with a contractual or business relationship if it can be shown that the interference was justified, or permissible. Bona fide competitive behavior is a permissible interference even if it results in the breaking of a contract.

For example, if Jerrod's Meats advertises so effectively that it induces Sam's Restaurant to break its contract with Burke's Meat Company, Burke's Meat Company will be unable to recover against Jerrod's Meats on a wrongful interference theory. After all, the public policy that favors free competition through advertising outweighs any possible instability that such competitive activity might cause in contractual relations. Although luring customers away from a competitor through aggressive marketing and advertising strategies obviously interferes with the competitor's relationship with its customers, courts typically allow such activities in the spirit of competition.

Intentional Torts against Property

Intentional torts against property include trespass to land, trespass to personal property, conversion, and disparagement of property. These torts are wrongful actions that interfere with individuals' legally recognized rights with regard to their land or personal property. The law distinguishes real property from personal property (see Chapter 25). *Real property* is land and things permanently attached to the land. *Personal property* consists of all other items, which are basically movable. Thus, a house and lot are real property, whereas the furniture inside a house is personal property. Cash and securities are also personal property.

Trespass to Land

The tort of **trespass to land** occurs any time a person, without permission, enters onto, above, or below the surface of land that is owned by another; causes anything to enter onto the land; or remains on the land or permits anything to remain on it. Actual harm to the land is not an essential element of this tort because the tort is designed to protect the right of an owner to exclusive possession. Common types of trespass to land include walking or driving on another's land; shooting a gun over another's land; throwing rocks at or spraying water on a building that belongs to someone else; building a dam across a river, thereby causing water to back up on someone else's land; and constructing one's building so that it extends onto an adjoining landowner's property.

Trespass Criteria, Rights, and Duties

Before a person can be a trespasser, the real property owner (or other person in actual and exclusive possession of the property, such as a person who is leasing the property) must establish that person as a trespasser. For example, "posted" trespass signs expressly establish as a trespasser a person who ignores these signs and enters onto the property. Any person who enters onto another's property to commit an illegal act (such as a thief entering a lumberyard at night to steal lumber) is established impliedly as a trespasser, without posted signs.

At common law, a trespasser is liable for damages caused to the property and generally cannot hold the owner liable for injuries that the trespasser sustains on the premises. This common law rule is being abandoned in many jurisdictions, however, in favor of a "reasonable duty" rule that varies depending on the status of the parties. For example, a landowner may have a duty to post a notice that the property is patrolled by guard dogs. Also, under the "attractive nuisance" doctrine, a landowner may be held liable for injuries sustained by young children on the landowner's property if the children were attracted to the premises by some object, such as a swimming pool or an abandoned building. Finally, an owner can remove a trespasser from the premises—or detain a trespasser on the premises for a reasonable time—through the use of reasonable force without being liable for assault, battery, or false imprisonment.

Defenses against Trespass to Land Trespass to land involves wrongful interference with another person's real property rights. If it can be shown that the trespass was warranted, however, as when a trespasser enters to assist someone in danger, a defense exists. Another defense exists when the trespasser can show that he or she had a license to come onto the land. A *licensee* is one who is invited (or allowed to enter) onto the property of another for the licensee's benefit. A person who enters another's property to read an electric meter, for example, is a licensee. When you purchase a ticket to attend a movie or sporting event, you are licensed to go onto the property of another to view that movie or event. Note that licenses to enter onto another's property are *revocable* by the property owner. If a property owner asks a meter reader to leave and the meter reader refuses to do so, the meter reader at that point becomes a trespasser.

Trespass to Personal Property

Whenever any individual, without consent, takes or harms the personal property of another or otherwise interferes with the lawful owner's possession and enjoyment of personal property, **trespass to personal property** occurs. This tort may also be called *trespass to chattels* or *trespass to personalty.* In this context, harm means not only destruction of the property, but also anything that diminishes its value, condition, or quality. Trespass to personal property involves intentional meddling with a possessory interest (an interest arising from possession), including barring an owner's access to personal property. If Kelly takes Ryan's business law book as a practical joke and hides it so that Ryan is unable to find it for several days prior to the final examination, Kelly has engaged in a trespass to personal property.

If it can be shown that trespass to personal property was warranted, then a complete defense exists. Most states, for example, allow automobile repair shops to hold a customer's car (under what is called an *artisan's lien,* discussed in Chapter 15) when the customer refuses to pay for repairs already completed.

Conversion

Whenever a person wrongfully possesses or uses the personal property of another as if the property belonged to her or him, the tort of **conversion** occurs. Any act that deprives an owner of personal property of the use of that property without that owner's permission and without just cause can be conversion. Often, when conversion occurs, a trespass to personal property also occurs because the original taking of the personal property from the owner was a trespass, and wrongfully retaining it is conversion. Conversion requires a more serious interference with the personal property than trespass, in terms of the duration and extensiveness of use.

Conversion is the civil side of crimes related to theft, but it is not limited to theft. Even when the rightful owner consented to the initial taking of the property so there was no theft or trespass, a failure to return the personal property may still be conversion. For example, Chen borrows Marik's iPod to use while traveling home from school for the holidays. When Chen returns to school, Marik asks for his iPod back, but Chen says that he gave it to his little brother for Christmas. In this situation, Marik can sue Chen for conversion, and Chen will have to either return the iPod or pay damages equal to its value.

Similarly, even if a person mistakenly believed that she or he was entitled to the goods, a tort of conversion may still have occurred. In other words, good intentions are not a defense against conversion; in fact, conversion can be an entirely innocent act. Someone who buys stolen goods, for example, has committed the tort of conversion even if he or she did not know the goods were stolen. Note that even the taking of electronic records and data may form the basis of a common law conversion claim.[14] So can the wrongful taking of a domain name or the misappropriation of a net tax loss that harms a company.[15] Thus, the personal property need not be tangible (physical) property.

Disparagement of Property

Disparagement of property occurs when economically injurious falsehoods are made about another's product or property rather than about another's reputation (as in the tort of defamation). *Disparagement of property* is a general term for torts that can be more specifically referred to as *slander of quality* or *slander of title.*

---

14. See *Thyroff v. Nationwide Mutual Insurance Co.,* 8 N.Y.3d 283, 864 N.E.2d 1272 (2007).

15. See *Kremen v. Cohen,* 325 F.3d 1035 (9th Cir. 2003); and *Fremont Indemnity Co. v. Fremont General Corp.,* 148 Cal.App.4th 97, 55 Cal.Rptr.3d 621 (2d Dist. 2007).

CHAPTER 13

Strict Liability and Product Liability

The intentional torts and torts of negligence discussed in Chapter 12 involve acts that depart from a reasonable standard of care and cause injuries. In this chapter, we look at another category of tort—**strict liability,** or *liability without fault.* Under the doctrine of strict liability, a person who engages in certain activities can be held responsible for any harm that results to others even if the person used the utmost care.

We open this chapter with an examination of this doctrine. We then look at an area of tort law of particular importance to businesspersons—product liability. **Product liability** refers to the liability incurred by manufacturers and sellers of products when product defects cause injury or property damage to consumers, users, or **bystanders** (people in the vicinity of the product).

Strict Liability

The modern concept of strict liability traces its origins, in part, to the 1868 English case of *Rylands v. Fletcher.*[1] In the coal-mining area of Lancashire, England, the Rylands, who were mill owners, had constructed a reservoir on their land. Water from the reservoir broke through a filled-in shaft of an abandoned coal mine nearby and flooded the connecting passageways in an active coal mine owned by Fletcher. Fletcher sued the Rylands, and the court held that the defendants (the Rylands) were liable, even though the circumstances did not fit within existing tort liability theories. The court held that a "person who for his own purposes brings on his land and collects and keeps there anything likely to do mischief if it escapes . . . is *prima facie* [on initial examination] answerable for all the damage which is the natural consequence of its escape."

British courts liberally applied the doctrine that emerged from the *Rylands v. Fletcher* case. Initially, few U.S. courts accepted this doctrine, presumably because the courts were worried about its effect on the expansion of American business. Today, however, the doctrine of strict liability is the norm rather than the exception.

Abnormally Dangerous Activities

Strict liability for damages proximately caused by an abnormally dangerous, or ultrahazardous, activity is one application of strict liability. Courts apply the doctrine of strict liability in these situations because of the extreme risk of the activity. Abnormally dangerous activities are those that involve a high risk of serious harm to persons or property that cannot be completely guarded against by the exercise of reasonable care—activities such as blasting or storing explosives. Even if blasting with dynamite is performed with all reasonable care, there is still a risk of injury. Balancing that risk against the potential for harm, it seems reasonable to ask the person engaged in the activity to pay for injuries caused by that activity. Although there is no fault, there is still responsibility because of the dangerous nature of the undertaking.

Other Applications of Strict Liability

Persons who keep wild animals are strictly liable for any harm inflicted by the animals. The basis for applying strict liability is that wild animals, should they

1. 3 L.R.–E & I App. [Law Reports, English & Irish Appeal Cases] (H.L. [House of Lords] 1868).

escape from confinement, pose a serious risk of harm to persons in the vicinity. An owner of domestic animals (such as dogs, cats, cows, or sheep) may be strictly liable for harm caused by those animals if the owner knew, or should have known, that the animals were dangerous or had a propensity to harm others.

A significant application of strict liability is in the area of product liability—liability of manufacturers and sellers for harmful or defective products. Liability here is a matter of social policy and is based on two factors: (1) the manufacturing company can better bear the cost of injury because it can spread the cost throughout society by increasing prices of goods, and (2) the manufacturing company is making a profit from its activities and therefore should bear the cost of injury as an operating expense. We discuss product liability in greater detail throughout the remainder of this chapter.

Product Liability

Those who make, sell, or lease goods can be held liable for physical harm or property damage caused by those goods to a consumer, user, or bystander. This is called product liability. Because one particular product may cause harm to a number of consumers, product liability actions are sometimes filed by a group of plaintiffs acting together. (For a discussion of a law that requires claims filed by a large group of plaintiffs to be heard in federal courts, see this chapter's *Emerging Trends* feature on pages 324 and 325.)

Product liability may be based on the theories of negligence, misrepresentation, and strict liability. We look here at product liability based on negligence and on misrepresentation.

Product Liability Based on Negligence

In Chapter 12, *negligence* was defined as the failure to exercise the degree of care that a reasonable, prudent person would have exercised under the circumstances. If a manufacturer fails to exercise "due care" to make a product safe, a person who is injured by the product may sue the manufacturer for negligence.

Due Care Must Be Exercised Due care must be exercised in designing the product, selecting the materials, using the appropriate production process, assembling and testing the product, and placing adequate warnings on the label informing the user of dangers of which an ordinary person might not be aware. The duty of care also extends to the inspection and testing of any purchased components that are used in the product sold by the manufacturer.

To succeed in a product liability suit against a manufacturer based on negligence, does a plaintiff have to prove the specific defect that caused the plaintiff's injury? That was the question in the following case.

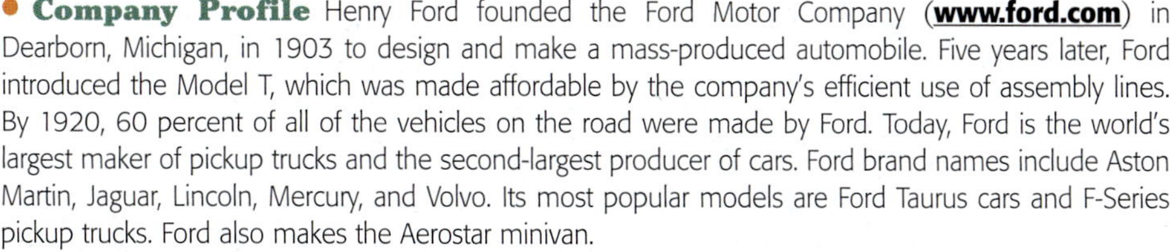

CASE 13.1 Jarvis v. Ford Motor Co.

United States Court of Appeals, Second Circuit, 2002. 283 F.3d 33.

• **Company Profile** Henry Ford founded the Ford Motor Company (**www.ford.com**) in Dearborn, Michigan, in 1903 to design and make a mass-produced automobile. Five years later, Ford introduced the Model T, which was made affordable by the company's efficient use of assembly lines. By 1920, 60 percent of all of the vehicles on the road were made by Ford. Today, Ford is the world's largest maker of pickup trucks and the second-largest producer of cars. Ford brand names include Aston Martin, Jaguar, Lincoln, Mercury, and Volvo. Its most popular models are Ford Taurus cars and F-Series pickup trucks. Ford also makes the Aerostar minivan.

• **Background and Facts** In 1991, Kathleen Jarvis bought a new Aerostar. Six days later, she started the van in the driveway of her home in Woodstock, New York. After she turned on the ignition, the engine suddenly revved and the vehicle took off. Jarvis pumped the brake with both feet, but the van would not stop. She steered to avoid people walking in the road before the van entered a ditch and turned over. As a result of the accident, Jarvis suffered a head injury and could not return to her job. She filed a suit in a federal district court against Ford, asserting product liability based, in part, on negligence.

CASE CONTINUES

CASE 13.1 CONTINUED Jarvis alleged that a defect in the van had caused the sudden acceleration. Her proof included her testimony, the testimony of other Aerostar owners who had experienced similar problems, and evidence that hundreds of additional Aerostar owners had experienced sudden acceleration. She also presented an expert who theorized that the van's cruise control had malfunctioned and who proposed an inexpensive remedy for this problem. Ford argued that Jarvis had failed to prove the defect that caused the cruise control to malfunction. A jury issued a verdict in Jarvis's favor, but the court granted Ford's motion for judgment as a matter of law. Jarvis appealed to the U.S. Court of Appeals for the Second Circuit.

IN THE LANGUAGE OF THE COURT
***SOTOMAYOR,* Circuit Judge.**

* * * *

* * * A plaintiff's failure to prove why a product malfunctioned does not necessarily prevent a plaintiff from showing that the product was defective. * * * While the burden is upon the plaintiff to prove that the product was defective and that the defect existed while the product was in the manufacturer's possession, [the] plaintiff is not required to prove the specific defect, especially where the product is complicated in nature. *Proof of necessary facts may be circumstantial. Though the happening of the accident is not proof of a defective condition, a defect may be inferred from proof that the product did not perform as intended by the manufacturer* * * * . [Emphasis added.]

* * * *

The district court erred in requiring proof of a specific defect in the Aerostar's cruise control and in not considering Jarvis's circumstantial evidence of a defect. The malfunction in the design of the Aerostar that Jarvis has alleged is that it suddenly accelerated, opening full throttle without Jarvis depressing the accelerator pedal, and that her efforts to stop the vehicle by pumping the brakes were unavailing. If Jarvis's six-day-old Aerostar performed in this manner, a jury could reasonably conclude that it was defective when put on the market by Ford, and that the defect made it reasonably certain that the vehicle would be dangerous when put to normal use, as required [in a cause of action based on] negligent design. Although Ford argued that the accident was caused instead by driver error, this theory would have been rejected if the jury had believed Jarvis's testimony that she had her feet on the brake and not on the accelerator, as Ford claimed. * * * Construing the evidence in Jarvis's favor and crediting her version of events, a reasonable jury could find that Ford breached its duty of care. Even accepting as true that sudden acceleration in the 1991 Aerostar would occur, at most, very infrequently when measured against all Aerostar ignition starts [as Ford claimed], the consequences of sudden acceleration could easily be catastrophic, the design of which Jarvis complains has no particular utility to balance its potential for harm, and, according to Jarvis's expert, the malfunction in the cruise control could be avoided by an inexpensive switch that would shut off power to the cruise control when not in use.

• **Decision and Remedy** *The U.S. Court of Appeals for the Second Circuit vacated (set aside, voided) the judgment of the lower court and remanded the case with instructions to reinstate the jury's verdict that Ford was negligent in the design of the cruise control mechanism in the 1991 Aerostar. A plaintiff in a product liability action based on negligence is not required to prove a specific defect when a defect may be inferred from proof that the product did not perform as the manufacturer intended.*[a]

• **The Legal Environment Dimension** *If plaintiffs were required to prove the specific defect that caused their injury, as the trial court in this case had ruled, what impact would this have on product liability claims based on negligence? Would there be more or fewer of these types of lawsuits filed?*

• **The Global Dimension** *Assume that other nations do not have laws concerning product liability based on negligence. Can a U.S. manufacturer sell a negligently designed product in a foreign market without risk of liability? Should it? Why or why not?*

---

a. This is also the principle in a strict product liability action, according to the *Restatement (Third) of Torts: Products Liability*, which will be discussed later in this chapter.

Privity of Contract Not Required A product liability action based on negligence does not require the injured plaintiff and the negligent defendant-manufacturer to be in **privity of contract.** In other words, the plaintiff and the defendant need not be directly involved in a contractual relationship (that is, in privity). Thus, any person who is injured by a product may bring a negligence suit even though he or she was not the one who actually purchased the product. A manufacturer, seller, or lessor is liable for failure to exercise due care to *any person* who sustains an injury proximately caused by a negligently made (defective) product. Relative to the long history of the common law, this exception to the privity requirement is a fairly recent development, dating to the early part of the twentieth century.[2]

Product Liability Based on Misrepresentation

When a fraudulent misrepresentation has been made to a user or consumer and that misrepresentation ultimately results in an injury, the basis of liability may be the tort of fraud. In this situation, the misrepresentation must have been made knowingly or with reckless disregard for the facts. For example, the intentional mislabeling of packaged cosmetics and the intentional concealment of a product's defects would constitute fraudulent misrepresentation. The misrepresentation must be of a material fact, and the seller must have had the intent to induce the buyer's reliance on the misrepresentation. Misrepresentation on a label or advertisement is enough to show an intent to induce the reliance of anyone who may use the product. In addition, the buyer must have relied on the misrepresentation.

Strict Product Liability

Under the doctrine of *strict liability* (discussed previously), people may be liable for the results of their acts regardless of their intentions or their exercise of reasonable care. In addition, liability does not depend on privity of contract. The injured party does not have to be the buyer or a third party beneficiary (see page 226), as required under contract warranty theory. In the 1960s, courts applied the doctrine of strict liability in several landmark cases involving manufactured goods, and it has since become a common method of holding manufacturers liable.

Strict Product Liability and Public Policy

The law imposes strict product liability as a matter of public policy. This public policy rests on the threefold assumption that (1) consumers should be protected against unsafe products; (2) manufacturers and distributors should not escape liability for faulty products simply because they are not in privity of contract with the ultimate user of those products; and (3) manufacturers, sellers, and lessors of products are in a better position to bear the costs associated with injuries caused by their products—costs that they can ultimately pass on to all consumers in the form of higher prices.

California was the first state to impose strict product liability in tort on manufacturers. In a landmark 1962 decision, *Greenman v. Yuba Power Products, Inc.*,[3] the California Supreme Court set out the reason for applying tort law rather than contract law (including laws governing warranties) in cases involving consumers who were injured by defective products. According to the *Greenman* court, the "purpose of such liability is to [e]nsure that the costs of injuries resulting from defective products are borne by the manufacturers . . . rather than by the injured persons who are powerless to protect themselves." Today, the majority of states recognize strict product liability, although some state courts limit its application to situations involving personal injuries (rather than property damage).

The Requirements for Strict Product Liability

The courts often look to the *Restatements of the Law* for guidance, even though the *Restatements* are not binding authorities. Section 402A of the *Restatement (Second) of Torts,* which was originally issued in 1964, has become a widely accepted statement of the liabilities of sellers of goods (including manufacturers, processors, assemblers, packagers, bottlers, wholesalers, distributors, retailers, and lessors).

The bases for an action in strict liability, which are set forth in Section 402A of the *Restatement (Second) of Torts* and commonly applied by the courts, can be summarized as a series of six requirements, which are listed here. Depending on the jurisdiction, if these requirements are met, a manufacturer's liability to an injured party can be virtually unlimited.

2. A landmark case in this respect is *MacPherson v. Buick Motor Co.*, 217 N.Y. 382, 111 N.E. 1050 (1916).

3. 59 Cal.2d 57, 377 P.2d 897, 27 Cal.Rptr. 697 (1962).

EMERGING TRENDS IN THE LEGAL ENVIRONMENT OF BUSINESS

Removing Class-Action Lawsuits to the Federal Courts

Many product liability actions are class actions. A *class action* is a lawsuit in which a single person or a small group of people represents the interests of a larger group. Women allegedly injured by silicone breast implants, for example, sued the manufacturers as a class, as did many of those allegedly injured by asbestos and tobacco. The idea behind class actions is that an individual consumer who has been injured by a product is unlikely to have the financial means to pursue complex litigation against a large corporation. A class action allows all those injured by a product to pool their resources and obtain competent legal counsel to bring a single lawsuit on their behalf.

Federal courts have always had specific requirements for class actions. For example, the class (the group of plaintiffs) must be so large that individual suits would be impracticable, and the case must involve legal or factual issues common to all members of the class. Until 2005, however, any state or federal court could hear class actions.

The Class Action Fairness Act of 2005

The Class Action Fairness Act (CAFA) of 2005[a] significantly changed the way class actions are tried. Though it affects all class actions, the CAFA was primarily designed to shift large, interstate product liability and tort class-action suits from the state courts to the federal courts. Under the act, federal district courts now have original (trial) jurisdiction over any civil action in which there are one hundred plaintiffs from multiple states and the damages sought exceed $5 million.

Under the CAFA, a state court can retain jurisdiction over a case *only* if more than two-thirds of the plaintiffs and at least one principal defendant are citizens of the state and the injuries were incurred in that state. If more than one-third but less than two-thirds of the plaintiffs live in a state, the act allows a federal judge to decide (based on specified considerations) whether the trial should be held in state or federal court.

In addition, the act makes it easier for a defendant to remove (transfer) a case from a state court to a federal court, even if the defendant is a citizen of the state where the action was filed. In cases involving multiple defendants, the CAFA also allows one defendant to remove the case to federal court without the consent of all the defendants (as was previously required). In sum, the act encourages all class actions to be heard in federal courts, which have historically been less sympathetic to consumers' product liability claims than state courts have been.

Goals of the Act

One of the main goals of the CAFA was to prevent plaintiffs' lawyers from "forum shopping," or looking for the state court that is most likely to be sympathetic to their claims. Corporate lawyers and business groups have long complained that class actions are often brought in states and counties where the judges and juries have a reputation for awarding large verdicts against corporate defendants. Sometimes, cases are even brought in states where only a small number of the plaintiffs reside. According to these critics, the CAFA will prevent such practices and help cut down on frivolous lawsuits. Not only will the business community benefit, but consumers will gain as well because businesses will no longer have to bear the costs of frivolous suits and will therefore be able to lower prices. President George W. Bush said that the act marks a critical step toward ending the "lawsuit culture in our country."[b]

Critics of the act contend, however, that class actions are the only way that individual consumers

a. Pub. L. No. 109-2, 119 St. 4 (February 18, 2005), codified at 28 U.S.C. Sections 1711 *et seq.*

b. Presidential press release, "President Signs Class-Action Fairness Act of 2005," February 18, 2005.

1. The product must be in a *defective condition* when the defendant sells it.
2. The defendant must normally be engaged in the *business of selling* (or otherwise distributing) that product.
3. The product must be *unreasonably dangerous* to the user or consumer because of its defective condition (in most states).
4. The plaintiff must incur *physical harm* to self or property by use or consumption of the product.
5. The defective condition must be the *proximate cause* of the injury or damage.
6. The goods *must not have been substantially changed* from the time the product was sold to the time the injury was sustained.

Proving a Defective Condition Under these requirements, in any action against a manufacturer, seller, or lessor the plaintiff need not show why or in what manner the product became defective. The plain-

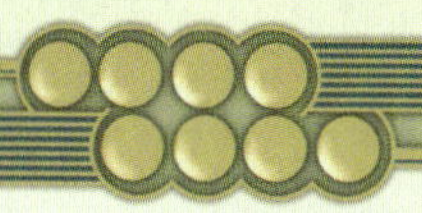

can obtain redress for injuries suffered from defective products. They say that by making it more difficult to pursue class actions, the CAFA is making it harder for injured parties to hold large corporations accountable for their wrongful acts and harmful products.

Even with the CAFA, Removing a Class Action to Federal Court Is Not Always Easy

The CAFA contains numerous ambiguities that the courts are still interpreting as they try to establish the new "rules of engagement" under the act. PepsiCo, Inc., found this out when it tried to remove a class-action suit from a New Jersey state court to a federal district court under the CAFA. The plaintiff had brought the suit against PepsiCo "for herself and on behalf of all persons in New Jersey who, within the past four years, purchased beverages with the tendency to contain benzene." The federal court held, however, that the case did not meet the CAFA's requirement that the amount in controversy exceed $5 million.[c]

Alabama Power Company suffered a similar fate when it also tried to remove a class action to a federal district court. When it appealed to the U.S. Court of Appeals for the Eleventh Circuit, the court denied the company's request in a seventy-seven-page ruling that addressed not only the $5 million threshold requirement but a number of other unresolved issues raised by the CAFA as well.[d]

In essence, the Eleventh Circuit raised the burden of proof for defendants seeking to remove cases to federal court. To do so, defendants must now prove that the amount-in-controversy requirement is a legal certainty. Prior to this ruling, the tradition was the use of a "preponderance of the evidence" standard.

IMPLICATIONS FOR THE BUSINESSPERSON

1. Product liability actions may still be tried in state courts. The CAFA applies only to class actions in which the plaintiffs seek damages of more than $5 million.
2. Businesspersons should be aware that even though a law appears to change only procedural rules, such as where and how a dispute is litigated, it may have consequences that affect substantive rights, including a party's ability to litigate.

FOR CRITICAL ANALYSIS

1. Do you agree that the CAFA will be effective in curtailing frivolous lawsuits? What other methods can you suggest to stop plaintiffs from filing suits that have no merit?
2. Critics of the CAFA argue that this legislation deprives Americans of "their day in court" when they are wronged by powerful corporations. Under what circumstances could this criticism be justified?

RELEVANT WEB SITES

To locate information on the Web concerning the issues discussed in this feature, go to this text's Web site at **academic.cengage.com/blaw/cross**, select "Chapter 13, and click on "Emerging Trends."

c. *Lamond v. PepsiCo, Inc.*, 2007 WL 1695401 (D.N.J. 2007).

d. *Lowery v. Alabama Power Co.*, 483 F.3d 1184 (11th Cir. 2007).

tiff does, however, have to prove that the product was defective at the time it left the hands of the seller or lessor and that this defective condition makes it "unreasonably dangerous" to the user or consumer. Unless evidence can be presented to support the conclusion that the product was defective when it was sold or leased, the plaintiff will not succeed. If the product was delivered in a safe condition and subsequent mishandling made it harmful to the user, the seller or lessor is normally not strictly liable.

Unreasonably Dangerous Products The *Restatement* recognizes that many products cannot be made entirely safe for all uses; thus, sellers or lessors are liable only for products that are *unreasonably* dangerous. A court could consider a product so defective as to be an **unreasonably dangerous product** in either of the following situations:

1. The product was dangerous beyond the expectation of the ordinary consumer.

2. A less dangerous alternative was *economically* feasible for the manufacturer, but the manufacturer failed to produce it.

As will be discussed next, a product may be unreasonably dangerous due to a flaw in the manufacturing process, a design defect, or an inadequate warning.

Product Defects

Because Section 402A of the *Restatement (Second) of Torts* did not clearly define such terms as *defective* and *unreasonably dangerous*, these terms have been subject to different interpretations by different courts. In 1997, to address these concerns, the American Law Institute (ALI) issued the *Restatement (Third) of Torts: Products Liability.* This *Restatement* defines the three types of product defects that have traditionally been recognized in product liability law—manufacturing defects, design defects, and inadequate warnings.

Manufacturing Defects According to Section 2(a) of the *Restatement (Third) of Torts,* a product "contains a manufacturing defect when the product departs from its intended design even though all possible care was exercised in the preparation and marketing of the product." Basically, a manufacturing defect is a departure from a product's design specifications. A glass bottle that is made too thin and explodes in a consumer's face is an example of a manufacturing defect. Liability is imposed on the manufacturer (and on the wholesaler and retailer) regardless of whether the manufacturer's quality control efforts were "reasonable." The idea behind holding defendants strictly liable for manufacturing defects is to encourage greater investment in product safety and stringent quality control standards. Cases involving allegations of a manufacturing defect are often decided based on the opinions and testimony of experts.[4]

Design Defects Unlike a product with a manufacturing defect, a product with a design defect is made in conformity with the manufacturer's design specifications but nevertheless results in injury to the user because the design itself was improper. The product's design creates an unreasonable risk to the user. A product "is defective in design when the foreseeable risks of harm posed by the product could have been reduced or avoided by the adoption of a reasonable alternative design by the seller or other distributor, or a predecessor in the commercial chain of distribution, and the omission of the alternative design renders the product not reasonably safe."[5]

Test for Design Defects. To successfully assert a design defect, a plaintiff has to show that a reasonable alternative design was available and that the defendant's failure to adopt the alternative design rendered the product not reasonably safe. In other words, a manufacturer or other defendant is liable only when the harm was reasonably preventable. In one case, for example, Gillespie, who cut off several of his fingers while operating a table saw, alleged that the blade guards on the saw were defectively designed. At the trial, however, an expert testified that the alternative design for blade guards used for table saws could not have been used for the particular cut that Gillespie was performing at the time he was injured. The court found that Gillespie's claim that the blade guards were defective failed because there was no proof that a guard with a "better" design would have prevented his injury.[6]

Factors to Be Considered. According to the *Restatement,* a court can consider a broad range of factors, including the magnitude and probability of the foreseeable risks, and the relative advantages and disadvantages of the product as it was designed and as it could have been designed. Basically, most courts engage in a risk-utility analysis, determining whether the risk of harm from the product as designed outweighs its utility to the user and to the public.

For example, suppose that a nine-year-old child finds rat poison in a cupboard at the local boys' club and eats it, thinking that it is candy. The child dies, and his parents file a suit against the manufacturer alleging that the rat poison was defectively designed because it looked like candy and was supposed to be placed in cupboards. In this situation, a court would probably consider factors such as the foreseeability that a child would think the rat poison was candy, the gravity of the potential harm from consumption, the availability of an alternative design, and the usefulness of the product. If the parents could offer sufficient evidence for a reasonable person to conclude that the harm was reasonably preventable, then the manufacturer could be held liable.

4. See, for example, *Derienzo v. Trek Bicycle Corp.,* 376 F.Supp.2d 537 (S.D.N.Y. 2005).

5. *Restatement (Third) of Torts: Products Liability,* Section 2(b).

6. *Gillespie v. Sears, Roebuck & Co.,* 386 F.3d 21 (1st Cir. 2004).

In the following case, a smoker who developed lung cancer sued a cigarette manufacturer claiming, among other things, that there was a defect in the design of its cigarettes. The jury instruction given by the trial court and quoted by the appellate court shows the numerous factors that judges and juries consider in determining design defects.

CASE 13.2 Bullock v. Philip Morris USA, Inc.

Court of Appeal of California, Second District, Division 3, 2008.
159 Cal.App. 4th 655, 71 Cal.Rptr 3d 775.
www.courtinfo.ca.gov/courts/courtsofappeal[a]

• **Company Profile** Philip Morris started as a tobacco products shop in London in 1847. Philip Morris & Co., Ltd., was incorporated in New York in 1902. It introduced the famous Marlboro cigarette in 1924. From 1954 on, it established itself on a worldwide basis. It is the largest seller of cigarettes in the United States. The company, along with other cigarette makers, has been the object of numerous lawsuits.

• **Background and Facts** Jodie Bullock smoked cigarettes manufactured by Philip Morris for forty-five years from 1956, when she was seventeen years old, until she was diagnosed with lung cancer in 2001. By the late 1950s, scientific professionals in the United States had proven that cigarette smoking caused lung cancer. Nonetheless, Philip Morris issued full-page announcements stating there was no proof that cigarette smoking caused cancer and that "numerous scientists" questioned "the validity of the statistics themselves." Philip Morris's chief executive officer, Joseph Cullman, III, stated on the television news program *Face the Nation* (CBS, January 3, 1971), "We do not believe that cigarettes are hazardous; we don't accept that." Jodie Bullock sued Philip Morris in April 2001 seeking to recover damages for personal injuries based on product liability, among other claims. At trial, the jury found that there was a defect in the design of the cigarettes and that they were negligently designed. It awarded Bullock $850,000 in compensatory damages, including $100,000 in noneconomic damages for pain and suffering, and later awarded her $28 billion in punitive damages. Philip Morris appealed.

IN THE LANGUAGE OF THE COURT
***CROSKEY,* J. [Judge]**

* * * *

Philip Morris heavily advertised its cigarettes on television in the 1950's and 1960's, until the federal government banned cigarette advertising on television in 1970. Television advertising had a particularly strong influence on youths under the age of 18, for whom there was a positive correlation between television viewing time and the incidence of smoking. Philip Morris's print advertisements for Marlboro and other cigarette brands in 1956, when Bullock began smoking at the age of 17, and generally in the years from 1954 to 1969, depicted handsome men and glamorous young women. Some advertisements featured slogans such as "Loved for Gentleness" and "'The gentlest cigarette you can smoke.'"

* * * *

Philip Morris contends (1) the evidence failed to establish a design defect under the risk-benefit test because there is no substantial evidence that a safer alternative cigarette design was available, that the failure to use a safer design was a cause of Bullock's lung cancer, or that Bullock would have smoked a safer cigarette if it were available; (2) the evidence failed to establish a design defect under the consumer expectations test or liability based on a failure to warn because there is no substantial evidence that the ordinary consumer was unaware of the dangers of cigarette smoking.

* * * *

A product is defective in design for purposes of tort liability if the benefits of the design do not outweigh the risk of danger inherent in the design, or if the product, used in an intended or

a. To access this court opinion, click on "Opinions 2nd District" and then click on recent "Published Opinions." Go to "January 30, 2008" and click on the name of the case.

CASE CONTINUES

CASE 13.2 CONTINUED *reasonably foreseeable manner, has failed to perform as safely as an ordinary consumer would expect.* [Emphasis added.]

Philip Morris challenges the finding of liability for design defect based on a risk-benefit theory by challenging the sufficiency of the evidence that a safer alternative design existed and the sufficiency of the evidence that its failure to use a safer alternative design caused Bullock's injuries. Philip Morris's argument is based on the premise that a plaintiff alleging a design defect based on a risk-benefit theory must prove that the defendant could have used a safer alternative design. The jury, however, was not so instructed. The court instructed the jury to determine whether the benefits of the design outweighed the risks by considering several factors, but did not instruct that any single factor was essential:

"In determining whether the benefits of the design outweigh its risks, you should consider, among other things, the gravity of the danger posed by the design, the likelihood that the danger would cause damage, the existence or nonexistence of warnings, the time of the manufacture, the financial cost of an improved design, and the adverse consequences to the product and the consumer that would result from an alternate design."

* * * We review the sufficiency of the evidence to support a verdict under the law stated in the instructions given, rather than under some other law on which the jury was not instructed. * * * Accordingly, we conclude that Philip Morris has shown no error with respect to the finding of liability for a design defect based on the risk-benefit test.

• **Decision and Remedy** *The Court of Appeal of California for the Second District affirmed the trial court's judgment as to the finding of liability. Philip Morris failed to show any error with respect to its liability for product liability based on a design defect.*

• **What If the Facts Were Different?** *Assume that Philip Morris had never publicly denied the scientific link between smoking and lung cancer. In other words, the company simply sold cigarettes without saying anything about the medical consequences of smoking. Do you think the jury award would have been the same? If yes, how?*

• **The Ethical Dimension** *Under what circumstances, if any, could Philip Morris have justified its continuing campaign to discredit the scientific arguments that linked smoking with lung cancer?*

Inadequate Warnings A product may also be deemed defective because of inadequate instructions or warnings. A product will be considered defective "when the foreseeable risks of harm posed by the product could have been reduced or avoided by the provision of reasonable instructions or warnings by the seller or other distributor, or a predecessor in the commercial chain of distribution, and the omission of the instructions or warnings renders the product not reasonably safe."[7]

Important factors for a court to consider include the risks of a product, the "content and comprehensibility" and "intensity of expression" of warnings and instructions, and the "characteristics of expected user groups."[8] A "reasonableness" test applies to determine if the warnings adequately alert consumers to the product's risks. For example, children would likely respond readily to bright, bold, simple warning labels, whereas educated adults might need more detailed information.

If a warning is provided with a product, can its manufacturer or seller assume that the warning will be read and obeyed? That was a question in the following case.

7. *Restatement (Third) of Torts: Products Liability,* Section 2(c).

8. *Restatement (Third) of Torts: Products Liability,* Section 2, Comment h.

EXTENDED CASE 13.3 Crosswhite v. Jumpking, Inc.

United States District Court, District of Oregon, 2006. 411 F.Supp.2d 1228.

***AIKEN*, J. [Judge]**

* * * *

On May 11, 2002, plaintiff, Gary Crosswhite, was jumping on a trampoline with another boy. The trampoline was owned by Jack and Misty Urbach * * * . The 14-foot round-shaped "backyard" trampoline was manufactured by defendant * * * , Jumpking [Inc.], and purchased by the Urbachs from Costco, Inc. sometime in 1999.

While on the trampoline, plaintiff attempted to execute a back-flip and accidentally landed on his head and neck. The force of the fall caused a fracture in plaintiff's cervical spine resulting in paraplegia. Plaintiff was sixteen years old at the time of his injury. Plaintiff alleges that his injuries were caused by * * * inadequate warnings and instructions [among other things]. Plaintiff brings this lawsuit [in a federal district court] against Jumpking alleging * * * strict liability [and other product liability claims].

Plaintiff, represented by counsel, filed this lawsuit on September 1, 2004. Over one year later, on November 10, 2005, defendant filed the summary judgment motion at bar.

* * * *

* * * *A product is not in a defective condition when it is safe for normal handling.* * * * *If the injury results from abnormal handling* * * * *the seller is not liable. Where, however, the seller has reason to anticipate that danger may result from a particular use,* * * * *the seller may be required to give adequate warning of the danger* * * * *and a product sold without such warning is in a defective condition.* [Emphasis added.]

* * * To prevent the product from being unreasonably dangerous, the seller may be required to give directions or warning, on the container, as to its use. However, where warning is given, the seller may reasonably assume that it will be read and heeded; and a product bearing such a warning is not in a defective condition, nor is it unreasonably dangerous.

Defendant's trampoline is manufactured with nine warning labels that are affixed to various trampoline components. In addition to these nine warning labels, defendant also provides a large laminated warning placard that is designed to be attached by the consumer to the metal frame near the ladder upon which jumpers mount the trampoline. Defendant further provides consumers with a detailed *User Manual* and a videotape that instructs both users and supervisors about safe and responsible trampoline use.

Uniform trampoline safety standards are published by the American Society for Testing and Materials (ASTM). The ASTM standard sets forth specific warning language to accompany trampolines. The record supports defendant's allegation that the trampoline at issue, including the warning that accompanied it, complied with all ASTM standards relevant at the time. Moreover, the ASTM standards at that time did not require warnings against users performing somersaults (flips) and/or jumping with multiple people to appear on the trampoline itself, however, defendant did affix those warnings to the trampoline as well as on a large warning placard attached to the trampoline at the point of entry or mounting. Specifically, one warning attached to the trampoline frame leg stated:

! WARNING
Do not land on head or neck.
Paralysis or death can result, even if you
land in the middle of the trampoline mat (bed).
To reduce the chance of landing on your head or neck, do not do flips.

Accompanying these warning labels is a "stick-figure" drawing of an individual landing on his head. The drawing is located above the warning language and is enclosed in a circular "x-ed" or "crossed-out" notation, commonly understood to mean that the conduct described should be avoided.

Another pair of warning labels affixed to the trampoline legs read:

CASE CONTINUES

CHAPTER 14

Intellectual Property and Internet Law

Most people think of wealth in terms of houses, land, cars, stocks, and bonds. Wealth, however, also includes **intellectual property,** which consists of the products that result from intellectual, creative processes. Although it is an abstract term for an abstract concept, intellectual property is nonetheless wholly familiar to virtually everyone. *Trademarks, service marks, copyrights,* and *patents* are all forms of intellectual property. The book you are reading is copyrighted. The software you use, the movies you see, and the music you listen to are all forms of intellectual property. We provide a comprehensive synopsis of these forms of intellectual property, as well as intellectual property that consists of *trade secrets,* in *Concept Summary 14.1* on page 358. In this chapter, we examine each of these forms in some detail.

Intellectual property has taken on increasing significance globally as well as in the United States. Today, the value of the world's intellectual property probably exceeds the value of physical property, such as machines and houses. For many U.S. companies, ownership rights in intangible intellectual property are more important to their prosperity than are their tangible assets. As you will read in this chapter, a pressing issue for businesspersons today is how to protect these valuable rights in the online world.

The need to protect creative works was voiced by the framers of the U.S. Constitution over two hundred years ago: Article I, Section 8, of the U.S. Constitution authorized Congress "[t]o promote the Progress of Science and useful Arts, by securing for limited Times to Authors and Inventors the exclusive Right to their respective Writings and Discoveries." Laws protecting patents, trademarks, and copyrights are explicitly designed to protect and reward inventive and artistic creativity. Although intellectual property law limits the economic freedom of some individuals, it does so to protect the freedom of others to enjoy the fruits of their labors—in the form of profits.

Trademarks and Related Property

A **trademark** is a distinctive mark, motto, device, or implement that a manufacturer stamps, prints, or otherwise affixes to the goods it produces so that they can be identified on the market and their origins made known. In other words, a trademark is a source indicator. At common law, the person who used a symbol or mark to identify a business or product was protected in the use of that trademark. Clearly, by using another's trademark, a business could lead consumers to believe that its goods were made by the other business. The law seeks to avoid this kind of confusion. In this section, we examine various aspects of the law governing trademarks.

In the following classic case concerning Coca-Cola, the defendants argued that the Coca-Cola trademark was entitled to no protection under the law because the term did not accurately represent the product.

CASE 14.1 The Coca-Cola Co. v. The Koke Co. of America

Supreme Court of the United States, 1920. 254 U.S. 143, 41 S.Ct. 113, 65 L.Ed. 189.
www.findlaw.com/casecode/supreme.html[a]

• **Company Profile** John Pemberton, an Atlanta pharmacist, invented a caramel-colored, carbonated soft drink in 1886. His bookkeeper, Frank Robinson, named the beverage Coca-Cola after two of the ingredients, coca leaves and kola nuts. Asa Candler bought the Coca-Cola Company (**www.cocacolacompany.com**) in 1891, and within seven years, he made the soft drink available in all of the United States, as well as in parts of Canada and Mexico. Candler continued to sell Coke aggressively and to open up new markets, reaching Europe before 1910. In doing so, however, he attracted numerous competitors, some of which tried to capitalize directly on the Coke name.

• **Background and Facts** The Coca-Cola Company sought to enjoin (prevent) the Koke Company of America and other beverage companies from, among other things, using the word *Koke* for their products. The Koke Company of America and other beverage companies contended that the Coca-Cola trademark was a fraudulent representation and that Coca-Cola was therefore not entitled to any help from the courts. The Koke Company and the other defendants alleged that the Coca-Cola Company, by its use of the Coca-Cola name, represented that the beverage contained cocaine (from coca leaves), which it no longer did. The trial court granted the injunction against the Koke Company, but the appellate court reversed the lower court's ruling. Coca-Cola then appealed to the United States Supreme Court.

IN THE LANGUAGE OF THE COURT
Mr. Justice *HOLMES* delivered the opinion of the Court.

* * * *

* * * Before 1900 the beginning of [Coca-Cola's] good will was more or less helped by the presence of cocaine, a drug that, like alcohol or caffeine or opium, may be described as a deadly poison or as a valuable [pharmaceutical item, depending on the speaker's purposes]. The amount seems to have been very small,[b] but it may have been enough to begin a bad habit and after the Food and Drug Act of June 30, 1906, if not earlier, long before this suit was brought, it was eliminated from the plaintiff's compound.

* * * Since 1900 the sales have increased at a very great rate corresponding to a like increase in advertising. The name now characterizes a beverage to be had at almost any soda fountain. It means a single thing coming from a single source, and well known to the community. It hardly would be too much to say that the drink characterizes the name as much as the name the drink. In other words *Coca-Cola probably means to most persons the plaintiff's familiar product to be had everywhere rather than a compound of particular substances.* * * * Before this suit was brought the plaintiff had advertised to the public that it must not expect and would not find cocaine, and had eliminated everything tending to suggest cocaine effects except the name and the picture of [coca] leaves and nuts, which probably conveyed little or nothing to most who saw it. It appears to us that it would be going too far to deny the plaintiff relief against a palpable [readily evident] fraud because possibly here and there an ignorant person might call for the drink with the hope for incipient cocaine intoxication. The plaintiff's position must be judged by the facts as they were when the suit was begun, not by the facts of a different condition and an earlier time. [Emphasis added.]

• **Decision and Remedy** *The district court's injunction was allowed to stand. The competing beverage companies were enjoined from calling their products Koke.*

---

a. This is the "U.S. Supreme Court Opinions" page within the Web site of the "FindLaw Internet Legal Resources" database. This page provides several options for accessing an opinion. Because you know the citation for this case, you can go to the "Citation Search" box, type in the appropriate volume and page numbers for the *United States Reports* ("254" and "143," respectively, for the *Coca-Cola* case), and click on "get it."

b. In reality, until 1903 the amount of active cocaine in each bottle of Coke was equivalent to one "line" of cocaine.

CASE CONTINUES

CASE 14.1 CONTINUED • **Impact of This Case on Today's Law** *In this early case, the United States Supreme Court made it clear that trademarks and trade names (and nicknames for those marks and names, such as the nickname "Coke" for "Coca-Cola") that are in common use receive protection under the common law. This holding is significant historically because it is the predecessor to the federal statute later passed to protect trademark rights—the Lanham Act of 1946, to be discussed next. In many ways, this act represented a codification of common law principles governing trademarks.*

• **What If the Facts Were Different?** *Suppose that Coca-Cola had been trying to make the public believe that its product contained cocaine. Would the result in this case likely have been different? Why or why not?*

Statutory Protection of Trademarks

Statutory protection of trademarks and related property is provided at the federal level by the Lanham Act of 1946.[1] The Lanham Act was enacted, in part, to protect manufacturers from losing business to rival companies that used confusingly similar trademarks. The Lanham Act incorporates the common law of trademarks and provides remedies for owners of trademarks who wish to enforce their claims in federal court. Many states also have trademark statutes.

Trademark Dilution In 1995, Congress amended the Lanham Act by passing the Federal Trademark Dilution Act,[2] which extended the protection available to trademark owners by allowing them to bring a suit in federal court for trademark **dilution.** Until the passage of this amendment, federal trademark law prohibited only the unauthorized use of the same mark on competing—or on noncompeting but "related"—goods or services when such use would likely confuse consumers as to the origin of those goods and services. Trademark dilution laws protect "distinctive" or "famous" trademarks (such as Jergens, McDonald's, Dell, and Apple) from certain unauthorized uses even when the use is on noncompeting goods or is unlikely to confuse. More than half of the states have also enacted trademark dilution laws.

Use of a Similar Mark May Constitute Trademark Dilution A famous mark may be diluted not only by the use of an *identical* mark but also by the use of a *similar* mark. In 2003, however, the United States Supreme Court ruled that to constitute dilution, the similar mark must reduce the value of the famous mark or lessen its ability to identify goods and services. Therefore, lingerie maker Victoria's Secret could not establish a dilution claim against a small adult store named "Victor's Little Secret" because there was not enough evidence that Victoria's Secret's mark would be diminished in value.[3]

A similar mark is more likely to lessen the value of a famous mark when the companies using the marks provide related goods or compete against each other in the same market. For example, a woman was operating a coffee shop under the name "Sambuck's Coffeehouse" in Astoria, Oregon, even though she knew that "Starbucks" is one of the largest coffee chains in the nation. When Starbucks Corporation filed a dilution lawsuit, the federal court ruled that use of the "Sambuck's" mark constituted trademark dilution because it created confusion for consumers. Not only was there a "high degree" of similarity between the marks, but also both companies provided coffee-related services and marketed their services through "stand-alone" retail stores. Therefore, the use of the similar mark (Sambuck's) reduced the value of the famous mark (Starbucks).[4]

Trademark Registration

Trademarks may be registered with the state or with the federal government. To register for protection under federal trademark law, a person must file an application with the U.S. Patent and Trademark Office in Washington, D.C. Under current law, a mark can be registered (1) if it is currently in commerce or (2) if the applicant intends to put it into commerce within six months.

In special circumstances, the six-month period can be extended by thirty months, giving the applicant a total of three years from the date of notice of trademark approval to make use of the mark and file the required use statement. Registration is postponed until the mark is actually used. Nonetheless, during this waiting period, any applicant can legally protect his or her

1. 15 U.S.C. Sections 1051–1128.
2. 15 U.S.C. Section 1125.

3. *Moseley v. V Secret Catalogue, Inc.,* 537 U.S. 418, 123 S.Ct. 1115, 155 L.Ed.2d 1 (2003). (A different case involving Victoria's Secret's trademark is presented as Case 14.2 on pages 339–341.)
4. *Starbucks Corp. v. Lundberg,* 2005 WL 3183858 (D.Or. 2005).

trademark against a third party who previously has neither used the mark nor filed an application for it. Registration is renewable between the fifth and sixth years after the initial registration and every ten years thereafter (every twenty years for those trademarks registered before 1990).

Trademark Infringement

Registration of a trademark with the U.S. Patent and Trademark Office gives notice on a nationwide basis that the trademark belongs exclusively to the registrant. The registrant is also allowed to use the symbol ® to indicate that the mark has been registered. Whenever that trademark is copied to a substantial degree or used in its entirety by another, intentionally or unintentionally, the trademark has been *infringed* (used without authorization). When a trademark has been infringed, the owner of the mark has a cause of action against the infringer. To sue for trademark infringement, a person need not have registered the trademark, but registration does furnish proof of the date of inception of the trademark's use.

A central objective of the Lanham Act is to reduce the likelihood that consumers will be confused by similar marks. For that reason, only those trademarks that are deemed sufficiently distinctive from all competing trademarks will be protected.

Distinctiveness of Mark

A trademark must be sufficiently distinct to enable consumers to identify the manufacturer of the goods easily and to distinguish between those goods and competing products.

Strong Marks Fanciful, arbitrary, or suggestive trademarks are generally considered to be the most distinctive (strongest) trademarks. Marks that are fanciful, arbitrary, or suggestive are protected as inherently distinctive without demonstrating secondary meaning. These marks receive automatic protection because they serve to identify a particular product's source, as opposed to describing the product itself.

Fanciful trademarks include invented words, such as "Xerox" for one manufacturer's copiers and "Kodak" for another company's photographic products. Arbitrary trademarks are those that use common words in an uncommon way that is nondescriptive, such as "English Leather" used as a name for an after-shave lotion (and not for leather processed in England). Suggestive trademarks imply something about a product without describing the product directly. For example, the trademark "Dairy Queen" suggests an association between the products and milk, but it does not directly describe ice cream.

Secondary Meaning Descriptive terms, geographic terms, and personal names are not inherently distinctive and do not receive protection under the law until they acquire a secondary meaning. A secondary meaning may arise when customers begin to associate a specific term or phrase (such as London Fog) with specific trademarked items (coats with "London Fog" labels). Whether a secondary meaning becomes attached to a term or name usually depends on how extensively the product is advertised, the market for the product, the number of sales, and other factors.

Once a secondary meaning is attached to a term or name, a trademark is considered distinctive and is protected. The United States Supreme Court has held that even a color can qualify for trademark protection, once customers associate that color with the product.[5] In 2006, a federal court held that trademark law protects the particular color schemes used by the sports teams of four state universities, including Ohio State University and Louisiana State University.[6]

At issue in the following case was whether a certain mark was suggestive or descriptive.

5. *Qualitex Co. v. Jacobson Products Co.*, 514 U.S. 159, 115 S.Ct. 1300, 131 L.Ed.2d 248 (1995).

6. *Board of Supervisors of Louisiana State University v. Smack Apparel Co.*, 438 F.Supp.2d 653 (E.D.La.2006).

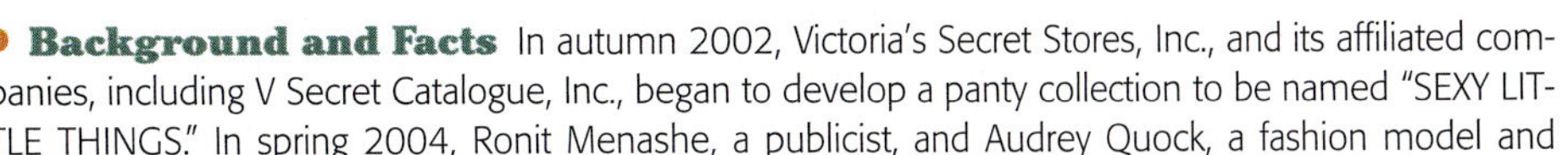

CASE 14.2 Menashe v. V Secret Catalogue, Inc.

United States District Court, Southern District of New York, 2006. 409 F.Supp.2d 412.

• **Background and Facts** In autumn 2002, Victoria's Secret Stores, Inc., and its affiliated companies, including V Secret Catalogue, Inc., began to develop a panty collection to be named "SEXY LITTLE THINGS." In spring 2004, Ronit Menashe, a publicist, and Audrey Quock, a fashion model and actress, began to plan a line of women's underwear also called "SEXY LITTLE THINGS." Menashe and

CASE CONTINUES

CASE 14.2 CONTINUED Quock designed their line, negotiated for its manufacture, registered the domain name **www.sexylittlethings.com**, and filed an intent-to-use (ITU) application with the U.S. Patent and Trademark Office (USPTO). In July, Victoria's Secret's collection appeared in its stores in Ohio, Michigan, and California, and, in less than three months, was prominently displayed in all its stores, in its catalogues, and on its Web site. By mid-November, more than 13 million units of the line had been sold, accounting for 4 percent of the company's sales for the year. When the firm applied to register "SEXY LITTLE THINGS" with the USPTO, it learned of Menashe and Quock's ITU application. The firm warned the pair that their use of the phrase constituted trademark infringement. Menashe and Quock filed a suit in a federal district court against V Secret Catalogue and others, asking the court to, among other things, declare "non-infringement of the trademark."

IN THE LANGUAGE OF THE COURT
***BAER,* District Judge.**

* * * *

Plaintiffs claim that Victoria's Secret has no right of priority in the Mark because "SEXY LITTLE THINGS" for lingerie is a descriptive term that had not attained secondary meaning by the time Plaintiffs filed their ITU application. Consequently, Plaintiffs assert that they have priority based on * * * their ITU application on September 13, 2004. Victoria's Secret counters that the Mark is suggestive and thus qualifies for trademark protection without proof of secondary meaning. Therefore, Victoria's Secret has priority by virtue of its *bona fide* use of the Mark in commerce beginning July 28, 2004.

* * * *

To merit trademark protection, a mark must be capable of distinguishing the products it marks from those of others. * * * A descriptive term * * * conveys an immediate idea of the ingredients, qualities or characteristics of the goods. In contrast, a suggestive term requires imagination, thought and perception to reach a conclusion as to the nature of the goods. *Suggestive marks are automatically protected because they are inherently distinctive, i.e., their intrinsic nature serves to identify a particular source of a product.* Descriptive marks are not inherently distinctive and may only be protected on a showing of secondary meaning, i.e., that the purchasing public associates the mark with a particular source. [Emphasis added.]

* * * To distinguish suggestive from descriptive marks [a court considers] whether the purchaser must use some imagination to connect the mark to some characteristic of the product * * * and * * * whether the proposed use would deprive competitors of a way to describe their goods.

* * * I find "SEXY LITTLE THINGS" to be suggestive. First, while the term describes the erotically stimulating quality of the trademarked lingerie, it also calls to mind the phrase "sexy little thing" popularly used to refer to attractive lithe young women. Hence, the Mark prompts the purchaser to mentally associate the lingerie with its targeted twenty- to thirty-year-old consumers. *Courts have classified marks that both describe the product and evoke other associations as inherently distinctive.* * * * [Also] it is hard to believe that Victoria's Secret's use of the Mark will deprive competitors of ways to describe their lingerie products. Indeed, Victoria's Secret's own descriptions of its lingerie in its catalogues and Web site illustrate that there are numerous ways to describe provocative underwear. [Emphasis added.]

* * * *

* * * Victoria's Secret used "SEXY LITTLE THINGS" as a trademark in commerce beginning on July 28, 2004. Commencing on that date, the prominent use of the Mark in four stores * * * satisfies the "use in commerce" requirement * * * . Similarly, Victoria's Secret's prominent use of the Mark in its catalogues beginning on September 4, 2004, and on its Web site beginning on or about September 9, 2004, together with pictures and descriptions of the goods meets the * * * test * * * . I find that because Victoria's Secret made *bona fide* trademark use of "SEXY LITTLE THINGS" in commerce before Plaintiffs filed their ITU application, and has continued to use that Mark in commerce, Victoria's Secret has acquired priority in the Mark.

• **Decision and Remedy** *The district court ruled that Menashe and Quock were not entitled to a judgment of "non-infringement" and dismissed their complaint. The court concluded that "SEXY*

CASE 14.2 CONTINUED *LITTLE THINGS" was a suggestive mark and that Victoria's Secret had used it in commerce before the plaintiffs filed their ITU application. For this reason, Victoria's Secret had "priority in the Mark."*

- **The E-Commerce Dimension** *Under the reasoning of the court in this case, would the use of a purported trademark solely on a Web site satisfy the "use in commerce" requirement? Explain.*

- **The Legal Environment Dimension** *Why is it important to allow those who have applied for trademark protection—in this case, ITU applicants Menashe and Quock—to defend preemptively against the use of the mark by another party? (Hint: Why were Menashe and Quock seeking a court declaration of "non-infringement of a trademark"?)*

Generic Terms Generic terms that refer to an entire class of products, such as *bicycle* and *computer,* receive no protection, even if they acquire secondary meanings. A particularly thorny problem arises when a trademark acquires generic use. For example, *aspirin* and *thermos* were originally the names of trademarked products, but today the words are used generically. Other examples are *escalator, trampoline, raisin bran, dry ice, lanolin, linoleum, nylon,* and *corn flakes.*

Sometimes, a company's use of a particular phrase becomes so closely associated with that company that the firm claims it should be protected under trademark law. In one case, for example, America Online, Inc. (AOL), sued AT&T Corporation, claiming that AT&T's use of "You Have Mail" on its WorldNet Service infringed AOL's trademark rights in the same phrase. The court ruled, however, that because each of the three words in the phrase was a generic term, the phrase as a whole was generic. Although the phrase had become widely associated with AOL's e-mail notification service, and thus might have acquired a secondary meaning, this issue was of no significance in the case. The court stated that it would not consider whether the mark had acquired any secondary meaning because "generic marks with secondary meaning are still not entitled to protection."[7]

Trade Dress

The term **trade dress** refers to the image and overall appearance of a product. Trade dress is a broad concept and can include either all or part of the total image or overall impression created by a product or its packaging. For example, the distinctive decor, menu, layout, and style of service of a particular restaurant may be regarded as trade dress. Trade dress can also include the layout and appearance of a catalogue, the use of a lighthouse as part of the design of a golf hole, the fish shape of a cracker, or the G-shaped design of a Gucci watch.

Basically, trade dress is subject to the same protection as trademarks. In cases involving trade dress infringement, as in trademark infringement cases, a major consideration is whether consumers are likely to be confused by the allegedly infringing use.

Service, Certification, and Collective Marks

A **service mark** is essentially a trademark that is used to distinguish the *services* (rather than the products) of one person or company from those of another. For example, each airline has a particular mark or symbol associated with its name. Titles and character names used in radio and television are frequently registered as service marks.

Other marks protected by law include certification marks and collective marks. A **certification mark** is used by one or more persons, other than the owner, to certify the region, materials, mode of manufacture, quality, or other characteristic of specific goods or services. When used by members of a cooperative, association, or other organization, it is referred to as a **collective mark.** Examples of certification marks are the phrases "Good Housekeeping Seal of Approval" and "UL Tested." Collective marks appear at the ends of motion picture credits to indicate the various associations and organizations that participated in the making of the films. The union marks found on the tags of certain products are also collective marks.

Counterfeit Goods

Counterfeit goods copy or otherwise imitate trademarked goods but are not genuine. The importation of goods that bear a counterfeit (fake) trademark poses a growing problem for U.S. businesses, consumers, and law enforcement. In addition to having

7. *America Online, Inc. v. AT&T Corp.*, 243 F.3d 812 (4th Cir. 2001).

CASE 14.4 CONTINUED

We have * * * concluded that Leadsinger's use is intended for commercial gain, and it is well accepted that when "the intended use is for commercial gain," the likelihood of market harm "may be presumed." We have not hesitated to apply this presumption in the past, and we are not reluctant to apply it here. Moreover, "the importance of [the market effect] factor [varies], not only with the amount of harm, but also with the relative strength of the showing on the other factors." The showing on all other factors under Section 107 is strong: the purpose and character of Leadsinger's use is commercial; song lyrics fall within the core of copyright protection; and Leadsinger uses song lyrics in their entirety. On this basis, we affirm the district court's dismissal of Leadsinger's request for a declaration based on the fair use doctrine.

- **Decision and Remedy** *The U.S. Court of Appeals for the Ninth Circuit affirmed the district court's decision to dismiss Leadsinger's complaint without the possibility of amending its complaint.*

- **The Global Dimension** *Could Leadsinger have attempted to show that its karaoke programs were used extensively abroad to help others learn English? If successful in this line of reasoning, might Leadsinger have prevailed on appeal? Explain your answer.*

- **The Legal Environment Dimension** *What was the underlying basis of Leadsinger's attempt to avoid paying additional licensing fees to BMG?*

Copyright Protection for Software

In 1980, Congress passed the Computer Software Copyright Act, which amended the Copyright Act of 1976 to include computer programs in the list of creative works protected by federal copyright law.[30] The 1980 statute, which classifies computer programs as "literary works," defines a computer program as a "set of statements or instructions to be used directly or indirectly in a computer in order to bring about a certain result."

The unique nature of computer programs, however, has created problems for the courts in applying and interpreting the 1980 act. Generally, the courts have held that copyright protection extends not only to those parts of a computer program that can be read by humans, such as the "high-level" language of a source code, but also to the binary-language object code, which is readable only by the computer.[31] Additionally, such elements as the overall structure, sequence, and organization of a program have been deemed copyrightable, but generally not the "look and feel" of computer programs.[32] The "look and feel" of computer programs refers to their general appearance, command structure, video images, menus, windows, and other screen displays.

Copyrights in Digital Information

Copyright law is probably the most important form of intellectual property protection on the Internet. This is because much of the material on the Internet consists of works of authorship (including multimedia presentations, software, and database information), which are the traditional focus of copyright law. Copyright law is also important because the nature of the Internet requires that data be "copied" to be transferred online. Traditionally, many of the controversies arising in this area of the law have involved copies.

The Copyright Act of 1976

When Congress drafted the principal U.S. law governing copyrights, the Copyright Act of 1976, cyberspace did not exist for most of us. At that time, the primary threat to copyright owners was from persons making unauthorized *tangible* copies of works. Because of the nature of cyberspace, however, one of the early controversies was determining at what point an intangible, electronic "copy" of a work has

30. Pub. L. No. 96-517 (1980), amending 17 U.S.C. Sections 101, 117.

31. See *Stern Electronics, Inc. v. Kaufman*, 669 F.2d 852 (2d Cir. 1982); and *Apple Computer, Inc. v. Franklin Computer Corp.*, 714 F.2d 1240 (3d Cir. 1983).

32. *Whelan Associates, Inc. v. Jaslow Dental Laboratory, Inc.*, 797 F.2d 1222 (3d Cir. 1986).

been made. The courts have held that loading a file or program into a computer's random access memory, or RAM, constitutes the making of a "copy" for purposes of copyright law.[33] RAM is a portion of a computer's memory into which a file, for example, is loaded so that it can be accessed. Thus, a copyright is infringed when a party downloads software into RAM without owning the software or otherwise having a right to download it.[34] Today, technology has vastly increased the potential for copyright infringement. For a discussion of whether search engines that use thumbnail images of copyrighted materials are liable for infringement, see this chapter's *Insight into E-Commerce* feature on pages 354 and 355.

Further Developments in Copyright Law

In the last fifteen years, Congress has enacted legislation designed specifically to protect copyright holders in a digital age. Particularly significant are the No Electronic Theft Act of 1997[35] and the Digital Millennium Copyright Act of 1998.[36]

The No Electronic Theft Act Prior to 1997, criminal penalties could be imposed under copyright law only if unauthorized copies were exchanged for financial gain. Yet much piracy of copyrighted materials was "altruistic" in nature; that is, unauthorized copies were made and distributed not for financial gain but simply for reasons of generosity—to share the copies with others. To combat altruistic piracy and for other reasons, Congress passed the No Electronic Theft (NET) Act of 1997.

NET extended criminal liability for the piracy of copyrighted materials to persons who exchange unauthorized copies of copyrighted works, such as software, even though they realize no profit from the exchange. The act also altered the traditional "fair use" doctrine by imposing penalties on those who make unauthorized electronic copies of books, magazines, movies, or music for *personal* use. The criminal penalties for violating the act are relatively severe; they include fines as high as $250,000 and incarceration for up to five years.

33. *MAI Systems Corp. v. Peak Computer, Inc.*, 991 F.2d 511 (9th Cir. 1993).

34. *DSC Communications Corp. v. Pulse Communications, Inc.*, 170 F.3d 1354 (Fed.Cir. 1999).

35. Pub. L. No. 105-147 (1997). Codified at 17 U.S.C. Sections 101, 506; 18 U.S.C. Sections 2311, 2319, 2319A, 2320; and 28 U.S.C. Sections 994 and 1498.

36. 17 U.S.C. Sections 512, 1201–1205, 1301–1332; and 28 U.S.C. Section 4001.

The Digital Millennium Copyright Act of 1998 The passage of the Digital Millennium Copyright Act (DMCA) of 1998 gave significant protection to owners of copyrights in digital information.[37] Among other things, the act established civil and criminal penalties for anyone who circumvents (bypasses, or gets around—by using a special decryption program, for example) encryption software or other technological antipiracy protection. Also prohibited are the manufacture, import, sale, and distribution of devices or services for circumvention.

The DMCA provides for exceptions to fit the needs of libraries, scientists, universities, and others. In general, the law does not restrict the "fair use" of circumvention methods for educational and other noncommercial purposes. For example, circumvention is allowed to test computer security, to conduct encryption research, to protect personal privacy, and to enable parents to monitor their children's use of the Internet. The exceptions are to be reconsidered every three years.

The DMCA also limits the liability of Internet service providers (ISPs). Under the act, an ISP is not liable for any copyright infringement by its customer *unless* the ISP is aware of the subscriber's violation. An ISP may be held liable only if it fails to take action to shut the subscriber down after learning of the violation. A copyright holder must act promptly, however, by pursuing a claim in court, or the subscriber has the right to be restored to online access.

MP3 and File-Sharing Technology

Soon after the Internet became popular, a few enterprising programmers created software to compress large data files, particularly those associated with music. The reduced file sizes make transmitting music over the Internet feasible. The most widely known compression and decompression system is MP3, which enables music fans to download songs or entire CDs onto their computers or onto portable listening devices, such as Rio or iPod. The MP3 system also made it possible for music fans to access other music fans' files by engaging in file-sharing via the Internet.

Peer-to-Peer (P2P) Networking File-sharing via the Internet is accomplished through what is called **peer-to-peer (P2P) networking.** The concept is simple. Rather than going through a central Web server,

37. This act implemented the World Intellectual Property Organization Copyright Treaty of 1996, which will be discussed later in this chapter.

browser.[40] Companies need not locate songs for users on other members' computers. Instead, the software automatically annotates files with descriptive information so that the music can easily be categorized and cross-referenced (by artist and title, for instance). When a user performs a search, the software is able to locate a list of peers that have the file available for downloading. Also, to expedite the P2P transfer, the software distributes the download task over the entire list of peers simultaneously. By downloading even one file, the user becomes a point of distribution for that file, which is then automatically shared with others on the network.

Because the file-sharing software was decentralized and did not use search indices that would enable the companies to locate infringing material, they had no ability to supervise or control which music (or other media files) their users exchanged. In addition, it was difficult for courts to apply the traditional doctrines of contributory and vicarious liability to these new technologies.

The Supreme Court's *Grokster* Decision

In 2005, the United States Supreme Court expanded the liability of file-sharing companies in its decision in *Metro-Goldwyn-Mayer Studios, Inc. v. Grokster, Ltd.*[41] In that case, organizations in the music and film industry (the plaintiffs) sued several companies that distribute file-sharing software used in P2P networks, including Grokster, Ltd., and StreamCast Networks, Inc. (the defendants). The plaintiffs claimed that the defendants were contributorily and vicariously liable for the infringement of their end users. The Supreme Court held that "one who distributes a device [software] with the object of promoting its use to infringe the copyright, as shown by clear expression or other affirmative steps taken to foster infringement, is liable for the resulting acts of infringement by third parties."

Although the Supreme Court did not specify what kind of affirmative steps are necessary to establish liability, it did note that there was ample evidence that the defendants had acted with the intent to cause copyright violations. (Grokster, Ltd., later settled this dispute out of court and stopped distributing its software.) Essentially, this means that file-sharing companies that have taken affirmative steps to promote copyright infringement can be held secondarily liable for millions of infringing acts that their users commit daily. Because the Court did not define exactly what is necessary to impose liability, however, a substantial amount of legal uncertainty remains concerning this issue. Although some file-sharing companies have been shut down, illegal file-sharing—and lawsuits against file-sharing companies and the individuals who use them—has continued in the years since this decision.

Section 6 Trade Secrets

The law of trade secrets protects some business processes and information that are not, or cannot be, patented, copyrighted, or trademarked against appropriation by competitors. **Trade secrets** include customer lists, plans, research and development, pricing information, marketing methods, production techniques, and generally anything that makes an individual company unique and that would have value to a competitor.

Unlike copyright and trademark protection, protection of trade secrets extends both to ideas and to their expression. (For this reason, and because a trade secret involves no registration or filing requirements, trade secret protection may be well suited for software.) Of course, the secret formula, method, or other information must be disclosed to some persons, particularly to key employees. Businesses generally attempt to protect their trade secrets by having all employees who use the process or information agree in their contracts, or in confidentiality agreements, never to divulge it.

State and Federal Law on Trade Secrets

Under Section 757 of the *Restatement of Torts*, "One who discloses or uses another's trade secret, without a privilege to do so, is liable to the other if (1) he [or she] discovered the secret by improper means, or (2) his [or her] disclosure or use constitutes a breach of confidence reposed in him [or her] by the other in disclosing the secret to him [or her]." The theft of confidential business data by industrial espionage, as when a business taps into a competitor's computer, is a theft of trade secrets without any contractual violation and is actionable in itself.

Until thirty years ago, virtually all law with respect to trade secrets was common law. In an effort to reduce the unpredictability of the common law in this area, a

40. Note that in 2005, KaZaA entered a settlement agreement with four major music companies that had alleged copyright infringement. KaZaA agreed to offer only legitimate, fee-based music downloads in the future.

41. 545 U.S. 913, 125 S.Ct. 2764, 162 L.Ed.2d 781 (2005).

model act, the Uniform Trade Secrets Act, was presented to the states for adoption in 1979. Parts of the act have been adopted in more than thirty states. Typically, a state that has adopted parts of the act has adopted only those parts that encompass its own existing common law. Additionally, in 1996 Congress passed the Economic Espionage Act,[42] which made the theft of trade secrets a federal crime. We examined the provisions and significance of this act in Chapter 7, in the context of crimes related to business.

Trade Secrets in Cyberspace

New computer technology is undercutting a business firm's ability to protect its confidential information, including trade secrets.[43] For example, a dishonest employee could e-mail trade secrets in a company's computer to a competitor or a future employer. If e-mail is not an option, the employee might walk out with the information on a flash pen drive.

International Protection for Intellectual Property

For many years, the United States has been a party to various international agreements relating to intellectual property rights. For example, the Paris Convention of 1883, to which about 170 countries are signatory, allows parties in one country to file for patent and trademark protection in any of the other member countries. Other international agreements in this area include the Berne Convention, the TRIPS agreement, and the Madrid Protocol.

The Berne Convention

Under the Berne Convention (an international copyright agreement) of 1886, as amended, if an American writes a book, every country that has signed the convention must recognize the American author's copyright in the book. Also, if a citizen of a country that has not signed the convention first publishes a book in one of the 170 countries that have signed, all other countries that have signed the convention must recognize that author's copyright. Copyright notice is not needed to gain protection under the Berne Convention for works published after March 1, 1989.

The laws of many countries, as well as international laws, are being updated to reflect changes in technology and the expansion of the Internet. Copyright holders and other owners of intellectual property generally agree that changes in the law are needed to stop the increasing international piracy of their property. The World Intellectual Property Organization (WIPO) Copyright Treaty of 1996, a special agreement under the Berne Convention, attempts to update international law governing copyright protection to include more safeguards against copyright infringement via the Internet. The United States signed the WIPO treaty in 1996 and implemented its terms in the Digital Millennium Copyright Act of 1998, which was discussed earlier in this chapter.

The Berne Convention and other international agreements have given some protection to intellectual property on a global level. Another significant worldwide agreement to increase such protection is the Trade-Related Aspects of Intellectual Property Rights agreement—or, more simply, the TRIPS agreement.

The TRIPS Agreement

Representatives from more than one hundred nations signed the TRIPS agreement in 1994. It was one of several documents that were annexed to the agreement that created the World Trade Organization, or WTO, in 1995. The TRIPS agreement established, for the first time, standards for the international protection of intellectual property rights, including patents, trademarks, and copyrights for movies, computer programs, books, and music. The TRIPS agreement provides that each member country must include in its domestic laws broad intellectual property rights and effective remedies (including civil and criminal penalties) for violations of those rights.

Members Cannot Discriminate against Foreign Intellectual Property Owners Generally, the TRIPS agreement forbids member nations from discriminating against foreign owners of intellectual property rights (in the administration, regulation, or adjudication of such rights). In other words, a member nation cannot give its own nationals (citizens) favorable treatment without offering the same treatment to nationals of all member countries. For instance, if a U.S. software manufacturer brings a suit for the infringement of intellectual property rights under a member nation's national laws, the U.S. manufacturer is entitled to receive the same treatment as a domestic manufacturer. Each member

42. 18 U.S.C. Sections 1831–1839.

43. Note that in at least one case, a court has held that customers' e-mail addresses may constitute trade secrets. See *T-N-T Motorsports, Inc. v. Hennessey Motorsports, Inc.*, 965 S.W.2d 18 (Tex.App.—Houston [1 Dist.] 1998); rehearing overruled (1998); petition dismissed (1998).

Artisan's Liens An **artisan's lien** is a device created at common law through which a creditor can recover payment from a debtor for labor and materials furnished in the repair of personal property. In contrast to a mechanic's lien, an artisan's lien is *possessory*. This means that the lienholder ordinarily must have retained possession of the property and have expressly or impliedly agreed to provide the services on a cash, not a credit, basis. The lien remains in existence as long as the lienholder maintains possession, and the lien is terminated once possession is voluntarily surrendered—unless the surrender is only temporary.

For example, Whitney leaves her diamond ring at the jewelry shop to be repaired and to have her initials engraved on the band. In the absence of an agreement, the jeweler can keep the ring until Whitney pays for the services that the jeweler provides. Should Whitney fail to pay, the jeweler has a lien on Whitney's ring for the amount of the bill and can sell the ring in satisfaction of the lien.

Modern statutes permit the holder of an artisan's lien to foreclose and sell the property subject to the lien to satisfy payment of the debt. As with a mechanic's lien, the lienholder is required to give notice to the owner of the property prior to foreclosure and sale. The sale proceeds are used to pay the debt and the costs of the legal proceedings, and the surplus, if any, is paid to the former owner.

Judicial Liens When a debt is past due, a creditor can bring a legal action against the debtor to collect the debt. If the creditor is successful in the action, the court awards the creditor a judgment against the debtor (usually for the amount of the debt plus any interest and legal costs incurred in obtaining the judgment). Frequently, however, the creditor is unable to collect the awarded amount.

To ensure that a judgment in the creditor's favor will be collectible, the creditor is permitted to request that certain nonexempt property of the debtor be seized to satisfy the debt. (As will be discussed later in this chapter, under state or federal statutes, some kinds of property are exempt from attachment by creditors.) If the court orders the debtor's property to be seized prior to a judgment in the creditor's favor, the court's order is referred to as a *writ of attachment.* If the court orders the debtor's property to be seized following a judgment in the creditor's favor, the court's order is referred to as a *writ of execution.*

Writ of Attachment. In the context of judicial liens, **attachment** refers to a court-ordered seizure and taking into custody of property prior to the securing of a judgment for a past-due debt. Normally, attachment is a *prejudgment* remedy, occurring either at the time a lawsuit is filed or immediately thereafter. In order to attach *before* a judgment, a creditor must comply with the specific state's statutory restrictions. The due process clause of the Fourteenth Amendment to the U.S. Constitution also applies and requires that the debtor be given notice and an opportunity to be heard (see Chapter 5).

The creditor must have an enforceable right to payment of the debt under law and must follow certain procedures. Otherwise, the creditor can be liable for damages for wrongful attachment. Typically, the creditor must file with the court an *affidavit* (a written or printed statement, made under oath or sworn to) stating that the debtor has failed to pay and delineating the statutory grounds under which attachment is sought. The creditor must also post a bond to cover at least the court costs, the value of the property attached, and the value of the loss of use of that property suffered by the debtor. When the court is satisfied that all the requirements have been met, it issues a **writ of attachment,** which directs the sheriff or other officer to seize nonexempt property. If the creditor prevails at trial, the seized property can be sold to satisfy the judgment.

Writ of Execution. If a creditor obtains a judgment against the debtor and the debtor will not or cannot pay the judgment, the creditor is entitled to go back to the court and request a writ of execution. A **writ of execution** is an order that directs the sheriff to seize (levy) and sell any of the debtor's nonexempt real or personal property that is within the court's geographic jurisdiction (usually the county in which the courthouse is located). The proceeds of the sale are used to pay the judgment, accrued interest, and the costs of the sale. Any excess is paid to the debtor. The debtor can pay the judgment and redeem the nonexempt property at any time before the sale takes place. (Because of exemption laws and bankruptcy laws, however, many judgments are virtually uncollectible.)

Garnishment

An order for **garnishment** permits a creditor to collect a debt by seizing property of the debtor that is being held by a third party. In a garnishment proceeding, the third party—the person or entity on whom the garnishment judgment is served—is called the *garnishee.* Typically, the garnishee is the debtor's employer, and the creditor is seeking a judgment so that part of the debtor's usual paycheck will be paid to the creditor. In some situations, however, the garnishee is a third party that holds funds belonging to the debtor (such as a bank) or who has possession of, or exercises control over, funds or other types of property belonging to the debtor. Almost all types of property can be garnished, including tax refunds, pensions, and trust funds—so long as the property is not exempt from garnishment and is in the possession of a third party.

Garnishment Proceedings State law governs garnishment actions, so the specific procedures vary from state to state. According to the laws in many states, the judgment creditor needs to obtain only one order of garnishment, which will then apply continuously to the judgment debtor's weekly wages until the entire debt is paid. Garnishment can be a prejudgment remedy, requiring a hearing before a court, or a postjudgment remedy.

Laws Limiting the Amount of Wages Subject to Garnishment Both federal and state laws limit the amount that can be taken from a debtor's weekly take-home pay through garnishment proceedings.[2] Federal law provides a minimal framework to protect debtors from losing all their income to pay judgment debts.[3] State laws also provide dollar exemptions, and these amounts are often larger than those provided by federal law. Under federal law, an employer cannot dismiss an employee because his or her wages are being garnished.

The question in the following case was whether payments to an independent contractor for services performed could be garnished.

2. A few states (for example, Texas) do not permit garnishment of wages by private parties except under a child-support order.

3. For example, the federal Consumer Credit Protection Act, 15 U.S.C. Sections 1601–1693r, provides that a debtor can retain either 75 percent of his or her disposable earnings per week or an amount equivalent to thirty hours of work paid at federal minimum wage rates, whichever is greater.

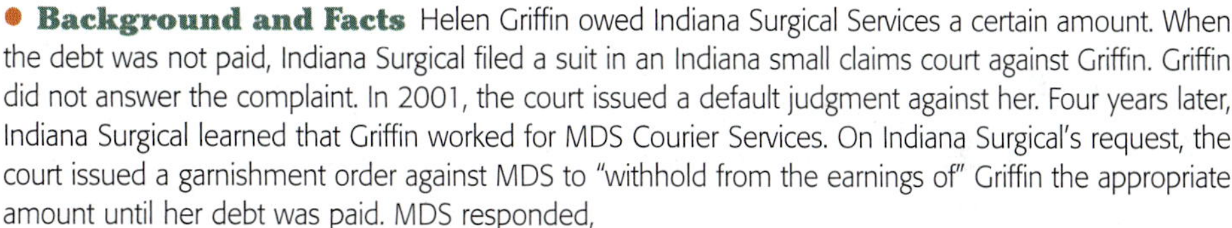

CASE 15.1 Indiana Surgical Specialists v. Griffin

Court of Appeals of Indiana, 2007. 867 N.E.2d 260.

• **Background and Facts** Helen Griffin owed Indiana Surgical Services a certain amount. When the debt was not paid, Indiana Surgical filed a suit in an Indiana small claims court against Griffin. Griffin did not answer the complaint. In 2001, the court issued a default judgment against her. Four years later, Indiana Surgical learned that Griffin worked for MDS Courier Services. On Indiana Surgical's request, the court issued a garnishment order against MDS to "withhold from the earnings of" Griffin the appropriate amount until her debt was paid. MDS responded,

> MDS Courier Services, Inc. employs drivers on a "contract" basis, therefore, drivers are not actual employees, but rather "contracted" to do a particular job. Because of this, we are not responsible for any payroll deductions including garnishments.

Indiana Surgical asked the court to hold MDS in contempt. Dawn Klingenberger, an MDS manager, testified that Griffin was a subcontractor of MDS, called as needed, compensated per job at "thirty-five percent of whatever she does," and paid on a biweekly basis. The court ruled that "the judgment debtor is a subcontractor, and not an employee," and that her earnings could not be garnished. Indiana Surgical appealed to a state intermediate appellate court.

IN THE LANGUAGE OF THE COURT

MAY, Judge.

* * * *

Indiana Surgical argues the trial court erred by declining to enforce the garnishment order issued to MDS on the ground Griffin was a "subcontractor" and not an employee of MDS. Indiana Surgical asserts the trial court's "distinction between wages subject to withholding and other earnings" is not supported in law. Under the facts of this case, we agree.

Garnishment refers to "any legal or equitable proceedings through which the earnings of an individual are required to be withheld by a garnishee, by the individual debtor, or by any other person for the payment of a judgment" [under Indiana Code Section 24-4.5-5-105(1)(b)].

CASE CONTINUES

CASE 15.1 CONTINUED

Earnings are [defined in Indiana Code Section 24-4.5-1-301(9) as] "compensation paid or payable for personal services, whether denominated as wages, salary, commission, bonus, or otherwise, and includes periodic payments under a pension or retirement program."[a] In discussing the [provision in the Consumer Credit Protection Act that is the] federal counterpart to the Indiana statute, the [United States] Supreme Court stated: "*There is every indication that Congress, in an effort to avoid the necessity of bankruptcy, sought to regulate garnishment in its usual sense as a levy on periodic payments of compensation needed to support the wage earner and his family on a week-to-week, month-to-month basis.*" [Emphasis added.]

Griffin received "periodic payments of compensation" for her personal services as a courier. These payments were earnings that could be garnished through a garnishment order. The trial court erred to the extent it held otherwise. We reverse and remand for further proceedings including, but not limited to, a determination of MDS's liability for payments made to Griffin after Indiana Surgical acquired an equitable lien upon service of process in [garnishment proceedings]. In light of our holding, the trial court should also determine whether MDS should be held in contempt of the garnishment order.

• **Decision and Remedy** *The state intermediate appellate court held that payments for the services of an independent contractor fall within the applicable definition of "earnings" and thus Griffin's earnings as an independent contractor could be garnished. The court reversed the decision of the lower court and remanded the case.*

• **The Ethical Dimension** *Should some persons be exempt from garnishment orders? Explain.*

• **The Legal Environment Dimension** *Building contractors and subcontractors are typically classified as independent contractors. Could payments to these parties also fall within the definition of "earnings" applied in this case? Discuss.*

a. Indiana's definition of earnings is included in the part of the Indiana Code known as the Uniform Consumer Credit Code, which was derived from the federal Consumer Credit Protection Act. The federal provision defining earnings is identical.

Creditors' Composition Agreements

Creditors may contract with the debtor for discharge of the debtor's liquidated debts (debts that are definite, or fixed, in amount) on payment of a sum less than that owed. These agreements are referred to as *composition agreements* or **creditors' composition agreements** and are usually held to be enforceable unless they are formed under duress.

Mortgages

A **mortgage** is a written instrument giving a creditor an interest in (lien on) the debtor's real property as security for the payment of a debt. Financial institutions grant mortgage loans for the purchase of property—usually a dwelling (real property will be discussed in Chapter 25). Given the relatively large sums that many individuals borrow to purchase a home, defaults are not uncommon. In fact, during 2007 and 2008 the number of defaults on mortgages increased dramatically. (For a discussion of the so-called subprime mortgage crisis, see the *Focus on Ethics* feature at the end of Unit 6.) Mortgages are recorded with the county in the state where the property is located. Recording ensures that the creditor is officially on record as holding an interest in the property. As a further precaution, most creditors require mortgage life insurance for debtors who do not pay at least 20 percent of the purchase price as a down payment at the time of the transaction.

Mortgage Foreclosure In the event of a debtor's default, the entire mortgage debt becomes due and payable. If the debtor cannot pay, the mortgage holder has the right to foreclose on the mortgaged property. The usual method of foreclosure is by judicial sale of the property, although the statutory methods of foreclosure vary from state to state. If the proceeds of the foreclosure sale are sufficient to cover both the costs of the foreclosure and the mortgage debt, any surplus goes to the debtor. If the sale proceeds are insufficient to cover the foreclosure costs and the mortgage debt, however, the **mortgagee** (the creditor-lender) can seek to recover the difference from the **mortgagor** (the debtor) by obtaining a *deficiency judgment.*

The mortgagee obtains a deficiency judgment in a separate legal action that is pursued subsequent to the foreclosure action. The deficiency judgment entitles the creditor to recover from other property owned by the debtor. Some states do not permit deficiency judgments for certain types of real estate interests.

Redemption Rights Before the foreclosure sale, a defaulting mortgagor can redeem the property by paying the full amount of the debt, plus any interest and costs that have accrued. This is known as the **right of redemption.** Some states even allow a mortgagor to redeem the property within a certain period of time after the foreclosure sale—called a *statutory period of redemption.* In states that allow redemption after the sale, the deed to the property usually is not delivered to the purchaser until the statutory period has expired. *Concept Summary 15.1* provides a synopsis of the remedies available to creditors.

Suretyship and Guaranty

When a third person promises to pay a debt owed by another in the event that the debtor does not pay, either a *suretyship* or a *guaranty* relationship is created. Exhibit 15–1 on the following page illustrates these relationships. The third person's credit becomes the security for the debt owed. At common law, there were significant differences in the liability of a surety and a guarantor, as will be discussed in the following subsections. Today, however, the distinctions outlined here have been abolished in some states.

Suretyship

A contract of **suretyship** is a promise made by a third person to be responsible for the debtor's obligation. It is an express contract between the **surety** (the third party) and the creditor. In the strictest sense, the surety is primarily liable for the debt of the principal. This means that the creditor can demand payment from the surety from the moment the debt is due and that the creditor need not exhaust all legal remedies against the principal debtor before holding the surety responsible for payment. Thus, a suretyship contract is

CONCEPT SUMMARY 15.1
Remedies Available to Creditors

Remedy	Description
LIENS	1. *Mechanic's lien*—A lien placed on an owner's real estate for labor, services, or materials furnished for improvements made to the realty. 2. *Artisan's lien*—A lien placed on an owner's personal property for labor performed or value added to that property. 3. *Judicial liens*— a. Writ of attachment—A court-ordered seizure of property prior to a court's final determination of the creditor's rights to the property. Creditors must strictly comply with applicable state statutes to obtain a writ of attachment. b. Writ of execution—A court order directing the sheriff to seize (levy) and sell a debtor's nonexempt real or personal property to satisfy a court's judgment in the creditor's favor.
GARNISHMENT	A collection remedy that allows the creditor to attach a debtor's funds (such as wages owed or bank accounts) and property that are held by a third person.
CREDITORS' COMPOSITION AGREEMENT	A contract between a debtor and her or his creditors by which the debtor's debts are discharged by payment of a sum less than the sum that is actually owed.
MORTGAGE FORECLOSURE	On the debtor's default, the entire mortgage debt is due and payable, allowing the creditor to foreclose on the realty by selling it to satisfy the debt.

EXHIBIT 15–1 • Suretyship and Guaranty Parties

In a suretyship or guaranty arrangement, a third party promises to be responsible for a debtor's obligations. A third party who agrees to be responsible for the debt even if the primary debtor does not default is known as a surety; a third party who agrees to be *secondarily* responsible for the debt—that is, responsible only if the primary debtor defaults—is known as a guarantor. Normally, a promise of guaranty (a collateral, or secondary, promise) must be in writing to be enforceable.

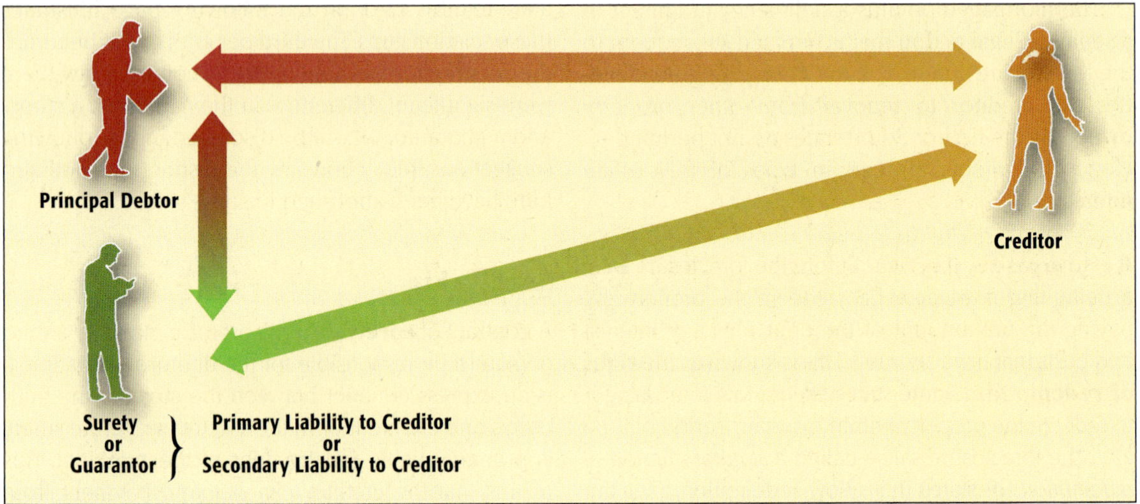

not a form of indemnity; that is, it is not merely a promise to make good any loss that a creditor may incur as a result of the debtor's failure to pay. Moreover, a surety agreement does not have to be in writing to be enforceable, although usually such agreements are in writing.

For example, Jason Oller wants to borrow funds from the bank to buy a used car. Because Jason is still in college, the bank will not lend him the funds unless his father, Stuart Oller, who has dealt with the bank before, will cosign the note (add his signature to the note, thereby becoming jointly liable for payment of the debt). When Mr. Oller cosigns the note, he becomes primarily liable to the bank. On the note's due date, the bank can seek payment from Jason Oller, Stuart Oller, or both jointly.

Guaranty

A guaranty contract is similar to a suretyship contract in that it includes a promise to answer for the debt or default of another. There are some significant differences between these two types of contracts, however.

Suretyship versus Guaranty With a suretyship arrangement, the surety is *primarily* liable for the debtor's obligation. With a guaranty arrangement, the **guarantor**—the third person making the guaranty—is *secondarily* liable. The guarantor can be required to pay the obligation only after the principal debtor defaults, and usually only after the creditor has made an attempt to collect from the debtor.

For example, a corporation, BX Enterprises, needs to borrow to meet its payroll. The bank is skeptical about the creditworthiness of BX and requires Dawson, its president, who is a wealthy businessperson and owner of 70 percent of BX Enterprises, to sign an agreement making herself personally liable for payment if BX does not pay off the loan. As a guarantor of the loan, Dawson cannot be held liable until BX Enterprises is in default.

Under the Statute of Frauds, a guaranty contract between the guarantor and the creditor must be in writing to be enforceable unless the *main purpose* exception applies.[4] A suretyship agreement, by contrast, need not be in writing to be enforceable. In other words, surety agreements can be oral, whereas guaranty contracts must be written.

The Extent and Time of the Guarantor's Liability The guaranty contract terms determine the extent and time of the guarantor's liability. For

4. Briefly, the main purpose exception provides that if the main purpose of the guaranty agreement is to benefit the guarantor, then the contract need not be in writing to be enforceable.

example, the guaranty can be *continuing,* designed to cover a series of transactions by the debtor. Also, the guaranty can be *unlimited* or *limited* as to time and amount. In addition, the guaranty can be *absolute* or *conditional.* When a guaranty is absolute, the guarantor becomes liable immediately on the debtor's default. With a conditional guaranty, the guarantor becomes liable only on the happening of a certain event. For example, Days Inns of America, Inc., entered into a contract that licensed P&N Enterprises, Inc., to operate a guest lodging facility in Connecticut. The president of P&N Enterprises, Paul Yeh, signed the licensing contract and also signed a guaranty contract, in his individual capacity. Yeh personally guaranteed P&N's obligations under the license agreement, "provided that P&N's tangible net worth was less than $1,000,000 at the time of payment or performance." The condition of that promise (the guaranty) was the tangible net worth requirement.[5]

Defenses of the Surety and the Guarantor

The defenses of the surety and the guarantor are basically the same. Therefore, the following discussion applies to both, although it refers only to the surety.

Actions Releasing the Surety Certain actions will release the surety from the obligation. If the principal obligation is paid by the debtor or by another person on behalf of the debtor, the surety is discharged from the obligation. Similarly, if valid tender of payment is made, and the creditor for some reason rejects it with knowledge of the surety's existence, then the surety is released from any obligation on the debt.

In addition, if a creditor surrenders the collateral to the debtor or impairs the collateral while knowing of the surety and without the surety's consent, the surety is released to the extent of any loss suffered as a result of the creditor's actions. The primary reason for this requirement is to protect a surety who agreed to become obligated only because the debtor's collateral was in the possession of the creditor.

Finally, making any material modification in the terms of the original contract between the principal debtor and the creditor can operate to discharge a surety's obligations. For example, a gratuitous surety will be completely discharged if the principal debtor and the creditor materially modify the contract without first obtaining the surety's consent. (A *gratuitous surety* is one who receives no consideration in return for acting as a surety, such as a father who agrees to assume responsibility for his daughter's debt obligation.) A surety who is compensated (such as a venture capitalist who will profit from a loan made to the principal debtor) will be discharged from the contract only if the modification is actually or potentially detrimental to the surety.

Defenses of the Principal Debtor Generally, the surety can use any defenses available to the principal debtor to avoid liability on the obligation to the creditor. The ability of the surety to assert any defenses the debtor may have against the creditor is the most important concept in suretyship. It means that most of the defenses available to the debtor are also those of the surety. A few exceptions do exist, however. The surety cannot assert the principal debtor's incapacity or bankruptcy as a defense, nor can the surety assert the statute of limitations as a defense.

Obviously, a surety may also have his or her own defenses—for example, incapacity or bankruptcy. If the creditor fraudulently induced the surety to guarantee the debt, the surety can assert fraud as a defense. In most states, the creditor has a legal duty to inform the surety, prior to the formation of the suretyship contract, of material facts known by the creditor that would substantially increase the surety's risk. Failure to so inform is fraud and makes the suretyship obligation voidable.

Rights of the Surety and the Guarantor

Generally, when the surety or guarantor pays the debt owed to the creditor, the surety or guarantor is entitled to certain rights. Because the rights of the surety and the guarantor are basically the same, the following discussion applies to both.

The Right of Subrogation First, the surety has the legal **right of subrogation.** Simply stated, this means that any right the creditor had against the debtor now becomes the right of the surety. Included are creditor rights in bankruptcy and rights to judgments obtained by the creditor. In short, the surety now stands in the shoes of the creditor and may pursue any remedies that were available to the creditor against the debtor.

5. *Days Inns of America, Inc. v. P&N Enterprises, Inc.,* 2006 WL 2801248 (D.Conn. 2006). For another example of a conditional guaranty, see *Express Recovery Services, Inc. v. Rice,* 2005 UT App 495, 125 P.3d 108 (2005).

The Right of Reimbursement Second, the surety has a **right of reimbursement** from the debtor. Basically, the surety is entitled to receive from the debtor all outlays made on behalf of the suretyship arrangement. Such outlays can include expenses incurred as well as the actual amount of the debt paid to the creditor.

The Right of Contribution Third, in the situation of **co-sureties** (two or more sureties on the same obligation owed by the debtor), a surety who pays more than her or his proportionate share on a debtor's default is entitled to recover from the co-sureties the amount paid above the surety's obligation. This is the **right of contribution.** Generally, a co-surety's liability either is determined by agreement or, in the absence of agreement, is set at the maximum liability under the suretyship contract.

Suppose that two co-sureties are obligated under a suretyship contract to guarantee the debt of a debtor. Together, the sureties' maximum liability is $25,000. Surety A's maximum liability is $15,000, and surety B's is $10,000. The debtor owes $10,000 and is in default. Surety A pays the creditor the entire $10,000. In the absence of agreement, surety A can recover $4,000 from surety B ($10,000/$25,000 × $10,000 = $4,000, surety B's obligation).

Protection for Debtors

The law protects debtors as well as creditors. Certain property of the debtor, for example, is exempt under state law from creditors' actions. Consumer protection statutes (see Chapter 23) also protect debtors' rights. Of course, bankruptcy laws, which will be discussed shortly, are designed specifically to assist debtors in need of help.

In most states, certain types of real and personal property are exempt from execution or attachment. State exemption statutes usually include both real and personal property.

Exempted Real Property

Probably the most familiar exemption is the **homestead exemption.** Each state permits the debtor to retain the family home, either in its entirety or up to a specified dollar amount, free from the claims of unsecured creditors or trustees in bankruptcy. (Note that federal bankruptcy laws after 2005 place a cap of $125,000 for debtors in bankruptcy who have recently moved and are seeking to use state homestead exemptions.)

Suppose that Beere owes Veltman $40,000. The debt is the subject of a lawsuit, and the court awards Veltman a judgment of $40,000 against Beere. Beere's homestead is valued at $50,000, and the homestead exemption is $25,000. There are no outstanding mortgages or other liens on his homestead. To satisfy the judgment debt, Beere's family home is sold at public auction for $45,000. The proceeds of the sale are distributed as follows:

1. Beere is given $25,000 as his homestead exemption.
2. Veltman is paid $20,000 toward the judgment debt, leaving a $20,000 deficiency judgment (that is, "leftover debt") that can be satisfied from any other nonexempt property (personal or real) that Beere may own, if permitted by state law.

In a few states, statutes allow the homestead exemption only if the judgment debtor has a family. If a judgment debtor does not have a family, a creditor may be entitled to collect the full amount realized from the sale of the debtor's home.

Exempted Personal Property

Personal property that is most often exempt from satisfaction of judgment debts includes the following:

1. Household furniture up to a specified dollar amount.
2. Clothing and certain personal possessions, such as family pictures or a Bible.
3. A vehicle (or vehicles) for transportation (at least up to a specified dollar amount).
4. Certain classified animals, usually livestock but including pets.
5. Equipment that the debtor uses in a business or trade, such as tools or professional instruments, up to a specified dollar amount.

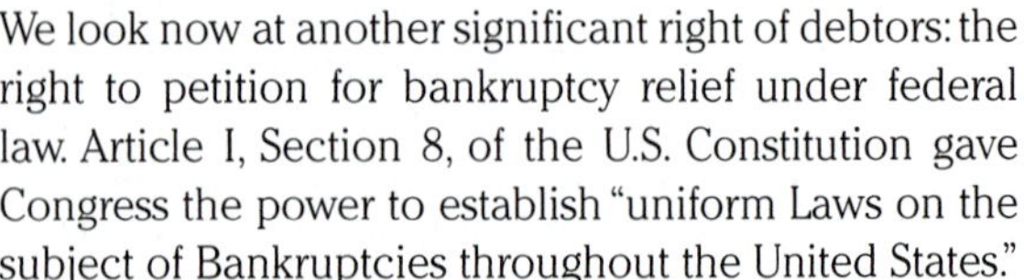

Bankruptcy and Reorganization

We look now at another significant right of debtors: the right to petition for bankruptcy relief under federal law. Article I, Section 8, of the U.S. Constitution gave Congress the power to establish "uniform Laws on the subject of Bankruptcies throughout the United States."

Bankruptcy law in the United States has two goals—to protect a debtor by giving him or her a fresh start, free from creditors' claims, and to ensure equitable treatment to creditors who are competing for a debtor's assets. Federal bankruptcy legislation was first enacted in 1898 and has undergone several modifications since that time, most recently in 2005 as a result of the 2005 Bankruptcy Reform Act. The 2005 act significantly overhauled certain provisions of the Bankruptcy Code for the first time in twenty-five years.

Bankruptcy Proceedings

Bankruptcy proceedings are held in federal bankruptcy courts, which are under the authority of the U.S. district courts, and rulings from bankruptcy courts can be appealed to the district courts. Although bankruptcy law is federal law, state laws on secured transactions, liens, judgments, and exemptions also play a role in federal bankruptcy proceedings.

Essentially, a bankruptcy court fulfills the role of an administrative court for the federal district court concerning matters in bankruptcy. The bankruptcy court holds proceedings dealing with the procedures required to administer the estate of the debtor in bankruptcy (the *estate* consists of the debtor's assets, as will be discussed shortly). A bankruptcy court can conduct a jury trial if the appropriate district court has authorized it and the parties to the bankruptcy consent.

Types of Bankruptcy Relief

Title 11 of the *United States Code* encompasses the Bankruptcy Code, which has eight chapters. Chapters 1, 3, and 5 of the Code contain general definitional provisions, as well as provisions governing case administration, creditors, the debtor, and the estate. These three chapters normally apply to all kinds of bankruptcies. The next five chapters of the Code set forth the different types of relief that debtors may seek. Chapter 7 provides for **liquidation** proceedings (the selling of all nonexempt assets and the distribution of the proceeds to the debtor's creditors). Chapter 9 governs the adjustment of a municipality's debts. Chapter 11 governs reorganizations. Chapters 12 and 13 provide for the adjustment of debts by parties with regular incomes (family farmers and family fishermen under Chapter 12 and individuals under Chapter 13).[6] A debtor (except for a municipality) does not have to be insolvent[7] to file for bankruptcy relief under any chapter of the Bankruptcy Code. Anyone obligated to a creditor can declare bankruptcy.

Special Treatment of Consumer-Debtors

To ensure that consumer-debtors are fully informed of the various types of relief available, the Code requires that the clerk of the bankruptcy court provide certain information to all consumer-debtors before they file for bankruptcy. A **consumer-debtor** is a debtor whose debts result primarily from the purchase of goods for personal, family, or household use. First, the clerk must give consumer-debtors written notice of the general purpose, benefits, and costs of each chapter of the Bankruptcy Code under which they might proceed. Second, the clerk must provide consumer-debtors with informational materials on the types of services available from credit counseling agencies.

Liquidation Proceedings

Liquidation under Chapter 7 of the Bankruptcy Code is generally the most familiar type of bankruptcy proceeding and is often referred to as an *ordinary,* or *straight, bankruptcy.* Put simply, a debtor in a liquidation bankruptcy turns all assets over to a **trustee.** The trustee sells the nonexempt assets and distributes the proceeds to creditors. With certain exceptions, the remaining debts are then **discharged** (extinguished), and the debtor is relieved of the obligation to pay the debts.

Any "person"—defined as including individuals, partnerships, and corporations[8]—may be a debtor in a liquidation proceeding. Railroads, insurance companies, banks, savings and loan associations, investment companies licensed by the Small Business Administration, and credit unions cannot be debtors in a liquidation bankruptcy, however. Other chapters of the Bankruptcy Code or other federal or state statutes apply to them. A husband and wife may file jointly for bankruptcy under a single petition.

6. There are no Chapters 2, 4, 6, 8, or 10 in Title 11. Such "gaps" are not uncommon in the *United States Code.* This is because chapter numbers (or other subdivisional unit numbers) are sometimes reserved for future use when a statute is enacted. (A gap may also appear if a law has been repealed.)

7. The inability to pay debts as they become due is known as *equitable* insolvency. A *balance sheet* insolvency, which exists when a debtor's liabilities exceed assets, is not the test. Thus, it is possible for debtors to petition for bankruptcy voluntarily or to be forced into involuntary bankruptcy even though their assets far exceed their liabilities. This may occur when a debtor's cash flow problems become severe.

8. The definition of *corporation* includes unincorporated companies and associations. It also covers labor unions.

A straight bankruptcy may be commenced by the filing of either a voluntary or an involuntary **petition in bankruptcy**—the document that is filed with a bankruptcy court to initiate bankruptcy proceedings. If a debtor files the petition, it is a voluntary bankruptcy. If one or more creditors file a petition to force the debtor into bankruptcy, it is called an involuntary bankruptcy. We discuss both voluntary and involuntary bankruptcy proceedings under Chapter 7 in the following subsections.

Voluntary Bankruptcy

To bring a voluntary petition in bankruptcy, the debtor files official forms designated for that purpose in the bankruptcy court. Under the Bankruptcy Reform Act of 2005, before debtors can file a petition, they must receive credit counseling from an approved nonprofit agency within the 180-day period preceding the date of filing. The act outlined detailed criteria for the **U.S. trustee** (a government official who performs appointment and other administrative tasks that a bankruptcy judge would otherwise have to perform) to approve nonprofit budget and counseling agencies and required the U.S. trustee to make the list of approved agencies publicly available. A debtor filing a Chapter 7 petition must include a certificate proving that he or she received individual or group briefing from an approved counseling agency within the last 180 days (roughly six months).

The Code requires a consumer-debtor who has opted for liquidation bankruptcy proceedings to confirm the accuracy of the petition's contents. The debtor must also state in the petition, at the time of filing, that he or she understands the relief available under other chapters of the Code and has chosen to proceed under Chapter 7. If an attorney is representing the consumer-debtor, the attorney must file an affidavit stating that she or he has informed the debtor of the relief available under each chapter of the Bankruptcy Code. In addition, the Code requires the attorney to reasonably attempt to verify the accuracy of the consumer-debtor's petition and schedules (described below). Failure to do so is considered perjury.

Chapter 7 Schedules The voluntary petition must contain the following schedules:

1. A list of both secured and unsecured creditors, their addresses, and the amount of debt owed to each.
2. A statement of the financial affairs of the debtor.
3. A list of all property owned by the debtor, including property that the debtor claims is exempt.
4. A list of current income and expenses.
5. A certificate of credit counseling (as discussed previously).
6. Proof of payments received from employers within sixty days prior to the filing of the petition.
7. A statement of the amount of monthly income, itemized to show how the amount is calculated.
8. A copy of the debtor's federal income tax return for the most recent year ending immediately before the filing of the petition.

As previously noted, the official forms must be completed accurately, sworn to under oath, and signed by the debtor. To conceal assets or knowingly supply false information on these schedules is a crime under the bankruptcy laws.

With the exception of tax returns, failure to file the required schedules within forty-five days after the filing of the petition (unless an extension of up to forty-five days is granted) will result in an automatic dismissal of the petition. The debtor has up to seven days before the date of the first creditors' meeting to provide a copy of the most recent tax returns to the trustee.

Additional Information May Be Required At the request of the court, the trustee, or any party in interest, the debtor must file tax returns at the end of each tax year while the case is pending and provide copies to the court. This requirement also applies to Chapter 11 and 13 bankruptcies (discussed later in this chapter). Also, if requested by the trustee, the debtor must provide a photo document establishing his or her identity (such as a driver's license or passport) or other such personal identifying information.

Substantial Abuse Prior to 2005, a bankruptcy court could dismiss a Chapter 7 petition for relief (discharge of debts) if the use of Chapter 7 would constitute a "substantial abuse" of that chapter. The Bankruptcy Reform Act of 2005 established a new system of "means testing" (the debtor's income) to determine whether a debtor's petition is presumed to be a "substantial abuse" of Chapter 7.

When Abuse Will Be Presumed. If the debtor's family income is greater than the median family income in the state in which the petition is filed, the trustee or any party in interest (such as a creditor) can bring a motion to dismiss the Chapter 7 petition. State median incomes vary from state to state and are calculated and reported by the U.S. Bureau of the Census.

The debtor's current monthly income is calculated using the last six months' average income, less certain "allowed expenses" reflecting the basic needs of the debtor. The monthly amount is then multiplied by twelve. If the resulting income exceeds the state median income by $6,000 or more,[9] abuse is presumed, and the trustee or any creditor can file a motion to dismiss the petition. A debtor can rebut (refute) the presumption of abuse "by demonstrating special circumstances that justify additional expenses or adjustments of current monthly income for which there is no reasonable alternative." (An example might be anticipated medical costs not covered by health insurance.) These additional expenses or adjustments must be itemized and their accuracy attested to under oath by the debtor.

9. This amount ($6,000) is the equivalent of $100 per month for five years, indicating that the debtor could pay at least $100 per month under a Chapter 13 five-year repayment plan.

When Abuse Will Not Be Presumed. If the debtor's income is below the state median (or if the debtor has successfully refuted the means-test presumption), abuse will not be presumed. In these situations, the court may still find substantial abuse, but the creditors will not have standing (see Chapter 2) to file a motion to dismiss. Basically, this leaves intact the prior law on substantial abuse, allowing the court to consider such factors as the debtor's bad faith or circumstances indicating substantial abuse.

Can a debtor seeking relief under Chapter 7 exclude voluntary contributions to a retirement plan as a reasonably necessary expense in calculating her income? The Code does not disallow the contributions, but whether their exclusion constitutes substantial abuse requires a review of the debtor's circumstances, as in the following case.

EXTENDED CASE 15.2 Hebbring v. U.S. Trustee

United States Court of Appeals, Ninth Circuit, 2006. 463 F.3d 902.

***WARDLAW,* Circuit Judge.**

* * * *

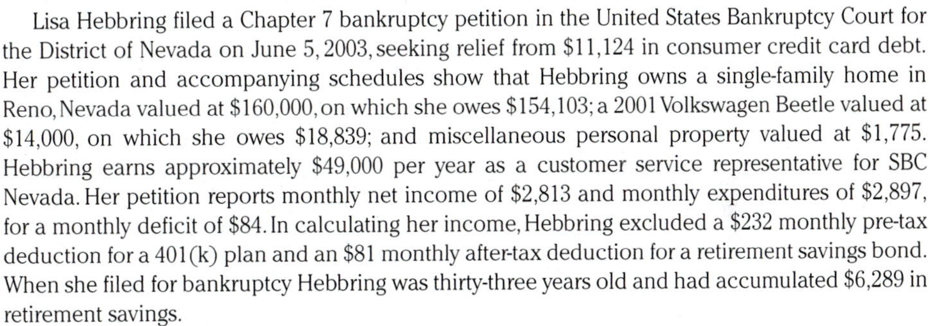

Lisa Hebbring filed a Chapter 7 bankruptcy petition in the United States Bankruptcy Court for the District of Nevada on June 5, 2003, seeking relief from $11,124 in consumer credit card debt. Her petition and accompanying schedules show that Hebbring owns a single-family home in Reno, Nevada valued at $160,000, on which she owes $154,103; a 2001 Volkswagen Beetle valued at $14,000, on which she owes $18,839; and miscellaneous personal property valued at $1,775. Hebbring earns approximately $49,000 per year as a customer service representative for SBC Nevada. Her petition reports monthly net income of $2,813 and monthly expenditures of $2,897, for a monthly deficit of $84. In calculating her income, Hebbring excluded a $232 monthly pre-tax deduction for a 401(k) plan and an $81 monthly after-tax deduction for a retirement savings bond. When she filed for bankruptcy Hebbring was thirty-three years old and had accumulated $6,289 in retirement savings.

The United States Trustee ("Trustee") moved to dismiss Hebbring's petition for substantial abuse, see 11 U.S.C. [Section] 707(b), arguing that she should not be allowed to deduct voluntary retirement contributions from her income and that her recent paystubs showed that her gross income was higher than she had claimed. As a result, the Trustee contended, Hebbring's monthly net income was actually $3,512, leaving her $615 per month in disposable income, sufficient to repay 100% of her unsecured debt over three years.

* * * *

The bankruptcy court granted the Trustee's motion to dismiss * * * [and ultimately Hebbring appealed the dismissal to the U.S. Court of Appeals for the Ninth Circuit].

* * * *

* * * In determining whether a petition constitutes a substantial abuse of Chapter 7, we examine the totality of the circumstances, focusing principally on whether the debtor will have sufficient future disposable income to fund a Chapter 13 plan that would pay a substantial portion of his unsecured debt. To calculate a debtor's disposable income, we begin with current monthly income and subtract amounts reasonably necessary to be expended * * * for the maintenance or support of the debtor or a dependent of the debtor.

* * * [Some] courts * * * have adopted a case-by-case approach, under which contributions to a retirement plan may be found reasonably necessary depending on the debtor's circumstances.

CASE CONTINUES

CASE 15.2 CONTINUED

We believe this * * * approach better comports [is consistent] with Congress's intent, as expressed in the language, purpose, and structure of the Bankruptcy Code. By not defining the phrase "reasonably necessary" or providing any examples of expenses that categorically are or are not reasonably necessary, the Code suggests courts should examine each debtor's specific circumstances to determine whether a claimed expense is reasonably necessary for that debtor's maintenance or support. We find no evidence that Congress intended courts to employ a *per se* rule against retirement contributions, which may be crucial for debtors' support upon retirement, particularly for older debtors who have little or no savings. Where Congress intended courts to use a *per se* rule rather than a case-by-case approach in classifying financial interests or obligations under the Bankruptcy Code, it has explicitly communicated its intent. *Congress's decision not to categorically exclude any specific expense, including retirement contributions, from being considered reasonably necessary is probative* [an indication] *of its intent.* [Emphasis added.]

Requiring a fact-specific analysis to determine whether an expense is reasonably necessary is sound policy because it comports with the Code's approach to identifying substantial abuse of the Chapter 7 relief provisions. * * * Congress chose [not] to define "substantial abuse" * * * . Congress thus left a flexible standard enabling courts to address each petition on its own merit. That Congress granted courts the discretion to identify substantial abuse necessarily suggests it intended courts to have the discretion to answer the subsidiary question of whether particular expenses are reasonably necessary.

In light of these considerations, and in the absence of any indication that Congress sought to prohibit debtors from voluntarily contributing to retirement plans *per se,* we conclude that bankruptcy courts have discretion to determine whether retirement contributions are a reasonably necessary expense for a particular debtor based on the facts of each individual case. In making this fact-intensive determination, courts should consider a number of factors, including but not limited to: the debtor's age, income, overall budget, expected date of retirement, existing retirement savings, and amount of contributions; the likelihood that stopping contributions will jeopardize the debtor's fresh start by forcing the debtor to make up lost contributions after emerging from bankruptcy; and the needs of the debtor's dependents. *Courts must allow debtors to seek bankruptcy protection while voluntarily saving for retirement if such savings appear reasonably necessary for the maintenance or support of the debtor or the debtor's dependents.* [Emphasis added.]

* * * *

Here, the bankruptcy court * * * found * * * that Hebbring's retirement contributions are not a reasonably necessary expense based on her age and specific financial circumstances. * * * When she filed her bankruptcy petition, Hebbring was only thirty-three years old and was contributing approximately 8% of her gross income toward her retirement. Although Hebbring had accumulated only $6,289 in retirement savings, she was earning $49,000 per year and making mortgage payments on a house. In light of these circumstances, the bankruptcy court's conclusion that Hebbring's retirement contributions are not a reasonably necessary expense is not clearly erroneous.

* * * *

For the foregoing reasons, the district court's order affirming the bankruptcy court's order dismissing this case is AFFIRMED.

QUESTIONS

1. Is it fair for the court to treat retirement contributions differently depending on a person's age?
2. Is it likely to have made a difference to the result in this case that the debtor's retirement contributions were automatically and electronically deducted from her pay? Explain.

Additional Grounds for Dismissal As noted, a debtor's voluntary petition for Chapter 7 relief may be dismissed for substantial abuse or for failing to provide the necessary documents (such as schedules and tax returns) within the specified time. In addition, a motion to dismiss a Chapter 7 filing might be granted in two other situations under the Bankruptcy Reform Act of 2005. First, if the debtor has been convicted of a violent crime or a drug-trafficking offense, the victim can file a motion to dismiss the voluntary petition.[10] Second, if the debtor fails to pay postpetition domestic-support obligations (which include child and spousal support), the court may dismiss the debtor's Chapter 7 petition.

Order for Relief If the voluntary petition for bankruptcy is found to be proper, the filing of the petition will itself constitute an **order for relief.** (An order for relief is a court's grant of assistance to a petitioner.) Once a consumer-debtor's voluntary petition has been filed, the clerk of the court or other appointee must give the trustee and creditors notice of the order for relief by mail not more than twenty days after entry of the order.

Involuntary Bankruptcy

An involuntary bankruptcy occurs when the debtor's creditors force the debtor into bankruptcy proceedings. An involuntary case cannot be commenced against a farmer[11] or a charitable institution. For an involuntary action to be filed against other debtors, the following requirements must be met: If the debtor has twelve or more creditors, three or more of these creditors having unsecured claims totaling at least $13,475 must join in the petition. If a debtor has fewer than twelve creditors, one or more creditors having a claim of $13,475 may file.

If the debtor challenges the involuntary petition, a hearing will be held, and the bankruptcy court will enter an order for relief if it finds either of the following:

1. The debtor is generally not paying debts as they become due.
2. A general receiver, assignee, or custodian took possession of, or was appointed to take charge of, substantially all of the debtor's property within 120 days before the filing of the petition.

If the court grants an order for relief, the debtor will be required to supply the same information in the bankruptcy schedules as in a voluntary bankruptcy.

An involuntary petition should not be used as an everyday debt-collection device, and the Code provides penalties for the filing of frivolous petitions against debtors. Judgment may be granted against the petitioning creditors for the costs and attorneys' fees incurred by the debtor in defending against an involuntary petition that is dismissed by the court. If the petition is filed in bad faith, damages can be awarded for injury to the debtor's reputation. Punitive damages may also be awarded.

Automatic Stay

The moment a petition, either voluntary or involuntary, is filed, an **automatic stay,** or suspension, of virtually all actions by creditors against the debtor or the debtor's property normally goes into effect. In other words, once a petition has been filed, creditors cannot contact the debtor by phone or mail or start any legal proceedings to recover debts or to repossess property. A secured creditor or other party in interest, however, may petition the bankruptcy court for relief from the automatic stay. The Code provides that if a creditor knowingly violates the automatic stay (a willful violation), any injured party, including the debtor, is entitled to recover actual damages, costs, and attorneys' fees, and may be awarded punitive damages as well.

Underlying the Code's automatic-stay provision for a secured creditor is a concept known as *adequate protection.* The **adequate protection doctrine,** among other things, protects secured creditors from losing their security as a result of the automatic stay. The bankruptcy court can provide adequate protection by requiring the debtor or trustee to make periodic cash payments or a one-time cash payment (or to provide additional collateral or replacement liens) to the extent that the stay may actually cause the value of the property to decrease.

Exceptions to the Automatic Stay There are several exceptions to the automatic stay. The 2005 Bankruptcy Reform Act created a new exception for domestic-support obligations, which include any debt owed to or recoverable by a spouse, former spouse, or child of the debtor; a child's parent or guardian; or a governmental unit. In addition, proceedings against the debtor related to divorce, child custody or visitation, domestic violence, and support enforcement are not stayed. Also excepted are investigations by a securities regulatory agency, the creation or perfection of statutory liens for property

10. Note that the court may not dismiss a case on this ground if the debtor's bankruptcy is necessary to satisfy a claim for a domestic-support obligation.

11. The definition of *farmer* includes persons who receive more than 50 percent of their gross income from farming operations, such as tilling the soil, dairy farming, ranching, or the production or raising of crops, poultry, or livestock. Corporations and partnerships may qualify under certain conditions.

taxes or special assessments on real property, eviction actions on judgments obtained prior to filing the petition, and withholding from the debtor's wages for repayment of a retirement account loan.

Limitations on the Automatic Stay Under the Code, if a creditor or other party in interest requests relief from the stay, the stay will automatically terminate sixty days after the request, unless the court grants an extension[12] or the parties agree otherwise. Also, the automatic stay on secured debts will terminate thirty days after the petition is filed if the debtor had filed a bankruptcy petition that was dismissed within the prior year. Any party in interest can request the court to extend the stay by showing that the filing is in good faith.

If two or more bankruptcy petitions were dismissed during the prior year, the Code presumes bad faith, and the automatic stay does not go into effect until the court determines that the filing was made in good faith. In addition, if the petition is subsequently dismissed because the debtor failed to file the required documents within thirty days of filing, for example, the stay is terminated. Finally, the automatic stay on secured property terminates forty-five days after the creditors' meeting (to be discussed shortly) unless the debtor redeems or reaffirms certain debts (*reaffirmation* is discussed later in this chapter). In other words, the debtor cannot keep the secured property (such as a financed automobile), even if she or he continues to make payments on it, without reinstating the rights of the secured party to collect on the debt.

Property of the Estate

On the commencement of a liquidation proceeding under Chapter 7, an *estate in property* is created. The estate consists of all the debtor's legal and equitable interests in property currently held, wherever located, together with community property (property jointly owned by a husband and wife in certain states—see Chapter 25), property transferred in a transaction voidable by the trustee, proceeds and profits from the property of the estate, and certain after-acquired property. Interests in certain property—such as gifts, inheritances, property settlements (from divorce), and life insurance death proceeds—to which the debtor becomes entitled *within 180 days after filing* may also become part of the estate. Withholdings for employee benefit plan contributions are excluded from the estate. Generally, though, the filing of a bankruptcy petition fixes a dividing line: property acquired prior to the filing of the petition becomes property of the estate, and property acquired after the filing of the petition, except as just noted, remains the debtor's.

Creditors' Meeting and Claims

Within a reasonable time after the order for relief has been granted (not less than twenty days or more than forty days), the trustee must call a meeting of the creditors listed in the schedules filed by the debtor. The bankruptcy judge does not attend this meeting, but the debtor is required to attend and to submit to examination under oath by the creditors and the trustee. At the meeting, the trustee ensures that the debtor is aware of the potential consequences of bankruptcy and of his or her ability to file for bankruptcy under a different chapter of the Bankruptcy Code.

To be entitled to receive a portion of the debtor's estate, each creditor normally files a *proof of claim* with the bankruptcy court clerk within ninety days of the creditors' meeting.[13] The proof of claim lists the creditor's name and address, as well as the amount that the creditor asserts is owed to the creditor by the debtor. A proof of claim is necessary if there is any dispute concerning the claim. Generally, any legal obligation of the debtor is a claim (except claims for breach of employment contracts or real estate leases for terms longer than one year).

Exemptions

The trustee takes control over the debtor's property, but an individual debtor is entitled to exempt certain property from the bankruptcy. The Bankruptcy Code exempts the following property:[14]

1. Up to $20,200 in equity in the debtor's residence and burial plot (the homestead exemption).
2. Interest in a motor vehicle up to $3,225.
3. Interest, up to $525 for a particular item, in household goods and furnishings, wearing apparel, appliances, books, animals, crops, and musical

12. The court might grant an extension, for example, on a motion by the trustee that the property is of value to the estate.

13. This ninety-day rule applies in Chapter 12 and Chapter 13 bankruptcies as well.

14. The dollar amounts stated in the Bankruptcy Code are adjusted automatically every three years on April 1 based on changes in the Consumer Price Index. The adjusted amounts are rounded to the nearest $25. The amounts stated in this chapter are in accordance with those computed on April 1, 2007.

instruments (the aggregate total of all items is limited, however, to $10,775).[15]

4. Interest in jewelry up to $1,350.
5. Interest in any other property up to $1,075, plus any unused part of the $20,200 homestead exemption up to $10,125.
6. Interest in any tools of the debtor's trade up to $2,025.
7. Life insurance contracts owned by the debtor.
8. Certain interests in accrued dividends and interest under life insurance contracts owned by the debtor, not to exceed $10,775.
9. Professionally prescribed health aids.
10. The right to receive Social Security and certain welfare benefits, alimony and support, certain retirement funds and pensions, and education savings accounts held for specific periods of time.
11. The right to receive certain personal-injury and other awards up to $20,200.

Individual states have the power to pass legislation precluding debtors from using the federal exemptions within the state; a majority of the states have done this. In those states, debtors may use only state, not federal, exemptions. In the rest of the states, an individual debtor (or a husband and wife filing jointly) may choose either the exemptions provided under state law or the federal exemptions.

The Homestead Exemption

The 2005 Bankruptcy Reform Act significantly changed the law for those debtors seeking to use state homestead exemption statutes. Under prior law, the homestead exemptions of six states, including Florida and Texas, allowed debtors petitioning for bankruptcy to shield *unlimited* amounts of equity in their homes from creditors. The Code now places limits on the amount that can be claimed as exempt in bankruptcy. Also, a debtor must have lived in a state for two years prior to filing the petition to be able to use the state homestead exemption (the prior law required only six months).

In general, if the debtor acquired the homestead within three and a half years preceding the date of filing, the maximum equity exempted is $136,875, even if state law would permit a higher amount. Moreover, the debtor may not claim the homestead exemption if he or she has committed any criminal act, intentional tort, or willful or reckless misconduct that caused serious physical injury or death to another individual in the preceding five years. Similarly, a debtor who has been convicted of a felony may not be able to claim the exemption.

The Trustee

Promptly after the order for relief in the liquidation proceeding has been entered, a trustee is appointed. The basic duty of the trustee is to collect the debtor's available estate and reduce it to cash for distribution, preserving the interests of both the debtor and unsecured creditors. This requires that the trustee be accountable for administering the debtor's estate. To enable the trustee to accomplish this duty, the Code gives the trustee certain powers, stated in both general and specific terms. These powers must be exercised within two years of the order for relief.

The trustee has additional duties with regard to means testing debtors and protecting domestic-support creditors. The trustee is required to promptly review all materials filed by the debtor to determine if there is substantial abuse. Within ten days after the first meeting of the creditors, the trustee must file a statement indicating whether the case is presumed to be an abuse under the means test. The trustee must provide all creditors with a copy of this statement. When there is a presumption of abuse, the trustee must either file a motion to dismiss the petition (or convert it to a Chapter 13 case) or file a statement setting forth the reasons why a motion would not be appropriate. If the debtor owes a domestic-support obligation (such as child support), the trustee is required to provide written notice of the bankruptcy to the claim holder (a former spouse, for example).

The Trustee's Powers The trustee occupies a position *equivalent* in rights to that of certain other parties. For example, the trustee has the same rights as a creditor who could have obtained a judicial lien or levy execution on the debtor's property. This means that a trustee has priority over an unperfected secured party as to the debtor's property.[16] This right of a

15. The 2005 Bankruptcy Reform Act clarified that "household goods and furnishings" includes, for example, one computer, one radio, one television, and one videocassette recorder. Other items, such as works of art, electronic entertainment equipment with a fair market value of more than $500, and antiques and jewelry (except wedding rings) valued at more than $500, are not included.

16. Nevertheless, in most states a creditor with an unperfected purchase-money security interest may prevail against a trustee if the creditor perfects (files) within twenty days of the debtor's receipt of the collateral. This is normally true even if the debtor files a bankruptcy petition before the creditor perfects.

trustee, which is equivalent to that of a lien creditor, is known as the *strong-arm power.* A trustee also has power equivalent to that of a *bona fide purchaser* of real property from the debtor.

The Right to Possession of the Debtor's Property The trustee has the power to require persons holding the debtor's property at the time the petition is filed to deliver the property to the trustee. (Usually, though, the trustee takes constructive, rather than actual, possession of the debtor's property. For example, to obtain control of a debtor's business inventory, a trustee might change the locks on the doors to the business and hire a security guard.)

Avoidance Powers The trustee also has specific powers of *avoidance*—that is, the trustee can set aside a sale or other transfer of the debtor's property, taking it back as a part of the debtor's estate. These powers include any voidable rights available to the debtor, preferences, certain statutory liens, and fraudulent transfers by the debtor. Each of these powers is discussed in more detail below. Note that under the 2005 act, the trustee no longer has the power to avoid any transfer that was a bona fide payment of a domestic-support debt.

The debtor shares most of the trustee's avoidance powers. Thus, if the trustee does not take action to enforce one of the rights mentioned above, the debtor in a liquidation bankruptcy can still enforce that right.[17]

Voidable Rights A trustee steps into the shoes of the debtor. Thus, any reason that a debtor can use to obtain the return of her or his property can be used by the trustee as well. These grounds include fraud, duress, incapacity, and mutual mistake.

For example, Ben sells his boat to Tara. Tara gives Ben a check, knowing that she has insufficient funds in her bank account to cover the check. Tara has committed fraud. Ben has the right to avoid that transfer and recover the boat from Tara. Once an order for relief under Chapter 7 of the Code has been entered for Ben, the trustee can exercise the same right to recover the boat from Tara, and the boat becomes a part of the debtor's estate.

17. Under a Chapter 11 bankruptcy (to be discussed later), for which no trustee other than the debtor generally exists, the debtor has the same avoidance powers as a trustee under Chapter 7. Under Chapters 12 and 13 (also to be discussed later), a trustee must be appointed.

Preferences A debtor is not permitted to transfer property or to make a payment that favors—or gives a **preference** to—one creditor over others. The trustee is allowed to recover payments made both voluntarily and involuntarily to one creditor in preference over another. If a **preferred creditor** (one who has received a preferential transfer from the debtor) has sold the property to an innocent third party, the trustee cannot recover the property from the innocent party. The preferred creditor, however, generally can be held accountable for the value of the property.

To have made a preferential payment that can be recovered, an *insolvent* debtor generally must have transferred property, for a *preexisting* debt, within *ninety days* prior to the filing of the bankruptcy petition. The transfer must have given the creditor more than the creditor would have received as a result of the bankruptcy proceedings. The trustee need not prove insolvency, as the Code presumes that the debtor is insolvent during this ninety-day period.

Preferences to Insiders. Sometimes, the creditor receiving the preference is an **insider**—an individual, a partner, a partnership, a corporation, or an officer or a director of a corporation (or a relative of one of these) who has a close relationship with the debtor. In this situation, the avoidance power of the trustee is extended to transfers made within *one year* before filing; however, the *presumption* of insolvency is confined to the ninety-day period. Therefore, the trustee must prove that the debtor was insolvent at the time of a transfer that occurred prior to the ninety-day period.

Transfers That Do Not Constitute Preferences. Not all transfers are preferences. To be a preference, the transfer must be made for something other than current consideration. Most courts generally assume that payment for services rendered within fifteen days prior to the payment is not a preference. If a creditor receives payment in the ordinary course of business from an individual or business debtor, such as payment of last month's telephone bill, the trustee in bankruptcy cannot recover the payment. To be recoverable, a preference must be a transfer for an antecedent (preexisting) debt, such as a year-old printing bill. In addition, the Code permits a consumer-debtor to transfer any property to a creditor up to a total value of $5,475, without the transfer's constituting a preference (this amount was increased from $600 to $5,000 by the 2005 act and is increased periodically under the law). Payment of domestic-support debts does not constitute a preference.

Liens on Debtor's Property The trustee has the power to avoid certain statutory liens against the debtor's property, such as a landlord's lien for unpaid rent. The trustee can avoid statutory liens that first became effective against the debtor when the bankruptcy petition was filed or when the debtor became insolvent. The trustee can also avoid any lien against a good faith purchaser that was not perfected or enforceable on the date of the bankruptcy filing.

Fraudulent Transfers The trustee may avoid fraudulent transfers or obligations if they were made within two years of the filing of the petition or if they were made with actual intent to hinder, delay, or defraud a creditor. Transfers made for less than a reasonably equivalent consideration are also vulnerable if by making them, the debtor became insolvent or intended to incur debts that he or she could not pay. Similarly, a transfer that left a debtor engaged in business with an unreasonably small amount of capital may be considered fraudulent. When a fraudulent transfer is made outside the Code's two-year limit, creditors may seek alternative relief under state laws. Some state laws often allow creditors to recover for transfers made up to three years prior to the filing of a petition.

Distribution of Property

The Code provides specific rules for the distribution of the debtor's property to secured and unsecured creditors. (We will examine these distributions shortly.) Anything remaining after the priority classes of creditors have been satisfied is turned over to the debtor. Exhibit 15–2 illustrates the collection and distribution of property in most voluntary bankruptcies.

In a bankruptcy case in which the debtor has no assets (called "no-asset cases"), creditors are notified of the debtor's petition for bankruptcy but are instructed not to file a claim. In no-asset cases, the unsecured creditors will receive no payment, and most, if not all, of these debts will be discharged.

Distribution to Secured Creditors The Code provides that a consumer-debtor must file with the clerk a statement of intention with respect to the secured collateral. The statement must be filed within thirty days of filing a liquidation petition or before the date of the first meeting of the creditors (whichever is first). The statement must indicate whether the debtor will redeem the collateral (make a single payment equal to the current value of the property), reaffirm the debt (continue making payments on the debt), or surrender the property to the secured party.[18] The trustee is obligated to enforce the debtor's statement within forty-five days after the meeting of the creditors. As noted previously, failure of the debtor to redeem or reaffirm within forty-five days terminates the automatic stay.

18. Also, if applicable, the debtor must specify whether the collateral will be claimed as exempt property.

EXHIBIT 15–2 • Collection and Distribution of Property in Most Voluntary Bankruptcies

This exhibit illustrates the property that might be collected in a debtor's voluntary bankruptcy and how it might be distributed to creditors. Involuntary bankruptcies and some voluntary bankruptcies could include additional types of property and other creditors.

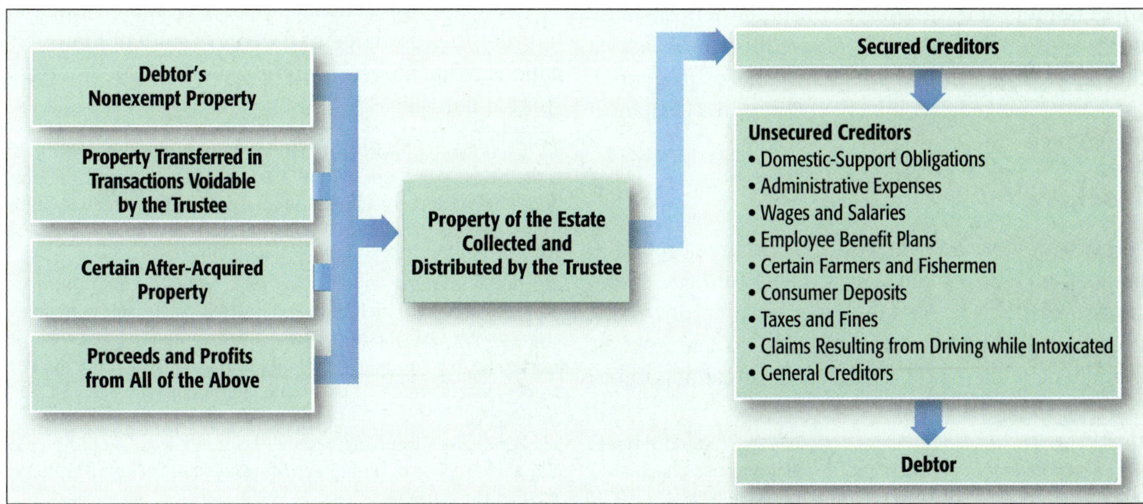

If the collateral is surrendered to the perfected secured party, the secured creditor can either accept the property in full satisfaction of the debt or foreclose on the collateral and use the proceeds to pay off the debt. Thus, the perfected secured party has priority over unsecured parties as to the proceeds from the disposition of the collateral. When the proceeds from sale of the collateral exceed the amount of the perfected secured party's claim, the secured party also has priority to an amount that will cover the reasonable fees and costs incurred. Any excess over this amount is returned to the trustee and used to satisfy the claims of unsecured creditors. If the collateral is insufficient to cover the secured debt owed, the secured creditor becomes an unsecured creditor for the difference.

Distribution to Unsecured Creditors Bankruptcy law establishes an order of priority for classes of debts owed to *unsecured* creditors, and they are paid in the order of their priority. Each class must be fully paid before the next class is entitled to any of the remaining proceeds. If there are insufficient proceeds to pay fully all the creditors in a class, the proceeds are distributed *proportionately* to the creditors in that class, and classes lower in priority receive nothing.

The 2005 act elevated domestic-support (mainly child-support) obligations to the highest priority of unsecured claims—so these are the first debts to be paid. After that, administrative expenses related to the bankruptcy (such as court costs, trustee fees, and attorneys' fees) are paid; next come any expenses that a debtor in an involuntary bankruptcy incurs in the ordinary course of business. Unpaid wages, salaries, and commissions earned within ninety days prior to the petition are paid next, followed by certain claims for contributions to employee benefit plans, claims by some farmers and fishermen, consumer deposits, and certain taxes. Claims of general creditors rank last in the order of priority, which is why these unsecured creditors often receive little, if anything, in a Chapter 7 bankruptcy.

Discharge

From the debtor's point of view, the primary purpose of liquidation is to obtain a fresh start through a discharge of debts.[19] As mentioned earlier, once the debtor's assets have been distributed to creditors as permitted by the Code, the debtor's remaining debts are then discharged, meaning that the debtor is not obligated to pay them. Any judgments on the debts are voided, and creditors are enjoined (prevented) from bringing any actions to collect them. A discharge does not affect the liability of a co-debtor.

Certain debts, however, are not dischargeable in bankruptcy. Also, certain debtors may not qualify to have all debts discharged in bankruptcy. These situations are discussed next.

Exceptions to Discharge Discharge of a debt may be denied because of the nature of the claim or the conduct of the debtor. A court will not discharge claims that are based on a debtor's willful or malicious conduct or fraud,[20] or claims related to property or funds that the debtor obtained by false pretenses, embezzlement, or larceny. Any monetary judgment against the debtor for driving while intoxicated cannot be discharged in bankruptcy. When a debtor fails to list a creditor on the bankruptcy schedules (and thus the creditor is not notified of the bankruptcy), that creditor's claims are not dischargeable.

Claims that are not dischargeable in a liquidation bankruptcy include amounts due to the government for taxes, fines, or penalties.[21] Additionally, amounts borrowed by the debtor to pay these taxes will not be discharged. Domestic-support obligations and property settlements arising from a divorce or separation cannot be discharged. Certain student loans and educational debts are not dischargeable (unless payment of the loans imposes an undue hardship on the debtor and the debtor's dependents),[22] nor are amounts due on a retirement account loan. Consumer debts for purchasing luxury items worth more than $550 and cash advances totaling more than $825 generally are not dischargeable.

In the following case, the court considered whether to order the discharge of a debtor's student loan obligations. What does a debtor have to prove to show "undue hardship"?

19. Discharges are granted under Chapter 7 only to individuals, not to corporations or partnerships. The latter may use Chapter 11, or they may terminate their existence under state law.

20. Even if a debtor who is sued for fraud settles the lawsuit, the United States Supreme Court has held that the amount due under the settlement agreement may not be discharged in bankruptcy because of the underlying fraud. See *Archer v. Warner,* 538 U.S. 314, 123 S.Ct. 1462, 155 L.Ed.2d 454 (2003).

21. Taxes accruing within three years prior to bankruptcy are nondischargeable, including federal and state income taxes, employment taxes, taxes on gross receipts, property taxes, excise taxes, customs duties, and any other taxes for which the government claims the debtor is liable in some capacity. See 11 U.S.C. Sections 507(a)(8), 523(a)(1).

22. For a case discussing whether a student loan should be discharged because of undue hardship, see *In re Savage,* 311 Bankr. 835 (1st Cir. 2004).

CASE 15.3 In re Mosley

United States Court of Appeals, Eleventh Circuit, 2007. 494 F.3d 1320.

• **Background and Facts** Keldric Mosley incurred student loans while attending Georgia's Alcorn State University between 1989 and 1994. At Alcorn, Mosley joined the U.S. Army Reserve Officers' Training Corps. During training in 1993, Mosley fell from a tank and injured his hip and back. Medical problems from his injuries led him to resign his commission. He left Alcorn to live with his mother in Atlanta from 1994 to 1999. He worked briefly for several employers, but depressed and physically limited by his injury, he was unable to keep any of the jobs. He tried to return to school but could not obtain financial aid because of the debt he had incurred at Alcorn. In 1999, a federal bankruptcy court granted him a discharge under Chapter 7, but it did not include the student loans. In 2000, after a week at the Georgia Regional Hospital, a state-supported mental-health facility, Mosley was prescribed medication through the U.S. Department of Veterans Affairs for depression, back pain, and other problems. By 2004, his monthly income consisted primarily of $210 in disability benefits from the Veterans Administration. Homeless and in debt for $45,000 to Educational Credit Management Corporation, Mosley asked the bankruptcy court to reopen his case. The court granted him a discharge of his student loans on the basis of undue hardship. Educational Credit appealed to the U.S. Court of Appeals for the Eleventh Circuit.

IN THE LANGUAGE OF THE COURT
***JOHN R. GIBSON,* Circuit Judge.**

* * * *

* * * To establish undue hardship [the courts require:]

> (1) that the debtor cannot maintain, based on current income and expenses, a "minimal" standard of living * * * if forced to repay the loans; (2) that additional circumstances exist indicating that this state of affairs is likely to persist for a significant portion of the repayment period of the student loans; and (3) that the debtor has made good faith efforts to repay the loans.

Educational Credit does not contest that Mosley has satisfied the first requirement, an inability to maintain a minimal standard of living, as he lives below the poverty line and has for several years. It contends that the bankruptcy court improperly relaxed Mosley's evidentiary burden [duty to produce enough evidence to prove an assertion] on the second and third requirements * * * .The bankruptcy court concluded that Mosley established undue hardship with his credible testimony that he has tried to obtain work but, for ten years, his "substantial physical and emotional ailments" have prevented him from holding a steady job. * * * Educational Credit argues that corroborating medical evidence independent from the debtor's testimony is required * * * where medical disabilities are the "additional circumstances" * * * .

* * * *

We * * * decline to adopt a rule requiring Mosley to submit independent medical evidence to corroborate his testimony that his depression and back problems were additional circumstances likely to render him unable to repay his student loans. We see no inconsistency between * * * holding that the debtor's detailed testimony was sufficient evidence of undue hardship and the * * * cases cited by Educational Credit where debtors' less detailed testimony was held to be insufficient.

Educational Credit also argues that Mosley's medical prognosis [prediction about how a situation will develop in the future] is a subject requiring specialized medical knowledge * * * and that Mosley was not competent to give his opinion on this matter. Mosley, however, did not purport to give an opinion on his medical prognosis, but rather testified from personal knowledge about how his struggles with depression, back pain, and the side effects of his medication have made it difficult for him to obtain work.

We now turn to Educational Credit's argument that the record does not support a conclusion of undue hardship because Mosley's testimony did not establish * * * that he likely will be unable to repay his student loans in the future and that he has made good faith efforts to repay the loans.

CASE CONTINUES

CASE 15.3 CONTINUED

* * * In showing that "additional circumstances" make it unlikely that he will be able to repay his loans for a significant period of time, Mosley testified that his depression and chronic back pain have frustrated his efforts to work, and thus his ability to repay his loans, as well as to provide himself with shelter, food, and transportation, for several years. * * * Mosley's testimony * * * is * * * unrefuted and is corroborated by his Social Security earnings statements. He testified that his back problems preclude him from heavy lifting, which rules out most of the jobs available [through the Georgia Department of Labor where] he seeks work. Exacerbating [aggravating] the problem, his medications make it difficult for him to function. He did not finish college and has been unable to complete the training necessary to learn a trade. Mosley relies on public assistance programs for health care and food, and * * * there is no reason to believe that Mosley's condition will improve in the future.

The bankruptcy court also correctly concluded that Mosley's testimony established the * * * requirement that he has made good faith efforts to repay his student loans. * * * *Good faith is measured by the debtor's efforts to obtain employment, maximize income, and minimize expenses; his default should result, not from his choices, but from factors beyond his reasonable control.* Mosley has attempted to find work, as demonstrated by the series of jobs he held while living with his mother from 1994 to 1999 and his participation in the [state] labor pool since 2000. Because of his medical conditions, Mosley has been largely unsuccessful, and thus has not had the means even to attempt to make payments. * * * His income has been below the poverty line for years. He lives without a home and car and cannot further minimize his expenses. [Emphasis added.]

- **Decision and Remedy** *The U.S. Court of Appeals for the Eleventh Circuit affirmed the lower court's discharge of the debtor's student loans. The debtor's medical problems, lack of skills, and "dire living conditions" made it unlikely that he would be able to hold a job and repay the loans. Furthermore, the debtor "has made good faith efforts to repay his student loans and would suffer undue hardship if they were excepted from discharge."*

- **The Ethical Dimension** *Should a debtor be required to attempt to negotiate a repayment plan with a creditor to demonstrate good faith? Why or why not?*

- **The Global Dimension** *If this debtor were to relocate to a country with a lower cost of living than the United States, should his change in circumstances be a ground for revoking the discharge? Explain your answer.*

Objections to Discharge In addition to the exceptions to discharge previously discussed, a bankruptcy court may also deny the discharge of the *debtor* (as opposed to the debt). In the latter situation, the assets of the debtor are still distributed to the creditors, but the debtor remains liable for the unpaid portion of all claims. Grounds for the denial of discharge of the debtor include the following:

1. The debtor's concealment or destruction of property with the intent to hinder, delay, or defraud a creditor.
2. The debtor's fraudulent concealment or destruction of financial records.
3. The granting of a discharge to the debtor within eight years of the filing of the petition. (This period was increased from six to eight years by the 2005 act.)
4. The debtor's failure to complete the required consumer education course (unless such a course is unavailable).
5. Proceedings in which the debtor could be found guilty of a felony (basically, a court may not discharge any debt until the completion of felony proceedings against the debtor).

Revocation of Discharge On petition by the trustee or a creditor, the bankruptcy court can, within one year, revoke the discharge decree. The discharge decree will be revoked if it is discovered that the debtor acted fraudulently or dishonestly during the bankruptcy proceedings. The revocation renders the discharge void, allowing creditors not satisfied by the distribution of the debtor's estate to proceed with their claims against the debtor.

Reaffirmation of Debt

An agreement to pay a debt dischargeable in bankruptcy is called a **reaffirmation agreement.** A debtor may wish to pay a debt—for example, a debt owed to a family member, physician, bank, or some other creditor—even though the debt could be discharged in bankruptcy. Also, as noted previously, under the 2005 act a debtor cannot retain secured property while continuing to pay without entering into a reaffirmation agreement.

Reaffirmation Procedures To be enforceable, reaffirmation agreements must be made before the debtor is granted a discharge. The agreement must be signed and filed with the court (along with certain required disclosures, described next). Court approval is required unless the debtor is represented by an attorney during the negotiation of the reaffirmation and submits the proper documents and certifications. Even when the debtor is represented by an attorney, court approval may be required if it appears that the reaffirmation will result in undue hardship on the debtor.[23] When court approval is required, a separate hearing will take place. The court will approve the reaffirmation only if it finds that the agreement will not result in undue hardship to the debtor and that the reaffirmation is consistent with the debtor's best interests.

Reaffirmation Disclosures To discourage creditors from engaging in abusive reaffirmation practices, the 2005 act added more requirements for reaffirmation. The Code now provides specific language for several pages of disclosures that must be given to debtors entering reaffirmation agreements. Among other things, these disclosures explain that the debtor is not required to reaffirm any debt, but that liens on secured property, such as mortgages and cars, will remain in effect even if the debt is not reaffirmed.

The reaffirmation agreement must disclose the amount of the debt reaffirmed, the rate of interest, the date payments begin, and the right to rescind. The disclosures also caution the debtor: "Only agree to reaffirm a debt if it is in your best interest. Be sure you can afford the payments you agree to make." The original disclosure documents must be signed by the debtor, certified by the debtor's attorney, and filed with the court at the same time as the reaffirmation agreement. A reaffirmation agreement that is not accompanied by the original signed disclosures will not be effective.

23. Under the provisions of the 2005 act, if the debtor's monthly income minus the debtor's monthly expenses as shown on her or his completed and signed statement is less than the scheduled payments on the reaffirmed debt, undue hardship will be presumed. The debtor can rebut the presumption by providing a statement that explains and identifies additional sources of funds from which the debtor will make the agreed-on payments.

Reorganizations

The type of bankruptcy proceeding most commonly used by corporate debtors is the Chapter 11 *reorganization*. In a reorganization, the creditors and the debtor formulate a plan under which the debtor pays a portion of the debts and is discharged of the remainder. The debtor is allowed to continue in business. Although this type of bankruptcy is generally a corporate reorganization, any debtors (including individuals but excluding stockbrokers and commodities brokers) who are eligible for Chapter 7 relief are eligible for relief under Chapter 11.[24] In 1994, Congress established a "fast-track" Chapter 11 procedure for small-business debtors whose liabilities do not exceed $2.19 million and who do not own or manage real estate. This allows bankruptcy proceedings without the appointment of committees and can save time and costs.

The same principles that govern the filing of a liquidation (Chapter 7) petition apply to reorganization (Chapter 11) proceedings. The case may be brought either voluntarily or involuntarily. The same guidelines govern the entry of the order for relief. The automatic-stay and adequate protection provisions are applicable in reorganizations as well. The 2005 Bankruptcy Reform Act's exceptions to the automatic stay also apply to Chapter 11 proceedings, as do the new provisions regarding substantial abuse and additional grounds for dismissal (or conversion) of bankruptcy petitions. Additionally, the 2005 act contained specific rules and limitations for *individual* debtors who file a Chapter 11 petition. For example, an individual debtor's postpetition acquisitions and earnings become the property of the bankruptcy estate.

Must Be in the Best Interests of the Creditors

Under Section 305(a) of the Bankruptcy Code, a court, after notice and a hearing, may dismiss or suspend all proceedings in a case at any time if dismissal or suspension would better serve the interests of the creditors. Section 1112 also allows a court, after notice and a hearing, to dismiss a case under reorganization "for cause." Cause includes the absence of a reasonable likelihood of rehabilitation, the inability to effect a plan, and an unreasonable delay by the

24. In addition, railroads are eligible for Chapter 11 relief.

interested party objects to the modification, the court must hold a hearing to determine whether the modified plan will be approved.

Discharge After the debtor has completed all payments, the court grants a discharge of all debts provided for by the repayment plan. Except for allowed claims not provided for by the plan, certain long-term debts provided for by the plan, certain tax claims, payments on retirement accounts, and claims for domestic-support obligations, all other debts are dischargeable. Under prior law, a discharge of debts under a Chapter 13 repayment plan was sometimes referred to as a "superdischarge" because it allowed the discharge of fraudulently incurred debt and claims resulting from malicious or willful injury.

The 2005 Bankruptcy Reform Act, however, deleted most of the "superdischarge" provisions, especially for debts based on fraud. Today, debts for trust fund taxes, taxes for which returns were never filed or filed late (within two years of filing), domestic-support payments, student loans, and injury or property damage from driving under the influence of alcohol or drugs are nondischargeable. The law also excludes fraudulent tax obligations, criminal fines and restitution, fraud by a person acting in a fiduciary capacity, and restitution for willfully and maliciously causing personal injury or death.

Even if the debtor does not complete the plan, a hardship discharge may be granted if failure to complete the plan was due to circumstances beyond the debtor's control and if the value of the property distributed under the plan was greater than what would have been paid in a liquidation. A discharge can be revoked within one year if it was obtained by fraud.

Family Farmers and Fishermen

In 1986, to help relieve economic pressure on small farmers, Congress created Chapter 12 of the Bankruptcy Code. In 2005, Congress extended this protection to family fishermen,[31] modified its provisions somewhat, and made it a permanent chapter in the Bankruptcy Code (previously, the statutes authorizing Chapter 12 had to be periodically renewed by Congress).

For purposes of Chapter 12, a *family farmer* is one whose gross income is at least 50 percent farm dependent and whose debts are at least 50 percent farm related. The total debt for a family farmer must not exceed $3,544,525. A partnership or closely held corporation (see Chapter 18) at least 50 percent owned by the farm family can also qualify as a family farmer.

A *family fisherman* is defined as one whose gross income is at least 50 percent dependent on commercial fishing operations[32] and whose debts are at least 80 percent related to commercial fishing. The total debt for a family fisherman must not exceed $1,642,500. As with family farmers, a partnership or closely held corporation can also qualify.

Filing the Petition The procedure for filing a family-farmer or family-fisherman bankruptcy plan is very similar to the procedure for filing a repayment plan under Chapter 13. The debtor must file a plan not later than ninety days after the order for relief. The filing of the petition acts as an automatic stay against creditors' and co-obligors' actions against the estate.

A farmer or fisherman who has already filed a reorganization or repayment plan may convert it to a Chapter 12 plan. The debtor may also convert a Chapter 12 plan to a liquidation plan.

Content and Confirmation of the Plan The content of a plan under Chapter 12 is basically the same as that of a Chapter 13 repayment plan. The plan can be modified by the debtor but, except for cause, must be confirmed or denied within forty-five days of filing.

Court confirmation of the plan is the same as for a repayment plan. In summary, the plan must provide for payment of secured debts at the value of the collateral. If the secured debt exceeds the value of the collateral, the remaining debt is unsecured. For unsecured debtors, the plan must be confirmed if either (1) the value of the property to be distributed under the plan equals the amount of the claim, or (2) the plan provides that all of the debtor's disposable income to be received in a three-year period (or longer, by court approval) will be applied to making payments. Disposable income is all income received less amounts needed to support the farmer or fisherman and his or her family and to continue the farming or commercial fishing operation. Completion of payments under the plan discharges all debts provided for by the plan. See *Concept Summary 15.2* for a comparison of bankruptcy procedures under Chapters 7, 11, 12, and 13.

31. Although the Code uses the terms *fishermen* and *fisherman*, Chapter 12 provisions apply equally to men and women.

32. Commercial fishing operations include catching, harvesting, or aquaculture raising fish, shrimp, lobsters, urchins, seaweed, shellfish, or other aquatic species or products.

CONCEPT SUMMARY 15.2
Forms of Bankruptcy Relief Compared

Issue	Chapter 7	Chapter 11	Chapters 12 and 13
Purpose	Liquidation.	Reorganization.	Adjustment.
Who Can Petition	Debtor (voluntary) or creditors (involuntary).	Debtor (voluntary) or creditors (involuntary).	Debtor (voluntary) only.
Who Can Be a Debtor	Any "person" (including partnerships, corporations, and municipalities) *except* railroads, insurance companies, banks, savings and loan institutions, investment companies licensed by the Small Business Administration, and credit unions. Farmers and charitable institutions also cannot be involuntarily petitioned. If the court finds the petition to be a substantial abuse of the use of Chapter 7, the debtor may be required to convert to a Chapter 13 repayment plan.	Any debtor eligible for Chapter 7 relief; railroads are also eligible. Individuals have specific rules and limitations.	*Chapter 12*—Any family farmer (one whose gross income is at least 50 percent farm dependent and whose debts are at least 50 percent farm related) or family fisherman (one whose gross income is at least 50 percent dependent on commercial fishing operations and whose debts are at least 80 percent related to commercial fishing) or any partnership or closely held corporation at least 50 percent owned by a family farmer or fisherman, when total debt does not exceed a specified amount ($3,544,525 for farmers and $1,642,500 for fishermen). *Chapter 13*—Any individual (not partnerships or corporations) with regular income who owes fixed unsecured debts of less than $336,900 or fixed secured debts of less than $1,010,650.
Procedure Leading to Discharge	Nonexempt property is sold with proceeds to be distributed (in order) to priority groups. Dischargeable debts are terminated.	Plan is submitted; if it is approved and followed, debts are discharged.	Plan is submitted and must be approved if the value of the property to be distributed equals the amount of the claims or if the debtor turns over disposable income for a three-year or five-year period; if the plan is followed, debts are discharged.
Advantages	On liquidation and distribution, most debts are discharged, and the debtor has an opportunity for a fresh start.	Debtor continues in business. Creditors can either accept the plan, or it can be "crammed down" on them. The plan allows for the reorganization and liquidation of debts over the plan period.	Debtor continues in business or possession of assets. If the plan is approved, most debts are discharged after the plan period.

CHAPTER 16
Sole Proprietorships, Franchises, and Partnerships

Anyone who starts a business must first decide which form of business organization will be most appropriate for the new endeavor. In making this decision, the **entrepreneur** (one who initiates and assumes the financial risk of a new enterprise) needs to consider a number of factors, especially (1) ease of creation, (2) the liability of the owners, (3) tax considerations, and (4) the need for capital. In studying this unit on the business environment, keep these factors in mind as you read about the various business organizational forms available to entrepreneurs. You may also find it helpful to refer to Exhibit 18–3 on pages 469–470 in Chapter 18, which compares the major business forms in use today with respect to these and other factors.

Traditionally, entrepreneurs have relied on three major business forms—the sole proprietorship, the partnership, and the corporation. In this chapter, we examine the sole proprietorship and the franchise, which, though not really a separate business organizational form, is widely used today by entrepreneurs. Then we examine the second traditional business form, the partnership.

Sole Proprietorships

The simplest form of business organization is a **sole proprietorship.** In this form, the owner is the business; thus, anyone who does business without creating a separate business organization has a sole proprietorship. More than two-thirds of all American businesses are sole proprietorships. They are usually small enterprises—about 99 percent of the sole proprietorships in the United States have revenues of less than $1 million per year. Sole proprietors can own and manage any type of business from an informal, home-office undertaking to a large restaurant or construction firm.

Advantages of the Sole Proprietorship

A major advantage of the sole proprietorship is that the proprietor owns the entire business and receives all of the profits (because she or he assumes all of the risk). In addition, starting a sole proprietorship is often easier and less costly than starting any other kind of business, as few legal formalities are required.[1] No documents need to be filed with the government to start a sole proprietorship (though a state business license may be required to operate certain businesses).

This type of business organization also provides more flexibility than does a partnership or a corporation. The sole proprietor is free to make any decision he or she wishes concerning the business—such as whom to hire, when to take a vacation, and what kind of business to pursue. In addition, the proprietor can sell or transfer all or part of the business to another party at any time and does not need approval from anyone else (as would be required from partners in a partnership or normally from shareholders in a corporation).

A sole proprietor pays only personal income taxes (including Social Security and Medicare taxes) on the business's profits, which are reported as personal

1. Although starting a sole proprietorship involves fewer legal formalities than other business organizational forms, even small sole proprietorships may need to comply with zoning requirements, obtain licenses, and the like.

income on the proprietor's personal income tax return. Sole proprietors are also allowed to establish certain tax-exempt retirement accounts.

Disadvantages of the Sole Proprietorship

The major disadvantage of the sole proprietorship is that, as sole owner, the proprietor alone bears the burden of any losses or liabilities incurred by the business enterprise. In other words, the sole proprietor has unlimited liability, or legal responsibility, for all obligations that arise in doing business. Any lawsuit against the business or its employees can lead to unlimited personal liability for the owner of a sole proprietorship. Creditors can go after the owner's personal assets to satisfy any business debts. This unlimited liability is a major factor to be considered in choosing a business form.

The sole proprietorship also has the disadvantage of lacking continuity on the death of the proprietor. When the owner dies, so does the business—it is automatically dissolved. Another disadvantage is that in raising capital, the proprietor is limited to his or her personal funds and any personal loans that he or she can obtain.

The personal liability of the owner of a sole proprietorship was at issue in the following case. The case involved the federal Cable Communications Act, which prohibits a commercial establishment from broadcasting television programs to its patrons without authorization. The court had to decide whether the owner of a sole proprietorship that installed a satellite television system was personally liable for violating this act by identifying a restaurant as a "residence" for billing purposes.

CASE 16.1 Garden City Boxing Club, Inc. v. Dominguez

United States District Court, Northern District of Illinois, Eastern Division, 2006. __ F.Supp.2d __.

Background and Facts Garden City Boxing Club, Inc. (GCB), which is based in San Jose, California, owned the exclusive right to broadcast via closed-circuit television several prizefights, including the match between Oscar De La Hoya and Fernando Vargas on September 14, 2002. GCB sold the right to receive the broadcasts to bars and other commercial venues. The fee was $20 multiplied by an establishment's maximum fire code occupancy. Antenas Enterprises in Chicago, Illinois, sells and installs satellite television systems under a contract with DISH Network. After installing a system, Antenas sends the buyer's address and other identifying information to DISH. In January 2002, Luis Garcia, an Antenas employee, identified a new customer as Jose Melendez at 220 Hawthorn Commons in Vernon Hills. The address was a restaurant—Mundelein Burrito—but Garcia designated the account as residential. Mundelein's patrons watched the De La Hoya–Vargas match on September 14, as well as three other fights on other dates, for which the restaurant paid only the residential rate to DISH and nothing to GCB. GCB filed a suit in a federal district court against Luis Dominguez, the sole proprietor of Antenas, to collect the fee.

IN THE LANGUAGE OF THE COURT
LEINENWEBER, J. [Judge]

* * * *

Section 605(a) [of the Cable Communications Act] states "[a]n authorized intermediary of a communication violates the Act when it divulges communication through an electronic channel to one other than the addressee." Mundelein Burrito was clearly a commercial establishment. The structure of the building, an exterior identification sign, and its location in a strip mall made this obvious. Mundelein Burrito paid only the residential fee for the four fights it broadcast to its patrons. It was not an authorized addressee of any of the four fights. By improperly listing Mundelein Burrito as a residence, Antenas Enterprises allowed the unauthorized broadcast of the Event, and three additional fights, to Mundelein Burrito. Antenas Enterprises is liable under [Section] 605 of the Act.

* * * *

CASE CONTINUES

EXHIBIT 16–1 • Terms Commonly Included in a Partnership Agreement

Basic Structure	1. Name of the partnership. 2. Names of the partners. 3. Location of the business and the state law under which the partnership is organized. 4. Purpose of the partnership. 5. Duration of the partnership.
Capital Contributions	1. Amount of capital that each partner is contributing. 2. The agreed-on value of any real or personal property that is contributed instead of cash. 3. How losses and gains on contributed capital will be allocated, and whether contributions will earn interest.
Sharing of Profits and Losses	1. Percentage of the profits and losses of the business that each partner will receive. 2. When distributions of profit will be made and how net profit will be calculated.
Management and Control	1. How management responsibilities will be divided among the partners. 2. Name(s) of the managing partner or partners, and whether other partners have voting rights.
Accounting and Partnership Records	1. Name of the bank in which the partnership will maintain its business and checking accounts. 2. Statement that an accounting of partnership records will be maintained and that any partner or her or his agent can review these records at any time. 3. The dates of the partnership's fiscal year and when the annual audit of the books will take place.
Dissociation and Dissolution	1. Events that will cause the dissociation of a partner or dissolve the partnership, such as the retirement, death, or incapacity of any partner. 2. How partnership property will be valued and apportioned on dissociation and dissolution. 3. Whether an arbitrator will determine the value of partnership property on dissociation and dissolution and whether that determination will be binding.
Arbitration	Whether arbitration is required for any dispute relating to the partnership agreement.

Partnership by Estoppel Sometimes, persons who are not partners nevertheless hold themselves out as partners and make representations that third parties rely on in dealing with them. In such a situation, a court may conclude that a **partnership by estoppel** exists and impose liability—but not partnership *rights*—on the alleged partner or partners. Similarly, a partnership by estoppel may be imposed when a partner represents, expressly or impliedly, that a nonpartner is a member of the firm. Whenever a third person has reasonably and detrimentally relied on the representation that a nonpartner was part of the partnership, partnership by estoppel is deemed to exist. When this occurs, the nonpartner is regarded as an agent whose acts are binding on the partnership [UPA 308].

For example, Moreno owns a small shop. Knowing that Midland Bank will not make a loan on his credit alone, Moreno represents that Lorman, a financially secure businesswoman, is a partner in Moreno's business. Lorman knows of Moreno's misrepresentation but fails to correct it. Midland Bank, relying on the strength of Lorman's reputation and credit, extends a loan to Moreno. Moreno will be liable to the bank for repaying the loan. In many states, Lorman would also be held liable to the bank. Because Lorman has impliedly consented to the misrepresentation, she will normally be estopped (prevented) from denying that she is Moreno's partner. A court will treat Lorman as if she were in fact a partner in Moreno's business insofar as this loan is concerned.

Partnership Operation

The rights and duties of partners are governed largely by the specific terms of their partnership agreement. In the absence of provisions to the contrary in the partnership agreement, the law imposes the rights and duties discussed in the following subsections. The character and nature of the partnership business generally influence the application of these rights and duties.

Rights of Partners The rights of partners in a partnership relate to the following areas: management, interest in the partnership, compensation, inspection of books, accounting, and property.

Management. In a general partnership, "All partners have equal rights in the management and conduct of partnership business" [UPA 401(f)]. Unless the partners agree otherwise, each partner has one vote in management matters *regardless of the proportional size of his or her interest in the firm.* In a large partnership, partners often agree to delegate daily management responsibilities to a management committee made up of one or more of the partners.

The majority rule controls decisions on ordinary matters connected with partnership business, unless otherwise specified in the agreement. Decisions that significantly affect the nature of the partnership or that are not apparently for carrying on the ordinary course of the partnership business, or business of the kind, however, require the *unanimous* consent of the partners [UPA 301(2), 401(i), 401(j)]. Unanimous consent is likely to be required for a decision to undertake any of the following actions:[10]

1. Altering the essential nature of the firm's business as expressed in the partnership agreement or altering the capital structure of the partnership.
2. Admitting new partners or engaging in a completely new business.
3. Assigning partnership property to a trust for the benefit of creditors.
4. Disposing of the partnership's goodwill.
5. Confessing judgment against the partnership or submitting partnership claims to arbitration. (A **confession of judgment** is an act by a debtor permitting a judgment to be entered against him or her by a creditor, for an agreed sum, without the institution of legal proceedings.)
6. Undertaking any act that would make further conduct of partnership business impossible.
7. Amending the terms of the partnership agreement.

10. The previous version of the UPA specifically listed most of these actions as requiring unanimous consent. The current version of the UPA omits the list entirely to allow the courts more flexibility. The Official Comments explain that most of these acts, except for submitting a claim to arbitration, will likely still remain outside the apparent authority of an individual partner.

Interest in the Partnership. Each partner is entitled to the proportion of business profits and losses that is designated in the partnership agreement. If the agreement does not apportion profits (indicate how the profits will be shared), the UPA provides that profits will be shared equally. If the agreement does not apportion losses, losses will be shared in the same ratio as profits [UPA 401(b)].

For example, Rico and Brett form a partnership. The partnership agreement provides for capital contributions of $60,000 from Rico and $40,000 from Brett, but it is silent as to how they will share profits or losses. In this situation, they will share both profits and losses equally. If their partnership agreement had provided that they would share profits in the same ratio as capital contributions, however, 60 percent of the profits would go to Rico, and 40 percent would go to Brett. If the agreement was silent as to losses, losses would be shared in the same ratio as profits (60 percent and 40 percent, respectively).

Compensation. Devoting time, skill, and energy to partnership business is a partner's duty and generally is not a compensable service. Partners can, of course, agree otherwise. For example, the managing partner of a law firm often receives a salary in addition to her or his share of profits for performing special duties, such as managing the office or personnel.

Inspection of Books. Partnership books and records must be kept accessible to all partners. Each partner has the right to receive (and the corresponding duty to produce) full and complete information concerning the conduct of all aspects of partnership business [UPA 403]. Each firm retains books for recording and securing such information. Partners contribute the information, and a bookkeeper typically has the duty to preserve it. The books must be kept at the firm's principal business office (unless the partners agree otherwise). Every partner, whether active or inactive, is entitled to inspect all books and records on demand and can make copies of the materials. The personal representative of a deceased partner's estate has the same right of access to partnership books and records that the decedent would have had [UPA 403].

Accounting of Partnership Assets or Profits. An accounting of partnership assets or profits is required to determine the value of each partner's share in the partnership. An accounting can be performed voluntarily, or it can be compelled by court order. At common law, an accounting was generally not available to partners prior to the dissolution of the partnership. Under UPA 405(b), in contrast, a partner has the right to bring an action for an accounting during the term of the partnership, as well as on the firm's dissolution and winding up.[11] The UPA also provides partners with access to the courts during the term of the partnership to resolve various claims against the partnership and the other partners.

Property Rights. Property acquired *by* a partnership is the property of the partnership and not of the partners individually [UPA 203]. Partnership property includes all property that was originally contributed to the partnership and anything later purchased by the partnership or in the partnership's name (except in rare circumstances) [UPA 204]. A partner may use or possess partnership property only on behalf of the partnership [UPA 401(g)]. A partner is *not* a co-owner of partnership property and has no right to sell, mortgage, or transfer partnership property to another [UPA 501].[12]

In other words, partnership property is owned by the partnership as an entity and not by the individual partners. Thus, a creditor of an individual partner cannot seek to use partnership property to satisfy the partner's debt. Such a creditor can, however, petition a court for a **charging order** to attach the individual partner's *interest* in the partnership (her or his proportionate share of the profits and losses and right to receive distributions) to satisfy the partner's obligation [UPA 502]. (A partner can also assign her or his right to a share of the partnership profits to another to satisfy a debt.)

Duties and Liabilities of Partners

The duties and liabilities of partners that we examine here are basically derived from agency law. Each partner is an agent of every other partner and acts as both a principal and an agent in any business transaction within the scope of the partnership agreement. Each partner is also a general agent of the partnership in carrying out the usual business of the firm "or business of the kind carried on by the partnership" [UPA 301(1)]. Thus, every act of a partner concerning partnership business and "business of the kind" and every contract signed in the partnership's name bind the firm. The UPA affirms general principles of agency law that pertain to the authority of a partner to bind a partnership in contract or tort.

Fiduciary Duties The fiduciary duties that a partner owes to the partnership and the other partners are the duty of care and the duty of loyalty [UPA 404(a)].

Duty of Care. A partner's duty of care is limited to refraining from "grossly negligent or reckless conduct, intentional misconduct, or a knowing violation of law" [UPA 404(c)].[13] A partner is not liable to the partnership for simple negligence or honest errors in judgment in conducting partnership business, but is liable for any grossly negligent or reckless conduct that causes damage to the firm.

Duty of Loyalty. The duty of loyalty requires a partner to account to the partnership for "any property, profit, or benefit" derived by the partner in the conduct of the partnership's business or from the use of its property. A partner must also refrain from dealing with the firm as an adverse party or competing with the partnership in business [UPA 404(b)]. The duty of loyalty can be breached by self-dealing, misusing partnership property, disclosing trade secrets, or usurping a partnership business opportunity.

A classic example is the 1928 case of *Meinhard v. Salmon.*[14] Salmon leased a building on Fifth Avenue in New York City for twenty years. The building had been a hotel, and Salmon wanted to convert it into a commercial building and lease it out to shops and offices. Salmon formed a partnership with Meinhard, who put up half of the capital. Both men received a percentage of the profits and shared the losses equally, but Salmon had the sole power to manage the building. A few months before the lease was set to expire, the property owner approached Salmon about leasing several adjacent properties and constructing a $3 million building on them.

Salmon did not inform Meinhard about this business opportunity and instead signed a new lease in the name of his own business (in which Meinhard was not

11. Under the previous version of the UPA, a partner could bring an action for an accounting only if the partnership agreement provided for an accounting, the partner was wrongfully excluded from the business or its property or books, another partner was in breach of his or her fiduciary duty, or other circumstances rendered it "just and reasonable."

12. Under the previous version of the UPA, partners were *tenants in partnership.* This meant that every partner was a co-owner with all other partners of the partnership property. The current UPA does not recognize this concept.

13. The previous version of the UPA touched only briefly on the duty of loyalty and left the details of the partners' fiduciary duties to be developed under the law of agency.

14. 249 N.Y. 458, 164 N.E. 545 (N.Y.App. 1928).

an owner). The new lease covered the adjacent properties and the original development. In the lawsuit that followed, the court held that Salmon had breached his fiduciary duty by failing to inform Meinhard of a business opportunity and secretly taking advantage of the opportunity himself. The court granted Meinhard a 50 percent interest in the new lease.

Breach and Waiver of Fiduciary Duties. A partner's fiduciary duties may not be waived or eliminated in the partnership agreement, and in fulfilling them, each partner must act consistently with the obligation of good faith and fair dealing [UPA 103(b), 404(d)]. Note that a partner may pursue his or her own interests without automatically violating these duties [UPA 404(e)]. The key is whether the partner has disclosed the interest to the other partners.

For example, a partner who owns a shopping mall may vote against a partnership proposal to open a competing mall, provided that the partner has fully disclosed her interest in the shopping mall to the other partners at the firm. Similarly, suppose that in the case *Meinhard v. Salmon* discussed previously, Salmon had informed Meinhard about the opportunity of leasing and developing the additional properties. If Meinhard was not interested in extending the partnership's lease to cover the nearby properties, then Salmon would have been able to take advantage of the opportunity on his own. A partner cannot make secret profits or put self-interest before his or her duty to the interest of the partnership, however.

Authority of Partners The UPA affirms general principles of agency law that pertain to a partner's authority to bind a partnership in contract. A partner may also subject the partnership to tort liability under agency principles. When a partner is carrying on partnership business or business of the kind with third parties in the usual way, apparent authority exists, and both the partner and the firm share liability.

The partnership will not be liable, however, if the third parties *know* that the partner has no such authority. For example, Patricia, a partner in the partnership of Heise, Green, and Stevens, applies for a loan on behalf of the partnership without authorization from the other partners. The bank manager knows that Patricia has no authority to do so. If the bank manager grants the loan, Patricia will be personally bound, but the firm will not be liable.

A partnership may file a "statement of partnership authority" to limit a partner's capacity to act as the firm's agent or transfer property on its behalf [UPA 105, 303]. Any limit on a partner's authority, however, normally does not affect a third party who does not know about the statement. Statements limiting the partners' authority to transfer real property that are filed with the appropriate state records office (the office that records real property transfers—see Chapter 25) will bind third parties, whether or not they know about the limitation.

The agency concepts relating to apparent authority, actual authority, and ratification that will be discussed in Chapter 19 also apply to partnerships. The extent of *implied authority* is generally broader for partners than for ordinary agents, however.

The Scope of Implied Powers. The character and scope of the partnership business and the customary nature of the particular business operation determine the implied powers of partners. For example, a partnership business that has goods in inventory and makes profits buying and selling those goods is known as a *trading partnership.* In a trading partnership, each partner has a wide range of implied powers, such as to advertise products, hire employees, and extend the firm's credit by issuing or signing checks.

In an ordinary partnership, the partners can exercise all implied powers reasonably necessary and customary to carry on that particular business. Such powers include the authority to make warranties on goods in the sales business and the power to enter into contracts consistent with the firm's regular course of business. Most partners also have the implied authority to make admissions and representations concerning partnership affairs. A partner might also have the implied power to convey (transfer) real property in the firm's name when such conveyances are part of the ordinary course of partnership business.

Authorized versus Unauthorized Actions. If a partner acts within the scope of authority, the partnership is legally bound to honor the partner's commitments to third parties. For example, a partner's authority to sell partnership products carries with it the implied authority to transfer title and to make usual warranties. Hence, in a partnership that operates a retail tire store, any partner negotiating a contract with a customer for the sale of a set of tires can warrant that "each tire will be warranted for normal wear for 40,000 miles."

This same partner, however, does not have the authority to sell office equipment, fixtures, or the partnership's retail facility without the consent of all of the other partners. In addition, because partnerships are formed to generate profits, a partner generally does not have the authority to make charitable contributions without the consent of the other partners. Such actions are not binding on the partnership unless they are ratified by all of the other partners.

Liability of Partners One significant disadvantage associated with a traditional partnership is that the partners are *personally* liable for the debts of the partnership. Moreover, the liability is essentially unlimited because the acts of one partner in the ordinary course of business subject the other partners to personal liability [UPA 305]. The following subsections explain the rules on a partner's liability.

Joint Liability. Each partner in a partnership is jointly liable for the partnership's obligations. **Joint liability** means that a third party must sue all of the partners as a group, but each partner can be held liable for the full amount. Under the prior version of the UPA, which is still in effect in a few states, partners were subject to joint liability on partnership debts and contracts, but not on partnership debts arising from torts.[15] If, for example, a third party sues a partner on a partnership contract, the partner has the right to demand that the other partners be sued with her or him. In fact, if the third party does not sue all of the partners, the assets of the partnership cannot be used to satisfy the judgment. Under the theory of joint liability, the partnership's assets must be exhausted before creditors can reach the partners' individual assets.[16]

Joint and Several Liability. In the majority of the states, under UPA 306(a), partners are both jointly and severally (separately, or individually) liable for all partnership obligations, including contracts, torts, and breaches of trust. **Joint and several liability** means that a third party has the option of suing all of the partners together (jointly) or one or more of the partners separately (severally). This is true even if a partner did not participate in, ratify, or know about whatever it was that gave rise to the cause of action. Normally, though, the partnership's assets must be exhausted before a creditor can enforce a judgment against a partner's separate assets [UPA 307(d)].

A judgment against one partner severally (separately) does not extinguish the others' liability. Those not sued in the first action normally may be sued subsequently, unless the first action was conclusive on the question of liability. Suppose that Renalt brings a malpractice (professional negligence) action against one partner in a firm and then discovers that another partner was involved in the negligence. Normally, he may also file a lawsuit against the second partner (unless the court held that no one at the firm breached the standard of care with regard to Renalt).

If a plaintiff is successful in a suit against a partner or partners, he or she may collect on the judgment only against the assets of those partners named as defendants. A partner who commits a tort is required to indemnify (reimburse) the partnership for any damages it pays. The question in the following case was whether a partnership must indemnify a partner for liability that results from negligent conduct occurring in the ordinary course of the partnership's business.

15. Under the previous version of the UPA, the partners were subject to *joint and several liability,* which is discussed next, on debts arising from torts. States that still follow this rule include Connecticut, West Virginia, and Wyoming.

16. For a case applying joint liability to partnerships, see *Shar's Cars, LLC v. Elder,* 97 P.3d 724 (Utah App. 2004).

CASE 16.3 Moren v. Jax Restaurant

Minnesota Court of Appeals, 2004. 679 N.W.2d 165.
www.lawlibrary.state.mn.us/archive/cap1st.html[a]

• **Background and Facts** "Jax Restaurant" is a partnership that operates Jax Restaurant in Foley, Minnesota. One afternoon in October 2000, Nicole Moren, one of the partners, finished her shift at the restaurant at 4:00 P.M. and picked up her two-year-old son, Remington, from day care. About 5:30 P.M., Moren returned to the restaurant with Remington after Amy Benedetti, the other partner and Moren's sister, asked for help. Moren's husband offered to pick up Remington in twenty minutes. Because Moren

a. In the "Published" section, click on "M–O." On that page, scroll to the name of the case and click on the docket number to access the opinion. The Minnesota State Law Library maintains this Web site.

CASE 16.3 CONTINUED did not want Remington running around the restaurant, she brought him into the kitchen with her, set him on top of the counter, and began rolling out pizza dough using a dough-pressing machine. While she was making pizzas, Remington reached his hand into the dough press. His hand was crushed, causing permanent injuries. Through his father, Remington filed a suit in a Minnesota state court against the partnership, alleging negligence. The partnership filed a complaint against Moren, arguing that it was entitled to indemnity (compensation or reimbursement) from Moren for her negligence. The court issued a summary judgment in favor of Moren on the complaint. The partnership appealed this judgment to a state intermediate appellate court.

IN THE LANGUAGE OF THE COURT
***CRIPPEN*, Judge.**

* * * *

Under Minnesota's Uniform Partnership Act [the most recent version of the UPA], a partnership is an entity distinct from its partners, and as such, a partnership may sue and be sued in the name of the partnership. [Under the UPA] *"[a] partnership is liable for loss or injury caused to a person * * * as a result of a wrongful act or omission, or other actionable conduct, of a partner acting in the ordinary course of business of the partnership or with authority of the partnership."* Accordingly, a "partnership shall * * * indemnify [reimburse] a partner for liabilities incurred by the partner in the ordinary course of the business of the partnership * * * ." Stated conversely, an "act of a partner which is not apparently for carrying on in the ordinary course the partnership business or business of the kind carried on by the partnership binds the partnership only if the act was authorized by the other partners." Thus, under the plain language of the UPA, *a partner has a right to indemnity from the partnership, but the partnership's claim of indemnity from a partner is not authorized or required.* [Emphasis added.]

The [lower] court correctly concluded that Nicole Moren's conduct was in the ordinary course of business of the partnership and, as a result, indemnity by the partner to the partnership was inappropriate. It is undisputed that one of the cooks scheduled to work that evening did not come in, and that Moren's partner asked her to help in the kitchen. It also is undisputed that Moren was making pizzas for the partnership when her son was injured. Because her conduct at the time of the injury was in the ordinary course of business of the partnership, under the UPA, her conduct bound the partnership and it owes indemnity to her for her negligence.

* * * *

Appellant * * * claims that because Nicole Moren's action of bringing Remington into the kitchen was partly motivated by personal reasons, her conduct was outside the ordinary course of business. Because it has not been previously addressed, there is no Minnesota authority regarding this issue. * * * We conclude that the conduct of Nicole Moren was no less in the ordinary course of business because it also served personal purposes. It is undisputed that Moren was acting for the benefit of the partnership by making pizzas when her son was injured, and even though she was simultaneously acting in her role as a mother, her conduct remained in the ordinary course of the partnership business.

- **Decision and Remedy** *The state intermediate appellate court affirmed the lower court's judgment. "Minnesota law requires a partnership to indemnify its partners for the result of their negligence." The appellate court also reasoned that "the conduct of a partner may be partly motivated by personal reasons and still occur in the ordinary course of business of the partnership." Thus "liability for Nicole Moren's negligence rested with the partnership, even if the partner's conduct partly served her personal interests."*

- **What If the Facts Were Different?** *Suppose that Moren's predominant motive in bringing her son to the restaurant had been to benefit herself by feeding him free pizza. Would the result have been different? Why or why not?*

- **The Legal Environment Dimension** *What seems to have occurred in this case that might have served as an alternative basis for imposing liability on the partnership? (Hint: Who besides Moren had the authority to act on behalf of the partnership?)*

Liability of Incoming Partners. A partner newly admitted to an existing partnership is not personally liable for any partnership obligation incurred before the person became a partner [UPA 306(b)]. In other words, the new partner's liability to existing creditors of the partnership is limited to her or his capital contribution to the firm. Suppose that Smartclub is a partnership with four members. Alex Jaff, a newly admitted partner, contributes $100,000 to the partnership. Smartclub has about $600,000 in debt at the time Jaff joins the firm. Although Jaff's capital contribution of $100,000 can be used to satisfy Smartclub's obligations, Jaff is not personally liable for partnership debts that were incurred before he became a partner. Thus, his personal assets cannot be used to satisfy the partnership's antecedent (prior) debt. If, however, the managing partner at Smartclub borrows funds for the partnership after Jaff becomes a partner, Jaff will be personally liable for those amounts.

Dissociation of a Partner

Dissociation occurs when a partner ceases to be associated in the carrying on of the partnership business. Although a partner always has the *power* to dissociate from the firm, he or she may not have the *right* to dissociate. Dissociation normally entitles the partner to have his or her interest purchased by the partnership, and terminates his or her actual authority to act for the partnership and to participate with the partners in running the business. Otherwise, the partnership can continue to do business without the dissociating partner.[17]

Events Causing Dissociation Under UPA 601, a partner can be dissociated from a partnership in any of the following ways:

1. By the partner's voluntarily giving notice of an "express will to withdraw." (Note that when a partner gives notice of her or his intent to withdraw, the remaining partners must decide whether to continue or give up the partnership business. If they do not agree to continue the partnership, the voluntary dissociation of a partner will dissolve the firm [UPA 801(1)].)
2. By the occurrence of an event agreed to in the partnership agreement.
3. By a unanimous vote of the other partners under certain circumstances, such as when a partner transfers substantially all of her or his interest in the partnership, or when it becomes unlawful to carry on partnership business with that partner.
4. By order of a court or arbitrator if the partner has engaged in wrongful conduct that affects the partnership business, breached the partnership agreement or violated a duty owed to the partnership or the other partners, or engaged in conduct that makes it "not reasonably practicable to carry on the business in partnership with the partner" [UPA 601(5)].
5. By the partner's declaring bankruptcy, assigning his or her interest in the partnership for the benefit of creditors, or becoming physically or mentally incapacitated, or by the partner's death. Note that although the bankruptcy or death of a partner represents that partner's "dissociation" from the partnership, it is not an *automatic* ground for the partnership's dissolution (*dissolution* will be discussed shortly).

Wrongful Dissociation As mentioned, a partner has the power to dissociate from a partnership at any time, but a partner's dissociation can be wrongful in a few circumstances [UPA 602]. When a partner's dissociation is in breach of a partnership agreement, for instance, it is wrongful. For example, a partnership agreement states that it is a breach of the partnership agreement for any partner to assign partnership property to a creditor without the consent of the others. If a partner, Janik, makes such an assignment, she has not only breached the agreement but has also wrongfully dissociated from the partnership. Similarly, if a partner refuses to perform duties required by the partnership agreement—such as accounting for profits earned from the use of partnership property—this breach can be treated as wrongful dissociation.

With regard to a partnership for a definite term or a particular undertaking, dissociation that occurs before the expiration of the term or the completion of the undertaking can be wrongful. In such partnerships, the dissociation normally is considered wrongful if the partner withdraws by express will, is expelled by a court or an arbitrator, or declares bankruptcy [UPA 602].

17. Under the previous version of the UPA, when a partner withdrew from a partnership, the partnership was considered dissolved, its business had to be wound up, and the proceeds had to be distributed to creditors and among partners. The new UPA provisions dramatically changed the law governing partnership breakups and dissolution by no longer requiring that the partnership end if one partner dissociates.

A partner who wrongfully dissociates is liable to the partnership and to the other partners for damages caused by the dissociation. This liability is in addition to any other obligation of the partner to the partnership or to the other partners. Thus, a wrongfully dissociating partner would be liable to the partnership not only for any damage caused by the breach of the partnership agreement, but also for costs incurred to replace the partner's expertise or to obtain new financing.

Effects of Dissociation Dissociation (rightful or wrongful) terminates some of the rights of the dissociated partner, requires that the partnership purchase his or her interest, and alters the liability of the parties to third parties.

Rights and Duties. On a partner's dissociation, his or her right to participate in the management and conduct of the partnership business terminates [UPA 603]. The partner's duty of loyalty also ends. A partner's other fiduciary duties, including the duty of care, continue only with respect to events that occurred before dissociation, unless the partner participates in winding up the partnership's business (to be discussed shortly). For example, Debbie Pearson is a partner who is leaving an accounting firm, Bubb & Pearson. Pearson can immediately compete with the firm for new clients. She must exercise care in completing ongoing client transactions, however, and must account to the firm for any fees received from the old clients based on those transactions.

After a partner's dissociation, his or her interest in the partnership must be purchased according to the rules in UPA 701. The **buyout price** is based on the amount that would have been distributed to the partner if the partnership had been wound up on the date of dissociation. Offset against the price are amounts owed by the partner to the partnership, including damages for wrongful dissociation.

In the following case, the court had to decide how the buyout price of a partner's interest should be determined on his dissociation from his family's ranch business, which had been operated as a partnership for more than twenty years.

CASE 16.4 Warnick v. Warnick

Supreme Court of Wyoming, 2006. 2006 WY 58, 133 P.3d 997.

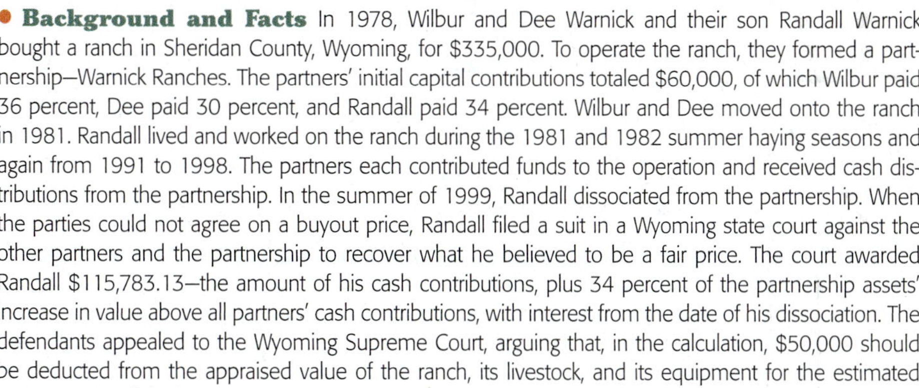

• **Background and Facts** In 1978, Wilbur and Dee Warnick and their son Randall Warnick bought a ranch in Sheridan County, Wyoming, for $335,000. To operate the ranch, they formed a partnership—Warnick Ranches. The partners' initial capital contributions totaled $60,000, of which Wilbur paid 36 percent, Dee paid 30 percent, and Randall paid 34 percent. Wilbur and Dee moved onto the ranch in 1981. Randall lived and worked on the ranch during the 1981 and 1982 summer haying seasons and again from 1991 to 1998. The partners each contributed funds to the operation and received cash distributions from the partnership. In the summer of 1999, Randall dissociated from the partnership. When the parties could not agree on a buyout price, Randall filed a suit in a Wyoming state court against the other partners and the partnership to recover what he believed to be a fair price. The court awarded Randall $115,783.13—the amount of his cash contributions, plus 34 percent of the partnership assets' increase in value above all partners' cash contributions, with interest from the date of his dissociation. The defendants appealed to the Wyoming Supreme Court, arguing that, in the calculation, $50,000 should be deducted from the appraised value of the ranch, its livestock, and its equipment for the estimated expenses of selling these assets.

IN THE LANGUAGE OF THE COURT

***BURKE*, Justice.**

* * * *

The district court was charged with calculating the amount owed to Randall Warnick pursuant to the applicable provisions of [Wyoming Statutes Section 17-21-701 (Wyoming's version of UPA 701)]. That amount, or *the buyout price, is the amount that would have been paid to the dissociating partner following a settlement of partnership accounts upon the*

CASE CONTINUES

CASE 16.4 CONTINUED

winding up of the partnership, if, on the date of dissociation, the assets of the partnership were sold at a price equal to the greater of the liquidation value or the value based on a sale of the business as a going concern without the dissociating partner. [Emphasis added.]

* * * *

* * * Warnick Ranches claims that the [lower] court erred in the first step of its calculation of the buyout price by overvaluing the ranch assets. The asserted error is the [lower] court's failure to deduct estimated sales expenses of $50,000 from the value of the partnership assets.

Critical to our determination in this case is the recognition that the assets of this partnership were not, in fact, liquidated. Instead, the record reflects that the assets were retained by Warnick Ranches. Randall Warnick's dissociation from the partnership did not require the winding up of the partnership. * * * Accordingly, the deduction urged by Warnick Ranches is for hypothetical costs.

* * * *

* * * Contrary to the interpretation asserted by Warnick Ranches, liquidation value is not the amount of the seller's residual cash following a sale. We find that the meaning of liquidation value in the statute is best understood by comparing it to the other method provided. *When contrasted with "going concern value" it is clear that "liquidation value" simply means the sale of the separate assets rather than the value of the business as a whole.* [Emphasis added.]

Additionally, under either valuation method, * * * [Section] 17-21-701(b) directs that the sale price be determined "on the basis of the amount that would be paid by a willing buyer to a willing seller, neither being under any compulsion to buy or sell, and with knowledge of all relevant facts." * * * This "willing buyer" and "willing seller" language does not present a novel legal concept, as it sets forth precisely what has long been the legal definition or test of "fair market value."

* * * *

Considering the language of [Section 17-21-701(b)] as a whole, we conclude that "liquidation value" does not have the meaning that Warnick Ranches desires, i.e. the amount a seller would "net" upon liquidation. Rather, "liquidation value" represents the sale price of the assets based upon fair market value. It is one thing to say that a business is worth little more than its hard assets. It is quite another * * * to deduct the substantial cost of a liquidation which all parties agree will not take place. Where it is contemplated that a business will continue, it is not appropriate to assume an immediate liquidation with its attendant transactional costs and taxes.

- **Decision and Remedy** *The Wyoming Supreme Court affirmed the judgment of the lower court, holding that "purely hypothetical costs of sale are not a required deduction in valuing partnership assets" to determine the buyout price of a dissociated partner.*

- **The Ethical Dimension** *Was it unethical for Randall to file a suit against his parents to obtain what he regarded as a fair price for his interest? Why or why not?*

- **The Legal Environment Dimension** *How and why might the value of a partnership interest in a going concern differ from the value of the same interest as a result of a liquidation?*

Liability to Third Parties. For two years after a partner dissociates from a continuing partnership, the partnership may be bound by the acts of the dissociated partner based on apparent authority [UPA 702]. In other words, the partnership may be liable to a third party with whom a dissociated partner enters into a transaction if the third party reasonably believed that the dissociated partner was still a partner. Similarly, a dissociated partner may be liable for partnership obligations entered into during a two-year period following dissociation [UPA 703].

To avoid this possible liability, a partnership should notify its creditors, customers, and clients of a partner's dissociation. Also, either the partnership or the dissociated partner can file a statement of dissociation in the appropriate state office to limit the dissociated partner's authority to ninety days after the filing [UPA 704]. Filing this statement helps to minimize the firm's potential liability for the former partner and vice versa.

Partnership Termination

The same events that cause dissociation can result in the end of the partnership if the remaining partners no longer wish to (or are unable to) continue the partnership business. Not every type of dissociation will cause dissolution of the partnership, though. Only certain departures of a partner will trigger dissolution, and generally the partnership can continue if the remaining partners consent [UPA 801].

The termination of a partnership is referred to as **dissolution,** which essentially means the commencement of the winding up process. **Winding up** is the actual process of collecting, liquidating, and distributing the partnership assets.[18] We discuss here the dissolution and winding up of partnership business.

Dissolution Dissolution of a partnership generally can be brought about by the acts of the partners, by operation of law, and by judicial decree [UPA 801]. Any partnership (including one for a fixed term) can be dissolved by the partners' agreement. Similarly, if the partnership agreement states that it will dissolve on a certain event, such as a partner's death or bankruptcy, then the occurrence of that event will dissolve the partnership. A partnership for a fixed term or a particular undertaking is dissolved by operation of law at the expiration of the term or on the completion of the undertaking.

Any event that makes it unlawful for the partnership to continue its business will result in dissolution [UPA 801(4)]. Under the UPA, a court may order dissolution when it becomes obviously impractical for the firm to continue—for example, if the business can only be operated at a loss [UPA 801(5)]. Additionally, a partner's impropriety involving partnership business (for example, fraud perpetrated on the other partners) or improper behavior reflecting unfavorably on the firm may provide grounds for a judicial decree of dissolution. Finally, if dissension between partners becomes so persistent and harmful as to undermine the confidence and cooperation necessary to carry on the firm's business, a court may grant a decree of dissolution.

18. Although "winding down" would seem to describe more accurately the process of settling accounts and liquidating the assets of a partnership, English and U.S. statutory and case law have traditionally used "winding up" to denote this final stage of a partnership's existence.

Winding Up and Distribution of Assets After dissolution, the partnership continues for the limited purpose of the winding up process.[19] The partners cannot create new obligations on behalf of the partnership. They have authority only to complete transactions begun but not finished at the time of dissolution and to wind up the business of the partnership [UPA 803, 804(1)].

Winding up includes collecting and preserving partnership assets, discharging liabilities (paying debts), and accounting to each partner for the value of his or her interest in the partnership. Partners continue to have fiduciary duties to one another and to the firm during this process. UPA 401(h) provides that a partner is entitled to compensation for services in winding up partnership affairs (and reimbursement for expenses incurred in the process) above and apart from his or her share in the partnership profits.

Both creditors of the partnership and creditors of the individual partners can make claims on the partnership's assets. In general, partnership creditors share proportionately with the partners' individual creditors in the partners' assets, which include their interests in the partnership. A partnership's assets are distributed according to the following priorities [UPA 807]:

1. Payment of debts, including those owed to partner and nonpartner creditors.
2. Return of capital contributions and distribution of profits to partners.[20]

If the partnership's liabilities are greater than its assets, the partners bear the losses—in the absence of a contrary agreement—in the same proportion in which they shared the profits (rather than, for example, in proportion to their contributions to the partnership's capital).

Partnership Buy-Sell Agreements Usually, when people enter into partnerships, they are getting along with one another. To prepare for the possibility that the situation might change and they may become unable to work together amicably, the partners should make express arrangements during the formation of

19. Note that at any time after dissolution but before winding up is completed, all of the partners may decide to continue the partnership business and waive the right to have the business wound up [UPA 802].

20. Under the previous version of the UPA, creditors of the partnership had priority over creditors of the individual partners. Also, in distributing partnership assets, third party creditors were paid before partner creditors, and capital contributions were returned before profits.

the partnership to provide for its smooth dissolution. A **buy-sell agreement,** sometimes called simply a *buy-out agreement,* provides for one or more partners to buy out the other or others, should the situation warrant. Agreeing beforehand on who buys what, under what circumstances, and, if possible, at what price may eliminate costly negotiations or litigation later. Alternatively, the agreement may specify that one or more partners will determine the value of the interest being sold and that the other or others will decide whether to buy or sell.

Under UPA 701(a), if a partner's dissociation does not result in a dissolution of the partnership, a buyout of the partner's interest is mandatory. The UPA contains an extensive set of buyout rules that apply when the partners do not have a buyout agreement. Basically, a withdrawing partner receives the same amount through a buyout that he or she would receive if the business were winding up [UPA 701(b)].

REVIEWING Sole Proprietorships, Franchises, and Partnerships

Carlos Del Rey decided to open a Mexican fast-food restaurant and signed a franchise contract with a national chain called La Grande Enchilada. The contract required the franchisee to strictly follow the franchisor's operating manual and stated that failure to do so would be grounds for terminating the franchise contract. The manual set forth detailed operating procedures and safety standards, and provided that a La Grande Enchilada representative would inspect the restaurant monthly to ensure compliance. Nine months after Del Rey began operating his restaurant, a spark from the grill ignited an oily towel in the kitchen. No one was injured, but by the time firefighters were able to put out the fire, the kitchen had sustained extensive damage. The cook told the fire department that the towel was "about two feet from the grill" when it caught fire, which was in compliance with the franchisor's manual that required towels be placed at least one foot from the grills. Nevertheless, the next day La Grande Enchilada notified Del Rey that his franchise would terminate in thirty days for failure to follow the prescribed safety procedures. Using the information presented in the chapter, answer the following questions.

1. What type of franchise was Del Rey's La Grande Enchilada restaurant?
2. If Del Rey operates the restaurant as a sole proprietorship, who bears the loss for the damaged kitchen? Explain.
3. Assume that Del Rey files a lawsuit against La Grande Enchilada, claiming that his franchise was wrongfully terminated. What is the main factor that a court would consider in determining whether the franchise was wrongfully terminated?
4. Would a court be likely to rule that La Grande Enchilada had good cause to terminate Del Rey's franchise in this situation? Why or why not?

TERMS AND CONCEPTS

articles of partnership 409
buyout price 417
buy-sell agreement 420
charging order 412
confession of judgment 411
dissociation 416
dissolution 419
entrepreneur 400
franchise 402
franchisee 402
franchisor 402
information return 409
joint and several liability 414
joint liability 414
partnership 407
partnership by estoppel 410
sole proprietorship 400
winding up 419

QUESTIONS AND CASE PROBLEMS

16–1. Maria, Pablo, and Vicky are recent college graduates who would like to go into business for themselves. They are considering purchasing a franchise. If they enter into a franchising arrangement, they would have the support of a large company that could answer any questions they might have. Also, a firm that has been in business for many years would be experienced in dealing with some of the problems that novice businesspersons might encounter. These and other attributes of franchises can lessen some of the risks of the marketplace. What other aspects of franchising—positive and negative—should Maria, Pablo, and Vicky consider before committing themselves to a particular franchise?

16–2. QUESTION WITH SAMPLE ANSWER

National Foods, Inc., sells franchises to its fast-food restaurants, known as Chicky-D's. Under the franchise agreement, franchisees agree to hire and train employees strictly according to Chicky-D's standards. Chicky-D's regional supervisors are required to approve all job candidates before they are hired and all general policies affecting those employees. Chicky-D's reserves the right to terminate a franchise for violating the franchisor's rules. In practice, however, Chicky-D's regional supervisors routinely approve new employees and individual franchisees' policies. After several incidents of racist comments and conduct by Tim, a recently hired assistant manager at a Chicky-D's, Sharon, a counterperson at the restaurant, resigns. Sharon files a suit in a federal district court against National. National files a motion for summary judgment, arguing that it is not liable for harassment by franchise employees. Will the court grant National's motion? Why or why not?

- **For a sample answer to Question 16–2, go to Appendix I at the end of this text.**

16–3. Daniel is the owner of a chain of shoe stores. He hires Rubya to be the manager of a new store, which is to open in Grand Rapids, Michigan. Daniel, by written contract, agrees to pay Rubya a monthly salary and 20 percent of the profits. Without Daniel's knowledge, Rubya represents himself to Classen as Daniel's partner, showing Classen the agreement to share profits. Classen extends credit to Rubya. Rubya defaults. Discuss whether Classen can hold Daniel liable as a partner.

16–4. Meyer, Knapp, and Cavanna establish a partnership to operate a window-washing service. Meyer contributes $10,000 to the partnership, and Knapp and Cavanna contribute $1,000 each. The partnership agreement is silent as to how profits and losses will be shared. One month after the partnership begins operation, Knapp and Cavanna vote, over Meyer's objection, to purchase another truck for the firm. Meyer believes that because he contributed $10,000, the partnership cannot make any major commitment to purchase over his objection. In addition, Meyer claims that in the absence of any provision in the agreement, profits must be divided in the same ratio as capital contributions. Discuss Meyer's contentions.

16–5. Partnership Status. Charlie Waugh owned and operated an auto parts junkyard in Georgia. Charlie's son, Mack, started working in the business part-time as a child and full-time when he left school at the age of sixteen. Mack oversaw the business's finances, depositing the profits in a bank. Charlie gave Mack a one-half interest in the business, telling him that if "something happened" to Charlie, the entire business would be his. In 1994, Charlie and his wife, Alene, transferred to Mack the land on which the junkyard was located. Two years later, however, Alene and her daughters, Gail and Jewel, falsely convinced Charlie, whose mental competence had deteriorated, that Mack had cheated him. Mack was ordered off the land. Shortly thereafter, Charlie died. Mack filed a suit in a Georgia state court against the rest of the family, asserting, in part, that he and Charlie had been partners and that he was entitled to Charlie's share of the business. Was the relationship between Charlie and Mack a partnership? Is Mack entitled to Charlie's "share"? Explain. [*Waugh v. Waugh,* 265 Ga.App. 799, 595 S.E.2d 647 (2004)]

16–6. Franchise Termination. Walik Elkhatib, a Palestinian Arab, emigrated to the United States in 1971 and became an American citizen. Eight years later, Elkhatib bought a Dunkin' Donuts, Inc., franchise in Bellwood, Illinois. Dunkin' Donuts began offering breakfast sandwiches with bacon, ham, or sausage through its franchises in 1984, but Elkhatib refused to sell these items at his store on the ground that his religion forbade the handling of pork. In 1995, Elkhatib opened a second franchise in Berkeley, Illinois, at which he also refused to sell pork products. The next year, Elkhatib began selling meatless sandwiches at both locations. In 1998, Elkhatib opened a third franchise in Westchester, Illinois. When he proposed to relocate this franchise, Dunkin' Donuts refused to approve the new location and added that it would not renew any of his franchise agreements because he did not carry the full sandwich line. Elkhatib filed a suit in a federal district court against Dunkin' Donuts and others. The defendants filed a motion for summary judgment. Did Dunkin' Donuts act in good faith in its relationship with Elkhatib? Explain. [*Elkhatib v. Dunkin' Donuts, Inc.,* __ F.Supp.2d __ (N.D.Ill. 2004)]

16–7. CASE PROBLEM WITH SAMPLE ANSWER

At least six months before the 1996 Summer Olympic Games in Atlanta, Georgia, Stafford Fontenot, Steve Turner, Mike Montelaro, Joe Sokol, and Doug Brinsmade agreed to sell Cajun food at the Games and began making preparations. Calling themselves

"Prairie Cajun Seafood Catering of Louisiana," on May 19 the group applied for a license with the Fulton County, Georgia, Department of Public Health–Environmental Health Services. Later, Ted Norris received for the sale of a mobile kitchen an $8,000 check drawn on the "Prairie Cajun Seafood Catering of Louisiana" account and two promissory notes, one for $12,000 and the other for $20,000. The notes, which were dated June 12, listed only Fontenot "d/b/a [doing business as] Prairie Cajun Seafood" as the maker. On July 31, Fontenot and his friends signed a partnership agreement, which listed specific percentages of profits and losses. They drove the mobile kitchen to Atlanta, but business was "disastrous." When the notes were not paid, Norris filed a suit in a Louisiana state court against Fontenot, seeking payment. What are the elements of a partnership? Was there a partnership among Fontenot and the others? Who is liable on the notes? Explain. [*Norris v. Fontenot,* 867 So.2d 179 (La.App. 3 Cir. 2004)]

- **To view a sample answer for Problem 16–7, go to this book's Web site at academic.cengage.com/blaw/cross, select "Chapter 16," and click on "Case Problem with Sample Answer."**

16–8. Indications of Partnership. In August 2003, Tammy Duncan began working as a waitress at Bynum's Diner, which was owned by her mother, Hazel Bynum, and her stepfather, Eddie Bynum, in Valdosta, Georgia. Less than a month later, the three signed an agreement under which Eddie was to relinquish his management responsibilities, allowing Tammy to be co-manager. At the end of this six-month period, Eddie would revisit this agreement and could then extend it for another six-month period. The diner's bank account was to remain in Eddie's name. There was no provision with regard to the diner's profit, if any, and the parties did not change the business's tax information. Tammy began doing the bookkeeping, as well as waiting tables and performing other duties. On October 30, she slipped off a ladder and injured her knees. At the end of the six-month term, Tammy quit working at the diner. The Georgia State Board of Workers' Compensation determined that she had been the diner's employee and awarded her benefits under the diner's workers' compensation policy with Cypress Insurance Co. Cypress filed a suit in a Georgia state court against Tammy, arguing that she was not an employee, but a co-owner. What are the essential elements of a partnership? Was Tammy a partner in the business of the diner? Explain. [*Cypress Insurance Co. v. Duncan,* 281 Ga.App. 469, 636 S.E.2d 159 (2006)]

16–9. Sole Proprietorship. James Ferguson operates "Jim's 11-E Auto Sales" in Jonesborough, Tennessee, as a sole proprietorship. In 1999, Consumers Insurance Co. issued a policy to "Jim Ferguson, Jim's 11E Auto Sales" covering "Owned 'Autos' Only." *Auto* was defined to include "a land motor vehicle," which was not further explained in the policy. Coverage extended to damage caused by the owner or driver of an underinsured motor vehicle. In 2000, Ferguson bought and titled in his own name a 1976 Harley-Davidson motorcycle, intending to repair and sell the cycle through his dealership. In October 2001, while riding the motorcycle, Ferguson was struck by an auto driven by John Jenkins. Ferguson filed a suit in a Tennessee state court against Jenkins, who was underinsured with respect to Ferguson's medical bills, and Consumers. The insurer argued, among other things, that because the motorcycle was bought and titled in Ferguson's own name, and he was riding it at the time of the accident, it was his personal vehicle and thus was not covered under the dealership's policy. What is the relationship between a sole proprietor and a sole proprietorship? How might this status affect the court's decision in this case? [*Ferguson v. Jenkins,* 204 S.W.3d 779 (Tenn.App. 2006)]

16–10. A QUESTION OF ETHICS

*In August 2004, Ralph Vilardo contacted Travel Center, Inc., in Cincinnati, Ohio, to buy a trip to Florida in December for his family to celebrate his fiftieth wedding anniversary. Vilardo paid $6,900 to David Sheets, the sole proprietor of Travel Center. Vilardo also paid $195 to Sheets for a separate trip to Florida in February 2005. Sheets assured Vilardo that everything was set, but in fact no arrangements were made. Later, two unauthorized charges for travel services totaling $1,182.35 appeared on Vilardo's credit-card statement. Vilardo filed a suit in an Ohio state court against Sheets and his business, alleging, among other things, fraud and violations of the state consumer protection law. Vilardo served Sheets and Travel Center with copies of the complaint, the summons, a request for admissions, and other documents filed with the court, including a motion for summary judgment. Each of these filings asked for a response within a certain time period. Sheets responded once on his own behalf with a denial of all of Vilardo's claims. Travel Center did not respond. [*Vilardo v. Sheets, *__ Ohio App.3d __, __ N.E.2d __ (12 Dist. 2006)]*

(a) Almost four months after Vilardo filed his complaint, Sheets decided that he was unable to adequately represent himself and retained an attorney who asked the court for more time. Should the court grant this request? Why or why not? Ultimately, what should the court rule in this case?

(b) Sheets admitted that "Travel Center, Inc." was a sole proprietorship. He also argued that liability might be imposed on his business but not on himself. How would you rule with respect to this argument? Why? Would there be anything unethical about allowing Sheets to avoid liability on this basis? Explain.

LAW ON THE WEB

For updated links to resources available on the Web, as well as a variety of other materials, visit this text's Web site at

academic.cengage.com/blaw/cross

For some of the advantages and disadvantages of doing business as a partnership, go to the following page, which is part of the U.S. Small Business Administration's Web site. Click on "Forms of Ownership" and then scroll down to "Partnerships."

www.sba.gov/smallbusinessplanner/start/chooseastructure/index.html

For information about FTC regulations on franchising, as well as state laws regulating franchising, go to

www.ftc.gov/bcp/franchise/netfran.htm

A good source of information on the purchase and sale of franchises is Franchising.org, which is online at

www.franchising.org

Legal Research Exercises on the Web

Go to **academic.cengage.com/blaw/cross**, the Web site that accompanies this text. Select "Chapter 16" and click on "Internet Exercises." There you will find the following Internet research exercises that you can perform to learn more about the topics covered in this chapter.

Internet Exercise 16–1: Legal Perspective
Liability of Dissociated Partners

Internet Exercise 16–2: Economic Perspective
Taxation of Partnerships

Internet Exercise 16–3: Management Perspective
Franchises

CHAPTER 17

Limited Liability Companies and Limited Partnerships

In the preceding chapter, we examined sole proprietorships, franchises, and general partnerships. Before we discuss corporations, one of the most prevalent business forms, we pause to examine a relatively new form of business organization called the **limited liability company (LLC).** We also examine business forms designed to limit the liability of partners. The LLC is a hybrid form that combines the limited liability aspects of the corporation and the tax advantages of a partnership. Increasingly, LLCs are becoming an organizational form of choice among businesspersons—a trend encouraged by state statutes permitting their use.

In this chapter, we begin by examining the LLC. We then look at a similar type of entity that is also relatively new—the *limited liability partnership* (LLP). The chapter concludes with a discussion of the *limited partnership* (LP), a special type of partnership in which some of the partners have limited liability, and the *limited liability limited partnership* (LLLP).

Limited Liability Companies

Limited liability companies (LLCs) are governed by state LLC statutes. These laws vary, of course, from state to state. In an attempt to create more uniformity among the states in this respect, in 1995 the National Conference of Commissioners on Uniform State Laws issued the Uniform Limited Liability Company Act (ULLCA). To date, fewer than one-fourth of the states have adopted the ULLCA, and thus the law governing LLCs remains far from uniform.[1] Some provisions are common to most state statutes, however, and we base our discussion of LLCs in this section on these common elements.

Evolution of the LLC

In 1977, Wyoming became the first state to pass legislation authorizing the creation of an LLC. Although LLCs emerged in the United States only in 1977, they have been used for more than a century in other foreign jurisdictions, including several European and South American nations. For example, the South American *limitada* is a form of business organization that operates more or less as a partnership but provides limited liability for the owners.

Taxation of the LLC In the United States, after Wyoming's adoption of an LLC statute, it still was not known how the Internal Revenue Service (IRS) would treat the LLC for tax purposes. In 1988, however, the IRS ruled that Wyoming LLCs would be taxed as partnerships instead of corporations, providing that certain requirements were met. Prior to this ruling, only one additional state—Florida, in 1982—had authorized LLCs. The 1988 ruling encouraged other states to enact LLC statutes, and in less than a decade, all states had done so.

IRS rules that went into effect on January 1, 1997, also encouraged more widespread use of LLCs in the business world. Under these rules, an unincorporated business will automatically be taxed as a partnership

1. Note that the ULLCA was revised in 2006, but no state has yet adopted the revised version of this uniform act.

unless it indicates otherwise on the tax form. The exceptions involve publicly traded companies, companies formed under a state incorporation statute, and certain foreign-owned companies. If a business chooses to be taxed as a corporation, it can indicate this preference by checking a box on the Internal Revenue Service (IRS) form.

Foreign Entities May Be LLC Members Part of the impetus behind creating LLCs in this country is that foreign investors are allowed to become LLC members. Thus, in an era increasingly characterized by global business efforts and investments, the LLC offers U.S. firms and potential investors from other countries flexibility and the opportunity for limited liability and increased tax benefits.

The Nature of the LLC

LLCs share many characteristics with corporations. Like corporations, LLCs are creatures of the state. In other words, they must be formed and operated in compliance with state law. Like the shareholders of a corporation, the owners of an LLC, who are called **members,** enjoy limited liability [ULLCA 303].[2] Also like corporations, LLCs are legal entities apart from their owners. As a legal person, the LLC can sue or be sued, enter into contracts, and hold title to property [ULLCA 201]. The terminology used to describe LLCs formed in other states or nations is also similar to that used in corporate law. For example, an LLC formed in one state but doing business in another state is referred to in the second state as a *foreign LLC.*

2. Members of an LLC can also bring derivative actions, which you will read about in Chapter 18, on behalf of the LLC [ULLCA 101]. As with a corporate shareholder's derivative suit, any damages recovered go to the LLC, not to the members personally. See, for example, *PacLink Communications International, Inc. v. Superior Court,* 90 Cal.App.4th 958, 109 Cal.Rptr.2d 436 (2001).

LLC Formation

As mentioned, LLCs are creatures of statute and thus must follow state statutory requirements. To form an LLC, **articles of organization** must be filed with a central state agency—usually the secretary of state's office [ULLCA 202]. Typically, the articles are required to include such information as the name of the business, its principal address, the name and address of a registered agent, the names of the owners, and information on how the LLC will be managed [ULLCA 203]. The business's name must include the words *Limited Liability Company* or the initials *LLC* [ULLCA 105(a)]. In addition to filing the articles of organization, a few states require that a notice of the intention to form an LLC be published in a local newspaper. Although a majority of the states permit one-member LLCs, some states require at least two members.

Businesspersons sometimes enter into contracts on behalf of a business organization that is not yet formed. For example, as you will read in Chapter 18, persons forming a corporation may enter into contracts during the process of incorporation but before the corporation becomes a legal entity. These contracts are referred to as preincorporation contracts. Once the corporation is formed and adopts the preincorporation contract (by means of a *novation,* discussed in Chapter 9), it can then enforce the contract terms.

In the following case, the question was whether the same principle extends to LLCs. A person in the process of forming an LLC entered into a preorganization contract under which it would be obligated to purchase the Park Plaza Hotel in Hollywood, California. Once the LLC legally existed, the owners of the hotel refused to sell the property to the LLC, claiming that the contract was unenforceable.

EXTENDED CASE 17.1 **02 Development, LLC v. 607 South Park, LLC**

Court of Appeal, Second District, Division 1, California, 2008.
159 Cal.App.4th 609, 71 Cal.Rptr.3d 608.

***ROTHSCHILD,* J. [Judge]**

02 Development, LLC (02 Development), a California limited liability company, appeals from a summary judgment in favor of 607 South Park, LLC (607 South Park), also a California limited liability company, on 02 Development's complaint for breach of a real estate purchase agreement.

BACKGROUND

In March 2004, 607 South Park entered into a written agreement to sell the Park Plaza Hotel to "Creative Environments of Hollywood, Inc., as General Partner of 607 Park View Associates, Ltd., a

CASE CONTINUES

CASE 17.1 CONTINUED

California limited partnership" (Creative Environments) for $8.7 million. In February 2005, Creative Environments and 02 Development executed a contract purporting to assign Creative Environments' rights in the hotel purchase agreement to 02 Development.

02 Development did not exist when the parties executed the assignment agreement. Robert Epstein executed the assignment agreement for 02 Development, and in May 2005 he created 02 Development by executing and filing the appropriate articles of organization [for the LLC] with the California Secretary of State.

02 Development later sued 607 South Park for breach of the hotel purchase agreement. The operative second amended complaint alleged that 607 South Park both refused to perform under the contract and denied that 02 Development held any rights under the purchase and assignment agreements.

607 South Park moved for summary judgment on two grounds: (1) There was no enforceable contract between 607 South Park and 02 Development because 02 Development did not exist when the assignment agreement was executed; and (2) 607 South Park's repudiation of the alleged contract did not cause 02 Development any harm because 02 Development was not ready, willing, and able to fund the purchase of the hotel. In support of the second ground, 607 South Park presented evidence that neither Epstein nor 02 Development had the $8.7 million needed to close the purchase of the hotel or had commitments from anyone else to provide the necessary financing. 607 South Park presented no other evidence concerning 02 Development's ability to fund the purchase of the hotel.

In opposition to the motion, 02 Development argued that a business entity can enforce pre-organization contracts made for its benefit. 02 Development also argued that to prove causation it needed to prove only that it would have been able to fund the purchase of the hotel when required to do so under the contract. Thus, contrary to 607 South Park's argument, 02 Development contended that it did not need to prove that it already had the necessary funds, or already had binding commitments from third parties to provide the funds, when 607 South Park anticipatorily repudiated the contract. All that 02 Development needed to prove was that it would have been able to obtain the necessary funding (or funding commitments) in order to close the transaction on time.

The trial court granted the motion and entered judgment in favor of 607 South Park. 02 Development timely appealed.

* * * *

DISCUSSION

02 Development argues that both grounds for 607 South Park's summary judgment motion fail as a matter of law and that the trial court therefore erred in granting the motion. We agree.

I. Enforceability of Pre-Organization Contracts

It is hornbook law [black letter law] that a corporation can enforce preincorporation contracts made in its behalf, as long as the corporation "has adopted the contract or otherwise succeeded to it." * * * California law does not deviate from that well-established norm. *607 South Park does not argue that limited liability companies should be treated differently from corporations in this respect, and we are aware of no authority that would support such a position.* 607 South Park's first ground for its summary judgment motion—that there is no enforceable contract between 607 South Park and 02 Development because 02 Development did not exist when the assignment agreement was executed—therefore fails as a matter of law. [Emphasis added.]

607 South Park's principal contention to the contrary is that a nonexistent business entity cannot be a party to a contract. The contention is true but irrelevant. *When the assignment agreement was executed, 02 Development did not exist, so it was not then a party to the agreement. But once 02 Development came into existence, it could enforce any pre-organization contract made in its behalf, such as the assignment agreement, if it adopted or ratified it.* [Emphasis added.]

* * * *

II. Causation

In the trial court, 607 South Park contended that in order to prove causation, 02 Development would have to prove either that it had the $8.7 million necessary to fund the transaction or that it had legally binding commitments from third parties to provide the necessary funding. * * * 607 South Park disavows [this contention] on appeal.

CASE 17.1 CONTINUED

Instead, 607 South Park now argues that its motion was based on the proposition that 02 Development "must present admissible evidence that it would have been financially able to close the transaction." But 607 South Park's evidence in support of its motion showed only that 02 Development had neither the $8.7 million to fund the transaction nor legally binding commitments from third parties to provide the funding. *607 South Park presented no evidence that 02 Development would have been unable to arrange for the necessary funding to close the transaction on time if 607 South Park had given it the opportunity instead of repudiating the contract in advance.* Because 607 South Park introduced no evidence to support an argument based on the proposition of law that 607 South Park is now advocating, the burden of production never shifted to 02 Development to present contrary evidence. For all of these reasons, the trial court erred when it granted 607 South Park's motion for summary judgment. [Emphasis added.]

DISPOSITION

The judgment is reversed, and the trial court is directed to enter an order denying 607 South Park's motion for summary judgment.

QUESTIONS

1. Why was it unimportant to the appellate court that 02 Development did not have to prove that it had funding commitments for $8.7 million?
2. What might have been some of the possible reasons that 607 South Park did not agree to sell the property to 02 Development?

Jurisdictional Requirements

One of the significant differences between LLCs and corporations has to do with federal jurisdictional requirements. Under the federal jurisdiction statute, a corporation is deemed to be a citizen of the state where it is incorporated and maintains its principal place of business. The statute does not mention the state citizenship of partnerships, LLCs, and other unincorporated associations, but the courts have tended to regard these entities as citizens of every state in which their members are citizens.

The state citizenship of an LLC may come into play when a party sues the LLC based on diversity of citizenship. Remember from Chapter 2 that when parties to a lawsuit are from different states and the amount in controversy exceeds $75,000, a federal court can exercise diversity jurisdiction. *Total* diversity of citizenship must exist, however. For example, Fong, a citizen of New York, wishes to bring a suit against Skycel, an LLC formed under the laws of Connecticut. One of Skycel's members also lives in New York. Fong will not be able to bring a suit against Skycel in federal court on the basis of diversity jurisdiction because the defendant LLC is also a citizen of New York. The same would be true if Fong was bringing a suit against multiple defendants and one of the defendants lived in New York.

Advantages and Disadvantages of the LLC

The LLC offers many advantages, and relatively few disadvantages, to businesspersons.

Advantages A key advantage of the LLC is that the members are not personally liable for the debts or obligations of the entity: their risk of loss is limited to the amount of their investments. An LLC also offers flexibility in regard to both taxation and management, as will be discussed shortly. Another advantage is that an LLC is an enduring business entity that exists beyond the illness or death of its members. In addition, as mentioned earlier, an LLC can include foreign investors.

An LLC that has *two or more members* can choose to be taxed as either a partnership or a corporation. As will be discussed in Chapter 18, a corporate entity must pay income taxes on its profits, and the shareholders pay personal income taxes on profits distributed as dividends. An LLC that wants to distribute profits to the members may prefer to be taxed as a partnership to avoid the double taxation that occurs with corporate entities. Unless an LLC indicates that it wishes to be taxed as a corporation, the IRS automatically taxes it as a partnership. This means that, as in a partnership, the LLC as an entity pays no taxes but "passes through" its profits to the members, who then personally pay taxes on the profits. If an LLC's members want to reinvest profits in the business, however, rather than distribute the profits to members, they may prefer to be taxed as a corporation. Corporate income tax rates may be lower than personal tax rates.

An LLC that has only *one member* cannot be taxed as a partnership, however. For federal income tax purposes, one-member LLCs are automatically taxed as sole proprietorships unless they indicate that they wish to be taxed as corporations. With respect to state taxes, most states follow the IRS rules, but a few states tax LLCs even though they do not tax partnerships.

Disadvantages The main disadvantage of the LLC is that state LLC statutes are not uniform. Therefore, businesses that operate in more than one state may not receive consistent treatment. Generally, though, most states will apply to a foreign LLC (an LLC formed in another state) the law of the state where the LLC was formed.

The LLC Operating Agreement

As mentioned, an advantage of the LLC form of business is the flexibility it offers in terms of operation and management. The members get to decide who will participate in the management and operation of their business, and how other issues will be resolved. Members normally do this by forming an **operating agreement** [ULLCA 103(a)]. Operating agreements typically contain provisions relating to management, how profits will be divided, the transfer of membership interests, whether the LLC will be dissolved on the death or departure of a member, and other important issues.

In many states, an operating agreement need not be in writing and indeed need not even be formed for an LLC to exist. Generally, though, LLC members should protect their interests by forming a written operating agreement. As with any business arrangement, disputes may arise over any number of issues. If there is no agreement covering the topic under dispute, such as how profits will be divided, the state LLC statute will govern the outcome. For example, most LLC statutes provide that if the members have not specified how profits will be divided, they will be divided equally among the members.

Generally, when an issue is not covered by an operating agreement or by an LLC statute, the principles of partnership law are applied. The following case illustrates what can happen in the absence of a written operating agreement when one of the members of the LLC has a "bad intent."

CASE 17.2 Kuhn v. Tumminelli

Superior Court of New Jersey, Appellate Division, 2004. 366 N.J.Super. 431, 841 A.2d 496.
lawlibrary.rutgers.edu/search.shtml#party[a]

• **Background and Facts** Clifford Kuhn, Jr., and Joseph Tumminelli formed Touch of Class Limousine Service, doing business as Touch of Elegance Limousine Service, under the New Jersey Limited Liability Company Act in 1999. They did not sign a written operating agreement, but orally agreed that Kuhn would provide the financial backing and procure customers, and that Tumminelli would manage the day-to-day operations of the company. Tumminelli embezzled $283,000 from the company after cashing customers' checks at Quick Cash, Inc., a local check-cashing service. Quick Cash deposited the checks in its bank account with First Union National Bank, N.A., which collected on the checks from the drawee banks, Bank of America Corporation and Chase Manhattan Bank, N.A. Kuhn filed a suit in a New Jersey state court against Tumminelli, the banks, and others to recover the embezzled funds. The court ordered Tumminelli to pay Kuhn and to transfer his interest in Touch of Class to Kuhn, but issued a summary judgment in favor of the other defendants. Kuhn appealed to a state intermediate appellate court, arguing, among other things, that Quick Cash and the banks were liable because Tumminelli did not have the authority to cash the company's checks and convert the funds.

a. In the "Which courts do you want to search?" section, click on the small box next to "Appellate Division." In the "Enter Names Here" section, in the "First Name:" box, type "Kuhn"; in the "Second Name:" box, type "Tumminelli"; then click on "Submit Form." In the result, click on the appropriate link to access the opinion. Rutgers University School of Law in Camden, New Jersey, maintains this Web site.

CASE 17.2 CONTINUED

IN THE LANGUAGE OF THE COURT
***LEFELT*, J.A.D. [Judge, Appellate Division]**

* * * *

New Jersey enacted the Limited Liability Company Act in 1994. Its purpose was to enable members and managers of LLCs to take advantage of both the limited liability afforded to shareholders and directors of corporations and the pass-through tax advantages available to partnerships.

Under the LLC Act, *when a limited liability company is managed by its members, unless otherwise provided in the operating agreement, each member shall have the authority to bind the limited liability company.* Moreover, except as otherwise provided in an operating agreement, a member or manager may lend money to, borrow money from, act as a surety, guarantor or endorser for, * * * an LLC. [Emphasis added.]

In the absence of a written operating agreement providing to the contrary, Tumminelli as a 50% owner of the LLC had broad authority to bind the LLC * * * and specific authority * * * to endorse and presumably cash checks payable to the LLC. If more limited authority was desired, Kuhn and Tumminelli had to so provide in a written operating agreement.

* * * *

* * * The LLC Act contemplates that its provisions will control unless the members agree otherwise in an operating agreement. *When executing an operating agreement, which must be written if the LLC has more than one member, the members are free to structure the company in a variety of ways and are free to restrict and expand the rights, responsibilities and authority of its managers and members.* [Emphasis added.]

The LLC Act is, therefore, quite flexible and permits the LLC members great discretion to establish the company structure and procedures, with the statute controlling in the absence of a contrary operating agreement. The legislative intent is revealed by the directive that the LLC Act is to be liberally construed to give the maximum effect to the principle of freedom of contract and to the enforceability of operating agreements.

* * * *

Tumminelli was authorized under the LLC Act to endorse the checks. In fact, considering Tumminelli's position at the LLC, his responsibilities, and daily functions along with the statutory grant of authority, it can be inferred that Tumminelli had actual authority to receive the checks, endorse the checks, and cash them at Quick Cash, especially because Kuhn knew that Tumminelli was paying business expenses in cash.

* * * Under Kuhn's argument, even if a person had been authorized to endorse and cash a check, if that person converts the funds to an unauthorized use, a depository bank would be liable, as if the check had been paid on a forged endorsement.

We disagree that an authorized endorsement can become unauthorized by a subsequent unauthorized use of the funds. Rather, we view the circumstances as constituting two acts, the endorsement necessary to obtain the funds and the subsequent use of the funds. These acts are not inseparable. *The misappropriation of the funds is unauthorized, but does not convert an authorized endorsement into a forgery.* [Emphasis added.]

It defies reason to allow an event that occurs after the endorsement to affect the validity of the endorsement. The use to which the agent later puts the check does not affect the agent's authorization to endorse it. The validity of an endorsement does not depend upon the agent's subjective motivation at the time of the endorsement. * * * How can a bank or anyone else protect themselves against someone's bad intent?

If the agent is otherwise authorized * * * the fact that the agent had an improper purpose in making or endorsing the instrument in the authorized form does not prevent a bona fide purchaser in due course, or a subsequent transferee from one, from having the same rights in the instrument and against the principal as if the agent's act were authorized.

• **Decision and Remedy** *The state intermediate appellate court affirmed the lower court's judgment in favor of Quick Cash and the banks. Tumminelli had the authority to accept, indorse, and cash checks on behalf of Touch of Class, under the LLC Act and in the absence of a written*

CASE CONTINUES

CASE 17.2 CONTINUED *operating agreement, which might have specified otherwise. His "bad intent" to convert the funds to his own use did not affect this authority.*

- **What If the Facts Were Different?** *Suppose that Kuhn and Tumminelli had signed a written operating agreement that required both members' indorsements when cashing customers' checks. Assuming that Quick Cash would have known of this requirement, would the result in this case have been different? If so, how?*

- **The Legal Environment Dimension** *What does the outcome in this case suggest to potential members of LLCs who want to avoid the negative consequences of debt and litigation to which Kuhn was subject?*

Management of an LLC

Basically, the members have two options for managing an LLC—the members may decide in their operating agreement to be either a "member-managed" LLC or a "manager-managed" LLC. Most state LLC statutes and the ULLCA provide that unless the articles of organization specify otherwise, an LLC is assumed to be member managed [ULLCA 203(a)(6)].

Participation in Management In a *member-managed* LLC, all of the members participate in management, and decisions are made by majority vote [ULLCA 404(a)]. In a *manager-managed* LLC, the members designate a group of persons to manage the firm. The management group may consist of only members, both members and nonmembers, or only nonmembers. Managers in a manager-managed LLC owe fiduciary duties to the LLC and its members, including the duty of loyalty and the duty of care [ULLCA 409(a), 409(h)], just as corporate directors and officers owe fiduciary duties to the corporation and its shareholders.

Operating Procedures The members of an LLC can include provisions governing decision-making procedures in their operating agreement. For instance, the agreement can include procedures for choosing or removing managers. Although most LLC statutes are silent on this issue, the ULLCA provides that members may choose and remove managers by majority vote [ULLCA 404(b)(3)].

The members are also free to include in the agreement provisions designating when and for what purposes they will hold formal members' meetings. Most state LLC statutes have no provisions regarding members' meetings, which is in contrast to most state laws governing corporations, as you will read in Chapter 18.

Members may also specify in their agreement how voting rights will be apportioned. If they do not, LLC statutes in most states provide that voting rights are apportioned according to each member's capital contributions.[3] Some states provide that, in the absence of an agreement to the contrary, each member has one vote.

Dissociation and Dissolution of an LLC

Recall from Chapter 16 that in the context of partnerships, *dissociation* occurs when a partner ceases to be associated in the carrying on of the partnership business. The same concept applies to LLCs. A member of an LLC has the *power* to dissociate from the LLC at any time, but he or she may not have the *right* to dissociate. Under the ULLCA, the events that trigger a member's dissociation from an LLC are similar to the events causing a partner to be dissociated under the Uniform Partnership Act (UPA). These include voluntary withdrawal, expulsion by other members or by court order, bankruptcy, incompetence, and death. Generally, even if a member dies or otherwise dissociates from an LLC, the other members may continue to carry on the LLC business, unless the operating agreement has contrary provisions.

Effect of Dissociation When a member dissociates from an LLC, he or she loses the right to participate in management and the right to act as an agent for the LLC. His or her duty of loyalty to the LLC also terminates, and the duty of care continues only with respect

3. This is similar to partnership law in the sense that partners in a partnership generally have equal rights in management and equal voting rights unless otherwise specified in a partnership agreement [UPA 401(f)].

to events that occurred before dissociation. Generally, the dissociated member also has a right to have his or her interest in the LLC bought out by the other members of the LLC. The LLC's operating agreement may contain provisions establishing a buyout price, but if it does not, the member's interest is usually purchased at a fair value. In states that have adopted the ULLCA, the LLC must purchase the interest at "fair" value within 120 days after the dissociation.

If the member's dissociation violates the LLC's operating agreement, it is considered legally wrongful, and the dissociated member can be held liable for damages caused by the dissociation. Suppose that Chadwick and Barrel are members in an LLC. Chadwick manages the accounts, and Barrel, who has many connections in the community and is a skilled investor, brings in the business. If Barrel wrongfully dissociates from the LLC, the LLC's business will suffer, and Chadwick can hold Barrel liable for the loss of business resulting from her withdrawal.

Dissolution Regardless of whether a member's dissociation was wrongful or rightful, normally the dissociated member has no right to force the LLC to dissolve. The remaining members can opt to either continue or dissolve the business. Members can also stipulate in their operating agreement that certain events will cause dissolution, or they can agree that they have the power to dissolve the LLC by vote. As with partnerships, a court can order an LLC to be dissolved in certain circumstances, such as when the members have engaged in illegal or oppressive conduct, or when it is no longer feasible to carry on the business.

When an LLC is dissolved, any members who did not wrongfully dissociate may participate in the winding up process. To wind up the business, members must collect, liquidate, and distribute the LLC's assets. Members may preserve the assets for a reasonable time to optimize their return, and they continue to have the authority to perform reasonable acts in conjunction with winding up. In other words, the LLC will be bound by the reasonable acts of its members during the winding up process. Once all of the LLC's assets have been sold, the proceeds are distributed to pay off debts to creditors first (including debts owed to members who are creditors of the LLC). The member's capital contributions are returned next, and any remaining amounts are then distributed to members in equal shares or according to their operating agreement.

Section 2 Limited Liability Partnerships

The **limited liability partnership (LLP)** is a hybrid form of business designed mostly for professionals who normally do business as partners in a partnership. The major advantage of the LLP is that it allows a partnership to continue as a pass-through entity for tax purposes but limits the personal liability of the partners.

The first state to enact an LLP statute was Texas, in 1991. Other states quickly followed suit, and by 1997, virtually all of the states had enacted LLP statutes. LLPs must be formed and operated in compliance with state statutes, which may include provisions of the UPA. The appropriate form must be filed with a central state agency, usually the secretary of state's office, and the business's name must include either "Limited Liability Partnership" or "LLP" [UPA 1001, 1002]. In addition, an LLP must file an annual report with the state to remain qualified as an LLP in that state [UPA 1003]. In most states, it is relatively easy to convert a traditional partnership into an LLP because the firm's basic organizational structure remains the same. Additionally, all of the statutory and common law rules governing partnerships still apply (apart from those modified by the LLP statute). Normally, LLP statutes are simply amendments to a state's already existing partnership law.

The LLP is especially attractive for two categories of enterprises: professional services and family businesses. Professional service firms include law firms and accounting firms. *Family limited liability partnerships* are basically business organizations in which the majority of the partners are related to each other.

Liability in an LLP

Traditionally, many professionals, such as attorneys and accountants, have worked together using the partnership business form. As previously discussed, a major disadvantage of the general partnership is the unlimited personal liability of its owner-partners. Each partner in a general partnership is exposed to potential liability for the malpractice of another partner.

The LLP allows professionals to avoid personal liability for the malpractice of other partners. A partner in an LLP is still liable for her or his own wrongful acts, such as negligence, however. Also liable is the partner who supervised the party who committed a wrongful act. This is generally true for all types of partners and partnerships, not just LLPs.

Although LLP statutes vary from state to state, generally each state statute limits the liability of partners in some way. For example, Delaware law protects each innocent partner from the "debts and obligations of the partnership arising from negligence, wrongful acts, or misconduct." In North Carolina, Texas, and Washington, D.C., the statutes protect innocent partners from obligations arising from "errors, omissions, negligence, incompetence, or malfeasance." The UPA more broadly exempts partners from personal liability for any partnership obligation, "whether arising in contract, tort, or otherwise" [UPA 306(c)].

Even though the language of these statutes may seem to apply specifically to attorneys, virtually any group of professionals can use the LLP (depending on the state statute). LLPs are especially popular in the accounting field. All of the "Big Four" firms—the four largest international accountancy and professional services firms—are organized as LLPs, including PricewaterhouseCoopers LLP and Deloitte Development LLP.

Family Limited Liability Partnerships

A **family limited liability partnership (FLLP)** is a limited liability partnership in which the majority of the partners are persons related to each other, essentially as spouses, parents, grandparents, siblings, cousins, nephews, or nieces. A person acting in a fiduciary capacity for persons so related can also be a partner. All of the partners must be natural persons or persons acting in a fiduciary capacity for the benefit of natural persons.

Probably the most significant use of the FLLP form of business organization is in agriculture. Family-owned farms sometimes find this form to their benefit. The FLLP offers the same advantages as other LLPs with certain additional advantages, such as, in Iowa, an exemption from real estate transfer taxes when partnership real estate is transferred among partners.[4]

Limited Partnerships

We now look at a business organizational form that limits the liability of *some* of its owners—the **limited partnership.** Limited partnerships originated in medieval Europe and have been in existence in the United States since the early 1800s. In many ways, limited partnerships are like the general partnerships (discussed in Chapter 16), but they differ from general partnerships in several ways. Because of this, they are sometimes referred to as *special partnerships.*

A limited partnership consists of at least one **general partner** and one or more **limited partners.** A general partner assumes management responsibility for the partnership and has full responsibility for the partnership and for all its debts. A limited partner contributes cash or other property and owns an interest in the firm but does not undertake any management responsibilities and is not personally liable for partnership debts beyond the amount of his or her investment. A limited partner can forfeit limited liability by taking part in the management of the business. A comparison of the characteristics of general partnerships and limited partnerships appears in Exhibit 17–1.[5]

Until 1976, the law governing limited partnerships in all states except Louisiana was the Uniform Limited Partnership Act (ULPA). Since 1976, most states and the District of Columbia have adopted the revised version of the ULPA, known as the Revised Uniform Limited Partnership Act (RULPA). Because the RULPA is the dominant law governing limited partnerships in the United States, we refer to the RULPA in the following discussion. Note, however, that in 2001 the National Conference of Commissioners on Uniform State Laws adopted a new, more flexible version of this law (ULPA 2001), which has been adopted in a minority of states.

Formation of a Limited Partnership

In contrast to the informal, private, and voluntary agreement that usually suffices for a general partnership, the formation of a limited partnership is formal and public. The parties must follow specific statutory requirements and file a certificate with the state. In this regard, a limited partnership resembles a corporation more than it does a general partnership. A limited partnership must have at least one general partner and one limited partner, as mentioned previously. Additionally, the partners must sign a **certificate of limited partnership,** which requires information similar to that found in articles of incorporation

4. Iowa Statutes Section 428A.2.

5. Under the UPA, a general partnership can be converted into a limited partnership and vice versa [UPA 902, 903]. The UPA also provides for the merger of a general partnership with one or more general or limited partnerships [UPA 905].

EXHIBIT 17–1 • A Comparison of General Partnerships and Limited Partnerships

Characteristic	General Partnership (UPA)	Limited Partnership (RULPA)
Creation	By agreement of two or more persons to carry on a business as co-owners for profit.	By agreement of two or more persons to carry on a business as co-owners for profit. Must include one or more general partners and one or more limited partners. Filing of a certificate with the secretary of state is required.
Sharing of Profits and Losses	By agreement; or, in the absence of agreement, profits are shared equally by the partners, and losses are shared in the same ratio as profits.	Profits are shared as required in the certificate agreement, and losses are shared likewise, up to the amount of the limited partners' capital contributions. In the absence of a provision in the certificate agreement, profits and losses are shared on the basis of percentages of capital contributions.
Liability	Unlimited personal liability of all partners.	Unlimited personal liability of all general partners; limited partners liable only to the extent of their capital contributions.
Capital Contribution	No minimum or mandatory amount; set by agreement.	Set by agreement.
Management	By agreement, or in the absence of agreement, all partners have an equal voice.	General partner or partners only. Limited partners have no voice or else are subject to liability as general partners (but *only* if a third party has reason to believe that the limited partner is a general partner). A limited partner may act as an agent or employee of the partnership and vote on amending the certificate or on the sale or dissolution of the partnership.
Duration	Terminated by agreement of the partners, but can continue to do business even when a partner dissociates from the partnership.	Terminated by agreement in the certificate or by retirement, death, or mental incompetence of a general partner in the absence of the right of the other general partners to continue the partnership. Death of a limited partner, unless he or she is the only remaining limited partner, does not terminate the partnership.
Distribution of Assets on Liquidation—Order of Priorities	1. Payment of debts, including those owed to partner and nonpartner creditors. 2. Return of capital contributions and distribution of profit to partners.	1. Outside creditors and partner creditors. 2. Partners and former partners entitled to distributions or partnership assets. 3. Unless otherwise agreed, return of capital contributions and distribution of profit to partners.

(see Chapter 18), such as the name, mailing address, and capital contribution of each general and limited partner. The certificate must be filed with the designated state official—under the RULPA, the secretary of state. The certificate is usually open to public inspection.

Rights and Liabilities of Partners

General partners, unlike limited partners, are personally liable to the partnership's creditors; thus, at least one general partner is necessary in a limited partnership so that someone has personal liability. This policy

CASE 17.3 CONTINUED

* * * *

MSEL claims the correct standard * * * is the hypothetical transaction analysis * * *. [The] Canevas argue that * * * the offer from Kellar represented the fair market value * * *.

* * * *

* * * *[There are] sound policy reasons why an offer cannot be the fair market value.* * * * What if a businessman, for personal reasons, offers 10 times the real value of the business? What if the partnership, for personal reasons, such as sentimental value, refuses to sell for that absurdly high offer? *These arbitrary, emotional offers and rejections cannot provide a rational and reasonable basis for determining the fair market value.* [Emphasis added.]

Conversely, the hypothetical transaction standard does provide a rational and reasonable basis for determining the fair market value * * * by removing the irrationalities, strategies, and emotions * * *.

* * * *

Since it was error for the [lower] court to value Midnight Star at $6.2 million, it was also error to force the general partners to buy the business for $6.2 million or sell the business.

* * * *

* * * Instead of ordering the majority partners to purchase the whole partnership for the appraised value, the majority partners should only be required to pay any interests the withdrawing partner is due. * * * The majority partners should only be required to pay the Canevas the value of their 6.5 partnership units * * *.

- **Decision and Remedy** *The South Dakota Supreme Court reversed the judgment of the lower court and remanded the case to allow MSEL and Costner to pay the Canevas the value of their 6.5 partnership units after a revaluation of the partnership. The court concluded that under the partnership agreement, during liquidation, the firm's property could be distributed in kind among the partners if it was first offered for sale to a third party. The court also concluded that the correct value of the business was the accountant's figure, which was based on a fair market value analysis using a hypothetical buyer.*

- **The Legal Environment Dimension** *Why did the court hold that a forced sale of the property of the limited partnership was not appropriate in this case?*

- **The Ethical Dimension** *Under what circumstances might a forced sale of the property of a limited partnership on its dissolution be appropriate?*

Limited Liability Limited Partnerships

A **limited liability limited partnership (LLLP)** is a type of limited partnership. An LLLP differs from a limited partnership in that a general partner in an LLLP has the same liability as a limited partner in a limited partnership. In other words, the liability of all partners is limited to the amount of their investments in the firm.

A few states provide expressly for LLLPs. In states that do not provide for LLLPs but do allow for limited partnerships and limited liability partnerships, a limited partnership should probably still be able to register with the state as an LLLP.

REVIEWING Limited Liability Companies and Limited Partnerships

A bridge on a prominent public roadway in the city of Papagos, Arizona, was deteriorating and in need of repair. The city posted notices seeking proposals for an artistic bridge design and reconstruction. Davidson Masonry, LLC, which was owned and managed by Carl Davidson and his wife,

REVIEWING Limited Liability Companies and Limited Partnerships, Continued

Marilyn Rowe, decided to submit a bid for a decorative concrete project that incorporated artistic metalwork. They contacted Shana Lafayette, a local sculptor who specialized in large-scale metal forms, to help them design the bridge. The city selected their bridge design and awarded them the contract for a commission of $184,000. Davidson Masonry and Lafayette then entered into an agreement to work together on the bridge project. Davidson Masonry agreed to install and pay for concrete and structural work, and Lafayette agreed to install the metalwork at her expense. They agreed that overall profits would be split, with 25 percent going to Lafayette and 75 percent going to Davidson Masonry. Lafayette designed numerous metal sculptures of salmon that were incorporated into colorful decorative concrete forms designed by Rowe, while Davidson performed the structural engineering. Using the information presented in the chapter, answer the following questions.

1. Would Davidson Masonry automatically be taxed as a partnership or a corporation?
2. Is Davidson Masonry member managed or manager managed?
3. Suppose that during construction, Lafayette had entered into an agreement to rent space in a warehouse that was close to the bridge so that she could work on her sculptures near the site where they would eventually be installed. She entered into the contract without the knowledge or consent of Davidson Masonry. In this situation, would a court be likely to hold that Davidson Masonry was bound by the contract that Lafayette entered? Why or why not?
4. Now suppose that Rowe has an argument with her husband and wants to withdraw from being a member of Davidson Masonry. What is the term for such a withdrawal and what effect does it have on the LLC?

TERMS AND CONCEPTS

articles of organization 425
certificate of limited partnership 432
family limited liability partnership (FLLP) 432
general partner 432
limited liability company (LLC) 424
limited liability limited partnership (LLLP) 436
limited liability partnership (LLP) 431
limited partner 432
limited partnership 432
member 425
operating agreement 428

QUESTIONS AND CASE PROBLEMS

17-1. John, Lesa, and Tabir form a limited liability company. John contributes 60 percent of the capital, and Lesa and Tabir each contribute 20 percent. Nothing is decided about how profits will be divided. John assumes that he will be entitled to 60 percent of the profits, in accordance with his contribution. Lesa and Tabir, however, assume that the profits will be divided equally. A dispute over the question arises, and ultimately a court has to decide the issue. What law will the court apply? In most states, what will result? How could this dispute have been avoided in the first place? Discuss fully.

17-2. Asher and Breem form a limited partnership with Asher as the general partner and Breem as the limited partner. Breem puts up $15,000, and Asher contributes some office equipment that he owns. A certificate of limited partnership is properly filed, and business is begun.

LLRX.com, a Web site for legal professionals, provides information on LLCs on its Web journal. Go to

www.llrx.com/features/llc.htm

You can find information on filing fees for LLCs at

www.bizcorp.com

Legal Research Exercises on the Web

Go to **academic.cengage.com/blaw/cross**, the Web site that accompanies this text. Select "Chapter 17" and click on "Internet Exercises." There you will find the following Internet research exercises that you can perform to learn more about the topics covered in this chapter.

Internet Exercise 17–1: Legal Perspective
Limited Liability Companies

Internet Exercise 17–2: Management Perspective
Limited Partnerships and Limited Liability Partnerships

CHAPTER 18

Corporations

The corporation is a creature of statute. A **corporation** is an artificial being, existing only in law and neither tangible nor visible. Its existence generally depends on state law, although some corporations, especially public organizations, are created under federal law. Each state has its own body of corporate law, and these laws are not entirely uniform.

The Model Business Corporation Act (MBCA) is a codification of modern corporation law that has been influential in the codification of state corporation statutes. Today, the majority of state statutes are guided by the most recent version of the MBCA, often referred to as the Revised Model Business Corporation Act (RMBCA). Excerpts from the RMBCA are included in Appendix G of this text. Keep in mind, however, that there is considerable variation among the regulations of the states that have used the MBCA or the RMBCA as a basis for their statutes, and several states do not follow either act. Consequently, individual state corporation laws should be relied on to determine corporate law rather than the MBCA or RMBCA.

In this chapter, we examine the corporate form of business enterprise. Under modern law, except as limited by charters, statutes, or constitutions, *a corporation can engage in any act and enter into any contract available to a natural person in order to accomplish the purposes for which it was created.* When a corporation is created, the express and implied powers necessary to achieve its purpose also come into existence.

The Nature and Classification of Corporations

A corporation is a legal entity created and recognized by state law. It can consist of one or more *natural persons* (as opposed to the artificial *legal person* of the corporation) identified under a common name. The corporation substitutes itself for its shareholders in conducting corporate business and in incurring liability, yet its authority to act and the liability for its actions are separate and apart from the individuals who own it.

Corporate Personnel

When an individual purchases a share of stock in a corporation, that person becomes a shareholder and an owner of the corporation. The shareholders elect a *board of directors* who are responsible for the overall management of the corporation. The directors make all policy decisions and hire the *corporate officers* and other employees to run the daily business operations of the corporation.

The body of shareholders can change constantly without affecting the continued existence of the corporation. A shareholder can sue the corporation, and the corporation can sue a shareholder. Additionally, under certain circumstances, a shareholder can sue on behalf of a corporation. The rights and duties of all corporate personnel will be examined later in this chapter.

The Limited Liability of Shareholders

One of the key advantages of the corporate form is the limited liability of its owners (shareholders). Corporate shareholders normally are not personally liable for the obligations of the corporation beyond the extent of their investments. In certain limited situations, however, the "corporate veil" can be pierced and liability for the corporation's obligations extended to shareholders—a concept that will be explained later in this chapter. Additionally, to enable the firm to obtain credit, shareholders in small companies sometimes voluntarily assume personal liability, as guarantors, for corporate obligations.

Corporate Taxation

Corporate profits are taxed by various levels of government. Corporations can do one of two things with corporate profits—retain them or pass them on to shareholders in the form of dividends. The corporation normally receives no tax deduction for dividends distributed to shareholders. Dividends are again taxable (except when they represent distributions of capital) to the shareholder receiving them. This double-taxation feature of the corporation is one of its major disadvantages.[1]

Profits that are not distributed are retained by the corporation. These **retained earnings,** if invested properly, will yield higher corporate profits in the future and thus cause the price of the company's stock to rise. Individual shareholders can then reap the benefits of these retained earnings in the capital gains they receive when they sell their shares.

In recent years, some U.S. corporations have been using holding companies to reduce—or at least defer—their U.S. income taxes. At its simplest, a **holding company** (sometimes referred to as a *parent company*) is a company whose business activity consists of holding shares in another company. Typically, the holding company is established in a low-tax or no-tax offshore jurisdiction. Among the best known are the Cayman Islands, Dubai, Hong Kong, Luxembourg, Monaco, and Panama.

Sometimes, a major U.S. corporation sets up an investment holding company in a low-tax offshore environment. The corporation then transfers its cash, bonds, stocks, and other investments to the holding company. In general, any profits received by the holding company on these investments are taxed at the rate of the offshore jurisdiction in which the company is registered, not the U.S. tax rates applicable to the U.S. corporation or its shareholders. Thus, deposits of cash, for example, may earn interest that is taxed at only a minimal rate. Once the profits are brought "onshore," though, they are taxed at the federal corporate income tax rate, and any payments received by the shareholders are also taxable at the full U.S. rates.

1. Congress enacted a law in 2003 that mitigated this double-taxation feature to some extent by providing a reduced federal tax rate on qualifying dividends. The Jobs Growth Tax Relief Reconciliation Act of 2003, Pub. L. No. 108-27, May 28, 2003, is codified at 26 U.S.C.A. Section 6429.

Torts and Criminal Acts

A corporation is liable for the torts committed by its agents or officers within the course and scope of their employment. This principle applies to a corporation exactly as it applies to the ordinary agency relationships, which will be discussed in Chapter 19. It follows the doctrine of *respondeat superior.*

Under modern criminal law (see Chapter 7), a corporation may also be held liable for the criminal acts of its agents and employees, provided the punishment is one that can be applied to the corporation. Although corporations cannot be imprisoned, they can be fined. (Of course, corporate directors and officers can be imprisoned, and in recent years, many have faced criminal penalties for their own actions or for the actions of employees under their supervision.)

The question in the following case was whether a corporation could be convicted for its employee's criminal negligence.

CASE 18.1 Commonwealth v. Angelo Todesca Corp.

Supreme Judicial Court of Massachusetts, 2006. 446 Mass. 128, 842 N.E.2d 930.
www.findlaw.com/11stategov/ma/maca.html[a]

• **Background and Facts** Brian Gauthier worked as a truck driver for Angelo Todesca Corporation, a trucking and paving company. During 2000, Gauthier drove a ten-wheel tri-axle dump truck, which was designated AT-56. Angelo's safety manual required its trucks to be equipped with back-up alarms, which were to sound automatically whenever the vehicles were in reverse gear. In November,

a. In the "Supreme Court Opinions" section, in the "2006" row, click on "March." When that page opens, scroll to the name of the case and click on its docket number to access the opinion.

CASE 18.1 CONTINUED Gauthier discovered that AT-56's alarm was missing. Angelo ordered a new alarm. Meanwhile, Gauthier continued to drive AT-56. On December 1, Angelo assigned Gauthier to haul asphalt to a work site in Centerville, Massachusetts. At the site, as Gauthier backed up AT-56 to dump its load, he struck a police officer who was directing traffic through the site and facing away from the truck. The officer died of his injuries. The commonwealth of Massachusetts charged Gauthier and Angelo in a Massachusetts state court with, among other wrongful acts, motor vehicle homicide. Angelo was convicted and fined $2,500. On Angelo's appeal, a state intermediate appellate court reversed Angelo's conviction. The state appealed to the Massachusetts Supreme Judicial Court, the state's highest court.

IN THE LANGUAGE OF THE COURT
***SPINA*, J. [Justice]**

* * * *

* * * [On this appeal, the] defendant maintains that a corporation never can be criminally liable for motor vehicle homicide * * * because * * * a "corporation" cannot "operate" a vehicle. *The Commonwealth, however, argues that corporate liability is necessarily vicarious [indirect, or secondary], and that a corporation can be held accountable for criminal acts committed by its agents, including negligent operation of a motor vehicle causing the death of another* * * * . [Emphasis added.]

We agree with the Commonwealth. Because a corporation is not a living person, it can act only through its agents. By the defendant's reasoning, a corporation never could be liable for any crime. A "corporation" can no more serve alcohol to minors, or bribe government officials, or falsify data on loan applications, than operate a vehicle negligently: only human agents, acting for the corporation, are capable of these actions. Nevertheless, * * * *a corporation may be criminally liable for such acts when performed by corporate employees, acting within the scope of their employment and on behalf of the corporation.* [Emphasis added.]

The defendant further contends that it cannot be found vicariously liable for the victim's death because corporate criminal liability requires criminal conduct by the agent, which is lacking in this case. Operating a truck without a back-up alarm, the defendant notes, is not a criminal act: no State or Federal statute requires that a vehicle be equipped with such a device. Although the defendant is correct that criminal conduct of an agent is necessary before criminal liability may be imputed to the corporation, it mischaracterizes the agent's conduct in this case. Gauthier's criminal act, and the conduct imputed to the defendant, was not simply backing up without an alarm, as the defendant contends; rather, the criminal conduct was Gauthier's negligent operation of the defendant's truck, resulting in the victim's death * * * . Clearly, a corporation cannot be criminally liable for acts of employee negligence that are not criminal; however, [a Massachusetts state statute] criminalizes negligence in a very specific context (the operation of a motor vehicle on a public way) and with a specific outcome (resulting in death). Furthermore, nothing in that statute requires that the negligence be based on a statutory violation; the fact that a back-up alarm is not required by statute, then, is irrelevant to the issue whether vehicular homicide committed by an employee can be imputed to the corporation. If a corporate employee violates [this statute] while engaged in corporate business that the employee has been authorized to conduct, we can see no reason why the corporation cannot be vicariously liable for the crime.

- **Decision and Remedy** *The Massachusetts Supreme Judicial Court affirmed Angelo's conviction. The court recognized that a corporation is not a "living person" and "can act only through its agents," which may include its employees. The court reasoned that if an employee commits a crime, "while engaged in corporate business that the employee has been authorized to conduct," a corporation can be held liable for the crime.*

- **What If the Facts Were Different?** *If Gauthier had been an independent contractor rather than Angelo's employee, would the result in this case have been different? Explain.*

- **The Legal Environment Dimension** *Under what circumstances might an employee's supervisor, or even a corporate officer or director, be held liable for the employee's crime?*

Corporate Sentencing Guidelines

Recall from Chapter 7 that the U.S. Sentencing Commission has created standardized sentencing guidelines for federal crimes. The commission subsequently created specific sentencing guidelines for crimes committed by corporate employees (white-collar crimes). The net effect of the guidelines has been a significant increase in the penalties for crimes committed by corporate personnel. Penalties depend on such factors as the seriousness of the offense, the amount involved, and the extent to which top company executives are implicated. Corporate lawbreakers can face fines amounting to hundreds of millions of dollars, though the guidelines allow judges to impose less severe penalties in certain circumstances.

When a company has taken substantial steps to prevent, investigate, and punish wrongdoing, such as by establishing and enforcing crime prevention standards, a court may impose less serious penalties. Many states' corporate laws now require corporations to have adequate systems for detecting and reporting misconduct that can be attributed to corporations. Corporate sentencing guidelines that became effective in 2004 require corporations to train employees on how to comply with relevant laws. Additionally, corporate directors have a fiduciary duty to prevent employee misconduct, which means that if they discover an employee has committed a crime, they have a duty to promptly report it. The Sarbanes-Oxley Act also requires corporate attorneys to report possible corporate misconduct (both civil and criminal) to officials within the corporation. (For a detailed discussion of corporate governance and compliance issues, see Chapter 28.)

Classification of Corporations

Corporations can be classified in several ways. The classification of a corporation normally depends on its location, purpose, and ownership characteristics, as described in the following subsections.

Domestic, Foreign, and Alien Corporations

A corporation is referred to as a **domestic corporation** by its home state (the state in which it incorporates). A corporation formed in one state but doing business in another is referred to in the second state as a **foreign corporation.** A corporation formed in another country (say, Mexico) but doing business in the United States is referred to in the United States as an **alien corporation.**

A corporation does not have an automatic right to do business in a state other than its state of incorporation. In some instances, it must obtain a *certificate of authority* in any state in which it plans to do business. Once the certificate has been issued, the corporation generally can exercise in that state all of the powers conferred on it by its home state. If a foreign corporation does business in a state without obtaining a certificate of authority, the state can impose substantial fines and sanctions on the corporation, and sometimes even on its officers, directors, or agents.

Note that most state statutes specify certain activities, such as soliciting orders via the Internet, that are not considered "doing business" within the state. Thus, a foreign corporation normally does not need a certificate of authority to sell goods or services via the Internet or by mail.

Public and Private Corporations A public corporation is one formed by the government to meet some political or governmental purpose. Cities and towns that incorporate are common examples. In addition, many federal government organizations, such as the U.S. Postal Service, the Tennessee Valley Authority, and AMTRAK, are public corporations. Note that a public corporation is not the same as a *publicly held* corporation (often called a *public company*). A publicly held corporation is any corporation whose shares are publicly traded in a securities market, such as the New York Stock Exchange or the over-the-counter market.

In contrast to public corporations (*not* public companies), private corporations are created either wholly or in part for private benefit. Most corporations are private. Although they may serve a public purpose, as a public electric or gas utility does, they are owned by private persons rather than by the government.[2]

Nonprofit Corporations Corporations formed for purposes other than making a profit are called *nonprofit* or *not-for-profit* corporations. Private hospitals, educational institutions, charities, and religious organizations, for example, are frequently organized as nonprofit corporations. The nonprofit corporation is a convenient form of organization that allows various groups to own property and to form contracts without exposing the individual members to personal liability.

2. The United States Supreme Court first recognized the property rights of private corporations and clarified the distinction between public and private corporations in the landmark case *Trustees of Dartmouth College v. Woodward,* 17 U.S. (4 Wheaton) 518, 4 L.Ed. 629 (1819).

Close Corporations In terms of numbers, not size, most corporate enterprises in the United States fall into the category of close corporations. A **close corporation** is one whose shares are held by members of a family or by relatively few persons. Close corporations are also referred to as *closely held, family*, or *privately held* corporations. Usually, the members of the small group constituting a close corporation are personally known to each other. Because the number of shareholders is so small, there is no trading market for the shares.

In practice, a close corporation is often operated like a partnership. Some states have enacted special statutory provisions that apply to close corporations. These provisions expressly permit close corporations to depart significantly from certain formalities required by traditional corporation law.[3]

Additionally, a provision added to the RMBCA in 1991 gives a close corporation considerable flexibility in determining its rules of operation [RMBCA 7.32]. If all of a corporation's shareholders agree in writing, the corporation can operate without directors, bylaws, annual or special shareholders' or directors' meetings, stock certificates, or formal records of shareholders' or directors' decisions.[4]

Management of Close Corporations. A close corporation has a single shareholder or a closely knit group of shareholders, who usually hold the positions of directors and officers. Management of a close corporation resembles that of a sole proprietorship or a partnership. As a corporation, however, the firm must meet all specific legal requirements set forth in state statutes.

To prevent a majority shareholder from dominating a close corporation, the corporation may require that more than a simple majority of the directors approve any action taken by the board. Typically, this would apply only to extraordinary actions, such as changing the amount of dividends or dismissing an employee-shareholder, and not to ordinary business decisions.

Transfer of Shares in Close Corporations. By definition, a close corporation has a small number of shareholders. Thus, the transfer of one shareholder's shares to someone else can cause serious management problems. The other shareholders may find themselves required to share control with someone they do not know or like.

Suppose that three brothers, Terry, Damon, and Henry Johnson, are the only shareholders of Johnson's Car Wash, Inc. Terry and Damon do not want Henry to sell his shares to an unknown third person. To avoid this situation, the corporation could restrict the transferability of shares to outside persons. Shareholders could be required to offer their shares to the corporation or the other shareholders before selling them to an outside purchaser. In fact, a few states have statutes that prohibit the transfer of close corporation shares unless certain persons—including shareholders, family members, and the corporation—are first given the opportunity to purchase the shares for the same price.

Control of a close corporation can also be stabilized through the use of a *shareholder agreement.* A shareholder agreement can provide that when one of the original shareholders dies, her or his shares of stock in the corporation will be divided in such a way that the proportionate holdings of the survivors, and thus their proportionate control, will be maintained. Courts are generally reluctant to interfere with private agreements, including shareholder agreements.

S Corporations A close corporation that meets the qualifying requirements specified in Subchapter S of the Internal Revenue Code can operate as an **S corporation.** If a corporation has S corporation status, it can avoid the imposition of income taxes at the corporate level while retaining many of the advantages of a corporation, particularly limited liability.

Qualification Requirements for S Corporations. Among the numerous requirements for S corporation status, the following are the most important:

1. The corporation must be a domestic corporation.
2. The corporation must not be a member of an affiliated group of corporations.
3. The shareholders of the corporation must be individuals, estates, or certain trusts. Nonqualifying trusts and partnerships cannot be shareholders. Corporations can be shareholders under certain circumstances.
4. The corporation must have no more than one hundred shareholders.
5. The corporation must have only one class of stock, although all shareholders do not need to have the same voting rights.

---

3. For example, in some states (such as Maryland), a close corporation need not have a board of directors.

4. Shareholders cannot agree, however, to eliminate certain rights of shareholders, such as the right to inspect corporate books and records or the right to bring *derivative actions* (lawsuits on behalf of the corporation—see page 467).

6. No shareholder of the corporation may be a nonresident alien.

Benefits of S Corporations. At times, it is beneficial for a regular corporation to elect S corporation status. Benefits include the following:

1. When the corporation has losses, the S election allows the shareholders to use the losses to offset other taxable income.
2. When the shareholder's tax bracket is lower than the tax bracket for regular corporations, the S election causes the corporation's entire income to be taxed in the shareholder's bracket (because it is taxed as personal income), whether or not it is distributed. This is particularly attractive when the corporation wants to accumulate earnings for some future business purpose.

In the past, many close corporations opted for S corporation status to obtain these tax benefits. Today, however, the limited liability partnership and the limited liability company (discussed in Chapter 17) offer similar advantages plus additional benefits, including more flexibility in forming and operating the business. Hence, the S corporation has lost some of its appeal.

Professional Corporations Professionals such as physicians, lawyers, dentists, and accountants can incorporate. Professional corporations are typically identified by the letters *P.C.* (professional corporation), *S.C.* (service corporation), or *P.A.* (professional association). In general, the laws governing professional corporations are similar to those governing ordinary business corporations, but there are a few differences with regard to liability that deserve mention.

First, there is generally no limitation on liability for acts of malpractice or obligations incurred because of a breach of duty to a client or patient of the professional corporation. In other words, each shareholder in a professional corporation can be held liable for any malpractice liability incurred by the others within the scope of the corporate business. The reason for this rule is that professionals, in contrast to shareholders in other types of corporations, should not be allowed to avoid liability for their wrongful acts simply by incorporating. Second, in many states, professional persons are liable not only for their own negligent acts, but also for the misconduct of persons under their direct supervision who render professional services on behalf of the corporation. Third, a shareholder in a professional corporation is generally protected from contractual liability and cannot be held liable for the torts—other than malpractice or a breach of duty to clients or patients—that are committed by other professionals at the firm.

Corporate Formation

Up to this point, we have discussed some of the general characteristics of corporations. We now examine the process by which corporations come into existence. Incorporating a business is much simpler today than it was twenty years ago, and many states allow businesses to incorporate online.

One of the most common reasons for creating a corporation is the need for additional capital to finance expansion. Many of the Fortune 500 companies started as sole proprietorships or partnerships and then converted to a corporate entity. A sole proprietor in need of funds can seek partners who will bring capital with them. Although a partnership may be able to secure more funds from potential lenders than the sole proprietor could, the amount is still limited. When a firm wants significant growth, continuing to add partners can result in so many partners that the firm can no longer operate effectively. Therefore, incorporation may be the best choice for an expanding business organization because a corporation can obtain more capital by issuing shares of stock. (Corporate financing is discussed later in this chapter.)

Promotional Activities

In the past, preliminary steps were taken to organize and promote the business prior to incorporating. Contracts were made with investors and others on behalf of the future corporation. Today, however, due to the relative ease of forming a corporation in most states, persons incorporating their business rarely, if ever, engage in preliminary promotional activities. Nevertheless, it is important for businesspersons to understand that they are personally liable for all preincorporation contracts made with investors, accountants, or others on behalf of the future corporation. This personal liability continues until the corporation assumes the preincorporation contracts by *novation* (discussed in Chapter 10).

Incorporation Procedures

Exact procedures for incorporation differ among states, but the basic steps are as follows: (1) select a state of incorporation, (2) secure the corporate name, (3) prepare the articles of incorporation, and (4) file the articles of incorporation with the secretary of state. These steps are discussed in more detail in the following subsections.

Selecting the State of Incorporation The first step in the incorporation process is to select a state in which to incorporate. Because state laws differ, individuals may look for the states that offer the most advantageous tax or incorporation provisions. Another consideration is the fee that a particular state charges to incorporate as well as the annual fees and the fees for specific transactions (such as stock transfers).

Delaware has historically had the least restrictive laws, as well as provisions that favor corporate management. Consequently, many corporations, including a number of the largest, have incorporated there. Delaware's statutes permit firms to incorporate in that state and conduct business and locate their operating headquarters elsewhere. Most other states now permit this as well. Generally, though, closely held corporations, particularly those of a professional nature, incorporate in the state where their principal shareholders live and work. For reasons of convenience and cost, businesses often choose to incorporate in the state in which most of the corporation's business will be conducted.

Securing the Corporate Name The choice of a corporate name is subject to state approval to ensure against duplication or deception. State statutes usually require that the secretary of state run a check on the proposed name in the state of incorporation. In some states, the persons incorporating a firm must do the check themselves at their own expense. Specialized Internet search engines are available for checking corporate names, and many companies will perform this service for a fee. Once cleared, a name can be reserved for a short time, for a fee, pending the completion of the articles of incorporation. All states require the corporation name to include the word *Corporation (Corp.), Incorporated (Inc.), Company (Co.),* or *Limited (Ltd.).*

A new corporation's name cannot be the same as (or deceptively similar to) the name of an existing corporation doing business within the state (see Chapter 14). The name should also be one that can be used as the business's Internet domain name. Suppose that an existing corporation is named Digital Synergy, Inc. A new corporation cannot choose the name Digital Synergy Company because that name is deceptively similar to the first, and the state will be unlikely to allow it. In addition, the new firm would not want to choose the name Digital Synergy Company since it would be unable to acquire an Internet domain name using the name of the business.

If those incorporating a firm contemplate doing business in other states—or over the Internet—they need to check on existing corporate names in those states as well. Otherwise, if the firm does business under a name that is the same as or deceptively similar to an existing company's name, it may be liable for trade name infringement.

Preparing the Articles of Incorporation The primary document needed to incorporate a business is the **articles of incorporation.** The articles include basic information about the corporation and serve as a primary source of authority for its future organization and business functions. The person or persons who execute (sign) the articles are called *incorporators.* Generally, the articles of incorporation *must* include the following information [RMBCA 2.02].

1. The name of the corporation.
2. The number of shares the corporation is authorized to issue.
3. The name and address of the corporation's initial registered agent.
4. The name and address of each incorporator.

In addition, the articles *may* set forth other information, such as the names and addresses of the initial board of directors, the duration and purpose of the corporation, a par value of shares of the corporation, and any other information pertinent to the rights and duties of the corporation's shareholders and directors. Articles of incorporation vary widely depending on the jurisdiction and the size and type of the corporation. Frequently, the articles do not provide much detail about the firm's operations, which are spelled out in the company's **bylaws** (internal rules of management adopted by the corporation at its first organizational meeting).

Shares of the Corporation. The articles must specify the number of shares of stock the corporation is authorized to issue [RMBCA 2.02(a)]. For instance, a company might state that the aggregate number of shares that the corporation has the authority to issue is

CASE 18.2 CONTINUED

• **Decision and Remedy** *The court issued a judgment against Discount, and in the trustee's favor, for $108,732.64, which represented the amount of the claims listed in Aqua's bankruptcy schedules. The court also agreed to add the administrative expenses and all other claims allowed against Aqua once those amounts were determined.*

• **The Ethical Dimension** *Was the Jacobsons' disregard for corporate formalities unethical? Why or why not?*

• **The Global Dimension** *If the scope of the Jacobsons' business had been global, should the court have issued a different judgment? Explain.*

The Commingling of Personal and Corporate Assets

The potential for corporate assets to be used for personal benefit is especially great in a close corporation, in which the shares are held by a single person or by only a few individuals, usually family members. In such a situation, the separate status of the corporate entity and the sole shareholder (or family-member shareholders) must be carefully preserved. Certain practices invite trouble for the one-person or family-owned corporation: the commingling of corporate and personal funds; the failure to remit taxes, including payroll and sales taxes; and the shareholders' continuous personal use of corporate property (for example, vehicles).

For example, Donald Park incorporated three sports companies—SSP, SSI, and SSII. His mother was the president of SSP and SSII but did not participate in their operations. Park handled most of the corporations' activities out of his apartment and drew funds from their accounts as needed to pay his personal expenses. None of the three corporations had any employees, issued stock or paid dividends, maintained corporate records, or followed other corporate formalities. Park—misrepresenting himself as the president of SSP and the vice president of SSII—obtained loans on behalf of SSP from Dimmitt & Owens Financial, Inc. When the loans were not paid, Dimmitt filed a suit in a federal district court, seeking, among other things, to impose personal liability on Park. Because Park had commingled corporate funds with his personal funds and failed to follow corporate formalities, the court "pierced the corporate veil" and held him personally responsible for the debt.[7]

Loans to the Corporation

Corporation laws usually do not specifically prohibit a shareholder from lending funds to her or his corporation. When an officer, director, or majority shareholder lends the corporation funds and takes back security in the form of corporate assets, however, the courts will scrutinize the transaction closely. Any such transaction must be made in good faith and for fair value.

Directors, Officers, and Shareholders

Corporate directors, officers, and shareholders all play different roles within the corporate entity. Sometimes, actions that may benefit the corporation as a whole do not coincide with the separate interests of the individuals making up the corporation. In such situations, it is important to know the rights and duties of all participants in the corporate enterprise, and the ways in which conflicts among corporate participants are resolved.

Role of Directors

The board of directors is the ultimate authority in every corporation. Directors have responsibility for all policymaking decisions necessary to the management of all corporate affairs. Just as shareholders cannot act individually to bind the corporation, the directors must act as a body in carrying out routine corporate business. The board selects and removes the corporate officers, determines the capital structure of the corporation, and declares dividends. Each director has one vote, and customarily the majority rules. The general areas of responsibility of the board of directors are shown in Exhibit 18–1.

Directors are sometimes inappropriately characterized as *agents* because they act on behalf of the corporation. No individual director, however, can act as an agent to bind the corporation; and as a group, directors collectively control the corporation in a way that no agent is able to control a principal. In addition, although

7. *Dimmitt & Owens Financial, Inc. v. Superior Sports Products, Inc.*, 196 F.Supp.2d 731 (N.D.Ill. 2002).

EXHIBIT 18–1 • Directors' Management Responsibilities

Authorize Major Corporate Policy Decisions	Select and Remove Corporate Officers and Other Managerial Employees, and Determine Their Compensation	Make Financial Decisions
Examples: —Oversee major contract negotiations and management-labor negotiations. —Initiate negotiations on sale or lease of corporate assets outside the regular course of business. —Decide whether to pursue new product lines or business opportunities.	*Examples:* —Search for and hire corporate executives and determine the elements of their compensation packages, including stock options. —Supervise managerial employees and make decisions regarding their termination.	*Examples:* —Make decisions regarding the issuance of authorized shares and bonds. —Decide when to declare dividends to be paid to shareholders.

directors occupy positions of trust and control over the corporation, they are not *trustees* because they do not hold title to property for the use and benefit of others.

Few qualifications are required for directors. Only a handful of states impose minimum age and residency requirements. A director may be a shareholder, but that is not necessary (unless the articles of incorporation or bylaws require ownership).

Election of Directors Subject to statutory limitations, the number of directors is set forth in the corporation's articles or bylaws. Historically, the minimum number of directors has been three, but today many states permit fewer. Normally, the incorporators appoint the first board of directors at the time the corporation is created, or the corporation itself names the directors in the articles. The initial board serves until the first annual shareholders' meeting. Subsequent directors are elected by a majority vote of the shareholders.

A director usually serves for a term of one year—from annual meeting to annual meeting. Longer and staggered terms are permissible under most state statutes. A common practice is to elect one-third of the board members each year for a three-year term. In this way, there is greater management continuity.

Removal of Directors. A director can be removed *for cause*—that is, for failing to perform a required duty—either as specified in the articles or bylaws or by shareholder action. Even the board of directors itself may be given power to remove a director for cause, subject to shareholder review. In most states, a director cannot be removed without cause unless the shareholders have reserved the right to do so at the time of election.

Vacancies on the Board of Directors. Vacancies can occur on the board of directors because of death or resignation or when a new position is created through amendment of the articles or bylaws. In these situations, either the shareholders or the board itself can fill the position, depending on state law or on the provisions of the bylaws. Note, however, that even when the bylaws appear to authorize an election, a court can invalidate an election if the directors were attempting to diminish the shareholders' influence in it.

For example, the bylaws of Liquid Audio, a Delaware corporation, authorized a board of five directors. Two directors on the board were elected each year. Another company had offered to buy all of Liquid Audio's stock, but the board of directors rejected this offer. An election was coming up, and the directors feared that the shareholders would elect new directors who would go through with the sale. The directors therefore amended the bylaws to increase the number of directors to seven, thereby diminishing the shareholders' influence in the vote. The shareholders filed an action challenging the election. The Delaware Supreme Court ruled that the directors' action was illegal because they had attempted to diminish the shareholders' right to vote effectively in an election of directors.[8]

8. *MM Companies, Inc. v. Liquid Audio, Inc.,* 813 A.2d 1118 (Del.Sup.Ct. 2003).

Compensation of Directors In the past, corporate directors rarely were compensated, but today they are often paid at least nominal sums and may receive more substantial compensation in large corporations because of the time, work, effort, and especially risk involved. Most states permit the corporate articles or bylaws to authorize compensation for directors. In fact, the Revised Model Business Corporation Act (RMBCA) states that unless the articles or bylaws provide otherwise, the board of directors may set their own compensation [RMBCA 8.11]. Directors also gain through indirect benefits, such as business contacts and prestige, and other rewards, such as stock options.

In many corporations, directors are also chief corporate officers (president or chief executive officer, for example) and receive compensation in their managerial positions. A director who is also an officer of the corporation is referred to as an **inside director,** whereas a director who does not hold a management position is an **outside director.** Typically, a corporation's board of directors includes both inside and outside directors.

Board of Directors' Meetings The board of directors conducts business by holding formal meetings with recorded minutes. The dates of regular meetings are usually established in the articles or bylaws or by board resolution, and no further notice is customarily required. Special meetings can be called, with notice sent to all directors. Today, most states allow directors to participate in board of directors' meetings from remote locations via telephone or Web conferencing, provided that all the directors can simultaneously hear each other during the meeting [RMBCA 8.20].

Unless the articles of incorporation or bylaws specify a greater number, a majority of the board of directors normally constitutes a quorum [RMBCA 8.24]. (A **quorum** is the minimum number of members of a body of officials or other group that must be present for business to be validly transacted.) Some state statutes specifically allow corporations to set a quorum as less than a majority but not less than one-third of the directors.[9]

Once a quorum is present, the directors transact business and vote on issues affecting the corporation. Each director present at the meeting has one vote.[10] Ordinary matters generally require a simple majority vote; certain extraordinary issues may require a greater-than-majority vote. In other words, the affirmative vote of a majority of the directors present at a meeting binds the board of directors with regard to most decisions.

Rights of Directors A corporate director must have certain rights to function properly in that position. The *right to participation* means that directors are entitled to participate in all board of directors' meetings and have a right to be notified of these meetings. As mentioned earlier, the dates of regular board meetings are usually preestablished and no notice of these meetings is required. If special meetings are called, however, notice is required unless waived by the director [RMBCA 8.23].

A director also has a *right of inspection,* which means that each director can access the corporation's books and records, facilities, and premises. Inspection rights are essential for directors to make informed decisions and to exercise the necessary supervision over corporate officers and employees. This right of inspection is virtually absolute and cannot be restricted (by the articles, bylaws, or any act of the board of directors).

When a director becomes involved in litigation by virtue of her or his position or actions, the director may also have a *right to indemnification* (reimbursement) for the legal costs, fees, and damages incurred. Most states allow corporations to indemnify and purchase liability insurance for corporate directors [RMBCA 8.51].

Committees of the Board of Directors

When a board of directors has a large number of members and must deal with a myriad of complex business issues, meetings can become unwieldy. Therefore, the boards of large, publicly held corporations typically create committees, appoint directors to serve on individual committees, and delegate certain tasks to these committees. Committees focus on individual subjects and increase the efficiency of the board. The most common types of committees include the following:

1. *Executive committee.* The board members often elect an executive committee of directors to handle the interim management decisions between board of directors' meetings. The executive committee is limited to making management deci-

9. See, for example, Delaware Code Annotated Title 8, Section 141(b); and New York Business Corporation Law, Section 707.
10. Except in Louisiana, which allows a director to vote by proxy under certain circumstances.

sions about ordinary business matters and conducting preliminary investigations into proposals. It cannot declare dividends, authorize the issuance of shares, amend the bylaws, or initiate any actions that require shareholder approval.

2. *Audit committee.* The audit committee is responsible for the selection, compensation, and oversight of the independent public accountants who audit the corporation's financial records. The Sarbanes-Oxley Act of 2002 requires all publicly held corporations to have an audit committee.
3. *Nominating committee.* This committee chooses the candidates for the board of directors that management wishes to submit to the shareholders in the next election. The committee cannot select directors to fill vacancies on the board, however [RMBCA 8.25].
4. *Compensation committee.* The compensation committee reviews and decides the salaries, bonuses, stock options, and other benefits that are given to the corporation's top executives. The committee may also determine the compensation of directors.
5. *Litigation committee.* This committee decides whether the corporation should pursue requests by shareholders to file a lawsuit against some party that has allegedly harmed the corporation. The committee members investigate the allegations and weigh the costs and benefits of litigation.

In addition to appointing committees, the board of directors can also delegate some of its functions to corporate officers. In doing so, the board is not relieved of its overall responsibility for directing the affairs of the corporation. Instead, corporate officers and managerial personnel are empowered to make decisions relating to ordinary, daily corporate activities within well-defined guidelines.

Corporate Officers and Executives

Officers and other executive employees are hired by the board of directors. At a minimum, most corporations have a president, one or more vice presidents, a secretary, and a treasurer. In most states, an individual can hold more than one office, such as president and secretary, and can be both an officer and a director of the corporation. In addition to carrying out the duties articulated in the bylaws, corporate and managerial officers act as agents of the corporation, and the ordinary rules of agency (discussed in Chapter 19) normally apply to their employment.

Corporate officers and other high-level managers are employees of the company, so their rights are defined by employment contracts. Regardless of the terms of an employment contract, however, the board of directors normally can remove a corporate officer at any time with or without cause—although the officer may then seek damages from the corporation for breach of contract.

The duties of corporate officers are the same as those of directors because both groups are involved in decision making and are in similar positions of control. Hence, officers and directors are viewed as having the same fiduciary duties of care and loyalty in their conduct of corporate affairs, a subject to which we now turn.

Duties and Liabilities of Directors and Officers

Directors and officers are deemed to be fiduciaries of the corporation because their relationship with the corporation and its shareholders is one of trust and confidence. As fiduciaries, directors and officers owe ethical—and legal—duties to the corporation and the shareholders as a whole. These fiduciary duties include the duty of care and the duty of loyalty.

Duty of Care Directors and officers must exercise due care in performing their duties. The standard of *due care* has been variously described in judicial decisions and codified in many state corporation codes. Generally, directors and officers are required to act in good faith, to exercise the care that an ordinarily prudent person would exercise in similar circumstances, and to do what they believe is in the best interests of the corporation [RMBCA 8.30(a), 8.42(a)]. Directors and officers whose failure to exercise due care results in harm to the corporation or its shareholders can be held liable for negligence (unless the business judgment rule applies).

Duty to Make Informed and Reasonable Decisions. Directors and officers are expected to be informed on corporate matters and to conduct a reasonable investigation of the situation before making a decision. This means that they must do what is necessary to keep adequately informed: attend meetings and presentations, ask for information from those who have it, read reports, and review other written materials. In other words, directors and officers must investigate, study, and discuss matters and evaluate alternatives before making a decision. They cannot decide on the spur of the moment without adequate research.

Although directors and officers are expected to act in accordance with their own knowledge and training, they are also normally entitled to rely on information given to them by certain other persons. Most states and Section 8.30(b) of the RMBCA allow a director to make decisions in reliance on information furnished by competent officers or employees, professionals such as attorneys and accountants, and committees of the board of directors (on which the director does not serve). The reliance must be in good faith, of course, to insulate a director from liability if the information later proves to be inaccurate or unreliable.

Duty to Exercise Reasonable Supervision. Directors are also expected to exercise a reasonable amount of supervision when they delegate work to corporate officers and employees. Suppose that Dale, a corporate bank director, fails to attend any board of directors' meetings for five years. In addition, Dale never inspects any of the corporate books or records and generally fails to supervise the efforts of the bank president and the loan committee. Meanwhile, Brennan, the bank president, who is a corporate officer, makes various improper loans and permits large overdrafts. In this situation, Dale (the corporate director) can be held liable to the corporation for losses resulting from the unsupervised actions of the bank president and the loan committee.

Dissenting Directors. Directors are expected to attend board of directors' meetings, and their votes should be entered into the minutes. Sometimes, an individual director disagrees with the majority's vote (which becomes an act of the board of directors). Unless a dissent is entered in the minutes, the director is presumed to have assented. If a decision later leads to the directors being held liable for mismanagement, dissenting directors are rarely held individually liable to the corporation. For this reason, a director who is absent from a given meeting sometimes registers with the secretary of the board a dissent to actions taken at the meeting.

The Business Judgment Rule. Directors and officers are expected to exercise due care and to use their best judgment in guiding corporate management, but they are not insurers of business success. Under the **business judgment rule,** a corporate director or officer will not be liable to the corporation or to its shareholders for honest mistakes of judgment and bad business decisions. Courts give significant deference to the decisions of corporate directors and officers, and consider the reasonableness of a decision at the time it was made, without the benefit of hindsight. Thus, corporate decision makers are not subjected to second-guessing by shareholders or others in the corporation.

The business judgment rule will apply as long as the director or officer (1) took reasonable steps to become informed about the matter, (2) had a rational basis for his or her decision, and (3) did not have a conflict of interest between his or her personal interest and that of the corporation. In fact, unless there is evidence of bad faith, fraud, or a clear breach of fiduciary duties, most courts will apply the rule and protect directors and officers who make bad business decisions from liability for those choices. Consequently, if there is a reasonable basis for a business decision, a court is unlikely to interfere with that decision, even if the corporation suffers as a result.

Duty of Loyalty *Loyalty* can be defined as faithfulness to one's obligations and duties. In the corporate context, the duty of loyalty requires directors and officers to subordinate their personal interests to the welfare of the corporation.

For example, directors may not use corporate funds or confidential corporate information for personal advantage. Similarly, they must refrain from putting their personal interests above those of the corporation. For instance, a director should not oppose a transaction that is in the corporation's best interest simply because pursuing it may cost the director her or his position. Cases dealing with the duty of loyalty typically involve one or more of the following:

1. Competing with the corporation.
2. Usurping (taking personal advantage of) a corporate opportunity.
3. Having an interest that conflicts with the interest of the corporation.
4. Engaging in *insider trading* (using information that is not public to make a profit trading securities, as discussed in Chapter 28).
5. Authorizing a corporate transaction that is detrimental to minority shareholders.
6. Selling control over the corporation.

The following classic case illustrates the conflict that can arise between a corporate official's personal interest and his or her duty of loyalty.

CASE 18.3 Guth v. Loft, Inc.

Supreme Court of Delaware, 1939. 23 Del.Ch. 255, 5 A.2d 503.

Background and Facts Loft, Inc., made and sold candies, syrups, beverages, and food from its offices and plant in Long Island City, New York. Loft operated 115 retail outlets in several states and also sold its products wholesale. Charles Guth was Loft's president. Guth and his family owned Grace Company, which made syrups for soft drinks in a plant in Baltimore, Maryland. Coca-Cola Company supplied Loft with cola syrup. Unhappy with what he felt was Coca-Cola's high price, Guth entered into an agreement with Roy Megargel to acquire the trademark and formula for Pepsi-Cola and form Pepsi-Cola Corporation. Neither Guth nor Megargel could finance the new venture, however, and Grace was insolvent. Without the knowledge of Loft's board, Guth used Loft's capital, credit, facilities, and employees to further the Pepsi enterprise. At Guth's direction, Loft made the concentrate for the syrup, which was sent to Grace to add sugar and water. Loft charged Grace for the concentrate but allowed forty months' credit. Grace charged Pepsi for the syrup but also granted substantial credit. Grace sold the syrup to Pepsi's customers, including Loft, which paid on delivery or within thirty days. Loft also paid for Pepsi's advertising. Finally, losing profits at its stores as a result of switching from Coca-Cola, Loft filed a suit in a Delaware state court against Guth, Grace, and Pepsi, seeking their Pepsi stock and an accounting. The court entered a judgment in the plaintiff's favor. The defendants appealed to the Delaware Supreme Court.

IN THE LANGUAGE OF THE COURT

***LAYTON,* Chief Justice, delivering the opinion of the Court:**

* * * *

Corporate officers and directors are not permitted to use their position of trust and confidence to further their private interests. * * * They stand in a fiduciary relation to the corporation and its stockholders. A public policy, existing through the years, and derived from a profound knowledge of human characteristics and motives, has established *a rule that demands of a corporate officer or director, peremptorily [not open for debate] and inexorably [unavoidably], the most scrupulous observance of his duty, not only affirmatively to protect the interests of the corporation committed to his charge, but also to refrain from doing anything that would work injury to the corporation* * * * .The rule that requires an undivided and unselfish loyalty to the corporation demands that there shall be no conflict between duty and self-interest. [Emphasis added.]

* * * *

* * * *If there is presented to a corporate officer or director a business opportunity which the corporation is financially able to undertake [that] is* * * * *in the line of the corporation's business and is of practical advantage to it* * * * *and, by embracing the opportunity, the self-interest of the officer or director will be brought into conflict with that of his corporation, the law will not permit him to seize the opportunity for himself.* * * * In such circumstances, * * * the corporation may elect to claim all of the benefits of the transaction for itself, and the law will impress a trust in favor of the corporation upon the property, interests and profits so acquired. [Emphasis added.]

* * * *

* * * The appellants contend that no conflict of interest between Guth and Loft resulted from his acquirement and exploitation of the Pepsi-Cola opportunity [and] that the acquisition did not place Guth in competition with Loft * * * . [In this case, however,] Guth was Loft, and Guth was Pepsi. He absolutely controlled Loft. His authority over Pepsi was supreme. As Pepsi, he created and controlled the supply of Pepsi-Cola syrup, and he determined the price and the terms. What he offered, as Pepsi, he had the power, as Loft, to accept. Upon any consideration of human characteristics and motives, he created a conflict between self-interest and duty. He made himself the judge in his own cause. * * * Moreover, a reasonable probability of injury to Loft resulted from the situation forced upon it. Guth was in the same position to impose his terms upon Loft as had been the Coca-Cola Company.

* * * The facts and circumstances demonstrate that Guth's appropriation of the Pepsi-Cola opportunity to himself placed him in a competitive position with Loft with respect to a

CASE CONTINUES

UNIT FOUR FOCUS ON ETHICS

though, if a company can show that it has an effective compliance program in place to detect and prevent wrongdoing by corporate personnel. The Sarbanes-Oxley Act of 2002 required the sentencing commission to revise these guidelines, and now the penalties for white-collar crimes, such as federal mail and wire fraud, have increased dramatically.

Fiduciary Duties to Creditors It is a long-standing principle that corporate directors ordinarily owe fiduciary duties only to a corporation's shareholders. Directors who favor the interests of other corporate "stakeholders," such as creditors, over those of the shareholders have been held liable for breaching these duties. The picture changes, however, when a corporation approaches insolvency. At this point, the shareholders' equity interests in the corporation may be worthless, while the interests of creditors become paramount. In this situation, do the fiduciary duties of loyalty and care extend to the corporation's creditors as well as to the shareholders? The answer to this question, according to some courts, is yes. In a leading case on this issue, a Delaware court noted that "[t]he possibility of insolvency can do curious things to incentives, exposing creditors to risks of opportunistic behavior and creating complexities for directors." The court held that when a corporation is on the brink of insolvency, the directors assume a fiduciary duty to other stakeholders that sustain the corporate entity, including creditors.[5]

Franchise Relationships

Franchise relationships present several significant ethical issues. One issue has to do with the franchisor's quality control over the franchisee's activities. On the one hand, if the franchisor ignores the problem of quality control, the reputation of the franchisor's business may suffer. On the other hand, if a franchisor's control over the operations of the franchisee is too extensive, the franchisor may be liable for the torts of the franchisee's employees under agency theory (see Chapter 19). Even when an independent business entity purchases a franchise and the franchise agreement specifies that no agency relationship exists, the courts may find otherwise.

Another issue today is how to adapt certain protections for franchisees to the online world. This issue has become increasingly important as more and more prospective franchisees are going online to find information about particular franchises. Recall from Chapter 16 that the Franchise Rule of the Federal Trade Commission (FTC) imposes certain disclosure requirements on franchisors and that states also have rules. Does a franchisor advertising on the Internet have to comply with fifty different state franchise regulations? Generally, how can the interests of franchisees be protected in the cyber environment?

In view of these problems, the FTC has proposed a rule that would require online franchisors to state very clearly that franchisees would not be entitled to exclusive territorial rights. Notwithstanding these changes, however, one problem would remain: given the speed with which online franchises can be created, it may be difficult—if not impossible—for the FTC to effectively regulate these relationships.

DISCUSSION QUESTIONS

1. Do you agree that when a corporation is approaching insolvency, the directors' fiduciary obligations should extend to the corporation's creditors as well as to the shareholders? In this situation, should the fiduciary duties owed to creditors take priority over the duties to shareholders? Why or why not?
2. As explained, if a franchisor exercises "too much control" over a franchisee's business operations, a court may deem the franchisor to be liable as an employer for the torts committed by the franchisee's employees. How can holding franchisors liable in such circumstances be squared with the doctrine of freedom of contract (see Chapter 9)?

5. *Credit Lyonnais Bank Nederland N.V. v. Pathe Communications Corp.*, 1991 WL 277613 (Del.Ch. 1991). See also *Production Resources Group, LLC v. NCT Group, Inc.*, 863 A.2d 772 (Del.Ch. 2004); and *In re Amcast Industrial Corp.*, 365 Bankr. 91 (S.D. Ohio 2007).

UNIT FIVE

The Employment Environment

CONTENTS

In one case, for example, Graham marketed CD-ROM discs containing compilations of software programs that are available free to the public. Graham hired James to create a file-retrieval program that allowed users to access the software on the CDs. James built into the final version of the program a notice stating that he was the author of the program and owned the copyright. Graham removed the notice. When James sold the program to another CD-ROM publisher, Graham filed a suit claiming that James's file-retrieval program was a "work for hire" and that Graham owned the copyright to the program. The court, however, decided that James—a skilled computer programmer who controlled the manner and method of his work—was an independent contractor and not an employee for hire. Thus, James owned the copyright to the file-retrieval program.[3]

Section 2 Formation of the Agency Relationship

Agency relationships normally are *consensual;* in other words, they come about by voluntary consent and agreement between the parties. Generally, the agreement need not be in writing,[4] and consideration is not required.

A person must have contractual capacity to be a principal.[5] Those who cannot legally enter into contracts directly should not be allowed to do so indirectly through an agent. Any person can be an agent, however, regardless of whether he or she has the capacity to contract. Because an agent derives the authority to enter into contracts from the principal and because a contract made by an agent is legally viewed as a contract of the principal, it is immaterial whether the agent personally has the legal capacity to make that contract. Thus, even a minor or a person who is legally incompetent can be appointed as an agent.

An agency relationship can be created for any legal purpose. An agency relationship created for a purpose that is illegal or contrary to public policy is unenforceable. If LaSalle (as principal) contracts with Burke (as agent) to sell illegal narcotics, the agency relationship is unenforceable because selling illegal narcotics is a felony and is contrary to public policy. It is also illegal for physicians and other licensed professionals to employ unlicensed agents to perform professional actions.

Generally, an agency relationship can arise in four ways: by agreement of the parties, by ratification, by estoppel, and by operation of law. We look here at each of these possibilities.

Agency by Agreement

Most agency relationships are based on an express or implied agreement that the agent will act for the principal and that the principal agrees to have the agent so act. An agency agreement can take the form of an express written contract. For example, Henchen enters into a written agreement with Vogel, a real estate agent, to sell Henchen's house. An agency relationship exists between Henchen and Vogel for the sale of the house and is detailed in a document that both parties sign.

Many express agency relationships are created by oral agreement and are not based on a written contract. Suppose that Henchen asks Grace, a gardener, to contract with others for the care of his lawn on a regular basis. If Grace agrees, an agency relationship exists between Henchen and Grace for the lawn care.

An agency agreement can also be implied by conduct. For example, a hotel expressly allows only Hans Cooper to park cars, but Hans has no employment contract there. The hotel's manager tells Hans when to work, as well as where and how to park the cars. The hotel's conduct manifests a willingness to have Hans park its customers' cars, and Hans can infer from the hotel's conduct that he has authority to act as a parking valet. Thus, there is an implied agreement that Hans is an agent for the hotel and provides valet parking services for hotel guests.

Agency by Ratification

On occasion, a person who is in fact not an agent may make a contract on behalf of another (a principal). If the principal approves or affirms that contract by word or by action, an agency relationship is created by ratification. Ratification involves a question of intent, and intent can be expressed by either words or conduct.

---

3. *Graham v. James,* 144 F.3d 229 (2d Cir. 1998).

4. There are two main exceptions to the statement that agency agreements need not be in writing. An agency agreement must be in writing (1) whenever agency authority empowers the agent to enter into a contract that the Statute of Frauds requires to be in writing (this is called the *equal dignity rule,* to be discussed on page 490) and (2) whenever an agent is given power of attorney.

5. Note that some states allow a minor to be a principal. When a minor is permitted to be a principal, however, any resulting contracts will be voidable by the minor principal but *not* by the adult third party.

The basic requirements for ratification will be discussed later in this chapter.

Agency by Estoppel

When a principal causes a third person to believe that another person is the principal's agent, and the third person acts to his or her detriment in reasonable reliance on that belief, the principal is "estopped to deny" (prevented from denying) the agency relationship. In such a situation, the principal's actions have created the *appearance* of an agency that does not in fact exist. The third person must prove that he or she *reasonably* believed that an agency relationship existed, however.[6]

Suppose that Jayden accompanies Grant, a seed sales representative, to call on a customer, Palko, who owns a seed store. Jayden has performed independent sales work but has never signed an employment agreement with Grant. Grant boasts to Palko that he wishes he had three more assistants "just like Jayden." By making this representation, Grant creates the impression that Jayden is his agent and has authority to solicit orders. Palko has reason to believe from Grant's statements that Jayden is an agent for Grant. Palko then places seed orders with Jayden. If Grant does not correct the impression that Jayden is an agent, Grant will be bound to fill the orders just as if Jayden were really his agent. Grant's representation to Palko has created the impression that Jayden is Grant's agent and has authority to solicit orders.

Note that the acts or declarations of a purported *agent* in and of themselves do not create an agency by estoppel. Rather, it is the deeds or statements *of the principal* that create an agency by estoppel. If Jayden walked into Palko's store and claimed to be Grant's agent, when in fact he was not, and Grant had no knowledge of Jayden's representations, Grant would not be bound to any deal struck by Jayden and Palko.

Under what other circumstances might a third party reasonably believe that a person is an agent of and has the authority to act for a principal when the person does not actually have this authority? The following case provides an illustration.

6. These concepts also apply when a person who is in fact an agent undertakes an action that is beyond the scope of her or his authority, as will be discussed later in this chapter.

CASE 19.2 Motorsport Marketing, Inc. v. Wiedmaier, Inc.

Missouri Court of Appeals, Western District, 2006. 195 S.W.3d 492.
www.courts.mo.gov[a]

Background and Facts Wiedmaier, Inc., owns and operates Wiedmaier Truck Stop in St. Joseph, Missouri. The owners are Marsha Wiedmaier and her husband, Jerry. Their son Michael does not own an interest in the firm, but in 2002 and 2003, he worked for it as a fuel truck operator. Motorsport Marketing, Inc., sells racing collectibles and memorabilia to retail outlets. In April 2003, Michael faxed a credit application to Motorsport's sales manager, Lesa James. Michael's mother, Marsha, signed the form as "Secretary-Owner" of Wiedmaier; after she signed, Michael added himself to the list of owners. A credit line was approved. Michael formed Extreme Diecast, LLC, and told Motorsport that it was part of Wiedmaier. He then began ordering Motorsport merchandise. By early 2004, however, Michael had stopped making payments on the account, quit his job, and moved to Columbus, Ohio. Patrick Rainey, the president of Motorsport, contacted Marsha about the account, but she refused to pay. Motorsport filed a suit in a Missouri state court against Wiedmaier and others to collect the unpaid amount. The court entered a judgment in favor of Motorsport, assessing liability against the defendants for the outstanding balance of $93,388.58, plus $13,406.38 in interest and $25,165.93 in attorneys' fees. The defendants appealed to a state intermediate appellate court.

IN THE LANGUAGE OF THE COURT
VICTOR C. HOWARD, **Presiding Judge.**

* * * *

* * *

a. In the "Quick Links" box, click on "Opinion & Minutes." When that page opens, click on the "Missouri Court of Appeals, Western District opinions" link. At the bottom of the next page, click on the "Search Opinions" link. In that page's "Search for" box, type "Wiedmaier" and click on "Search." In the result, click on the name of the case to access the opinion. The Missouri state courts maintain this Web site.

CASE CONTINUES

CASE 19.2 CONTINUED

To establish the apparent authority of a purported agent, Motorsport must show that

> *(1) the principal manifested his consent to the exercise of such authority or knowingly permitted the agent to assume the exercise of such authority; (2) the person relying on this exercise of authority knew of the facts and, acting in good faith, had reason to believe, and actually believed, the agent possessed such authority; and (3) the person relying on the appearance of authority changed his position and will be injured or suffer loss if the transaction executed by the agent does not bind the principal.* * * * [Emphasis added.]

We find that Motorsport has shown that each of the criteria for establishing Michael's apparent agency has been satisfied. First, * * * [t]he credit application constituted a direct communication from Wiedmaier, Inc. (through Marsha) to Motorsport causing Motorsport to reasonably believe that Michael had authority to act for Wiedmaier, Inc.

Second, Motorsport, relying on Michael's exercise of authority and acting in good faith, had reason to believe, and actually believed, that Michael possessed such authority. Motorsport received a credit application from Wiedmaier, Inc. signed by owner Marsha Wiedmaier, listing Michael as an owner. Motorsport had no reason to believe that Michael was not an owner of Wiedmaier or was otherwise unauthorized to act on Wiedmaier, Inc.'s behalf.

Wiedmaier, Inc. argues that even if Motorsport's reliance on Michael's apparent authority was reasonably prudent on April 10, 2003, when Michael submitted the credit application, such reliance could not have been and was not reasonably prudent from and after June 23, 2003. At that time, Michael personally made the first payment on the account with a check drawn on the account of Extreme Diecast. * * * At the very least, Wiedmaier, Inc. argues, Motorsport had "red flags waving all around it suggesting that Michael was something other than the agent of Wiedmaier, Inc."

We find that this argument is without merit. * * * It is a common practice for a truck stop to have a separate division with a separate name to handle its diecast and other related merchandise, and * * * Michael represented that this is exactly what Extreme Diecast was. * * * This evidence explains what Wiedmaier, Inc. characterizes as "red flags" concerning Michael's authority to act on behalf of Wiedmaier, Inc., and negates any alleged duty on Motorsport's part to investigate Michael's authority.

Third, Motorsport changed its position and will be injured or suffer loss if the transaction executed by Michael does not bind Wiedmaier, Inc. Motorsport extended credit to Wiedmaier, Inc. based on its interaction with Michael and based on its belief that it was dealing with Wiedmaier, Inc. Marsha Wiedmaier has refused to pay the account balance. If the transaction executed by Michael does not bind Wiedmaier, Inc., Motorsport will suffer the loss of the balance due on the account.

- **Decision and Remedy** *The state intermediate appellate court affirmed the judgment of the lower court, echoing the conclusion that "Michael acted as an apparent agent of Wiedmaier, Inc., in its dealings with Motorsport." In other words, Motorsport reasonably believed that Michael acted as Wiedmaier's agent in ordering merchandise.*

- **What If the Facts Were Different?** *Suppose that Motorsport's sales manager had telephoned Marsha Wiedmaier. Further suppose that Marsha had vouched for Michael's creditworthiness but informed Motorsport that she and her husband owned Wiedmaier and that Michael worked for them. How might the outcome of this case have been different in that situation?*

- **The E-Commerce Dimension** *Should the court have applied the law differently in this case if Michael had done business with Motorsport entirely online? Explain.*

Agency by Operation of Law

The courts may find an agency relationship in the absence of a formal agreement in other situations as well. This may occur in family relationships. For example, suppose that one spouse purchases certain basic necessaries (such as food or clothing) and charges them to the other spouse's charge account. The courts will often rule that the latter is liable for payment for the necessaries, either because of a social policy of promoting the general welfare of the spouse or because of a legal duty to supply necessaries to family members.

Agency by operation of law may also occur in emergency situations, when the agent's failure to act outside the scope of her or his authority would cause the principal substantial loss. If the agent is unable to contact the principal, the courts will often grant this emergency power. For example, a railroad engineer may contract on behalf of his or her employer for medical care for an injured motorist hit by the train. *Concept Summary 19.1* reviews the various ways that agencies are formed.

Duties of Agents and Principals

Once the principal-agent relationship has been created, both parties have duties that govern their conduct. As discussed previously, the principal-agent relationship is *fiduciary*—one of trust. In a fiduciary relationship, each party owes the other the duty to act with the utmost good faith. In this section, we examine the various duties of agents and principals.

Agent's Duties to the Principal

Generally, the agent owes the principal five duties—performance, notification, loyalty, obedience, and accounting.

Performance An implied condition in every agency contract is the agent's agreement to use reasonable diligence and skill in performing the work. When an agent fails to perform his or her duties, liability for breach of contract may result. The degree of skill or care required of an agent is usually that expected of a reasonable person under similar circumstances. Generally, this is interpreted to mean ordinary care. If an agent has represented herself or himself as possessing special skills, however, the agent is expected to exercise the degree of skill or skills claimed. Failure to do so constitutes a breach of the agent's duty.

Not all agency relationships are based on contract. In some situations, an agent acts gratuitously—that is, without payment. A gratuitous agent cannot be liable for breach of contract, as there is no contract; he or she is subject only to tort liability. Once a gratuitous agent has begun to act in an agency capacity, he or she has the duty to continue to perform in that capacity in an acceptable manner and is subject to the same standards of care and duty to perform as other agents.

For example, Bower's friend Alcott is a real estate broker. Alcott offers to sell Bower's farm at no charge. If Alcott never attempts to sell the farm, Bower has no legal cause of action to force her to do so. If Alcott does find a buyer, however, but negligently fails to follow through with the sales contract, causing the buyer to seek other property, then Bower can sue Alcott for negligence.

Notification An agent is required to notify the principal of all matters that come to her or his attention

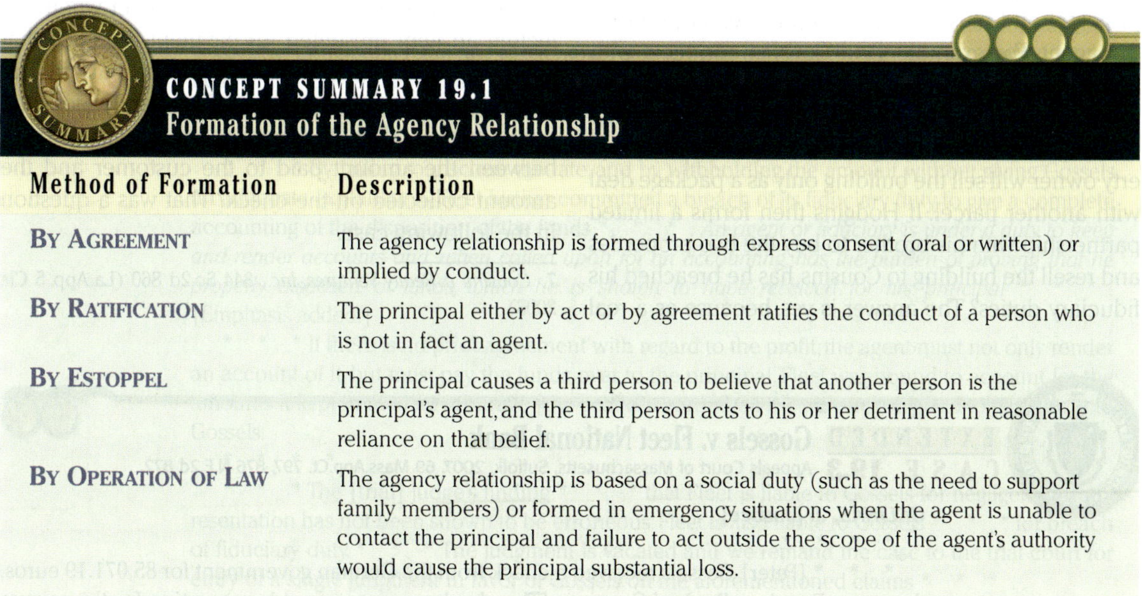

CONCEPT SUMMARY 19.1
Formation of the Agency Relationship

Method of Formation	Description
By Agreement	The agency relationship is formed through express consent (oral or written) or implied by conduct.
By Ratification	The principal either by act or by agreement ratifies the conduct of a person who is not in fact an agent.
By Estoppel	The principal causes a third person to believe that another person is the principal's agent, and the third person acts to his or her detriment in reasonable reliance on that belief.
By Operation of Law	The agency relationship is based on a social duty (such as the need to support family members) or formed in emergency situations when the agent is unable to contact the principal and failure to act outside the scope of the agent's authority would cause the principal substantial loss.

collect payments from customers on behalf of the principal. Suppose that she does accept payments from Corgley Enterprises, however, and submits them to the principal's accounting department for processing. If the principal does nothing to stop Bain from continuing this practice, a pattern develops over time, and the principal confers apparent authority on Bain to accept payments from Corgley.

At issue in the following case was a question of apparent authority or, as the court referred to it, "ostensible agency."

CASE 19.4 Ermoian v. Desert Hospital

Court of Appeal of California, Fourth District, Division 2, 2007.
152 Cal.App.4th 475, 61 Cal.Rptr.3d 754.

• **Background and Facts** In 1990, Desert Hospital in California established a comprehensive perinatal services program (CPSP) to provide obstetrical care to women who were uninsured (*perinatal* is often defined as relating to the period from about the twenty-eighth week of pregnancy to around one month after birth). The CPSP was set up in an office suite across from the hospital and named "Desert Hospital Outpatient Maternity Services Clinic." The hospital contracted with a corporation controlled by Dr. Morton Gubin, which employed Dr. Masami Ogata, to provide obstetrical services. In January 1994, Jackie Shahan went to the hospital's emergency room because of cramping and other symptoms. The emergency room physician told Shahan that she was pregnant and referred her to the clinic. Shahan visited the clinic throughout her pregnancy. On May 15, Shahan's baby, named Amanda, was born with brain abnormalities that left her severely mentally retarded and unable to care for herself. Her conditions could not have been prevented, treated, or cured *in utero.* Amanda filed a suit in a California state court against the hospital and others, alleging "wrongful life." She claimed that the defendants negligently failed to inform her mother of her abnormalities before her birth, depriving her mother of the opportunity to make an informed choice to terminate the pregnancy. The court ruled in the defendants' favor, holding, among other things, that the hospital was not liable because Drs. Gubin and Ogata were not its employees. Amanda appealed to a state intermediate appellate court, contending in part that the physicians were the hospital's "ostensible agents."

IN THE LANGUAGE OF THE COURT

KING, J. [Judge]

* * * *

Agency may be either actual or ostensible [apparent]. Actual agency exists when the agent is really employed by the principal. Here, there was evidence that the physicians were not employees of the Hospital, but were physicians with a private practice who contracted with the Hospital to perform obstetric services at the clinic. The written contract between the Hospital and Dr. Gubin's corporation (which employed Dr. Ogata) describes Dr. Gubin and his corporation as "independent contractors with, and not as employees of, [the] Hospital." [Maria Sterling, a registered nurse at the clinic and Shahan's CPSP case coordinator] testified that Drs. Gubin and Ogata, not the Hospital, provided the obstetric services to the clinic's patients. Donna McCloudy, a director of nursing [who set up the CPSP] at the Hospital, testified that while the Hospital provided some aspects of the CPSP services, "independent physicians * * * provided the obstetrical care * * * ." Based upon such evidence, the [trial] court reasonably concluded that the physicians were not the employees or actual agents of the Hospital for purposes of vicarious [indirect] liability.

Ostensible [apparent] agency on the other hand, may be implied from the facts of a particular case, and if a principal by his acts has led others to believe that he has conferred authority upon an agent, he cannot be heard to assert, as against third parties who have relied thereon in good faith, that he did not intend to confer such power * * * . The doctrine establishing the principles of liability for the acts of an ostensible agent rests on the doctrine of estoppel. *The essential elements are representations by the principal, justifiable reliance thereon by a third party, and change of position or injury resulting from such reliance.* Before recovery can be had against the principal for the acts of an ostensible agent, the person dealing with an agent must do so with belief in the

CASE 19.4 CONTINUED

agent's authority and this belief must be a reasonable one. Such belief must be generated by some act or neglect by the principal sought to be charged and the person relying on the agent's apparent authority must not be guilty of neglect. [Emphasis added.]

* * * *

Here, the Hospital held out the clinic and the personnel in the clinic as part of the Hospital. Furthermore, it was objectively reasonable for Shahan to believe that Drs. Gubin and Ogata were employees of the Hospital. The clinic was located across the street from the Hospital. It used the same name as the Hospital and labeled itself as an outpatient clinic. Numerous professionals at the clinic were employees of the Hospital. [Carol Cribbs, a comprehensive perinatal health worker at the clinic] and Sterling indicated to Shahan that they were employees of the Hospital and that the program was run by the Hospital. Sterling personally set up all of Shahan's appointments at the main Hospital rather than giving Shahan a referral for the various tests. Shahan was referred by individuals in the emergency room specifically to Dr. Gubin. When she called for an appointment she was told by the receptionist that she was calling the Hospital outpatient clinic which was the clinic of Dr. Gubin. On days when Shahan would see either Dr. Gubin or Dr. Ogata at the clinic, she would also see either Cribbs or Sterling, whom she knew were employed by the Hospital.

* * * At her first appointment she signed a document titled "patient rights and responsibilities," which would unambiguously lead a patient to the conclusion that the clinic "was a one-stop shop for the patient," and that all individuals at the clinic were connected with the Hospital. All of Shahan's contacts with the physicians were at the Hospital-run clinic. Most, if not all, of the physician contacts occurred in conjunction with the provision of other services by either Sterling or Cribbs. The entire appearance created by the Hospital, and those associated with it, was that the Hospital was the provider of the obstetrical care to Shahan.

• **Decision and Remedy** *The state intermediate appellate court decided that, contrary to the lower court's finding, Drs. Gubin and Ogata were "ostensible agents of the Hospital." The appellate court affirmed the lower court's ruling, however, on Amanda's "wrongful life" claim, concluding that the physicians were not negligent in failing to advise Shahan to have an elective abortion.*

• **The Ethical Dimension** *Does a principal have an ethical responsibility to inform an unaware third party that an apparent (ostensible) agent does not in fact have authority to act on the principal's behalf?*

• **The E-Commerce Dimension** *Could Amanda have established Drs. Gubin and Ogata's apparent authority if Desert Hospital had maintained a Web site that advertised the services of the CPSP clinic and stated clearly that the physicians were not its employees? Explain.*

Emergency Powers

When an unforeseen emergency demands action by the agent to protect or preserve the property and rights of the principal, but the agent is unable to communicate with the principal, the agent has emergency power. For example, Fulsom is an engineer for Pacific Drilling Company. While Fulsom is acting within the scope of his employment, he is severely injured in an accident at an oil rig many miles from home. Dudley, the rig supervisor, directs Thompson, a physician, to give medical aid to Fulsom and to charge Pacific for the medical services. Dudley, an agent, has no express or implied authority to bind the principal, Pacific Drilling, for Thompson's medical services. Because of the emergency situation, however, the law recognizes Dudley as having authority to act appropriately under the circumstances.

Ratification

Ratification occurs when the principal affirms, or accepts responsibility for, an agent's *unauthorized* act. When ratification occurs, the principal is bound to the agent's act, and the act is treated as if it had been authorized by the principal *from the outset.* Ratification can be either express or implied.

If the principal does not ratify the contract, the principal is not bound, and the third party's agreement with the agent is viewed as merely an unaccepted offer. Because the third party's agreement is an unaccepted offer, the third party can revoke it at any time,

CHAPTER 20

Employment Relationships

Traditionally, employment relationships in the United States were governed primarily by the common law. Today, in contrast, the workplace is regulated extensively by federal and state statutes. Recall from Chapter 1 that common law doctrines apply only to areas *not* covered by statutory law. Common law doctrines have thus been displaced to a significant extent by statutory law. In this chapter, we look at the most significant laws regulating employment relationships. We examine other important laws regulating the workplace, including those covering employment discrimination, immigration, and labor unions, in Chapters 21 and 22.

Keep in mind, however, that certain aspects of employment relationships are still governed by common law rules, including the rules under contract, tort, and agency law discussed in previous chapters of this text. Given that many employees (those who deal with third parties) normally are deemed to be agents of their employer, agency concepts are especially relevant in the employment context, as is the distinction between employees and independent contractors. Generally, the laws discussed in this chapter and in Chapter 21 apply only to the employer-employee relationship and not to independent contractors. Here, we begin our discussion by examining one other common law doctrine that has not been entirely displaced by statutory law—that of employment at will.

Employment at Will

Traditionally, employment relationships have generally been governed by the common law doctrine of **employment at will.** Under this doctrine, either the employer or the employee may terminate an employment contract at any time and for any reason, unless the contract specifically provides to the contrary. This doctrine is still in widespread use, and only one state (Montana) does not apply it. Nonetheless, as has occurred in many other areas of employment law, federal and state statutes have partially displaced the common law and now prevent this doctrine from being applied in a number of circumstances. Today, an employer may not fire an employee if to do so would violate a federal or state statute, such as one prohibiting termination of employment for discriminatory reasons (see Chapter 21).

Exceptions to the Employment-at-Will Doctrine

Under the employment-at-will doctrine, as mentioned, an employer may hire and fire employees at will (regardless of the employees' performance) without liability, unless the decision violates the terms of an employment contract or statutory law. Because of the harsh effects of the employment-at-will doctrine for employees, courts have carved out various exceptions to this doctrine. These exceptions are based on contract theory, tort theory, and public policy.

Exceptions Based on Contract Theory Some courts have held that an *implied* employment contract exists between the employer and the employee. If the employee is fired outside the terms of the implied contract, he or she may succeed in an action for breach of contract even though no written employment contract exists.

For example, an employer's manual or personnel bulletin may state that, as a matter of policy, workers will be dismissed only for good cause. If the employee is aware of this policy and continues to work for the employer, a court may find that there is an implied contract based on the terms stated in the manual or bulletin. Generally, the key consideration in determining whether an employment manual creates an implied contractual obligation is the employee's reasonable expectations.

Oral promises that an employer makes to employees regarding discharge policy may also be considered part of an implied contract. If the employer fires a worker in a manner contrary to what was promised, a court may hold that the employer has violated the implied contract and is liable for damages. Most state courts will consider this claim and judge it by traditional contract standards. In some cases, courts have held that an implied employment contract existed even though the employees agreed in writing to be employees at will.[1] In a few states, courts have gone further and held that all employment contracts contain an implied covenant of good faith. In those states, if an employer fires an employee for an arbitrary or unjustified reason, the employee can claim that the covenant of good faith was breached and the contract violated.

Exceptions Based on Tort Theory In some situations, the discharge of an employee may give rise to an action for wrongful discharge under tort theories. Abusive discharge procedures may result in intentional infliction of emotional distress or defamation. In addition, some courts have permitted workers to sue their employers under the tort theory of fraud. Under this theory, an employer may be held liable for making false promises to a prospective employee if the person detrimentally relies on the employer's representations by taking the job.

Suppose that an employer induces a prospective employee to leave a lucrative position and move to another state by offering "a long-term job with a thriving business." In fact, the employer is having significant financial problems. Furthermore, the employer is planning a merger that will result in the elimination of the position offered to the prospective employee. If the person takes the job in reliance on the employer's representations and is laid off shortly thereafter, he or she may be able to bring an action against the employer for fraud.[2]

Exceptions Based on Public Policy Another common law exception to the employment-at-will doctrine is made on the basis of public policy. Courts may apply this exception when an employer fires a worker for reasons that violate a fundamental public policy of the jurisdiction.

Generally, the courts require that the public policy involved be expressed clearly in the statutory law governing the jurisdiction. The public policy against employment discrimination, for instance, is expressed clearly in federal and state statutes. Thus, if a worker is fired for discriminatory reasons but has no cause of action under statutory law (because, for example, the workplace has too few employees to be covered by the statute, discussed in Chapter 21) that worker may succeed in a suit against the employer for wrongful discharge in violation of public policy.[3] Firing an employee for filing a workers' compensation claim (discussed later in this chapter) is another example of the strong public policy that must exist for a court to find an exception to the employment-at-will doctrine.[4]

Occasionally, a discharge can violate public policy if it is done in retaliation for an employee's refusing to engage in criminal conduct or reporting an employer's unlawful conduct to authorities (commonly referred to as *whistleblowing*). Does the public policy exception apply to a nursing home employee who is fired for reporting the abuse of a patient as required by a state statute? That was the question in the following case.

1. See, for example, *Kuest v. Regent Assisted Living, Inc.*, 111 Wash.App. 36, 43 P.3d 23 (2002).

2. See, for example, *Lazar v. Superior Court of Los Angeles Co.*, 12 Cal.4th 631, 909 P.2d 981, 49 Cal.Rptr.2d 377 (1996); and *Helmer v. Bingham Toyota Isuzu*, 129 Cal.App. 4th 1121, 29 Cal.Rptr.3d 136 (2005).

3. See, for example, *Wholey v. Sears Roebuck*, 370 Md. 38, 803 A.2d 482 (2002).

4. Note that some states, such as Ohio, have limited an employee's ability to sue for wrongful discharge based on the public policy exception. See, for example, *Bickers v. W.&S. Life Insurance Co.*, 116 Ohio St.3d 351, 879 N.E.2d 201 (2007).

CASE 20.1 Wendeln v. The Beatrice Manor, Inc.

Supreme Court of Nebraska, 2006. 271 Neb. 373, 712 N.W.2d 226.

• **Background and Facts** Rebecca Wendeln, a twenty-one-year-old certified nursing assistant, worked as a staffing coordinator at The Beatrice Manor, Inc., in Beatrice, Nebraska. One of the patients at Beatrice Manor was wheelchair-bound. Moving the patient required two persons and a gait belt (an ambulatory aid used to transfer or mobilize patients). In December 2001, two medical aides told Wendeln that the patient had been improperly moved and had been injured. Wendeln reported the incident to the Nebraska Department of Health and Human Services, as required under the state Adult Protective Services Act (APSA). A few days later, Wendeln's supervisor angrily confronted her about the report. Intimidated, Wendeln asked for a day off, which was granted. On her return, she was fired. She filed a suit in a Nebraska state court against Beatrice Manor, alleging, among other things, that her discharge was a violation of the state's public policy. A jury returned a verdict in her favor, awarding damages of $79,000. Beatrice Manor appealed to the Nebraska Supreme Court.

IN THE LANGUAGE OF THE COURT
***McCORMACK,* J. [Justice]**

* * * *

* * * Beatrice Manor asserts that * * * "[t]here is no clear legislative enactment declaring an important public policy with such clarity as to provide a basis for [Wendeln's] civil action for wrongful discharge."

The clear rule in Nebraska is that unless constitutionally, statutorily, or contractually prohibited, an employer, without incurring liability, may terminate an at-will employee at any time with or without reason. We recognize, however, a public policy exception to the at-will employment doctrine. *Under the public policy exception, we will allow an employee to claim damages for wrongful discharge when the motivation for the firing contravenes public policy.* * * * However, * * * it [is] important that abusive discharge claims of employees at-will be limited to manageable and clear standards. Thus, the right of an employer to terminate employees at will should be restricted only by exceptions created by statute or to those instances where a very clear mandate of public policy has been violated. [Emphasis added.]

* * * An employee could state a cause of action for retaliatory discharge based upon the allegation that the employee was terminated from her employment because she filed a workers' compensation claim. * * * Nebraska law neither specifically prohibit[s] an employer from discharging an employee for filing a workers' compensation claim, nor specifically [makes] it a crime for an employer to do so. Nevertheless, * * * the general purpose and unique nature of the Nebraska Workers' Compensation Act itself provides a mandate for public policy. * * * The Nebraska Workers' Compensation Act was meant to create * * * rights for employees and * * * such [a] beneficent purpose would be undermined by failing to adopt a rule which allows a retaliatory discharge claim for employees discharged for filing a workers' compensation claim. This is because were we not to recognize such a public policy exception to the employment-at-will doctrine, the * * * rights granted by the Nebraska Workers' Compensation Act could simply be circumvented by the employer's threatening to discharge the employee if he or she exercised those rights.

* * * *

* * * [In Nebraska] the law imposes an affirmative obligation upon an employee to prevent abuse or neglect of nursing home residents, and the employee fulfills that obligation by reporting the abuse [and may be subject to criminal sanctions for failing to do so. *An] employer's termination of employment for fulfillment of the legal obligation exposes the employer to a wrongful termination action under the fundamental and well-defined public policy of protecting nursing home residents from abuse and neglect.* * * * By applying the public policy exception * * *, employees [are] relieved of the onerous burden of choosing between equally destructive alternatives: report and be terminated, or fail to report and be prosecuted. [Emphasis added.]

* * * The purpose of the APSA would be circumvented if employees mandated by the APSA to report suspected patient abuse could be threatened with discharge for making such a report.

CASE 20.1 CONTINUED

The [Nebraska] Legislature articulates public policy when it declares certain conduct to be in violation of the criminal law. The APSA makes a clear public policy statement by utilizing the threat of criminal sanction to ensure the implementation of the reporting provisions set forth to protect the vulnerable adults with which the APSA is concerned. Thus, we determine that a public policy exception to the employment-at-will doctrine applies to allow a cause of action for retaliatory discharge when an employee is fired for making a report of abuse as mandated by the APSA.

- **Decision and Remedy** *The state supreme court affirmed the trial court's judgment. The appellate court emphasized that under the employment-at-will doctrine an employer may fire an at-will employee at any time with or without cause. The court recognized an exception to this principle, however, "for wrongful discharge when the motivation for the firing contravenes public policy." Under this exception, an employee has a cause of action for retaliatory discharge when she is fired for reporting abuse of a nursing home patient, as state law requires.*

- **The Ethical Dimension** *Is it fair to sanction an employer for discharging an employee who reports on the employer's unsafe or illegal actions to government authorities or others? Discuss.*

- **The Global Dimension** *In many countries, discharging an employee is more difficult and costly for the employer than it is in the United States. Why?*

Wrongful Discharge

Whenever an employer discharges an employee in violation of an employment contract or a statutory law protecting employees, the employee may bring an action for **wrongful discharge.** Even if an employer's actions do not violate any express employment contract or statute, the employer may still be subject to liability under a common law doctrine, such as a tort theory or agency. For example, an employer discharges a female employee and publicly discloses private facts about her sex life to her co-workers. In that situation, the employee could bring a wrongful discharge claim against the employer based on the tort of invasion of privacy (see Chapter 12).

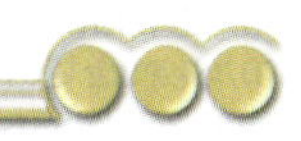

Wage and Hour Laws

In the 1930s, Congress enacted several laws regulating the wages and working hours of employees. In 1931, Congress passed the Davis-Bacon Act,[5] which requires the payment of "prevailing wages" to employees of contractors and subcontractors working on government construction projects. In 1936, the Walsh-Healey Act[6] was passed. This act requires that a minimum wage, as well as overtime pay at 1.5 times regular pay rates, be paid to employees of manufacturers or suppliers entering into contracts with agencies of the federal government.

In 1938, with the passage of the Fair Labor Standards Act[7] (FLSA), Congress extended wage-hour requirements to cover all employers engaged in interstate commerce or in the production of goods for interstate commerce. Here we examine the FLSA's provisions in regard to child labor, maximum hours, and minimum wages, and overtime exceptions.

Child Labor

The FLSA prohibits oppressive child labor. Children under fourteen years of age are allowed to do certain types of work, such as deliver newspapers, work for their parents, and be employed in the entertainment and (with some exceptions) agricultural areas. Children who are fourteen or fifteen years of age are allowed to work, but not in hazardous occupations. There are also numerous restrictions on how many hours per day and per week they can work. For example, minors under the age of sixteen cannot work during school hours, for more than three hours on a school day (or eight hours on a nonschool day), for more than eighteen hours during a school week (or forty hours during a nonschool week), or before 7 A.M. or after 7 P.M. (9 P.M. during the summer). Most states require persons under sixteen years of age to obtain work permits.

5. 40 U.S.C. Sections 276a–276a-5.
6. 41 U.S.C. Sections 35–45.
7. 29 U.S.C. Sections 201–260.

EMERGING TRENDS IN THE LEGAL ENVIRONMENT OF BUSINESS

Paying Overtime in the Virtual Workforce

According to WorldatWork, a research organization for human resources professionals, nearly 46 million U.S. workers perform at least part of their job at home, and close to 13 million of them are full-time *telecommuters,* meaning that they work at home or off-site by means of an electronic linkup to the central workplace. Just because employees work at a remote location does not mean that they are automatically exempt from overtime-pay requirements (or minimum-wage laws). Federal (and sometimes state and local) wage and hour laws often apply to the virtual workforce, as many businesses are finding out the unfortunate way—through litigation.

Telecommuters and Overtime-Pay Requirements

As described in the text, the U.S. Department of Labor revised its regulations in 2004 to clarify how overtime exemptions apply to employees in various occupations. The new regulations established a primary duty test to be used in classifying workers.[a] In general, workers whose primary duty involves the exercise of discretion and independent judgment are more likely to be exempt from the overtime-pay requirements. So are those whose positions require advanced knowledge or specialized instructions, such as computer systems analysts and software engineers.

Although the regulations appear detailed, they do not specifically address how these exemptions apply to telecommuters. Since the new rules went into effect in 2004, telecommuters have filed a barrage of lawsuits claiming that their employers violated the Fair Labor Standards Act by failing to pay them for overtime work and to compensate them for work-related tasks.

a. See 29 C.F.R. Sections 541.203 and 541.400.

An Increasing Number of Cases and Settlements

To date, more cases have been filed in California than in any other state—mostly by telecommuting information technology workers, pharmaceutical sales representatives, and insurance company employees. Suits are also pending in Colorado, the District of Columbia, Illinois, Missouri, New Jersey, New York, and Ohio.

Some defendants with large numbers of employees have decided to settle before the case goes to trial. Computer Sciences Corporation in El Segundo, California, for example, paid $24 million to settle a case brought by telecommuters and call-center

disability, death, hospitalization, and unemployment. The key federal law on this subject is the Social Security Act of 1935.[14]

Social Security

The Social Security Act of 1935 provides for old-age (retirement), survivors', and disability insurance. The act is therefore often referred to as OASDI. Both employers and employees must "contribute" under the Federal Insurance Contributions Act (FICA)[15] to help pay for benefits that will partially make up for the employees' loss of income on retirement.

The basis for the employee's and the employer's contribution is the employee's annual wage base—the maximum amount of the employee's wages that is subject to the tax. The employer withholds the employee's FICA contribution from the employee's wages and then matches this contribution. The annual wage base increases each year to take into account the rising cost of living. In 2008, employers were required to withhold 6.2 percent of each employee's wages, up to a maximum wage base of $102,000, and to match this contribution.

Retired workers are eligible to receive monthly payments from the Social Security Administration, which administers the Social Security Act. Social Security benefits are fixed by statute but increase automatically with increases in the cost of living.

Medicare

Medicare, a federal government health-insurance program, is administered by the Social Security Administration for people sixty-five years of age and older and for some under age sixty-five who have a disability. It originally had two parts, one pertaining to hospital costs and the other to nonhospital medical costs, such as visits to physicians' offices. People who have Medicare hospital insurance can obtain additional federal medical insurance if they pay small monthly premiums, which increase as the cost of medical care rises.

As with Social Security contributions, both the employer and the employee "contribute" to Medicare, but unlike Social Security, there is no cap on the

14. 42 U.S.C. Sections 301–1397e.
15. 26 U.S.C. Sections 3101–3125.

employees,[b] and International Business Machines Corporation (IBM) settled a similar suit for $65 million.[c] Other defendants have refused to settle. Farmers Insurance Exchange went to trial but lost and faced a significant jury verdict. On appeal to the U.S. Court of Appeals for the Ninth Circuit, however, the company prevailed.[d] In contrast, Advanced Business Integrators, Inc., had to pay nearly $50,000 in overtime compensation to a computer consultant who had spent the majority of his work time at customers' sites training their employees in the use of his employer's software.[e]

b. *Computer Sciences Corp.,* No. 03-08201 (C.D.Cal., settled in 2005).

c. *International Business Machines Corp.,* No. 06-00430 (N.D.Cal., settled in 2006).

d. *In re Farmers Insurance Exchange, Claims Representatives' Overtime Pay Litigation,* 481 F.3d 1119 (9th Cir. 2007).

e. *Eicher v. Advanced Business Integrators, Inc.,* 151 Cal.App.4th 1363, 61 Cal.Rptr.3d 114 (2007).

IMPLICATIONS FOR THE BUSINESSPERSON

1. The litigation discussed here illustrates the importance of properly tracking hours worked for compensation purposes. Even though recording the hours worked by telecommuters may be difficult, allowing employees to work from home without an accounting of how many hours they actually work may lead to class-action claims for overtime pay.
2. Businesspersons may consider whether a particular job is appropriate for telecommuting and then allow only exempt employees to telecommute.

FOR CRITICAL ANALYSIS

1. Why might telecommuting employees sometimes accept being wrongly classified as "executives" or "professionals" under the overtime-pay requirements and thus be exempt from overtime pay?
2. If more class-action lawsuits claiming overtime pay for telecommuters are successful, what do you think will be the effect on telecommuting? Why?

RELEVANT WEB SITES

To locate information on the Web concerning the issues discussed in this feature, go to this text's Web site at **academic.cengage.com/blaw/cross**, select "Chapter 20," and click on "Emerging Trends."

amount of wages subject to the Medicare tax. In 2008, both the employer and the employee were required to pay 1.45 percent of *all* wages and salaries to finance Medicare. Thus, for Social Security and Medicare together, in 2008 the employer and employee each paid 7.65 percent of the first $102,000 of income (6.2 percent for Social Security + 1.45 percent for Medicare), for a combined total of 15.3 percent. In addition, all wages and salaries above $102,000 were taxed at a combined (employer and employee) rate of 2.9 percent for Medicare. Self-employed persons pay both the employer and the employee portions of the Social Security and Medicare taxes (15.3 percent of income up to $102,000 and 2.9 percent of income above that amount in 2008).

Private Pension Plans

The Employee Retirement Income Security Act (ERISA) of 1974[16] is the major federal act regulating employee retirement plans set up by employers to supplement Social Security benefits. This statute empowers the Labor Management Services Administration of the U.S. Department of Labor to enforce its provisions governing employers who have private pension funds for their employees. ERISA does not require an employer to establish a pension plan. When a plan exists, however, ERISA provides standards for its management.

A key provision of ERISA concerns vesting. **Vesting** gives an employee a legal right to receive pension benefits at some future date when she or he stops working. Before ERISA was enacted, some employees who had worked for companies for as long as thirty years received no pension benefits when their employment terminated because those benefits had not vested. ERISA establishes complex vesting rules. Generally, however, all of an employee's contributions to a pension plan vest immediately, and the employee's rights to the employer's contributions vest after five years of employment.

In an attempt to prevent mismanagement of pension funds, ERISA has established rules on how they must be invested. Managers must choose investments

16. 29 U.S.C. Sections 1001 *et seq.*

cautiously and must diversify the plan's investments to minimize the risk of large losses. ERISA also includes detailed record-keeping and reporting requirements.

Unemployment Compensation

To ease the financial impact of unemployment, the United States has a system of unemployment insurance. The Federal Unemployment Tax Act (FUTA) of 1935[17] created a state-administered system that provides unemployment compensation to eligible individuals. Under this system, employers pay into a fund, and the proceeds are paid out to qualified unemployed workers. FUTA and state laws require employers that fall under the provisions of the act to pay unemployment taxes at regular intervals.

FUTA generally determines covered employment and imposes certain requirements on state unemployment programs, but the states determine individual eligibility requirements and benefit amounts. To be eligible for unemployment compensation, a worker must be willing and able to work and be actively seeking employment. Workers who have been fired for misconduct or who have left their jobs without good cause normally are not eligible for benefits.

COBRA

Federal legislation also addresses the issue of health insurance for workers who have lost their jobs and are no longer eligible for group health-insurance plans. Employers who have twenty or more employees and provide a group health plan must comply with the requirements of the Consolidated Omnibus Budget Reconciliation Act (COBRA) of 1985.[18] COBRA basically gives employees a right to continue the group health benefits provided by their employers for a limited time after the voluntary or involuntary loss of employment. The act also applies to workers who are no longer eligible for coverage under the employer's health plan because their hours have been decreased. Spouses, former spouses, and dependent children who were covered under the plan also have the right to continue health coverage.

Procedures under COBRA An employer must notify an employee of COBRA's provisions if the worker faces termination or a reduction of hours that would affect her or his eligibility for coverage under the plan. The worker has sixty days (beginning with the date that the group coverage would stop) to decide whether to continue with the employer's group insurance plan. If the worker chooses to discontinue the coverage, then the employer has no further obligation. If the worker chooses to continue coverage, the employer is obligated to keep the policy active for up to eighteen months but is not required to pay for the coverage.[19]

Usually, the worker (or beneficiary) must pay the premiums for continued coverage, plus an additional 2 percent administrative fee. The coverage provided must be the same as that enjoyed by the worker prior to the termination or reduction of employment. If family members were originally included, for example, COBRA prohibits their exclusion.

Employer's Obligations under COBRA The employer is relieved of the responsibility to provide COBRA coverage if the worker fails to pay the premium, becomes eligible for Medicare, or is covered under another health plan (such as a spouse's or new employer's). The employer is also relieved of the obligation if the employer completely cancels its group benefit plan for all employees. An employer that fails to comply with COBRA risks substantial penalties, such as a tax of up to 10 percent of the annual cost of the group plan or $500,000, whichever is less.

Employer-Sponsored Group Health Plans

The Health Insurance Portability and Accountability Act (HIPAA),[20] which was discussed in Chapter 5 in the context of its privacy protections, contains provisions that affect employer-sponsored group health plans. HIPAA does not require employers to provide health insurance, but it does establish requirements for those that do. One provision of HIPAA limits an employer's ability to exclude persons from coverage for "preexisting conditions" to conditions for which medical treatment was received within the previous six months (excluding pregnancy). Another provision requires that an employee be given credit for previous health coverage (including COBRA coverage) to decrease any waiting period before coverage becomes effective.

17. 26 U.S.C. Sections 3301–3310.
18. 29 U.S.C. Sections 1161–1169.
19. Certain events, such as a disability, can extend the period of COBRA coverage. Also, COBRA does not prohibit health plans from offering continuation health coverage that goes beyond COBRA periods.
20. 29 U.S.C.A. Sections 1181 *et seq.*

In addition, employers that are plan sponsors have significant responsibilities regarding the manner in which they collect, use, and disclose the health information of employees and their families. Employers must comply with numerous administrative, technical, and procedural safeguards (such as training employees, designating privacy officials, and distributing privacy notices) to ensure that employees' health information is not disclosed to unauthorized parties. Failure to comply with HIPAA regulations can result in civil penalties of up to $100 per person per violation (with a cap of $25,000 per year). The employer is also subject to criminal prosecution for certain types of HIPAA violations and can face up to $250,000 in criminal fines and imprisonment for up to ten years if convicted.

Family and Medical Leave

In 1993, Congress passed the Family and Medical Leave Act (FMLA)[21] to protect employees who need time off work for family or medical reasons. A majority of the states also have legislation allowing for a leave from employment for family or medical reasons, and many employers maintain private family-leave plans for their workers.

Coverage and Application of the FMLA

The FMLA requires employers who have fifty or more employees to provide an employee with up to twelve weeks of unpaid family or medical leave during any twelve-month period. Generally, an employee may take family leave to care for a newborn baby, an adopted child, or a foster child, and medical leave when the employee or the employee's spouse, child, or parent has a "serious health condition" requiring care.[22] Employees suffering from certain chronic health conditions, such as asthma, diabetes, and pregnancy, may take FMLA leave for their own incapacities that require absences of fewer than three days.

The employer must continue the worker's health-care coverage and guarantee employment in the same position or a comparable position when the employee returns to work. An important exception to the FMLA, however, allows the employer to avoid reinstating a *key employee*—defined as an employee whose pay falls within the top 10 percent of the firm's workforce. (The employer must continue to maintain health benefits for the key employee during the leave, however.) Also, the act does not apply to part-time or newly hired employees (those who have worked for less than one year).

The FMLA expressly covers private and public (government) employees. Nevertheless, some states argued that public employees could not sue their state employers in federal courts to enforce their FMLA rights unless the states consented to be sued.[23] This argument came before the United States Supreme Court in the following case.

21. 29 U.S.C. Sections 2601, 2611–2619, 2651–2654.

22. The foster care must be state sanctioned before such an arrangement falls within the coverage of the FMLA.

23. Under the Eleventh Amendment to the U.S. Constitution, a state is immune from suit in a federal court unless the state agrees to be sued.

EXTENDED CASE 20.3

Nevada Department of Human Resources v. Hibbs

Supreme Court of the United States, 2003. 538 U.S. 721, 123 S.Ct. 1972, 155 L.Ed.2d 953.

Chief Justice *REHNQUIST* Delivered the Opinion of the Court.

* * * *

Petitioners include the Nevada Department of Human Resources (Department) * * * . Respondent William Hibbs (hereinafter respondent) worked for the Department's Welfare Division. In April and May 1997, he sought leave under the FMLA to care for his ailing wife, who was recovering from a car accident and neck surgery. The Department granted his request for the full 12 weeks of FMLA leave and authorized him to use the leave intermittently as needed between May and December 1997. Respondent did so until August 5, 1997, after which he did not return to work. In October 1997, the Department informed respondent that he had exhausted his FMLA leave, that no further leave would be granted, and that he must report to work by November 12, 1997. Respondent failed to do so and was terminated.

CASE CONTINUES

CASE 20.3 CONTINUED

Respondent sued petitioners in [a] United States District Court * * * . The District Court awarded petitioners summary judgment on the grounds that the FMLA claim was barred by the [U.S. Constitution's] Eleventh Amendment * * * . Respondent appealed * * * . The Ninth Circuit reversed.

We granted *certiorari* * * * .

* * * *

The history of the many state laws limiting women's employment opportunities is chronicled in—and, until relatively recently, was sanctioned by—this Court's own opinions. For example, in [previous cases] the Court upheld state laws prohibiting women from practicing law and tending bar * * * . State laws frequently subjected women to distinctive restrictions, terms, conditions, and benefits for those jobs they could take. In [one case] for example, this Court approved a state law limiting the hours that women could work for wages, and observed that 19 States had such laws at the time. Such laws were based on the related beliefs that (1) woman is, and should remain, the center of home and family life, and (2) a proper discharge of a woman's maternal functions—having in view not merely her own health, but the well-being of the race—justifies legislation to protect her from the greed as well as the passion of man. Until [1971] it remained the prevailing doctrine that government, both federal and state, could withhold from women opportunities accorded men so long as any basis in reason—such as the above beliefs—could be conceived for the discrimination.

Congress responded to this history of discrimination by abrogating [revoking] States' sovereign immunity in Title VII of the Civil Rights Act of 1964 * * * .[a] But state gender discrimination did not cease. * * * According to evidence that was before Congress when it enacted the FMLA, States continue[d] to rely on invalid gender stereotypes in the employment context, specifically in the administration of leave benefits.

* * * *

Congress * * * heard testimony that parental leave for fathers * * * is rare. Even * * * where child-care leave policies do exist, men, both in the public and private sectors, receive notoriously discriminatory treatment in their requests for such leave. Many States offered women extended "maternity" leave that far exceeded the typical 4- to 8-week period of physical disability due to pregnancy and childbirth, but very few States granted men a parallel benefit: Fifteen States provided women up to one year of extended maternity leave, while only four provided men with the same. This and other differential leave policies were not attributable to any differential physical needs of men and women, but rather to the pervasive sex-role stereotype that caring for family members is women's work.

* * * *

* * * Because employers continued to regard the family as the woman's domain, they often denied men similar accommodations or discouraged them from taking leave. These mutually reinforcing stereotypes created a self-fulfilling cycle of discrimination that forced women to continue to assume the role of primary family caregiver, and fostered employers' stereotypical views about women's * * * value as employees.

* * * *

By creating an across-the-board, routine employment benefit for all eligible employees, Congress sought to ensure that family-care leave would no longer be stigmatized as an inordinate drain on the workplace caused by female employees, and that employers could not evade leave obligations simply by hiring men. *By setting a minimum standard of family leave for all eligible employees, irrespective of gender, the FMLA attacks the formerly state-sanctioned stereotype that only women are responsible for family caregiving, thereby reducing employers' incentives to engage in discrimination by basing hiring and promotion decisions on stereotypes.* [Emphasis added.]

* * * *

* * * The FMLA is narrowly targeted at the fault line between work and family—precisely where sex-based overgeneralization has been and remains strongest—and affects only one aspect of the employment relationship.

* * * *

a. This statute will be discussed in detail in Chapter 21.

CASE 20.3 CONTINUED

For the above reasons, we conclude that [the FMLA] is congruent [harmonious] and proportional to its remedial object, and can be understood as responsive to, or designed to prevent, unconstitutional behavior. The judgment of the Court of Appeals [holding that the Eleventh Amendment did not bar the plaintiff's suit] is therefore *Affirmed.*

QUESTIONS

1. What did the Court hold with respect to the primary issue in this case?
2. How might a law foster discrimination even when the law is not obviously discriminatory?

Remedies for Violations of the FMLA

Remedies for violations of the FMLA can include (1) damages for lost benefits, denied compensation, and actual monetary losses (such as the cost of providing for care of the family member) up to an amount equivalent to the employee's wages for twelve weeks; (2) job reinstatement; and (3) promotion, if a promotion had been denied. A successful plaintiff is entitled to court costs, attorneys' fees, and—in cases involving bad faith on the part of the employer—two times the amount of damages awarded by a judge or jury. Supervisors may also be subject to personal liability, as employers, for violations of the act when the supervisor exercises sufficient control over the employee's leave.[24]

Employers generally are required to notify employees when an absence will be counted against leave authorized under the act. If an employer fails to provide such notice, and the employee consequently suffers an injury because he or she did not receive notice, the employer may be sanctioned.[25]

Interaction with Other Laws

The FMLA does not affect any other federal or state law that prohibits discrimination. Nor does it supersede any state or local law that provides more generous family- or medical-leave protection. For example, if a California state law allows employees who are disabled by pregnancy to take up to four months of unpaid leave, an employer in California would have to comply with that law (in addition to the provisions of the FMLA). Also, an employer who is obligated to provide more extensive leave under a collective bargaining agreement must do so, regardless of the FMLA.

Section 6 Employee Privacy Rights

In the last thirty years, concerns about the privacy rights of employees have arisen in response to the sometimes invasive tactics used by employers to monitor and screen workers. Perhaps the greatest privacy concern in today's employment arena has to do with electronic monitoring of employees' activities. Clearly, employers need to protect themselves from liability for their employees' online activities. They also have a legitimate interest in monitoring the productivity of their workers. At the same time, employees expect to have a certain zone of privacy in the workplace. Indeed, many lawsuits have alleged that employers' intrusive monitoring practices violate employees' privacy rights.

Electronic Monitoring in the Workplace

According to the American Management Association, more than two-thirds of employers engage in some form of electronic monitoring of their employees. Types of monitoring include monitoring workers' Web site connections, reviewing employees' e-mail and computer files, video recording of employee job performance, and recording and reviewing telephone conversations and voice mail.

Various specially designed software products have made it easier for an employer to track employees' Internet use. Software allows an employer to track almost every move an employee makes on the Internet, including the specific Web sites visited and

24. See, for example, *Rupnow v. TRC, Inc.*, 999 F.Supp. 1047 (N.D. Ohio 1998); and *Mueller v. J. P. Morgan Chase & Co.*, 2007 WL 915160 (N.D. Ohio 2007).

25. *Ragsdale v. Wolverine World Wide, Inc.*, 535 U.S. 81, 122 S.Ct. 1155, 152 L.Ed.2d 167 (2002); and *Mondaine v. American Drug Stores, Inc.*, 408 F. Supp.2d 1169 (D.Kan. 2006).

the time spent surfing the Web. Filtering software, which was discussed in Chapter 5, can be used to prevent access to certain Web sites, such as sites containing sexually explicit images. Other filtering software may be used to screen incoming e-mail for viruses and to block junk e-mail (spam).

Although the use of filtering software by public employers (government agencies) has led to charges that blocking access to Web sites violates employees' rights to free speech, this issue does not arise in private businesses. This is because the First Amendment's protection of free speech applies only to *government* restraints on speech, not restraints imposed in the private sector.

Employee Privacy Protection under Constitutional and Tort Law Recall from Chapter 5 that the United States Supreme Court has inferred a personal right to privacy from the constitutional guarantees provided by the First, Third, Fourth, Fifth, and Ninth Amendments to the Constitution. Tort law (see Chapter 12), state constitutions, and a number of state and federal statutes also provide for privacy rights.

When determining whether an employer should be held liable for violating an employee's privacy rights, the courts generally weigh the employer's interests against the employee's reasonable expectation of privacy. Normally, if employees are informed that their communications are being monitored, they cannot reasonably expect those communications to be private. If employees are not informed that certain communications are being monitored, however, the employer may be held liable for invading their privacy. For this reason, today most employers that engage in electronic monitoring notify their employees about the monitoring.

For the most part, courts have held that an employer's monitoring of electronic communications in the workplace does not violate employees' privacy rights. Even if employees are not informed that their e-mail will be monitored, courts have generally concluded that employees have no expectation of privacy if the employer provided the e-mail system.[26] Courts have even found that employers have a right to monitor the e-mail of an independent contractor (such as an insurance agent) when the employer provided the e-mail service and was authorized to access stored messages.[27]

26. For a leading case on this issue, see *Smyth v. Pillsbury Co.*, 914 F.Supp. 97 (E.D.Pa. 1996).

27. See *Fraser v. Nationwide Mutual Insurance Co.*, 352 F.3d 107 (3d Cir. 2004).

The Electronic Communications Privacy Act The major statute with which employers must comply is the Electronic Communications Privacy Act (ECPA) of 1986.[28] This act amended existing federal wiretapping law to cover electronic forms of communications, such as communications via cellular telephones or e-mail. The ECPA prohibits the intentional interception of any wire or electronic communication or the intentional disclosure or use of the information obtained by the interception. Excluded from coverage, however, are any electronic communications through devices that are "furnished to the subscriber or user by a provider of wire or electronic communication service" and that are being used by the subscriber or user, or by the provider of the service, "in the ordinary course of its business."

This "business-extension exception" to the ECPA permits an employer to monitor employees' electronic communications in the ordinary course of business. It does not, however, permit an employer to monitor employees' personal communications. Under another exception to the ECPA, however, an employer may avoid liability under the act if the employees consent to having their electronic communications intercepted by the employer. Thus, an employer may be able to avoid liability under the ECPA by simply requiring employees to sign forms indicating that they consent to such monitoring.

Other Types of Monitoring

In addition to monitoring their employees' online activities, employers also engage in other types of employee screening and monitoring practices. The practices discussed below have often been challenged as violations of employee privacy rights.

Lie-Detector Tests At one time, many employers required employees or job applicants to take polygraph examinations (lie-detector tests). To protect the privacy interests of employees and job applicants, in 1988 Congress passed the Employee Polygraph Protection Act.[29] The act prohibits employers from (1) requiring or causing employees or job applicants to take lie-detector tests or suggesting or requesting that they do so; (2) using, accepting, referring to, or asking about the results of lie-detector tests taken by employees or applicants; and (3) taking or threatening negative employment-related action against employees or

28. 18 U.S.C. Sections 2510–2521.

29. 29 U.S.C. Sections 2001 *et seq.*

applicants based on results of lie-detector tests or on their refusal to take the tests.

Employers excepted from these prohibitions include federal, state, and local government employers; certain security service firms; and companies manufacturing and distributing controlled substances. Other employers may use polygraph tests when investigating losses attributable to theft, including embezzlement and the theft of trade secrets.

Drug Testing In the interests of public safety and to reduce unnecessary costs, many employers, including the government, require their employees to submit to drug testing.

Public Employers. Government (public) employers, of course, are constrained in drug testing by the Fourth Amendment to the U.S. Constitution, which prohibits unreasonable searches and seizures (see Chapter 5). Drug testing of public employees is allowed by statute for transportation workers and is normally upheld by the courts when drug use in a particular job may threaten public safety.[30] The Federal Aviation Administration also requires drug and alcohol testing of all employees and contractors (including employees of foreign air carriers) who perform safety-related functions.[31] When there is a reasonable basis for suspecting public employees of drug use, courts often find that drug testing does not violate the Fourth Amendment.

Private Employers. The Fourth Amendment does not apply to drug testing conducted by private employers.[32] Hence, the privacy rights and drug testing of private-sector employees are governed by state law, which varies from state to state. When testing is not allowed by state statute, employees sometimes file suit against their employers for the tort of invasion of privacy, although such claims have not met with much success.

Many states have statutes that allow drug testing by private employers but put restrictions on when and how the testing may be performed. A collective bargaining agreement may also provide protection against drug testing (or authorize drug testing under certain conditions). The permissibility of a private employee's drug test often hinges on whether the employer's testing was reasonable. Random drug tests and even "zero-tolerance" policies (that deny a "second chance" to employees who test positive for drugs) have been held to be reasonable.[33]

AIDS and HIV Testing A number of employers test their workers for acquired immune deficiency syndrome (AIDS) or the presence of human immunodeficiency virus (HIV), the virus that causes AIDS. Some state laws restrict such testing, and federal statutes—particularly the Americans with Disabilities Act of 1990[34] (see Chapter 21)—offer some protection to employees or job applicants who have AIDS or have tested positive for HIV. Employees may not be discharged and job applicants may not be discriminated against based on the results of AIDS tests. Employers are also required to safeguard a person's protected medical information and cannot disclose an employee's test results to unauthorized parties under HIPAA, which was discussed earlier in this chapter.

---

30. Omnibus Transportation Employee Testing Act of 1991, Pub. L. No. 102-143, Title V, 105 Stat. 917 (1991).
31. Antidrug and Alcohol Misuse Prevention Program for Personnel Engaged in Specified Aviation Activities, 71 *Federal Register* 1666 (January 10, 2006), enacted pursuant to 49 U.S.C. Section 45102(a)(1).
32. See *Chandler v. Miller,* 520 U.S. 305, 117 S.Ct. 1295, 137 L.Ed.2d 513 (1997).
33. See *CITGO Asphalt Refining Co. v. Paper, Allied-Industrial, Chemical, and Energy Workers International Union Local No. 2-991,* 385 F.3d 809 (3d Cir. 2004).
34. 42 U.S.C. Sections 12102–12118.

REVIEWING Employment Relationships

Rick Saldona began working as a traveling salesperson for Aimer Winery in 1979. Sales constituted 90 percent of Saldona's work time. Saldona worked an average of fifty hours per week but received no overtime pay. In June 2009, Saldona's new supervisor, Caesar Braxton, claimed

REVIEWING CONTINUES

An abundance of helpful information on disability-based discrimination, including the text of the Americans with Disabilities Act of 1990, can be found at the following Web site:

www.jan.wvu.edu/links/adalinks.htm

An excellent source for information on various forms of employment discrimination is the Equal Employment Opportunity Commission's Web site at

www.eeoc.gov

Legal Research Exercises on the Web

Go to **academic.cengage.com/blaw/cross**, the Web site that accompanies this text. Select "Chapter 21" and click on "Internet Exercises." There you will find the following Internet research exercises that you can perform to learn more about the topics covered in this chapter.

Internet Exercise 21–1: Legal Perspective
Americans with Disabilities

Internet Exercise 21–2: Management Perspective
Equal Employment Opportunity

Internet Exercise 21–3: Social Perspective
Religious and National-Origin Discrimination

CHAPTER 22

Immigration and Labor Law

During the nineteenth century, two separate forces began to affect the employment environment in the United States—a rise in immigration and the Industrial Revolution. Both led to significant changes in the legal environment of the workplace, which we will examine in this chapter. Legislation was enacted to prohibit employers from hiring illegal immigrants. Immigration law has evolved over the years into a myriad of complex rules that employers need to follow when hiring foreign-born workers. The laws on immigration are also in a state of transition, as politicians and others debate what reforms are needed to best serve the interests of both employers and workers.

During the Industrial Revolution, fewer Americans were self-employed than ever before, and employers generally set the terms of employment. Moreover, with increasing industrialization, the size of workplaces and the number of on-the-job hazards increased. Workers came to believe that to counter the power and freedom of their employers and to protect themselves, they needed to organize into unions. Employers discouraged—sometimes forcibly—collective activities such as unions. In support of unionization, Congress enacted such legislations as the Railway Labor Act of 1926.[1] These laws were often restricted to particular industries. Beginning in 1932, Congress enacted a number of statutes that increased employees' rights generally. At the heart of these rights is the right to join unions and engage in *collective bargaining* with management to negotiate working conditions, salaries, and benefits for a group of workers.

This chapter begins with a discussion of immigration law from its beginnings to its current state, and its importance to today's business owners and employers. We then describe the development of labor law and the legal recognition of the right to form unions. Next, the chapter examines the process of unionizing a company, the collective bargaining required of a unionized employer, and the strikes and lockouts that may result if bargaining fails. We also look at the labor practices that are considered unfair under federal law, and briefly discuss the rights of nonunion employees.

1. 45 U.S.C. Sections 151–188.

Section 1 The Law Governing Immigration

The United States is known as a nation of immigrants. Until 1875, there was no legislation restricting immigration, and the United States Supreme Court had declared state laws regulating immigration to be unconstitutional. The late nineteenth century saw the first federal immigration restrictions, beginning with a law excluding convicts and prostitutes. This coincided with a huge surge in immigration from new sources (including China, Ireland, and Southern and Eastern Europe). In 1890, more than 40 percent of New York City's population was foreign born. Immigration peaked at the beginning of the twentieth century. After that time, immigration waned, but recent years have seen a marked increase in illegal immigration from Latino countries, especially Mexico.

The rapid growth in immigration saw an increase in exclusionary laws. In 1924, Congress created a permanent national origin quota system that based legal immigration on the proportion of persons from a foreign country enumerated in the 1890 census. This was modified in the 1952 McCarran-Walter Act,[2] which continued the quota system, set standards for deportation, and first created preferences for aliens with special skills. The national origin and racial quotas were eliminated in 1965. The next major statute was the Immigration Reform and Control Act of 1986 (IRCA),[3] which provided amnesty to certain groups of illegal aliens then living in the United States and also established a system of sanctions against employers for hiring illegal immigrants lacking work authorization.

Both legal and illegal immigration have been surging in recent decades, as illustrated in Exhibit 22–1. The expansion of immigration has made an understanding of related legal requirements for business steadily more important. Employers must take steps to avoid hiring illegal immigrants or face serious penalties.

Law and Illegal Immigration

Today, there are an estimated 11 to 12 million illegal immigrants living in the United States. The overwhelming majority of these immigrants hold jobs, and they are the subject of considerable political controversy.

2. 8 U.S.C. Sections 1101 *et seq.*

3. This act amended various provisions of the McCarran-Walter Act, including 8 U.S.C. Sections 1160, 1187, 1188, 1255a, 1324a, 1324b, 1364, and 1365.

EXHIBIT 22–1 • Foreign-Born Population and Illegal Aliens, 1960–2010 (in Millions)

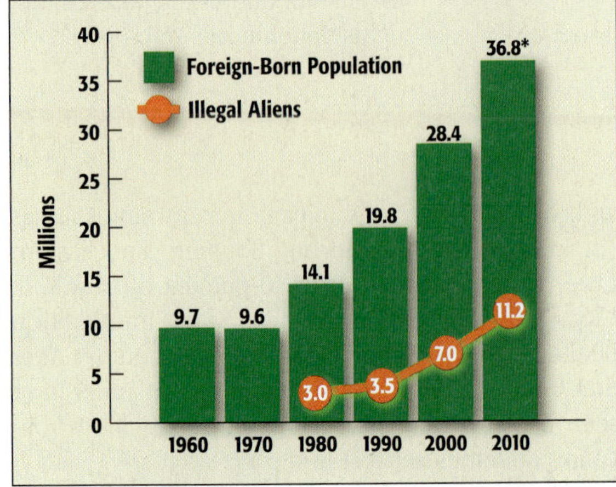

*Authors' estimates.
Source: U.S. Census Bureau, Center for Immigration Studies.

Many contend that the immigrants take jobs from American citizens or hold down wages for such jobs. The 1986 immigration reform just mentioned (IRCA) was intended to prevent this and made it illegal to hire, recruit, or refer for a fee someone not authorized to work in the country. The federal government—through Immigration and Customs Enforcement officers—conducts random compliance audits, and the federal government has further engaged in enforcement actions against employers who hire illegal immigrants. This section sets out the compliance requirements for companies.

I-9 Employment Verification

To comply with current law (based on the 1986 act), employers must perform **I-9 verifications** for new hires and this includes even those hired as "contractors" or "day workers" if they work under the employer's direct supervision. Form I-9, Employment Eligibility Verification, available from the U.S. Citizenship and Immigration Services,[4] must be completed within three days of the worker's commencement of employment. The three-day period is to allow the employer to verify the documents and the form's accuracy. The I-9 form requires employers to review and verify documents establishing the prospective worker's identity and eligibility for employment in the United States. Acceptable documents include a U.S. passport establishing a person's citizenship or others, such as a Permanent Resident Card or Alien Registration Receipt Card, that authorize a foreign citizen to work in the country.

The employer must attest, under penalty of perjury, that an employee produced documents establishing his or her identity and legal employability. The employee must state that he or she is a U.S. citizen or otherwise authorized to work in the United States. The employer is the party legally responsible for any problems with the I-9 verification process. Companies need to establish compliance procedures and keep completed I-9 forms on file for at least three years for potential future government inspection.

The 1986 act only prohibits "knowing" violations, but these include cases in which an employer "should have known" that the worker was unauthorized. Good

4. The U.S. Citizenship and Immigration Services is a federal agency that is part of the U.S. Department of Homeland Security.

faith is a defense under the statute, and employers are legally entitled to rely on documentation of authorization to work that reasonably appears on its face to be genuine, even if it is later established to be counterfeit. Good faith is not a defense, however, to the failure to possess the proper paperwork. Moreover, if an employer subsequently learns that an employee is not authorized to work in this country, it must promptly discharge that employee or be in violation of the law.

EXHIBIT 22–2 • Worksite Enforcement Arrests by the U.S. Immigration and Customs Enforcement

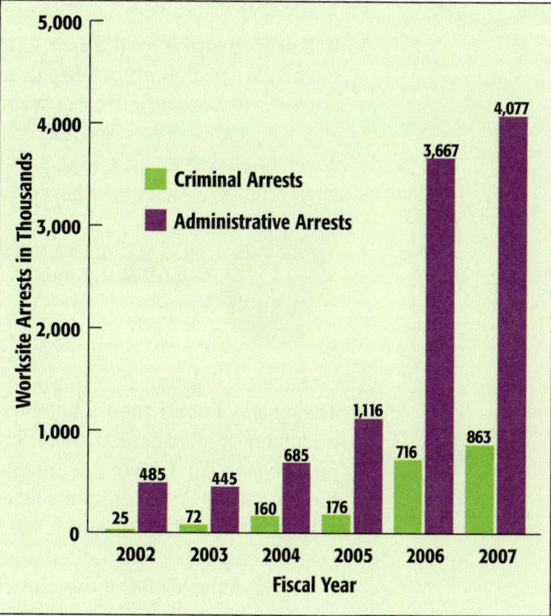

Source: U.S. Immigration and Customs Enforcement, 2008.

Enforcement

The U.S. Immigration and Customs Enforcement (ICE) was established in 2003 as the largest investigative arm of the U.S. Department of Homeland Security. ICE has a General Inspection Program that conducts random compliance audits. Other audits may occur after the agency receives a written complaint alleging an employer's violations. Government inspections involve a review of an employer's file of I-9 forms. The government need not obtain a subpoena or a warrant to conduct such an inspection.

Administrative Actions After investigation and discovery of a possible violation, ICE will bring an administrative action and issue a Notice of Intent to Fine, which sets out the charges against the employer. The employer has a right to a hearing on the enforcement action, if it files a request within thirty days. This hearing is conducted before an *administrative law judge* (see Chapter 6), and the employer has a right to counsel and to *discovery* (see Chapter 2). The typical defense in such actions is good faith or substantial compliance with the documentation provisions.

In past years, the threat of enforcement was regarded as minimal, but the federal government has substantially increased its enforcement activities. This is demonstrated by ICE data presented in Exhibit 22–2. In 2007, ICE raided and identified hundreds of illegal workers at plants owned by companies including Koch Foods, Fresh Del Monte Produce, Tarrasco Steel, and Jones Industrial Network.

Criminal Actions ICE has increasingly sought criminal punishment for acts such as harboring an alien or illegally inducing illegal immigration. In January 2008, an employee of George's Processing, Inc., was convicted by a Missouri federal jury after an ICE raid resulted in the arrest of 136 illegal aliens at the plant. The convicted management employee was in the human resources department of the company and was involved in the hiring process. Evidence suggested that she helped applicants complete their I-9 forms, with knowledge that they had fraudulently obtained identity documents. The potential penalty for this crime is ten years in prison without parole.

A company may present a defense demonstrating that the employee alleged to be in violation was truly an independent contractor rather than an employee and therefore not subject to the I-9 requirements. Even for independent contractors, though, a party's actual knowledge that a worker was unauthorized is illegal. Ultimately, the administrative law judge reviewing the case makes a ruling and assesses penalties if he or she finds a violation. This hearing may be appealed administratively or to a federal court.

Individuals who believe they have suffered as a result of illegal hiring have no direct cause of action to sue an employer under current law. They may sue under the Racketeer Influenced and Corrupt Organizations Act (RICO), though, using the violations as a predicate illegal act.[5] The following case illustrates such an action.

5. RICO was discussed in Chapter 7.

CASE 22.1 Trollinger v. Tyson Foods, Inc.

United States District Court, Eastern District of Tennessee, 2007. ___ F.Supp.2d ___.

• **Background and Facts** Tyson Foods, Inc., is one of the nation's largest poultry processors, with more than 100,000 employees. One of its plants was located in Shelbyville, Tennessee. In December 2001, Tyson was indicted for conspiring to smuggle illegal aliens into the country and employ them. Soon after the indictment was filed, four former workers at the Shelbyville facility filed this action against Tyson under the Racketeer Influenced and Corrupt Organizations Act (RICO), alleging that Tyson engaged in an illegal scheme to depress wages by hiring illegal immigrants. Tyson moved to dismiss the complaint.

IN THE LANGUAGE OF THE COURT
COLLIER, J. [Judge]

* * * *

* * * The Complaint alleges Defendants engaged in a long-term pattern and practice of violating [the Immigration Reform and Control Act]. * * * The Complaint states Tyson signs Employment Eligibility Verification Forms (I-9 forms) in mass quantities before any documents are inspected, more than three days after new hires have been employed, and based on a review of copies of documents rather than reviewing the original documents. The Complaint further alleges Tyson prohibits its employees from taking into account obvious facts which indicate that documents do not relate to the people tendering them; rehires persons whom it previously hired under different names, usually after a short absence; hires workers who appear decades younger than the pictures on their stolen identity documents; uses temporary employment placement services to hire illegal immigrants and then "loan" them to Tyson for a fee; and gives employees leave to "get good documents" after Tyson learns the initial documents submitted by the illegal alien actually belong to someone else.

* * * *

In the context of the present illegal immigration problem in the United States, it is widely, if not universally, known that illegal immigration from Mexico is done in substantial part through smuggling. It is also of note that Tyson's processing plants are all located in areas where the predominant illegal alien population is from Mexico. *This knowledge along with the above allegations satisfies the requirement that the Complaint alleges Defendants had a subjective belief that large numbers of its illegal alien employees had been brought into the United States illegally.* [Emphasis added.]

• **Decision and Remedy** *The court denied Tyson's motion to dismiss the complaint.*

• **What If the Facts Were Different?** *Assume that Tyson's human resource managers were acting on their own, in clear violation of that company's written employment policy. Would the judge have ruled differently? Why or why not?*

• **The Global Dimension** *Many businesses in U.S. communities near the border with Mexico rely on the purchasing power of immigrants, both legal and illegal. What incentives, if any, do these businesses have in helping enforce U.S. immigration laws?*

Penalties

In general, the federal government (through ICE) enforces the current immigration laws. An employer who violates the law by hiring an unauthorized alien is subject to substantial penalties. A first offense can result in a civil fine of up to $2,200 for each unauthorized employee. Fines rise to $5,000 per employee for a second offense and up to $11,000 for subsequent offenses by the same employer. Criminal penalties apply to employers who have engaged in a "pattern or practice of violations," and these penalties include additional fines and imprisonment. A company may also be barred from future government contracts for violations.

ICE regulations provide a list of circumstances that may warrant the mitigation or aggravation of penalties. Considerations include whether the company is a small business and the relative cooperation of the employer in the investigation. In determining the amount of the penalty, ICE also considers the seriousness of the violation (such as intentional falsification of documents) and the employer's past compliance.

Anti-Discrimination Provisions

The passage of the Immigration Reform and Control Act (ICRA) led to concerns about discrimination based on national origin. Some employers reportedly refused to hire Latinos out of concern for violating the statute. Amendments to the act established prohibitions on unfair immigration-related employment practices. The ICRA now provides that it is an unfair immigration-related practice for an employer to discriminate against any individual (other than an unauthorized alien) with respect to hiring or discharging the individual from employment.[6] Companies must exercise reasonable care to evaluate the required I-9 documents in a fair and consistent manner. They may not require greater proof from some prospective employees or reject apparently sufficient documentation of work authorization or citizenship.

A prospective employee who believes that he or she has been subject to discrimination may file a charge with the Office of Special Counsel for Immigration Related Unfair Employment Practices (OSC). The OSC investigates the charge and may file a complaint with an administrative law judge if it finds the complaint has merit. If the OSC fails to file such a complaint within 120 days, the private party may bring a private action for discrimination. The standards and procedures for evaluating the action parallel those of Title VII of the Civil Rights Act, which was discussed in Chapter 21.

Law and Legal Immigration

The immigration laws of this country are very elaborate, and individuals can seek authorization to enter the country under numerous different authorities. These include provisions for refugees who can demonstrate certain persecution from their home country's government. This section focuses on the rules for those who immigrate in order to work in the United States. U.S. businesses can benefit from hiring immigrants who have abilities surpassing those of available domestic workers. Our immigration laws have long made provisions for businesses to hire especially qualified foreign workers. The Immigration Act of 1990 placed caps on the number of visas (entry permits) that can be issued to immigrants each year.

Most temporary visas are set aside for workers who can be characterized as "persons of extraordinary ability," members of the professions holding advanced degrees, or other skilled workers and professionals. To hire these individuals, employers must submit a petition with the Citizenship and Immigration Services, which determines whether the job candidate meets the legal standards. Each visa is for a specific job, and there are legal limits on the employee's ability to switch jobs once in the United States.

Self-Authorized Immigrant Job Candidates

A company seeking to hire a noncitizen worker may do so, if the worker is self-authorized. This means that the worker is either (a) a lawful permanent resident or (b) has a valid temporary Employment Authorization Document (EAD). Lawful permanent residents can prove their status to an employer by presenting an **I-551 Alien Registration Receipt,** known as a "green card," or a properly stamped foreign passport.

When an Immigrant Is Not Self-Authorized

Many workers are not already self-authorized, though, and employers may obtain a labor certification, or green card, for those immigrants whom they wish to hire. Fifty thousand new green card immigrants are authorized each year. To take advantage of this authority, the job must be for a permanent, full-time position.

To gain such authorization for hiring a foreign worker, the employer must show that no American worker is qualified, willing, and able to take the job. This requires publication of the bona fide job opening in suitable newspapers or professional journals within six months of the hiring action. The government has detailed regulations governing the nature of this publication.[7] Any U.S. applicants must be interviewed and

6. 8 U.S.C. Section 1324b.

7. The most relevant regulations can be found at 20 C.F.R. 655 (for temporary employment) and 20 C.F.R. 656 (for permanent employment).

hired for the position if they meet its stated qualifications. The qualifications are also evaluated for their business necessity. A group of administrative law judges rejected one company's notice for hiring kitchen supervisors, because the company required that the applicants speak Spanish.[8]

The employer must also determine from a state agency what the "prevailing wage" for the position is in the location and must offer the immigrating worker at least 100 percent of that prevailing wage. The prevailing wage rate is defined as the average wage paid to similarly employed workers in the requested occupation in the area of intended employment. Fringe benefits are also considered in this calculation.

A separate authorization system provides for the temporary entry and hiring of nonimmigrant visa workers. These are individuals who enter the country for a period of time and who are restricted to an activity consistent with their visas. Applicants must express an intention to depart the country at the expiration of their requested stay, though they may apply for an extension of the stay.

The H-1B Visa Program The most common and controversial visa program today involves the H-1B visa system. These individuals may stay and work in the country for three to six years and work only for the sponsoring employer. The recipients of these visas include many high-tech workers. Sixty-five thousand slots for new immigrants were set aside for H-1B visas; the number was temporarily increased to 195,000, but that law expired and the cap returned to 65,000 in 2004. The available slots go quickly, and many businesses, such as Microsoft, have lobbied Congress to expand the number of H1-B visas offered to immigrants. In recent years, the total allotment of H1-B visas has been filled within the first few weeks of the year, leaving no slots available for the remaining eleven months.

The criteria for such a visa include the potential employee's "specialty occupation," which is defined as having highly specialized knowledge and the attainment of a bachelor's or higher degree or its equivalent. Qualifying jobs may include computer programmers, electronics specialists, complex business managers, engineers, professionals, and other jobs. In one 2006 ruling, ICE found that the position of "accountant" did not qualify as a specialty occupation because the American Council for Accountancy and Taxation did not require a degree for an individual to be credentialed as such.

Labor Certification Before an employer can submit an H-1B application, it must obtain a Labor Certification application filed on a form known as ETA 9035. The employer must agree to provide a wage level at least equal to those offered to other individuals with similar experience and qualifications and attest that the hiring will not adversely affect other workers similarly employed. The employer must inform U.S. workers of the intent to hire a foreign worker by posting the form. The U.S. Department of Labor reviews the applications and may reject them for incompleteness or inaccuracies.

In 2002, a former employee of Sun Microsystems complained to the Justice Department that the company was discriminating against American workers in favor of H-1B visa holders. Sun had laid off nearly 4,000 domestic workers while applying for thousands of temporary visa employees. The court ultimately found that Sun had violated only minor technical requirements and ordered it only to change its posting practices for applicants for open positions.

H-2, O, L, and E Visas Other specialty temporary nonimmigrant visas are available for other categories of employees. H-2 visas provide for workers performing agricultural labor of a seasonal nature. O visas provide entry for persons who have "extraordinary ability in the sciences, arts, education, business or athletics which has been demonstrated by sustained national or international acclaim." L visas allow companies to bring some of their foreign managers or executives to work inside the country. E visas permit the entry of certain foreign investors or entrepreneurs.

Immigration Reform on the Horizon

For many years, the president, members of Congress, business owners, and citizens have debated proposals for immigration reform. Some of the proposals would have allowed illegal immigrants to remain legally in this country and would have allowed many of them to eventually become citizens. At the other extreme, anti-immigration proposals would have required all illegal immigrants to leave this country and go through the full procedures for obtaining a legal way to return in order to work. At the writing of this edition, too many factors were at play to predict what immigration reform would look like in the years to come.

8. *In the matter of Malnati Organization, Inc.*, 2007-INA-00035 (Bd. Alien Lab. Cert. App. 2007).

One thing is certain: problems with immigration will remain. The average wage differential between Mexico and the United States is more than 400 percent. This wage differential is larger than between any other two countries in the world that share a contiguous border. Thus, the incentives facing those south of the border will remain the same until economic growth in Mexico (and other Latin American countries) boosts average wage rates to be closer to those in the United States.

SECTION 2 Federal Labor Laws

Federal labor laws governing union-employer relations have developed considerably since the first law was enacted in 1932. Initially, the laws were concerned with protecting the rights and interests of workers. Subsequent legislation placed some restraints on unions and granted rights to employers. We look here at four major federal statutes regulating union-employer relations.

Norris-LaGuardia Act

Congress protected peaceful strikes, picketing, and boycotts in 1932 in the Norris-LaGuardia Act.[9] The statute restricted the power of federal courts to issue injunctions against unions engaged in peaceful strikes. In effect, this act declared a national policy permitting employees to organize.

National Labor Relations Act

One of the foremost statutes regulating labor is the National Labor Relations Act (NLRA) of 1935.[10] The purpose of the NLRA was to secure for employees the rights to organize; to bargain collectively through representatives of their own choosing; and to engage in concerted activities for organizing, collective bargaining, and other purposes. The NLRA specifically defined a number of employer practices as unfair to labor:

1. Interference with the efforts of employees to form, join, or assist labor organizations or to engage in concerted activities for their mutual aid or protection.
2. An employer's domination of a labor organization or contribution of financial or other support to it.
3. Discrimination in the hiring of or the awarding of tenure to employees for reason of union affiliation.
4. Discrimination against employees for filing charges under the act or giving testimony under the act.
5. Refusal to bargain collectively with the duly designated representative of the employees.

To ensure that employees' rights would be protected, the NLRA established the National Labor Relations Board (NLRB). The NLRB has the authority to investigate employees' charges of unfair labor practices and to file complaints against employers in response to these charges. When violations are found, the NLRB may also issue **cease-and-desist orders**—orders compelling employers to stop engaging in the unfair practices. Cease-and-desist orders can be enforced by a federal appellate court if necessary. Disputes over alleged unfair labor practices are first decided by the NLRB and may then be appealed to a federal court.

To be protected under the NLRA, an individual must be an employee or a job applicant (otherwise, the NLRA's ban on discrimination in regard to hiring would mean little). Additionally, the United States Supreme Court has held that individuals who are hired by a union to organize a company (union organizers) are to be considered employees of the company for NLRA purposes.[11]

Labor-Management Relations Act

The Labor-Management Relations Act (LMRA) of 1947[12] was passed to proscribe certain unfair union practices, such as the *closed shop*. A **closed shop** is a firm that requires union membership by its workers as a condition of employment. Although the act made the closed shop illegal, it preserved the legality of the union shop. A **union shop** is a firm that does not require union membership as a prerequisite for employment but can, and usually does, require that workers join the union after a specified amount of time on the job.

The LMRA also prohibited unions from refusing to bargain with employers, engaging in certain types of picketing, and *featherbedding* (causing employers to hire more employees than necessary). In addition, the act allowed individual states to pass their own **right-to-work laws**—laws making it illegal for

9. 29 U.S.C. Sections 101–110, 113–115.
10. 20 U.S.C. Sections 151–169.
11. *NLRB v. Town & Country Electric, Inc.*, 516 U.S. 85, 116 S.Ct. 450, 133 L.Ed.2d 371 (1995).
12. 29 U.S.C. Sections 141 *et seq.*

union membership to be required for *continued* employment in any establishment. Thus, union shops are technically illegal in the twenty-two states that have right-to-work laws.

Labor-Management Reporting and Disclosure Act

The Labor-Management Reporting and Disclosure Act (LMRDA) of 1959[13] established an employee bill of rights and reporting requirements for union activities. The act strictly regulates unions' internal business procedures, including elections. For example, the LMRDA requires unions to hold regularly scheduled elections of officers using secret ballots. Former convicts are prohibited from holding union office. Moreover, union officials are accountable for union property and funds. Members have the right to attend and to participate in union meetings, to nominate officers, and to vote in most union proceedings.

The act also outlawed *hot-cargo agreements* and *secondary boycotts,* as will be discussed later in this chapter.

Coverage and Procedures

Coverage of the federal labor laws is broad and extends to all employers whose business activity either involves or affects interstate commerce. Some workers are specifically excluded from these laws. Railroads and airlines are not covered by the NLRA but are covered by a separate act, the Railway Labor Act, which closely parallels the NLRA. Other types of workers, such as agricultural workers and domestic servants, are excluded from the NLRA and have no coverage under separate legislation.

When a union or employee believes that the employer has violated federal labor law (or vice versa), the union or employee files a charge with a regional office of the NLRB. The form for an employee to use to file an unfair labor practice charge against an employer is shown in Exhibit 22–3. The charge is investigated, and if it is found worthy, the regional director files a complaint. An administrative law judge (ALJ) initially hears the complaint and rules on it (see Chapter 6). The board reviews the ALJ's findings and decision. If the NLRB finds a violation, it may issue remedial orders (including requiring rehiring of discharged workers). The NLRB decision may be appealed to a U.S. court of appeals.

13. 29 U.S.C. Sections 401 *et seq.*

The Decision to Form or Select a Union

The key starting point for labor relations law is the decision by a company's employees to form a union, which is usually referred to in the law as their bargaining representative. Many workplaces have no union, and workers bargain individually with the employer. If the workers decide that they want the added power of collective union representation, they must follow certain steps to have a union certified. Usually, the employer will resist these efforts to unionize.

Preliminary Organizing

Suppose that a national union, such as the Communication Workers of America (CWA), wants to organize workers who produce semiconductor chips. The union would visit a manufacturing plant of a company—SemiCo in this example. If some SemiCo workers are interested in joining the union, they must begin organizing. An essential part of the process is to decide exactly which workers will be covered in the planned union. Will all manufacturing workers be covered or just those engaged in a single stage in the manufacturing process?

The first step in forming a union is to get the relevant workers to sign **authorization cards.** These cards usually state that the worker desires to have a certain union, such as the CWA, represent the workforce. If a majority of the workers sign authorization cards, the organizers can present the cards to the employer and ask for formal recognition of the union. The employer is not required to recognize the union at this point, but it may do so voluntarily on a showing of majority support. (Under legislation that was proposed in 2007, the employer would have been required to recognize the union as soon as a majority of the workers had signed authorization cards—without holding an election, as described next.)[14]

If the employer refuses to voluntarily recognize the union after a majority of the workers sign authorization cards—or if fewer than 50 percent of the workers sign authorization cards—the union organizers can

14. The U.S. House of Representatives passed the Employee Free Choice Act, also known as the Card Check Bill (H.R. 800), in March 2007, but the bill (S 1041) was defeated in the U.S. Senate in June 2007. Because this pro-labor measure enjoyed wide support, similar legislation is likely to be proposed in the future.

EXHIBIT 22-3 • Unfair Labor Practice Complaint Form

FORM EXEMPT UNDER 44 U.S.C 3512

FORM NLRB-501
(9-07)

UNITED STATES OF AMERICA
NATIONAL LABOR RELATIONS BOARD
CHARGE AGAINST EMPLOYER

DO NOT WRITE IN THIS SPACE	
Case	Date Filed / /

INSTRUCTIONS:
File an original together with four copies and a copy for each additional charged party named in item 1 with NLRB Regional Director for the region in which the alleged unfair labor practice occurred or is occurring.

1. EMPLOYER AGAINST WHOM CHARGE IS BROUGHT

a. Name of Employer

b. Number of workers employed

c. Address *(Street, city, state, and ZIP code)*

d. Employer Representative

e. Telephone No.
( ) -

Fax No.
( ) -

f. Type of Establishment *(factory, mine, wholesaler, etc.)*

g. Identify principal product or service

h. The above-named employer has engaged in and is engaging in unfair labor practices within the meaning of section 8(a), subsections (1) and *(list subsections)* ______________________ of the National Labor Relations Act, and these unfair labor practices are practices affecting commerce within the meaning of the Act, or these unfair labor practices are unfair practices affecting commerce within the meaning of the Act and the Postal Reorganization Act.

2. Basis of the Charge *(set forth a clear and concise statement of the facts constituting the alleged unfair labor practices)*

3. Full name of party filing charge *(if labor organization, give full name, including local name and number)*

4a. Address *(Street and number, city, state, and ZIP code)*

4b. Telephone No.
( ) -

Fax No.
( ) -

5. Full name of national or international labor organization of which it is an affiliate or constituent unit *(to be filled in when charge is filed by a labor organization)*

6. DECLARATION

I declare that I have read the above charge and that the statements are true to the best of my knowledge and belief.

By ______________________
(signature of representative or person making charge)

____
(Print/type name and title or office, if any)

(fax) ( ) -

Address ______________________ ( ) - ______ / /
(Telephone No.) *(date)*

WILLFUL FALSE STATEMENTS ON THIS CHARGE CAN BE PUNISHED BY FINE AND IMPRISONMENT (U.S. CODE, TITLE 18, SECTION 1001)

PRIVACY ACT STATEMENT

Solicitation of the information on this form is authorized by the National Labor Relations Act (NLRA), 29 U.S.C. § 151 *et seq.* The principal use of the information is to assist the National Labor Relations Board (NLRB) in processing unfair labor practice and related proceedings or litigation. The routine uses for the imformation are fully set forth in the Federal Register, 71 Fed. Reg. 74942-43 (Dec. 13, 2006). The NLRB will further explain these uses upon request. Disclosure of this information to the NLRB is voluntary; however, failure to supply the information will cause the NLRB to decline to invoke its processes.

labor practices. In this situation, the employer may still hire replacements but must give the strikers back their jobs once the strike is over.

Lockouts

Lockouts are the employer's counterpart to the worker's right to strike. A **lockout** occurs when the employer shuts down to prevent employees from working. Lockouts are usually used when the employer believes that a strike is imminent.

Lockouts may be a legal employer response. In the leading Supreme Court case on this issue, a union and an employer had reached a stalemate in collective bargaining. The employer feared that the union would delay a strike until the busy season and thereby cause the employer to suffer more greatly from the strike. The employer called a lockout before the busy season to deny the union this leverage, and the Supreme Court held that this action was legal.[18]

Some lockouts are illegal, however. An employer may not use its lockout weapon as a tool to break the union and pressure employees into decertification. Consequently, an employer must show some economic justification for instituting a lockout.

Section 7 Unfair Labor Practices

The preceding sections have discussed unfair labor practices involved in the significant acts of union elections, collective bargaining, and strikes. Many unfair labor practices may occur within the normal working relationship as well. The most important of these practices are discussed in the following sections. Exhibit 22–4 lists the basic unfair labor practices.

Employer's Refusal to Recognize the Union and to Negotiate

As noted above, once a union has been certified as the exclusive representative of a bargaining unit, an employer must recognize and bargain in good faith with the union over issues affecting all employees who are within the bargaining unit. Failure to do so is an unfair labor practice. Because the National Labor Relations Act embraces a policy of majority rule, certification of the union as the bargaining unit's representative binds *all* of the employees in that bargaining unit. Thus, the union must fairly represent all the members of the bargaining unit.

Certification does not mean that a union will continue indefinitely as the exclusive representative of the bargaining unit. If the union loses the majority support of those it represents, an employer is not obligated to continue recognition of, or negotiation with, the union. As a practical matter, a newly elected representative needs time to establish itself among the workers and to begin to formulate and implement its programs. Therefore, as a matter of labor policy, a union is immune from attack by employers and from repudiation by the employees for a period of one year after certification. During this period, it is *presumed* that the union enjoys majority support among the employees; the employer cannot refuse to deal with the union as the employees' exclusive representative, even if the employees prefer not to be represented by that union.

EXHIBIT 22–4 • Basic Unfair Labor Practices

Employers *It is unfair to . . .*	**Unions** *It is unfair to . . .*
1. Refuse to recognize a union and refuse to bargain in good faith. **2.** Interfere with, restrain, or coerce employees in their efforts to form a union and bargain collectively. **3.** Dominate a union. **4.** Discriminate against union workers. **5.** Punish employees for engaging in concerted activity.	**1.** Refuse to bargain in good faith. **2.** Picket to coerce unionization without the support of a majority of the employees. **3.** Demand the hiring of unnecessary excess workers. **4.** Discriminate against nonunion workers. **5.** Agree to participate in a secondary boycott. **6.** Engage in an illegal strike. **7.** Charge excessive membership fees.

18. *American Ship Building Co. v. NLRB,* 380 U.S. 300, 85 S.Ct. 955, 13 L.Ed.2d 855 (1965).

Beyond the one-year period, the presumption of majority support continues, but it is *rebuttable*. An employer may rebut (attempt to refute) the presumption with objective evidence that a majority of employees do not wish to be represented by the union. If the evidence is sufficient to support a *good faith belief* that the union no longer enjoys majority support among the employees, the employer may refuse to continue to recognize and negotiate with the union.[19]

Employer's Interference in Union Activities

The NLRA declares it to be an unfair labor practice for an employer to interfere with, restrain, or coerce employees in the exercise of their rights to form a union and bargain collectively. Unlawful employer interference may take a variety of forms.

Courts have found it an unfair labor practice for an employer to make threats that may interfere with an employee's decision to join a union. Even asking employees about their views on the union may be considered coercive. Employees responding to such questioning must be able to remain anonymous and must receive assurances against employer reprisals. Employers also may not prohibit certain forms of union activity in the workplace. If an employee has a grievance with the company, the employer cannot prevent the union's participation in support of the employee, for example.

If an employer has unlawfully interfered with the operation of a union, the NLRB or a reviewing court may issue a cease-and-desist order halting the practice. The company typically is required to post the order on a bulletin board and renounce its past unlawful conduct.

Employer's Domination of a Union

In the early days of unionization, employers fought back by forming employer-sponsored unions to represent employees. These "company unions" were seldom more than the puppets of management. The NLRA outlawed company unions and any other form of employer domination of workers' unions.

Under the law against employer domination, an employer can have no say in which employees belong to the union or which employees serve as union officers. Nor may supervisors or other management personnel participate in union meetings.

Company actions that support a union may be considered improper potential domination. For this reason, a company cannot give union workers pay for time spent on union activities, because this is considered undue support for the union. The company may not provide financial aid to a union and may not solicit workers to join a union.

Employer's Discrimination against Union Employees

The NLRA prohibits employers from discriminating against workers because they are union officers or are otherwise associated with a union. When workers must be laid off, the company cannot consider union participation as a criterion for deciding whom to fire.

The provisions prohibiting discrimination also apply to hiring decisions. Suppose that certain employees of SemiCo are represented by a union, but the company is attempting to weaken the union's strength. The company is prohibited from requiring potential new hires to guarantee that they will not join the union.

Discriminatory punishment of union members or officers can be difficult to prove. The company will claim to have good reasons for its action. The NLRB has specified a series of factors to be considered in determining whether an action had an unlawful, discriminatory motivation. These include giving inconsistent reasons for the action, applying rules inconsistently and more strictly against union members, failing to give an expected warning prior to discharge or other discipline, and acting contrary to worker seniority.

The decision to close a facility cannot be made with a discriminatory motive. If a company has several facilities and only one is unionized, the company cannot shut down the union plant simply because of the union. The company could shut down the union plant if it were demonstrably less efficient than the other facilities, however.

Union's Unfair Labor Practices

Certain union activities are declared to be unfair labor practices by the Taft-Hartley Act. Secondary boycotts, discussed above, are one such union unfair labor practice.

Coercion Another significant union unfair labor practice is coercion or restraint on an employee's

19. An employer cannot agree to a collective bargaining agreement and later refuse to abide by it, however, on the ground of a good faith belief that the union did not have majority support when the agreement was negotiated. See *Auciello Iron Works, Inc. v. NLRB*, 517 U.S. 781, 116 S.Ct. 1754, 135 L.Ed.2d 64 (1996).

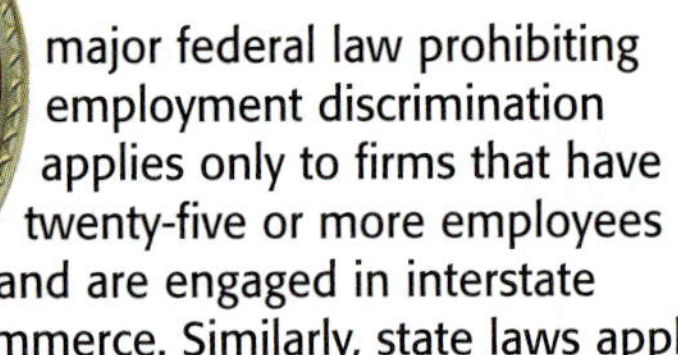

major federal law prohibiting employment discrimination applies only to firms that have twenty-five or more employees and are engaged in interstate commerce. Similarly, state laws apply only to firms with a threshold number of employees, such as eight or ten employees. Even if an employer is subject to such statutes, these laws do not apply to many types of employment disputes, such as whether an employment contract was formed.

Exceptions to the At-Will Doctrine Sometimes, the only hope for plaintiffs in many employment disputes is that a court will make an exception to the at-will doctrine—on the basis of public policy, for example. The public-policy exception, though, remains just that—an exception. Often, courts are reluctant to make such an exception unless it can be justified by a clearly expressed public policy.

DISCUSSION QUESTIONS

1. How much obedience and loyalty does an agent-employee owe a principal-employer? What if the employer engages in an activity—or requests that the employee engage in an activity—that violates the employee's ethical standards but does not necessarily violate any public policy or law? In such a situation, does an employee's duty to abide by her or his own ethical standards override the employee's duty of loyalty to the employer?
2. When an agent acts in violation of his or her ethical or legal duty to the principal, should that action terminate the agent's authority to act on behalf of the principal? Why or why not?
3. If an agent injures a third party during the course of employment, under the doctrine of *respondeat superior,* the employer may be held liable for the agent's actions even though the employer did not authorize the action and was not even aware of it. Do you think that it is fair to hold employers liable in such situations? Do you think that it would be more equitable to hold that the employee alone should bear the responsibility for his or her tortious (legally wrongful) actions to third parties, even when the actions are committed within the scope of employment?

UNIT SIX

The Regulatory Environment

CONTENTS

CHAPTER 23

Consumer Protection

All statutes, agency rules, and common law judicial decisions that serve to protect the interests of consumers are classified as **consumer law.** Traditionally, in disputes involving consumers, it was assumed that the freedom to contract carried with it the obligation to live by the deal made. Over time, this attitude has changed considerably. Today, myriad federal and state laws protect consumers from unfair trade practices, unsafe products, discriminatory or unreasonable credit requirements, and other problems related to consumer transactions. Nearly every agency and department of the federal government has an office of consumer affairs, and most states have one or more such offices to help consumers. Also, typically the attorney general's office assists consumers at the state level.

In this chapter, we examine some of the major laws and regulations protecting consumers. Because of the wide variation among state consumer protection laws, our primary focus in this chapter is on federal legislation. Realize, though, that state laws often provide more sweeping and significant protections for the consumer than do federal laws. Exhibit 23–1 indicates many of the areas of consumer law that are regulated by federal statutes.

Deceptive Advertising

One of the earliest federal consumer protection laws—and still one of the most important—was the Federal Trade Commission Act of 1914 (mentioned in Chapter 6).[1] The act created the Federal Trade Commission (FTC) to carry out the broadly stated goal of preventing unfair and deceptive trade practices, including deceptive advertising.[2]

1. 15 U.S.C. Sections 41–58.
2. 15 U.S.C. Section 45.

EXHIBIT 23–1 • Selected Areas of Consumer Law Regulated by Statutes

CONSUMER LAW

Advertising	*Example*—The Federal Trade Commission Act of 1914
Labeling and Packaging	*Example*—The Fair Packaging and Labeling Act of 1966
Sales	*Example*—The FTC Mail-Order Rule of 1975
Food and Drugs	*Example*—The Federal Food, Drug and Cosmetic Act of 1938
Product Safety	*Example*—The Consumer Product Safety Act of 1972
Credit Protection	*Example*—The Consumer Credit Protection Act of 1968

Generally, **deceptive advertising** occurs if a reasonable consumer would be misled by the advertising claim. Vague generalities and obvious exaggerations are permissible. These claims are known as *puffery*. When a claim takes on the appearance of literal authenticity, however, it may create problems. Advertising that *appears* to be based on factual evidence but in fact is not reasonably supported by some evidence will be deemed deceptive.

Some advertisements contain "half-truths," meaning that the presented information is true but incomplete and therefore leads consumers to a false conclusion. For example, the makers of Campbell's soups advertised that "most" Campbell's soups were low in fat and cholesterol and thus were helpful in fighting heart disease. What the ad did not say was that Campbell's soups are high in sodium, and high-sodium diets may increase the risk of heart disease. The FTC ruled that Campbell's claims were thus deceptive. Advertising that contains an endorsement by a celebrity may be deemed deceptive if the celebrity does not actually use the product.

In the following case brought by the FTC, *WIRED* magazine had already put the product in question on its list of top ten "Snake-Oil Gadgets."

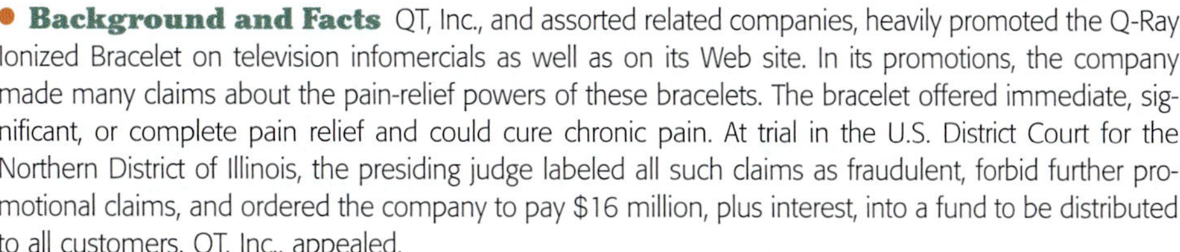

CASE 23.1 Federal Trade Commission v. QT, Inc.

United States Court of Appeals, Seventh Circuit, 2008. 512 F.3d 858.
www.ca7.uscourts.gov[a]

Background and Facts QT, Inc., and assorted related companies, heavily promoted the Q-Ray Ionized Bracelet on television infomercials as well as on its Web site. In its promotions, the company made many claims about the pain-relief powers of these bracelets. The bracelet offered immediate, significant, or complete pain relief and could cure chronic pain. At trial in the U.S. District Court for the Northern District of Illinois, the presiding judge labeled all such claims as fraudulent, forbid further promotional claims, and ordered the company to pay $16 million, plus interest, into a fund to be distributed to all customers. QT, Inc., appealed.

IN THE LANGUAGE OF THE COURT
***EASTERBROOK,* Chief Judge.**

* * * According to the district court's findings, almost everything that defendants have said about the bracelet is false. Here are some highlights:

- Defendants promoted the bracelet as a miraculous cure for chronic pain, but it has no therapeutic effect.
- Defendants told consumers that claims of "immediate, significant or complete pain relief" had been "test-proven"; they hadn't.

* * * *

- Defendants represented that the therapeutic effect wears off in a year or two, despite knowing that the bracelet's properties do not change. This assertion is designed to lead customers to buy new bracelets. Likewise the false statement that the bracelet has a "memory cycle specific to each individual wearer" so that only the bracelet's original wearer can experience pain relief is designed to increase sales by eliminating the second-hand market and "explaining" the otherwise-embarrassing fact that the buyer's friends and neighbors can't perceive any effect.

The magistrate judge [the judge presiding over the trial] did not commit a clear error, or abuse his discretion, in concluding that the defendants set out to bilk unsophisticated persons who found themselves in pain from arthritis and other chronic conditions.

Defendants maintain that the magistrate judge subjected their statements to an excessively rigorous standard of proof.

a. In the box for the case number, type "07" and "1662" and then click on "List Case." Follow the links to access the opinion. The U.S. Court of Appeals for the Seventh Circuit maintains this Web site.

CASE CONTINUES

CASE 23.1 CONTINUED

* * * *The Federal Trade Commission Act forbids false and misleading statements, and a statement that is plausible but has not been tested in the most reliable way cannot be condemned out of hand.* [Emphasis added.]

* * * For the Q-Ray Ionized Bracelet, * * * all statements about how the product works—Q-Rays, ionization, enhancing the flow of bio-energy, and the like—are blather. Defendants might as well have said: "Beneficent creatures from the 17th Dimension use this bracelet as a beacon to locate people who need pain relief, and whisk them off to their homeworld every night to provide help in ways unknown to our science."

* * * *Proof is what separates an effect new to science from a swindle.* Defendants themselves told customers that the bracelet's efficacy had been "test-proven"; * * * but defendants have no proof of the Q-Ray Ionized Bracelet's efficacy. The "tests" on which they relied were bunk. * * * What remain are testimonials, which are not a form of proof * * *. That's why the "testimonial" of someone who keeps elephants off the streets of a large city by snapping his fingers is the basis of a joke rather than proof of cause and effect. [Emphasis added.]

* * * *

Physicians know how to treat pain. Why pay $200 for a Q-Ray Ionized Bracelet when you can get relief from an aspirin tablet that costs 1¢?

- **Decision and Remedy** *The U.S. Court of Appeals for the Seventh Circuit affirmed the district court's decision. QT, Inc., was required to stop its deceptive advertising and to pay the $16 million, plus interest, so that its customers could be reimbursed.*

- **What If the Facts Were Different?** *Assume that the defendant had actually done scientific studies, but they were inconclusive. How might the judge have ruled in that situation?*

- **The Ethical Dimension** *Most people have seen infomercials. Do the fraudulent promotional claims of QT, Inc., in such infomercials mean that all products "pitched" on television are suspect? Why or why not?*

Bait-and-Switch Advertising

The FTC has issued rules that govern specific advertising techniques. One of the most important rules is contained in the FTC's "Guides Against Bait Advertising,"[3] issued in 1968. The rule seeks to prevent **bait-and-switch advertising—**that is, advertising a very low price for a particular item that will likely be unavailable to the consumer, who will then be encouraged to purchase a more expensive item. The low price is the "bait" to lure the consumer into the store. The salesperson is instructed to "switch" the consumer to a different, more expensive item. Under the FTC guidelines, bait-and-switch advertising occurs if the seller refuses to show the advertised item, fails to have a reasonable quantity of the item in stock, fails to promise to deliver the advertised item within a reasonable time, or discourages employees from selling the item.

Online Deceptive Advertising

Deceptive advertising may occur in the online environment as well. The FTC has been quite active in monitoring online advertising and has identified hundreds of Web sites that have made false or deceptive advertising claims for products ranging from medical treatments for various diseases to exercise equipment and weight-loss aids.

The FTC has issued guidelines to help online businesses comply with existing laws prohibiting deceptive advertising.[4] These guidelines include three basic requirements. First, all ads—both online and offline—must be truthful and not misleading. Second, any claims made in an ad must be substantiated; that is, advertisers must have evidence to back up their claims. Third, ads cannot be "unfair," which the FTC defines as "caus[ing] or . . . likely to cause substantial consumer injury that consumers could not reasonably avoid and that is not outweighed by the benefit to consumers or competition."

The guidelines also call for "clear and conspicuous" disclosure of any qualifying or limiting information. The FTC suggests that advertisers should assume that consumers will not read an entire Web page. Therefore, to satisfy the "clear and conspicuous" requirement, online advertisers should place the dis-

3. 16 C.F.R. Part 238.

4. *Advertising and Marketing on the Internet: Rules of the Road,* September 2000.

closure as close as possible to the claim being qualified or include the disclosure within the claim itself. If such placement is not feasible, the next-best location is on a section of the page to which a consumer can easily scroll. Generally, hyperlinks to a disclosure are recommended only for lengthy disclosures or for disclosures that must be repeated in a variety of locations on the Web page.

FTC Actions against Deceptive Advertising

The FTC receives complaints from many sources, including competitors of alleged violators, consumers, consumer organizations, trade associations, Better Business Bureaus, government organizations, and state and local officials. When the agency receives numerous and widespread complaints about a particular problem, it will investigate. If the FTC concludes that a given advertisement is unfair or deceptive, it drafts a formal complaint, which is sent to the alleged offender. The company may agree to settle the complaint without further proceedings; if not, the FTC can conduct a hearing in which the company can present its defense (see Chapter 6).

If the FTC succeeds in proving that an advertisement is unfair or deceptive, it usually issues a **cease-and-desist order** requiring the company to stop the challenged advertising. It might also impose a sanction known as **counteradvertising** by requiring the company to advertise anew—in print, on the Internet, on radio, and on television—to inform the public about the earlier misinformation. The FTC may institute **multiple product orders,** which require a firm to cease and desist from false advertising in regard to all of its products, not just the product that was the subject of the action.

In some instances, the FTC may seek other remedies. In the following case, for example, after receiving more than five hundred consumer complaints, the FTC sought restitution of the amounts that the consumers had paid.

EXTENDED CASE 23.2

Federal Trade Commission v. Verity International, Ltd.

United States Court of Appeals, Second Circuit, 2006. 443 F.3d 48.

***JOHN M. WALKER, JR.*, Chief Judge.**

The incessant demand for pornography, some have said, is an engine of technological development. The telephonic system at dispute in this appeal is an example of that phenomenon—it was designed and implemented to ensure that consumers paid charges for accessing pornography and other adult entertainment. The system identified the user of an online adult-entertainment service by the telephone line used to access that service and then billed the telephone-line subscriber for the cost of that service as if it was a charge for an international phone call to Madagascar. This system had the benefit that the user's credit card never had to be processed, but it had a problem as well: It was possible for someone to access an adult-entertainment service over a telephone line without authorization from the telephone-line subscriber who understood herself contractually bound to pay all telephone charges, including those that disguised fees for the adult entertainment.

The Federal Trade Commission ("FTC") took a dim view of this billing system and brought suit [in a federal district court] to shut it down as a deceptive and unfair trade practice within the meaning of [Section] 5(a)(1) of the Federal Trade Commission Act ("FTC Act"). The FTC sued Verity International, Ltd. ("Verity") and Automatic Communications, Ltd. ("ACL"), corporations that operated this billing system, as well as Robert Green and Marilyn Shein, who controlled these corporations.

* * * *

* * * [The] court entered * * * [a judgment] against the defendants-appellants for a total of $17.9 million. * * * The defendants-appellants timely appealed * * * [to the U.S. Court of Appeals for the Second Circuit].

* * * *

* * * *To prove a deceptive act or practice under [Section] 5(a)(1) [of the FTC Act], the FTC must show three elements: (1) a representation, omission, or practice, that (2) is likely to mislead consumers acting reasonably under the circumstances, and [that] (3)* * * * *is material.* [Emphasis added.]

CASE CONTINUES

CASE 23.2 CONTINUED

The FTC contends that the first element is satisfied by proof that the defendants-appellants caused telephone-line subscribers to receive explicit and implicit representations that they could not successfully avoid paying charges for adult entertainment that had been accessed over their phone lines—what we call a "representation of uncontestability [cannot be disputed]." * * * The defendants-appellants caused charges for adult entertainment to appear on * * * phone bills as telephone calls, thereby capitalizing on the common and well-founded perception held by consumers that they must pay their telephone bills, irrespective of whether they made or authorized the calls. * * * [This] conveyed a representation of uncontestability.

* * * [As for the second element, the] FTC contends that the representation of uncontestability was false and therefore likely to mislead consumers who did not use or authorize others to use the adult entertainment in question; the defendants-appellants contend that the representation was rendered true by * * * agency principles.

*Under common law agency principles, a person is liable to pay for services that she does not herself contract for if another person has * * * authority to consent on her behalf to pay for the services.* [Emphasis added.]

* * * [But a] computer * * * is not primarily understood as a payment mechanism, and in the ordinary habits of human behavior, one does not reasonably infer that because a person is authorized to use a computer, the subscriber to the telephone line connected to that computer has authorized the computer user to purchase online content * * * .

* * * The FTC proved the second element of its * * * claim.

Finally [with respect to the third element] * * * telephone-line subscribers found the representation material to their decision whether to pay the billed charges because of the worry of telephone-line disconnection, the perception of the futility of challenging the charges, the desire to avoid credit-score injury, or some combination of these factors.

* * * *

The district court measured the appropriate amount of [the judgment] as "the full amount lost by consumers." This was error. The appropriate measure * * * is the benefit unjustly received by the defendants.

* * * *

* * * [Phone service providers] received some fraction of the money * * * before any payments were made to the defendants-appellants.

* * * *

* * * [Also] some fraction of consumers * * * actually used or authorized others to use the services at issue * * * .

* * * *

We affirm all components of the district court's * * * order of relief except for the monetary judgment * * * . The case is remanded to the district court for further proceedings consistent with this opinion.

QUESTIONS

1. How might the defendants have avoided the charges against them in this case?
2. As an administrative agency, what powers might the FTC use to determine more precisely the number of consumers who paid their phone bills but did not use, or authorize others to use, the defendants' services?

Telemarketing and Electronic Advertising

The Telephone Consumer Protection Act (TCPA)[5] prohibits telephone solicitation using an automatic telephone dialing system or a prerecorded voice. Most states also have statutes regulating telephone solicitation. The TCPA also makes it illegal to transmit ads via fax without first obtaining the recipient's permission. (Similar issues have arisen with respect to junk e-mail, called *spam*—see Chapters 7 and 12.)

The Federal Communications Commission (FCC) enforces the TCPA. The FCC imposes substantial fines

5. 47 U.S.C. Sections 227 *et seq.*

($11,000 each day) on companies that violate the junk fax provisions of the act and has even fined one company as much as $5.4 million.[6] The TCPA also provides for a private right of action under which consumers can recover actual losses resulting from a violation of the act or receive $500 in damages for each violation, whichever is greater. If a court finds that a defendant willfully or knowingly violated the act, the court has the discretion to treble (triple) the amount of damages awarded.

The Telemarketing and Consumer Fraud and Abuse Prevention Act of 1994[7] directed the FTC to establish rules governing telemarketing and to bring actions against fraudulent telemarketers. The FTC's Telemarketing Sales Rule of 1995[8] requires a telemarketer to identify the seller's name, describe the product being sold, and disclose all material facts related to the sale (such as the total cost of the goods being sold). The rule makes it illegal for telemarketers to misrepresent information or facts about their goods or services. A telemarketer must also remove a consumer's name from its list of potential contacts if the customer so requests. An amendment to the Telemarketing Sales Rule established the national Do Not Call Registry, which became effective in October 2003. Telemarketers must refrain from calling those consumers who have placed their names on the list.

SECTION 2 Labeling and Packaging Laws

A number of federal and state laws deal specifically with the information given on labels and packages. In general, labels must be accurate, and they must use words that are easily understood by the ordinary consumer. For example, a box of cereal cannot be labeled "giant" if that would exaggerate the amount of cereal contained in the box.

In some instances, labels must specify the raw materials used in the product, such as the percentage of cotton, nylon, or other fiber used in a garment. In other instances, the product must carry a warning. Cigarette packages and advertising, for example, must include one of several warnings about the health hazards associated with smoking.[9]

Federal Statutes

There are numerous federal laws regulating the labeling and packaging of products. These include the Wool Products Labeling Act of 1939,[10] the Fur Products Labeling Act of 1951,[11] the Flammable Fabrics Act of 1953,[12] and the Fair Packaging and Labeling Act of 1966.[13] The Comprehensive Smokeless Tobacco Health Education Act of 1986,[14] for example, requires that producers, packagers, and importers of smokeless tobacco label their product with one of several warnings about the use of smokeless tobacco.

Food Labeling

Because the quality and safety of food are so important to consumers, several statutes deal specifically with food labeling. The Fair Packaging and Labeling Act requires that food product labels identify (1) the product; (2) the net quantity of the contents and, if the number of servings is stated, the size of the serving; (3) the manufacturer; and (4) the packager or distributor. The act includes additional requirements concerning descriptions on packages, savings claims, components of nonfood products, and standards for the partial filling of packages.

Food products must bear labels detailing the nutritional content, including how much fat the food contains and what kind of fat it is. The Nutrition Labeling and Education Act of 1990[15] requires standard nutrition facts (including fat content) on food labels; regulates the use of such terms as *fresh* and *low fat;* and authorizes certain health claims, subject to the federal Food and Drug Administration's approval. The FTC enforces these rules.

Sales

A number of statutes protect consumers by requiring the disclosure of certain terms in sales transactions and providing rules governing unsolicited merchandise and various forms of sales, such as door-to-door sales, mail-order sales, and referral sales. The FTC has regulatory authority in this area, as do other federal

6. See *Missouri ex rel. Nixon v. American Blast Fax, Inc.*, 323 F.3d 649 (8th Cir. 2003); *cert.* denied, 540 U.S. 1104, 124 S.Ct. 1043, 157 L.Ed.2d 888 (2004).
7. 15 U.S.C. Sections 6101–6108.
8. 16 C.F.R. Sections 310.1–310.8.
9. 15 U.S.C. Sections 1331–1341.
10. 15 U.S.C. Section 68.
11. 15 U.S.C. Section 69.
12. 15 U.S.C. Section 1191.
13. 15 U.S.C. Sections 1451 *et seq.*
14. 15 U.S.C. Sections 4401–4408.
15. 21 U.S.C. Section 343.1.

agencies. The Federal Reserve Board of Governors, for example, has issued **Regulation Z,**[16] which governs credit provisions associated with sales contracts, as discussed later in this chapter.

Many states have also enacted laws governing consumer sales transactions. Moreover, states have protected consumers to a certain extent through adopting the Uniform Commercial Code (discussed in Chapter 11) and, in a few states, the Uniform Consumer Credit Code.

Door-to-Door Sales

Door-to-door sales are singled out for special treatment in the laws of most states, largely because of the potential for high-pressure sales tactics. Repeat purchases are not as likely as they are in stores, so the seller has less incentive to cultivate the goodwill of the purchaser. Furthermore, the seller is unlikely to present alternative products and their prices. Thus, a number of states have passed "cooling-off" laws that permit the buyers of goods sold door to door to cancel their contracts within a specified period of time, usually two to three business days after the sale.

An FTC regulation also requires sellers to give consumers three days to cancel any door-to-door sale, and this rule applies in addition to any state law. The FTC rule further requires that consumers be notified in Spanish of this right if the oral negotiations for the sale were in that language.

Telephone and Mail-Order Sales

The FTC Mail or Telephone Order Merchandise Rule of 1993, which amended the FTC Mail-Order Rule of 1975,[17] provides specific protections for consumers who purchase goods over the phone or through the mail. The 1993 rule extended the 1975 rule to include sales orders transmitted using computers, fax machines, or other means involving a telephone line. Among other things, the rule requires merchants to ship orders within the time promised in their catalogues or advertisements and to notify consumers when orders cannot be shipped on time. Merchants must also issue a refund within a specified period of time when a consumer cancels an order.

In addition, under the Postal Reorganization Act of 1970,[18] a consumer who receives *unsolicited* merchandise sent by U.S. mail can keep it, throw it away, or dispose of it in any manner that she or he sees fit. The recipient will not be obligated to the sender. Suppose that Serena receives a copy of the "Cookbook of the Month" from a company via U.S. mail, even though she did not order the cookbook. She gives it to her friend, Vaya, who loves to cook. The following month, Serena receives a bill for $49.99 from the company that sent the cookbook. Under the 1970 act, because the cookbook was sent to her unsolicited through the U.S. mail, Serena is not obligated to pay the bill.

Online Sales

Protecting consumers from fraudulent and deceptive sales practices conducted via the Internet has proved to be a challenging task. Nonetheless, the FTC and other federal agencies have brought a number of enforcement actions against those who perpetrate online fraud. Additionally, the federal statute prohibiting wire fraud that was discussed in Chapter 7 applies to online transactions.

Some states have amended their consumer protection statutes to cover Internet transactions as well. For example, the California legislature revised its Business and Professions Code to include transactions conducted over the Internet or by "any other electronic means of communication." Previously, that code covered only telephone, mail-order catalogue, radio, and television sales. Now any entity selling over the Internet in California must explicitly create an on-screen notice indicating its refund and return policies, where its business is physically located, its legal name, and a number of other details. Various states are also setting up information sites to help consumers protect themselves.

Credit Protection

Because of the extensive use of credit by American consumers, credit protection has become an especially important area of consumer protection legislation. A key statute regulating the credit and credit-card industries is Title I of the Consumer Credit Protection Act (CCPA),[19] which is commonly referred to as the Truth-in-Lending Act (TILA).

The Truth-in-Lending Act

The TILA is basically a *disclosure law.* It is administered by the Federal Reserve Board and requires sellers and

16. 12 C.F.R. Sections 226.1–226.30.
17. 16 C.F.R. Sections 435.1–435.2.
18. 39 U.S.C. Section 3009.
19. 15 U.S.C. Sections 1601–1693r.

lenders to disclose credit terms or loan terms so that individuals can shop around for the best financing arrangements. TILA requirements apply only to persons who, in the ordinary course of business, lend funds, sell on credit, or arrange for the extension of credit. Thus, sales or loans made between two consumers do not come under the protection of the act. Additionally, this law protects only debtors who are natural persons (as opposed to the artificial "person" of a corporation); it does not extend to other legal entities.

The disclosure requirements are contained in Regulation Z, which was promulgated (publicized) by the Federal Reserve Board. If the contracting parties are subject to the TILA, the requirements of Regulation Z apply to any transaction involving an installment sales contract that calls for payment to be made in more than four installments. Transactions subject to Regulation Z typically include installment loans, retail and installment sales, car loans, home-improvement loans, and certain real estate loans if the amount of financing is less than $25,000.

Under the provisions of the TILA, all of the terms of a credit instrument must be clearly and conspicuously disclosed. The TILA provides for contract rescission (cancellation) if a creditor fails to follow *exactly* the procedures required by the act.[20] TILA requirements are strictly enforced.

Equal Credit Opportunity In 1974, Congress enacted the Equal Credit Opportunity Act (ECOA)[21] as an amendment to the TILA. The ECOA prohibits the denial of credit solely on the basis of race, religion, national origin, color, gender, marital status, or age. The act also prohibits credit discrimination on the basis of whether an individual receives certain forms of income, such as public-assistance benefits.

Under the ECOA, a creditor may not require the signature of an applicant's spouse, other than as a joint applicant, on a credit instrument if the applicant qualifies under the creditor's standards of creditworthiness for the amount and terms of the credit request. For example, Tonja, an African American, applied for financing with a used-car dealer. The dealer looked at Tonja's credit report and, without submitting the application to the lender, decided that she would not qualify. Instead of informing Tonja that she did not qualify, the dealer told her that she needed a cosigner on the loan to purchase the car. According to a federal appellate court, the dealer qualified as a creditor in this situation because the dealer unilaterally denied the credit and thus could be held liable under the ECOA.[22]

Credit-Card Rules The TILA also contains provisions regarding credit cards. One provision limits the liability of a cardholder to $50 per card for unauthorized charges made before the creditor is notified that the card has been lost. Another provision prohibits a credit-card company from billing a consumer for any unauthorized charges if the credit card was improperly issued by the company. Suppose that a consumer receives an unsolicited credit card in the mail and the card is later stolen and used by the thief to make purchases. In this situation, the consumer to whom the card was sent will not be liable for the unauthorized charges.

Other provisions of the act set out specific procedures for both the credit-card company and its cardholder to use in settling disputes related to credit-card purchases. These procedures would be used if, for example, a cardholder thinks that an error has occurred in billing or wishes to withhold payment for a faulty product purchased by credit card.

Consumer Leases The Consumer Leasing Act (CLA) of 1988[23] amended the TILA to provide protection for consumers who lease automobiles and other goods. The CLA applies to those who lease or arrange to lease consumer goods in the ordinary course of their business. The act applies only if the goods are priced at $25,000 or less and if the lease term exceeds four months. The CLA and its implementing regulation, Regulation M,[24] require lessors to disclose in writing (or by electronic record) all of the material terms of the lease.

The Fair Credit Reporting Act

In 1970, to protect consumers against inaccurate credit reporting, Congress enacted the Fair Credit Reporting Act (FCRA).[25] The act provides that consumer credit reporting agencies may issue credit reports to users only for specified purposes, including the extension of credit, the issuance of insurance policies, and compliance with a court order, and in

20. Note, however, that amendments to the TILA enacted in 1995 prevent borrowers from rescinding loans because of minor clerical errors in closing documents [15 U.S.C. Sections 1605, 1631, 1635, 1640, and 1641].
21. 15 U.S.C. Sections 1691–1691f.
22. *Treadway v. Gateway Chevrolet Oldsmobile, Inc.*, 362 F.3d 971 (7th Cir. 2004).
23. 15 U.S.C. Sections 1667–1667e.
24. 12 C.F.R. Part 213.
25. 15 U.S.C. Sections 1681–1681t.

response to a consumer's request for a copy of his or her own credit report. The act further provides that whenever a consumer is denied credit or insurance on the basis of her or his credit report, or is charged more than others ordinarily would be for credit or insurance, the consumer must be notified of that fact and of the name and address of the credit reporting agency that issued the credit report.

Under the FCRA, consumers may request the source of any information being given out by a credit agency, as well as the identity of anyone who has received an agency's report. Consumers are also permitted to access the information about them contained in a credit reporting agency's files. If a consumer discovers that an agency's files contain inaccurate information about his or her credit standing, the agency, on the consumer's written request, must investigate the matter and delete any unverifiable or erroneous information within a reasonable period of time. As part of its investigation, the agency should systematically examine its records and contact the creditor whose information the consumer disputes.[26] An agency that fails to comply with the act is liable for actual damages, plus additional damages not to exceed $1,000 and attorneys' fees.[27] The FCRA allows an award of punitive damages for a "willful" violation.[28]

Fair and Accurate Credit Transactions Act

In an effort to combat identity theft (discussed in Chapter 7), Congress passed the Fair and Accurate Credit Transactions Act (FACT Act) of 2003.[29] The act established a national fraud alert system so that consumers who suspect that they have been or may be victimized by identity theft can place an alert on their credit files. The act also requires the major credit reporting agencies to provide consumers with free copies of their own credit reports every twelve months. Another provision requires account numbers on credit-card receipts to be shortened (truncated) so that merchants, employees, or others who may have access to the receipts do not have the consumers' names and full credit-card numbers. The act further mandates that financial institutions work with the Federal Trade Commission to identify "red flag" indicators of identity theft and to develop rules for disposing of sensitive credit information.

The FACT Act gives consumers who have been victimized by identity theft some assistance in rebuilding their credit reputations. For example, credit reporting agencies must stop reporting allegedly fraudulent account information once the consumer establishes that identify theft has occurred. Business owners and creditors are required to provide consumers with copies of any records that can help the consumer prove that the particular account or transaction is fraudulent (records showing that an account was created by a fraudulent signature, for example). In addition, the act allows consumers to report the accounts affected by identity theft directly to creditors in order to help prevent the spread of erroneous credit information.

The Fair Debt Collection Practices Act

In 1977, Congress enacted the Fair Debt Collection Practices Act (FDCPA)[30] in an attempt to curb what were perceived to be abuses by collection agencies. The act applies only to specialized debt-collection agencies that regularly attempt to collect debts on behalf of someone else, usually for a percentage of the amount owed. Creditors attempting to collect debts are not covered by the act unless, by misrepresenting themselves, they cause debtors to believe they are collection agencies.

Requirements under the Act The act explicitly prohibits a collection agency from using any of the following tactics:

1. Contacting the debtor at the debtor's place of employment if the debtor's employer objects.
2. Contacting the debtor during inconvenient or unusual times (for example, calling the debtor at three o'clock in the morning) or at any time if the debtor is being represented by an attorney.
3. Contacting third parties other than the debtor's parents, spouse, or financial adviser about payment of a debt unless a court authorizes such action.

26. See, for example, *Johnson v. MBNA America Bank, N.A.*, 357 F.3d 426 (4th Cir. 2004).
27. 15 U.S.C. Section 1681n.
28. Under the FCRA, if an insurance company *raises* a customer's rates because of a credit score, the insurance company is required to notify the individual. In 2007, the United States Supreme Court held that even the failure to notify *new* customers that they are paying higher insurance rates as a result of their credit scores is an adverse action that can be considered a *willful* violation of the FCRA. *Safeco Insurance Co. of America v. Burr*, ___ U.S. ___, 127 S.Ct. 2201, 167 L.Ed.2d 1045 (2007).
29. Pub. L. No. 108-159, 117 Stat. 1952 (December 4, 2003).
30. 15 U.S.C. Section 1692.

4. Using harassment or intimidation (for example, using abusive language or threatening violence) or employing false or misleading information (for example, posing as a police officer).
5. Communicating with the debtor at any time after receiving notice that the debtor is refusing to pay the debt, except to advise the debtor of further action to be taken by the collection agency.

The FDCPA also requires a collection agency to include a **validation notice** whenever it initially contacts a debtor for payment of a debt or within five days of that initial contact. The notice must state that the debtor has thirty days in which to dispute the debt and to request a written verification of the debt from the collection agency. The debtor's request for debt validation must be in writing.

The following case involved contacting a third party other than the debtor's parents, spouse, or financial adviser about the payment of a debt. A consumer alleged that a debt collection company violated Colorado's fair debt collection statute when it hired a third party—an automated mailing service—to send her the required validation notice. Although the case was brought under Colorado's fair debt collection statute, the state statute parallels the relevant portions of the FDCPA and both prohibit communications between a debt collector and third parties.

CASE 23.3 Flood v. Mercantile Adjustment Bureau, LLC

Supreme Court of Colorado, 2008. 176 P.3d 769.
www.courts.state.co.us/supct/supctopinion.htm[a]

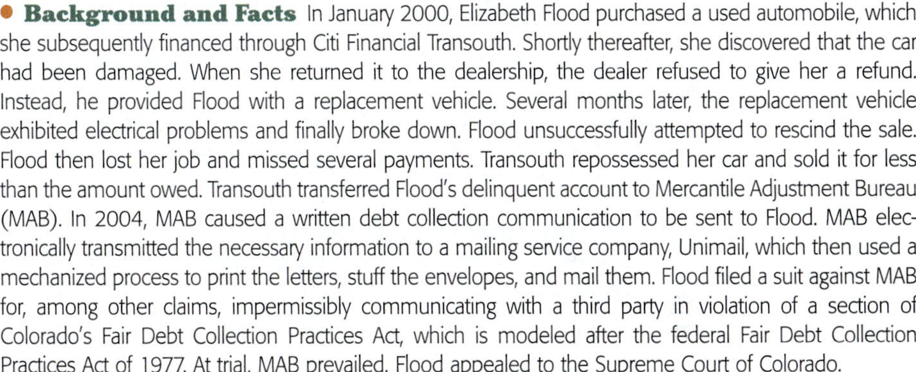

Background and Facts In January 2000, Elizabeth Flood purchased a used automobile, which she subsequently financed through Citi Financial Transouth. Shortly thereafter, she discovered that the car had been damaged. When she returned it to the dealership, the dealer refused to give her a refund. Instead, he provided Flood with a replacement vehicle. Several months later, the replacement vehicle exhibited electrical problems and finally broke down. Flood unsuccessfully attempted to rescind the sale. Flood then lost her job and missed several payments. Transouth repossessed her car and sold it for less than the amount owed. Transouth transferred Flood's delinquent account to Mercantile Adjustment Bureau (MAB). In 2004, MAB caused a written debt collection communication to be sent to Flood. MAB electronically transmitted the necessary information to a mailing service company, Unimail, which then used a mechanized process to print the letters, stuff the envelopes, and mail them. Flood filed a suit against MAB for, among other claims, impermissibly communicating with a third party in violation of a section of Colorado's Fair Debt Collection Practices Act, which is modeled after the federal Fair Debt Collection Practices Act of 1977. At trial, MAB prevailed. Flood appealed to the Supreme Court of Colorado.

IN THE LANGUAGE OF THE COURT
HOBBES, **Justice**

* * * *

[Two previous courts] ruled that the debt collection communication that Mercantile Adjustment Bureau, LLC ("MAB") sent to Elizabeth Flood complied with the notice provisions of section 12-14-109 [of Colorado's Fair Debts Collection Practices Act], and that MAB did not violate section 12-14-105(2) [of that act] when it utilized an automated mailing service to print and mail the communication.

* * * *

* * * Flood * * * alleged that MAB impermissibly communicated with a third party, in violation of section 12-14-105(2), by outsourcing the printing and mailing of its collection communications to Unimail [a mailing service company].

* * * *

In the case before us, the relevant provisions of the Colorado statute parallel the federal statute. Because the Colorado statute is patterned on the federal statute, we look to federal case law for persuasive guidance bearing on the construction of our state's law.

a. Click on "Supreme Court Case Announcements by Date," then click on "2008," and then on "01/22/08."

CASE CONTINUES

CASE 23.3 CONTINUED

* * * *

Flood * * * argues that MAB violated the [Colorado statute] by using an automated mailing service to prepare and mail its debt collection communications. With certain exceptions, [the statute] prohibits communications between a debt collector and third parties. Our analysis * * * leads us to conclude that the [Colorado legislature] did not intend for section 12-14-105(2) [of the Colorado act] to prohibit a debt collector from using an automated mailing service. The federal statute contains a nearly identical provision. *The purpose of [this federal provision] is to "protect a consumer's reputation and privacy, as well as to prevent loss of jobs resulting from a debt collector's communication with a consumer's employer concerning the collection of a debt."* [Emphasis added.]

The record here shows that MAB utilized an entirely automated printing and mailing service. The county court found that MAB electronically transmitted the information included in its collection communications to Unimail. Unimail then printed the collection communications, which were mechanically stuffed into envelopes. The county court concluded that the use of such a highly automated procedure did not violate section 12-14-105(2) because it did not threaten the consumer with the risk of being coerced or embarrassed into paying a debt because the debt collector contacted an employer, family member, friend, or other third party.

We agree with the holding of the county court. The use of an automated mailing service, such as Unimail, by a debt collector is a *de minimus* [trivial] communication with a third party that cannot reasonably be perceived as a threat to the consumer's privacy or reputation.

Accordingly, we hold that MAB's use of Unimail to automatically print and mail its debt collection communications did not violate section 12-14-105(2). Thus, we affirm that part of the district court's judgment upholding the county court's judgment on this issue.

• **Decision and Remedy** *The Supreme Court of Colorado held that Mercantile Adjustment Bureau did not violate Colorado's statute prohibiting communications with a third party about an outstanding debt. The state supreme court affirmed the lower court's opinion on this issue, but reversed the decision on other grounds (the letter sent contained contradictory language and failed to effectively convey the required notices regarding the debtor's rights).*

• **What If the Facts Were Different?** *Assume that Unimail had spotcheckers who randomly pulled printed communications to debtors prior to mailing. These checkers read the letters to make sure that they were accurate. Would the court have still ruled in favor of Mercantile Adjustment Bureau? Why or why not?*

• **The Legal Environment Dimension** *Why might this ruling actually benefit debtors in the long run?*

Enforcement of the Act The enforcement of the FDCPA is primarily the responsibility of the Federal Trade Commission. The act provides that a debt collector who fails to comply with the act is liable for actual damages, plus additional damages not to exceed $1,000[31] and attorneys' fees.

Cases brought under the FDCPA sometimes raise questions as to who qualifies as a debt collector or debt-collection agency subject to the act. For example, in the past courts were issuing conflicting opinions on whether attorneys who attempted to collect debts owed to their clients were subject to the FDCPA's provisions. In 1995, however, the United States Supreme Court resolved this issue when it held that an attorney who regularly tries to obtain payment of consumer debts through legal proceedings meets the FDCPA's definition of "debt collector."[32]

Garnishment of Wages

Despite the increasing number of protections afforded debtors, creditors are not without means of securing

31. According to the U.S. Court of Appeals for the Sixth Circuit, the $1,000 limit on damages applies to each lawsuit, not to each violation. See *Wright v. Finance Service of Norwalk, Inc.*, 22 F.3d 647 (6th Cir. 1994).

32. *Heintz v. Jenkins*, 514 U.S. 291, 115 S.Ct. 1489, 131 L.Ed.2d 395 (1995).

payment on debts. One of these is the right to garnish a debtor's wages after the debt has gone unpaid for a prolonged period. Recall from Chapter 15 that in a *garnishment* process, a creditor directly attaches, or seizes, a portion of the debtor's assets (such as wages) that are in the possession of a third party (such as an employer).

State law governs the garnishment process, but the law varies among the states as to how easily garnishment can be obtained. Indeed, a few states, such as Texas, prohibit garnishment of wages except for child support and court-approved spousal maintenance. Constitutional due process and federal legislation under the TILA also provide certain protections against abuse.[33] In general, the debtor is entitled to notice and an opportunity to be heard. Moreover, wages cannot be garnished beyond 25 percent of the debtor's after-tax earnings, and the garnishment must leave the debtor with at least a specified minimum income.

SECTION 5 Consumer Health and Safety

The laws discussed earlier regarding the labeling and packaging of products go a long way toward promoting consumer health and safety. There is a significant distinction, however, between regulating the information dispensed about a product and regulating the actual content of the product. The classic example is tobacco products. Producers of tobacco products are required to warn consumers about the hazards associated with the use of their products, but the sale of tobacco products has not been subjected to significant restrictions or banned outright despite the obvious dangers to health.[34] We now examine various laws that regulate the actual products made available to consumers.

The Federal Food, Drug and Cosmetic Act

The first federal legislation regulating food and drugs was enacted in 1906 as the Pure Food and Drugs Act. That law, as amended in 1938, exists today as the Federal Food, Drug and Cosmetic Act (FDCA).[35] The act protects consumers against adulterated and misbranded foods and drugs. As to foods, in its present form, the act establishes food standards, specifies safe levels of potentially hazardous food additives, and sets classifications of foods and food advertising. Most of these statutory requirements are monitored and enforced by the Food and Drug Administration (FDA).

The FDCA also charges the FDA with the responsibility of ensuring that drugs are safe before they are marketed to the public. Under an extensive set of procedures established by the FDA, drugs must be shown to be effective as well as safe, and the use of some food additives suspected of being carcinogenic is prohibited. A 1976 amendment to the FDCA[36] authorizes the FDA to regulate medical devices, such as pacemakers and other health devices and equipment, and to withdraw from the market any such device that is mislabeled.

The question in the following case was whether the U.S. Constitution provides terminally ill patients with a right of access to experimental drugs that have passed limited safety trials but have not been proved safe and effective.

33. 15 U.S.C. Sections 1671–1677.

34. We are ignoring recent civil litigation concerning the liability of tobacco product manufacturers for injuries that arise from the use of tobacco. See, for example, *Philip Morris USA v. Williams*, ___U.S.___, 127 S.Ct. 1057, 166 L.Ed.2d 940 (2007).

35. 21 U.S.C. Sections 301–393.

36. 21 U.S.C. Sections 352(o), 360(j), 360(k), and 360c–360k.

CASE 23.4 Abigail Alliance for Better Access to Developmental Drugs v. von Eschenbach

United States Court of Appeals, District of Columbia Circuit, 2007. 495 F.3d 695.

• **Background and Facts** The Food and Drug Administration (FDA) and Congress have created programs to provide terminally ill patients with access to promising experimental drugs before the completion of the clinical-testing process—which can be lengthy. The Abigail Alliance for Better Access to Developmental Drugs (Alliance), an organization of terminally ill patients and their supporters, asked the FDA to expand this access. The FDA responded that, among other things, "a reasonably precise estimate of response rate" and "enough experience to detect serious adverse effects" are "critical" in determining

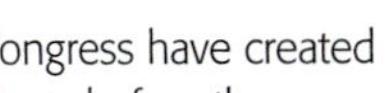

CASE CONTINUES

CASE 23.4 CONTINUED when experimental drugs should be made available. Accordingly, "it does not serve patients well to make drugs too widely available before there is a reasonable assessment of such risks to guide patient decisions, and experience in managing them." Accepting Alliance's proposal "would upset the appropriate balance * * * by giving almost total weight to the goal of early availability and giving little recognition to the importance of marketing drugs with reasonable knowledge for patients and physicians of their likely clinical benefit and their toxicity." Alliance filed a suit in a federal district court against FDA commissioner Andrew von Eschenbach and others, arguing that the Constitution provides terminally ill patients with a fundamental right of access to experimental drugs. The court ruled in the defendants' favor. Alliance appealed to the U.S. Court of Appeals for the District of Columbia Circuit.

IN THE LANGUAGE OF THE COURT
***GRIFFITH,* Circuit Judge:**

* * * *

* * * [The due process clause of the Fifth Amendment to the Constitution] provides heightened protection against government interference with certain fundamental rights [by subjecting that interference to strict scrutiny] * * * .

* * * *

* * * *The Due Process Clause specially protects those fundamental rights * * * which are, objectively, deeply rooted in this Nation's history and tradition* * * * . [Emphasis added.]

* * * *

Drug regulation in the United States began with the Colonies and the States * * * . In the early history of our Nation, we observe not a tradition of protecting a right of access to drugs, but rather governments responding to the risks of new compounds as they become aware of and able to address those risks.

* * * *

The current regime of federal drug regulation began to take shape with the Food, Drug, and Cosmetic Act [FDCA] of 1938. The Act required that drug manufacturers provide proof that their products were safe before they could be marketed.

* * * Congress amended the FDCA in 1962 to explicitly require that the FDA only approve drugs deemed effective for public use. Thus, the Alliance argues that, prior to 1962, patients were free to make their own decisions whether a drug might be effective. * * * Alliance's argument ignores our Nation's history of drug safety regulation * * * . Nor can the Alliance override current FDA regulations simply by insisting that drugs which have completed [some] testing are safe enough for terminally ill patients. Current law bars public access to drugs undergoing clinical testing on safety grounds. *The fact that a drug * * * is safe for limited clinical testing in a controlled and closely monitored environment after detailed scrutiny of each trial participant does not mean that a drug is safe for use beyond supervised trials.* [Emphasis added.]

* * * *

* * * We conclude that the Alliance has not provided evidence of a right to procure and use experimental drugs that is deeply rooted in our Nation's history and traditions.

* * * *

Because the Alliance's claimed right is not fundamental, the Alliance's claim of a right of access to experimental drugs is subject only to rational basis scrutiny. *The rational basis test requires that the Alliance prove that the government's restrictions bear no rational relationship to a legitimate state interest.* [Emphasis added.]

* * * *

Applying the rational basis standard to the Alliance's complaint, we cannot say that the government's interest does not bear a rational relation to a legitimate state interest. * * * For the terminally ill, as for anyone else, a drug is unsafe if its potential for inflicting death or physical injury is not offset by the possibility of therapeutic benefit.

* * * Thus, we must conclude that * * * the Government has a rational basis for ensuring that there is a scientifically and medically acceptable level of knowledge about the risks and benefits of such a drug.

• **Decision and Remedy** *The U.S. Court of Appeals for the District of Columbia Circuit affirmed the lower court's decision, holding that terminally ill patients do not have a fundamental con-*

CASE 23.4 CONTINUED *stitutional right of access to experimental drugs. Furthermore, "the FDA's policy of limiting access to investigational drugs is rationally related to the legitimate state interest of protecting patients, including the terminally ill, from potentially unsafe drugs with unknown therapeutic effects."*

- **The Global Dimension** *Should the court have ruled that as long as a drug has been approved for use in any country, terminally ill patients in the United States should be given access to it? Explain.*

- **The Legal Environment Dimension** *In light of the analysis in this case, what option is left to those who believe that terminally ill patients—not the government—should make the decision about whether to accept the risk associated with experimental drugs?*

The Consumer Product Safety Act

Consumer product-safety legislation began in 1953 with the passage of the Flammable Fabrics Act, which prohibits the sale of highly flammable clothing or materials. Over the next two decades, Congress enacted legislation regarding the design or composition of specific classes of products. Then, in 1972, Congress enacted the Consumer Product Safety Act,[37] creating the first comprehensive scheme of regulation over matters of consumer safety. The act also established the Consumer Product Safety Commission (CPSC), which has far-reaching authority over consumer safety.

The CPSC's Authority The CPSC conducts research on the safety of individual consumer products and maintains a clearinghouse on the risks associated with various products. The Consumer Product Safety Act authorizes the CPSC to set standards for consumer products and to ban the manufacture and sale of any product that it deems to be potentially hazardous to consumers. The CPSC also has authority to remove from the market any products it believes to be imminently hazardous and to require manufacturers to report on any products already sold or intended for sale if the products have proved to be dangerous. The CPSC also has authority to administer other product-safety legislation, such as the Child Protection and Toy Safety Act of 1969[38] and the Federal Hazardous Substances Act of 1960.[39]

The CPSC's authority is sufficiently broad to allow it to ban any product that it believes poses an "unreasonable risk" to consumers. This includes the authority to ban the importation of hazardous products into the United States. Some of the products that the CPSC has banned include various types of fireworks, cribs, and toys, as well as many products containing asbestos or vinyl chloride.

37. 15 U.S.C. Sections 2051–2083.

38. This act consists of amendments to 15 U.S.C. Sections 1261, 1262, and 1274.

39. 15 U.S.C. Sections 1261–1277.

Notification Requirements The Consumer Product Safety Act requires the distributors of consumer products to notify the CPSC immediately if they receive information that a product "contains a defect which . . . creates a substantial risk to the public" or "an unreasonable risk of serious injury or death."

For example, Aroma Housewares Company had been distributing a particular model of juicer for just over a year when it began receiving letters from customers. They complained that during operation the juicer had suddenly exploded, sending pieces of glass and razor-sharp metal across the room. The company received twenty-three letters from angry consumers about the exploding juicer but waited more than six months before notifying the CPSC that the product posed a significant risk to the public. In a suit filed by the federal government, the court held that when a company first receives information regarding a threat, the company is required to report the problem within twenty-four hours to the CPSC. The court also found that even if the company had to investigate the allegations, it should not have taken more than ten days to verify the information and report the problem. The court therefore held that the company had violated the law and ordered it to pay damages.[40]

40. *United States v. Miram Enterprises, Inc.*, 185 F.Supp.2d 1148 (S.D.Ca. 2002).

REVIEWING Consumer Protection

Leota Sage saw a local motorcycle dealer's newspaper advertisement for a MetroRider EZ electric scooter for $1,699. When she went to the dealership, however, she learned that the EZ model had been sold out. The salesperson told Sage that he still had the higher-end MetroRider FX model in stock for $2,199 and would offer her one for $1,999. Sage was disappointed but decided to purchase the FX model. When Sage said that she wished to purchase the scooter on credit, she was directed to the dealer's credit department. As she filled out the credit forms, the clerk told Sage, who is an African American, that she would need a cosigner to obtain a loan. Sage could not understand why she would need a cosigner and asked to speak to the store manager. The manager apologized, told her that the clerk was mistaken, and said that he would "speak to" the clerk about that. The manager completed Sage's credit application, and Sage then rode the scooter home. Seven months later, Sage received a letter from the manufacturer informing her that a flaw had been discovered in the scooter's braking system and that the model had been recalled. Using the information presented in the chapter, answer the following questions.

1. Had the dealer engaged in deceptive advertising? Why or why not?
2. Suppose that Sage had ordered the scooter through the dealer's Web site but the dealer had been unable to deliver it by the date promised. What would the FTC have required the merchant to do in that situation?
3. Assuming that the clerk had required a cosigner based on Sage's race or gender, what act prohibits such credit discrimination?
4. What organization has the authority to ban the sale of scooters based on safety concerns?

TERMS AND CONCEPTS

bait-and-switch advertising 582
cease-and-desist order 583
consumer law 580
counteradvertising 583
deceptive advertising 581
multiple product order 583
Regulation Z 586
validation notice 589

QUESTIONS AND CASE PROBLEMS

23–1. Andrew, a resident of California, received an advertising circular in the U.S. mail announcing a new line of regional cookbooks distributed by the Every-Kind Cookbook Co. Andrew didn't want any books and threw the circular away. Two days later, Andrew received in the mail an introductory cookbook entitled *Lower Mongolian Regional Cookbook,* as announced in the circular, on a "trial basis" from Every-Kind. Andrew was not interested but did not go to the trouble to return the cookbook. Every-Kind demanded payment of $20.95 for the *Lower Mongolian Regional Cookbook.* Discuss whether Andrew can be required to pay for the book.

23–2. Maria Ochoa receives two new credit cards on May 1. She had solicited one of them from Midtown Department Store, and the other arrived unsolicited from High-Flying Airlines. During the month of May, Ochoa makes numerous credit-card purchases from Midtown Department Store, but she does not use the High-Flying Airlines card. On May 31, a burglar breaks into Ochoa's home and steals both credit cards, along with other items. Ochoa notifies the Midtown Department Store of the theft on June 2, but she fails to notify High-Flying Airlines. Using the Midtown credit card, the burglar makes a $500 purchase on June 1 and a $200 purchase on June 3. The burglar then charges a vacation flight on the High-Flying Airlines card for $1,000 on June 5. Ochoa receives the bills for these charges and refuses to pay them. Discuss Ochoa's liability in these situations.

23-3. QUESTION WITH SAMPLE ANSWER

On June 28, a salesperson for Renowned Books called on the Gonchars at their home. After a very persuasive sales pitch by the agent, the Gonchars agreed in writing to purchase a twenty-volume set of historical encyclopedias from Renowned Books for a total of $299. A down payment of $35 was required, with the remainder of the cost to be paid in monthly payments over a one-year period. Two days later, the Gonchars, having second thoughts, contacted the book company and stated that they had decided to rescind the contract. Renowned Books said this would be impossible. Has Renowned Books violated any consumer law by not allowing the Gonchars to rescind their contract? Explain.

- **For a sample answer to Question 23–3, go to Appendix I at the end of this text.**

23-4. Fair Debt Collection. CrossCheck, Inc., provides check-authorization services to retail merchants. When a customer presents a check, the merchant contacts CrossCheck, which estimates the probability that the check will clear the bank. If the check is within an acceptable statistical range, CrossCheck notifies the merchant. If the check is dishonored, the merchant sends it to CrossCheck, which pays it. CrossCheck then attempts to redeposit the check. If this fails, CrossCheck takes further steps to collect the amount. CrossCheck attempts to collect on more than two thousand checks per year and spends $2 million on these efforts, which involve about 7 percent of its employees and 6 percent of its total expenses. William Winterstein took his truck to C&P Auto Service Center, Inc., for a tune-up and paid for the service with a check. C&P contacted CrossCheck and, on its recommendation, accepted the check. When the check was dishonored, C&P mailed it to CrossCheck, which reimbursed C&P and sent a letter to Winterstein requesting payment. Winterstein filed a suit in a federal district court against CrossCheck, asserting that the letter violated the Fair Debt Collection Practices Act. CrossCheck filed a motion for summary judgment. On what ground might the court grant the motion? Explain. [*Winterstein v. CrossCheck, Inc.*, 149 F.Supp.2d 466 (N.D.Ill. 2001)]

23-5. Fair Credit Reporting Act. Source One Associates, Inc., is based in Poughquag, New York. Peter Easton, Source One's president, is responsible for its daily operations. Between 1995 and 1997, Source One received requests from persons in Massachusetts seeking financial information about individuals and businesses. To obtain this information, Easton first obtained the targeted individuals' credit reports through Equifax Consumer Information Services by claiming that the reports would be used only in connection with credit transactions involving the consumers. From the reports, Easton identified financial institutions at which the targeted individuals held accounts. He then called the institutions to learn the account balances by impersonating either officers of the institutions or the account holders. The information was then provided to Source One's customers for a fee. Easton did not know why the customers wanted the information. The state ("commonwealth") of Massachusetts filed a suit in a Massachusetts state court against Source One and Easton, alleging, among other things, violations of the Fair Credit Reporting Act (FCRA). Did the defendants violate the FCRA? Explain. [*Commonwealth v. Source One Associates, Inc.*, 436 Mass. 118, 763 N.E.2d 42 (2002)]

23-6. Deceptive Advertising. "Set Up & Ready to Make Money in Minutes Guaranteed!" the ads claimed. "The Internet Treasure Chest (ITC) will give you everything you need to start your own exciting Internet business including your own worldwide Web site all for the unbelievable price of only $59.95." The ITC "contains virtually everything you need to quickly and easily get your very own worldwide Internet business up, running, stocked with products, able to accept credit cards and ready to take orders almost immediately." What ITC's marketers—Damien Zamora and end70 Corp.—did not disclose were the significant additional costs required to operate the business: domain name registration fees, monthly Internet access and hosting charges, monthly fees to access the ITC product warehouse, and other "upgrades." The Federal Trade Commission filed a suit in a federal district court against end70 and Zamora, seeking an injunction and other relief. Are the defendants' claims "deceptive advertising"? If so, what might the court order the defendants to do to correct any misrepresentations? [*Federal Trade Commission v. end70 Corp.*, __ F.Supp.2d __ (N.D.Tex. 2003)]

23-7. CASE PROBLEM WITH SAMPLE ANSWER

One of the products that McDonald's Corp. sells is the Happy Meal®, which consists of a McDonald's food entree, a small order of french fries, a small drink, and a toy. In the early 1990s, McDonald's began to aim its Happy Meal marketing at children aged one to three. In 1995, McDonald's began making nutritional information for its food products available in documents known as "McDonald's Nutrition Facts." Each document lists each food item that the restaurant serves and provides a nutritional breakdown, but the Happy Meal is not included. Marc Cohen filed a suit in an Illinois state court against McDonald's, alleging, among other things, that the defendant had violated a state law prohibiting consumer fraud and deceptive business practices by failing to adhere to the National Labeling and Education Act (NLEA) of 1990. The NLEA sets out different requirements for products specifically intended for children under the age of four—generally, the products cannot declare the percent of daily value of nutritional components. Would this requirement be readily understood by a consumer who is not familiar with nutritional standards? Why or why not? Should a state court impose such regulations? Explain. [*Cohen v. McDonald's Corp.*, 347 Ill.App.3d 627, 808 N.E.2d 1, 283 Ill.Dec. 451 (1 Dist. 2004)]

- **To view a sample answer for Problem 23–7, go to this book's Web site at academic.cengage.com/blaw/cross, select "Chapter 23," and click on "Case Problem with Sample Answer."**

23–8. Debt Collection. 55th Management Corp. in New York City owns residential property that it leases to various tenants. In June 2000, claiming that one of the tenants, Leslie Goldman, owed more than $13,000 in back rent, 55th retained Jeffrey Cohen, an attorney, to initiate nonpayment proceedings. Cohen filed a petition in a New York state court against Goldman, seeking recovery of the unpaid rent and at least $3,000 in attorneys' fees. After receiving notice of the petition, Goldman filed a suit in a federal district court against Cohen. Goldman contended that the notice of the petition constituted an initial contact that, under the Fair Debt Collection Practices Act (FDCPA), required a validation notice. Because Cohen did not give Goldman a validation notice at the time, or within five days, of the notice of the petition, Goldman argued that Cohen was in violation of the FDCPA. Should the filing of a suit in a state court be considered "communication," requiring a debt collector to provide a validation notice under the FDCPA? Why or why not? [*Goldman v. Cohen*, 445 F.3d 152 (2d Cir. 2006)]

23–9. A QUESTION OF ETHICS

*After graduating from law school—and serving time in prison for attempting to collect debts by posing as an FBI agent—Barry Sussman theorized that if a debt-collection business collected only debts that it owned as a result of buying checks written on accounts with insufficient funds (NSF checks), it would not be subject to the Federal Debt Collection Practices Act (FDCPA). Sussman formed Check Investors, Inc., to act on his theory. Check Investors bought more than 2.2 million NSF checks, with an estimated face value of about $348 million, for pennies on the dollar. Check Investors added a fee of $125 or $130 to the face amount of each check (which exceeds the legal limit in most states) and aggressively pursued its drawer to collect. The firm's employees were told to accuse drawers of being criminals and to threaten them with arrest and prosecution. The threats were false. Check Investors never took steps to initiate a prosecution. The employees contacted the drawers' family members and used "saturation phoning"—phoning a drawer numerous times in a short period. They used abusive language, referring to drawers as "deadbeats," "retards," "thieves," and "idiots." Between January 2000 and January 2003, Check Investors netted more than $10.2 million from its efforts. [*Federal Trade Commission v. Check Investors, Inc.*, *502 F.3d 159 (3d Cir. 2007)]*

(a) The Federal Trade Commission filed a suit in a federal district court against Check Investors and others, alleging, in part, violations of the FDCPA. Was Check Investors a "debt collector," collecting "debts," within the meaning of the FDCPA? If so, did its methods violate the FDCPA? Were its practices unethical? What might Check Investors argue in its defense? Discuss.

(b) Are "deadbeats" the primary beneficiaries of laws such as the FDCPA? If not, how would you characterize debtors who default on their obligations?

23–10. VIDEO QUESTION

Go to this text's Web site at **academic.cengage.com/blaw/cross** and select "Chapter 23." Click on "Video Questions" and view the video titled *Advertising Communication Law: Bait and Switch*. Then answer the following questions.

(a) Is the auto dealership's advertisement for the truck in the video deceptive? Why or why not?

(b) Is the advertisement for the truck an offer to which the dealership is bound? Does it matter if Betty detrimentally relied on the advertisement?

(c) Is Tony committed to buying Betty's trade-in truck for $3,000 because that is what he told her over the phone?

LAW ON THE WEB

For updated links to resources available on the Web, as well as a variety of other materials, visit this text's Web site at

academic.cengage.com/blaw/cross

For a government-sponsored Web site containing reports on consumer issues, go to

www.consumer.gov

The Federal Trade Commission (FTC) offers extensive information on consumer protection laws, consumer problems, enforcement issues, and other topics relevant to consumer law at its Web site. Go to

www.ftc.gov

and click on "Consumer Protection."

To learn more about the FTC's "cooling-off" rule, you can access it directly by going to the following URL:

www.ftc.gov/bcp/edu/pubs/consumer/products/pro03.shtm

Legal Research Exercises on the Web

Go to **academic.cengage.com/blaw/cross**, the Web site that accompanies this text. Select "Chapter 23" and click on "Internet Exercises." There you will find the following Internet research exercises that you can perform to learn more about the topics covered in this chapter.

Internet Exercise 23–1: Legal Perspective
The Food and Drug Administration

Internet Exercise 23–2: Management Perspective
Internet Advertising and Marketing

CHAPTER 24

Environmental Law

Concerns over the degradation of the environment have increased over time in response to the environmental effects of population growth, urbanization, and industrialization. Environmental protection is not without a price, however. For many businesses, the costs of complying with environmental regulations are high, and for some they may seem too high. A constant tension exists between the desire to increase profits and productivity and the need to protect the environment. In this chapter, we discuss **environmental law,** which consists of all laws and regulations designed to protect and preserve our environmental resources.

Common Law Actions

Common law remedies against environmental pollution originated centuries ago in England. Those responsible for operations that created dirt, smoke, noxious odors, noise, or toxic substances were sometimes held liable under common law theories of nuisance or negligence. Today, injured individuals continue to rely on the common law to obtain damages and injunctions against business polluters.

Nuisance

Under the common law doctrine of **nuisance,** persons may be held liable if they use their property in a manner that unreasonably interferes with others' rights to use or enjoy their own property. Courts typically balance the equities between the harm caused by the pollution and the costs of stopping it. Courts have often denied injunctive relief on the ground that the hardships that would be imposed on the polluter and on the community are greater than the hardships suffered by the plaintiff. For example, a factory that causes neighboring landowners to suffer from smoke, soot, and vibrations may be left in operation if it is the core of the local economy. The injured parties may be awarded only monetary damages, which may include compensation for the decline in the value of their property caused by the factory's operation.

A property owner may be given relief from pollution if he or she can identify a distinct harm separate from that affecting the general public. This harm is referred to as a "private" nuisance. Under the common law, individuals were denied *standing* (access to the courts—see Chapter 2) unless they suffered a harm distinct from the harm suffered by the public at large. Some states still require this. For example, in one case a group of individuals who made their living by commercial fishing in a major river in New York filed a suit seeking damages and an injunction against a company that was polluting the river. The New York court found that the plaintiffs had standing because they were particularly harmed by the pollution in the river.[1] A public authority (such as a state's attorney general), however, can sue to abate a "public" nuisance.

Negligence and Strict Liability

An injured party may sue a business polluter in tort under the negligence and strict liability theories discussed in Chapters 12 and 13. The basis for a negligence action is a business's alleged failure to use reasonable care toward a party whose injury was foreseeable and was caused by the lack of reasonable

1. *Lee v. General Electric Co.*, 538 N.Y.S.2d 844, 145 A.D.2d 291 (1989).

care. For example, employees might sue an employer whose failure to use proper pollution controls contaminated the air, causing the employees to suffer respiratory illnesses. A developing area of tort law involves **toxic torts**—actions against toxic polluters.

Businesses that engage in ultrahazardous activities—such as the transportation of radioactive materials—are strictly liable for any injuries the activities cause. In a strict liability action, the injured party need not prove that the business failed to exercise reasonable care.

Federal, State, and Local Regulation

All levels of government in the United States regulate some aspect of the environment. In this section, we look at the various ways in which the federal, state, and local governments control business activities and land use in the interests of environmental preservation and protection.

Federal Regulation

Congress has passed a number of statutes to control the impact of human activities on the environment. Exhibit 24–1 on the next page lists and summarizes the major federal environmental statutes, most of which are discussed in this chapter. Some of these statutes were passed in an attempt to improve air and water quality. Others specifically regulate toxic chemicals, including pesticides, herbicides, and hazardous wastes.

Environmental Regulatory Agencies The primary federal agency regulating environmental law is the Environmental Protection Agency (EPA), which was created in 1970 to coordinate federal environmental responsibilities. Other federal agencies with authority for regulating specific environmental matters include the Department of the Interior, the Department of Defense, the Department of Labor, the Food and Drug Administration, and the Nuclear Regulatory Commission. These regulatory agencies—and all other agencies of the federal government—must take environmental factors into consideration when making significant decisions.

Most federal environmental laws provide that private parties can sue to enforce environmental regulations if government agencies fail to do so—or can sue to protest agency enforcement actions if they believe that these actions go too far. Typically, a threshold hurdle in such suits is meeting the requirements for standing to sue (see Chapter 2).

State and local regulatory agencies also play a significant role in carrying out federal environmental legislation. Typically, the federal government relies on state and local governments to implement federal environmental statutes and regulations such as those regulating air quality.

Environmental Impact Statements The National Environmental Policy Act (NEPA) of 1969[2] requires that an **environmental impact statement (EIS)** be prepared for every major federal action that significantly affects the quality of the environment. An EIS must analyze (1) the impact on the environment that the action will have, (2) any adverse effects on the environment and alternative actions that might be taken, and (3) irreversible effects the action might generate.

An action qualifies as "major" if it involves a substantial commitment of resources (monetary or otherwise). An action is "federal" if a federal agency has the power to control it. Construction by a private developer of a ski resort on federal land, for example, may require an EIS. Building or operating a nuclear plant, which requires a federal permit, or constructing a dam as part of a federal project requires an EIS. If an agency decides that an EIS is unnecessary, it must issue a statement supporting this conclusion. EISs have become instruments for private individuals, consumer interest groups, businesses, and others to challenge federal agency actions on the basis that the actions improperly threaten the environment.

State and Local Regulation

Many states regulate the degree to which the environment may be polluted. Thus, for example, even when state zoning laws permit a business's proposed development, the proposal may have to be altered to lessen the development's impact on the environment. State laws may restrict a business's discharge of chemicals into the air or water or regulate its disposal of toxic wastes. States may also regulate the disposal or recycling of other wastes, including glass, metal, and plastic containers and paper. Additionally, states may restrict the emissions from motor vehicles.

City, county, and other local governments oversee certain aspects of the environment. For instance, local

2. 42 U.S.C. Sections 4321–4370d.

CASE 24.1 CONTINUED

* * * *

EPA maintains that it possesses authority to remove EGUs [electrical generating units] from * * * [the] list under the "fundamental principle of administrative law that an agency has inherent authority to reverse an earlier administrative determination or ruling where an agency has a principled basis for doing so."

EPA states in its brief that it has previously removed sources listed * * * without satisfying the requirements of [the statute]. But previous statutory violations cannot excuse the one now before the court. "We do not see how merely applying an unreasonable statutory interpretation for several years can transform it into a reasonable interpretation."

- **Decision and Remedy** *The U.S. Court of Appeals for the District of Columbia Circuit ruled in favor of New Jersey and the other plaintiffs. The EPA was required to rescind its delisting of mercury.*

- **What If the Facts Were Different?** *Assume that the EPA had carried out scientific tests that showed mercury was relatively harmless as a by-product of electricity generation. How might this have affected the court's ruling?*

- **The Global Dimension** *Because air pollution knows no borders, how did this ruling affect our neighboring countries?*

Air Pollution Control Standards The EPA sets primary and secondary levels of ambient standards—that is, the maximum levels of certain pollutants—and the states formulate plans to achieve those standards. Different standards apply depending on whether the sources of pollution are located in clean areas or polluted areas and whether they are already existing sources or major new sources. Major new sources include existing sources modified by a change in a method of operation that increases emissions. Performance standards for major sources require the use of the *maximum achievable control technology,* or MACT, to reduce emissions. The EPA issues guidelines as to what equipment meets this standard.[6]

The pollution-control schemes established under the Clean Air Act are known as New Source Performance Standards (NSPS) and Prevention of Significant Deterioration (PSD). The NSPS and PSD provisions' definitions of the term *modification* were at the center of the dispute in the following case.

6. The EPA has also issued rules to regulate hazardous air pollutants emitted by landfills. 40 C.F.R. Sections 60.750–759.

EXTENDED CASE 24.2 Environmental Defense v. Duke Energy Corp.

Supreme Court of the United States, 2007. __ U.S. __, 127 S.Ct. 1423, 167 L.Ed.2d 295.
www.law.cornell.edu/supct/index.html[a]

Justice *SOUTER* delivered the opinion of the Court.

* * * *

* * * Section 111(a) of the [Clean Air Amendments of] 1970 * * * defined [modification] within the NSPS [New Source Performance Standards] scheme as "any physical change in, or change in the method of operation of, a stationary source which increases the amount of any air pollutant emitted by such source or which results in the emission of any air pollutant not previously emitted."

EPA's 1975 regulations implementing NSPS * * * [identified] "a modification within the meaning of [S]ection 111" * * * as a change that "increase[s] * * * the emission rate," which "shall be expressed as [kilograms per hour] of any pollutant discharged into the atmosphere."

a. In the "Archive of Decisions" section, in the "By party" subsection, click on "1990-present." In the result, in the "2006-2007" row, click on "1st party." On the next page, scroll to the name of the case and click on it. On that page, click on the appropriate link to access the opinion. Cornell University Law School maintains this Web site.

CASE 24.2 CONTINUED

* * * The Clean Air Act Amendments of 1977 included the PSD [Prevention of Significant Deterioration] provisions, which * * * required a PSD permit before a "major emitting facility" could be "constructed" * * * ."The term 'construction' * * * includes the modification (as defined in [S]ection 111(a)) * * * ."

* * * *

* * * EPA's 1980 PSD regulations require a permit for a modification (with the same statutory definition) only when it is a major one and only when it would increase the actual annual emission of a pollutant above the actual average for the two prior years.

* * * *

* * * Duke Energy Corporation runs 30 coal-fired electric generating units at eight plants in North and South Carolina. The units were placed in service between 1940 and 1975, and each includes a boiler containing thousands of steel tubes arranged in sets. Between 1988 and 2000, Duke replaced or redesigned 29 tube assemblies in order to extend the life of the units and allow them to run longer each day.

The United States filed this action [in a federal district court] in 2000, claiming, among other things, that Duke violated the PSD provisions by doing this work without permits. Environmental Defense [and other private organizations] filed a complaint charging similar violations.

* * * [T]he District Court [ruled that] a PSD "major modification" can occur "only if the project increases the hourly rate of emissions" [and issued a judgment in Duke's favor] * * * .

* * * *

[On the plaintiffs' appeal, the U.S.] Court of Appeals for the Fourth Circuit affirmed * * * . "Identical statutory definitions of the term 'modification'" in the NSPS and PSD provisions * * * "[have] affirmatively mandated that this term be interpreted identically" in the regulations * * * . [The plaintiffs appealed to the United States Supreme Court.]

* * * *

In applying the 1980 PSD regulations to Duke's conduct, the Court of Appeals thought that, by defining the term "modification" identically in its NSPS and PSD provisions, the Act required EPA to conform its PSD interpretation of that definition to any such interpretation it reasonably adhered to under NSPS. *But principles of statutory construction are not so rigid.* * * * *Most words have different shades of meaning and consequently may be variously construed, not only when they occur in different statutes, but when used more than once in the same statute or even in the same section.* Thus, the natural presumption that identical words used in different parts of the same act are intended to have the same meaning * * * readily yields whenever there is such variation in the connection in which the words are used as reasonably to warrant the conclusion that they were employed in different parts of the act with different intent. *A given term in the same statute may take on distinct characters from association with distinct statutory objects calling for different implementation strategies.* [Emphasis added.]

* * * *

The Court of Appeals's reasoning that the PSD regulations must conform to their NSPS counterparts led the court to read those PSD regulations in a way that seems to us too far a stretch * * * .

* * * The regulatory language simply cannot be squared with a regime under which "hourly rate of emissions" is dispositive [a controlling factor].

* * * *

The judgment of the Court of Appeals is vacated, and the case is remanded for further proceedings consistent with this opinion.

QUESTIONS

1. What would support an argument that the Court should have given the term *modification* a definition that would be common to both regulations?
2. Did the U.S. Court of Appeals for the Fourth Circuit's attempt to equate the NSPS and PSD regulations implicitly—without analysis or discussion—invalidate those regulations? Explain.

CASE 24.3 CONTINUED *into navigable waters under a federal license requires state approval. Water flowing through a hydropower dam operated under a federal license constitutes such a "discharge."*

- **What If the Facts Were Different?** *Would the result in this case have been different if the quality of the water flowing through the turbines of Warren's dams improved before returning to the river? Why or why not?*

- **The Global Dimension** *Should the Court have ruled differently if the discharge had been into international or foreign waters rather than into the waters of the United States? Explain.*

Standards for Equipment Regulations, for the most part, specify that the *best available control technology,* or BACT, be installed. The EPA issues guidelines as to what equipment meets this standard; essentially, the guidelines require the most effective pollution-control equipment available. New sources must install BACT equipment before beginning operations. Existing sources are subject to timetables for the installation of BACT equipment and must immediately install equipment that utilizes the *best practical control technology,* or BPCT. The EPA also issues guidelines as to what equipment meets this standard.

Wetlands The Clean Water Act prohibits the filling or dredging of wetlands unless a permit is obtained from the Army Corps of Engineers. The EPA defines **wetlands** as "those areas that are inundated or saturated by surface or ground water at a frequency and duration sufficient to support, and that under normal circumstances do support, a prevalence of vegetation typically adapted for life in saturated soil conditions." The EPA's broad interpretation of what constitutes a wetland for purposes of regulation by the federal government has generated substantial controversy.

The Migratory Bird Rule. One of the most controversial regulations was the "migratory bird rule" issued by the Army Corps of Engineers. Under this rule, any bodies of water that could affect interstate commerce, including seasonal ponds or waters "used or suitable for use by migratory birds" that fly over state borders, were "navigable waters" subject to federal regulation under the Clean Water Act as wetlands. The rule was challenged in a case brought by a group of communities that wanted to build a landfill in a tract of land northwest of Chicago. The Army Corps of Engineers refused to grant a permit for the landfill on the ground that the shallow ponds on the property formed a habitat for migratory birds.

Ultimately, the United States Supreme Court held that the Army Corps of Engineers had exceeded its authority under the Clean Water Act. The Court stated that it was not prepared to hold that isolated and seasonable ponds, puddles, and "prairie potholes" become "navigable waters of the United States" simply because they serve as a habitat for migratory birds.[10]

Seasonal Bodies of Water. The United States Supreme Court revisited the issue of wetlands in 2006, again scaling back the reach of the Clean Water Act. Two disputes had arisen as to whether certain properties in Michigan could be developed by the owners or were protected as wetlands, and the Court consolidated the cases on appeal. One involved property deemed to be wetlands because it was near an unnamed ditch that flowed into the Sutherland-Oemig Drain, which ultimately connected to Lake St. Clair. The other involved acres of marshy land, some of which was adjacent to a creek that flowed into a river, which flowed into yet another river, eventually reaching Saginaw Bay. Although the lower courts had concluded that both properties were wetlands under the Clean Water Act, the Supreme Court reversed these decisions. The Court held that the act covers "only those wetlands with a continuous surface connection to bodies that are waters of the United States in their own right." The Court further held that navigable waters under the act include only relatively permanent, standing or flowing bodies of water—not intermittent or temporary flows of water.[11]

10. *Solid Waste Agency of Northern Cook County v. U.S. Army Corps of Engineers,* 531 U.S. 159, 121 S.Ct. 675, 148 L.Ed.2d 576 (2001).

11. *Rapanos v. United States,* 547 U.S. 715, 126 S.Ct. 2208, 165 L.Ed.2d 159 (2006).

Violations of the Clean Water Act Under the Clean Water Act, violators are subject to a variety of civil and criminal penalties. Depending on the violation, civil penalties range from $10,000 to $25,000 per day, but not more than $25,000 per violation. Criminal penalties, which apply only if an act was intentional, range from a fine of $2,500 per day and imprisonment for up to one year to a fine of $1 million and fifteen years' imprisonment. Injunctive relief and damages can also be imposed. The polluting party can be required to clean up the pollution or pay for the cost of the clean-up.

Drinking Water

Another statute governing water pollution is the Safe Drinking Water Act.[12] Passed in 1974, this act requires the EPA to set maximum levels for pollutants in public water systems. Operators of public water supply systems must come as close as possible to meeting the EPA's standards by using the best available technology that is economically and technologically feasible. The EPA is particularly concerned about contamination from underground sources. Pesticides and wastes leaked from landfills or disposed of in underground injection wells are among the more than two hundred pollutants known to exist in groundwater used for drinking in at least thirty-four states. Many of these substances are associated with cancer and may cause damage to the central nervous system, liver, and kidneys.

The act was amended in 1996 to give the EPA greater flexibility in setting regulatory standards governing drinking water. These amendments also imposed requirements on suppliers of drinking water. Each supplier must send to every household it supplies with water an annual statement describing the source of its water, the level of any contaminants contained in the water, and any possible health concerns associated with the contaminants.

Ocean Dumping

The Marine Protection, Research, and Sanctuaries Act of 1972[13] (known popularly as the Ocean Dumping Act) regulates the transportation and dumping of material (pollutants) into ocean waters. It prohibits entirely the ocean dumping of radiological, chemical, and biological warfare agents and high-level radioactive waste.

The act also established a permit program for transporting and dumping other materials, and designated certain areas as marine sanctuaries. Each violation of any provision or permit requirement in the Ocean Dumping Act may result in a civil penalty of up to $50,000. A knowing violation is a criminal offense that may result in a $50,000 fine, imprisonment for not more than a year, or both. A court may also grant an injunction to prevent an imminent or continuing violation.

Oil Pollution

In response to the worst oil spill in North American history—more than 10 million gallons of oil that leaked into Alaska's Prince William Sound from the *Exxon Valdez* supertanker—Congress passed the Oil Pollution Act of 1990.[14] Under this act, any onshore or offshore oil facility, oil shipper, vessel owner, or vessel operator that discharges oil into navigable waters or onto an adjoining shore may be liable for clean-up costs, as well as damages. The act created an oil clean-up and economic compensation fund, and required oil tankers using U.S. ports to be double hulled by the year 2011 (to limit the severity of accidental spills).

Under the act, damage to natural resources, private property, and the local economy, including the increased cost of providing public services, is compensable. The penalties range from $2 million to $350 million, depending on the size of the vessel and on whether the oil spill came from a vessel or an offshore facility. The party held responsible for the clean-up costs can bring a civil suit for contribution from other potentially liable parties.

Toxic Chemicals

Originally, most environmental clean-up efforts were directed toward reducing smog and making water safe for fishing and swimming. Today, control of toxic chemicals used in agriculture and in industry has become increasingly important.

Pesticides and Herbicides

The Federal Insecticide, Fungicide, and Rodenticide Act (FIFRA) of 1947[15] regulates pesticides and herbicides. Under FIFRA, pesticides and herbicides must be

12. 42 U.S.C. Sections 300f to 300j-25.
13. 16 U.S.C. Sections 1401–1445.
14. 33 U.S.C. Sections 2701–2761.
15. 7 U.S.C. Sections 136–136y.

(1) registered before they can be sold, (2) certified and used only for approved applications, and (3) used in limited quantities when applied to food crops. The EPA can cancel or suspend registration of substances that are identified as harmful and may also inspect factories where the chemicals are made. Under 1996 amendments to FIFRA, there must be no more than a one-in-a-million risk to people of developing cancer from any kind of exposure to the substance, including eating food that contains pesticide residues.[16]

It is a violation of FIFRA to sell a pesticide or herbicide that is either unregistered or has had its registration canceled or suspended. It is also a violation to sell a pesticide or herbicide with a false or misleading label or to destroy or deface any labeling required under the act. For example, it is an offense to sell a substance that has a chemical strength different from the concentration declared on the label. Penalties for commercial dealers include imprisonment for up to one year and a fine up to $25,000 (producers can be fined up to $50,000). Farmers and other private users of pesticides or herbicides who violate the act are subject to a $1,000 fine and incarceration for up to thirty days.

Can a state regulate the sale and use of federally registered pesticides? Tort suits against pesticide manufacturers were common long before the enactment of FIFRA in 1947 and continued to be a feature of the legal landscape at the time FIFRA was amended. Until it heard the following case, however, the United States Supreme Court had never considered whether the statute preempts claims arising under state law.

16. 21 U.S.C. Section 346a.

CASE 24.4 Bates v. Dow Agrosciences, LLC

Supreme Court of the United States, 2005. 544 U.S. 431, 125 S.Ct. 1788, 161 L.Ed.2d 687.
www.findlaw.com/casecode/supreme.html[a]

Background and Facts The Environmental Protection Agency (EPA) conditionally registered Strongarm, a new weed-killing pesticide, on March 8, 2000.[b] Dow Agrosciences, LLC, immediately sold Strongarm to Texas peanut farmers, who normally plant their crops around May 1. The label stated, "Use of Strongarm is recommended in all areas where peanuts are grown." When the farmers applied Strongarm to their fields, the pesticide damaged their crops while failing to control the growth of weeds. After unsuccessfully attempting to negotiate with Dow, the farmers announced their intent to sue Strongarm's maker for violations of Texas state law. Dow filed a suit in a federal district court against the peanut farmers, asserting that FIFRA preempted their claims. The court issued a summary judgment in Dow's favor. The farmers appealed to the U.S. Court of Appeals for the Fifth Circuit, which affirmed the lower court's judgment. The farmers appealed to the United States Supreme Court.

IN THE LANGUAGE OF THE COURT
Justice *STEVENS* delivered the opinion of the Court.

* * * *

Under FIFRA * * * , [a] pesticide is misbranded if its label contains a statement that is false or misleading in any particular, including a false or misleading statement concerning the efficacy of the pesticide. *A pesticide is also misbranded if its label does not contain adequate instructions for use, or if its label omits necessary warnings or cautionary statements.* [Emphasis added.]

* * * *

* * * [Section] 136v provides:

> (a) * * * A State may regulate the sale or use of any federally registered pesticide or device in the State, but only if and to the extent [that] the regulation does not permit any sale or use prohibited by [FIFRA].
> (b) * * * Such State shall not impose or continue in effect any requirements for labeling or packaging in addition to or different from those required under [FIFRA].

* * * *

* * * *Nothing in the text of FIFRA would prevent a State from making the violation of a federal labeling or packaging requirement a state offense,* thereby imposing its own sanctions on pes-

a. In the "Browsing" section, click on "2005 Decisions." In the result, click on the name of the case to access the opinion.
b. Strongarm might more commonly be called an herbicide, but FIFRA classifies it as a pesticide.

CASE 24.4 CONTINUED

ticide manufacturers who violate federal law. The imposition of state sanctions for violating state rules that merely duplicate federal requirements is equally consistent with the text of [Section] 136v. [Emphasis added.]

* * * *

* * * For a particular state rule to be preempted, it must satisfy two conditions. First, it must be a requirement "for labeling or packaging"; rules governing the design of a product, for example, are not preempted. Second, it must impose a labeling or packaging requirement that is "in addition to or different from those required under [FIFRA]." A state regulation requiring the word "poison" to appear in red letters, for instance, would not be preempted if an EPA regulation imposed the same requirement.

* * * Rules that require manufacturers to design reasonably safe products, to use due care in conducting appropriate testing of their products, to market products free of manufacturing defects, and to honor their express warranties or other contractual commitments plainly do not qualify as requirements for "labeling or packaging." None of these common-law rules requires that manufacturers label or package their products in any particular way. Thus, petitioners' claims for defective design, defective manufacture, negligent testing, and breach of express warranty are not preempted.

* * * *

Dow * * * argues that [this] "parallel requirements" reading of [Section] 136v(b) would "give juries in 50 States the authority to give content to FIFRA's misbranding prohibition, establishing a crazy-quilt of anti-misbranding requirements * * * ." Conspicuously absent from the submissions by Dow * * * is any plausible alternative interpretation of "in addition to or different from" that would give that phrase meaning. Instead, they appear to favor reading those words out of the statute * * * . This amputated version of [Section] 136v(b) would no doubt have clearly and succinctly commanded the pre-emption of *all* state requirements concerning labeling. *That Congress added the remainder of the provision is evidence of its intent to draw a distinction between state labeling requirements that are preempted and those that are not.* [Emphasis added.]

* * * *

In sum, under our interpretation, [Section] 136v(b) * * * preempts competing state labeling standards—imagine 50 different labeling regimes prescribing the color, font size, and wording of warnings—that would create significant inefficiencies for manufacturers. The provision also preempts any statutory or common-law rule that would impose a labeling requirement that diverges from those set out in FIFRA * * * . *It does not, however, preempt any state rules that are fully consistent with federal requirements.* [Emphasis added.]

• **Decision and Remedy** *The United States Supreme Court vacated the lower court's judgment. A state can regulate the sale and use of federally registered pesticides to the extent that it does not permit anything that FIFRA prohibits, but a state cannot impose any requirements for labeling or packaging in addition to or different from those that FIFRA requires. The Court remanded the case, however, for further proceedings subject to this standard, concerning certain state law claims "on which we have not received sufficient briefing."*

• **What If the Facts Were Different?** *Suppose that FIFRA required Strongarm's label to include the word* CAUTION, *and the Texas peanut farmers filed their claims under a state regulation that required the label to use the word* DANGER. *Would the result have been different?*

• **The Legal Environment Dimension** *According to the Court's interpretation, what is required for a state regulation or rule to be preempted under FIFRA? Why is this significant?*

Toxic Substances

The first comprehensive law covering toxic substances was the Toxic Substances Control Act of 1976.[17] The act was passed to regulate chemicals and chemical compounds that are known to be toxic—such as asbestos and polychlorinated biphenyls, popularly known as PCBs—and to institute investigation of any possible harmful effects from new chemical compounds. The regulations authorize the EPA to require that manufacturers, processors, and other entities planning to use

17. 15 U.S.C. Sections 2601–2692.

chemicals first determine their effects on human health and the environment. The EPA can regulate substances that may pose an imminent hazard or an unreasonable risk of injury to health or the environment. The EPA may require special labeling, limit the use of a substance, set production quotas, or prohibit the use of a substance altogether.

Hazardous Wastes

Some industrial, agricultural, and household wastes pose more serious threats than others. If not properly disposed of, these toxic chemicals may present a substantial danger to human health and the environment. If released into the environment, they may contaminate public drinking water resources.

Resource Conservation and Recovery Act

In 1976, Congress passed the Resource Conservation and Recovery Act (RCRA)[18] in reaction to a growing concern about the effects of hazardous waste materials on the environment. The RCRA required the EPA to establish regulations to determine which forms of solid waste should be considered hazardous and to establish regulations to monitor and control hazardous waste disposal. The act also requires all producers of hazardous waste materials to label and package properly any hazardous waste to be transported. The RCRA was amended in 1984 and 1986 to decrease the use of land containment in the disposal of hazardous waste and to require smaller generators of hazardous waste to comply with the act.

Under the RCRA, a company may be assessed a civil penalty of up to $25,000 for each violation.[19] The penalty is based on the seriousness of the violation, the probability of harm, and the extent to which the violation deviates from RCRA requirements. Criminal penalties include fines up to $50,000 for each day of violation, imprisonment for up to two years (in most instances), or both. Criminal fines and the time of imprisonment can be doubled for certain repeat offenders.

Superfund

In 1980, Congress passed the Comprehensive Environmental Response, Compensation, and Liability Act (CERCLA),[20] commonly known as Superfund. The basic purpose of Superfund is to regulate the cleanup of disposal sites in which hazardous waste is leaking into the environment. A special federal fund was created for that purpose.

Superfund provides that when a release or a threatened release of hazardous chemicals from a site occurs, the EPA can clean up the site and recover the cost of the clean-up from the following persons: (1) the person who generated the wastes disposed of at the site, (2) the person who transported the wastes to the site, (3) the person who owned or operated the site at the time of the disposal, or (4) the current owner or operator. A person falling within one of these categories is referred to as a **potentially responsible party (PRP).**

Liability under Superfund is usually joint and several—that is, a PRP who generated *only a fraction of the hazardous waste* disposed of at the site may nevertheless be liable for *all* of the clean-up costs. CERCLA authorizes a party who has incurred clean-up costs to bring a "contribution action" against any other person who is liable or potentially liable for a percentage of the costs.

18. 42 U.S.C. Sections 6901–6986.
19. 42 U.S.C. Section 6928(a).
20. 42 U.S.C. Sections 9601–9675.

REVIEWING Environmental Law

In the late 1980s, residents of Lake Caliopa, Minnesota, began noticing an unusually high number of lung ailments among their population. A group of concerned local citizens pooled their resources and commissioned a study of the frequency of these health conditions per capita as compared to national averages. The study concluded that residents of Lake Caliopa experienced four to seven times the frequency of asthma, bronchitis, and emphysema as the population nationwide.

REVIEWING Environmental Law, Continued

During the study period, citizens began expressing concerns about the large volumes of smog emitted by the Cotton Design apparel manufacturing plant on the outskirts of town. The plant had opened its production facility two miles east of town beside the Tawakoni River in 1997 and employed seventy full-time workers by 2008.

Just downstream on the Tawakoni River, the city of Lake Caliopa operated a public water works facility, which supplied all city residents with water. In August 2008, the Minnesota Pollution Control Agency required Cotton Design to install new equipment to control air and water pollution. In May 2009, thirty citizens brought a class-action lawsuit in a Minnesota state court against Cotton Design for various respiratory ailments allegedly caused or compounded by smog from Cotton Design's factory. Using the information presented in the chapter, answer the following questions.

1. Under the common law, what would each plaintiff be required to identify in order to be given relief by the court?
2. Are air-quality regulations typically overseen by federal, state, or local governments?
3. What standard for limiting emissions into the air does Cotton Design's pollution-control equipment have to meet?
4. What information must the city send to every household that the city supplies with water?

TERMS AND CONCEPTS

environmental impact statement (EIS) 599
environmental law 598
nuisance 598
potentially responsible party (PRP) 612
toxic tort 599
wetlands 608

QUESTIONS AND CASE PROBLEMS

24–1. Some scientific knowledge indicates that there is no safe level of exposure to a cancer-causing agent. In theory, even one molecule of such a substance has the potential for causing cancer. Section 112 of the Clean Air Act requires that all cancer-causing substances be regulated to ensure a margin of safety. Some environmental groups have argued that all emissions of such substances must be eliminated to attain such a margin of safety. Total elimination would likely shut down many major U.S. industries. Should the Environmental Protection Agency totally forbid all emissions of cancer-causing chemicals? Discuss.

24–2. QUESTION WITH SAMPLE ANSWER

Fruitade, Inc., is a processor of a soft drink called Freshen Up. Fruitade uses returnable bottles, which it cleans with a special acid to allow for further beverage processing. The acid is diluted with water and then allowed to pass into a navigable stream. Fruitade crushes its broken bottles and throws the crushed glass into the stream. Discuss fully any environmental laws that Fruitade has violated.

• **For a sample answer to Question 24–2, go to Appendix I at the end of this text.**

24–3. Moonbay is a home-building corporation that primarily develops retirement communities. Farmtex owns a number of feedlots in Sunny Valley. Moonbay purchased 20,000 acres of farmland in the same area and began building and selling homes on this acreage. In the meantime, Farmtex continued to expand its feedlot business, and eventually only 500 feet separated the two operations. Because of the odor and flies from the feedlots, Moonbay found it difficult to sell the homes in its development. Moonbay wants to enjoin (prevent) Farmtex from operating its feedlot in the vicinity of the retirement home development. Under what common law theory would Moonbay file this action? Has Farmtex violated any federal environmental laws? Discuss.

24–4. Clean Water Act. Attique Ahmad owned the Spin-N-Market, a convenience store and gas station. The gas pumps were fed by underground tanks, one of which had a leak at its top that allowed water to enter. Ahmad emptied the tank by pumping its contents into a storm drain and a sewer system. Through the storm drain, gasoline flowed into a creek, forcing the city to clean the water. Through the sewer system, gasoline flowed into a sewage treatment plant, forcing the city to evacuate the plant and two nearby schools. Ahmad was charged with discharging a pollutant without a permit, which is a criminal violation of the Clean Water Act. The act provides that a person who "knowingly violates" the act commits a felony. Ahmad claimed that he had believed he was discharging only water. Did Ahmad commit a felony? Why or why not? Discuss fully. [*United States v. Ahmad,* 101 F.3d 386 (5th Cir. 1996)]

24–5. Environmental Impact Statement. Greers Ferry Lake is in Arkansas, and its shoreline is under the management of the U.S. Army Corps of Engineers, which is part of the U.S. Department of Defense (DOD). The Corps's 2000 Shoreline Management Plan (SMP) rezoned numerous areas along the lake, authorized the Corps to issue permits for the construction of new boat docks in the rezoned areas, increased by 300 percent the area around habitable structures that could be cleared of vegetation, and instituted a Wildlife Enhancement Permit to allow limited modifications of the shoreline. In relation to the SMP's adoption, the Corps issued a Finding of No Significant Impact, which declared that no environmental impact statement (EIS) was necessary. The Corps issued thirty-two boat dock construction permits under the SMP before Save Greers Ferry Lake, Inc., filed a suit in a federal district court against the DOD, asking the court to, among other things, stop the Corps from acting under the SMP and order it to prepare an EIS. What are the requirements for an EIS? Is an EIS needed in this case? Explain. [*Save Greers Ferry Lake, Inc. v. Department of Defense,* 255 F.3d 498 (8th Cir. 2001)]

24–6. CERCLA. Beginning in 1926, Marietta Dyestuffs Co. operated an industrial facility in Marietta, Ohio, to make dyes and other chemicals. In 1944, Dyestuffs became part of American Home Products Corp. (AHP), which sold the Marietta facility to American Cyanamid Co. in 1946. In 1950, AHP sold the rest of the Dyestuffs assets and all of its stock to Goodrich Co., which immediately liquidated the acquired corporation. Goodrich continued to operate the dissolved corporation's business, however. Cyanamid continued to make chemicals at the Marietta facility, and in 1993, it created Cytec Industries, Inc., which expressly assumed all environmental liabilities associated with Cyanamid's ownership and operation of the facility. Cytec spent nearly $25 million on clean-up costs and filed a suit in a federal district court against Goodrich to recover, under CERCLA, a portion of the costs attributable to the clean-up of hazardous wastes that may have been discarded at the site between 1926 and 1946. Cytec filed a motion for summary judgment in its favor. Should the court grant Cytec's motion? Explain. [*Cytec Industries, Inc. v. B. F. Goodrich Co.,* 196 F.Supp.2d 644 (S.D. Ohio 2002)]

24–7. CASE PROBLEM WITH SAMPLE ANSWER

William Gurley was the president and majority stockholder in Gurley Refining Co. (GRC). GRC bought used oil, treated it, and sold it. The refining process created a by-product residue of oily waste. GRC disposed of this waste by dumping it at, among other locations, a landfill in West Memphis, Arkansas. In February 1992, after detecting hazardous chemicals at the site, the Environmental Protection Agency (EPA) asked Gurley about his assets, the generators of the material disposed of at the landfill, site operations, and the structure of GRC. Gurley refused to respond, except to suggest that the EPA ask GRC. In October, the EPA placed the site on its clean-up list and again asked Gurley for information. When he still refused to respond, the EPA filed a suit in a federal district court against him, asking the court to impose a civil penalty. In February 1999, Gurley finally answered the EPA's questions. Under CERCLA, a court may impose a civil penalty "not to exceed $25,000 for each day of noncompliance against any person who unreasonably fails to comply" with an information request. Should the court assess a penalty in this case? Why or why not? [*United States v. Gurley,* 384 F.3d 316 (6th Cir. 2004)]

- **To view a sample answer for Problem 24–7, go to this book's Web site at academic.cengage.com/blaw/cross, select "Chapter 24," and click on "Case Problem with Sample Answer."**

24–8. Clean Water Act. The Anacostia River, which flows through Washington, D.C., is one of the ten most polluted rivers in the country. For bodies of water such as the Anacostia, the Clean Water Act requires states (which, under the act, include the District of Columbia) to set a "total maximum daily load" (TMDL) for pollutants. A TMDL is to be set "at a level necessary to implement the applicable water-quality standards with seasonal variations." The Anacostia contains biochemical pollutants that consume oxygen, putting the river's aquatic life at risk for suffocation. In addition, the river is murky, stunting the growth of plants that rely on sunlight and impairing recreational use. The Environmental Protection Agency (EPA) approved one TMDL limiting the *annual* discharge of oxygen-depleting pollutants and a second limiting the *seasonal* discharge of pollutants contributing to turbidity. Neither TMDL limited daily discharges. Friends of the Earth, Inc. (FoE), asked a federal district court to review the TMDLs. What is FoE's best argument in this dispute? What is the EPA's likely response? What should the court rule, and why? [*Friends of the Earth, Inc. v. Environmental Protection Agency,* 446 F.3d 140 (D.C.Cir. 2006)]

24–9. Environmental Impact Statement. The fourth largest crop in the United States is alfalfa, of which 5 percent is exported to Japan. RoundUp Ready alfalfa is genetically engineered to resist glyphosate, the active ingredient in the herbicide RoundUp. The U.S. Department of Agriculture (USDA) regulates genetically engineered agricultural products through the Animal and Plant Health Inspection Service (APHIS). APHIS concluded that RoundUp Ready alfalfa does not have any harmful health effects on humans or livestock and deregulated it. Geertson Seed Farms and others filed a suit in a federal district court against Mike Johanns (the secretary of the USDA) and others, asserting that APHIS's decision required the preparation of an environmental impact statement (EIS). The plaintiffs argued, among other things, that the introduction of RoundUp Ready alfalfa might significantly decrease the availability of, or even eliminate, all nongenetically engineered varieties. The plaintiffs were concerned that the RoundUp Ready alfalfa might contaminate standard alfalfa because alfalfa is pollinated by bees, which can travel as far as two miles from a pollen source. If contamination occurred, farmers would not be able to market "contaminated" varieties as "organic," which would impact the sales of "organic" livestock and exports to Japan, which does not allow the import of glyphosate-tolerant alfalfa. Should an EIS be prepared in this case? Why or why not? [*Geertson Seed Farms v. Johanns,* __ F.Supp.2d __ (N.D.Cal. 2007)]

24–10. A QUESTION OF ETHICS

*In the Clean Air Act, Congress allowed California, which has particular problems with clean air, to adopt its own standard for emissions from cars and trucks, subject to the approval of the Environmental Protection Agency (EPA) according to certain criteria. Congress also allowed other states to adopt California's standard after the EPA's approval. In 2004, in an effort to address global warming, the California Air Resources Board amended the state's standard to attain "the maximum feasible and cost-effective reduction of GHG [greenhouse gas] emissions from motor vehicles." The regulation, which applies to new passenger vehicles and light-duty trucks for 2009 and later, imposes decreasing limits on emissions of carbon dioxide through 2016. While EPA approval was pending, Vermont and other states adopted similar standards. Green Mountain Chrysler Plymouth Dodge Jeep and other auto dealers, automakers, and associations of automakers filed a suit in a federal district court against George Crombie (secretary of the Vermont Agency of Natural Resources) and others, seeking relief from the state regulations. [*Green Mountain Chrysler Plymouth Dodge Jeep v. Crombie, *508 F.Supp.2d 295 (D.Vt. 2007)]*

(a) Under the Environmental Policy and Conservation Act (EPCA) of 1975, the National Highway Traffic Safety Administration sets fuel economy standards for new cars. The plaintiffs argued, among other things, that the EPCA, which prohibits states from adopting separate fuel economy standards, preempts Vermont's GHG regulation. Do the GHG rules equate to the fuel economy standards? Discuss.

(b) Do Vermont's rules tread on the efforts of the federal government to address global warming internationally? Who should regulate GHG emissions? The federal government? The state governments? Both? Neither? Why?

(c) The plaintiffs claimed that they would go bankrupt if they were forced to adhere to the state's GHG standards. Should they be granted relief on this basis? Does history support their claim? Explain.

LAW ON THE WEB

For updated links to resources available on the Web, as well as a variety of other materials, visit this text's Web site at

academic.cengage.com/blaw/cross

For information on the standards, guidelines, and regulations of the Environmental Protection Agency (EPA), go to the EPA's Web site at

www.epa.gov

To learn about the Resource Conservation and Recovery Act's "buy-recycled" requirements and other steps that the federal government has taken toward "greening the environment," go to

www.epa.gov/cpg

The Law Library of the Indiana University School of Law provides numerous links to online environmental law sources. Go to

www.law.indiana.edu/library/services/onl_env.shtml

Legal Research Exercises on the Web

Go to **academic.cengage.com/blaw/cross**, the Web site that accompanies this text. Select "Chapter 24" and click on "Internet Exercises." There you will find the following Internet research exercises that you can perform to learn more about the topics covered in this chapter.

Internet Exercise 24–1: Legal Perspective
Nuisance Law

Internet Exercise 24–2: Management Perspective
Complying with Environmental Regulation

Internet Exercise 24–3: Ethical Perspective
Environmental Justice

CHAPTER 25

Land-Use Control and Real Property

Property ownership confers certain rights. An owner generally has the right to possess the property; the right either to use the property or to derive profits from another's use of the property; and the right to *alienate*[1] the property—that is, to sell, bequeath (pass on through a will), or give to others the same rights of ownership. Not all forms of ownership provide such a complete bundle of rights, but one or more of these attributes are normally included when we say that property is "owned."

1. *Alienate* derives from the Latin word *alienus* (alien), which is from the Latin *alus* (other). In legal terms, alienate means to transfer the title to property.

Even for one who possesses the entire bundle of rights we have delineated, however, ownership is not absolute. The law places restrictions on how property may be used. It also imposes duties on the owners regarding how the land is to be maintained. In addition, individual owners may agree with others to restrict or limit the use of their property. Thus, property owners cannot always do with their property whatever they wish. Nuisance and environmental laws, for example, restrict how people carry out certain types of activities on their own land. Briefly stated, the rights of every property owner are subject to certain conditions and limitations.

In this chapter, we first look at the nature of ownership rights in real property. We then examine the legal requirements involved in the transfer of real property, including the kinds of rights that are transferred by various types of deeds; the procedures used in the sale of real estate; and a way in which real property can, under certain conditions, be transferred merely by possession. We also discuss the right of government to take, for compensation, private land for public use, as well as other types of restrictions on the ownership and use of property.

The Nature of Real Property

Real property (sometimes called *realty* or *real estate*) consists of land and the buildings, plants, and trees that it contains. Everything else is **personal property.** Personal property is movable; real property is immovable. Real property usually means land and structures, but it also includes airspace and subsurface rights, plant life and vegetation, and *fixtures* (as will be discussed shortly).

Land and Structures

Land includes the soil on the surface of the earth and the natural products or artificial structures that are attached to it. Land further includes all the waters contained on or under its surface and much, but not necessarily all, of the airspace above it. The exterior boundaries of land extend down to the center of the earth and up to the farthest reaches of the atmosphere (subject to certain qualifications).

Airspace and Subsurface Rights

The owner of real property has relatively exclusive rights to both the airspace above the land and the soil and minerals underneath it. Any limitations on either airspace rights or subsurface rights, called *encumbrances,* normally must be indicated on the document that transfers title at the time of purchase. The ways in which ownership rights in real property can be limited will be examined in detail later in this chapter.

Airspace Rights Early cases involving airspace rights dealt with such matters as whether a telephone wire could be run across a person's property when the wire did not touch any of the property[2] and whether a bullet shot over a person's land constituted trespass.[3] Today, disputes concerning airspace rights may involve the right of commercial and private planes to fly over property and the right of individuals and governments to seed clouds and produce artificial rain. Flights over private land normally do not violate property rights unless the flights are so low and so frequent that they directly interfere with the owner's enjoyment and use of the land.

Subsurface Rights In many states, land ownership can be separated from ownership of its subsurface. In other words, the owner of the surface may sell subsurface rights to another person. Subsurface rights can be extremely valuable, as these rights include the ownership of minerals, oil, or natural gas. But a subsurface owner's rights would be of little value if he or she could not use the surface to exercise those rights. Hence, a subsurface owner will have a right (called a *profit*, discussed later in this chapter) to go onto the surface of the land to, for example, find and remove minerals.

When the ownership is separated into surface and subsurface rights, each owner can pass title to what she or he owns without the consent of the other owner. Of course, conflicts may arise between surface and subsurface owners when attempts are made to excavate below the surface. One party's interest may become subservient (secondary) to the other party's interest either by statute or case law. At common law and generally today, if the owners of the subsurface rights excavate, they are absolutely liable if their excavation causes the surface to collapse. Depending on the circumstances, the excavators may also be liable for any damage to structures on the land. Many states have statutes that extend excavators' liability to include damage to structures on the property. Typically, these statutes provide exact guidelines as to the requirements for excavations of various depths.

2. *Butler v. Frontier Telephone Co.*, 186 N.Y. 486, 79 N.E. 716 (1906). Stringing a wire across someone's property violates the airspace rights of that person. Leaning walls and projecting eave spouts and roofs also violate the airspace rights of the property owner.

3. *Herrin v. Sutherland*, 74 Mont. 587, 241 P. 328 (1925). Shooting over a person's land normally constitutes trespass.

Plant Life and Vegetation

Plant life, both natural and cultivated, is also considered to be real property. In many instances, the natural vegetation, such as trees, adds greatly to the value of realty. When a parcel of land is sold and the land has growing crops on it, the sale includes the crops, unless otherwise specified in the sales contract. When crops are sold by themselves, however, they are considered to be personal property or goods rather than real property. Consequently, the sale of crops is a sale of goods and thus is governed by the Uniform Commercial Code (see Chapter 11) rather than by real property law.

Fixtures

Certain personal property can become so closely associated with the real property to which it is attached that the law views it as real property. Such property is known as a **fixture**—a thing affixed to realty. A thing is affixed to realty when it is attached to the realty by roots; embedded in it; or permanently attached by means of cement, plaster, bolts, nails, or screws. The fixture can be physically attached to real property or attached to another fixture; it can even be an item, such as a statue, that is not physically attached to the land, as long as the owner *intends* the property to be a fixture.

Fixtures are included in the sale of land if the sales contract does not provide otherwise. The sale of a house includes the land and the house and garage on it, as well as the cabinets, plumbing, and windows. Because these are permanently affixed to the property, they are considered to be a part of it. Unless otherwise agreed, however, the curtains and throw rugs are not included. Items such as drapes and window-unit air conditioners are difficult to classify. Thus, a contract for the sale of a house or commercial property should indicate which items of this sort are included in the sale.

The issue of whether an item is a fixture (and thus real estate) or not a fixture (and thus personal property) often arises with respect to land sales, real property taxation, insurance coverage, and divorces. Generally, when the courts need to determine whether a certain item is a fixture, they examine the intention of the party who placed the object on the real property. If the facts indicate that the person intended the item to be a fixture, then it normally will be considered a fixture.

Ownership and Other Interests in Real Property

Ownership of property is an abstract concept that cannot exist independently of the legal system. No one can actually possess, or *hold,* a piece of land, the air above, the earth below, and all the water contained on it. One can only possess *rights* in real property. Numerous rights are involved in real property ownership, which is why property ownership is often viewed as a bundle of rights. These rights include the right to possess the property and the right to dispose of the property—by sale, gift, rental, and lease, for example. Traditionally, ownership interests in real property were referred to as *estates in land,* which include fee simple estates, life estates, and leasehold estates. We examine these estates in land, forms of concurrent ownership, and certain other interests in real property that is owned by others in the following subsections.

Ownership in Fee Simple

A person who holds the entire bundle of rights is said to be the owner in **fee simple absolute.** In a fee simple absolute, the owner has the greatest aggregation of rights, privileges, and power possible. The owner can give the property away or dispose of the property by *deed* (the instrument used to transfer property, as discussed later in this chapter) or by a will. When there is no will, the fee simple passes to the owner's legal heirs on her or his death. A fee simple absolute is potentially infinite in duration and is assigned forever to a person and her or his heirs without limitation or condition.[4] The owner has the right of *exclusive* possession and use of the property.

The rights that accompany a fee simple absolute include the right to use the land for whatever purpose the owner sees fit. Of course, other laws, including applicable zoning, noise, and environmental laws, may limit the owner's ability to use the property in certain ways.

In the following case, the court had to decide whether the noise—rock and roll music, conversation, and clacking pool balls—coming from a local bar (called a "saloon" during the days of cowboys in the United States) unreasonably interfered with a neighboring property owner's rights.

4. Note that in *fee simple defeasible,* ownership in fee simple will automatically terminate if a stated event occurs, such as when property is conveyed (transferred) to a school board only as long as it is used for school purposes. In addition, the fee simple may be subject to a *condition subsequent,* meaning that if a stated event occurs, the prior owner of the property can bring an action to regain possession of the property.

CASE 25.1 Biglane v. Under the Hill Corp.

Mississippi Supreme Court, 2007. 949 So.2d 9.
www.mssc.state.ms.us[a]

• **Background and Facts** In 1967, Nancy and James Biglane bought and refurbished a building at 27 Silver Street in Natchez, Mississippi, and opened the lower portion as a gift shop. In 1973, Andre Farish and Paul O'Malley bought the building next door, at 25 Silver Street, and opened the Natchez Under the Hill Saloon. Later, the Biglanes converted the upper floors of their building into an apartment and moved in. Despite installing insulated walls and windows, locating the bedroom on the side of the building away from the Saloon, and placing the air-conditioning unit on the side nearest the Saloon, the Biglanes had a problem: the noise of the Saloon kept them wide awake at night. During the summer, the Saloon, which had no air-conditioning, opened its windows and doors, and live music echoed up and down the street. The Biglanes asked the Saloon to turn the music down, and it was: thicker windows were installed, the loudest band was replaced, and the other bands were asked to keep their output below a certain level of decibels. Still dissatisfied, the Biglanes filed a suit in a Mississippi state court against the Saloon. The court enjoined the defendant from opening doors or windows when music was playing and ordered it to prevent its patrons from loitering in the street. Both parties appealed to the Mississippi Supreme Court.

a. In the center of the page, click on the "Search this site" link. On the next page, click on "Plain English." When that page opens, in the "Enter the ISYS Plain English query:" box, type "2005-CA-01751-SCT" and click on "Search." In the result, click on the first item in the list that includes that number to access the opinion. The Mississippi Supreme Court maintains this Web site.

CASE CONTINUES

CASE 25.1 CONTINUED

IN THE LANGUAGE OF THE COURT
***DIAZ,* Justice, for the Court.**

* * * *

*An entity is subject to liability * * * when its conduct is a legal cause of an invasion of another's interest in the private use and enjoyment of land and that invasion is * * * intentional and unreasonable * * *.* [Emphasis added.]

* * * [The trial court] found ample evidence that the Biglanes frequently could not use or enjoy their property—significantly, that Mrs. Biglane often slept away from the apartment on weekends to avoid the noise and that she could not have her grandchildren over on the weekends because of the noise. The audiologist [one who diagnoses hearing problems] who testified for the Biglanes concluded that the noise levels were excessive and unreasonable * * *.

* * * *

* * * The trial court weighed the fact that the Biglanes knew or should have known that there was going to be some sort of noise associated with living within five feet of a * * * saloon which provides live music on the weekends.

* * * *

* * * *A reasonable use of one's property cannot be construed to include those uses which produce obnoxious noises, which in turn result in a material injury to owners of property in the vicinity, causing them to suffer substantial annoyance, inconvenience, and discomfort.* [Emphasis added.]

Accordingly, even a lawful business—which the Under the Hill Saloon certainly is—may * * * [not interfere] with its neighbors' enjoyment of their property. We recognize that each * * * case must be decided upon its own peculiar facts, taking into consideration the location and the surrounding circumstances. Ultimately, it is not necessary that other property owners should be driven from their dwellings, because it is enough that the enjoyment of life and property is rendered materially uncomfortable and annoying.

* * * *

In the case at hand, the trial court exercised its power to permit continued operation of the Saloon while setting conditions to its future operation. Namely, it found that the Saloon could not operate its business with its doors and windows opened during any time that amplified music is being played inside the saloon. The * * * court found that such a limitation is reasonable in that it should help contain the noise within the saloon, and should discourage the bar patrons from congregating or loitering in the streets outside of the saloon.

From a review of the record it is clear that the * * * court balanced the interests between the Biglanes and the Saloon in a quest for an equitable remedy that allowed the couple to enjoy their private apartment while protecting a popular business and tourist attraction from overregulation.

• **Decision and Remedy** *The Mississippi Supreme Court affirmed the lower court's injunction. The Saloon unreasonably interfered with the Biglanes' rights. "One landowner may not use his land so as to unreasonably annoy, inconvenience, or harm others."*

• **The Ethical Dimension** *At one point in their dispute, the Biglanes blocked off two parking lots that served the Saloon. Was this an unreasonable interference with the Saloon's rights? Explain.*

• **The Legal Environment Dimension** *Could repulsive odors emanating from a neighbor's property constitute unreasonable interference with a property owner's rights? Why or why not?*

Life Estates

A **life estate** is an estate that lasts for the life of some specified individual. A **conveyance,** or transfer of real property, "to A for his life" creates a life estate.[5] In a life estate, the life tenant's ownership rights cease to exist on the life tenant's death. The life tenant has the right to use the land, provided no **waste** (injury to the land) is committed. In other words, the life tenant cannot use the land in a manner that would adversely affect its value. The life tenant can use the land to harvest crops or, if mines and oil wells are already on the land, can

5. A less common type of life estate is created by the conveyance "to A for the life of B." This is known as an estate *pur autre vie*—that is, an estate for the duration of the life of another.

extract minerals and oil from it, but the life tenant cannot exploit the land by creating new wells or mines.

With few exceptions, the owner of a life estate has an exclusive right to possession during his or her lifetime. In addition, the life tenant has the right to mortgage the life estate and create other interests in the land, but none can extend beyond the life of the tenant.

Along with these rights, the life tenant also has some duties—to keep the property in repair and to pay property taxes. In sum, the owner of the life estate has the same rights as a fee simple owner except that she or he must maintain the value of the property during her or his tenancy, less the decrease in value resulting from the normal use of the property allowed by the life tenancy.

Concurrent Ownership

Persons who share ownership rights simultaneously in particular property (including real property and personal property) are said to be concurrent owners. There are two principal types of **concurrent ownership:** *tenancy in common* and *joint tenancy.* Concurrent ownership rights can also be held in a tenancy by the entirety or as community property, although these types of concurrent ownership are less common.

Tenancy in Common The term **tenancy in common** refers to a form of co-ownership in which each of two or more persons owns an undivided interest in the property. The interest is undivided because each tenant has rights in the whole property. On the death of a tenant in common, that tenant's interest in the property passes to her or his heirs.

For example, four friends purchase a condominium unit in Hawaii together as tenants in common. This means that each of them has an ownership interest (one-fourth) in the whole. If one of the four owners, Trey, dies a year after the purchase, his ownership interest passes to his heirs (his wife and children, for example) rather than to the other tenants in common.

Unless the co-tenants have agreed otherwise, a tenant in common can transfer her or his interest in the property to another without the consent of the remaining co-owners. Generally, it is presumed that a co-tenancy is a tenancy in common unless there is a clear intention to establish a joint tenancy (discussed next).

Joint Tenancy In a **joint tenancy,** each of two or more persons owns an undivided interest in the property, but a deceased joint tenant's interest passes to the surviving joint tenant or tenants. The right of a surviving joint tenant to inherit a deceased joint tenant's ownership interest—referred to as a *right of survivorship*—distinguishes a joint tenancy from a tenancy in common. Suppose that Jerrold and Eva are married and purchase a house as joint tenants. The title to the house clearly expresses the intent to create a joint tenancy because it says "to Jerrold and Eva as joint tenants with right of survivorship." Jerrold has three children from a prior marriage. If Jerrold dies, his interest in the house automatically passes to Eva rather than to his children from the prior marriage.

Although a joint tenant can transfer her or his rights by sale or gift to another without the consent of the other joint tenants, doing so terminates the joint tenancy. In such a situation, the person who purchases the property or receives it as a gift becomes a tenant in common, not a joint tenant. For example, three brothers, Brody, Saul, and Jacob, own a parcel as joint tenants. Brody is experiencing financial difficulties and sells his interest in the property to Beth. The sale terminates the joint tenancy, and now Beth, Saul, and Jacob hold the property as tenants in common.

A joint tenant's interest can also be levied against (seized by court order) to satisfy the tenant's judgment creditors. If this occurs, the joint tenancy terminates, and the remaining owners hold the property as tenants in common. (Judgment creditors can also seize the interests of tenants in a tenancy in common.)

Tenancy by the Entirety A **tenancy by the entirety** is a less common form of ownership that typically is created by a conveyance (transfer) of real property to a husband and wife. It differs from a joint tenancy in that neither spouse may separately transfer his or her interest during his or her lifetime unless the other spouse consents. In some states in which statutes give the wife the right to convey her property, this form of concurrent ownership has effectively been abolished. A divorce, either spouse's death, or mutual agreement will terminate a tenancy by the entirety.

Community Property Only a limited number of states[6] allow property to be owned by a married couple as **community property.** If property is held as community property, each spouse technically owns an undivided one-half interest in the property. This type of

6. These states include Alaska, Arizona, California, Idaho, Louisiana, Nevada, New Mexico, Texas, Washington, and Wisconsin. Puerto Rico allows property to be owned as community property as well.

ownership applies to most property acquired by the husband or the wife during the course of the marriage. It generally does not apply to property acquired prior to the marriage or to property acquired by gift or inheritance during the marriage. After a divorce, community property is divided equally in some states and according to the discretion of the court in other states.

Leasehold Estates

A **leasehold estate** is created when a real property owner or lessor (landlord) agrees to convey the right to possess and use the property to a lessee (tenant) for a certain period of time. In every leasehold estate, the tenant has a *qualified* right to exclusive, though *temporary*, possession (qualified by the landlord's right to enter onto the premises to ensure that the tenant is not causing damage to the property). The tenant can use the land—for example, by harvesting crops—but cannot injure it by such activities as cutting down timber for sale or extracting oil.

Here, we look at the types of leasehold estates, or tenancies, that can be created when real property is leased.

Fixed-Term Tenancy or Tenancy for Years

A **fixed-term tenancy,** also called a *tenancy for years,* is created by an express contract by which property is leased for a specified period of time, such as a month, a year, or a period of years. Signing a one-year lease to occupy an apartment, for instance, creates a tenancy for years. Note that the term need not be specified by date and can be conditioned on the occurrence of an event, such as leasing a cabin for the summer or an apartment during Mardi Gras. At the end of the period specified in the lease, the lease ends (without notice), and possession of the property returns to the lessor. If the tenant dies during the period of the lease, the lease interest passes to the tenant's heirs as personal property. Often, leases include renewal or extension provisions.

Periodic Tenancy A **periodic tenancy** is created by a lease that does not specify how long it is to last but does specify that rent is to be paid at certain intervals. This type of tenancy is automatically renewed for another rental period unless properly terminated. For example, Jewel, LLC, enters into a lease with Capital Properties. The lease states, "Rent is due on the tenth day of every month." This provision creates a periodic tenancy from month to month. This type of tenancy can also extend from week to week or from year to year. A periodic tenancy sometimes arises when a landlord allows a tenant under a tenancy for years to *hold over* (retain possession after the lease term ends) and continue paying monthly or weekly rent.

Under the common law, to terminate a periodic tenancy, the landlord or tenant must give at least one period's notice to the other party. If the tenancy is month to month, for example, one month's notice must be given. State statutes often require a different period for notice of termination in a periodic tenancy, however.

Tenancy at Will In a **tenancy at will,** either the landlord or the tenant can terminate the tenancy without notice. This type of tenancy can arise if a landlord rents property to a tenant "for as long as both agree" or allows a person to live on the premises without paying rent. Tenancy at will is rare today because most state statutes require a landlord to provide some period of notice to terminate a tenancy (as previously noted). States may also require a landowner to have sufficient cause (reason) to end a residential tenancy. Certain events, such as the death of either party or the voluntary commission of waste by the tenant, automatically terminate a tenancy at will.

Tenancy at Sufferance The mere possession of land without right is called a **tenancy at sufferance.** A tenancy at sufferance is not a true tenancy because it is created when a tenant *wrongfully* retains possession of property. Whenever a tenancy for years or a periodic tenancy ends and the tenant continues to retain possession of the premises without the owner's permission, a tenancy at sufferance is created.

Nonpossessory Interests

In contrast to the types of property interests just described, some interests in land do not include any rights to possess the property. These interests, known as **nonpossessory interests,** include *easements, profits,* and *licenses.* Nonpossessory interests are basically interests in real property owned by others. (See *Concept Summary 25.1* for a review of the interests that can exist in real property.)

An **easement** is the right of a person to make limited use of another person's real property without taking anything from the property. An easement, for

CONCEPT SUMMARY 25.1
Interests in Real Property

Type of Interest	Description
OWNERSHIP INTERESTS	1. *Fee simple absolute*—The most complete form of ownership. 2. *Life estate*—An estate that lasts for the life of a specified individual. 3. *Concurrent interests*—When two or more persons hold title to property together, concurrent ownership exists. a. A tenancy in common exists when two or more persons own an undivided interest in property; on a tenant's death, that tenant's property interest passes to his or her heirs. b. A joint tenancy exists when two or more persons own an undivided interest in property, with a right of survivorship; on the death of a joint tenant, that tenant's property interest transfers to the remaining tenant(s), not to the heirs of the deceased. c. A tenancy by the entirety is a form of co-ownership between a husband and wife that is similar to a joint tenancy, except that a spouse cannot transfer separately her or his interest during her or his lifetime. d. Community property is a form of co-ownership between a husband and wife in which each spouse technically owns an undivided one-half interest in property acquired during the marriage. This type of ownership occurs in only a few states.
LEASEHOLD INTERESTS	A leasehold interest, or estate, is an interest in real property that is held for only a limited period of time, as specified in the lease agreement. Types of tenancies relating to leased property include the following: 1. *Fixed-term tenancy (tenancy for years)*—Tenancy for a period of time stated by express contract. 2. *Periodic tenancy*—Tenancy for a period determined by the frequency of rent payments; automatically renewed unless proper notice is given. 3. *Tenancy at will*—Tenancy for as long as both parties agree; no notice of termination is required. 4. *Tenancy at sufferance*—Possession of land without legal right.
NONPOSSESSORY INTERESTS	Interests that involve the right to use real property but not to possess it. Easements, profits, and licenses are nonpossessory interests.

example, can be the right to walk across another's property. In contrast, a **profit** is the right to go onto land owned by another and take away some part of the land itself or some product of the land. For example, Akmed, the owner of Sandy View, gives Ann the right to go there and remove all the sand and gravel that she needs for her cement business. Ann has a profit.

Easements and profits can be classified as either *appurtenant* or *in gross*. Because easements and profits are similar and the same rules apply to both, we discuss them together.

Easement or Profit Appurtenant An easement or profit *appurtenant* arises when the owner of one piece of land has a right to go onto (or remove things from) an adjacent piece of land owned by another. The land that is benefited by the easement is called the *dominant estate*, and the land that is burdened is called the *servient estate*. Because easements appurtenant are intended to *benefit the land*, they run with (are conveyed with) the land when it is transferred.[7] Suppose that Owen has a right to drive his car

7. See, for example, *Webster v. Ragona*, 7 A.D.3d 850, 776 N.Y.S.2d 347 (2004).

across Green's land, which is adjacent to Owen's property. This right-of-way over Green's property is an easement appurtenant to Owen's land and can be used only by Owen. If Owen sells his land, the easement runs with the land to benefit the new owner.

Easement or Profit in Gross An easement or profit *in gross* exists when someone who does not own an adjacent tract of land has a right to use or take things from another's land. These easements are intended to *benefit a particular person or business,* not a particular piece of land, and cannot be transferred. For example, Avery owns a parcel of land with a marble quarry. Avery conveys to Classic Stone Corporation the right to come onto her land and remove up to five hundred pounds of marble per day. Classic Stone owns a profit in gross and cannot transfer this right to another. Similarly, when a utility company is granted an easement to run its power lines across another's property, it obtains an easement in gross.

Creation of an Easement or Profit Most easements and profits are created by an express grant in a contract, deed, or will. This allows the parties to include terms defining the extent and length of time of use. In some situations, an easement or profit can also be created without an express agreement.

An easement or profit may arise by *implication* when the circumstances surrounding the division of a parcel of property imply its creation. For example, Barrow divides a parcel of land that has only one well for drinking water. If Barrow conveys the half without a well to Dean, a profit by implication arises because Dean needs drinking water.

An easement may also be created by *necessity.* An easement by necessity does not require division of property for its existence. A person who rents an apartment, for example, has an easement by necessity in the private road leading up to the dwelling.

An easement arises by *prescription* when one person exercises an easement, such as a right-of-way, on another person's land without the landowner's consent, and the use is apparent and continues for a period of time equal to the applicable statute of limitations. (In much the same way, title to property may be obtained by *adverse possession,* which will be discussed later in this chapter.)

Termination of an Easement or Profit An easement or profit can be terminated or extinguished in several ways. The simplest way is to deed it back to the owner of the land that is burdened by it. Another way is to abandon it and create evidence of intent to relinquish the right to use it. Mere nonuse will not extinguish an easement or profit *unless the nonuse is accompanied by an overt act showing the intent to abandon.* Also, if the owner of an easement or profit becomes the owner of the property burdened by it, then it is merged into the property.

Licenses In the context of real property, a **license** is the revocable right of a person to come onto another person's land. It is a personal privilege that arises from the consent of the owner of the land and can be revoked by the owner. A ticket to attend a movie at a theater is an example of a license. Assume that a Broadway theater owner issues a ticket to see a play to Alena. If Alena is refused entry because she is improperly dressed, she has no right to force her way into the theater. The ticket is only a revocable license, not a conveyance of an interest in property.

In essence, a license grants a person the authority to enter the land of another and perform a specified act or series of acts without obtaining any permanent interest in the land. What happens when a person with a license exceeds the authority granted and undertakes an action that is not permitted? That was the central issue in the following case.

CASE 25.2 Roman Catholic Church of Our Lady of Sorrows v. Prince Realty Management, LLC

New York Supreme Court, Appellate Division, Second Department, 2008.
47 A.D.3d 909, 850 N.Y.S.2d 569.

• Background and Facts The Roman Catholic Church of Our Lady of Sorrows (the Church) and Prince Realty Management, LLC (Prince), own adjoining property in Queens County, New York. On August 19, 2005, the parties entered into an agreement by which the Church granted Prince a three-month license to use a three-foot strip of its property immediately adjacent to Prince's property. The license specifically authorized Prince to remove an existing chainlink fence on the licensed strip and to "put up plywood panels surrounding the construction site, including the [licensed strip]." The license also required that Prince

CASE 25.2 CONTINUED restore the boundary line between the properties with a new brick fence. The purpose of the license was to allow Prince to erect a temporary plywood fence in order to protect Prince's property during the construction of a new building. During the term of the license, Prince installed structures consisting of steel piles and beams on the licensed property. The Church objected to the installation of these structures, and repeatedly demanded that they be removed. The Church commenced an action to recover damages for breach of the license and for trespass. The trial court concluded that the Church had made a *prima facie* case showing that structures were placed upon its property by the defendant in violation of the license, and that Prince had failed to dispute the plaintiff's claim that it had violated the agreement. Prince appealed.

IN THE LANGUAGE OF THE COURT
***SKELOS*, J.P. [Justice Presiding]**

* * * *

The [trial court] properly granted the plaintiff summary judgment on its causes of action alleging breach of the license and trespass. *"A license, within the context of real property law, grants the licensee a revocable non-assignable privilege to do one or more acts upon the land of the licensor, without granting possession of any interest therein. A license is the authority to do a particular act or series of acts upon another's land, which would amount to a trespass without such permission."* Here, the evidentiary [related to the evidence] proof submitted by the plaintiff * * * established that the license granted the defendant a privilege to use a three-foot strip of its land for specified purposes, primarily consisting of the temporary erection of wooden fencing to protect the defendant's property during construction of a building, the removal of an existing chain link fence, and the installation of a new brick fence upon completion of the license. The plaintiff also submitted uncontroverted evidence that the defendant installed structures consisting of steel piles and beams on the licensed strip of property. Contrary to the defendant's contention, the license did not permit it to install structures of this nature on the plaintiff's property. Moreover, in opposition to the establishment of a *prima facie* case for summary judgment, the defendant offered no proof that the installation of these structures was reasonably related to its licensed use of the property. [Emphasis added.]

In addition, since the plaintiff established as a matter of law that the defendant violated the license by installing unauthorized structures on its property, the plaintiff also established as a matter of law that the defendant's installation of these structures constituted a trespass regardless of whether they were subsequently removed.

- **Decision and Remedy** *The New York appellate court held that a license did not permit the adjoining property owner (Prince) to install structures consisting of steel piles and beams on the licensed strip of property.*

- **The Ethical Dimension** *While the Church pastor requested that the steel piles and beams be removed, the defendant resisted, but eventually did remove them. Was it still appropriate for the Church to file this lawsuit? Explain your answer.*

- **The Legal Environment Dimension** *The Church sued for damages. What would be an appropriate calculation of those damages?*

SECTION 3 Transfer of Ownership

Ownership of real property can pass from one person to another in a number of ways. Commonly, ownership interests in land are transferred by sale, and the terms of the transfer are specified in a real estate sales contract. Often, real estate brokers or agents who are licensed by the state assist the buyers and sellers during the sales transaction. Real property ownership can also be transferred by gift, by will or inheritance, by possession, or by eminent domain. In the subsections that follow, we focus primarily on voluntary sales of real property. We then consider adverse possession, which is an involuntary method of transferring title to real property. *Eminent domain* will be discussed later in this chapter.

CASE 25.3 CONTINUED tank. In February 2004, Terry and Tabitha Whitehead bought the house for $67,000. A few months after they moved in, problems began to develop with the air-conditioning unit, the fireplace, and the plumbing in the bathrooms. In May 2005, they discovered rotten wood behind the tile in the bathroom and around the front porch. In October, the Whiteheads filed a suit in a Louisiana state court against Humphrey, seeking to rescind the sale. The court awarded the plaintiffs the cost of repairing the fireplace ($1,675) and replacing some of the bad wood ($7,695). The Whiteheads appealed to a state intermediate appellate court.

IN THE LANGUAGE OF THE COURT
***CARAWAY*, J. [Judge]**

* * * *

Terry Whitehead testified that when they were looking at the house to buy, the yard was a mess because all of the field lines for the sewer system had been dug up. However, he did not realize at that time that the septic tank was located under the driveway. As part of her pre-inspection of the house, Tabitha Whitehead testified that she flushed both of the toilets and they both worked.

The Whiteheads' initial problem concerned the master bathroom and began three or four months after they moved into the house. When the water backed up in the main bathroom in the spring of 2004, Tabitha called Roto-Rooter to correct the flow. It was then that she learned the septic tank was located under the driveway. This meant that the traffic across the driveway could cause problems with the tank and lines.

In May 2005 * * * [t]he Whiteheads * * * began using the rear bathroom and experienced the same backing-up problem. At that time, the Whiteheads consulted Cook's Plumbing which provided the Whiteheads with an estimate totaling $12,000 which included relocation of the septic system and correction of other problems.

This evidence reveals that prior to the sale, the vendor and vendee were alerted to an issue regarding the sewer system. Corrective actions were taken, and no problems concerning the flushing of the toilets and flowage through the underground system prevented the Whiteheads from completing their purchase. *From this evidence, the ruling of the trial court * * * can be upheld from the view that neither side understood that a latent defect remained unresolved.* [Emphasis added.]

* * * *

Accordingly, we find no manifest error in the trial court's factual determination that the Whiteheads discovered that the sewer system remained a problem with their residence in the spring of 2004, and therefore their failure to have filed suit within one year of that discovery caused [the limitations period] to run against that claim.

On the other hand, the trial court expressly found that Humphrey had knowledge of the rotten boards or sills underneath the house which were improperly repaired by Humphrey prior to the sale. * * * The evidence showed that the Whiteheads first discovered this problem in May 2005, five months prior to [their law]suit.

* * * *

The trial court's judgment refused to rescind the sale and awarded a reduction in price based upon the cost of repairs of the defects in the fireplace and the wooden sills. From our review of the nature of these two defects, we find that the court properly used its discretion in rejecting rescission, and appellants' assignment of error seeking rescission and return of the sale price is without merit.

- **Decision and Remedy** *The state intermediate appellate court affirmed the lower court's conclusions regarding the defects in the Whiteheads' home. Rescission was not warranted for the sewer problems because the Whiteheads waited too long after their discovery to file a claim against Humphrey. The other defects "could be repaired with relative ease" and the "costs of those repairs were a small fraction of the sale price."*

- **The Ethical Dimension** *Should the court have rescinded the sale despite the running of the limitations period on the Whiteheads' sewer claim? Why or why not?*

CASE 25.3 CONTINUED • **The Legal Environment Dimension** *In Louisiana, a seller who knows of a defect and does not inform a buyer can be liable for the buyer's attorneys' fees in a suit based on that defect. Did Humphrey qualify as such a "bad faith" seller in this case? Explain.*

Deeds

Possession and title to land are passed from person to person by means of a **deed**—the instrument of conveyance of real property. A deed is a writing signed by an owner of real property by which title to it is transferred to another.[8] Deeds must meet certain requirements, but unlike a contract, a deed does not have to be supported by legally sufficient consideration. Gifts of real property are common, and they require deeds even though there is no consideration for the gift. To be valid, a deed must include the following:

1. The names of the *grantor* (the giver or seller) and the *grantee* (the donee or buyer).
2. Words evidencing the intent to convey (for example, "I hereby bargain, sell, grant, or give"). No specific words are necessary, and if the deed does *not* specify the estate being transferred, it presumptively transfers it in fee simple absolute.
3. A legally sufficient description of the land. (The description must include enough detail to distinguish the property being conveyed from every other parcel of land. The property can be identified by reference to an official survey or recorded plat map, or each boundary can be described by *metes and bounds*. **Metes and bounds** is a system of measuring boundary lines by the distance between two points, often using physical features of the local geography. For example, "beginning at the southwesterly intersection of Court and Main Streets, then West 40 feet to the fence, then South 100 feet, then Northeast approximately 120 feet back to the beginning.")
4. The grantor's (and usually his or her spouse's) signature.
5. Delivery of the deed.

Warranty Deeds Different types of deeds provide different degrees of protection against defects of title. A **warranty deed** makes the greatest number of warranties and thus provides the most extensive protection against defects of title. In most states, special language is required to create a warranty deed.

Warranty deeds include a number of *covenants,* or promises, that the grantor makes to the grantee. These covenants include a covenant that the grantor has the title to, and the power to convey, the property; a covenant of quiet enjoyment (a warranty that the buyer will not be disturbed in her or his possession of the land); and a covenant that transfer of the property is made without knowledge of adverse claims of third parties.

Generally, the warranty deed makes the grantor liable for all defects of title by the grantor and previous titleholders. For example, Julio sells a two-acre lot and office building by warranty deed. Subsequently, a third person appears, shows that she has better title than Julio had, and forces the buyer off the property. Here, the covenant of quiet enjoyment has been breached, and the buyer can sue Julio to recover the purchase price of the land, plus any other damages incurred as a result.

Special Warranty Deed In contrast to the warranty deed, the **special warranty deed,** which is frequently referred to as a *limited warranty deed,* warrants only that the grantor or seller held good title during his or her ownership of the property. In other words, the grantor is not warranting that there were no defects of title when the property was held by previous owners.

If the special warranty deed discloses all liens or other encumbrances, the seller will not be liable to the buyer if a third person subsequently interferes with the buyer's ownership. If the third person's claim arises out of, or is related to, some act of the seller, however, the seller will be liable to the buyer for damages.

Quitclaim Deed A **quitclaim deed** offers the least amount of protection against defects in the title. Basically, a quitclaim deed conveys to the grantee whatever interest the grantor had; so, if the grantor had no interest, then the grantee receives no interest. Naturally, if the grantor had a defective title or no title at all, a conveyance by warranty deed or special warranty deed

8. Note that in some states when a person purchases real property, the bank or lender receives a *trust deed* on the property until the homeowner pays off the mortgage. Despite its name, a trust deed is not used to transfer property. Instead, it is similar to a mortgage in that the lender holds the property as security for a loan.

would not cure the defects. Such deeds, however, will give the buyer a cause of action to sue the seller.

A quitclaim deed can and often does serve as a release of the grantor's interest in a particular parcel of property. For instance, Sandor owns a strip of waterfront property on which he wants to build condominiums. Lanz has an easement on a portion of the property, which might interfere with Sandor's plans for the development. Sandor can negotiate with Lanz to deed the easement back to Sandor. Lanz's signing of a quitclaim deed would constitute such a transfer.

Grant Deed With a **grant deed,** the grantor simply states, "I grant the property to you" or "I convey, or bargain and sell, the property to you." By state statute, grant deeds carry with them an implied warranty that the grantor owns the property and has not previously transferred it to someone else or encumbered it, except as set out in the deed.

Sheriff's Deed A **sheriff's deed** is a document giving ownership rights to a buyer of property at a sheriff's sale, which is a sale held by a sheriff when the owner of the property has failed to pay a court judgment against her or him. Typically, the property was subject to a mortgage or tax payments, and the owner defaulted on the payments. After a statutory period of time during which the defaulting owner can redeem the property, the deed is delivered to the purchaser.

Recording Statutes

Once the seller delivers the deed to the buyer (at closing), legal title to the property is conveyed. Nevertheless, the buyer should promptly record the deed with the state records office to establish superior ownership rights against any third parties who might make a claim to the property. Every state has a **recording statute,** which allows deeds to be recorded in the public record. Recording a deed involves a fee, which the buyer typically pays because he or she is the one who will be protected by recording the deed.

Recording a deed gives notice to the public that a certain person is now the owner of a particular parcel of real estate. Putting everyone on notice as to the true owner is intended to prevent the previous owners from fraudulently conveying the land to other purchasers. Deeds are generally recorded in the county in which the property is located. Many state statutes require that the grantor sign the deed in the presence of two witnesses before it can be recorded.

Marketable Title The question of title to a particular parcel of property is especially important to the buyer. A grantor (seller) is obligated to transfer **marketable title,** or good title, to the grantee (buyer). Marketable title means that the grantor's ownership is free from encumbrances (except those disclosed by the grantor) and free of defects. If the buyer signs a real estate sales contract and then discovers that the seller does not have a marketable title, the buyer can withdraw from the contract. For example, Chan enters an agreement to buy Fortuna Ranch from Hal. Chan then discovers that Hal has previously given Pearl an unexpired option to purchase the ranch. In this situation, the title is not marketable because Pearl could exercise the option and Hal would be compelled to sell the ranch to her. Therefore, Chan can withdraw from the contract to buy the property.

Title Search Because each document affecting ownership of property is recorded, recording provides a chronological public record of all transactions concerning the property. Systematically examining this record for transactions creating interests or rights in a specific parcel of real property is called a **title search.** A prospective buyer or lender generally performs a title search to determine whether the seller truly owns the interest that he or she is attempting to convey and whether anyone else has an interest in the property. A title search should—but does not always—reveal encumbrances on the property, such as the existence of an easement or lien.

Methods of Ensuring Good Title To ensure that the title is marketable, a grantee has several options depending on the state. The grantee may hire an attorney to examine an *abstract of title* (history of what the public records show regarding the title to the property) and provide an opinion as to whether the title is marketable. If the title is defective, the attorney's opinion will specify the nature of the defects. The attorney is liable to the grantee for any loss caused by her or his negligence.

An alternative method available in a few states is the *Torrens system* of title registration. Under this system, the title is registered in a judicial proceeding; all parties claiming an interest in the property are notified of the proceeding and are given an opportunity to assert their claims. After the hearing, the court issues a certificate of title, which is similar to an automobile title, to the person found to be the owner. All encumbrances (such as liens for unpaid taxes, mechanic's liens, or restrictive covenants, discussed next) are noted on the certificate, and when the property is sold, the certificate is transferred to the grantee along with the deed.

The most common method of assuring title is through **title insurance,** which insures the grantee against loss from defects in title to real property. When financing the purchase of real property, many lenders require title insurance to protect their interests in the collateral for the loan. Title insurance is becoming less significant, though, because title information and records are now available electronically and thus are easy to access.

Restrictive Covenants

Deeds may include voluntary agreements between individuals that limit the use of the property. For example, easements, profits, and licenses, which were discussed earlier, may place limitations on a property owner's rights. Also, deeds sometimes include a **restrictive covenant,** which is a private restriction on the use of land. If the restriction is binding on the party who purchases the property originally as well as on subsequent purchasers—in other words, if its benefit or obligation passes with the land's ownership—it is said to "run with the land."

Covenants Running with the Land A restrictive covenant that runs with the land goes with the land and cannot be separated from it. Consider an example. Owen is the owner of Grasslands, a twenty-acre estate whose northern half contains a small reservoir. Owen wishes to convey the northern half to Arid City, but before he does, he digs an irrigation ditch connecting the reservoir with the lower ten acres, which he uses as farmland. When Owen conveys the northern ten acres to Arid City, he enters into an agreement with the city. The agreement, which is contained in the deed, states, "Arid City, its heirs and assigns, promises not to remove more than five thousand gallons of water per day from the Grasslands reservoir." Owen has created a restrictive covenant running with the land under which Arid City and all future owners of the northern ten acres of Grasslands are limited as to the amount of water they can draw from its reservoir.

Four requirements must be met for a covenant running with the land to be enforceable. If they are not met, the covenant will apply to the two original parties to a contract only and will not run with the land to future owners. The requirements are as follows:

1. The covenant running with the land must be created in a written agreement (usually it is in the deed).
2. The parties must intend that the covenant run with the land. In other words, the instrument that contains the covenant must state not only that the promisor is bound by the terms of the covenant but also that all the promisor's "successors, heirs, or assigns" will be bound.
3. The covenant must touch and concern the land—that is, the limitations on the activities of the owner of the burdened land must have some connection with the land. For example, a purchaser of land cannot be bound by a covenant requiring him or her to drive only Ford pickups, because such a restriction has no relation to the land purchased.
4. The successors to the original parties to the covenant must have notice of the covenant.

To satisfy the last requirement, the notice may be actual or constructive. For example, in the course of developing a fifty-lot suburban subdivision, Levitt records a declaration of restrictions that effectively limits construction on each lot to one single-family house. In each lot's deed is a reference to the declaration with a provision that the purchaser and his or her successors are bound to those restrictions. Thus, each purchaser assumes ownership with notice of the restrictions. If an owner attempts to build a duplex (or any structure that does not comply with the restrictions) on a lot, the other owners may obtain a court order enjoining the construction.

In fact, Levitt might simply have included the restrictions on the subdivision's map, filed the map in the appropriate public office, and included a reference to the map in each deed. In this way, each owner would have been held to have constructive notice of the restrictions.

Illegal Restrictive Covenants Restrictive covenants have sometimes been used to perpetuate neighborhood segregation, and in these cases they have been invalidated by the courts. In the United States Supreme Court case of *Shelley v. Kraemer,*[9] restrictive covenants proscribing resale to minority groups were declared unconstitutional and could no longer be enforced in courts of law. In addition, the Civil Rights Act of 1968 (also known as the Fair Housing Act) prohibits all discrimination based on

9. 334 U.S. 1, 68 S.Ct. 836, 92 L.Ed. 1161 (1948).

race, color, religion, gender, familial status, or national origin in the sale and leasing of housing.

Adverse Possession

A person who wrongfully possesses (by occupying or using) the real property of another may eventually acquire title to it through **adverse possession.** Adverse possession is a means of obtaining title to land without delivery of a deed and without the consent of—or payment to—the true owner. Thus, adverse possession is a method of involuntarily transferring title to the property from the true owner to the adverse possessor.

Essentially, when one person possesses the real property of another for a certain statutory period of time (three to thirty years, with ten years being most common), that person acquires title to the land. For property to be held adversely, four elements must be satisfied:

1. Possession must be *actual and exclusive*—that is, the possessor must physically occupy the property. This requirement is clearly met if the possessor lives on the property, but it may also be met if the possessor builds fences, erects structures, plants crops, or even grazes animals on the land.
2. The possession must be *open, visible, and notorious,* not secret or clandestine. The possessor must occupy the land for all the world to see. This requirement of obviousness ensures that the true owner is on notice that someone is possessing the owner's property wrongfully.
3. Possession must be *continuous and peaceable for the required period of time.* This requirement means that the possessor must not be interrupted in the occupancy by the true owner or by the courts. *Continuous* does not mean constant—it simply means that the possessor has continuously occupied the property in some fashion for the statutory time and has not used force to possess the land.
4. Possession must be *hostile and adverse.* In other words, the possessor cannot be living on the property with the owner's permission and must claim the property as against the whole world.

There are a number of public-policy reasons for the adverse possession doctrine. These include society's interest in resolving boundary disputes, in quieting (determining) title when title to property is in question, and in ensuring that real property remains in the stream of commerce. More fundamentally, policies behind the doctrine include punishing owners who do not take action when they see adverse possession and rewarding possessors for putting land to productive use.

SECTION 4 Public Control of Land Use

Land-use control is the control over the ownership and uses of real property by authorized public agencies. Land use is subject to regulation by the state within whose political boundaries the land is located. Most states authorize control over land use through various planning boards and zoning authorities at a city or county level. The federal government does not engage in land-use control under normal circumstances, except with respect to federally owned land.[10] The federal government does influence state and local regulation, however, through the allocation of federal funds. Stipulations on land use may be a condition to the states' receiving such funds.

Sources of Public Control

The states' power to control the use of land through legislation is derived from their *police power* and the doctrine of *eminent domain.* Under their police power, state governments enact legislation that promotes the health, safety, and welfare of their citizens. This legislation includes land-use controls. The power of **eminent domain** is the government's authority to take private property for public use or purpose without the owner's consent. Typically, this is accomplished through a judicial proceeding to obtain title to the land.

Police Power

As an exercise of its police power,[11] a state can regulate the use of land within its jurisdiction. A few states control land use at the state level. Hawaii, for instance, employs a statewide land-use classification scheme. Some states have a land-permit process that operates in conjunction with local control. Florida, for example, uses such a scheme in certain areas of "critical environmental concern" to permit or prohibit develop-

10. Federal (and state) laws concerning environmental matters—such as air and water quality, the protection of endangered species, and the preservation of natural wetlands—are also a source of land-use control.

11. As pointed out in Chapter 5, the police power of a state encompasses the right to regulate private activities to protect or promote the public order, health, safety, morals, and general welfare.

ment on the basis of available roads, sewers, and so on. Vermont also utilizes a statewide land-permit scheme.

Usually, however, a state authorizes its city or county governments to regulate the use of land within their local jurisdictions. A state confers this power through *enabling legislation.* Enabling legislation normally requires local governments to devise *general plans* before imposing other land-use controls. Enabling acts also typically authorize local bodies to enact *zoning laws* to regulate the use of land and the types of, and specifications for, structures. Local planning boards may regulate the development of subdivisions, in which private developers subdivide large tracts of land and construct commercial or residential units for resale to others. Local governments may also enact growth-management ordinances to control development in their jurisdictions.

Government Plans Most states require that land-use laws follow a local government's general plan. A **general plan** is a comprehensive, long-term scheme dealing with the physical development, and in some cases redevelopment, of a city or community. It addresses such concerns as types of housing, protection of natural resources, provision of public facilities and transportation, and other issues related to land use. A plan indicates the direction of growth in a community and the contributions that private developers must make toward providing such public facilities as roads. If a proposed use is not authorized by the general plan, the plan may be amended to permit the use. (A plan may also be amended to preclude a proposed use.)

Even when a proposed use complies with a general plan, it may not be allowed. Most jurisdictions have requirements in addition to those in the general plan. These requirements are included in specific plans—also called special, area, or community plans. Specific plans typically pertain to only a portion of a jurisdiction's area. For example, a specific plan may concern a downtown area subject to redevelopment efforts, an area with special environmental concerns, or an area with increased public transportation needs arising from population growth.

Zoning Laws In addition to complying with a general plan and any specific plans, a particular land use must comply with zoning laws. The term **zoning** refers to the dividing of an area into districts to which specific land-use regulations apply. A typical zoning law consists of a zoning map and a zoning ordinance. The zoning map indicates the characteristics of each parcel of land within an area and divides that area into districts. The zoning ordinance specifies the restrictions on land use within those districts.

Zoning ordinances generally include two types of restrictions. One type pertains to the kind of land use—such as commercial versus residential—to which property within a particular district may be put. The second type dictates the engineering features and architectural design of structures built within that district.

Use Restrictions. Districts are typically zoned for residential, commercial, industrial, or agricultural use. Each district may be further subdivided for degree or intensity of use. For example, a residential district may be subdivided to permit a certain number of apartment buildings and a certain number of units in each building. Commercial and industrial districts are often zoned to permit *heavy* or *light* activity. Heavy activity might include the operation of large factories. Light activity might include the operation of professional office buildings or small retail shops. Zoning that specifies the use to which property may be put is referred to as **use zoning.**

Structural Restrictions. Restrictions known as bulk regulations cover such details as minimum floor-space requirements and minimum lot-size restrictions. For example, a particular district's minimum floor-space requirements might specify that a one-story building contain a minimum of 1,240 square feet of floor space, and minimum lot-size restrictions might specify that each single-family dwelling be built on a lot that is at least one acre in size. Referred to collectively as **bulk zoning,** these regulations also dictate *setback* (the distance between a building and a street, sidewalk, or other boundary) and the height of buildings, with different requirements for buildings in different areas.

Restrictions related to structure may also be concerned with such matters as architectural control, the overall appearance of a community, and the preservation of historic buildings. An ordinance may require that all proposed construction be approved by a design review board composed of local architects. A community may restrict the size and placement of outdoor advertising, such as billboards and business signs. A property owner may be prohibited from tearing down or remodeling a historic landmark or building. In challenges against these types of restrictions, the courts have generally upheld the regulations.

EXHIBIT 27–1 • Backward and Forward Vertical Integration

A firm that is integrated backward moves down the chain of production. A firm that is integrated forward moves up the chain of production.

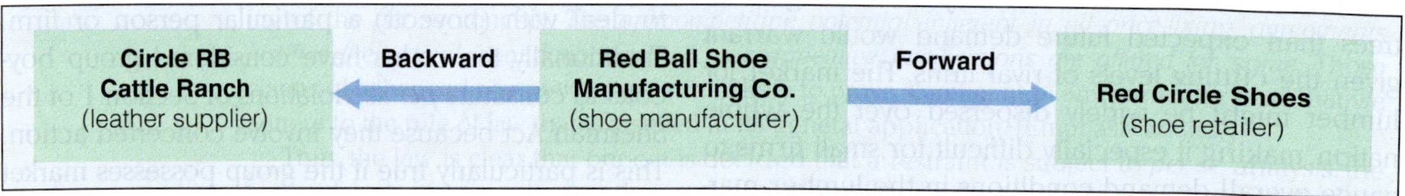

Even though firms operating at different functional levels do not directly compete with one another, each does compete with other firms operating at its own level of operation. Thus, agreements between firms standing in a vertical relationship may affect competition. For example, suppose that a contractual agreement between tire manufacturer Firestone and Billy Ray's Automotive Supplies, an independent retailer, conditions Billy Ray's future supply of Firestone tires on its willingness to resell only at a price set by Firestone. This agreement is a form of **vertical restraint**—an anticompetitive agreement between entities operating at different levels of the market structure. Other types of vertical restraints are often encountered, but not all of them necessarily harm competition. Indeed, many are procompetitive. Some vertical restraints are *per se* violations of Section 1; others are judged under a rule of reason.

Territorial or Customer Restrictions

In arranging for the distribution of its products, a manufacturing firm often wishes to insulate dealers from direct competition with other dealers selling its products. To this end, the manufacturer may institute territorial restrictions or attempt to prohibit wholesalers or retailers from reselling the products to certain classes of buyers, such as competing retailers.

A firm may have legitimate reasons for imposing such territorial or customer restrictions. For example, a computer manufacturer may wish to prevent a dealer from reducing costs and undercutting rivals by offering computers without promotion or customer service, while relying on a nearby dealer to provide these services. In this situation, the cost-cutting dealer reaps the benefits (sales of the product) paid for by other dealers who undertake promotion and arrange for customer service. By not providing customer service, the cost-cutting dealer may also harm the manufacturer's reputation.

Territorial and customer restrictions are judged under a rule of reason. In *United States v. Arnold, Schwinn & Co.*,[5] a case decided in 1967, a bicycle manufacturer, Schwinn, was assigning specific territories to its wholesale distributors and authorizing certain retail dealers only if they agreed to advertise Schwinn bicycles and give them the same prominence as other brands. The United States Supreme Court held that these vertical territorial and customer restrictions were *per se* violations of Section 1 of the Sherman Act. Ten years later, however, in the case that follows, the United States Supreme Court overturned the *Schwinn* decision.

5. 388 U.S. 365, 87 S.Ct. 1856, 18 L.Ed.2d 1249 (1967).

CASE 27.2 Continental T.V., Inc. v. GTE Sylvania, Inc.

Supreme Court of the United States, 1977. 433 U.S. 36, 97 S.Ct. 2549, 53 L.Ed.2d 568.
www.findlaw.com/casecode/supreme.html[a]

• **Background and Facts** GTE Sylvania, Inc., a manufacturer of television sets, adopted a franchise plan that limited the number of franchises granted in any given geographic area and that required each franchise to sell only Sylvania products from the location or locations at which it was franchised. Sylvania retained sole discretion to increase the number of retailers in an area, depending on the success or failure of existing retailers in developing their markets. Continental T.V., Inc., was a retailer under Sylvania's franchise plan. Shortly after proposing a new franchise that would compete with Continental, Sylvania terminated Continental's franchise, and a suit was brought in a federal district court for funds owed. Continental claimed that Sylvania's vertically restrictive franchise system violated Section 1 of the

a. In the "Citation Search" section, type "433" in the first box, type "36" in the second box, and click on "Get It" to access the case.

CASE 27.2 CONTINUED

Sherman Act. The district court held for Continental, and Sylvania appealed. The appellate court reversed the trial court's decision. Continental appealed to the United States Supreme Court.

IN THE LANGUAGE OF THE COURT

Mr. Justice *POWELL* delivered the opinion of the Court.

* * * *

Vertical restrictions reduce intrabrand competition by limiting the number of sellers of a particular product competing for the business of a given group of buyers.

Vertical restrictions promote interbrand competition by allowing the manufacturer to achieve certain efficiencies in the distribution of his products. * * * Established manufacturers can use them to induce retailers to engage in promotional activities or to provide service and repair facilities necessary to the efficient marketing of their products. * * * The availability and quality of such services affect a manufacturer's goodwill and the competitiveness of his product. [Emphasis added.]

* * * *

* * * When anticompetitive effects are shown to result from particular vertical restrictions, they can be adequately policed under the rule of reason * * * .

- **Decision and Remedy** *The United States Supreme Court upheld the appellate court's reversal of the district court's decision. Sylvania's vertical system, which was not price restrictive, did not constitute a* per se *violation of Section 1 of the Sherman Act.*

- **Impact of This Case on Today's Law** *The decision in this case generally is regarded as one of the most important antitrust cases since the 1940s. It marked a definite shift from rigid characterization of these kinds of vertical restraints as* per se *violations to a more flexible, economic analysis under the rule of reason. Today's courts follow the precedent laid down in this case and apply the rule of reason to territorial and customer restrictions.*

- **The E-Commerce Dimension** *How does the Internet benefit competition without encouraging violations of the antitrust laws?*

Resale Price Maintenance Agreements

An agreement between a manufacturer and a distributor or retailer in which the manufacturer specifies what the retail prices of its products must be is known as a **resale price maintenance agreement.** Such agreements were once considered to be *per se* violations of Section 1 of the Sherman Act, but in 1997 the United States Supreme Court ruled that *maximum* resale price maintenance agreements should be judged under the rule of reason.[6] In these agreements, the manufacturer sets a maximum price that retailers and distributors can charge for its products.

The question before the Court in the following case was whether *minimum* resale price maintenance agreements should be treated as *per se* unlawful.

6. *State Oil Co. v. Khan,* 522 U.S. 3, 118 S.Ct. 275, 139 L.Ed.2d 199 (1997).

EXTENDED CASE 27.3

Leegin Creative Leather Products, Inc. v. PSKS, Inc.

Supreme Court of the United States, 2007. __ U.S. __, 127 S.Ct. 2705, 168 L.Ed.2d 623.
supct.law.cornell.edu/supct/index.html[a]

Justice *KENNEDY* delivered the opinion of the Court.

* * * *

Petitioner, Leegin Creative Leather Products, Inc. (Leegin), designs, manufactures, and distributes leather goods and accessories. In 1991, Leegin began to sell [products] under the brand name "Brighton."

a. In the "Archive of Decisions" section, in the "By party" subsection, click on "1990-present." In the result, in the "2006–2007" row, click on "1st party." On the next page, scroll to the name of the case and click on it. On the next page, click on the appropriate link to access the opinion.

CASE CONTINUES

CASE 27.3 CONTINUED

Respondent, PSKS, Inc. (PSKS), operates Kay's Kloset, a women's apparel store in Lewisville, Texas. * * * It first started purchasing Brighton goods from Leegin in 1995.

* * * *

In December 2002, Leegin discovered Kay's Kloset had been marking down Brighton's entire line by 20 percent. * * * Leegin stopped selling [Brighton products] to the store.

PSKS sued Leegin in the United States District Court for the Eastern District of Texas. It alleged, among other claims, that Leegin had violated the antitrust laws by "enter[ing] into agreements with retailers to charge only those prices fixed by Leegin." * * * [The court] entered judgment against Leegin in the amount of $3,975,000.80.

The [U.S.] Court of Appeals for the Fifth Circuit affirmed. * * * We granted *certiorari* * * * .

* * * *

The rule of reason is the accepted standard for testing whether a practice restrains trade in violation of [Section] 1 [of the Sherman Act].

* * * *

Resort to per se *rules is confined to restraints * * * that would always or almost always tend to restrict competition and decrease output. To justify a* per se *prohibition a restraint must have manifestly anticompetitive effects, and lack * * * any redeeming virtue.* [Emphasis added.]

As a consequence, the *per se* rule is appropriate only after courts have had considerable experience with the type of restraint at issue, and only if courts can predict with confidence that it would be invalidated in all or almost all instances under the rule of reason.

* * * *

The reasoning of the Court's more recent jurisprudence has rejected the rationales on which [the application of the *per se* rule to minimum resale price maintenance agreements] was based. * * * [These rationales were] based on formalistic legal doctrine rather than demonstrable economic effect.

* * * Furthermore [the Court] treated vertical agreements a manufacturer makes with its distributors as analogous to a horizontal combination among competing distributors. * * * Our recent cases formulate antitrust principles in accordance with the appreciated differences in economic effect between vertical and horizontal agreements * * * .

* * * *

The justifications for vertical price restraints are similar to those for other vertical restraints. *Minimum resale price maintenance can stimulate interbrand competition * * * by reducing intrabrand competition* * * * . The promotion of interbrand competition is important because the primary purpose of the antitrust laws is to protect this type of competition. * * * *Resale price maintenance also has the potential to give consumers more options so that they can choose among low-price, low-service brands; high-price, high-service brands; and brands that fall in between.* [Emphasis added.]

* * * *

While vertical agreements setting minimum resale prices can have procompetitive justifications, they may have anticompetitive effects in other cases; and unlawful price fixing, designed solely to obtain monopoly profits, is an ever present temptation.

* * * *

Notwithstanding the risks of unlawful conduct, it cannot be stated with any degree of confidence that resale price maintenance always or almost always tends to restrict competition and decrease output. Vertical agreements establishing minimum resale prices can have either procompetitive or anticompetitive effects, depending upon the circumstances in which they are formed. * * * As the *[per se]* rule would proscribe a significant amount of procompetitive conduct, these agreements appear ill suited for *per se* condemnation.

* * * *

The judgment of the Court of Appeals is reversed, and the case is remanded for proceedings consistent with this opinion.

QUESTIONS

1. Should the Court have applied the doctrine of *stare decisis* to hold that minimum resale price maintenance agreements are still subject to the *per se* rule? Why or why not?

CASE 27.3 CONTINUED

2. What factors might the courts consider in applying the rule of reason to minimum resale price maintenance agreements?

Refusals to Deal

Group boycotts, as mentioned, are subject to sharp scrutiny under Section 1. In contrast, basic freedom of contract has been held to support the rule that manufacturers, acting unilaterally rather than in concert, as in a group boycott, are free to deal—or not to deal—with whomever they choose. Assume that in our hypothetical example Acme acts alone to set the price for the resale of its Blu-ray burners by refusing to deal with any wholesaler that resells them at a different price. Acme has not violated the Sherman Act; it has only exercised its right to deal with whomever it chooses.

In some instances, however, a refusal to deal will violate antitrust laws. These instances involve offenses proscribed under Section 2 of the Sherman Act and occur only if (1) the firm refusing to deal has, or is likely to acquire, monopoly power and (2) the refusal is likely to have an anticompetitive effect on a particular market.

Price Discrimination

Whenever a seller charges different buyers different prices for identical goods, the seller is engaging in **price discrimination.** Recall from the preceding chapter that such behavior may violate the Robinson-Patman Act, which was enacted in 1936 and amended Section 2 of the Clayton Act. A violation of Section 2 occurs if a seller discriminates in the prices it charges different customers for commodities of like quality and grade in interstate commerce and the practice results in injury to competition. The act prohibits indirect discrimination, such as variations in the terms of delivery and differences in sales returns, cash discounts, and the like, as well as direct price discrimination.

Customer Preferences Although the act appears to embrace the goals of fairness and equality in the marketplace, it has often been criticized as being economically unrealistic. For instance, a difference in packaging, labeling, or product quality normally does not exempt the pricing of the differing products from scrutiny under the act if the difference is deemed to be *negligible.* Thus, orange juice containers that differ by one-eighth inch are considered to be of like grade and quality, because they are *functionally* identical in terms of performance. Despite functional equivalence, however, customer perceptions may favor one type of container over another.

In the same vein, identical products sold under different labels are deemed to be of like quality, though some experts note that many customers exhibit strong preferences for better-known brand names even though the products are physically identical. In *Federal Trade Commission v. Borden Co.,*[7] the United States Supreme Court addressed the issue of a milk producer's charging different prices for milk sold under different labels. Borden sold evaporated milk under the Borden label, a well-known brand, and at the same time, it packed and marketed evaporated milk under private labels owned by its customers. Although the milk was physically indistinguishable, Borden charged a higher price for its brand-labeled milk. In spite of obvious customer preference for the Borden brand of milk, the Court concluded that the act applied to the pricing difference because the milk was of like quality and grade in terms of physical attributes. The Court held that preferences due to brand-name recognition created through national advertising should not be considered in resolving whether goods are of like grade and quality.

Time and Cost Considerations Despite these examples, some economic aspects are taken into account in judging the legality of pricing practices under the Robinson-Patman Act. For example, as noted in the preceding chapter, Section 2 is not violated even though the goods sold are identical if the seller can justify the price differential on the basis of differences in cost, such as the cost of transporting the goods to buyers in disparate locations. Similarly, consideration is given to the fact that prices are not static but fluctuate as market conditions change. Thus, price discrimination occurs only if sales at different price levels are made reasonably close together in time.

Closeness in time is determined by the economic circumstances of the sales. For example, sales of products that are not frequently sold and that involve considerable production costs may be considered close in time even if they occur years apart. Conversely, sales of

7. 383 U.S. 637, 86 S.Ct. 1092, 16 L.Ed.2d 153 (1966).

low-cost products sold in high volume may be considered close in time when they occur a day or even a few hours apart. Jet aircraft typify high-cost, low-volume products. Closeness in time for sales of aircraft could be two years or more. In contrast, sales of bakery goods occur on an almost continuous basis. Closeness in time for sales of such products could be several hours or, at most, a day.

Exclusionary Practices

Recall also from the preceding chapter that Section 3 of the Clayton Act prohibits sellers and lessors from selling or leasing goods, machinery, supplies, and the like "on the condition, agreement or understanding that the . . . purchaser or lessee thereof shall not use or deal in the goods . . . of a competitor or competitors of the seller." Two types of vertical arrangements involving exclusionary tactics—*exclusive-dealing contracts* and *tying arrangements*—are within the reach of Section 3 of the Clayton Act.

Exclusive-Dealing Contracts A contract under which a seller forbids a buyer to purchase products from the seller's competitors is called an **exclusive-dealing contract.** A seller is prohibited from making an exclusive-dealing contract under Section 3 if the effect of the contract is "to substantially lessen competition or tend to create a monopoly."

The United States Supreme Court's 1949 decision in the case of *Standard Oil Co. of California v. United States* provides a classic illustration of exclusive dealing.[8] In this case, the then largest gasoline seller in the nation made exclusive-dealing contracts with independent stations in seven western states. The contracts involved 16 percent of all retail outlets, whose sales were approximately 7 percent of all retail sales in that market. The Court noted that the market was substantially concentrated because the seven largest gasoline suppliers all used exclusive-dealing contracts with their independent retailers and together controlled 65 percent of the market. Looking at market conditions after the arrangements were instituted, the Court found that market shares were extremely stable, and entry into the market was apparently restricted. Thus, the Court held that the Clayton Act had been violated because competition was "foreclosed in a substantial share" of the relevant market.

Note that since the Supreme Court's 1949 decision in the *Standard Oil* case, a number of subsequent decisions have called the holding in this case into doubt.[9] Today, it is clear that to violate antitrust law, the effect of an exclusive-dealing agreement (or a tying arrangement, discussed next) must qualitatively and substantially harm competition. To prevail, a plaintiff must present affirmative evidence that the performance of the agreement will foreclose competition and harm consumers.

Tying Arrangements In a **tying arrangement,** or *tie-in sales agreement,* a seller conditions the sale of a product (the tying product) on the buyer's agreement to purchase another product (the tied product) produced or distributed by the same seller. The legality of a tie-in agreement depends on many factors, particularly the purpose of the agreement and the agreement's likely effect on competition in the relevant markets (the market for the tying product and the market for the tied product).

In 1936, for example, the United States Supreme Court held that International Business Machines and Remington Rand had violated Section 3 of the Clayton Act by requiring the purchase of their own machine cards (the tied product) as a condition to the leasing of their tabulation machines (the tying product). Because only these two firms sold completely automated tabulation machines, the Court concluded that each possessed market power sufficient to "substantially lessen competition" through the tying arrangements.[10]

Section 3 of the Clayton Act has been held to apply only to commodities, not to services. Tying arrangements, however, can also be considered agreements that restrain trade in violation of Section 1 of the Sherman Act. Thus, cases involving tying arrangements of services have been brought under Section 1 of the Sherman Act. Although earlier cases condemned tying arrangements as illegal *per se,* courts now evaluate tying agreements under the rule of reason.

When an arrangement ties patented and unpatented products, can the relevant market and the patent holder's power in that market be presumed without proof? That was the question in the following case.

8. 337 U.S. 293, 69 S.Ct. 1051, 93 L.Ed. 1371 (1949).

9. See, for example, *Illinois Tool Works, Inc. v. Independent Ink, Inc.*, which is presented as Case 27.4 on page 671; *Stop & Shop Supermarket Co. v. Blue Cross & Blue Shield of R.I.*, 373 F.3d 57 (1st Cir. 2004); *Texas Instruments, Inc. v. Hyundai Electronics Industries Co.*, 49 F.Supp.2d 893 (E.D.Tex. 1999); and *Yeager's Fuel, Inc. v. Pennsylvania Power & Light Co.*, 953 F.Supp. 617 (E.D.Pa. 1997).

10. *International Business Machines Corp. v. United States,* 298 U.S. 131, 56 S.Ct. 701, 80 L.Ed. 1085 (1936).

CASE 27.4 Illinois Tool Works, Inc. v. Independent Ink, Inc.

Supreme Court of the United States, 2006. 547 U.S. 28, 126 S.Ct. 1281, 164 L.Ed.2d 26.
www.findlaw.com/casecode/supreme.html[a]

• **Background and Facts** Illinois Tool Works, Inc., in Glenview, Illinois, owns Trident, Inc. The firms make printing systems that include three components: a patented inkjet printhead; a patented ink container that attaches to the printhead; and specially designed, but unpatented, ink. They sell the systems to original equipment manufacturers (OEMs) that incorporate the systems into printers that are sold to other companies to use in printing bar codes on packaging materials. As part of each deal, the OEMs agree to buy ink exclusively from Illinois and Trident and not to refill the patented containers with ink of any kind. Independent Ink, Inc., in Gardena, California, sells ink with the same chemical composition as Illinois and Trident's product at lower prices. Independent filed a suit in a federal district court against Illinois and Trident, alleging, among other things, that they were engaged in illegal tying in violation of the Sherman Act. Independent filed a motion for summary judgment, arguing that because the defendants owned patents in their products, market power could be presumed. The court issued a summary judgment in the defendants' favor, holding that market power could not be presumed. The U.S. Court of Appeals for the Federal Circuit reversed this judgment. Illinois and Trident appealed to the United States Supreme Court.

IN THE LANGUAGE OF THE COURT
Justice *STEVENS* delivered the opinion of the Court.

* * * *

American courts first encountered tying arrangements in the course of patent infringement litigation [in 1912].

In the years since [1912], four different rules of law have supported challenges to tying arrangements. They have been condemned as improper extensions of the patent monopoly under the patent misuse doctrine, as unfair methods of competition under [Section] 5 of the Federal Trade Commission Act, as contracts tending to create a monopoly under [Section] 3 of the Clayton Act, and as contracts in restraint of trade under [Section] 1 of the Sherman Act. In all of those instances, the justification for the challenge rested on either an assumption or a showing that the defendant's position of power in the market for the tying product was being used to restrain competition in the market for the tied product. * * * The essential characteristic of an invalid tying arrangement lies in the seller's exploitation of its control over the tying product to force the buyer into the purchase of a tied product that the buyer either [does] not want at all, or might [prefer] to purchase elsewhere on different terms.

Over the years, however, this Court's strong disapproval of tying arrangements has substantially diminished. Rather than relying on assumptions, in its more recent opinions the Court has required a showing of market power in the tying product.

* * * *

* * * The presumption that a patent confers market power arose outside the antitrust context as part of the patent misuse doctrine.

Without any analysis of actual market conditions, [the] patent misuse [doctrine] assumed that, by tying the purchase of unpatented goods to the sale of [a] patented good, the patentee was restraining competition or securing a limited monopoly of an unpatented material. In other words, [the doctrine] presumed the requisite economic power over the tying product such that the patentee could extend its economic control to unpatented products.

* * * *

Although the patent misuse doctrine and our antitrust jurisprudence became intertwined in [a case decided in 1947], subsequent events initiated their untwining.

* * * *

a. In the "Browsing" section, click on "2006 Decisions." When that page opens, scroll to the name of the case and click on it to read the opinion.

CASE CONTINUES

CASE 27.4 CONTINUED

Shortly thereafter, Congress * * * *excluded some conduct, such as a tying arrangement involving the sale of a patented product tied to an "essential" or "nonstaple" product that has no use except as part of the patented product or method, from the scope of the patent misuse doctrine. Thus,* * * * *Congress began chipping away at the assumption in the patent misuse context from whence it came.* [Emphasis added.]

It is Congress' most recent narrowing of the patent misuse defense * * * that is directly relevant to this case. * * * [In 1988] Congress amended the [patent laws] to eliminate [the patent-equals-market-power] presumption in the patent misuse context.

While the 1988 amendment does not expressly refer to the antitrust laws, it certainly invites a reappraisal of the *per se* rule * * * . Given the fact that the patent misuse doctrine provided the basis for the market power presumption, it would be anomalous to preserve the presumption in antitrust after Congress has eliminated its foundation.

After considering the congressional judgment reflected in the 1988 amendment, we conclude that tying arrangements involving patented products should be evaluated under [such factors as those that apply in a rule-of-reason analysis] rather than under the *per se* rule * * * . While some such arrangements are still unlawful, such as those that are the product of a true monopoly or a marketwide conspiracy, that conclusion must be supported by proof of power in the relevant market rather than by a mere presumption thereof.

• **Decision and Remedy** *The United States Supreme Court vacated the judgment of the lower court and remanded the case to the trial court to give Independent "a fair opportunity" to offer evidence of the relevant market and the defendants' power within it. The Supreme Court ruled that a plaintiff that alleges an illegal tying arrangement involving a patented product must prove that the defendant has market power in the tying product. A company that holds a patent in a product does not automatically possess market power in that product for antitrust purposes.*

• **The Ethical Dimension** *What are the ethical values underpinning antitrust laws, and why are those laws applied to tying arrangements in particular?*

• **The Legal Environment Dimension** *In light of the factors that a court considers under the rule of reason, how might the court rule on remand in the* Illinois *case? Explain.*

Mergers

Under Section 7 of the Clayton Act, a person or business organization cannot hold stock or assets in more than one business when "the effect . . . may be to substantially lessen competition." Section 7 is the statutory authority for preventing mergers that could result in monopoly power or a substantial lessening of competition in the marketplace. Section 7 applies to both horizontal and vertical mergers, as discussed in the following subsections.

A crucial consideration in most merger cases is **market concentration.** Determining market concentration involves allocating percentage market shares among the various companies in the relevant market. When a small number of companies share a large part of the market, the market is concentrated. For example, if the four largest grocery stores in Chicago accounted for 80 percent of all retail food sales, that specific market clearly would be concentrated in those four firms. Competition is not necessarily diminished solely as a result of market concentration, however, and other factors must be considered to determine if a merger violates Section 7. One factor of particular importance is whether the merger will make it more difficult for *potential* competitors to enter the relevant market.

Horizontal Mergers Mergers between firms that compete with each other in the same market are called **horizontal mergers.** If a horizontal merger creates an entity with a resulting significant market share, the merger may be presumed illegal. This is because of the United States Supreme Court's interpretation that Congress, in amending Section 7 of the Clayton Act in 1950, intended to prevent mergers that increase market concentration.[11] Three other factors are also considered: overall concentration of the rele-

11. *Brown Shoe v. United States,* 370 U.S. 294, 82 S.Ct. 1502, 8 L.Ed.2d 510 (1962).

vant market, the relevant market's history of tending toward concentration, and whether the apparent design of the merger is to establish market power or restrict competition.

Market Share and Market Concentration. The Court's intense focus on market share in horizontal merger decisions has made the definition of relevant markets especially critical in most Section 7 cases. As a result, the Federal Trade Commission (FTC) and the Department of Justice (DOJ) have established guidelines indicating which mergers will be challenged.

Under the guidelines, the first factor to be considered in determining whether a merger will be challenged is the degree of concentration in the relevant market. In determining market concentration, the FTC and the DOJ employ what is known as the **Herfindahl-Hirschman index (HHI).** The HHI is computed by summing the squares of the percentage market shares of the firms in the relevant market. For example, if there are four firms with shares of 30 percent, 30 percent, 20 percent, and 20 percent, respectively, then the HHI equals 2,600 (900 + 900 + 400 + 400 = 2,600). If the premerger HHI is less than 1,000, then the market is unconcentrated, and the merger is unlikely to be challenged. If the premerger HHI is between 1,000 and 1,800, the industry is moderately concentrated, and the merger will be challenged only if it increases the HHI by 100 points or more.[12] If the HHI is greater than 1,800, the market is highly concentrated. In a highly concentrated market, a merger that produces an increase in the HHI of between 50 and 100 points raises significant competitive concerns. Mergers that produce an increase in the HHI of more than 100 points in a highly concentrated market are deemed likely to enhance market power. HHI figures were a factor in the following case.

12. Compute the change in the index by doubling the product of the merging firms' premerger market shares. For example, a merger between a firm with a 5 percent share and one with a 6 percent share will increase the HHI by $2 \times (5 \times 6) = 60$.

CASE 27.5 Chicago Bridge & Iron Co. v. Federal Trade Commission

United States Court of Appeals, Fifth Circuit, 2008. 515 F.3d 447.
www.ca5.uscourts.gov[a]

Background and Facts Chicago Bridge & Iron Company, and its U.S. subsidiary of the same name, is a company that designs, engineers, and constructs industrial storage tanks for liquefied natural gas (LNG), liquefied petroleum gas (LPG), and liquid atmospheric gases, such as nitrogen, oxygen, and argon (LIN/LOX), as well as thermal vacuum chambers (TVCs) for testing aerospace satellites. In these four separate markets, Chicago Bridge and another company, Pitt-Des Moines, Inc., have been the dominant firms. In 2001, Chicago Bridge acquired all of Pitt-Des Moines's assets for $84 million. The Federal Trade Commission charged that Chicago Bridge's acquisition violated Section 7 of the Clayton Act and Section 5 of the Federal Trade Commission Act. An administrative law judge concurred, finding that the acquisition resulted in an undue increase in Chicago Bridge's market power that would not be constrained by timely entry of new competitors. At issue was the use of the Herfindahl-Hirschman index (HHI). The Federal Trade Commission calculated the HHI over a several-year period rather than on an annualized basis. Chicago Bridge appealed to the U.S. Court of Appeals for the Fifth Circuit.

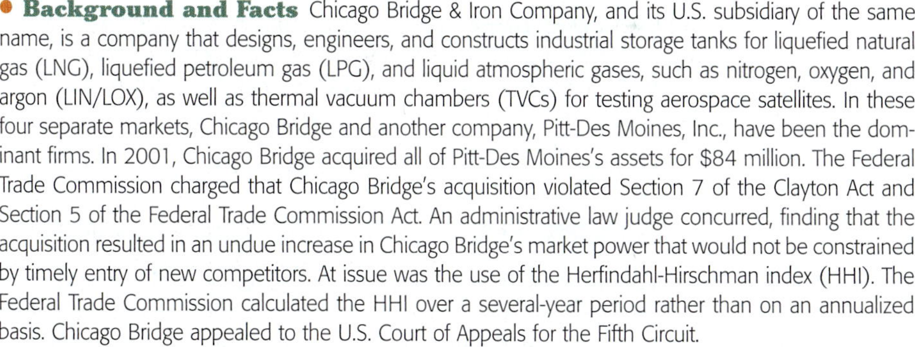

IN THE LANGUAGE OF THE COURT
***DENNIS,* Circuit Judge:**

* * * *

The HHIs are just one element in the Government's strong *prima facie* case. Market concentration figures should be examined in the context of the entire *prima facie* case. Here, the *prima facie* case establishes without dispute that the two dominant, and often only, players in these four domestic markets are merging. This indisputable fact "bolster[s]" the Government's market concentration figures. Where the post-merger HHI exceeds 1,800, and the merger produces an

a. On the left, click on "Opinions Page" and then in "Search for opinions where:" type "Chicago Bridge." Then click on the docket number listed.

CASE CONTINUES

CASE 27.5 CONTINUED increase in the HHI of more than 100 points, the merger guidelines create a presumption of adverse competitive consequences. The increases in HHIs in this case are extremely high. HHI increases of 2,635 for the LIN/LOX tank market, 3,911 for the LPG tank market, 4,956 for the LNG tank market, and 4,999 for the TVC tank market are predicted post-merger. An HHI of 10,000 denotes a complete monopoly. Post-acquisition HHIs for the four markets are: 5,845 for LIN/LOX, 8,380 for LPG, and 10,000 for the LNG and TVC markets.

* * * The Commission agrees with the ALJ [administrative law judge] that the use of HHIs based solely on sales from the 1996-2001 period is unreliable, and therefore extended the sales-data time period to an 11-year period, 1990-2001. When sales data are sporadic, a longer historical perspective may be necessary. * * * The Commission adequately explained why it chose an extended period: (1) the extended period provided more data points, which averages out the year-to-year fluctuations and "chance outcomes" and (2) [Chicago Bridge] presents no evidence that a structural change affected the market, and thus the same market conditions persist in the 1996-2001 time-period as the 11-year period, except the 11-year period has additional data points.

* * * *

In addition to its challenge of the selection of the time period, [Chicago Bridge] also argues that the "sporadic" nature of the sales data undermines all evidence of market power. * * * We agree that reliance on very limited data, such as two data points, may undermine an entire *prima facie* case. However, we find this to be a very limited exception * * * because the academic literature has not accepted any broad conclusion that small markets are all *per se* problematic.

* * * *

We find that the record contains substantial evidence to support the Commission's finding that the HHIs are not completely irrelevant in three of the four markets. Instead of ignoring HHIs, we agree with the Commission that they should be viewed with caution and within the larger picture of long-term trends and market structure. Long-term trends in the market and the Government's other evidence favor what the HHIs also indicate: the proposed merger will substantially lessen competition.

- **Decision and Remedy** *The U.S. Court of Appeals for the Fifth Circuit affirmed the Federal Trade Commission's decision that Chicago Bridge divest itself of its former competitor, Pitt-Des Moines.*

- **The Global Dimension** *Assume that just prior to Chicago Bridge's acquisition of its only U.S. competitor, a multinational-based company in Indonesia announced that it intended to enter all four of the markets mentioned in this case. How might this announcement affect the reasoning behind this case, if at all?*

- **The Legal Environment Dimension** *What are some of the problems with attempting to measure industry concentration?*

Other Factors. The guidelines stress that determining market share and market concentration is only the starting point in analyzing the potential anticompetitive effects of a merger. Before deciding to challenge a merger, the FTC and the DOJ will look at a number of other factors, including the ease of entry into the relevant market, economic efficiency, the financial condition of the merging firms, the nature and price of the product or products involved, and so on. If a firm is a leading one—having at least a 35 percent share and twice that of the next leading firm—any merger with another firm will be closely scrutinized.

Political Considerations in Defining the Relevant Market. Not considered in the above discussion are the sometimes unfathomable definitions of the relevant market determined by the federal government. To take an example, reconsider the proposed Whole Foods Market–Wild Oats Markets merger that the FTC sought to prevent in 2007 that was discussed in Chapter 26 on page 652. The FTC decided that the relevant product market was not all supermarkets but rather "premium natural and organic supermarkets." It then concluded that the proposed merger would seriously weaken competition in the narrowly defined market. In other words, the decision was evidently political rather than based on any theory of the economics of antitrust law.

Vertical Mergers A **vertical merger** occurs when a company at one stage of production acquires a company at a higher or lower stage of production. Courts in the past have almost exclusively focused on "foreclosure" in assessing vertical mergers. Foreclosure occurs because competitors of the merging firms lose opportunities to either sell or to buy products from the merging firms.

Today, whether a vertical merger will be deemed illegal depends on several factors, including market concentration, barriers to entry into the market, and the apparent intent of the merging parties. Mergers that do not prevent competitors of either of the merging firms from competing in a segment of the market will not be condemned as "foreclosing" competition and are legal.

Conglomerate Mergers **Conglomerate mergers** are mergers between firms that do not compete with each other because they are in different markets. There are three general types of conglomerate mergers: market-extension, product-extension, and diversification mergers. A market-extension merger occurs when a firm seeks to sell its product in a new market by merging with a firm already established in that market. A product-extension merger occurs when a firm seeks to add a closely related product to its existing line by merging with a firm already producing that product. For example, a manufacturer might seek to extend its product line of household products to include floor wax by acquiring a leading manufacturer of floor wax. Diversification occurs when a firm merges with another firm that offers a product or service wholly unrelated to the first firm's existing activities. An example of a diversification merger would be Google's acquisition of Holiday Inns.

REVIEWING Antitrust and Restraint of Trade

The Internet Corporation for Assigned Names and Numbers (ICANN) is a nonprofit entity organizing Internet domain names. It is governed by a board of directors elected by various groups with commercial interests in the Internet. One of ICANN's functions is to authorize an entity as a registry for certain "Top Level Domains" (TLDs). ICANN entered into an agreement with VeriSign to serve as registry for the ".com" TLD to provide registry services in accordance with ICANN's specifications. VeriSign complained that ICANN was restricting the services that it could make available as a registrar and blocking new services, imposing unnecessary conditions on those services, and setting prices at which the services were offered. VeriSign claimed that ICANN's control of the registry services for domain names violated Section 1 of the Sherman Act. Using the information presented in the chapter, answer the following questions.

1. Should ICANN's actions be judged under the rule of reason or be deemed a *per se* violation of Section 1 of the Sherman Act?
2. Should ICANN's actions be viewed as a horizontal or a vertical restraint of trade?
3. Does it matter that ICANN's leadership is chosen by those with a commercial interest in the Internet?
4. If the dispute is judged under the rule of reason, what might be ICANN's defense for having a standardized set of registry services that must be used?

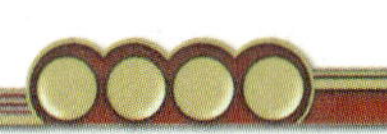

TERMS AND CONCEPTS

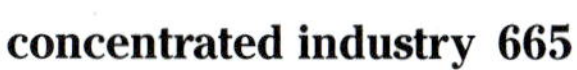

concentrated industry 665
conglomerate merger 675
exclusive-dealing contract 670
group boycott 665
Herfindahl-Hirschman index (HHI) 673
horizontal market division 664
horizontal merger 672
horizontal restraint 662
market concentration 672
***per se* violation 661**

price discrimination 669
price fixing 662
resale price maintenance agreement 667
rule of reason 662
tying arrangement 670
vertical merger 675
vertical restraint 666
vertically integrated firm 665

QUESTIONS AND CASE PROBLEMS

27–1. Most of the egg wholesalers supplying eggs to grocery stores in a particular area sell eggs to the retailers under various credit terms. The credit terms vary among the different buyers and sellers, but all of the wholesalers follow a common practice of reducing by 10 percent the price charged to a retailer if the retailer pays the wholesaler within three days of delivery. The various wholesalers agree that henceforth the 10 percent discount will be discontinued. If the agreement is indeed carried out by the wholesalers and the discount policy is discontinued, have the wholesalers violated any antitrust laws? Explain. If suit is brought against the wholesalers, what—if any—justification could they offer for the agreement?

27–2. Suppose that the wholesale egg suppliers in the preceding problem agree that the three largest suppliers should sell exclusively to the area's large chain-store groceries, leaving the remaining suppliers to sell solely to local individual "mom and pop" stores. Does the agreement violate any antitrust laws? Is it a defense that the larger suppliers, because of their scale of operations, enjoy a cost advantage that allows them to supply the large chain buyers more efficiently?

27–3. QUESTION WITH SAMPLE ANSWER

Discuss *fully* whether each of the following situations violates the Sherman Act:

(a) Trujillo Foods, Inc., is the leading seller of frozen Mexican foods in three southwestern states. The various retail outlets that sell Trujillo products are in close competition, and customers are very price conscious. Trujillo has conditioned its sales to retailers with the agreement that the retailers will not sell below a minimum price nor above a maximum price. The retailers are allowed to set any price within these limits.

(b) Franklin, Inc., Green, Inc., and Fill-It, Inc., are competitors in the manufacture and sale of microwave ovens sold primarily east of the Mississippi River. As a patriotic gesture and to assist the unemployed, the three competitors agree to lower their prices on all microwave models by 20 percent for a three-month period that includes the Fourth of July and Labor Day.

(c) Foam Beer, Inc., sells its beer to distributors all over the United States. Foam sends each of its distributors a recommended price list, explaining that past records indicate that selling beer at those prices should ensure the distributor a reasonable rate of return. The price list clearly states that the sale of beer by Foam to the distributor is not conditioned on the distributor's reselling the beer at the recommended price and that the distributor is free to set the price.

• **For a sample answer to Question 27–3, go to Appendix I at the end of this text.**

27–4. Tying Arrangement. Public Interest Corp. (PIC) owned and operated television station WTMV-TV in Lakeland, Florida. MCA Television, Ltd., owns and licenses syndicated television programs. The parties entered into a licensing contract with respect to several television shows. MCA conditioned the license on PIC's agreeing to take another show, *Harry and the Hendersons.* PIC agreed to this arrangement, although it would not have chosen to license *Harry* if it did not have to do so to secure the licenses for the other shows. More than two years into the contract, a dispute arose over PIC's payments, and negotiations failed to resolve the dispute. In a letter, MCA suspended PIC's broadcast rights for all of its shows and stated that "[a]ny telecasts of MCA programming by WTMV-TV . . . will be deemed unauthorized and shall constitute an infringement of MCA's copyrights." PIC nonetheless continued broadcasting MCA's programs, with the exception of *Harry.* MCA filed a suit in a federal district court against PIC, alleging breach of contract and copyright infringement. PIC filed a counterclaim, contending in part that MCA's deal was an illegal tying arrangement. Is PIC correct? Explain. [*MCA Television, Ltd. v. Public Interest Corp.*, 171 F.3d 1265 (11th Cir. 1999)]

27–5. Restraint of Trade. High fructose corn syrup (HFCS) is a sweetener made from corn and used in food products. There are two grades, HFCS 42 and HFCS 55. The five principal HFCS makers, including Archer Daniels Midland Co. (ADM), account for 90 percent of the sales. In 1988, shortly after Terrence Wilson became the head of ADM's corn-processing division, which was responsible for HFCS and other products, ADM announced that it was raising its price for HFCS 42 to 90 percent of the price of HFCS 55. It cost only 65 percent as much to manufacture HFCS 42, but the other makers followed suit. Over the next seven years, the makers sometimes bought HFCS from each other even when they could have produced the amount at a lower cost, and many sales to other customers were made at prices below the list prices. After Wilson was imprisoned for antitrust violations with regard to other ADM products, HFCS buyers filed a suit in a federal district court against the makers, alleging a *per se* violation of the Sherman Act and seeking billions of dollars in damages. How might the makers have violated antitrust law? What might be their defense? How should the court rule? Discuss. [*In re High Fructose Corn Syrup Antitrust Litigation,* 295 F.3d 651 (7th Cir. 2002)]

27–6. Restraint of Trade. Visa U.S.A., Inc., MasterCard International, Inc., American Express (Amex), and Discover are the four major credit- and charge-card networks in the United States. Visa and MasterCard are joint ventures, owned by the thousands of banks that are their members. The banks issue the cards, clear transactions, and collect fees from the merchants who accept the cards. By contrast, Amex and Discover themselves issue cards to customers, process transactions, and collect fees. Since 1995, Amex has asked banks to issue its cards. No bank has been willing to do so, however, because it would have to stop issuing Visa and MasterCard cards under those networks' rules barring member banks from issuing cards on rival networks. The U.S. Department of Justice filed a suit in a federal district court against Visa and MasterCard, alleging, in part, that the rules were illegal restraints of trade under the Sherman Act. Do the rules harm competition? If so, how? What relief might the court order to stop any anticompetitiveness? [*United States v. Visa U.S.A., Inc.,* 344 F.3d 229 (2d Cir. 2003)]

27–7. Sherman Act. Dentsply International, Inc., is one of a dozen manufacturers of artificial teeth for dentures and other restorative devices. Dentsply sells its teeth to twenty-three dealers of dental products. The dealers supply the teeth to dental laboratories, which fabricate dentures for sale to dentists. There are hundreds of other dealers who compete with each other on the basis of price and service. Some manufacturers sell directly to the laboratories. There are also thousands of laboratories that compete with each other on the basis of price and service. Because of advances in dental medicine, however, artificial tooth manufacturing is marked by low growth potential, and Dentsply dominates the industry. Dentsply's market share is greater than 75 percent and is about fifteen times larger than that of its next-closest competitor. Dentsply prohibits its dealers from marketing competitors' teeth unless they were selling the teeth before 1993. The federal government filed a suit in a federal district court against Dentsply, alleging, among other things, a violation of Section 2 of the Sherman Act. What must the government show to succeed in its suit? Are those elements present in this case? What should the court rule? Explain. [*United States v. Dentsply International, Inc.,* 399 F.3d 181 (3d Cir. 2005)]

27–8. CASE PROBLEM WITH SAMPLE ANSWER

Texaco, Inc., and Shell Oil Co. are competitors in the national and international oil and gasoline markets. They refine crude oil into gasoline and sell it to service station owners and others. Between 1998 and 2002, Texaco and Shell engaged in a joint venture, Equilon Enterprises, to consolidate their operations in the western United States and a separate venture, Motiva Enterprises, for the same purpose in the eastern United States. This ended their competition in the domestic refining and marketing of gasoline. As part of the ventures, Texaco and Shell agreed to pool their resources and share the risks and profits of their joint activities. The Federal Trade Commission and several states approved the formation of these entities without restricting the pricing of their gasoline, which the ventures began to sell at a single price under the original Texaco and Shell brand names. Fouad Dagher and other station owners filed a suit in a federal district court against Texaco and Shell, alleging that the defendants were engaged in illegal price fixing. Do the circumstances in this case fit the definition of a price-fixing agreement? Explain. [*Texaco Inc. v. Dagher,* 547 U.S. 1, 126 S.Ct. 1276, 164 L.Ed.2d 1 (2006)]

- **To view a sample answer for Problem 27–8, go to this book's Web site at academic.cengage.com/blaw/cross, select "Chapter 27," and click on "Case Problem with Sample Answer."**

27–9. SPECIAL CASE ANALYSIS

Go to Case 27.3, *Leegin Creative Leather Products, Inc. v. PSKS, Inc.,* __ U.S. __, 127 S.Ct. 2705, 168 L.Ed.2d 623 (2007), on pages 667–669. Read the excerpt and answer the following questions.

(a) **Issue:** What was the main issue in this case?
(b) **Rule of Law:** What rule of law did the Court apply?
(c) **Applying the Rule of Law:** Describe how the Court applied the rule of law to the facts of this case.
(d) **Conclusion:** What was the Court's conclusion in this case?

27–10. A QUESTION OF ETHICS

In the 1990s, DuCoa, L.P., made choline chloride, a B-complex vitamin essential for the growth and development of animals. The U.S. market for choline chloride was divided into thirds among DuCoa, Bioproducts, Inc., and Chinook Group, Ltd. To stabilize the market and keep the price of the vitamin higher than it would otherwise have been, the companies agreed to fix the price and allocate market share by deciding which of them would offer the lowest price to each customer. At times, however, the companies disregarded the agreement. During an increase in competitive activity in August 1997, Daniel Rose became president of DuCoa. The next month, a subordinate advised him of the conspiracy. By February 1998, Rose had begun to implement a strategy to persuade DuCoa's competitors to rejoin the conspiracy. By April, the three companies had reallocated their market shares and increased their prices. In June, the U.S. Department of Justice began to investigate allegations of price fixing in the vitamin market. Ultimately, a federal *district court convicted Rose of conspiracy to violate Section 1 of the Sherman Act. [*United States v. Rose, *449 F.3d 627 (5th Cir. 2006)]*

(a) The court "enhanced" Rose's sentence to thirty months' imprisonment, one year of supervised release, and a $20,000 fine based, among other things, on his role as "a manager or supervisor" in the conspiracy. Rose appealed this enhancement to the U.S. Court of Appeals for the Fifth Circuit. Was it fair to increase Rose's sentence on this ground? Why or why not?

(b) Was Rose's participation in the conspiracy unethical? If so, how might Rose have behaved ethically instead? If not, could any of the participants' conduct be considered unethical? Explain.

LAW ON THE WEB

For updated links to resources available on the Web, as well as a variety of other materials, visit this text's Web site at

academic.cengage.com/blaw/cross

You can access the Antitrust Division of the U.S. Department of Justice online at

www.usdoj.gov

To see the American Bar Association's Web page on antitrust law, go to

www.abanet.org/antitrust

The Federal Trade Commission offers an abundance of information on antitrust law, including *A Plain English Guide to Antitrust Laws,* which is available at

www.ftc.gov/bc/compguide/index.html

Legal Research Exercises on the Web

Go to **academic.cengage.com/blaw/cross**, the Web site that accompanies this text. Select "Chapter 27" and click on "Internet Exercises." There you will find the following Internet research exercises that you can perform to learn more about the topics covered in this chapter.

Internet Exercise 27–1: Legal Perspective
Mergers and Antitrust Law

Internet Exercise 27–2: Management Perspective
Avoiding Antitrust Problems

CHAPTER 28

Investor Protection and Corporate Governance

The stock market crash of October 29, 1929, and the ensuing economic depression caused the public to focus on the importance of securities markets for the economic well-being of the nation. Congress was pressured to regulate securities trading, and the result was the Securities Act of 1933[1] and the Securities Exchange Act of 1934.[2] Both acts were designed to provide investors with more information to help them make buying and selling decisions about securities—generally defined as any instruments evidencing corporate ownership (stock) or debts (bonds)—and to prohibit deceptive, unfair, and manipulative practices in the purchase and sale of securities.

This chapter discusses the nature of federal securities regulation and its effect on the business world. We begin by looking at the federal administrative agency that regulates securities transactions, the Securities and Exchange Commission. Next, we examine the major traditional laws governing securities offerings and trading. We then discuss corporate governance and the Sarbanes-Oxley Act, which significantly affects certain types of securities transactions. In the concluding pages of this chapter, we look at how securities laws are being adapted to the online environment.

1. 15 U.S.C. Sections 77a–77aa.
2. 15 U.S.C. Sections 78a–78mm.

SECTION 1 The Securities and Exchange Commission

The 1934 act created the Securities and Exchange Commission (SEC) as an independent regulatory agency that would administer the 1933 and 1934 acts. The SEC plays a key role in interpreting the provisions of these acts (and their amendments) and in creating regulations governing the purchase and sale of securities. The basic functions of the SEC are listed in Exhibit 28–1.

Organization of the SEC

The SEC's broad responsibilities are organized into four divisions—Corporate Finance, Market Regulation, Investment Management, and Enforcement. Each divi-

EXHIBIT 28–1 • Basic Functions of the SEC

1. **Interprets federal securities laws and investigates securities law violations.**
2. **Issues new rules and amends existing rules.**
3. **Oversees the inspection of securities firms, brokers, investment advisers, and ratings agencies.**
4. **Oversees private regulatory organizations in the securities, accounting, and auditing fields.**
5. **Coordinates U.S. securities regulation with federal, state, and foreign authorities.**

Investment Scams

An ongoing concern for the SEC is how to curb investment scams. One fraudulent investment scheme involved twenty thousand investors, who lost, in all, more than $3 million. Some cases have involved false claims about the earnings potential of home businesses, such as the claim that one could "earn $4,000 or more each month." Others have concerned claims of "guaranteed credit repair."

Using Chat Rooms to Manipulate Stock Prices

"Pumping and dumping" occurs when a person who has purchased a particular stock heavily promotes ("pumps up") that stock—thereby creating a great demand for it and driving up its price—and then sells ("dumps") it. The practice of pumping up a stock and then dumping it is quite old. In the online world, however, the process can occur much more quickly and efficiently.

A famous example in this area involved Jonathan Lebed, a fifteen-year-old from New Jersey, who became the first minor ever charged with securities fraud by the SEC. The SEC charged that Lebed bought thinly traded stocks. After purchasing a stock, he would flood stock-related chat rooms with messages touting the stock's virtues. He used numerous false names so that no one would know that a single person was posting the messages. He would say that the stock was the most "undervalued stock in history" and that its price would jump by 1,000 percent "very soon." When other investors bought the stock, the price would go up quickly, and Lebed would sell out. The SEC forced the teenager to repay almost $300,000 in gains plus interest but allowed him to keep about $500,000 of his profits.

The SEC has been bringing an increasing number of cases against those who manipulate stock prices in this way. Many of these online investment scams are perpetrated through mass e-mails (spam) and online newsletters, as well as chat rooms.

Hacking into Online Stock Accounts

The last few years have seen the emergence of a new form of "pumping and dumping" stock that involves hackers who break into existing online stock accounts and make unauthorized transfers. Millions of people now buy and sell investments online through online brokerage companies such as E*Trade and Ameritrade. Sophisticated hackers have learned to use online investing to their advantage.

By installing keystroke-monitoring software on computer terminals in public places, such as hotels, libraries, and airports, hackers can gain access to online account information. They simply wait for a person to access an online trading account and then monitor the next several dozen keystrokes to determine the customer's account number and password. Once they have the log-in information, they can access the customer's account and liquidate her or his existing stock holdings. The hackers then use the customer's funds to purchase thinly traded, microcap securities, also known as penny stocks. The goal is to boost the price of a stock that the hacker has already purchased at a lower price. Then, when the stock price goes up, the hacker sells all the stock and wires the funds to either an offshore account or a dummy corporation, making it difficult for the SEC to trace the transactions and prosecute the offender.

For example, Aleksey Kamardin, a twenty-one-year-old Florida student, purchased 55,000 shares of stock in Fuego Entertainment using an E*Trade account in his own name. Kamardin then hacked into other customers' accounts at E*Trade, Ameritrade, Schwab, and other brokerage companies, and used their funds to purchase a total of 458,000 shares of Fuego stock. When the stock price rose from $.88 per share to $1.28 per share, Kamardin sold all of his shares of Fuego, making a profit of $9,164.28 in about three hours. Kamardin did this with other thinly traded stocks as well, allegedly making $82,960 in about five weeks and prompting the SEC to file charges against him in January 2007.[41]

So far, the brokerage companies have been covering their customers' losses from this new wave of frauds, but the potential for loss is substantial. E*Trade and Ameritrade have also increased security measures and are changing their software to prevent further intrusions into customers' online stock accounts.

---

41. You can read the SEC's complaint against Kamardin by going to the SEC's Web site at **www.sec.gov**, clicking on the link to litigation releases, and selecting LR-19981. The case had not been resolved by the time this book went to press.

REVIEWING Investor Protection and Corporate Governance

Dale Emerson served as the chief financial officer for Reliant Electric Co., a distributor of electricity serving portions of Montana and North Dakota. Reliant was in the final stages of planning a takeover of Dakota Gasworks, Inc., a natural gas distributor that operated solely within North Dakota. Emerson went on a weekend fishing trip with his uncle, Ernest Wallace. Emerson mentioned to Wallace that he had been putting in a lot of extra hours at the office planning a takeover of Dakota Gasworks. On returning from the fishing trip, Wallace met with a broker from Chambers Investments and purchased $20,000 of Reliant stock. Three weeks later, Reliant made a tender offer to Dakota Gasworks stockholders and purchased 57 percent of Dakota Gasworks stock. Over the next two weeks, the price of Reliant stock rose 72 percent before leveling out. Wallace then sold his Reliant stock for a gross profit of $14,400. Using the information presented in the chapter, answer the following questions.

1. Would registration with the SEC be required for Dakota Gasworks securities? Why or why not?
2. Did Emerson violate Section 10(b) of the Securities Exchange Act of 1934 and SEC Rule 10b-5? Why or why not?
3. What theory or theories might a court use to hold Wallace liable for insider trading?
4. Under the Sarbanes-Oxley Act of 2002, who would be required to certify the accuracy of the financial statements Reliant filed with the SEC?

TERMS AND CONCEPTS

accredited investor 685
blue sky laws 701
bounty payment 697
corporate governance 697
free-writing prospectus 682
insider trading 688
investment company 685
investment contract 680
mutual fund 685
prospectus 681
red herring prospectus 682
SEC Rule 10b-5 688
stock options 698
tippee 693
tombstone ad 682

QUESTIONS AND CASE PROBLEMS

28–1. Estrada Hermanos, Inc., a corporation incorporated and doing business in Florida, decides to sell $1 million worth of its common stock to the public. The stock will be sold only within the state of Florida. José Estrada, the chair of the board, says the offering need not be registered with the Securities and Exchange Commission. His brother, Gustavo, disagrees. Who is right? Explain.

28-2. QUESTION WITH SAMPLE ANSWER

Huron Corp. has 300,000 common shares outstanding. The owners of these outstanding shares live in several different states. Huron has decided to split the 300,000 shares two for one. Will Huron Corp. have to file a registration statement and prospectus on the 300,000 new shares to be issued as a result of the split? Explain.

- **For a sample answer to Question 28–2, go to Appendix I at the end of this text.**

28-3. Violations of the 1934 Act. 2TheMart.com, Inc., was conceived in January 1999 to launch an auction Web site to compete with eBay, Inc. On January 19, 2TheMart announced that its Web site was in its "final development" stages and expected to be active by the end of July as a "preeminent" auction site, and that the company had "retained the services of leading Web site design and architecture consultants to design and construct" the site. Based on the announcement, investors rushed to buy 2TheMart's stock, causing a rapid increase in the price. On February 3, 2TheMart entered into an agreement with IBM to take preliminary steps to plan the site. Three weeks later, 2TheMart announced that the site was "currently in final development." On June 1, 2TheMart signed a contract with IBM to design, build, and test the site, with a target delivery date of October 8. When 2TheMart's site did not debut as announced, Mary Harrington and others who had bought the stock filed a suit in a federal district court against the firm's officers, alleging violations of the Securities Exchange Act of 1934. The defendants responded, in part, that any alleged misrepresentations were not material and asked the court to dismiss the suit. How should the court rule, and why? [*In re 2TheMart.com, Inc. Securities Litigation,* 114 F.Supp.2d 955 (C.D.Ca. 2000)]

28-4. Insider Reporting and Trading. Ronald Bleakney, an officer at Natural Microsystems Corp. (NMC), a Section 12 corporation, directed NMC sales in North America, South America, and Europe. In November 1998, Bleakney sold more than 7,500 shares of NMC stock. The following March, Bleakney resigned from the firm, and the next month, he bought more than 20,000 shares of its stock. NMC provided some guidance to employees concerning the rules of insider trading, and with regard to Bleakney's transactions, the corporation said nothing about potential liability. Richard Morales, an NMC shareholder, filed a suit against NMC and Bleakney to compel recovery, under Section 16(b) of the Securities Exchange Act of 1934, of Bleakney's profits from the purchase and sale of his shares. (When Morales died, his executor Deborah Donoghue became the plaintiff.) Bleakney argued that he should not be liable because he relied on NMC's advice. Should the court order Bleakney to return his profits to the corporation? Explain. [*Donoghue v. Natural Microsystems Corp.,* 198 F.Supp.2d 487 (S.D.N.Y. 2002)]

28-5. CASE PROBLEM WITH SAMPLE ANSWER

Scott Ginsburg was chief executive officer (CEO) of Evergreen Media Corp., which owned and operated radio stations. In 1996, Evergreen became interested in acquiring EZ Communications, Inc., which also owned radio stations. To initiate negotiations, Ginsburg met with EZ's CEO, Alan Box, on Friday, July 12. Two days later, Scott phoned his brother Mark, who, on Monday, bought 3,800 shares of EZ stock. Mark discussed the deal with their father Jordan, who bought 20,000 EZ shares on Thursday. On July 25, the day before the EZ bid was due, Scott phoned his parents' home, and Mark bought another 3,200 EZ shares. The same routine was followed over the next few days, with Scott periodically phoning Mark or Jordan, both of whom continued to buy EZ shares. Evergreen's bid was refused, but on August 5, EZ announced its merger with another company. The price of EZ stock rose 30 percent, increasing the value of Mark's and Jordan's shares by $664,024 and $412,875, respectively. The Securities and Exchange Commission (SEC) filed a civil suit in a federal district court against Scott. What was the most likely allegation? What is required to impose sanctions for this offense? Should the court hold Scott liable? Why or why not? [*SEC v. Ginsburg,* 362 F.3d 1292 (11th Cir. 2004)]

- **To view a sample answer for Problem 28–5, go to this book's Web site at academic.cengage.com/blaw/cross, select "Chapter 28," and click on "Case Problem with Sample Answer."**

28-6. Securities Laws. In 1997, WTS Transnational, Inc., required financing to develop a prototype of an unpatented fingerprint-verification system. At the time, WTS had no revenue, $655,000 in liabilities, and only $10,000 in assets. Thomas Cavanagh and Frank Nicolois, who operated an investment banking company called U.S. Milestone (USM), arranged the financing using Curbstone Acquisition Corp. Curbstone had no assets but had registered approximately 3.5 million shares of stock with the Securities and Exchange Commission (SEC). Under the terms of the deal, Curbstone acquired WTS, and the resulting entity was named Electro-Optical Systems Corp. (EOSC). New EOSC shares were issued to all of the WTS shareholders. Only Cavanagh and others affiliated with USM could sell EOSC stock to the public, however. Over the next few months, these individuals issued false press releases, made small deceptive purchases of EOSC shares at high prices, distributed hundreds of thousands of shares to friends and relatives, and sold their own shares at inflated prices through third party companies they owned. When the SEC began to investigate, the share price fell to its actual value, and innocent investors lost more than $15 million. Were any securities laws violated in this case? If so, what might be an appropriate remedy? [*SEC v. Cavanagh,* 445 F.3d 105 (2d Cir. 2006)]

28-7. Securities Trading. Between 1994 and 1998, Richard Svoboda, a credit officer for NationsBank N.A., in Dallas, Texas, evaluated and approved his employer's extensions of credit to clients. These responsibilities gave Svoboda access to nonpublic information about the clients' earnings, performance, acquisitions, and business plans in confidential memos, e-mail, credit applications, and other sources. Svoboda devised a scheme with Michael Robles, an independent accountant, to use this information to trade securities. Pursuant to their scheme, Robles traded in the securities of more than twenty different companies and profited by more than $1 million. Despite their agreement that Robles would do all of the trading, Svoboda also executed trades on his own and made profits of more than $200,000. Aware that their scheme violated NationsBank's policy, they attempted to conduct their trades so as to avoid suspicion. When NationsBank questioned Svoboda about his actions, he lied, refused to cooperate, and was fired. Did Svoboda or Robles commit any crimes? Are they subject to civil liability? If so, who could file a suit and on what ground? What are the possible sanctions? What might be a defense? How should a court rule? Discuss. [*SEC v. Svoboda,* 409 F.Supp.2d 331 (S.D.N.Y. 2006)]

28-8. SPECIAL CASE ANALYSIS

Go to Case 28.2, *Merrill Lynch, Pierce, Fenner & Smith, Inc. v. Dabit,* 547 U.S. 71, 126 S.Ct. 1503, 164 L.Ed.2d 179 (2006), on pages 690–691. Read the excerpt and answer the following questions.

(a) **Issue:** What was the main issue in this case?
(b) **Rule of Law:** What rule of law did the Court apply?
(c) **Applying the Rule of Law:** Describe how the Court applied the rule of law to the facts of this case.
(d) **Conclusion:** What was the Court's conclusion in this case?

28-9. A QUESTION OF ETHICS

*Melvin Lyttle told John Montana and Paul Knight about a "Trading Program" that purportedly would buy and sell securities in deals that were fully insured, as well as monitored and controlled by the Federal Reserve. Without checking the details or even verifying whether the Program existed, Montana and Knight, with Lyttle's help, began to sell interests in the Program to investors. For a minimum investment of $1 million, the investors were promised extraordinary rates of return—from 10 percent to as much as 100 percent per week—without risk. They were told, among other things, that the Program would "utilize banks that can ensure full bank integrity of The Transaction whose undertaking[s] are in complete harmony with international banking rules and protocol and who guarantee maximum security of a Funder's Capital Placement Amount." Nothing was required but the investors' funds and their silence—the Program was to be kept secret. Over a four-month period in 1999, Montana raised approximately $23 million from twenty-two investors. The promised gains did not accrue, however. Instead, Montana, Lyttle, and Knight depleted investors' funds in high-risk trades or spent the funds on themselves. [*SEC v. Montana, *464 F.Supp.2d 772 (S.D.Ind. 2006)]*

(a) The Securities and Exchange Commission (SEC) filed a suit in a federal district court against Montana and the others, seeking an injunction, civil penalties, and refund of profits with interest. The SEC alleged, among other things, violations of Section 10(b) of the Securities Exchange Act of 1934 and SEC Rule 10b-5. What is required to establish such violations? Describe how and why the facts in this case meet, or fail to meet, these requirements.
(b) It is often remarked, "There's a sucker born every minute!" Does that phrase describe the Program's investors? Ultimately, about half of the investors recouped the amount they invested. Should the others be considered at least partly responsible for their own losses? Why or why not?

28-10. VIDEO QUESTION

Go to this text's Web site at **academic.cengage.com/blaw/cross** and select "Chapter 28." Click on "Video Questions" and view the video titled *Mergers and Acquisitions.* Then answer the following questions.

(a) Was the purchase of Onyx Advertising a material fact that the Quigley Co. had a duty to disclose under SEC Rule 10b-5? Why or why not?
(b) Does it matter whether Quigley knew about or authorized the company spokesperson's statements? Explain.
(c) Would Onyx Advertising be able to maintain a suit against the Quigley Co. for violation of SEC Rule 10b-5? Why or why not?
(d) Who else might be able to bring a suit against the Quigley Co. for insider trading under SEC Rule 10b-5?

LAW ON THE WEB

For updated links to resources available on the Web, as well as a variety of other materials, visit this text's Web site at

academic.cengage.com/blaw/cross

To access the SEC's EDGAR database, go to

www.sec.gov/edgar.shtml

The Center for Corporate Law at the University of Cincinnati College of Law examines many of the laws discussed in this chapter, including the Securities Act of 1933 and the Securities Exchange Act of 1934. Go to

www.law.uc.edu/CCL

Legal Research Exercises on the Web

Go to **academic.cengage.com/blaw/cross**, the Web site that accompanies this text. Select "Chapter 28" and click on "Internet Exercises." There you will find the following Internet research exercises that you can perform to learn more about the topics covered in this chapter.

Internet Exercise 28–1: Legal Perspective
Electronic Delivery

Internet Exercise 28–2: Management Perspective
The SEC's Role

UNIT SIX FOCUS ON ETHICS

Ethics and the Regulatory Environment

If this text had been written a hundred years ago, it would have had little to say about federal government regulation. Today, in contrast, virtually every area of economic activity is regulated by the government.

Essentially, government regulation brings two ethical principles into conflict. On the one hand, deeply embedded in American culture is the idea that the government should play a limited role in directing our lives. Indeed, this nation was founded so that Americans could be free from the "heavy hand of government" experienced by the colonists under British rule. On the other hand, one of the basic functions of government is to protect the welfare of individuals and the environment in which they live.

Ultimately, virtually every law or rule regulating business represents a decision to give up certain rights in order to protect other perceived rights. In this *Focus on Ethics* feature, we look at some of the ethical aspects of government regulation.

Telemarketing and Consumers' Privacy Rights

A good example of how the rights of one group may conflict with those of another is the debate over the Do Not Call Registry discussed in Chapter 23. The do-not-call list allows consumers to register their telephone numbers with the FTC to protect themselves from unwanted phone solicitations. Consumers, who had long complained about receiving unsolicited sales calls, have welcomed the Do Not Call Registry and the reduced number of calls that they receive as a result.

Telemarketers, in contrast, have strongly objected to the list. Business has sagged for numerous companies, causing jobs to be lost. Many firms have continued to contact individuals on the registry, making themselves vulnerable to fines of up to $11,000 whenever they dial a phone number on the list. Thus, protecting consumers' privacy rights has entailed significant restrictions on an industry's ability to conduct its business.

Recently, some members of Congress have suggested that a Do Not Spam bill, similar to the Do Not Call legislation, be enacted. While the idea holds promise in principle, in practice it would be hard to enforce. Most spammers use offshore Internet servers to avoid being regulated by U.S. authorities. For the moment, there is no practical way to limit the large quantity of spam that fills e-mail inboxes each minute of every day."[1]

Consumer Safety

Recently, many consumers have become concerned about the safety of the products they buy, especially children's toys. Many of the toys—and other goods—sold in the United States are imported, often from China. Domestic manufacturers are unable or unwilling to compete with Chinese toy makers. Wal-Mart, for example, buys millions of Chinese toys each year. After some well-publicized safety lapses with such imports, many Americans have called for increased regulation of products from low-cost Chinese producers. Indeed, Wal-Mart criticized its Chinese suppliers. Later, though, Wal-Mart publicly apologized to the government of China for exaggerating the cause of the toy defects. It turned out that the Chinese suppliers had followed Wal-Mart's specifications, which were at the basis of the safety problems.

The economic and even ethical trade-off here is obvious: accept lower-priced, less-than-perfect products from foreign low-cost producers or impose stricter scrutiny on such imports and have the U.S. consumer pay a higher price.

Environmental Law

Questions of fairness inevitably arise in regard to environmental law. Has the government gone too far—or not far enough—in regulating businesses in the interest of protecting the environment? At what point do the costs of environmental regulations become too burdensome for society to bear? Consider the problem of toxic waste. Although everybody is in favor of cleaning up America's toxic waste dumps, nobody has the slightest idea what this task will ultimately cost. Moreover, there is no agreed-on standard as to how clean a site must be before it no longer poses any threat. Must 100 percent of the contamination be removed, or would removal of some lesser amount achieve a reasonable degree of environmental quality?

1. *Mainstream Marketing Services, Inc. v. Federal Trade Commission,* 358 F.3d 1228 (10th Cir. 2004).

(Continued)

UNIT SIX FOCUS ON ETHICS

Global Environmental Issues

Pollution does not respect geographic borders. Indeed, one of the reasons that the federal government became involved in environmental protection was that state regulation alone apparently could not solve the problem of air or water pollution. Pollutants generated in one state move in the air and water to other states. Neither does pollution respect national borders. Environmental issues, perhaps more than any others, bring home to everyone the fact that the world today is truly a global community. What one country does or does not do with respect to environmental preservation may be felt by citizens in countries thousands of miles away.

Another challenging—and controversial—issue is potential global warming. The fear is that emissions, largely from combustion of fossil fuels, will remain in the atmosphere and create a "greenhouse effect" by preventing heat from radiating outward. Concerns over this issue have led to many attempts to force all world polluters to "clean up their acts." For example, leaders of 160 nations have already agreed to reduce emissions of greenhouse gases in their respective countries. They did this when they ratified the Kyoto Protocol, which was drawn up at a world summit meeting held in Kyoto, Japan, in 1997. The Kyoto Protocol, which is often referred to as the global warming treaty, established different rates of reduction in emissions of greenhouse gases for different countries or regions. Most nations, however, including the United States, will not meet the treaty's objectives.

Economists have shown that economic development is the quickest way to reduce pollution worldwide. After a nation reaches a certain per capita income level, the more economic growth the nation experiences, the lower the pollution output. This occurs because richer nations have the resources to pay for pollution reduction. For example, industries in the United States pollute much less per unit of output than do industries in developing nations—because we are willing to pay for pollution abatement. Even among developed nations, the United States is a leader in curbing pollution. Indeed, from 2001 to 2009, the United States saw a much smaller increase in greenhouse gases than did the European Union (EU). Most members of the EU had signed the Kyoto Protocol.

Land-Use Regulations and the "Takings Clause"

Regulations to control land use, including environmental regulations, are prevalent throughout the United States. Generally, these laws reflect the public's interest in preserving natural resources and habitats for wildlife. At times, their goal is to enable the public to have access to and enjoy limited natural resources, such as coastal areas. Although few would disagree with the rationale underlying these laws, the owners of the private property directly affected by the laws often feel that they should be compensated for the limitations imposed on their right to do as they wish with their land.

Remember from Chapter 25 that the Fifth Amendment to the U.S. Constitution gives the government the power to "take" private property for public use. The Fifth Amendment attaches an important condition to this power, however: when private land is taken for public use, the landowner must be given "just compensation."

No General Rule In cases alleging that a "regulatory taking" has occurred, the courts have largely decided the issue on a case-by-case basis. In other words, there is no general rule that one can cite to indicate whether a specific situation will be deemed a taking. In one case, the city of Monterey, California, in the interests of protecting various forms of coastal wildlife, would not allow an owner of oceanfront property to build a residential development. In effect, the city's actions meant that the entire property had to be left in its natural state, thus making the owner's planned use of the land impossible. When the landowner challenged the city's action as an unconstitutional taking without compensation, the United States Supreme Court ultimately agreed, and the landowner had to be compensated.[2]

In another case, however, the Supreme Court held for the regulators. In an attempt to curb pollution in Lake Tahoe, located on the California-Nevada border, a regional government planning agency issued a moratorium on (a temporary suspension of) the construction of housing in certain areas around the lake. The moratorium was extended time and again until, some twenty years

2. *City of Monterey v. Del Monte Dunes at Monterey, Ltd.,* 526 U.S. 687, 119 S.Ct. 1624, 143 L.Ed.2d 882 (1999). See also *Vulcan Materials Co. v. The City of Tehuacana,* 369 F.3d 882 (5th Cir. 2004).

later, a number of landowners sued the agency. The landowners claimed that a regulatory taking had occurred for which they should be compensated. The Supreme Court disagreed. Because the agency's actions had not deprived the owners of their property for too long a time, no taking had occurred. How long was too long? The Court said that no categorical rule could be stated; the answer always depended on "the facts presented."[3]

A Question of Fairness The question of whether private landowners should be compensated when their land is essentially "taken" for public use by environmental and land-use regulations clearly involves issues of fairness. On the one hand, states, cities, and other local governments want to preserve their natural resources and need some authority to regulate land use to achieve this goal. On the other hand, private property owners complain that they alone should not have to bear the costs of creating a benefit, such as environmental preservation, given that all members of the public enjoy that benefit.

Mortgage Lending Practices and Ethics

Mortgage lenders usually extend credit to high-risk borrowers using higher-than-normal interest rates (called subprime mortgages) and adjustable-rate mortgages (ARMs). In fact, the widespread use of subprime and ARM mortgages in recent years has resulted in many borrowers being overextended and unable to pay their loan payments as they come due.

In addition, housing prices in the United States have dropped, which means that some borrowers are not able to sell their homes for the amount they owe on the mortgage. As a consequence, there was a sharp increase in the number of home foreclosures in 2007 and 2008. These foreclosures cause many to question the ethics of mortgage lenders that extend subprime and ARM loans to high-risk borrowers, knowing that the borrowers are likely to default if the interest rate goes up.

3. *Tahoe-Sierra Preservation Council v. Tahoe Regional Planning Agency,* 535 U.S. 302, 122 S.Ct. 1465, 152 L.Ed.2d 517 (2002).

FOCUS on ETHICS

Antitrust Law— The Baseball Exemption

The fact that, until relatively recently, baseball remained totally exempt from antitrust laws not only seemed unfair to many but also defied logic: Why was an exemption made for baseball but not for other professional sports? The answer to this perfectly reasonable question has always been the same: baseball was exempt because the United States Supreme Court, in 1922, said that it was. The Court held that baseball was a sport played only locally by local players. Because the activity purportedly did not involve interstate commerce, it did not meet the requirement for federal jurisdiction.

The exemption was challenged in the early 1970s, but the Supreme Court ruled that it was up to Congress, not the Court, to overturn the exemption. In 1998, Congress did address the issue and passed the Curt Flood Act—named for the St. Louis Cardinals' star outfielder who challenged the exemption in the early 1970s. The act, however, did not invalidate the 1922 Supreme Court decision but only limited some of the effects of baseball's exempt status. Essentially, the act allows players the option of suing team owners for anticompetitive practices if, for example, the owners collude to "blacklist" players, hold down players' salaries, or force players to play for specific teams.

Baseball is still not subject to antitrust laws to the extent that football, basketball, and other professional sports are. Critics of the exemption argue that it should be completely abolished because it makes no sense to continue to treat an enterprise generating revenues of $4 billion a year as a "local" activity.

The Emergence of Corporate Governance

The well-publicized corporate abuses that took place in the last ten years have fueled the impetus for businesspersons to create their own internal rules for corporate governance (discussed in Chapter 28). In a few situations, officers have blatantly stolen from the corporation and its shareholders. More frequently, though, officers receive benefits or "perks" of office that are excessive. To illustrate: Tyco International bought a $6,000 shower curtain and a $15,000 umbrella stand for its CEO's apartment.

Corporate officers may be given numerous benefits that they may or may not deserve. A leading

(Continued)

UNIT SIX FOCUS ON ETHICS

corporate officer can receive compensation of $50 million or more while her or his company's share price is actually declining. Even if corporate officers are scrupulously honest and have modest personal tastes, their behavior may still raise concerns: they may not be good managers, and they may make incompetent corporate choices. They may be a little lazy and fail to do the hard work necessary to investigate corporate decisions. Alternatively, officers may simply fail to appreciate the concerns of shareholders on certain matters, such as maximizing short-term versus long-term results.

Corporate governance controls are meant to ensure that officers receive only the benefits they earn. Governance monitors the actions taken by officers to make sure they are wise and in the best interests of the company. In this way, the corporation can be confident that it is acting ethically toward its shareholders.

Insider Trading

As you learned in Chapter 28, SEC Rule 10b-5 has broad applicability. The rule covers not only corporate insiders but even "outsiders" who trade on tips received from insiders. Investigating and prosecuting violations of SEC Rule 10b-5 is costly, both for the government and for those accused of insider trading. Some people doubt that such extensive regulation is necessary and even contend that insider trading should be legal. Would there be any benefit from the legalization of insider trading?

To evaluate this question, review the facts in *SEC v. Texas Gulf Sulphur Co.* (Case 28.1 in Chapter 28 on pages 689–690). If insider trading were legal, the discovery of the ore sample would probably have caused many more company insiders to purchase stock. Consequently, the price of Texas Gulf's stock would have increased fairly quickly. These increases presumably would have attracted the attention of outside investors, who would have realized sooner that something positive had happened to the company and would thus have purchased the stock. The higher demand for the stock would have more quickly translated into higher prices for the stock and hence, perhaps, a more efficient capital market. Nonetheless, the SEC and the courts have routinely upheld the rule that insider trading is illegal.

The Sarbanes-Oxley Act and Insider Trading

The attorney-client privilege generally prevents lawyers from disclosing confidential client information—even when the client has committed an unlawful act. The idea is to encourage clients to be open and honest with their attorneys to ensure competent representation. The Sarbanes-Oxley Act of 2002, however, requires attorneys to report any material violations of securities laws to the corporation's highest authority.[4] The act does not require that the lawyer break client confidences, though, because the lawyer is still reporting to officials within the corporation.

In August 2003, the SEC went one step further than the Sarbanes-Oxley Act to permit attorneys to disclose confidential information to the SEC without the corporate client's consent in certain circumstances.[5] Although the American Bar Association modified its ethics rules to allow attorneys to break confidence with a client to report possible corporate fraud, not all state ethics codes allow attorneys to disclose client information to the SEC. Thus, by reporting possible violations of securities law to the SEC, corporate lawyers may violate the state ethics code of their profession.

DISCUSSION QUESTIONS

1. Does the national Do Not Call Registry adversely affect the way that business is conducted in this country? If so, how? Should Congress enact a Do Not Spam law? Why or why not?
2. Do you believe that the law strikes a fair balance between the rights of landowners and the right of governments to control land use in the public interest? Why or why not?
3. Three decades ago, corporations and corporate directors were rarely prosecuted for crimes, and penalties for corporate crimes were relatively light. Today, this is no longer true. Under the corporate sentencing guidelines and the Sarbanes-Oxley Act, corporate wrongdoers can receive strict penalties. Do these developments mean that corporations are committing more crimes today than in the past? Will stricter laws be effective in curbing corporate criminal activity? How can a company avoid liability for crimes committed by its employees?

4. See Section 307 of the Sarbanes-Oxley Act.
5. See 17 C.F.R. Part 205.3.

APPENDIX A

How to Brief Cases and Analyze Case Problems

HOW TO BRIEF CASES

To fully understand the law with respect to business, you need to be able to read and understand court decisions. To make this task easier, you can use a method of case analysis that is called *briefing*. There is a fairly standard procedure that you can follow when you "brief" any court case. You must first read the case opinion carefully. When you feel you understand the case, you can prepare a brief of it.

Although the format of the brief may vary, typically it will present the essentials of the case under headings such as those listed below.

1. **Citation.** Give the full citation for the case, including the name of the case, the date it was decided, and the court that decided it.
2. **Facts.** Briefly indicate (a) the reasons for the lawsuit; (b) the identity and arguments of the plaintiff(s) and defendant(s), respectively; and (c) the lower court's decision—if appropriate.
3. **Issue.** Concisely phrase, in the form of a question, the essential issue before the court. (If more than one issue is involved, you may have two—or even more—questions here.)
4. **Decision.** Indicate here—with a "yes" or "no," if possible—the court's answer to the question (or questions) in the *Issue* section above.
5. **Reason.** Summarize as briefly as possible the reasons given by the court for its decision (or decisions) and the case or statutory law relied on by the court in arriving at its decision.

AN EXAMPLE OF A BRIEFED SAMPLE COURT CASE

As an example of the format used in briefing cases, we present here a briefed version of the sample court case that was presented in Exhibit 1–6 on page 24.

BERGER V. CITY OF SEATTLE
United States Court of Appeals,
Ninth Circuit, 2008.
512 F.3d 582.

FACTS The Seattle Center is an entertainment "zone" in downtown Seattle, Washington, that attracts nearly ten million tourists each year. The center encompasses theaters, arenas, museums, exhibition halls, conference rooms, outdoor stadiums, and restaurants, and features street performers. Under the authority of the city, the center's director issued rules in 2002 to address safety concerns and other matters. Among other things, street performers were required to obtain permits and wear badges. After members of the public filed numerous complaints of threatening behavior by street performer and balloon artist Michael Berger, Seattle Center staff cited Berger for several rules violations. He filed a suit in a federal district court against the city and others, alleging, in part, that the rules violated his free speech rights under the First Amendment to the U.S. Constitution. The court issued a judgment in the plaintiff's favor. The city appealed to the U.S. Court of Appeals for the Ninth Circuit.

ISSUE Did the rules issued by the Seattle Center under the city's authority meet the requirements for valid restrictions on speech under the First Amendment?

DECISION Yes. The U.S. Court of Appeals for the Ninth Circuit reversed the decision of the lower court and remanded the case for further proceedings. "Such content neutral and narrowly tailored rules * * * must be upheld."

REASON The court concluded first that the rules requiring permits and badges were "content neutral." Time, place, and manner restrictions do not violate the First Amendment if they burden all expression equally and do not allow officials to treat different messages differently. In this case, the rules met this test and thus did not discriminate based on content. The court also concluded that the rules were "narrowly tailored" to "promote a substantial government interest that would be achieved less effectively" otherwise. With the rules, the city was trying to "reduce territorial disputes among performers, deter patron harassment, and facilitate the identification and apprehension of offending performers." This was pursuant to the valid governmental objective of protecting the safety and convenience of the other performers and the public generally. The public's complaints about Berger and others showed that unregulated street performances posed a threat to these interests. The court was "satisfied that the city's permit scheme was designed to further valid governmental objectives."

REVIEW OF SAMPLE COURT CASE

Here, we provide a review of the briefed version to indicate the kind of information that is contained in each section.

CITATION The name of the case is *Berger v. City of Seattle.* Berger is the plaintiff; the City of Seattle is the defendant. The U.S. Court of Appeals for the Ninth Circuit decided this case in 2008. The citation states that this case can be found in volume 512 of the *Federal Reporter, Third Series,* on page 582.

FACTS The *Facts* section identifies the plaintiff and the defendant, describes the events leading up to this suit, the allegations made by the plaintiff in the initial suit, and (because this case is an appellate court decision) the lower court's ruling and the party appealing. The party appealing's argument on appeal is also sometimes included here.

ISSUE The *Issue* section presents the central issue (or issues) decided by the court. In this case, the U.S. Court of Appeals for the Ninth Circuit considered whether certain rules imposed on street performers by local government authorities satisfied the requirements for valid restrictions on speech under the First Amendment to the U.S. Constitution.

DECISION The *Decision* section includes the court's decision on the issues before it. The decision reflects the opinion of the judge or justice hearing the case. Decisions by appellate courts are frequently phrased in reference to the lower court's decision. In other words, the appellate court may "affirm" the lower court's ruling or "reverse" it. Here, the court determined that Seattle's rules were "content neutral" and "narrowly tailored" to "promote a substantial government interest that would otherwise be achieved less effectively." The court found in favor of the city and reversed the lower court's ruling in the plaintiff's (Berger's) favor.

REASON The *Reason* section includes references to the relevant laws and legal principles that the court applied in coming to its conclusion in the case. The relevant law in the *Berger* case included the requirements under the First Amendment for evaluating the purpose and effect of government regulation with respect to expression. This section also explains the court's application of the law to the facts in this case.

ANALYZING CASE PROBLEMS

In addition to learning how to brief cases, students of business law and the legal environment also find it helpful to know how to analyze case problems. Part of the study of business law and the legal environment usually involves analyzing case problems, such as those included in this text at the end of each chapter.

For each case problem in this book, we provide the relevant background and facts of the lawsuit and the issue before the court. When you are assigned one of these problems, your job will be to determine how the court should decide the issue, and why. In other words, you will need to engage in legal analysis and reasoning. Here, we offer some suggestions on how to make this task less daunting. We begin by presenting a sample problem:

> While Janet Lawson, a famous pianist, was shopping in Quality Market, she slipped and fell on a wet floor in one of the aisles. The floor had recently been mopped by one of the store's employees, but there were no signs warning customers that the floor in that area was wet. As a result of the fall, Lawson injured her right arm and was unable to perform piano concerts for the next six months. Had she been able to perform the scheduled concerts, she would have earned approximately $60,000 over that period of time. Lawson sued Quality Market for this amount, plus another $10,000 in medical expenses. She claimed that the store's failure to warn customers of the wet floor constituted negligence and therefore the market was liable for her injuries. Will the court agree with Lawson? Discuss.

UNDERSTAND THE FACTS

This may sound obvious, but before you can analyze or apply the relevant law to a specific set of facts, you must clearly understand those facts. In other words, you should read through the case problem carefully—more than once, if necessary—to make sure you understand the identity of the plaintiff(s) and defendant(s) in the case and the progression of events that led to the lawsuit.

In the sample case problem just given, the identity of the parties is fairly obvious. Janet Lawson is the one bringing the suit; therefore, she is the plaintiff. Quality Market, against whom she is bringing the suit, is the defendant. Some of the case problems you may work on have multiple plaintiffs or defendants. Often, it is helpful to use abbreviations for the parties. To indicate a reference to a plaintiff, for example, the *pi* symbol—π—is often used, and a defendant is denoted by a *delta*—Δ—a triangle.

The events leading to the lawsuit are also fairly straightforward. Lawson slipped and fell on a wet floor, and she contends that Quality Market should be liable for her injuries because it was negligent in not posting a sign warning customers of the wet floor.

When you are working on case problems, realize that the facts should be accepted as they are given. For example, in our sample problem, it should be accepted that the floor was wet and that there was no sign. In other words, avoid making conjectures, such as "Maybe the floor wasn't too wet," or "Maybe an employee was getting a sign to put up," or "Maybe someone stole the sign." Questioning the facts as they are presented only adds confusion to your analysis.

Legal Analysis and Reasoning

Once you understand the facts given in the case problem, you can begin to analyze the case. Recall from Chapter 1 that the IRAC method is a helpful tool to use in the legal analysis and reasoning process. IRAC is an acronym for **I**ssue, **R**ule, **A**pplication, **C**onclusion. Applying this method to our sample problem would involve the following steps:

1. First, you need to decide what legal **issue** is involved in the case. In our sample case, the basic issue is whether Quality Market's failure to warn customers of the wet floor constituted negligence. As discussed in Chapter 12, negligence is a *tort*—a civil wrong. In a tort lawsuit, the plaintiff seeks to be compensated for another's wrongful act. A defendant will be deemed negligent if he or she breached a duty of care owed to the plaintiff and the breach of that duty caused the plaintiff to suffer harm.
2. Once you have identified the issue, the next step is to determine what **rule of law** applies to the issue. To make this determination, you will want to review carefully the text of the chapter in which the relevant rule of law for the problem appears. Our sample case problem involves the tort of negligence, which is covered in Chapter 12. The applicable rule of law is the tort law principle that business owners owe a duty to exercise reasonable care to protect their customers ("business invitees"). Reasonable care, in this context, includes either removing—or warning customers of—*foreseeable* risks about which the owner *knew* or *should have known*. Business owners need not warn customers of "open and obvious" risks, however. If a business owner breaches this duty of care (fails to exercise the appropriate degree of care toward customers), and the breach of duty causes a customer to be injured, the business owner will be liable to the customer for the customer's injuries.
3. The next—and usually the most difficult—step in analyzing case problems is the **application** of the relevant rule of law to the specific facts of the case you are studying. In our sample problem, applying the tort law principle just discussed presents few difficulties. An employee of the store had mopped the floor in the aisle where Lawson slipped and fell, but no sign was present indicating that the floor was wet. That a customer might fall on a wet floor is clearly a foreseeable risk. Therefore, the failure to warn customers about the wet floor was a breach of the duty of care owed by the business owner to the store's customers.
4. Once you have completed Step 3 in the IRAC method, you should be ready to draw your **conclusion.** In our sample problem, Quality Market is liable to Lawson for her injuries, because the market's breach of its duty of care caused Lawson's injuries.

The fact patterns in the case problems presented in this text are not always as simple as those presented in our sample problem. Often, for example, a case has more than one plaintiff or defendant. A case may also involve more than one issue and have more than one applicable rule of law. Furthermore, in some case problems the facts may indicate that the general rule of law should not apply. For example, suppose that a store employee advised Lawson not to walk on the floor in the aisle because it was wet, but Lawson decided to walk on it anyway. This fact could alter the outcome of the case because the store could then raise the defense of *assumption of risk* (see Chapter 12). Nonetheless, a careful review of the chapter should always provide you with the knowledge you need to analyze the problem thoroughly and arrive at accurate conclusions.

then constitute notice to third parties of the buyer's rights under the contract for sale.

As amended in 1972.

Part 2 Form, Formation and Readjustment of Contract

§ 2–201. Formal Requirements; Statute of Frauds.

(1) Except as otherwise provided in this section a contract for the sale of goods for the price of $500 or more is not enforceable by way of action or defense unless there is some writing sufficient to indicate that a contract for sale has been made between the parties and signed by the party against whom enforcement is sought or by his authorized agent or broker. A writing is not insufficient because it omits or incorrectly states a term agreed upon but the contract is not enforceable under this paragraph beyond the quantity of goods shown in such writing.

(2) Between merchants if within a reasonable time a writing in confirmation of the contract and sufficient against the sender is received and the party receiving it has reason to know its contents, its satisfies the requirements of subsection (1) against such party unless written notice of objection to its contents is given within ten days after it is received.

(3) A contract which does not satisfy the requirements of subsection (1) but which is valid in other respects is enforceable

(a) if the goods are to be specially manufactured for the buyer and are not suitable for sale to others in the ordinary course of the seller's business and the seller, before notice of repudiation is received and under circumstances which reasonably indicate that the goods are for the buyer, has made either a substantial beginning of their manufacture or commitments for their procurement; or

(b) if the party against whom enforcement is sought admits in his pleading, testimony or otherwise in court that a contract for sale was made, but the contract is not enforceable under this provision beyond the quantity of goods admitted; or

(c) with respect to goods for which payment has been made and accepted or which have been received and accepted (Sec. 2–606).

§ 2–202. Final Written Expression: Parol or Extrinsic Evidence.

Terms with respect to which the confirmatory memoranda of the parties agree or which are otherwise set forth in a writing intended by the parties as a final expression of their agreement with respect to such terms as are included therein may not be contradicted by evidence of any prior agreement or of a contemporaneous oral agreement but may be explained or supplemented

(a) by course of dealing or usage of trade (Section 1–205) or by course of performance (Section 2–208); and

(b) by evidence of consistent additional terms unless the court finds the writing to have been intended also as a complete and exclusive statement of the terms of the agreement.

§ 2–203. Seals Inoperative.

The affixing of a seal to a writing evidencing a contract for sale or an offer to buy or sell goods does not constitute the writing a sealed instrument and the law with respect to sealed instruments does not apply to such a contract or offer.

§ 2–204. Formation in General.

(1) A contract for sale of goods may be made in any manner sufficient to show agreement, including conduct by both parties which recognizes the existence of such a contract.

(2) An agreement sufficient to constitute a contract for sale may be found even though the moment of its making is undetermined.

(3) Even though one or more terms are left open a contract for sale does not fail for indefiniteness if the parties have intended to make a contract and there is a reasonably certain basis for giving an appropriate remedy.

§ 2–205. Firm Offers.

An offer by a merchant to buy or sell goods in a signed writing which by its terms gives assurance that it will be held open is not revocable, for lack of consideration, during the time stated or if no time is stated for a reasonable time, but in no event may such period of irrevocability exceed three months; but any such term of assurance on a form supplied by the offeree must be separately signed by the offeror.

§ 2–206. Offer and Acceptance in Formation of Contract.

(1) Unless other unambiguously indicated by the language or circumstances

(a) an offer to make a contract shall be construed as inviting acceptance in any manner and by any medium reasonable in the circumstances;

(b) an order or other offer to buy goods for prompt or current shipment shall be construed as inviting acceptance either by a prompt promise to ship or by the prompt or current shipment of conforming or nonconforming goods, but such a shipment of nonconforming goods does not constitute an acceptance if the seller seasonably notifies the buyer that the shipment is offered only as an accommodation to the buyer.

(2) Where the beginning of a requested performance is a reasonable mode of acceptance an offeror who is not notified of acceptance within a reasonable time may treat the offer as having lapsed before acceptance.

§ 2–207. Additional Terms in Acceptance or Confirmation.

(1) A definite and seasonable expression of acceptance or a written confirmation which is sent within a reason-

able time operates as an acceptance even though it states terms additional to or different from those offered or agreed upon, unless acceptance is expressly made conditional on assent to the additional or different terms.

(2) The additional terms are to be construed as proposals for addition to the contract. Between merchants such terms become part of the contract unless:

(a) the offer expressly limits acceptance to the terms of the offer;

(b) they materially alter it; or

(c) notification of objection to them has already been given or is given within a reasonable time after notice of them is received.

(3) Conduct by both parties which recognizes the existence of a contract is sufficient to establish a contract for sale although the writings of the parties do not otherwise establish a contract. In such case the terms of the particular contract consist of those terms on which the writings of the parties agree, together with any supplementary terms incorporated under any other provisions of this Act.

§ 2–208. Course of Performance or Practical Construction.

(1) Where the contract for sale involves repeated occasions for performance by either party with knowledge of the nature of the performance and opportunity for objection to it by the other, any course of performance accepted or acquiesced in without objection shall be relevant to determine the meaning of the agreement.

(2) The express terms of the agreement and any such course of performance, as well as any course of dealing and usage of trade, shall be construed whenever reasonable as consistent with each other; but when such construction is unreasonable, express terms shall control course of performance and course of performance shall control both course of dealing and usage of trade (Section 1–303).

(3) Subject to the provisions of the next section on modification and waiver, such course of performance shall be relevant to show a waiver or modification of any term inconsistent with such course of performance.

§ 2–209. Modification, Rescission and Waiver.

(1) An agreement modifying a contract within this Article needs no consideration to be binding.

(2) A signed agreement which excludes modification or rescission except by a signed writing cannot be otherwise modified or rescinded, but except as between merchants such a requirement on a form supplied by the merchant must be separately signed by the other party.

(3) The requirements of the statute of frauds section of this Article (Section 2–201) must be satisfied if the contract as modified is within its provisions.

(4) Although an attempt at modification or rescission does not satisfy the requirements of subsection (2) or (3) it can operate as a waiver.

(5) A party who has made a waiver affecting an executory portion of the contract may retract the waiver by reasonable notification received by the other party that strict performance will be required of any term waived, unless the retraction would be unjust in view of a material change of position in reliance on the waiver.

§ 2–210. Delegation of Performance; Assignment of Rights.

(1) A party may perform his duty through a delegate unless otherwise agreed or unless the other party has a substantial interest in having his original promisor perform or control the acts required by the contract. No delegation of performance relieves the party delegating of any duty to perform or any liability for breach.

(2) Except as otherwise provided in Section 9–406, unless otherwise agreed, all rights of either seller or buyer can be assigned except where the assignment would materially change the duty of the other party, or increase materially the burden or risk imposed on him by his contract, or impair materially his chance of obtaining return performance. A right to damages for breach of the whole contract or a right arising out of the assignor's due performance of his entire obligation can be assigned despite agreement otherwise.

(3) The creation, attachment, perfection, or enforcement of a security interest in the seller's interest under a contract is not a transfer that materially changes the duty of or increases materially the burden or risk imposed on the buyer or impairs materially the buyer's chance of obtaining return performance within the purview of subsection (2) unless, and then only to the extent that, enforcement actually results in a delegation of material performance of the seller. Even in that event, the creation, attachment, perfection, and enforcement of the security interest remain effective, but (i) the seller is liable to the buyer for damages caused by the delegation to the extent that the damages could not reasonably by prevented by the buyer, and (ii) a court having jurisdiction may grant other appropriate relief, including cancellation of the contract for sale or an injunction against enforcement of the security interest or consummation of the enforcement.

(4) Unless the circumstances indicate the contrary a prohibition of assignment of "the contract" is to be construed as barring only the delegation to the assignee of the assignor's performance.

(5) An assignment of "the contract" or of "all my rights under the contract" or an assignment in similar general terms is an assignment of rights and unless the language or the circumstances (as in an assignment for security) indicate the contrary, it is a delegation of performance of the duties of the assignor and its acceptance by the assignee constitutes a promise by him to perform those duties. This promise is enforceable by either the assignor or the other party to the original contract.

(6) The other party may treat any assignment which delegates performance as creating reasonable grounds for

insecurity and may without prejudice to his rights against the assignor demand assurances from the assignee (Section 2–609).

As amended in 1999.

Part 3 General Obligation and Construction of Contract

§ 2–301. General Obligations of Parties.

The obligation of the seller is to transfer and deliver and that of the buyer is to accept and pay in accordance with the contract.

§ 2–302. Unconscionable Contract or Clause.

(1) If the court as a matter of law finds the contract or any clause of the contract to have been unconscionable at the time it was made the court may refuse to enforce the contract, or it may enforce the remainder of the contract without the unconscionable clause, or it may so limit the application of any unconscionable clause as to avoid any unconscionable result.

(2) When it is claimed or appears to the court that the contract or any clause thereof may be unconscionable the parties shall be afforded a reasonable opportunity to present evidence as to its commercial setting, purpose and effect to aid the court in making the determination.

§ 2–303. Allocations or Division of Risks.

Where this Article allocates a risk or a burden as between the parties "unless otherwise agreed", the agreement may not only shift the allocation but may also divide the risk or burden.

§ 2–304. Price Payable in Money, Goods, Realty, or Otherwise.

(1) The price can be made payable in money or otherwise. If it is payable in whole or in part in goods each party is a seller of the goods which he is to transfer.

(2) Even though all or part of the price is payable in an interest in realty the transfer of the goods and the seller's obligations with reference to them are subject to this Article, but not the transfer of the interest in realty or the transferor's obligations in connection therewith.

§ 2–305. Open Price Term.

(1) The parties if they so intend can conclude a contract for sale even though the price is not settled. In such a case the price is a reasonable price at the time for delivery if

(a) nothing is said as to price; or

(b) the price is left to be agreed by the parties and they fail to agree; or

(c) the price is to be fixed in terms of some agreed market or other standard as set or recorded by a third person or agency and it is not so set or recorded.

(2) A price to be fixed by the seller or by the buyer means a price for him to fix in good faith.

(3) When a price left to be fixed otherwise than by agreement of the parties fails to be fixed through fault of one party the other may at his option treat the contract as cancelled or himself fix a reasonable price.

(4) Where, however, the parties intend not to be bound unless the price be fixed or agreed and it is not fixed or agreed there is no contract. In such a case the buyer must return any goods already received or if unable so to do must pay their reasonable value at the time of delivery and the seller must return any portion of the price paid on account.

§ 2–306. Output, Requirements and Exclusive Dealings.

(1) A term which measures the quantity by the output of the seller or the requirements of the buyer means such actual output or requirements as may occur in good faith, except that no quantity unreasonably disproportionate to any stated estimate or in the absence of a stated estimate to any normal or otherwise comparable prior output or requirements may be tendered or demanded.

(2) A lawful agreement by either the seller or the buyer for exclusive dealing in the kind of goods concerned imposes unless otherwise agreed an obligation by the seller to use best efforts to supply the goods and by the buyer to use best efforts to promote their sale.

§ 2–307. Delivery in Single Lot or Several Lots.

Unless otherwise agreed all goods called for by a contract for sale must be tendered in a single delivery and payment is due only on such tender but where the circumstances give either party the right to make or demand delivery in lots the price if it can be apportioned may be demanded for each lot.

§ 2–308. Absence of Specified Place for Delivery.

Unless otherwise agreed

(a) the place for delivery of goods is the seller's place of business or if he has none his residence; but

(b) in a contract for sale of identified goods which to the knowledge of the parties at the time of contracting are in some other place, that place is the place for their delivery; and

(c) documents of title may be delivered through customary banking channels.

§ 2–309. Absence of Specific Time Provisions; Notice of Termination.

(1) The time for shipment or delivery or any other action under a contract if not provided in this Article or agreed upon shall be a reasonable time.

(2) Where the contract provides for successive performances but is indefinite in duration it is valid for a reasonable time but unless otherwise agreed may be terminated at any time by either party.

(3) Termination of a contract by one party except on the happening of an agreed event requires that reasonable notification be received by the other party and an agree-

ment dispensing with notification is invalid if its operation would be unconscionable.

§ 2–310. Open Time for Payment or Running of Credit; Authority to Ship Under Reservation.

Unless otherwise agreed

(a) payment is due at the time and place at which the buyer is to receive the goods even though the place of shipment is the place of delivery; and

(b) if the seller is authorized to send the goods he may ship them under reservation, and may tender the documents of title, but the buyer may inspect the goods after their arrival before payment is due unless such inspection is inconsistent with the terms of the contract (Section 2–513); and

(c) if delivery is authorized and made by way of documents of title otherwise than by subsection (b) then payment is due at the time and place at which the buyer is to receive the documents regardless of where the goods are to be received; and

(d) where the seller is required or authorized to ship the goods on credit the credit period runs from the time of shipment but post-dating the invoice or delaying its dispatch will correspondingly delay the starting of the credit period.

§ 2–311. Options and Cooperation Respecting Performance.

(1) An agreement for sale which is otherwise sufficiently definite (subsection (3) of Section 2–204) to be a contract is not made invalid by the fact that it leaves particulars of performance to be specified by one of the parties. Any such specification must be made in good faith and within limits set by commercial reasonableness.

(2) Unless otherwise agreed specifications relating to assortment of the goods are at the buyer's option and except as otherwise provided in subsections (1)(c) and (3) of Section 2–319 specifications or arrangements relating to shipment are at the seller's option.

(3) Where such specification would materially affect the other party's performance but is not seasonably made or where one party's cooperation is necessary to the agreed performance of the other but is not seasonably forthcoming, the other party in addition to all other remedies

(a) is excused for any resulting delay in his own performance; and

(b) may also either proceed to perform in any reasonable manner or after the time for a material part of his own performance treat the failure to specify or to cooperate as a breach by failure to deliver or accept the goods.

§ 2–312. Warranty of Title and Against Infringement; Buyer's Obligation Against Infringement.

(1) Subject to subsection (2) there is in a contract for sale a warranty by the seller that

(a) the title conveyed shall be good, and its transfer rightful; and

(b) the goods shall be delivered free from any security interest or other lien or encumbrance of which the buyer at the time of contracting has no knowledge.

(2) A warranty under subsection (1) will be excluded or modified only by specific language or by circumstances which give the buyer reason to know that the person selling does not claim title in himself or that he is purporting to sell only such right or title as he or a third person may have.

(3) Unless otherwise agreed a seller who is a merchant regularly dealing in goods of the kind warrants that the goods shall be delivered free of the rightful claim of any third person by way of infringement or the like but a buyer who furnishes specifications to the seller must hold the seller harmless against any such claim which arises out of compliance with the specifications.

§ 2–313. Express Warranties by Affirmation, Promise, Description, Sample.

(1) Express warranties by the seller are created as follows:

(a) Any affirmation of fact or promise made by the seller to the buyer which relates to the goods and becomes part of the basis of the bargain creates an express warranty that the goods shall conform to the affirmation or promise.

(b) Any description of the goods which is made part of the basis of the bargain creates an express warranty that the goods shall conform to the description.

(c) Any sample or model which is made part of the basis of the bargain creates an express warranty that the whole of the goods shall conform to the sample or model.

(2) It is not necessary to the creation of an express warranty that the seller use formal words such as "warrant" or "guarantee" or that he have a specific intention to make a warranty, but an affirmation merely of the value of the goods or a statement purporting to be merely the seller's opinion or commendation of the goods does not create a warranty.

§ 2–314. Implied Warranty: Merchantability; Usage of Trade.

(1) Unless excluded or modified (Section 2–316), a warranty that the goods shall be merchantable is implied in a contract for their sale if the seller is a merchant with respect to goods of that kind. Under this section the serving for value of food or drink to be consumed either on the premises or elsewhere is a sale.

(2) Goods to be merchantable must be at least such as

(a) pass without objection in the trade under the contract description; and

(b) in the case of fungible goods, are of fair average quality within the description; and

(c) are fit for the ordinary purposes for which such goods are used; and

(d) run, within the variations permitted by the agreement, of even kind, quality and quantity within each unit and among all units involved; and

(e) are adequately contained, packaged, and labeled as the agreement may require; and

(f) conform to the promises or affirmations of fact made on the container or label if any.

(3) Unless excluded or modified (Section 2–316) other implied warranties may arise from course of dealing or usage of trade.

§ 2–315. Implied Warranty: Fitness for Particular Purpose.

Where the seller at the time of contracting has reason to know any particular purpose for which the goods are required and that the buyer is relying on the seller's skill or judgment to select or furnish suitable goods, there is unless excluded or modified under the next section an implied warranty that the goods shall be fit for such purpose.

§ 2–316. Exclusion or Modification of Warranties.

(1) Words or conduct relevant to the creation of an express warranty and words or conduct tending to negate or limit warranty shall be construed wherever reasonable as consistent with each other; but subject to the provisions of this Article on parol or extrinsic evidence (Section 2–202) negation or limitation is inoperative to the extent that such construction is unreasonable.

(2) Subject to subsection (3), to exclude or modify the implied warranty of merchantability or any part of it the language must mention merchantability and in case of a writing must be conspicuous, and to exclude or modify any implied warranty of fitness the exclusion must be by a writing and conspicuous. Language to exclude all implied warranties of fitness is sufficient if it states, for example, that "There are no warranties which extend beyond the description on the face hereof."

(3) Notwithstanding subsection (2)

(a) unless the circumstances indicate otherwise, all implied warranties are excluded by expressions like "as is", "with all faults" or other language which in common understanding calls the buyer's attention to the exclusion of warranties and makes plain that there is no implied warranty; and

(b) when the buyer before entering into the contract has examined the goods or the sample or model as fully as he desired or has refused to examine the goods there is no implied warranty with regard to defects which an examination ought in the circumstances to have revealed to him; and

(c) an implied warranty can also be excluded or modified by course of dealing or course of performance or usage of trade.

(4) Remedies for breach of warranty can be limited in accordance with the provisions of this Article on liquidation or limitation of damages and on contractual modification of remedy (Sections 2–718 and 2–719).

§ 2–317. Cumulation and Conflict of Warranties Express or Implied.

Warranties whether express or implied shall be construed as consistent with each other and as cumulative, but if such construction is unreasonable the intention of the parties shall determine which warranty is dominant. In ascertaining that intention the following rules apply:

(a) Exact or technical specifications displace an inconsistent sample or model or general language of description.

(b) A sample from an existing bulk displaces inconsistent general language of description.

(c) Express warranties displace inconsistent implied warranties other than an implied warranty of fitness for a particular purpose.

§ 2–318. Third Party Beneficiaries of Warranties Express or Implied.

Note: If this Act is introduced in the Congress of the United States this section should be omitted. (States to select one alternative.)

Alternative A

A seller's warranty whether express or implied extends to any natural person who is in the family or household of his buyer or who is a guest in his home if it is reasonable to expect that such person may use, consume or be affected by the goods and who is injured in person by breach of the warranty. A seller may not exclude or limit the operation of this section.

Alternative B

A seller's warranty whether express or implied extends to any natural person who may reasonably be expected to use, consume or be affected by the goods and who is injured in person by breach of the warranty. A seller may not exclude or limit the operation of this section.

Alternative C

A seller's warranty whether express or implied extends to any person who may reasonably be expected to use, consume or be affected by the goods and who is injured by breach of the warranty. A seller may not exclude or limit the operation of this section with respect to injury to the person of an individual to whom the warranty extends.

As amended 1966.

§ 2–319. F.O.B. and F.A.S. Terms.

(1) Unless otherwise agreed the term F.O.B. (which means "free on board") at a named place, even though used only in connection with the stated price, is a delivery term under which

(a) when the term is F.O.B. the place of shipment, the seller must at that place ship the goods in the manner provided in this Article (Section 2–504) and bear the expense and risk of putting them into the possession of the carrier; or

(b) when the term is F.O.B. the place of destination, the seller must at his own expense and risk transport the goods to that place and there tender delivery of them in the manner provided in this Article (Section 2–503);

(c) when under either (a) or (b) the term is also F.O.B. vessel, car or other vehicle, the seller must in addition at his own expense and risk load the goods on board. If the term is F.O.B. vessel the buyer must name the vessel and in an appropriate case the seller must comply with the provisions of this Article on the form of bill of lading (Section 2–323).

(2) Unless otherwise agreed the term F.A.S. vessel (which means "free alongside") at a named port, even though used only in connection with the stated price, is a delivery term under which the seller must

(a) at his own expense and risk deliver the goods alongside the vessel in the manner usual in that port or on a dock designated and provided by the buyer; and

(b) obtain and tender a receipt for the goods in exchange for which the carrier is under a duty to issue a bill of lading.

(3) Unless otherwise agreed in any case falling within subsection (1)(a) or (c) or subsection (2) the buyer must seasonably give any needed instructions for making delivery, including when the term is F.A.S. or F.O.B. the loading berth of the vessel and in an appropriate case its name and sailing date. The seller may treat the failure of needed instructions as a failure of cooperation under this Article (Section 2–311). He may also at his option move the goods in any reasonable manner preparatory to delivery or shipment.

(4) Under the term F.O.B. vessel or F.A.S. unless otherwise agreed the buyer must make payment against tender of the required documents and the seller may not tender nor the buyer demand delivery of the goods in substitution for the documents.

§ 2–320. C.I.F. and C. & F. Terms.

(1) The term C.I.F. means that the price includes in a lump sum the cost of the goods and the insurance and freight to the named destination. The term C. & F. or C.F. means that the price so includes cost and freight to the named destination.

(2) Unless otherwise agreed and even though used only in connection with the stated price and destination, the term C.I.F. destination or its equivalent requires the seller at his own expense and risk to

(a) put the goods into the possession of a carrier at the port for shipment and obtain a negotiable bill or bills of lading covering the entire transportation to the named destination; and

(b) load the goods and obtain a receipt from the carrier (which may be contained in the bill of lading) showing that the freight has been paid or provided for; and

(c) obtain a policy or certificate of insurance, including any war risk insurance, of a kind and on terms then current at the port of shipment in the usual amount, in the currency of the contract, shown to cover the same goods covered by the bill of lading and providing for payment of loss to the order of the buyer or for the account of whom it may concern; but the seller may add to the price the amount of the premium for any such war risk insurance; and

(d) prepare an invoice of the goods and procure any other documents required to effect shipment or to comply with the contract; and

(e) forward and tender with commercial promptness all the documents in due form and with any indorsement necessary to perfect the buyer's rights.

(3) Unless otherwise agreed the term C. & F. or its equivalent has the same effect and imposes upon the seller the same obligations and risks as a C.I.F. term except the obligation as to insurance.

(4) Under the term C.I.F. or C. & F. unless otherwise agreed the buyer must make payment against tender of the required documents and the seller may not tender nor the buyer demand delivery of the goods in substitution for the documents.

§ 2–321. C.I.F. or C. & F.: "Net Landed Weights"; "Payment on Arrival"; Warranty of Condition on Arrival.

Under a contract containing a term C.I.F. or C. & F.

(1) Where the price is based on or is to be adjusted according to "net landed weights", "delivered weights", "out turn" quantity or quality or the like, unless otherwise agreed the seller must reasonably estimate the price. The payment due on tender of the documents called for by the contract is the amount so estimated, but after final adjustment of the price a settlement must be made with commercial promptness.

(2) An agreement described in subsection (1) or any warranty of quality or condition of the goods on arrival places upon the seller the risk of ordinary deterioration, shrinkage and the like in transportation but has no effect on the place or time of identification to the contract for sale or delivery or on the passing of the risk of loss.

(3) Unless otherwise agreed where the contract provides for payment on or after arrival of the goods the seller must before payment allow such preliminary inspection as is feasible; but if the goods are lost delivery of the documents and payment are due when the goods should have arrived.

§ 2–322. Delivery "Ex-Ship".

(1) Unless otherwise agreed a term for delivery of goods "ex-ship" (which means from the carrying vessel) or in equivalent language is not restricted to a particular ship and requires delivery from a ship which has reached a place at the named port of destination where goods of the kind are usually discharged.

(2) Under such a term unless otherwise agreed

(a) the seller must discharge all liens arising out of the carriage and furnish the buyer with a direction which puts the carrier under a duty to deliver the goods; and

(b) the risk of loss does not pass to the buyer until the goods leave the ship's tackle or are otherwise properly unloaded.

§ 2–323. Form of Bill of Lading Required in Overseas Shipment; "Overseas".

(1) Where the contract contemplates overseas shipment and contains a term C.I.F. or C. & F. or F.O.B. vessel, the seller unless otherwise agreed must obtain a negotiable bill of lading stating that the goods have been loaded on board or, in the case of a term C.I.F. or C. & F., received for shipment.

(2) Where in a case within subsection (1) a bill of lading has been issued in a set of parts, unless otherwise agreed if the documents are not to be sent from abroad the buyer may demand tender of the full set; otherwise only one part of the bill of lading need be tendered. Even if the agreement expressly requires a full set

(a) due tender of a single part is acceptable within the provisions of this Article on cure of improper delivery (subsection (1) of Section 2–508); and

(b) even though the full set is demanded, if the documents are sent from abroad the person tendering an incomplete set may nevertheless require payment upon furnishing an indemnity which the buyer in good faith deems adequate.

(3) A shipment by water or by air or a contract contemplating such shipment is "overseas" insofar as by usage of trade or agreement it is subject to the commercial, financing or shipping practices characteristic of international deep water commerce.

§ 2–324. "No Arrival, No Sale" Term.

Under a term "no arrival, no sale" or terms of like meaning, unless otherwise agreed,

(a) the seller must properly ship conforming goods and if they arrive by any means he must tender them on arrival but he assumes no obligation that the goods will arrive unless he has caused the non-arrival; and

(b) where without fault of the seller the goods are in part lost or have so deteriorated as no longer to conform to the contract or arrive after the contract time, the buyer may proceed as if there had been casualty to identified goods (Section 2–613).

§ 2–325. "Letter of Credit" Term; "Confirmed Credit".

(1) Failure of the buyer seasonably to furnish an agreed letter of credit is a breach of the contract for sale.

(2) The delivery to seller of a proper letter of credit suspends the buyer's obligation to pay. If the letter of credit is dishonored, the seller may on seasonable notification to the buyer require payment directly from him.

(3) Unless otherwise agreed the term "letter of credit" or "banker's credit" in a contract for sale means an irrevocable credit issued by a financing agency of good repute and, where the shipment is overseas, of good international repute. The term "confirmed credit" means that the credit must also carry the direct obligation of such an agency which does business in the seller's financial market.

§ 2–326. Sale on Approval and Sale or Return; Rights of Creditors.

(1) Unless otherwise agreed, if delivered goods may be returned by the buyer even though they conform to the contract, the transaction is

(a) a "sale on approval" if the goods are delivered primarily for use, and

(b) a "sale or return" if the goods are delivered primarily for resale.

(2) Goods held on approval are not subject to the claims of the buyer's creditors until acceptance; goods held on sale or return are subject to such claims while in the buyer's possession.

(3) Any "or return" term of a contract for sale is to be treated as a separate contract for sale within the statute of frauds section of this Article (Section 2–201) and as contradicting the sale aspect of the contract within the provisions of this Article or on parol or extrinsic evidence (Section 2–202).

As amended in 1999.

§ 2–327. Special Incidents of Sale on Approval and Sale or Return.

(1) Under a sale on approval unless otherwise agreed

(a) although the goods are identified to the contract the risk of loss and the title do not pass to the buyer until acceptance; and

(b) use of the goods consistent with the purpose of trial is not acceptance but failure seasonably to notify the seller of election to return the goods is acceptance, and if the goods conform to the contract acceptance of any part is acceptance of the whole; and

(c) after due notification of election to return, the return is at the seller's risk and expense but a merchant buyer must follow any reasonable instructions.

(2) Under a sale or return unless otherwise agreed

(a) the option to return extends to the whole or any commercial unit of the goods while in substantially their original condition, but must be exercised seasonably; and

(b) the return is at the buyer's risk and expense.

§ 2–328. Sale by Auction.

(1) In a sale by auction if goods are put up in lots each lot is the subject of a separate sale.

(2) A sale by auction is complete when the auctioneer so announces by the fall of the hammer or in other customary manner. Where a bid is made while the hammer is falling in acceptance of a prior bid the auctioneer

may in his discretion reopen the bidding or declare the goods sold under the bid on which the hammer was falling.

(3) Such a sale is with reserve unless the goods are in explicit terms put up without reserve. In an auction with reserve the auctioneer may withdraw the goods at any time until he announces completion of the sale. In an auction without reserve, after the auctioneer calls for bids on an article or lot, that article or lot cannot be withdrawn unless no bid is made within a reasonable time. In either case a bidder may retract his bid until the auctioneer's announcement of completion of the sale, but a bidder's retraction does not revive any previous bid.

(4) If the auctioneer knowingly receives a bid on the seller's behalf or the seller makes or procures such as bid, and notice has not been given that liberty for such bidding is reserved, the buyer may at his option avoid the sale or take the goods at the price of the last good faith bid prior to the completion of the sale. This subsection shall not apply to any bid at a forced sale.

Part 4 Title, Creditors and Good Faith Purchasers

§ 2–401. Passing of Title; Reservation for Security; Limited Application of This Section.

Each provision of this Article with regard to the rights, obligations and remedies of the seller, the buyer, purchasers or other third parties applies irrespective of title to the goods except where the provision refers to such title. Insofar as situations are not covered by the other provisions of this Article and matters concerning title became material the following rules apply:

(1) Title to goods cannot pass under a contract for sale prior to their identification to the contract (Section 2–501), and unless otherwise explicitly agreed the buyer acquires by their identification a special property as limited by this Act. Any retention or reservation by the seller of the title (property) in goods shipped or delivered to the buyer is limited in effect to a reservation of a security interest. Subject to these provisions and to the provisions of the Article on Secured Transactions (Article 9), title to goods passes from the seller to the buyer in any manner and on any conditions explicitly agreed on by the parties.

(2) Unless otherwise explicitly agreed title passes to the buyer at the time and place at which the seller completes his performance with reference to the physical delivery of the goods, despite any reservation of a security interest and even though a document of title is to be delivered at a different time or place; and in particular and despite any reservation of a security interest by the bill of lading

(a) if the contract requires or authorizes the seller to send the goods to the buyer but does not require him to deliver them at destination, title passes to the buyer at the time and place of shipment; but

(b) if the contract requires delivery at destination, title passes on tender there.

(3) Unless otherwise explicitly agreed where delivery is to be made without moving the goods,

(a) if the seller is to deliver a document of title, title passes at the time when and the place where he delivers such documents; or

(b) if the goods are at the time of contracting already identified and no documents are to be delivered, title passes at the time and place of contracting.

(4) A rejection or other refusal by the buyer to receive or retain the goods, whether or not justified, or a justified revocation of acceptance revests title to the goods in the seller. Such revesting occurs by operation of law and is not a "sale".

§ 2–402. Rights of Seller's Creditors Against Sold Goods.

(1) Except as provided in subsections (2) and (3), rights of unsecured creditors of the seller with respect to goods which have been identified to a contract for sale are subject to the buyer's rights to recover the goods under this Article (Sections 2–502 and 2–716).

(2) A creditor of the seller may treat a sale or an identification of goods to a contract for sale as void if as against him a retention of possession by the seller is fraudulent under any rule of law of the state where the goods are situated, except that retention of possession in good faith and current course of trade by a merchant-seller for a commercially reasonable time after a sale or identification is not fraudulent.

(3) Nothing in this Article shall be deemed to impair the rights of creditors of the seller

(a) under the provisions of the Article on Secured Transactions (Article 9); or

(b) where identification to the contract or delivery is made not in current course of trade but in satisfaction of or as security for a pre-existing claim for money, security or the like and is made under circumstances which under any rule of law of the state where the goods are situated would apart from this Article constitute the transaction a fraudulent transfer or voidable preference.

§ 2–403. Power to Transfer; Good Faith Purchase of Goods; "Entrusting".

(1) A purchaser of goods acquires all title which his transferor had or had power to transfer except that a purchaser of a limited interest acquires rights only to the extent of the interest purchased. A person with voidable title has power to transfer a good title to a good faith purchaser for value. When goods have been delivered under a transaction of purchase the purchaser has such power even though

(a) the transferor was deceived as to the identity of the purchaser, or

(b) the delivery was in exchange for a check which is later dishonored, or

(c) it was agreed that the transaction was to be a "cash sale", or

(d) the delivery was procured through fraud punishable as larcenous under the criminal law.

(2) Any entrusting of possession of goods to a merchant who deals in goods of that kind gives him power to transfer all rights of the entruster to a buyer in ordinary course of business.

(3) "Entrusting" includes any delivery and any acquiescence in retention of possession regardless of any condition expressed between the parties to the delivery or acquiescence and regardless of whether the procurement of the entrusting or the possessor's disposition of the goods have been such as to be larcenous under the criminal law.

(4) The rights of other purchasers of goods and of lien creditors are governed by the Articles on Secured Transactions (Article 9), Bulk Transfers (Article 6) and Documents of Title (Article 7).

As amended in 1988.

Part 5 Performance

§ 2–501. Insurable Interest in Goods; Manner of Identification of Goods.

(1) The buyer obtains a special property and an insurable interest in goods by identification of existing goods as goods to which the contract refers even though the goods so identified are non-conforming and he has an option to return or reject them. Such identification can be made at any time and in any manner explicitly agreed to by the parties. In the absence of explicit agreement identification occurs

(a) when the contract is made if it is for the sale of goods already existing and identified;

(b) if the contract is for the sale of future goods other than those described in paragraph (c), when goods are shipped, marked or otherwise designated by the seller as goods to which the contract refers;

(c) when the crops are planted or otherwise become growing crops or the young are conceived if the contract is for the sale of unborn young to be born within twelve months after contracting or for the sale of crops to be harvested within twelve months or the next normal harvest season after contracting whichever is longer.

(2) The seller retains an insurable interest in goods so long as title to or any security interest in the goods remains in him and where the identification is by the seller alone he may until default or insolvency or notification to the buyer that the identification is final substitute other goods for those identified.

(3) Nothing in this section impairs any insurable interest recognized under any other statute or rule of law.

§ 2–502. Buyer's Right to Goods on Seller's Insolvency.

(1) Subject to subsections (2) and (3) and even though the goods have not been shipped a buyer who has paid a part or all of the price of goods in which he has a special property under the provisions of the immediately preceding section may on making and keeping good a tender of any unpaid portion of their price recover them from the seller if:

(a) in the case of goods bought for personal, family, or household purposes, the seller repudiates or fails to deliver as required by the contract; or

(b) in all cases, the seller becomes insolvent within ten days after receipt of the first installment on their price.

(2) The buyer's right to recover the goods under subsection (1)(a) vests upon acquisition of a special property, even if the seller had not then repudiated or failed to deliver.

(3) If the identification creating his special property has been made by the buyer he acquires the right to recover the goods only if they conform to the contract for sale.

As amended in 1999.

§ 2–503. Manner of Seller's Tender of Delivery.

(1) Tender of delivery requires that the seller put and hold conforming goods at the buyer's disposition and give the buyer any notification reasonably necessary to enable him to take delivery. The manner, time and place for tender are determined by the agreement and this Article, and in particular

(a) tender must be at a reasonable hour, and if it is of goods they must be kept available for the period reasonably necessary to enable the buyer to take possession; but

(b) unless otherwise agreed the buyer must furnish facilities reasonably suited to the receipt of the goods.

(2) Where the case is within the next section respecting shipment tender requires that the seller comply with its provisions.

(3) Where the seller is required to deliver at a particular destination tender requires that he comply with subsection (1) and also in any appropriate case tender documents as described in subsections (4) and (5) of this section.

(4) Where goods are in the possession of a bailee and are to be delivered without being moved

(a) tender requires that the seller either tender a negotiable document of title covering such goods or procure acknowledgment by the bailee of the buyer's right to possession of the goods; but

(b) tender to the buyer of a non-negotiable document of title or of a written direction to the bailee to deliver is sufficient tender unless the buyer seasonably objects, and receipt by the bailee of notification of the buyer's rights fixes those rights as against the bailee and all third persons; but risk of loss of the goods and of any failure by the bailee to honor the non-negotiable document of title or to obey the direction remains on the seller until the buyer has had a reasonable time to present the document or direction, and a refusal by the bailee to honor the document or to obey the direction defeats the tender.

(5) Where the contract requires the seller to deliver documents

(a) he must tender all such documents in correct form, except as provided in this Article with respect to bills of lading in a set (subsection (2) of Section 2–323); and

(b) tender through customary banking channels is sufficient and dishonor of a draft accompanying the documents constitutes non-acceptance or rejection.

§ 2–504. Shipment by Seller.

Where the seller is required or authorized to send the goods to the buyer and the contract does not require him to deliver them at a particular destination, then unless otherwise agreed he must

(a) put the goods in the possession of such a carrier and make such a contract for their transportation as may be reasonable having regard to the nature of the goods and other circumstances of the case; and

(b) obtain and promptly deliver or tender in due form any document necessary to enable the buyer to obtain possession of the goods or otherwise required by the agreement or by usage of trade; and

(c) promptly notify the buyer of the shipment.

Failure to notify the buyer under paragraph (c) or to make a proper contract under paragraph (a) is a ground for rejection only if material delay or loss ensues.

§ 2–505. Seller's Shipment under Reservation.

(1) Where the seller has identified goods to the contract by or before shipment:

(a) his procurement of a negotiable bill of lading to his own order or otherwise reserves in him a security interest in the goods. His procurement of the bill to the order of a financing agency or of the buyer indicates in addition only the seller's expectation of transferring that interest to the person named.

(b) a non-negotiable bill of lading to himself or his nominee reserves possession of the goods as security but except in a case of conditional delivery (subsection (2) of Section 2–507) a non-negotiable bill of lading naming the buyer as consignee reserves no security interest even though the seller retains possession of the bill of lading.

(2) When shipment by the seller with reservation of a security interest is in violation of the contract for sale it constitutes an improper contract for transportation within the preceding section but impairs neither the rights given to the buyer by shipment and identification of the goods to the contract nor the seller's powers as a holder of a negotiable document.

§ 2–506. Rights of Financing Agency.

(1) A financing agency by paying or purchasing for value a draft which relates to a shipment of goods acquires to the extent of the payment or purchase and in addition to its own rights under the draft and any document of title securing it any rights of the shipper in the goods including the right to stop delivery and the shipper's right to have the draft honored by the buyer.

(2) The right to reimbursement of a financing agency which has in good faith honored or purchased the draft under commitment to or authority from the buyer is not impaired by subsequent discovery of defects with reference to any relevant document which was apparently regular on its face.

§ 2–507. Effect of Seller's Tender; Delivery on Condition.

(1) Tender of delivery is a condition to the buyer's duty to accept the goods and, unless otherwise agreed, to his duty to pay for them. Tender entitles the seller to acceptance of the goods and to payment according to the contract.

(2) Where payment is due and demanded on the delivery to the buyer of goods or documents of title, his right as against the seller to retain or dispose of them is conditional upon his making the payment due.

§ 2–508. Cure by Seller of Improper Tender or Delivery; Replacement.

(1) Where any tender or delivery by the seller is rejected because non-conforming and the time for performance has not yet expired, the seller may seasonably notify the buyer of his intention to cure and may then within the contract time make a conforming delivery.

(2) Where the buyer rejects a non-conforming tender which the seller had reasonable grounds to believe would be acceptable with or without money allowance the seller may if he seasonably notifies the buyer have a further reasonable time to substitute a conforming tender.

§ 2–509. Risk of Loss in the Absence of Breach.

(1) Where the contract requires or authorizes the seller to ship the goods by carrier

(a) if it does not require him to deliver them at a particular destination, the risk of loss passes to the buyer when the goods are duly delivered to the carrier even though the shipment is under reservation (Section 2–505); but

(b) if it does require him to deliver them at a particular destination and the goods are there duly tendered while in the possession of the carrier, the risk of loss passes to the buyer when the goods are there duly so tendered as to enable the buyer to take delivery.

(2) Where the goods are held by a bailee to be delivered without being moved, the risk of loss passes to the buyer

(a) on his receipt of a negotiable document of title covering the goods; or

(b) on acknowledgment by the bailee of the buyer's right to possession of the goods; or

(c) after his receipt of a non-negotiable document of title or other written direction to deliver, as provided in subsection (4)(b) of Section 2–503.

(3) In any case not within subsection (1) or (2), the risk of loss passes to the buyer on his receipt of the goods if

damages for non-delivery or repudiation by the seller is the difference between the market price at the time when the buyer learned of the breach and the contract price together with any incidental and consequential damages provided in this Article (Section 2–715), but less expenses saved in consequence of the seller's breach.

(2) Market price is to be determined as of the place for tender or, in cases of rejection after arrival or revocation of acceptance, as of the place of arrival.

§ 2–714. Buyer's Damages for Breach in Regard to Accepted Goods.

(1) Where the buyer has accepted goods and given notification (subsection (3) of Section 2–607) he may recover as damages for any non-conformity of tender the loss resulting in the ordinary course of events from the seller's breach as determined in any manner which is reasonable.

(2) The measure of damages for breach of warranty is the difference at the time and place of acceptance between the value of the goods accepted and the value they would have had if they had been as warranted, unless special circumstances show proximate damages of a different amount.

(3) In a proper case any incidental and consequential damages under the next section may also be recovered.

§ 2–715. Buyer's Incidental and Consequential Damages.

(1) Incidental damages resulting from the seller's breach include expenses reasonably incurred in inspection, receipt, transportation and care and custody of goods rightfully rejected, any commercially reasonable charges, expenses or commissions in connection with effecting cover and any other reasonable expense incident to the delay or other breach.

(2) Consequential damages resulting from the seller's breach include

(a) any loss resulting from general or particular requirements and needs of which the seller at the time of contracting had reason to know and which could not reasonably be prevented by cover or otherwise; and

(b) injury to person or property proximately resulting from any breach of warranty.

§ 2–716. Buyer's Right to Specific Performance or Replevin.

(1) Specific performance may be decreed where the goods are unique or in other proper circumstances.

(2) The decree for specific performance may include such terms and conditions as to payment of the price, damages, or other relief as the court may deem just.

(3) The buyer has a right of replevin for goods identified to the contract if after reasonable effort he is unable to effect cover for such goods or the circumstances reasonably indicate that such effort will be unavailing or if the goods have been shipped under reservation and satisfaction of the security interest in them has been made or tendered. In the case of goods bought for personal, family, or household purposes, the buyer's right of replevin vests upon acquisition of a special property, even if the seller had not then repudiated or failed to deliver.

As amended in 1999.

§ 2–717. Deduction of Damages From the Price.

The buyer on notifying the seller of his intention to do so may deduct all or any part of the damages resulting from any breach of the contract from any part of the price still due under the same contract.

§ 2–718. Liquidation or Limitation of Damages; Deposits.

(1) Damages for breach by either party may be liquidated in the agreement but only at an amount which is reasonable in the light of the anticipated or actual harm caused by the breach, the difficulties of proof of loss, and the inconvenience or nonfeasibility of otherwise obtaining an adequate remedy. A term fixing unreasonably large liquidated damages is void as a penalty.

(2) Where the seller justifiably withholds delivery of goods because of the buyer's breach, the buyer is entitled to restitution of any amount by which the sum of his payments exceeds

(a) the amount to which the seller is entitled by virtue of terms liquidating the seller's damages in accordance with subsection (1), or

(b) in the absence of such terms, twenty per cent of the value of the total performance for which the buyer is obligated under the contract or $500, whichever is smaller.

(3) The buyer's right to restitution under subsection (2) is subject to offset to the extent that the seller establishes

(a) a right to recover damages under the provisions of this Article other than subsection (1), and

(b) the amount or value of any benefits received by the buyer directly or indirectly by reason of the contract.

(4) Where a seller has received payment in goods their reasonable value or the proceeds of their resale shall be treated as payments for the purposes of subsection (2); but if the seller has notice of the buyer's breach before reselling goods received in part performance, his resale is subject to the conditions laid down in this Article on resale by an aggrieved seller (Section 2–706).

§ 2–719. Contractual Modification or Limitation of Remedy.

(1) Subject to the provisions of subsections (2) and (3) of this section and of the preceding section on liquidation and limitation of damages,

(a) the agreement may provide for remedies in addition to or in substitution for those provided in this Article and may limit or alter the measure of damages recoverable under this Article, as by limiting the buyer's remedies to return of the goods and repayment of the price or to repair and replacement of nonconforming goods or parts; and

(b) resort to a remedy as provided is optional unless the remedy is expressly agreed to be exclusive, in which case it is the sole remedy.

(2) Where circumstances cause an exclusive or limited remedy to fail of its essential purpose, remedy may be had as provided in this Act.

(3) Consequential damages may be limited or excluded unless the limitation or exclusion is unconscionable. Limitation of consequential damages for injury to the person in the case of consumer goods is prima facie unconscionable but limitation of damages where the loss is commercial is not.

§ 2–720. Effect of "Cancellation" or "Rescission" on Claims for Antecedent Breach.

Unless the contrary intention clearly appears, expressions of "cancellation" or "rescission" of the contract or the like shall not be construed as a renunciation or discharge of any claim in damages for an antecedent breach.

§ 2–721. Remedies for Fraud.

Remedies for material misrepresentation or fraud include all remedies available under this Article for non-fraudulent breach. Neither rescission or a claim for rescission of the contract for sale nor rejection or return of the goods shall bar or be deemed inconsistent with a claim for damages or other remedy.

§ 2–722. Who Can Sue Third Parties for Injury to Goods.

Where a third party so deals with goods which have been identified to a contract for sale as to cause actionable injury to a party to that contract

(a) a right of action against the third party is in either party to the contract for sale who has title to or a security interest or a special property or an insurable interest in the goods; and if the goods have been destroyed or converted a right of action is also in the party who either bore the risk of loss under the contract for sale or has since the injury assumed that risk as against the other;

(b) if at the time of the injury the party plaintiff did not bear the risk of loss as against the other party to the contract for sale and there is no arrangement between them for disposition of the recovery, his suit or settlement is, subject to his own interest, as a fiduciary for the other party to the contract;

(c) either party may with the consent of the other sue for the benefit of whom it may concern.

§ 2–723. Proof of Market Price: Time and Place.

(1) If an action based on anticipatory repudiation comes to trial before the time for performance with respect to some or all of the goods, any damages based on market price (Section 2–708 or Section 2–713) shall be determined according to the price of such goods prevailing at the time when the aggrieved party learned of the repudiation.

(2) If evidence of a price prevailing at the times or places described in this Article is not readily available the price prevailing within any reasonable time before or after the time described or at any other place which in commercial judgment or under usage of trade would serve as a reasonable substitute for the one described may be used, making any proper allowance for the cost of transporting the goods to or from such other place.

(3) Evidence of a relevant price prevailing at a time or place other than the one described in this Article offered by one party is not admissible unless and until he has given the other party such notice as the court finds sufficient to prevent unfair surprise.

§ 2–724. Admissibility of Market Quotations.

Whenever the prevailing price or value of any goods regularly bought and sold in any established commodity market is in issue, reports in official publications or trade journals or in newspapers or periodicals of general circulation published as the reports of such market shall be admissible in evidence. The circumstances of the preparation of such a report may be shown to affect its weight but not its admissibility.

§ 2–725. Statute of Limitations in Contracts for Sale.

(1) An action for breach of any contract for sale must be commenced within four years after the cause of action has accrued. By the original agreement the parties may reduce the period of limitation to not less than one year but may not extend it.

(2) A cause of action accrues when the breach occurs, regardless of the aggrieved party's lack of knowledge of the breach. A breach of warranty occurs when tender of delivery is made, except that where a warranty explicitly extends to future performance of the goods and discovery of the breach must await the time of such performance the cause of action accrues when the breach is or should have been discovered.

(3) Where an action commenced within the time limited by subsection (1) is so terminated as to leave available a remedy by another action for the same breach such other action may be commenced after the expiration of the time limited and within six months after the termination of the first action unless the termination resulted from voluntary discontinuance or from dismissal for failure or neglect to prosecute.

(4) This section does not alter the law on tolling of the statute of limitations nor does it apply to causes of action which have accrued before this Act becomes effective.

Article 2A
LEASES

Part 1 General Provisions

§ 2A–101. Short Title.

This Article shall be known and may be cited as the Uniform Commercial Code—Leases.

§ 2A–102. Scope.

This Article applies to any transaction, regardless of form, that creates a lease.

§ 2A–103. Definitions and Index of Definitions.

(1) In this Article unless the context otherwise requires:

(a) "Buyer in ordinary course of business" means a person who in good faith and without knowledge that the sale to him [or her] is in violation of the ownership rights or security interest or leasehold interest of a third party in the goods buys in ordinary course from a person in the business of selling goods of that kind but does not include a pawnbroker. "Buying" may be for cash or by exchange of other property or on secured or unsecured credit and includes receiving goods or documents of title under a pre-existing contract for sale but does not include a transfer in bulk or as security for or in total or partial satisfaction of a money debt.

(b) "Cancellation" occurs when either party puts an end to the lease contract for default by the other party.

(c) "Commercial unit" means such a unit of goods as by commercial usage is a single whole for purposes of lease and division of which materially impairs its character or value on the market or in use. A commercial unit may be a single article, as a machine, or a set of articles, as a suite of furniture or a line of machinery, or a quantity, as a gross or carload, or any other unit treated in use or in the relevant market as a single whole.

(d) "Conforming" goods or performance under a lease contract means goods or performance that are in accordance with the obligations under the lease contract.

(e) "Consumer lease" means a lease that a lessor regularly engaged in the business of leasing or selling makes to a lessee who is an individual and who takes under the lease primarily for a personal, family, or household purpose [, if the total payments to be made under the lease contract, excluding payments for options to renew or buy, do not exceed $______].

(f) "Fault" means wrongful act, omission, breach, or default.

(g) "Finance lease" means a lease with respect to which:

(i) the lessor does not select, manufacture or supply the goods;

(ii) the lessor acquires the goods or the right to possession and use of the goods in connection with the lease; and

(iii) one of the following occurs:

(A) the lessee receives a copy of the contract by which the lessor acquired the goods or the right to possession and use of the goods before signing the lease contract;

(B) the lessee's approval of the contract by which the lessor acquired the goods or the right to possession and use of the goods is a condition to effectiveness of the lease contract;

(C) the lessee, before signing the lease contract, receives an accurate and complete statement designating the promises and warranties, and any disclaimers of warranties, limitations or modifications of remedies, or liquidated damages, including those of a third party, such as the manufacturer of the goods, provided to the lessor by the person supplying the goods in connection with or as part of the contract by which the lessor acquired the goods or the right to possession and use of the goods; or

(D) if the lease is not a consumer lease, the lessor, before the lessee signs the lease contract, informs the lessee in writing (a) of the identity of the person supplying the goods to the lessor, unless the lessee has selected that person and directed the lessor to acquire the goods or the right to possession and use of the goods from that person, (b) that the lessee is entitled under this Article to any promises and warranties, including those of any third party, provided to the lessor by the person supplying the goods in connection with or as part of the contract by which the lessor acquired the goods or the right to possession and use of the goods, and (c) that the lessee may communicate with the person supplying the goods to the lessor and receive an accurate and complete statement of those promises and warranties, including any disclaimers and limitations of them or of remedies.

(h) "Goods" means all things that are movable at the time of identification to the lease contract, or are fixtures (Section 2A–309), but the term does not include money, documents, instruments, accounts, chattel paper, general intangibles, or minerals or the like, including oil and gas, before extraction. The term also includes the unborn young of animals.

(i) "Installment lease contract" means a lease contract that authorizes or requires the delivery of goods in separate lots to be separately accepted, even though the lease contract contains a clause "each delivery is a separate lease" or its equivalent.

(j) "Lease" means a transfer of the right to possession and use of goods for a term in return for consideration, but a sale, including a sale on approval or a sale or return, or retention or creation of a security interest is not a lease. Unless the context clearly indicates otherwise, the term includes a sublease.

(k) "Lease agreement" means the bargain, with respect to the lease, of the lessor and the lessee in fact as found in their language or by implication from other circumstances including course of dealing or usage of trade or course of performance as provided in this Article. Unless the context clearly indicates otherwise, the term includes a sublease agreement.

(l) "Lease contract" means the total legal obligation that results from the lease agreement as affected by this Article and any other applicable rules of law. Unless the context clearly indicates otherwise, the term includes a sublease contract.

(m) "Leasehold interest" means the interest of the lessor or the lessee under a lease contract.

(n) "Lessee" means a person who acquires the right to possession and use of goods under a lease. Unless the context clearly indicates otherwise, the term includes a sublessee.

(o) "Lessee in ordinary course of business" means a person who in good faith and without knowledge that the lease to him [or her] is in violation of the ownership rights or security interest or leasehold interest of a third party in the goods, leases in ordinary course from a person in the business of selling or leasing goods of that kind but does not include a pawnbroker. "Leasing" may be for cash or by exchange of other property or on secured or unsecured credit and includes receiving goods or documents of title under a pre-existing lease contract but does not include a transfer in bulk or as security for or in total or partial satisfaction of a money debt.

(p) "Lessor" means a person who transfers the right to possession and use of goods under a lease. Unless the context clearly indicates otherwise, the term includes a sublessor.

(q) "Lessor's residual interest" means the lessor's interest in the goods after expiration, termination, or cancellation of the lease contract.

(r) "Lien" means a charge against or interest in goods to secure payment of a debt or performance of an obligation, but the term does not include a security interest.

(s) "Lot" means a parcel or a single article that is the subject matter of a separate lease or delivery, whether or not it is sufficient to perform the lease contract.

(t) "Merchant lessee" means a lessee that is a merchant with respect to goods of the kind subject to the lease.

(u) "Present value" means the amount as of a date certain of one or more sums payable in the future, discounted to the date certain. The discount is determined by the interest rate specified by the parties if the rate was not manifestly unreasonable at the time the transaction was entered into; otherwise, the discount is determined by a commercially reasonable rate that takes into account the facts and circumstances of each case at the time the transaction was entered into.

(v) "Purchase" includes taking by sale, lease, mortgage, security interest, pledge, gift, or any other voluntary transaction creating an interest in goods.

(w) "Sublease" means a lease of goods the right to possession and use of which was acquired by the lessor as a lessee under an existing lease.

(x) "Supplier" means a person from whom a lessor buys or leases goods to be leased under a finance lease.

(y) "Supply contract" means a contract under which a lessor buys or leases goods to be leased.

(z) "Termination" occurs when either party pursuant to a power created by agreement or law puts an end to the lease contract otherwise than for default.

(2) Other definitions applying to this Article and the sections in which they appear are:

"Accessions". Section 2A–310(1).

"Construction mortgage". Section 2A–309(1)(d).

"Encumbrance". Section 2A–309(1)(e).

"Fixtures". Section 2A–309(1)(a).

"Fixture filing". Section 2A–309(1)(b).

"Purchase money lease". Section 2A–309(1)(c).

(3) The following definitions in other Articles apply to this Article:

"Accounts". Section 9–106.

"Between merchants". Section 2–104(3).

"Buyer". Section 2–103(1)(a).

"Chattel paper". Section 9–105(1)(b).

"Consumer goods". Section 9–109(1).

"Document". Section 9–105(1)(f).

"Entrusting". Section 2–403(3).

"General intangibles". Section 9–106.

"Good faith". Section 2–103(1)(b).

"Instrument". Section 9–105(1)(i).

"Merchant". Section 2–104(1).

"Mortgage". Section 9–105(1)(j).

"Pursuant to commitment". Section 9–105(1)(k).

"Receipt". Section 2–103(1)(c).

"Sale". Section 2–106(1).

"Sale on approval". Section 2–326.

"Sale or return". Section 2–326.

"Seller". Section 2–103(1)(d).

(4) In addition Article 1 contains general definitions and principles of construction and interpretation applicable throughout this Article.

As amended in 1990 and 1999.

§ 2A–104. Leases Subject to Other Law.

(1) A lease, although subject to this Article, is also subject to any applicable:

(a) certificate of title statute of this State: (list any certificate of title statutes covering automobiles, trailers, mobile homes, boats, farm tractors, and the like);

(b) certificate of title statute of another jurisdiction (Section 2A–105); or

(c) consumer protection statute of this State, or final consumer protection decision of a court of this State existing on the effective date of this Article.

(2) In case of conflict between this Article, other than Sections 2A–105, 2A–304(3), and 2A–305(3), and a statute or decision referred to in subsection (1), the statute or decision controls.

(3) Failure to comply with an applicable law has only the effect specified therein.

As amended in 1990.

§ 2A–105. Territorial Application of Article to Goods Covered by Certificate of Title.

Subject to the provisions of Sections 2A–304(3) and 2A–305(3), with respect to goods covered by a certificate of title issued under a statute of this State or of another jurisdiction, compliance and the effect of compliance or noncompliance with a certificate of title statute are governed by the law (including the conflict of laws rules) of the jurisdiction issuing the certificate until the earlier of (a) surrender of the certificate, or (b) four months after the goods are removed from that jurisdiction and thereafter until a new certificate of title is issued by another jurisdiction.

§ 2A–106. Limitation on Power of Parties to Consumer Lease to Choose Applicable Law and Judicial Forum.

(1) If the law chosen by the parties to a consumer lease is that of a jurisdiction other than a jurisdiction in which the lessee resides at the time the lease agreement becomes enforceable or within 30 days thereafter or in which the goods are to be used, the choice is not enforceable.

(2) If the judicial forum chosen by the parties to a consumer lease is a forum that would not otherwise have jurisdiction over the lessee, the choice is not enforceable.

§ 2A–107. Waiver or Renunciation of Claim or Right After Default.

Any claim or right arising out of an alleged default or breach of warranty may be discharged in whole or in part without consideration by a written waiver or renunciation signed and delivered by the aggrieved party.

§ 2A–108. Unconscionability.

(1) If the court as a matter of law finds a lease contract or any clause of a lease contract to have been unconscionable at the time it was made the court may refuse to enforce the lease contract, or it may enforce the remainder of the lease contract without the unconscionable clause, or it may so limit the application of any unconscionable clause as to avoid any unconscionable result.

(2) With respect to a consumer lease, if the court as a matter of law finds that a lease contract or any clause of a lease contract has been induced by unconscionable conduct or that unconscionable conduct has occurred in the collection of a claim arising from a lease contract, the court may grant appropriate relief.

(3) Before making a finding of unconscionability under subsection (1) or (2), the court, on its own motion or that of a party, shall afford the parties a reasonable opportunity to present evidence as to the setting, purpose, and effect of the lease contract or clause thereof, or of the conduct.

(4) In an action in which the lessee claims unconscionability with respect to a consumer lease:

(a) If the court finds unconscionability under subsection (1) or (2), the court shall award reasonable attorney's fees to the lessee.

(b) If the court does not find unconscionability and the lessee claiming unconscionability has brought or maintained an action he [or she] knew to be groundless, the court shall award reasonable attorney's fees to the party against whom the claim is made.

(c) In determining attorney's fees, the amount of the recovery on behalf of the claimant under subsections (1) and (2) is not controlling.

§ 2A–109. Option to Accelerate at Will.

(1) A term providing that one party or his [or her] successor in interest may accelerate payment or performance or require collateral or additional collateral "at will" or "when he [or she] deems himself [or herself] insecure" or in words of similar import must be construed to mean that he [or she] has power to do so only if he [or she] in good faith believes that the prospect of payment or performance is impaired.

(2) With respect to a consumer lease, the burden of establishing good faith under subsection (1) is on the party who exercised the power; otherwise the burden of establishing lack of good faith is on the party against whom the power has been exercised.

Part 2 Formation and Construction of Lease Contract

§ 2A–201. Statute of Frauds.

(1) A lease contract is not enforceable by way of action or defense unless:

(a) the total payments to be made under the lease contract, excluding payments for options to renew or buy, are less than $1,000; or

(b) there is a writing, signed by the party against whom enforcement is sought or by that party's authorized agent, sufficient to indicate that a lease contract has been made between the parties and to describe the goods leased and the lease term.

(2) Any description of leased goods or of the lease term is sufficient and satisfies subsection (1)(b), whether or not it is specific, if it reasonably identifies what is described.

(3) A writing is not insufficient because it omits or incorrectly states a term agreed upon, but the lease contract is not enforceable under subsection (1)(b) beyond the lease term and the quantity of goods shown in the writing.

(4) A lease contract that does not satisfy the requirements of subsection (1), but which is valid in other respects, is enforceable:

(a) if the goods are to be specially manufactured or obtained for the lessee and are not suitable for lease or sale to others in the ordinary course of the lessor's business, and the lessor, before notice of repudiation is received and under circumstances that reasonably indicate that the goods are for the lessee, has made either a substantial beginning of their manufacture or commitments for their procurement;

(b) if the party against whom enforcement is sought admits in that party's pleading, testimony or otherwise in court that a lease contract was made, but the lease contract is not enforceable under this provision beyond the quantity of goods admitted; or

(c) with respect to goods that have been received and accepted by the lessee.

(5) The lease term under a lease contract referred to in subsection (4) is:

(a) if there is a writing signed by the party against whom enforcement is sought or by that party's authorized agent specifying the lease term, the term so specified;

(b) if the party against whom enforcement is sought admits in that party's pleading, testimony, or otherwise in court a lease term, the term so admitted; or

(c) a reasonable lease term.

§ 2A–202. Final Written Expression: Parol or Extrinsic Evidence.

Terms with respect to which the confirmatory memoranda of the parties agree or which are otherwise set forth in a writing intended by the parties as a final expression of their agreement with respect to such terms as are included therein may not be contradicted by evidence of any prior agreement or of a contemporaneous oral agreement but may be explained or supplemented:

(a) by course of dealing or usage of trade or by course of performance; and

(b) by evidence of consistent additional terms unless the court finds the writing to have been intended also as a complete and exclusive statement of the terms of the agreement.

§ 2A–203. Seals Inoperative.

The affixing of a seal to a writing evidencing a lease contract or an offer to enter into a lease contract does not render the writing a sealed instrument and the law with respect to sealed instruments does not apply to the lease contract or offer.

§ 2A–204. Formation in General.

(1) A lease contract may be made in any manner sufficient to show agreement, including conduct by both parties which recognizes the existence of a lease contract.

(2) An agreement sufficient to constitute a lease contract may be found although the moment of its making is undetermined.

(3) Although one or more terms are left open, a lease contract does not fail for indefiniteness if the parties have intended to make a lease contract and there is a reasonably certain basis for giving an appropriate remedy.

§ 2A–205. Firm Offers.

An offer by a merchant to lease goods to or from another person in a signed writing that by its terms gives assurance it will be held open is not revocable, for lack of consideration, during the time stated or, if no time is stated, for a reasonable time, but in no event may the period of irrevocability exceed 3 months. Any such term of assurance on a form supplied by the offeree must be separately signed by the offeror.

§ 2A–206. Offer and Acceptance in Formation of Lease Contract.

(1) Unless otherwise unambiguously indicated by the language or circumstances, an offer to make a lease contract must be construed as inviting acceptance in any manner and by any medium reasonable in the circumstances.

(2) If the beginning of a requested performance is a reasonable mode of acceptance, an offeror who is not notified of acceptance within a reasonable time may treat the offer as having lapsed before acceptance.

§ 2A–207. Course of Performance or Practical Construction.

(1) If a lease contract involves repeated occasions for performance by either party with knowledge of the nature of the performance and opportunity for objection to it by the other, any course of performance accepted or acquiesced in without objection is relevant to determine the meaning of the lease agreement.

(2) The express terms of a lease agreement and any course of performance, as well as any course of dealing and usage of trade, must be construed whenever reasonable as consistent with each other; but if that construction is unreasonable, express terms control course of performance, course of performance controls both course of dealing and usage of trade, and course of dealing controls usage of trade.

(3) Subject to the provisions of Section 2A–208 on modification and waiver, course of performance is relevant to show a waiver or modification of any term inconsistent with the course of performance.

§ 2A–208. Modification, Rescission and Waiver.

(1) An agreement modifying a lease contract needs no consideration to be binding.

(2) A signed lease agreement that excludes modification or rescission except by a signed writing may not be otherwise modified or rescinded, but, except as between merchants, such a requirement on a form supplied by a merchant must be separately signed by the other party.

(3) Although an attempt at modification or rescission does not satisfy the requirements of subsection (2), it may operate as a waiver.

(4) A party who has made a waiver affecting an executory portion of a lease contract may retract the waiver by reasonable notification received by the other party that strict performance will be required of any term waived, unless the retraction would be unjust in view of a material change of position in reliance on the waiver.

§ 2A–209. Lessee under Finance Lease as Beneficiary of Supply Contract.

(1) The benefit of the supplier's promises to the lessor under the supply contract and of all warranties, whether express or implied, including those of any third party provided in connection with or as part of the supply contract, extends to the lessee to the extent of the lessee's leasehold interest under a finance lease related to the supply contract, but is subject to the terms warranty and of the supply contract and all defenses or claims arising therefrom.

(2) The extension of the benefit of supplier's promises and of warranties to the lessee (Section 2A–209(1)) does not: (i) modify the rights and obligations of the parties to the supply contract, whether arising therefrom or otherwise, or (ii) impose any duty or liability under the supply contract on the lessee.

(3) Any modification or rescission of the supply contract by the supplier and the lessor is effective between the supplier and the lessee unless, before the modification or rescission, the supplier has received notice that the lessee has entered into a finance lease related to the supply contract. If the modification or rescission is effective between the supplier and the lessee, the lessor is deemed to have assumed, in addition to the obligations of the lessor to the lessee under the lease contract, promises of the supplier to the lessor and warranties that were so modified or rescinded as they existed and were available to the lessee before modification or rescission.

(4) In addition to the extension of the benefit of the supplier's promises and of warranties to the lessee under subsection (1), the lessee retains all rights that the lessee may have against the supplier which arise from an agreement between the lessee and the supplier or under other law.

As amended in 1990.

§ 2A–210. Express Warranties.

(1) Express warranties by the lessor are created as follows:

(a) Any affirmation of fact or promise made by the lessor to the lessee which relates to the goods and becomes part of the basis of the bargain creates an express warranty that the goods will conform to the affirmation or promise.

(b) Any description of the goods which is made part of the basis of the bargain creates an express warranty that the goods will conform to the description.

(c) Any sample or model that is made part of the basis of the bargain creates an express warranty that the whole of the goods will conform to the sample or model.

(2) It is not necessary to the creation of an express warranty that the lessor use formal words, such as "warrant" or "guarantee," or that the lessor have a specific intention to make a warranty, but an affirmation merely of the value of the goods or a statement purporting to be merely the lessor's opinion or commendation of the goods does not create a warranty.

§ 2A–211. Warranties Against Interference and Against Infringement; Lessee's Obligation Against Infringement.

(1) There is in a lease contract a warranty that for the lease term no person holds a claim to or interest in the goods that arose from an act or omission of the lessor, other than a claim by way of infringement or the like, which will interfere with the lessee's enjoyment of its leasehold interest.

(2) Except in a finance lease there is in a lease contract by a lessor who is a merchant regularly dealing in goods of the kind a warranty that the goods are delivered free of the rightful claim of any person by way of infringement or the like.

(3) A lessee who furnishes specifications to a lessor or a supplier shall hold the lessor and the supplier harmless against any claim by way of infringement or the like that arises out of compliance with the specifications.

§ 2A–212. Implied Warranty of Merchantability.

(1) Except in a finance lease, a warranty that the goods will be merchantable is implied in a lease contract if the lessor is a merchant with respect to goods of that kind.

(2) Goods to be merchantable must be at least such as

(a) pass without objection in the trade under the description in the lease agreement;

(b) in the case of fungible goods, are of fair average quality within the description;

(c) are fit for the ordinary purposes for which goods of that type are used;

(d) run, within the variation permitted by the lease agreement, of even kind, quality, and quantity within each unit and among all units involved;

(e) are adequately contained, packaged, and labeled as the lease agreement may require; and

(f) conform to any promises or affirmations of fact made on the container or label.

(3) Other implied warranties may arise from course of dealing or usage of trade.

§ 2A–213. Implied Warranty of Fitness for Particular Purpose.

Except in a finance of lease, if the lessor at the time the lease contract is made has reason to know of any particular purpose for which the goods are required and that the lessee is relying on the lessor's skill or judgment to select or furnish suitable goods, there is in the lease contract an implied warranty that the goods will be fit for that purpose.

§ 2A–214. Exclusion or Modification of Warranties.

(1) Words or conduct relevant to the creation of an express warranty and words or conduct tending to negate or limit a warranty must be construed wherever reasonable as consistent with each other; but, subject to the provisions of Section 2A–202 on parol or extrinsic evidence, negation or limitation is inoperative to the extent that the construction is unreasonable.

(2) Subject to subsection (3), to exclude or modify the implied warranty of merchantability or any part of it the language must mention "merchantability", be by a writing, and be conspicuous. Subject to subsection (3), to exclude or modify any implied warranty of fitness the exclusion must be by a writing and be conspicuous. Language to exclude all implied warranties of fitness is sufficient if it is in writing, is conspicuous and states, for example, "There is no warranty that the goods will be fit for a particular purpose".

(3) Notwithstanding subsection (2), but subject to subsection (4),

(a) unless the circumstances indicate otherwise, all implied warranties are excluded by expressions like "as is" or "with all faults" or by other language that in common understanding calls the lessee's attention to the exclusion of warranties and makes plain that there is no implied warranty, if in writing and conspicuous;

(b) if the lessee before entering into the lease contract has examined the goods or the sample or model as fully as desired or has refused to examine the goods, there is no implied warranty with regard to defects that an examination ought in the circumstances to have revealed; and

(c) an implied warranty may also be excluded or modified by course of dealing, course of performance, or usage of trade.

(4) To exclude or modify a warranty against interference or against infringement (Section 2A–211) or any part of it, the language must be specific, be by a writing, and be conspicuous, unless the circumstances, including course of performance, course of dealing, or usage of trade, give the lessee reason to know that the goods are being leased subject to a claim or interest of any person.

§ 2A–215. Cumulation and Conflict of Warranties Express or Implied.

Warranties, whether express or implied, must be construed as consistent with each other and as cumulative, but if that construction is unreasonable, the intention of the parties determines which warranty is dominant. In ascertaining that intention the following rules apply:

(a) Exact or technical specifications displace an inconsistent sample or model or general language of description.

(b) A sample from an existing bulk displaces inconsistent general language of description.

(c) Express warranties displace inconsistent implied warranties other than an implied warranty of fitness for a particular purpose.

§ 2A–216. Third-Party Beneficiaries of Express and Implied Warranties.

Alternative A

A warranty to or for the benefit of a lessee under this Article, whether express or implied, extends to any natural person who is in the family or household of the lessee or who is a guest in the lessee's home if it is reasonable to expect that such person may use, consume, or be affected by the goods and who is injured in person by breach of the warranty. This section does not displace principles of law and equity that extend a warranty to or for the benefit of a lessee to other persons. The operation of this section may not be excluded, modified, or limited, but an exclusion, modification, or limitation of the warranty, including any with respect to rights and remedies, effective against the lessee is also effective against any beneficiary designated under this section.

Alternative B

A warranty to or for the benefit of a lessee under this Article, whether express or implied, extends to any natural person who may reasonably be expected to use, consume, or be affected by the goods and who is injured in person by breach of the warranty. This section does not displace principles of law and equity that extend a warranty to or for the benefit of a lessee to other persons. The operation of this section may not be excluded, modified, or limited, but an exclusion, modification, or limitation of the warranty, including any with respect to rights and remedies, effective against the lessee is also effective against the beneficiary designated under this section.

Alternative C

A warranty to or for the benefit of a lessee under this Article, whether express or implied, extends to any person who may reasonably be expected to use, consume, or be affected by the goods and who is injured by breach of the warranty. The operation of this section may not be excluded, modified, or limited with respect to injury to the person of an individual to whom the warranty extends, but an exclusion, modification, or limitation of the warranty, including any with respect to rights and remedies, effective against the lessee is also effective against the beneficiary designated under this section.

§ 2A–217. Identification.

Identification of goods as goods to which a lease contract refers may be made at any time and in any manner explicitly agreed to by the parties. In the absence of explicit agreement, identification occurs:

(a) when the lease contract is made if the lease contract is for a lease of goods that are existing and identified;

(b) when the goods are shipped, marked, or otherwise designated by the lessor as goods to which the lease contract refers, if the lease contract is for a lease of goods that are not existing and identified; or

(c) when the young are conceived, if the lease contract is for a lease of unborn young of animals.

§ 2A–218. Insurance and Proceeds.

(1) A lessee obtains an insurable interest when existing goods are identified to the lease contract even though the goods identified are nonconforming and the lessee has an option to reject them.

(2) If a lessee has an insurable interest only by reason of the lessor's identification of the goods, the lessor, until default or insolvency or notification to the lessee that identification is final, may substitute other goods for those identified.

(3) Notwithstanding a lessee's insurable interest under subsections (1) and (2), the lessor retains an insurable interest until an option to buy has been exercised by the lessee and risk of loss has passed to the lessee.

(4) Nothing in this section impairs any insurable interest recognized under any other statute or rule of law.

(5) The parties by agreement may determine that one or more parties have an obligation to obtain and pay for insurance covering the goods and by agreement may determine the beneficiary of the proceeds of the insurance.

§ 2A–219. Risk of Loss.

(1) Except in the case of a finance lease, risk of loss is retained by the lessor and does not pass to the lessee. In the case of a finance lease, risk of loss passes to the lessee.

(2) Subject to the provisions of this Article on the effect of default on risk of loss (Section 2A–220), if risk of loss is to pass to the lessee and the time of passage is not stated, the following rules apply:

(a) If the lease contract requires or authorizes the goods to be shipped by carrier

(i) and it does not require delivery at a particular destination, the risk of loss passes to the lessee when the goods are duly delivered to the carrier; but

(ii) if it does require delivery at a particular destination and the goods are there duly tendered while in the possession of the carrier, the risk of loss passes to the lessee when the goods are there duly so tendered as to enable the lessee to take delivery.

(b) If the goods are held by a bailee to be delivered without being moved, the risk of loss passes to the lessee on acknowledgment by the bailee of the lessee's right to possession of the goods.

(c) In any case not within subsection (a) or (b), the risk of loss passes to the lessee on the lessee's receipt of the goods if the lessor, or, in the case of a finance lease, the supplier, is a merchant; otherwise the risk passes to the lessee on tender of delivery.

§ 2A–220. Effect of Default on Risk of Loss.

(1) Where risk of loss is to pass to the lessee and the time of passage is not stated:

(a) If a tender or delivery of goods so fails to conform to the lease contract as to give a right of rejection, the risk of their loss remains with the lessor, or, in the case of a finance lease, the supplier, until cure or acceptance.

(b) If the lessee rightfully revokes acceptance, he [or she], to the extent of any deficiency in his [or her] effective insurance coverage, may treat the risk of loss as having remained with the lessor from the beginning.

(2) Whether or not risk of loss is to pass to the lessee, if the lessee as to conforming goods already identified to a lease contract repudiates or is otherwise in default under the lease contract, the lessor, or, in the case of a finance lease, the supplier, to the extent of any deficiency in his [or her] effective insurance coverage may treat the risk of loss as resting on the lessee for a commercially reasonable time.

§ 2A–221. Casualty to Identified Goods.

If a lease contract requires goods identified when the lease contract is made, and the goods suffer casualty without fault of the lessee, the lessor or the supplier before delivery, or the goods suffer casualty before risk of loss passes to the lessee pursuant to the lease agreement or Section 2A–219, then:

(a) if the loss is total, the lease contract is avoided; and

(b) if the loss is partial or the goods have so deteriorated as to no longer conform to the lease contract, the lessee may nevertheless demand inspection and at his [or her] option either treat the lease contract as avoided or, except in a finance lease that is not a consumer lease, accept the goods with due allowance from the rent payable for the balance of the lease term for the deterioration or the deficiency in quantity but without further right against the lessor.

Part 3 Effect of Lease Contract

§ 2A–301. Enforceability of Lease Contract.

Except as otherwise provided in this Article, a lease contract is effective and enforceable according to its terms between the parties, against purchasers of the goods and against creditors of the parties.

§ 2A–302. Title to and Possession of Goods.

Except as otherwise provided in this Article, each provision of this Article applies whether the lessor or a third party has title to the goods, and whether the lessor, the lessee, or a third party has possession of the goods, notwithstanding any statute or rule of law that possession or the absence of possession is fraudulent.

§ 2A–303. Alienability of Party's Interest Under Lease Contract or of Lessor's Residual Interest in Goods; Delegation of Performance; Transfer of Rights.

(1) As used in this section,"creation of a security interest" includes the sale of a lease contract that is subject to Article 9, Secured Transactions, by reason of Section 9–109(a)(3).

(2) Except as provided in subsections (3) and Section 9–407, a provision in a lease agreement which (i) prohibits the voluntary or involuntary transfer, including a transfer by sale, sublease, creation or enforcement of a security interest, or attachment, levy, or other judicial process, of an interest of a party under the lease contract or of the lessor's residual interest in the goods, or (ii) makes such a transfer an event of default, gives rise to the rights and remedies provided in subsection (4), but a transfer that is prohibited or is an event of default under the lease agreement is otherwise effective.

(3) A provision in a lease agreement which (i) prohibits a transfer of a right to damages for default with respect to the whole lease contract or of a right to payment arising out of the transferor's due performance of the transferor's entire obligation, or (ii) makes such a transfer an event of default, is not enforceable, and such a transfer is not a transfer that materially impairs the propsect of obtaining return performance by, materially changes the duty of, or materially increases the burden or risk imposed on, the other party to the lease contract within the purview of subsection (4).

(4) Subject to subsection (3) and Section 9–407:

(a) if a transfer is made which is made an event of default under a lease agreement, the party to the lease contract not making the transfer, unless that party waives the default or otherwise agrees, has the rights and remedies described in Section 2A-501(2);

(b) if paragraph (a) is not applicable and if a transfer is made that (i) is prohibited under a lease agreement or (ii) materially impairs the prospect of obtaining return performance by, materially changes the duty of, or materially increases the burden or risk imposed on, the other party to the lease contract, unless the party not making the transfer agrees at any time to the transfer in the lease contract or otherwise, then, except as limited by contract, (i) the transferor is liable to the party not making the transfer for damages caused by the transfer to the extent that the damages could not reasonably be prevented by the party not making the transfer and (ii) a court having jurisdiction may grant other appropriate relief, including cancellation of the lease contract or an injunction against the transfer.

(5) A transfer of "the lease" or of "all my rights under the lease", or a transfer in similar general terms, is a transfer of rights and, unless the language or the circumstances, as in a transfer for security, indicate the contrary, the transfer is a delegation of duties by the transferor to the transferee. Acceptance by the transferee constitutes a promise by the transferee to perform those duties. The promise is enforceable by either the transferor or the other party to the lease contract.

(6) Unless otherwise agreed by the lessor and the lessee, a delegation of performance does not relieve the transferor as against the other party of any duty to perform or of any liability for default.

(7) In a consumer lease, to prohibit the transfer of an interest of a party under the lease contract or to make a transfer an event of default, the language must be specific, by a writing, and conspicuous.

As amended in 1990 and 1999.

§ 2A–304. Subsequent Lease of Goods by Lessor.

(1) Subject to Section 2A–303, a subsequent lessee from a lessor of goods under an existing lease contract obtains, to the extent of the leasehold interest transferred, the leasehold interest in the goods that the lessor had or had power to transfer, and except as provided in subsection (2) and Section 2A–527(4), takes subject to the existing lease contract. A lessor with voidable title has power to transfer a good leasehold interest to a good faith subsequent lessee for value, but only to the extent set forth in the preceding sentence. If goods have been delivered under a transaction of purchase the lessor has that power even though:

(a) the lessor's transferor was deceived as to the identity of the lessor;

(b) the delivery was in exchange for a check which is later dishonored;

(c) it was agreed that the transaction was to be a "cash sale"; or

(d) the delivery was procured through fraud punishable as larcenous under the criminal law.

(2) A subsequent lessee in the ordinary course of business from a lessor who is a merchant dealing in goods of that kind to whom the goods were entrusted by the existing lessee of that lessor before the interest of the subsequent lessee became enforceable against that lessor obtains, to the extent of the leasehold interest transferred, all of that lessor's and the existing lessee's rights to the goods, and takes free of the existing lease contract.

(3) A subsequent lessee from the lessor of goods that are subject to an existing lease contract and are covered by a certificate of title issued under a statute of this State or of another jurisdiction takes no greater rights than those provided both by this section and by the certificate of title statute.

As amended in 1990.

§ 2A–305. Sale or Sublease of Goods by Lessee.

(1) Subject to the provisions of Section 2A–303, a buyer or sublessee from the lessee of goods under an existing lease contract obtains, to the extent of the interest transferred,

the leasehold interest in the goods that the lessee had or had power to transfer, and except as provided in subsection (2) and Section 2A–511(4), takes subject to the existing lease contract. A lessee with a voidable leasehold interest has power to transfer a good leasehold interest to a good faith buyer for value or a good faith sublessee for value, but only to the extent set forth in the preceding sentence. When goods have been delivered under a transaction of lease the lessee has that power even though:

(a) the lessor was deceived as to the identity of the lessee;

(b) the delivery was in exchange for a check which is later dishonored; or

(c) the delivery was procured through fraud punishable as larcenous under the criminal law.

(2) A buyer in the ordinary course of business or a sublessee in the ordinary course of business from a lessee who is a merchant dealing in goods of that kind to whom the goods were entrusted by the lessor obtains, to the extent of the interest transferred, all of the lessor's and lessee's rights to the goods, and takes free of the existing lease contract.

(3) A buyer or sublessee from the lessee of goods that are subject to an existing lease contract and are covered by a certificate of title issued under a statute of this State or of another jurisdiction takes no greater rights than those provided both by this section and by the certificate of title statute.

§ 2A–306. Priority of Certain Liens Arising by Operation of Law.

If a person in the ordinary course of his [or her] business furnishes services or materials with respect to goods subject to a lease contract, a lien upon those goods in the possession of that person given by statute or rule of law for those materials or services takes priority over any interest of the lessor or lessee under the lease contract or this Article unless the lien is created by statute and the statute provides otherwise or unless the lien is created by rule of law and the rule of law provides otherwise.

§ 2A–307. Priority of Liens Arising by Attachment or Levy on, Security Interests in, and Other Claims to Goods.

(1) Except as otherwise provided in Section 2A–306, a creditor of a lessee takes subject to the lease contract.

(2) Except as otherwise provided in subsection (3) and in Sections 2A–306 and 2A–308, a creditor of a lessor takes subject to the lease contract unless the creditor holds a lien that attached to the goods before the lease contract became enforceable.

(3) Except as otherwise provided in Sections 9–317, 9–321, and 9–323, a lessee takes a leasehold interest subject to a security interest held by a creditor of the lessor.

As amended in 1990 and 1999.

§ 2A–308. Special Rights of Creditors.

(1) A creditor of a lessor in possession of goods subject to a lease contract may treat the lease contract as void if as against the creditor retention of possession by the lessor is fraudulent under any statute or rule of law, but retention of possession in good faith and current course of trade by the lessor for a commercially reasonable time after the lease contract becomes enforceable is not fraudulent.

(2) Nothing in this Article impairs the rights of creditors of a lessor if the lease contract (a) becomes enforceable, not in current course of trade but in satisfaction of or as security for a pre-existing claim for money, security, or the like, and (b) is made under circumstances which under any statute or rule of law apart from this Article would constitute the transaction a fraudulent transfer or voidable preference.

(3) A creditor of a seller may treat a sale or an identification of goods to a contract for sale as void if as against the creditor retention of possession by the seller is fraudulent under any statute or rule of law, but retention of possession of the goods pursuant to a lease contract entered into by the seller as lessee and the buyer as lessor in connection with the sale or identification of the goods is not fraudulent if the buyer bought for value and in good faith.

§ 2A–309. Lessor's and Lessee's Rights When Goods Become Fixtures.

(1) In this section:

(a) goods are "fixtures" when they become so related to particular real estate that an interest in them arises under real estate law;

(b) a "fixture filing" is the filing, in the office where a mortgage on the real estate would be filed or recorded, of a financing statement covering goods that are or are to become fixtures and conforming to the requirements of Section 9–502(a) and (b);

(c) a lease is a "purchase money lease" unless the lessee has possession or use of the goods or the right to possession or use of the goods before the lease agreement is enforceable;

(d) a mortgage is a "construction mortgage" to the extent it secures an obligation incurred for the construction of an improvement on land including the acquisition cost of the land, if the recorded writing so indicates; and

(e) "encumbrance" includes real estate mortgages and other liens on real estate and all other rights in real estate that are not ownership interests.

(2) Under this Article a lease may be of goods that are fixtures or may continue in goods that become fixtures, but no lease exists under this Article of ordinary building materials incorporated into an improvement on land.

(3) This Article does not prevent creation of a lease of fixtures pursuant to real estate law.

(4) The perfected interest of a lessor of fixtures has priority over a conflicting interest of an encumbrancer or owner of the real estate if:

(a) the lease is a purchase money lease, the conflicting interest of the encumbrancer or owner arises before the goods become fixtures, the interest of the lessor is perfected by a fixture filing before the goods become fixtures or within ten days thereafter, and the lessee has an interest of record in the real estate or is in possession of the real estate; or

(b) the interest of the lessor is perfected by a fixture filing before the interest of the encumbrancer or owner is of record, the lessor's interest has priority over any conflicting interest of a predecessor in title of the encumbrancer or owner, and the lessee has an interest of record in the real estate or is in possession of the real estate.

(5) The interest of a lessor of fixtures, whether or not perfected, has priority over the conflicting interest of an encumbrancer or owner of the real estate if:

(a) the fixtures are readily removable factory or office machines, readily removable equipment that is not primarily used or leased for use in the operation of the real estate, or readily removable replacements of domestic appliances that are goods subject to a consumer lease, and before the goods become fixtures the lease contract is enforceable; or

(b) the conflicting interest is a lien on the real estate obtained by legal or equitable proceedings after the lease contract is enforceable; or

(c) the encumbrancer or owner has consented in writing to the lease or has disclaimed an interest in the goods as fixtures; or

(d) the lessee has a right to remove the goods as against the encumbrancer or owner. If the lessee's right to remove terminates, the priority of the interest of the lessor continues for a reasonable time.

(6) Notwithstanding paragraph (4)(a) but otherwise subject to subsections (4) and (5), the interest of a lessor of fixtures, including the lessor's residual interest, is subordinate to the conflicting interest of an encumbrancer of the real estate under a construction mortgage recorded before the goods become fixtures if the goods become fixtures before the completion of the construction. To the extent given to refinance a construction mortgage, the conflicting interest of an encumbrancer of the real estate under a mortgage has this priority to the same extent as the encumbrancer of the real estate under the construction mortgage.

(7) In cases not within the preceding subsections, priority between the interest of a lessor of fixtures, including the lessor's residual interest, and the conflicting interest of an encumbrancer or owner of the real estate who is not the lessee is determined by the priority rules governing conflicting interests in real estate.

(8) If the interest of a lessor of fixtures, including the lessor's residual interest, has priority over all conflicting interests of all owners and encumbrancers of the real estate, the lessor or the lessee may (i) on default, expiration, termination, or cancellation of the lease agreement but subject to the agreement and this Article, or (ii) if necessary to enforce other rights and remedies of the lessor or lessee under this Article, remove the goods from the real estate, free and clear of all conflicting interests of all owners and encumbrancers of the real estate, but the lessor or lessee must reimburse any encumbrancer or owner of the real estate who is not the lessee and who has not otherwise agreed for the cost of repair of any physical injury, but not for any diminution in value of the real estate caused by the absence of the goods removed or by any necessity of replacing them. A person entitled to reimbursement may refuse permission to remove until the party seeking removal gives adequate security for the performance of this obligation.

(9) Even though the lease agreement does not create a security interest, the interest of a lessor of fixtures, including the lessor's residual interest, is perfected by filing a financing statement as a fixture filing for leased goods that are or are to become fixtures in accordance with the relevant provisions of the Article on Secured Transactions (Article 9).

As amended in 1990 and 1999.

§ 2A–310. Lessor's and Lessee's Rights When Goods Become Accessions.

(1) Goods are "accessions" when they are installed in or affixed to other goods.

(2) The interest of a lessor or a lessee under a lease contract entered into before the goods became accessions is superior to all interests in the whole except as stated in subsection (4).

(3) The interest of a lessor or a lessee under a lease contract entered into at the time or after the goods became accessions is superior to all subsequently acquired interests in the whole except as stated in subsection (4) but is subordinate to interests in the whole existing at the time the lease contract was made unless the holders of such interests in the whole have in writing consented to the lease or disclaimed an interest in the goods as part of the whole.

(4) The interest of a lessor or a lessee under a lease contract described in subsection (2) or (3) is subordinate to the interest of

(a) a buyer in the ordinary course of business or a lessee in the ordinary course of business of any interest in the whole acquired after the goods became accessions; or

(b) a creditor with a security interest in the whole perfected before the lease contract was made to the extent that the creditor makes subsequent advances without knowledge of the lease contract.

(5) When under subsections (2) or (3) and (4) a lessor or a lessee of accessions holds an interest that is superior to all interests in the whole, the lessor or the lessee may (a) on default, expiration, termination, or cancellation of the lease contract by the other party but subject to the provisions of the lease contract and this Article, or (b) if necessary to enforce his [or her] other rights and remedies under this Article, remove the goods from the whole, free and clear of all interests in the whole, but he [or she] must reimburse any holder of an interest in the whole who is not the lessee and who has not otherwise agreed for the cost of repair of any physical injury but not for any diminution in value of the whole caused by the absence of the goods removed or by any necessity for replacing them. A person entitled to reimbursement may refuse permission to remove until the party seeking removal gives adequate security for the performance of this obligation.

§ 2A–311. Priority Subject to Subordination.

Nothing in this Article prevents subordination by agreement by any person entitled to priority.

As added in 1990.

Part 4 Performance of Lease Contract: Repudiated, Substituted and Excused

§ 2A–401. Insecurity: Adequate Assurance of Performance.

(1) A lease contract imposes an obligation on each party that the other's expectation of receiving due performance will not be impaired.

(2) If reasonable grounds for insecurity arise with respect to the performance of either party, the insecure party may demand in writing adequate assurance of due performance. Until the insecure party receives that assurance, if commercially reasonable the insecure party may suspend any performance for which he [or she] has not already received the agreed return.

(3) A repudiation of the lease contract occurs if assurance of due performance adequate under the circumstances of the particular case is not provided to the insecure party within a reasonable time, not to exceed 30 days after receipt of a demand by the other party.

(4) Between merchants, the reasonableness of grounds for insecurity and the adequacy of any assurance offered must be determined according to commercial standards.

(5) Acceptance of any nonconforming delivery or payment does not prejudice the aggrieved party's right to demand adequate assurance of future performance.

§ 2A–402. Anticipatory Repudiation.

If either party repudiates a lease contract with respect to a performance not yet due under the lease contract, the loss of which performance will substantially impair the value of the lease contract to the other, the aggrieved party may:

(a) for a commercially reasonable time, await retraction of repudiation and performance by the repudiating party;

(b) make demand pursuant to Section 2A–401 and await assurance of future performance adequate under the circumstances of the particular case; or

(c) resort to any right or remedy upon default under the lease contract or this Article, even though the aggrieved party has notified the repudiating party that the aggrieved party would await the repudiating party's performance and assurance and has urged retraction. In addition, whether or not the aggrieved party is pursuing one of the foregoing remedies, the aggrieved party may suspend performance or, if the aggrieved party is the lessor, proceed in accordance with the provisions of this Article on the lessor's right to identify goods to the lease contract notwithstanding default or to salvage unfinished goods (Section 2A–524).

§ 2A–403. Retraction of Anticipatory Repudiation.

(1) Until the repudiating party's next performance is due, the repudiating party can retract the repudiation unless, since the repudiation, the aggrieved party has cancelled the lease contract or materially changed the aggrieved party's position or otherwise indicated that the aggrieved party considers the repudiation final.

(2) Retraction may be by any method that clearly indicates to the aggrieved party that the repudiating party intends to perform under the lease contract and includes any assurance demanded under Section 2A–401.

(3) Retraction reinstates a repudiating party's rights under a lease contract with due excuse and allowance to the aggrieved party for any delay occasioned by the repudiation.

§ 2A–404. Substituted Performance.

(1) If without fault of the lessee, the lessor and the supplier, the agreed berthing, loading, or unloading facilities fail or the agreed type of carrier becomes unavailable or the agreed manner of delivery otherwise becomes commercially impracticable, but a commercially reasonable substitute is available, the substitute performance must be tendered and accepted.

(2) If the agreed means or manner of payment fails because of domestic or foreign governmental regulation:

(a) the lessor may withhold or stop delivery or cause the supplier to withhold or stop delivery unless the lessee provides a means or manner of payment that is commercially a substantial equivalent; and

(b) if delivery has already been taken, payment by the means or in the manner provided by the regulation discharges the lessee's obligation unless the regulation is discriminatory, oppressive, or predatory.

§ 2A–405. Excused Performance.

Subject to Section 2A–404 on substituted performance, the following rules apply:

(a) Delay in delivery or nondelivery in whole or in part by a lessor or a supplier who complies with paragraphs (b) and (c) is not a default under the lease contract if performance as agreed has been made impracticable by the occurrence of a contingency the nonoccurrence of which was a basic assumption on which the lease contract was made or by compliance in good faith with any applicable foreign or domestic governmental regulation or order, whether or not the regulation or order later proves to be invalid.

(b) If the causes mentioned in paragraph (a) affect only part of the lessor's or the supplier's capacity to perform, he [or she] shall allocate production and deliveries among his [or her] customers but at his [or her] option may include regular customers not then under contract for sale or lease as well as his [or her] own requirements for further manufacture. He [or she] may so allocate in any manner that is fair and reasonable.

(c) The lessor seasonably shall notify the lessee and in the case of a finance lease the supplier seasonably shall notify the lessor and the lessee, if known, that there will be delay or nondelivery and, if allocation is required under paragraph (b), of the estimated quota thus made available for the lessee.

§ 2A–406. Procedure on Excused Performance.

(1) If the lessee receives notification of a material or indefinite delay or an allocation justified under Section 2A–405, the lessee may by written notification to the lessor as to any goods involved, and with respect to all of the goods if under an installment lease contract the value of the whole lease contract is substantially impaired (Section 2A–510):

(a) terminate the lease contract (Section 2A–505(2)); or

(b) except in a finance lease that is not a consumer lease, modify the lease contract by accepting the available quota in substitution, with due allowance from the rent payable for the balance of the lease term for the deficiency but without further right against the lessor.

(2) If, after receipt of a notification from the lessor under Section 2A–405, the lessee fails so to modify the lease agreement within a reasonable time not exceeding 30 days, the lease contract lapses with respect to any deliveries affected.

§ 2A–407. Irrevocable Promises: Finance Leases.

(1) In the case of a finance lease that is not a consumer lease the lessee's promises under the lease contract become irrevocable and independent upon the lessee's acceptance of the goods.

(2) A promise that has become irrevocable and independent under subsection (1):

(a) is effective and enforceable between the parties, and by or against third parties including assignees of the parties, and

(b) is not subject to cancellation, termination, modification, repudiation, excuse, or substitution without the consent of the party to whom the promise runs.

(3) This section does not affect the validity under any other law of a covenant in any lease contract making the lessee's promises irrevocable and independent upon the lessee's acceptance of the goods.

As amended in 1990.

Part 5 Default

A. In General

§ 2A–501. Default: Procedure.

(1) Whether the lessor or the lessee is in default under a lease contract is determined by the lease agreement and this Article.

(2) If the lessor or the lessee is in default under the lease contract, the party seeking enforcement has rights and remedies as provided in this Article and, except as limited by this Article, as provided in the lease agreement.

(3) If the lessor or the lessee is in default under the lease contract, the party seeking enforcement may reduce the party's claim to judgment, or otherwise enforce the lease contract by self-help or any available judicial procedure or nonjudicial procedure, including administrative proceeding, arbitration, or the like, in accordance with this Article.

(4) Except as otherwise provided in Section 1–106(1) or this Article or the lease agreement, the rights and remedies referred to in subsections (2) and (3) are cumulative.

(5) If the lease agreement covers both real property and goods, the party seeking enforcement may proceed under this Part as to the goods, or under other applicable law as to both the real property and the goods in accordance with that party's rights and remedies in respect of the real property, in which case this Part does not apply.

As amended in 1990.

§ 2A–502. Notice After Default.

Except as otherwise provided in this Article or the lease agreement, the lessor or lessee in default under the lease contract is not entitled to notice of default or notice of enforcement from the other party to the lease agreement.

§ 2A–503. Modification or Impairment of Rights and Remedies.

(1) Except as otherwise provided in this Article, the lease agreement may include rights and remedies for default in addition to or in substitution for those provided in this Article and may limit or alter the measure of damages recoverable under this Article.

(2) Resort to a remedy provided under this Article or in the lease agreement is optional unless the remedy is expressly agreed to be exclusive. If circumstances cause

threaten to decline in value speedily. Instructions are not reasonable if on demand indemnity for expenses is not forthcoming.

(2) If a merchant lessee (subsection (1)) or any other lessee (Section 2A–512) disposes of goods, he [or she] is entitled to reimbursement either from the lessor or the supplier or out of the proceeds for reasonable expenses of caring for and disposing of the goods and, if the expenses include no disposition commission, to such commission as is usual in the trade, or if there is none, to a reasonable sum not exceeding 10 percent of the gross proceeds.

(3) In complying with this section or Section 2A–512, the lessee is held only to good faith. Good faith conduct hereunder is neither acceptance or conversion nor the basis of an action for damages.

(4) A purchaser who purchases in good faith from a lessee pursuant to this section or Section 2A–512 takes the goods free of any rights of the lessor and the supplier even though the lessee fails to comply with one or more of the requirements of this Article.

§ 2A–512. Lessee's Duties as to Rightfully Rejected Goods.

(1) Except as otherwise provided with respect to goods that threaten to decline in value speedily (Section 2A–511) and subject to any security interest of a lessee (Section 2A–508(5)):

(a) the lessee, after rejection of goods in the lessee's possession, shall hold them with reasonable care at the lessor's or the supplier's disposition for a reasonable time after the lessee's seasonable notification of rejection;

(b) if the lessor or the supplier gives no instructions within a reasonable time after notification of rejection, the lessee may store the rejected goods for the lessor's or the supplier's account or ship them to the lessor or the supplier or dispose of them for the lessor's or the supplier's account with reimbursement in the manner provided in Section 2A–511; but

(c) the lessee has no further obligations with regard to goods rightfully rejected.

(2) Action by the lessee pursuant to subsection (1) is not acceptance or conversion.

§ 2A–513. Cure by Lessor of Improper Tender or Delivery; Replacement.

(1) If any tender or delivery by the lessor or the supplier is rejected because nonconforming and the time for performance has not yet expired, the lessor or the supplier may seasonably notify the lessee of the lessor's or the supplier's intention to cure and may then make a conforming delivery within the time provided in the lease contract.

(2) If the lessee rejects a nonconforming tender that the lessor or the supplier had reasonable grounds to believe would be acceptable with or without money allowance, the lessor or the supplier may have a further reasonable time to substitute a conforming tender if he [or she] seasonably notifies the lessee.

§ 2A–514. Waiver of Lessee's Objections.

(1) In rejecting goods, a lessee's failure to state a particular defect that is ascertainable by reasonable inspection precludes the lessee from relying on the defect to justify rejection or to establish default:

(a) if, stated seasonably, the lessor or the supplier could have cured it (Section 2A–513); or

(b) between merchants if the lessor or the supplier after rejection has made a request in writing for a full and final written statement of all defects on which the lessee proposes to rely.

(2) A lessee's failure to reserve rights when paying rent or other consideration against documents precludes recovery of the payment for defects apparent on the face of the documents.

§ 2A–515. Acceptance of Goods.

(1) Acceptance of goods occurs after the lessee has had a reasonable opportunity to inspect the goods and

(a) the lessee signifies or acts with respect to the goods in a manner that signifies to the lessor or the supplier that the goods are conforming or that the lessee will take or retain them in spite of their nonconformity; or

(b) the lessee fails to make an effective rejection of the goods (Section 2A–509(2)).

(2) Acceptance of a part of any commercial unit is acceptance of that entire unit.

§ 2A–516. Effect of Acceptance of Goods; Notice of Default; Burden of Establishing Default after Acceptance; Notice of Claim or Litigation to Person Answerable Over.

(1) A lessee must pay rent for any goods accepted in accordance with the lease contract, with due allowance for goods rightfully rejected or not delivered.

(2) A lessee's acceptance of goods precludes rejection of the goods accepted. In the case of a finance lease, if made with knowledge of a nonconformity, acceptance cannot be revoked because of it. In any other case, if made with knowledge of a nonconformity, acceptance cannot be revoked because of it unless the acceptance was on the reasonable assumption that the nonconformity would be seasonably cured. Acceptance does not of itself impair any other remedy provided by this Article or the lease agreement for nonconformity.

(3) If a tender has been accepted:

(a) within a reasonable time after the lessee discovers or should have discovered any default, the lessee shall notify the lessor and the supplier, if any, or be barred from any remedy against the party notified;

(b) except in the case of a consumer lease, within a reasonable time after the lessee receives notice of litigation for infringement or the like (Section 2A–211) the lessee shall notify the lessor or be barred from any remedy over for liability established by the litigation; and

(c) the burden is on the lessee to establish any default.

(4) If a lessee is sued for breach of a warranty or other obligation for which a lessor or a supplier is answerable over the following apply:

(a) The lessee may give the lessor or the supplier, or both, written notice of the litigation. If the notice states that the person notified may come in and defend and that if the person notified does not do so that person will be bound in any action against that person by the lessee by any determination of fact common to the two litigations, then unless the person notified after seasonable receipt of the notice does come in and defend that person is so bound.

(b) The lessor or the supplier may demand in writing that the lessee turn over control of the litigation including settlement if the claim is one for infringement or the like (Section 2A–211) or else be barred from any remedy over. If the demand states that the lessor or the supplier agrees to bear all expense and to satisfy any adverse judgment, then unless the lessee after seasonable receipt of the demand does turn over control the lessee is so barred.

(5) Subsections (3) and (4) apply to any obligation of a lessee to hold the lessor or the supplier harmless against infringement or the like (Section 2A–211).

As amended in 1990.

§ 2A–517. Revocation of Acceptance of Goods.

(1) A lessee may revoke acceptance of a lot or commercial unit whose nonconformity substantially impairs its value to the lessee if the lessee has accepted it:

(a) except in the case of a finance lease, on the reasonable assumption that its nonconformity would be cured and it has not been seasonably cured; or

(b) without discovery of the nonconformity if the lessee's acceptance was reasonably induced either by the lessor's assurances or, except in the case of a finance lease, by the difficulty of discovery before acceptance.

(2) Except in the case of a finance lease that is not a consumer lease, a lessee may revoke acceptance of a lot or commercial unit if the lessor defaults under the lease contract and the default substantially impairs the value of that lot or commercial unit to the lessee.

(3) If the lease agreement so provides, the lessee may revoke acceptance of a lot or commercial unit because of other defaults by the lessor.

(4) Revocation of acceptance must occur within a reasonable time after the lessee discovers or should have discovered the ground for it and before any substantial change in condition of the goods which is not caused by the nonconformity. Revocation is not effective until the lessee notifies the lessor.

(5) A lessee who so revokes has the same rights and duties with regard to the goods involved as if the lessee had rejected them.

As amended in 1990.

§ 2A–518. Cover; Substitute Goods.

(1) After a default by a lessor under the lease contract of the type described in Section 2A–508(1), or, if agreed, after other default by the lessor, the lessee may cover by making any purchase or lease of or contract to purchase or lease goods in substitution for those due from the lessor.

(2) Except as otherwise provided with respect to damages liquidated in the lease agreement (Section 2A–504) or otherwise determined pursuant to agreement of the parties (Sections 1–102(3) and 2A–503), if a lessee's cover is by lease agreement substantially similar to the original lease agreement and the new lease agreement is made in good faith and in a commercially reasonable manner, the lessee may recover from the lessor as damages (i) the present value, as of the date of the commencement of the term of the new lease agreement, of the rent under the new lease agreement applicable to that period of the new lease term which is comparable to the then remaining term of the original lease agreement minus the present value as of the same date of the total rent for the then remaining lease term of the original lease agreement, and (ii) any incidental or consequential damages, less expenses saved in consequence of the lessor's default.

(3) If a lessee's cover is by lease agreement that for any reason does not qualify for treatment under subsection (2), or is by purchase or otherwise, the lessee may recover from the lessor as if the lessee had elected not to cover and Section 2A–519 governs.

As amended in 1990.

§ 2A–519. Lessee's Damages for Non-Delivery, Repudiation, Default, and Breach of Warranty in Regard to Accepted Goods.

(1) Except as otherwise provided with respect to damages liquidated in the lease agreement (Section 2A–504) or otherwise determined pursuant to agreement of the parties (Sections 1–102(3) and 2A–503), if a lessee elects not to cover or a lessee elects to cover and the cover is by lease agreement that for any reason does not qualify for treatment under Section 2A–518(2), or is by purchase or otherwise, the measure of damages for non-delivery or repudiation by the lessor or for rejection or revocation of acceptance by the lessee is the present value, as of the date of the default, of the then market rent minus the present value as of the same date of the original rent, computed for the remaining lease term of the original lease agreement, together with incidental and consequential damages, less expenses saved in consequence of the lessor's default.

(2) Market rent is to be determined as of the place for tender or, in cases of rejection after arrival or revocation of acceptance, as of the place of arrival.

(3) Except as otherwise agreed, if the lessee has accepted goods and given notification (Section 2A–516(3)), the measure of damages for non-conforming tender or delivery or other default by a lessor is the loss resulting in the ordinary course of events from the lessor's default as determined in any manner that is reasonable together with incidental and consequential damages, less expenses saved in consequence of the lessor's default.

(4) Except as otherwise agreed, the measure of damages for breach of warranty is the present value at the time and place of acceptance of the difference between the value of the use of the goods accepted and the value if they had been as warranted for the lease term, unless special circumstances show proximate damages of a different amount, together with incidental and consequential damages, less expenses saved in consequence of the lessor's default or breach of warranty.

As amended in 1990.

§ 2A–520. Lessee's Incidental and Consequential Damages.

(1) Incidental damages resulting from a lessor's default include expenses reasonably incurred in inspection, receipt, transportation, and care and custody of goods rightfully rejected or goods the acceptance of which is justifiably revoked, any commercially reasonable charges, expenses or commissions in connection with effecting cover, and any other reasonable expense incident to the default.

(2) Consequential damages resulting from a lessor's default include:

(a) any loss resulting from general or particular requirements and needs of which the lessor at the time of contracting had reason to know and which could not reasonably be prevented by cover or otherwise; and

(b) injury to person or property proximately resulting from any breach of warranty.

§ 2A–521. Lessee's Right to Specific Performance or Replevin.

(1) Specific performance may be decreed if the goods are unique or in other proper circumstances.

(2) A decree for specific performance may include any terms and conditions as to payment of the rent, damages, or other relief that the court deems just.

(3) A lessee has a right of replevin, detinue, sequestration, claim and delivery, or the like for goods identified to the lease contract if after reasonable effort the lessee is unable to effect cover for those goods or the circumstances reasonably indicate that the effort will be unavailing.

§ 2A–522. Lessee's Right to Goods on Lessor's Insolvency.

(1) Subject to subsection (2) and even though the goods have not been shipped, a lessee who has paid a part or all of the rent and security for goods identified to a lease contract (Section 2A–217) on making and keeping good a tender of any unpaid portion of the rent and security due under the lease contract may recover the goods identified from the lessor if the lessor becomes insolvent within 10 days after receipt of the first installment of rent and security.

(2) A lessee acquires the right to recover goods identified to a lease contract only if they conform to the lease contract.

C. Default by Lessee

§ 2A–523. Lessor's Remedies.

(1) If a lessee wrongfully rejects or revokes acceptance of goods or fails to make a payment when due or repudiates with respect to a part or the whole, then, with respect to any goods involved, and with respect to all of the goods if under an installment lease contract the value of the whole lease contract is substantially impaired (Section 2A–510), the lessee is in default under the lease contract and the lessor may:

(a) cancel the lease contract (Section 2A–505(1));

(b) proceed respecting goods not identified to the lease contract (Section 2A–524);

(c) withhold delivery of the goods and take possession of goods previously delivered (Section 2A–525);

(d) stop delivery of the goods by any bailee (Section 2A–526);

(e) dispose of the goods and recover damages (Section 2A–527), or retain the goods and recover damages (Section 2A–528), or in a proper case recover rent (Section 2A–529)

(f) exercise any other rights or pursue any other remedies provided in the lease contract.

(2) If a lessor does not fully exercise a right or obtain a remedy to which the lessor is entitled under subsection (1), the lessor may recover the loss resulting in the ordinary course of events from the lessee's default as determined in any reasonable manner, together with incidental damages, less expenses saved in consequence of the lessee's default.

(3) If a lessee is otherwise in default under a lease contract, the lessor may exercise the rights and pursue the remedies provided in the lease contract, which may include a right to cancel the lease. In addition, unless otherwise provided in the lease contract:

(a) if the default substantially impairs the value of the lease contract to the lessor, the lessor may exercise the rights and pursue the remedies provided in subsections (1) or (2); or

(b) if the default does not substantially impair the value of the lease contract to the lessor, the lessor may recover as provided in subsection (2).

As amended in 1990.

§ 2A–524. Lessor's Right to Identify Goods to Lease Contract.

(1) After default by the lessee under the lease contract of the type described in Section 2A–523(1) or 2A–523(3)(a) or, if agreed, after other default by the lessee, the lessor may:

(a) identify to the lease contract conforming goods not already identified if at the time the lessor learned of the default they were in the lessor's or the supplier's possession or control; and

(b) dispose of goods (Section 2A–527(1)) that demonstrably have been intended for the particular lease contract even though those goods are unfinished.

(2) If the goods are unfinished, in the exercise of reasonable commercial judgment for the purposes of avoiding loss and of effective realization, an aggrieved lessor or the supplier may either complete manufacture and wholly identify the goods to the lease contract or cease manufacture and lease, sell, or otherwise dispose of the goods for scrap or salvage value or proceed in any other reasonable manner.

As amended in 1990.

§ 2A–525. Lessor's Right to Possession of Goods.

(1) If a lessor discovers the lessee to be insolvent, the lessor may refuse to deliver the goods.

(2) After a default by the lessee under the lease contract of the type described in Section 2A–523(1) or 2A–523(3)(a) or, if agreed, after other default by the lessee, the lessor has the right to take possession of the goods. If the lease contract so provides, the lessor may require the lessee to assemble the goods and make them available to the lessor at a place to be designated by the lessor which is reasonably convenient to both parties. Without removal, the lessor may render unusable any goods employed in trade or business, and may dispose of goods on the lessee's premises (Section 2A–527).

(3) The lessor may proceed under subsection (2) without judicial process if that can be done without breach of the peace or the lessor may proceed by action.

As amended in 1990.

§ 2A–526. Lessor's Stoppage of Delivery in Transit or Otherwise.

(1) A lessor may stop delivery of goods in the possession of a carrier or other bailee if the lessor discovers the lessee to be insolvent and may stop delivery of carload, truckload, planeload, or larger shipments of express or freight if the lessee repudiates or fails to make a payment due before delivery, whether for rent, security or otherwise under the lease contract, or for any other reason the lessor has a right to withhold or take possession of the goods.

(2) In pursuing its remedies under subsection (1), the lessor may stop delivery until

(a) receipt of the goods by the lessee;

(b) acknowledgment to the lessee by any bailee of the goods, except a carrier, that the bailee holds the goods for the lessee; or

(c) such an acknowledgment to the lessee by a carrier via reshipment or as warehouseman.

(3) (a) To stop delivery, a lessor shall so notify as to enable the bailee by reasonable diligence to prevent delivery of the goods.

(b) After notification, the bailee shall hold and deliver the goods according to the directions of the lessor, but the lessor is liable to the bailee for any ensuing charges or damages.

(c) A carrier who has issued a nonnegotiable bill of lading is not obliged to obey a notification to stop received from a person other than the consignor.

§ 2A–527. Lessor's Rights to Dispose of Goods.

(1) After a default by a lessee under the lease contract of the type described in Section 2A–523(1) or 2A–523(3)(a) or after the lessor refuses to deliver or takes possession of goods (Section 2A–525 or 2A–526), or, if agreed, after other default by a lessee, the lessor may dispose of the goods concerned or the undelivered balance thereof by lease, sale, or otherwise.

(2) Except as otherwise provided with respect to damages liquidated in the lease agreement (Section 2A–504) or otherwise determined pursuant to agreement of the parties (Sections 1–102(3) and 2A–503), if the disposition is by lease agreement substantially similar to the original lease agreement and the new lease agreement is made in good faith and in a commercially reasonable manner, the lessor may recover from the lessee as damages (i) accrued and unpaid rent as of the date of the commencement of the term of the new lease agreement, (ii) the present value, as of the same date, of the total rent for the then remaining lease term of the original lease agreement minus the present value, as of the same date, of the rent under the new lease agreement applicable to that period of the new lease term which is comparable to the then remaining term of the original lease agreement, and (iii) any incidental damages allowed under Section 2A–530, less expenses saved in consequence of the lessee's default.

(3) If the lessor's disposition is by lease agreement that for any reason does not qualify for treatment under subsection (2), or is by sale or otherwise, the lessor may recover from the lessee as if the lessor had elected not to dispose of the goods and Section 2A–528 governs.

(4) A subsequent buyer or lessee who buys or leases from the lessor in good faith for value as a result of a disposition under this section takes the goods free of the original lease contract and any rights of the original lessee even though the lessor fails to comply with one or more of the requirements of this Article.

(5) The lessor is not accountable to the lessee for any profit made on any disposition. A lessee who has rightfully rejected or justifiably revoked acceptance shall account to the lessor for any excess over the amount of the lessee's security interest (Section 2A–508(5)).

As amended in 1990.

§ 2A–528. Lessor's Damages for Non-acceptance, Failure to Pay, Repudiation, or Other Default.

(1) Except as otherwise provided with respect to damages liquidated in the lease agreement (Section 2A–504) or otherwise determined pursuant to agreement of the parties (Section 1–102(3) and 2A–503), if a lessor elects to retain the goods or a lessor elects to dispose of the goods and the disposition is by lease agreement that for any reason does not qualify for treatment under Section 2A–527(2), or is by sale or otherwise, the lessor may recover from the lessee as damages for a default of the type described in Section 2A–523(1) or 2A–523(3)(a), or if agreed, for other default of the lessee, (i) accrued and unpaid rent as of the date of the default if the lessee has never taken possession of the goods, or, if the lessee has taken possession of the goods, as of the date the lessor repossesses the goods or an earlier date on which the lessee makes a tender of the goods to the lessor, (ii) the present value as of the date determined under clause (i) of the total rent for the then remaining lease term of the original lease agreement minus the present value as of the same date of the market rent as the place where the goods are located computed for the same lease term, and (iii) any incidental damages allowed under Section 2A–530, less expenses saved in consequence of the lessee's default.

(2) If the measure of damages provided in subsection (1) is inadequate to put a lessor in as good a position as performance would have, the measure of damages is the present value of the profit, including reasonable overhead, the lessor would have made from full performance by the lessee, together with any incidental damages allowed under Section 2A–530, due allowance for costs reasonably incurred and due credit for payments or proceeds of disposition.

As amended in 1990.

§ 2A–529. Lessor's Action for the Rent.

(1) After default by the lessee under the lease contract of the type described in Section 2A–523(1) or 2A–523(3)(a) or, if agreed, after other default by the lessee, if the lessor complies with subsection (2), the lessor may recover from the lessee as damages:

(a) for goods accepted by the lessee and not repossessed by or tendered to the lessor, and for conforming goods lost or damaged within a commercially reasonable time after risk of loss passes to the lessee (Section 2A–219), (i) accrued and unpaid rent as of the date of entry of judgment in favor of the lessor (ii) the present value as of the same date of the rent for the then remaining lease term of the lease agreement, and (iii) any incidental damages allowed under Section 2A–530, less expenses saved in consequence of the lessee's default; and

(b) for goods identified to the lease contract if the lessor is unable after reasonable effort to dispose of them at a reasonable price or the circumstances reasonably indicate that effort will be unavailing, (i) accrued and unpaid rent as of the date of entry of judgment in favor of the lessor, (ii) the present value as of the same date of the rent for the then remaining lease term of the lease agreement, and (iii) any incidental damages allowed under Section 2A–530, less expenses saved in consequence of the lessee's default.

(2) Except as provided in subsection (3), the lessor shall hold for the lessee for the remaining lease term of the lease agreement any goods that have been identified to the lease contract and are in the lessor's control.

(3) The lessor may dispose of the goods at any time before collection of the judgment for damages obtained pursuant to subsection (1). If the disposition is before the end of the remaining lease term of the lease agreement, the lessor's recovery against the lessee for damages is governed by Section 2A–527 or Section 2A–528, and the lessor will cause an appropriate credit to be provided against a judgment for damages to the extent that the amount of the judgment exceeds the recovery available pursuant to Section 2A–527 or 2A–528.

(4) Payment of the judgment for damages obtained pursuant to subsection (1) entitles the lessee to the use and possession of the goods not then disposed of for the remaining lease term of and in accordance with the lease agreement.

(5) After default by the lessee under the lease contract of the type described in Section 2A–523(1) or Section 2A–523(3)(a) or, if agreed, after other default by the lessee, a lessor who is held not entitled to rent under this section must nevertheless be awarded damages for non-acceptance under Sections 2A–527 and 2A–528.

As amended in 1990.

§ 2A–530. Lessor's Incidental Damages.

Incidental damages to an aggrieved lessor include any commercially reasonable charges, expenses, or commissions incurred in stopping delivery, in the transportation, care and custody of goods after the lessee's default, in connection with return or disposition of the goods, or otherwise resulting from the default.

§ 2A–531. Standing to Sue Third Parties for Injury to Goods.

(1) If a third party so deals with goods that have been identified to a lease contract as to cause actionable injury to a party to the lease contract (a) the lessor has a right of action against the third party, and (b) the lessee also has a right of action against the third party if the lessee:

(i) has a security interest in the goods;

(ii) has an insurable interest in the goods; or

(iii) bears the risk of loss under the lease contract or has since the injury assumed that risk as against the lessor and the goods have been converted or destroyed.

(2) If at the time of the injury the party plaintiff did not bear the risk of loss as against the other party to the lease contract and there is no arrangement between them for disposition of the recovery, his [or her] suit or settlement, subject to his [or her] own interest, is as a fiduciary for the other party to the lease contract.

(3) Either party with the consent of the other may sue for the benefit of whom it may concern.

§ 2A–532. Lessor's Rights to Residual Interest.

In addition to any other recovery permitted by this Article or other law, the lessor may recover from the lessee an amount that will fully compensate the lessor for any loss of or damage to the lessor's residual interest in the goods caused by the default of the lessee.

As added in 1990.

SECTION 303. Statement of Partnership Authority.

(a) A partnership may file a statement of partnership authority, which:

(1) must include:

(i) the name of the partnership;

(ii) the street address of its chief executive office and of one office in this State, if there is one;

(iii) the names and mailing addresses of all of the partners or of an agent appointed and maintained by the partnership for the purpose of subsection (b); and

(iv) the names of the partners authorized to execute an instrument transferring real property held in the name of the partnership; and

(2) may state the authority, or limitations on the authority, of some or all of the partners to enter into other transactions on behalf of the partnership and any other matter.

* * * *

(d) Except as otherwise provided in subsection (g), a filed statement of partnership authority supplements the authority of a partner to enter into transactions on behalf of the partnership as follows:

(1) Except for transfers of real property, a grant of authority contained in a filed statement of partnership authority is conclusive in favor of a person who gives value without knowledge to the contrary, so long as and to the extent that a limitation on that authority is not then contained in another filed statement. A filed cancellation of a limitation on authority revives the previous grant of authority.

(2) A grant of authority to transfer real property held in the name of the partnership contained in a certified copy of a filed statement of partnership authority recorded in the office for recording transfers of that real property is conclusive in favor of a person who gives value without knowledge to the contrary, so long as and to the extent that a certified copy of a filed statement containing a limitation on that authority is not then of record in the office for recording transfers of that real property. The recording in the office for recording transfers of that real property of a certified copy of a filed cancellation of a limitation on authority revives the previous grant of authority.

(e) A person not a partner is deemed to know of a limitation on the authority of a partner to transfer real property held in the name of the partnership if a certified copy of the filed statement containing the limitation on authority is of record in the office for recording transfers of that real property.

(f) Except as otherwise provided in subsections (d) and (e) and Sections 704 and 805, a person not a partner is not deemed to know of a limitation on the authority of a partner merely because the limitation is contained in a filed statement.

* * * *

SECTION 305. Partnership Liable for Partner's Actionable Conduct.

(a) A partnership is liable for loss or injury caused to a person, or for a penalty incurred, as a result of a wrongful act or omission, or other actionable conduct, of a partner acting in the ordinary course of business of the partnership or with authority of the partnership.

(b) If, in the course of the partnership's business or while acting with authority of the partnership, a partner receives or causes the partnership to receive money or property of a person not a partner, and the money or property is misapplied by a partner, the partnership is liable for the loss.

SECTION 306. Partner's Liability.

(a) Except as otherwise provided in subsections (b) and (c), all partners are liable jointly and severally for all obligations of the partnership unless otherwise agreed by the claimant or provided by law.

(b) A person admitted as a partner into an existing partnership is not personally liable for any partnership obligation incurred before the person's admission as a partner.

(c) An obligation of a partnership incurred while the partnership is a limited liability partnership, whether arising in contract, tort, or otherwise, is solely the obligation of the partnership. A partner is not personally liable, directly or indirectly, by way of contribution or otherwise, for such an obligation solely by reason of being or so acting as a partner. This subsection applies notwithstanding anything inconsistent in the partnership agreement that existed immediately before the vote required to become a limited liability partnership under Section 1001(b).

SECTION 307. Actions by and Against Partnership and Partners.

(a) A partnership may sue and be sued in the name of the partnership.

* * * *

(d) A judgment creditor of a partner may not levy execution against the assets of the partner to satisfy a judgment based on a claim against the partnership unless the partner is personally liable for the claim under Section 306 and:

(1) a judgment based on the same claim has been obtained against the partnership and a writ of execution on the judgment has been returned unsatisfied in whole or in part;

(2) the partnership is a debtor in bankruptcy;

(3) the partner has agreed that the creditor need not exhaust partnership assets;

(4) a court grants permission to the judgment creditor to levy execution against the assets of a partner based on a finding that partnership assets subject to

execution are clearly insufficient to satisfy the judgment, that exhaustion of partnership assets is excessively burdensome, or that the grant of permission is an appropriate exercise of the court's equitable powers; or

(5) liability is imposed on the partner by law or contract independent of the existence of the partnership.

(e) This section applies to any partnership liability or obligation resulting from a representation by a partner or purported partner under Section 308.

SECTION 308. Liability of Purported Partner.

(a) If a person, by words or conduct, purports to be a partner, or consents to being represented by another as a partner, in a partnership or with one or more persons not partners, the purported partner is liable to a person to whom the representation is made, if that person, relying on the representation, enters into a transaction with the actual or purported partnership. If the representation, either by the purported partner or by a person with the purported partner's consent, is made in a public manner, the purported partner is liable to a person who relies upon the purported partnership even if the purported partner is not aware of being held out as a partner to the claimant. If partnership liability results, the purported partner is liable with respect to that liability as if the purported partner were a partner. If no partnership liability results, the purported partner is liable with respect to that liability jointly and severally with any other person consenting to the representation.

(b) If a person is thus represented to be a partner in an existing partnership, or with one or more persons not partners, the purported partner is an agent of persons consenting to the representation to bind them to the same extent and in the same manner as if the purported partner were a partner, with respect to persons who enter into transactions in reliance upon the representation. If all of the partners of the existing partnership consent to the representation, a partnership act or obligation results. If fewer than all of the partners of the existing partnership consent to the representation, the person acting and the partners consenting to the representation are jointly and severally liable.

* * * *

Article 4
RELATIONS OF PARTNERS TO EACH OTHER AND TO PARTNERSHIP

SECTION 401. Partner's Rights and Duties.

* * * *

(b) Each partner is entitled to an equal share of the partnership profits and is chargeable with a share of the partnership losses in proportion to the partner's share of the profits.

* * * *

(f) Each partner has equal rights in the management and conduct of the partnership business.

(g) A partner may use or possess partnership property only on behalf of the partnership.

(h) A partner is not entitled to remuneration for services performed for the partnership, except for reasonable compensation for services rendered in winding up the business of the partnership.

(i) A person may become a partner only with the consent of all of the partners.

(j) A difference arising as to a matter in the ordinary course of business of a partnership may be decided by a majority of the partners. An act outside the ordinary course of business of a partnership and an amendment to the partnership agreement may be undertaken only with the consent of all of the partners.

* * * *

SECTION 403. Partner's Rights and Duties with Respect to Information.

(a) A partnership shall keep its books and records, if any, at its chief executive office.

(b) A partnership shall provide partners and their agents and attorneys access to its books and records. It shall provide former partners and their agents and attorneys access to books and records pertaining to the period during which they were partners. The right of access provides the opportunity to inspect and copy books and records during ordinary business hours. A partnership may impose a reasonable charge, covering the costs of labor and material, for copies of documents furnished.

* * * *

SECTION 404. General Standards of Partner's Conduct.

(a) The only fiduciary duties a partner owes to the partnership and the other partners are the duty of loyalty and the duty of care set forth in subsections (b) and (c).

(b) A partner's duty of loyalty to the partnership and the other partners is limited to the following:

(1) to account to the partnership and hold as trustee for it any property, profit, or benefit derived by the partner in the conduct and winding up of the partnership business or derived from a use by the partner of partnership property, including the appropriation of a partnership opportunity;

(2) to refrain from dealing with the partnership in the conduct or winding up of the partnership business as or on behalf of a party having an interest adverse to the partnership; and

(3) to refrain from competing with the partnership in the conduct of the partnership business before the dissolution of the partnership.

(c) A partner's duty of care to the partnership and the other partners in the conduct and winding up of the partnership business is limited to refraining from engaging in grossly negligent or reckless conduct, intentional misconduct, or a knowing violation of law.

(d) A partner shall discharge the duties to the partnership and the other partners under this [Act] or under the partnership agreement and exercise any rights consistently with the obligation of good faith and fair dealing.

(e) A partner does not violate a duty or obligation under this [Act] or under the partnership agreement merely because the partner's conduct furthers the partner's own interest.

* * * *

SECTION 405. Actions by Partnership and Partners.

(a) A partnership may maintain an action against a partner for a breach of the partnership agreement, or for the violation of a duty to the partnership, causing harm to the partnership.

(b) A partner may maintain an action against the partnership or another partner for legal or equitable relief, with or without an accounting as to partnership business, to:

(1) enforce the partner's rights under the partnership agreement;

(2) enforce the partner's rights under this [Act], including:

(i) the partner's rights under Sections 401, 403, or 404;

(ii) the partner's right on dissociation to have the partner's interest in the partnership purchased pursuant to Section 701 or enforce any other right under [Article] 6 or 7; or

(iii) the partner's right to compel a dissolution and winding up of the partnership business under or enforce any other right under [Article] 8; or

(3) enforce the rights and otherwise protect the interests of the partner, including rights and interests arising independently of the partnership relationship.

* * * *

Article 5
TRANSFEREES AND CREDITORS OF PARTNER

SECTION 501. Partner Not Co-Owner of Partnership Property.

A partner is not a co-owner of partnership property and has no interest in partnership property which can be transferred, either voluntarily or involuntarily.

SECTION 502. Partner's Transferable Interest in Partnership.

The only transferable interest of a partner in the partnership is the partner's share of the profits and losses of the partnership and the partner's right to receive distributions. The interest is personal property.

SECTION 503. Transfer of Partner's Transferable Interest.

(a) A transfer, in whole or in part, of a partner's transferable interest in the partnership:

(1) is permissible;

(2) does not by itself cause the partner's dissociation or a dissolution and winding up of the partnership business; and

(3) does not, as against the other partners or the partnership, entitle the transferee, during the continuance of the partnership, to participate in the management or conduct of the partnership business, to require access to information concerning partnership transactions, or to inspect or copy the partnership books or records.

* * * *

SECTION 504. Partner's Transferable Interest Subject to Charging Order.

(a) On application by a judgment creditor of a partner or of a partner's transferee, a court having jurisdiction may charge the transferable interest of the judgment debtor to satisfy the judgment. The court may appoint a receiver of the share of the distributions due or to become due to the judgment debtor in respect of the partnership and make all other orders, directions, accounts, and inquiries the judgment debtor might have made or which the circumstances of the case may require.

* * * *

Article 6
PARTNER'S DISSOCIATION

SECTION 601. Events Causing Partner's Dissociation.

A partner is dissociated from a partnership upon the occurrence of any of the following events:

(1) the partnership's having notice of the partner's express will to withdraw as a partner or on a later date specified by the partner;

(2) an event agreed to in the partnership agreement as causing the partner's dissociation;

(3) the partner's expulsion pursuant to the partnership agreement;

(4) the partner's expulsion by the unanimous vote of the other partners if:

(i) it is unlawful to carry on the partnership business with that partner;

(ii) there has been a transfer of all or substantially all of that partner's transferable interest in the partnership, other than a transfer for security purposes, or a court order charging the partner's interest, which has not been foreclosed;

(iii) within 90 days after the partnership notifies a corporate partner that it will be expelled because it has filed a certificate of dissolution or the equivalent, its charter has been revoked, or its right to conduct business has been suspended by the jurisdiction of its incorporation, there is no revocation of the certificate of dissolution or no reinstatement of its charter or its right to conduct business; or

(iv) a partnership that is a partner has been dissolved and its business is being wound up;

(5) on application by the partnership or another partner, the partner's expulsion by judicial determination because:

(i) the partner engaged in wrongful conduct that adversely and materially affected the partnership business;

(ii) the partner willfully or persistently committed a material breach of the partnership agreement or of a duty owed to the partnership or the other partners under Section 404; or

(iii) the partner engaged in conduct relating to the partnership business which makes it not reasonably practicable to carry on the business in partnership with the partner;

(6) the partner's:

(i) becoming a debtor in bankruptcy;

(ii) executing an assignment for the benefit of creditors;

(iii) seeking, consenting to, or acquiescing in the appointment of a trustee, receiver, or liquidator of that partner or of all or substantially all of that partner's property; or

(iv) failing, within 90 days after the appointment, to have vacated or stayed the appointment of a trustee, receiver, or liquidator of the partner or of all or substantially all of the partner's property obtained without the partner's consent or acquiescence, or failing within 90 days after the expiration of a stay to have the appointment vacated;

(7) in the case of a partner who is an individual:

(i) the partner's death;

(ii) the appointment of a guardian or general conservator for the partner; or

(iii) a judicial determination that the partner has otherwise become incapable of performing the partner's duties under the partnership agreement;

* * * *

SECTION 602. Partner's Power to Dissociate; Wrongful Dissociation.

(a) A partner has the power to dissociate at any time, rightfully or wrongfully, by express will pursuant to Section 601(1).

(b) A partner's dissociation is wrongful only if:

(1) it is in breach of an express provision of the partnership agreement; or

(2) in the case of a partnership for a definite term or particular undertaking, before the expiration of the term or the completion of the undertaking:

(i) the partner withdraws by express will, unless the withdrawal follows within 90 days after another partner's dissociation by death or otherwise under Section 601(6) through (10) or wrongful dissociation under this subsection;

(ii) the partner is expelled by judicial determination under Section 601(5);

(iii) the partner is dissociated by becoming a debtor in bankruptcy; or

(iv) in the case of a partner who is not an individual, trust other than a business trust, or estate, the partner is expelled or otherwise dissociated because it willfully dissolved or terminated.

(c) A partner who wrongfully dissociates is liable to the partnership and to the other partners for damages caused by the dissociation. The liability is in addition to any other obligation of the partner to the partnership or to the other partners.

SECTION 603. Effect of Partner's Dissociation.

(a) If a partner's dissociation results in a dissolution and winding up of the partnership business, [Article] 8 applies; otherwise, [Article] 7 applies.

(b) Upon a partner's dissociation:

(1) the partner's right to participate in the management and conduct of the partnership business terminates, except as otherwise provided in Section 803;

(2) the partner's duty of loyalty under Section 404(b)(3) terminates; and

(3) the partner's duty of loyalty under Section 404(b)(1) and (2) and duty of care under Section 404(c) continue only with regard to matters arising and events occurring before the partner's dissociation, unless the partner participates in winding up the partnership's business pursuant to Section 803.

Article 7

PARTNER'S DISSOCIATION WHEN BUSINESS NOT WOUND UP

SECTION 701. Purchase of Dissociated Partner's Interest.

(a) If a partner is dissociated from a partnership without resulting in a dissolution and winding up of the partnership business under Section 801, the partnership shall cause the dissociated partner's interest in the partnership to be purchased for a buyout price determined pursuant to subsection (b).

(b) The buyout price of a dissociated partner's interest is the amount that would have been distributable to the dissociating partner under Section 807(b) if, on the date of dissociation, the assets of the partnership were sold at a price equal to the greater of the liquidation value or the value based on a sale of the entire business as a going concern without the dissociated partner and the partnership were wound up as of that date. Interest must be paid from the date of dissociation to the date of payment.

(c) Damages for wrongful dissociation under Section 602(b), and all other amounts owing, whether or not presently due, from the dissociated partner to the partnership, must be offset against the buyout price. Interest must be paid from the date the amount owed becomes due to the date of payment.

* * * *

SECTION 702. Dissociated Partner's Power to Bind and Liability to Partnership.

(a) For two years after a partner dissociates without resulting in a dissolution and winding up of the partnership business, the partnership, including a surviving partnership under [Article] 9, is bound by an act of the dissociated partner which would have bound the partnership under Section 301 before dissociation only if at the time of entering into the transaction the other party:

(1) reasonably believed that the dissociated partner was then a partner;

(2) did not have notice of the partner's dissociation; and

(3) is not deemed to have had knowledge under Section 303(e) or notice under Section 704(c).

(b) A dissociated partner is liable to the partnership for any damage caused to the partnership arising from an obligation incurred by the dissociated partner after dissociation for which the partnership is liable under subsection (a).

SECTION 703. Dissociated Partner's Liability to Other Persons.

(a) A partner's dissociation does not of itself discharge the partner's liability for a partnership obligation incurred before dissociation. A dissociated partner is not liable for a partnership obligation incurred after dissociation, except as otherwise provided in subsection (b).

(b) A partner who dissociates without resulting in a dissolution and winding up of the partnership business is liable as a partner to the other party in a transaction entered into by the partnership, or a surviving partnership under [Article] 9, within two years after the partner's dissociation, only if the partner is liable for the obligation under Section 306 and at the time of entering into the transaction the other party:

(1) reasonably believed that the dissociated partner was then a partner;

(2) did not have notice of the partner's dissociation; and

(3) is not deemed to have had knowledge under Section 303(e) or notice under Section 704(c).

* * * *

SECTION 704. Statement of Dissociation.

(a) A dissociated partner or the partnership may file a statement of dissociation stating the name of the partnership and that the partner is dissociated from the partnership.

(b) A statement of dissociation is a limitation on the authority of a dissociated partner for the purposes of Section 303(d) and (e).

(c) For the purposes of Sections 702(a)(3) and 703(b)(3), a person not a partner is deemed to have notice of the dissociation 90 days after the statement of dissociation is filed.

* * * *

Article 8

WINDING UP PARTNERSHIP BUSINESS

SECTION 801. Events Causing Dissolution and Winding Up of Partnership Business.

A partnership is dissolved, and its business must be wound up, only upon the occurrence of any of the following events:

(1) in a partnership at will, the partnership's having notice from a partner, other than a partner who is dissociated under Section 601(2) through (10), of that partner's express will to withdraw as a partner, or on a later date specified by the partner;

(2) in a partnership for a definite term or particular undertaking:

(i) within 90 days after a partner's dissociation by death or otherwise under Section 601(6) through (10) or wrongful dissociation under Section 602(b), the express will of at least half of the remaining partners to wind up the partnership business, for which purpose a partner's rightful dissociation pursuant to Section 602(b)(2)(i) constitutes the expression of that partner's will to wind up the partnership business;

(ii) the express will of all of the partners to wind up the partnership business; or

(iii) the expiration of the term or the completion of the undertaking;

(3) an event agreed to in the partnership agreement resulting in the winding up of the partnership business;

(4) an event that makes it unlawful for all or substantially all of the business of the partnership to be continued, but a cure of illegality within 90 days after notice to the partnership of the event is effective retroactively to the date of the event for purposes of this section;

(5) on application by a partner, a judicial determination that:

(i) the economic purpose of the partnership is likely to be unreasonably frustrated;

(ii) another partner has engaged in conduct relating to the partnership business which makes it not reasonably practicable to carry on the business in partnership with that partner; or

(iii) it is not otherwise reasonably practicable to carry on the partnership business in conformity with the partnership agreement; or

* * * *

SECTION 802. Partnership Continues after Dissolution.

(a) Subject to subsection (b), a partnership continues after dissolution only for the purpose of winding up its business. The partnership is terminated when the winding up of its business is completed.

(b) At any time after the dissolution of a partnership and before the winding up of its business is completed, all of the partners, including any dissociating partner other than a wrongfully dissociating partner, may waive the right to have the partnership's business wound up and the partnership terminated. In that event:

(1) the partnership resumes carrying on its business as if dissolution had never occurred, and any liability incurred by the partnership or a partner after the dissolution and before the waiver is determined as if dissolution had never occurred; and

(2) the rights of a third party accruing under Section 804(1) or arising out of conduct in reliance on the dissolution before the third party knew or received a notification of the waiver may not be adversely affected.

SECTION 803. Right to Wind Up Partnership.

(a) After dissolution, a partner who has not wrongfully dissociated may participate in winding up the partnership's business, but on application of any partner, partner's legal representative, or transferee, the [designate the appropriate court], for good cause shown, may order judicial supervision of the winding up.

(b) The legal representative of the last surviving partner may wind up a partnership's business.

(c) A person winding up a partnership's business may preserve the partnership business or property as a going concern for a reasonable time, prosecute and defend actions and proceedings, whether civil, criminal, or administrative, settle and close the partnership's business, dispose of and transfer the partnership's property, discharge the partnership's liabilities, distribute the assets of the partnership pursuant to Section 807, settle disputes by mediation or arbitration, and perform other necessary acts.

SECTION 804. Partner's Power to Bind Partnership After Dissolution.

Subject to Section 805, a partnership is bound by a partner's act after dissolution that:

(1) is appropriate for winding up the partnership business; or

(2) would have bound the partnership under Section 301 before dissolution, if the other party to the transaction did not have notice of the dissolution.

SECTION 805. Statement of Dissolution.

(a) After dissolution, a partner who has not wrongfully dissociated may file a statement of dissolution stating the name of the partnership and that the partnership has dissolved and is winding up its business.

(b) A statement of dissolution cancels a filed statement of partnership authority for the purposes of Section 303(d) and is a limitation on authority for the purposes of Section 303(e).

(c) For the purposes of Sections 301 and 804, a person not a partner is deemed to have notice of the dissolution and the limitation on the partners' authority as a result of the statement of dissolution 90 days after it is filed.

* * * *

SECTION 807. Settlement of Accounts and Contributions among Partners.

(a) In winding up a partnership's business, the assets of the partnership, including the contributions of the partners required by this section, must be applied to discharge its obligations to creditors, including, to the extent permitted by law, partners who are creditors. Any surplus must be applied to pay in cash the net amount distributable to partners in accordance with their right to distributions under subsection (b).

(b) Each partner is entitled to a settlement of all partnership accounts upon winding up the partnership business. In settling accounts among the partners, profits and losses that result from the liquidation of the partnership assets must be credited and charged to the partners' accounts. The partnership shall make a distribution to a partner in an amount equal to any excess of the credits

and the liability of its limited partners, and (ii) a foreign limited partnership may not be denied registration by reason of any difference between those laws and the laws of this State.

Section 902. Registration.

Before transacting business in this State, a foreign limited partnership shall register with the Secretary of State. In order to register, a foreign limited partnership shall submit to the Secretary of State, in duplicate, an application for registration as a foreign limited partnership, signed and sworn to by a general partner and setting forth:

(1) the name of the foreign limited partnership and, if different, the name under which it proposes to register and transact business in this State;

(2) the State and date of its formation;

(3) the name and address of any agent for service of process on the foreign limited partnership whom the foreign limited partnership elects to appoint; the agent must be an individual resident of this State, a domestic corporation, or a foreign corporation having a place of business in, and authorized to do business in, this State;

(4) a statement that the Secretary of State is appointed the agent of the foreign limited partnership for service of process if no agent has been appointed under paragraph (3) or, if appointed, the agent's authority has been revoked or if the agent cannot be found or served with the exercise of reasonable diligence;

(5) the address of the office required to be maintained in the state of its organization by the laws of that state or, if not so required, of the principal office of the foreign limited partnership;

(6) the name and business address of each general partner; and

(7) the address of the office at which is kept a list of the names and addresses of the limited partners and their capital contributions, together with an undertaking by the foreign limited partnership to keep those records until the foreign limited partnership's registration in this State is cancelled or withdrawn.

Section 903. Issuance of Registration.

(a) If the Secretary of State finds that an application for registration conforms to law and all requisite fees have been paid, he [or she] shall:

> (1) endorse on the application the word "Filed", and the month, day, and year of the filing thereof;
>
> (2) file in his [or her] office a duplicate original of the application; and
>
> (3) issue a certificate of registration to transact business in this State.

(b) The certificate of registration, together with a duplicate original of the application, shall be returned to the person who filed the application or his [or her] representative.

Section 904. Name.

A foreign limited partnership may register with the Secretary of State under any name, whether or not it is the name under which it is registered in its state of organization, that includes without abbreviation the words "limited partnership" and that could be registered by a domestic limited partnership.

Section 905. Changes and Amendments.

If any statement in the application for registration of a foreign limited partnership was false when made or any arrangements or other facts described have changed, making the application inaccurate in any respect, the foreign limited partnership shall promptly file in the office of the Secretary of State a certificate, signed and sworn to by a general partner, correcting such statement.

Section 906. Cancellation of Registration.

A foreign limited partnership may cancel its registration by filing with the Secretary of State a certificate of cancellation signed and sworn to by a general partner. A cancellation does not terminate the authority of the Secretary of State to accept service of process on the foreign limited partnership with respect to [claims for relief] [causes of action] arising out of the transactions of business in this State.

Section 907. Transaction of Business Without Registration.

(a) A foreign limited partnership transacting business in this State may not maintain any action, suit, or proceeding in any court of this State until it has registered in this State.

(b) The failure of a foreign limited partnership to register in this State does not impair the validity of any contract or act of the foreign limited partnership or prevent the foreign limited partnership from defending any action, suit, or proceeding in any court of this State.

(c) A limited partner of a foreign limited partnership is not liable as a general partner of the foreign limited partnership solely by reason of having transacted business in this State without registration.

(d) A foreign limited partnership, by transacting business in this State without registration, appoints the Secretary of State as its agent for service of process with respect to [claims for relief] [causes of action] arising out of the transaction of business in this State.

Section 908. Action by [Appropriate Official].

The [designate the appropriate official] may bring an action to restrain a foreign limited partnership from transacting business in this State in violation of this Article.

Article 10
DERIVATIVE ACTIONS

Section 1001. Right of Action.

A limited partner may bring an action in the right of a limited partnership to recover a judgment in its favor if general partners with authority to do so have refused to bring the action or if an effort to cause those general partners to bring the action is not likely to succeed.

Section 1002. Proper Plaintiff.

In a derivative action, the plaintiff must be a partner at the time of bringing the action and (i) must have been a partner at the time of the transaction of which he [or she] complains or (ii) his [or her] status as a partner must have devolved upon him by operation of law or pursuant to the terms of the partnership agreement from a person who was a partner at the time of the transaction.

Section 1003. Pleading.

In a derivative action, the complaint shall set forth with particularity the effort of the plaintiff to secure initiation of the action by a general partner or the reasons for not making the effort.

Section 1004. Expenses.

If a derivative action is successful, in whole or in part, or if anything is received by the plaintiff as a result of a judgment, compromise, or settlement of an action or claim, the court may award the plaintiff reasonable expenses, including reasonable attorney's fees, and shall direct him [or her] to remit to the limited partnership the remainder of those proceeds received by him [or her].

Article 11
MISCELLANEOUS

Section 1101. Construction and Application.

This [Act] shall be so applied and construed to effectuate its general purpose to make uniform the law with respect to the subject of this [Act] among states enacting it.

Section 1102. Short Title.

This [Act] may be cited as the Uniform Limited Partnership Act.

Section 1103. Severability.

If any provision of this [Act] or its application to any person or circumstance is held invalid, the invalidity does not affect other provisions or applications of the [Act] which can be given effect without the invalid provision or application, and to this end the provisions of this [Act] are severable.

Section 1104. Effective Date, Extended Effective Date, and Repeal.

Except as set forth below, the effective date of this [Act] is ______ and the following acts [list existing limited partnership acts] are hereby repealed:

(1) The existing provisions for execution and filing of certificates of limited partnerships and amendments thereunder and cancellations thereof continue in effect until [specify time required to create central filing system], the extended effective date, and Sections 102, 103, 104, 105, 201, 202, 203, 204 and 206 are not effective until the extended effective date.

(2) Section 402, specifying the conditions under which a general partner ceases to be a member of a limited partnership, is not effective until the extended effective date, and the applicable provisions of existing law continue to govern until the extended effective date.

(3) Sections 501, 502 and 608 apply only to contributions and distributions made after the effective date of this [Act].

(4) Section 704 applies only to assignments made after the effective date of this [Act].

(5) Article 9, dealing with registration of foreign limited partnerships, is not effective until the extended effective date.

(6) Unless otherwise agreed by the partners, the applicable provisions of existing law governing allocation of profits and losses (rather than the provisions of Section 503), distributions to a withdrawing partner (rather than the provisions of Section 604), and distributions of assets upon the winding up of a limited partnership (rather than the provisions of Section 804) govern limited partnerships formed before the effective date of this [Act].

Section 1105. Rules for Cases Not Provided For in This [Act].

In any case not provided for in this [Act] the provisions of the Uniform Partnership Act govern.

Section 1106. Savings Clause.

The repeal of any statutory provision by this [Act] does not impair, or otherwise affect, the organization or the continued existence of a limited partnership existing at the effective date of this [Act], nor does the repeal of any existing statutory provision by this [Act] impair any contract or affect any right accrued before the effective date of this [Act].

APPENDIX G

The Revised Model Business Corporation Act (Excerpts)

Chapter 2. INCORPORATION

§ 2.01 Incorporators

One or more persons may act as the incorporator or incorporators of a corporation by delivering articles of incorporation to the secretary of state for filing.

§ 2.02 Articles of Incorporation

(a) The articles of incorporation must set forth:

(1) a corporate name * * * ;

(2) the number of shares the corporation is authorized to issue;

(3) the street address of the corporation's initial registered office and the name of its initial registered agent at that office; and

(4) the name and address of each incorporator.

(b) The articles of incorporation may set forth:

(1) the names and addresses of the individuals who are to serve as the initial directors;

(2) provisions not inconsistent with law regarding:

(i) the purpose or purposes for which the corporation is organized;

(ii) managing the business and regulating the affairs of the corporation;

(iii) defining, limiting, and regulating the powers of the corporation, its board of directors, and shareholders;

(iv) a par value for authorized shares or classes of shares;

(v) the imposition of personal liability on shareholders for the debts of the corporation to a specified extent and upon specified conditions;

(3) any provision that under this Act is required or permitted to be set forth in the bylaws; and

(4) a provision eliminating or limiting the liability of a director to the corporation or its shareholders for money damages for any action taken, or any failure to take any action, as a director, except liability for (A) the amount of a financial benefit received by a director to which he is not entitled; (B) an intentional infliction of harm on the corporation or the shareholders; (C) [unlawful distributions]; or (D) an intentional violation of criminal law.

(c) The articles of incorporation need not set forth any of the corporate powers enumerated in this Act.

§ 2.03 Incorporation

(a) Unless a delayed effective date is specified, the corporate existence begins when the articles of incorporation are filed.

(b) The secretary of state's filing of the articles of incorporation is conclusive proof that the incorporators satisfied all conditions precedent to incorporation except in a proceeding by the state to cancel or revoke the incorporation or involuntarily dissolve the corporation.

§ 2.04 Liability for Preincorporation Transactions

All persons purporting to act as or on behalf of a corporation, knowing there was no incorporation under this Act, are jointly and severally liable for all liabilities created while so acting.

§ 2.05 Organization of Corporation

(a) After incorporation:

(1) if initial directors are named in the articles of incorporation, the initial directors shall hold an organizational meeting, at the call of a majority of the directors, to complete the organization of the corporation by appointing officers, adopting bylaws, and carrying on any other business brought before the meeting;

(2) if initial directors are not named in the articles, the incorporator or incorporators shall hold an organizational meeting at the call of a majority of the incorporators:

(i) to elect directors and complete the organization of the corporation; or

(ii) to elect a board of directors who shall complete the organization of the corporation.

(b) Action required or permitted by this Act to be taken by incorporators at an organizational meeting may be taken without a meeting if the action taken is evidenced by one or more written consents describing the action taken and signed by each incorporator.

(c) An organizational meeting may be held in or out of this state.

* * * *

Chapter 3. PURPOSES AND POWERS

§ 3.01 Purposes

(a) Every corporation incorporated under this Act has the purpose of engaging in any lawful business unless a more limited purpose is set forth in the articles of incorporation.

(b) A corporation engaging in a business that is subject to regulation under another statute of this state may incorporate under this Act only if permitted by, and subject to all limitations of, the other statute.

§ 3.02 General Powers

Unless its articles of incorporation provide otherwise, every corporation has perpetual duration and succession in its corporate name and has the same powers as an individual to do all things necessary or convenient to carry out its business and affairs, including without limitation power:

(1) to sue and be sued, complain and defend in its corporate name;

(2) to have a corporate seal, which may be altered at will, and to use it, or a facsimile of it, by impressing or affixing it or in any other manner reproducing it;

(3) to make and amend bylaws, not inconsistent with its articles of incorporation or with the laws of this state, for managing the business and regulating the affairs of the corporation;

(4) to purchase, receive, lease, or otherwise acquire, and own, hold, improve, use, and otherwise deal with, real or personal property, or any legal or equitable interest in property, wherever located;

(5) to sell, convey, mortgage, pledge, lease, exchange, and otherwise dispose of all or any part of its property;

(6) to purchase, receive, subscribe for, or otherwise acquire; own, hold, vote, use, sell, mortgage, lend, pledge, or otherwise dispose of; and deal in and with shares or other interests in, or obligations of, any other entity;

(7) to make contracts and guarantees, incur liabilities, borrow money, issue its notes, bonds, and other obligations (which may be convertible into or include the option to purchase other securities of the corporation), and secure any of its obligations by mortgage or pledge of any of its property, franchises, or income;

(8) to lend money, invest and reinvest its funds, and receive and hold real and personal property as security for repayment;

(9) to be a promoter, partner, member, associate, or manager of any partnership, joint venture, trust, or other entity;

(10) to conduct its business, locate offices, and exercise the powers granted by this Act within or without this state;

(11) to elect directors and appoint officers, employees, and agents of the corporation, define their duties, fix their compensation, and lend them money and credit;

(12) to pay pensions and establish pension plans, pension trusts, profit sharing plans, share bonus plans, share option plans, and benefit or incentive plans for any or all of its current or former directors, officers, employees, and agents;

(13) to make donations for the public welfare or for charitable, scientific, or educational purposes;

(14) to transact any lawful business that will aid governmental policy;

(15) to make payments or donations, or do any other act, not inconsistent with law, that furthers the business and affairs of the corporation.

* * * *

Chapter 5. OFFICE AND AGENT

§ 5.01 Registered Office and Registered Agent

Each corporation must continuously maintain in this state:

(1) a registered office that may be the same as any of its places of business; and

(2) a registered agent, who may be:

(i) an individual who resides in this state and whose business office is identical with the registered office;

(ii) a domestic corporation or not-for-profit domestic corporation whose business office is identical with the registered office; or

(iii) a foreign corporation or not-for-profit foreign corporation authorized to transact business in this state whose business office is identical with the registered office.

* * * *

§ 5.04 Service on Corporation

(a) A corporation's registered agent is the corporation's agent for service of process, notice, or demand required or permitted by law to be served on the corporation.

(b) If a corporation has no registered agent, or the agent cannot with reasonable diligence be served, the corporation may be served by registered or certified mail, return receipt requested, addressed to the secretary of the corporation at its principal office. Service is perfected under this subsection at the earliest of:

(1) the date the corporation receives the mail;

(2) the date shown on the return receipt, if signed on behalf of the corporation; or

(3) five days after its deposit in the United States Mail, if mailed postpaid and correctly addressed.

(c) This section does not prescribe the only means, or necessarily the required means, of serving a corporation.

Chapter 6. SHARES AND DISTRIBUTIONS

* * * *

Subchapter B. Issuance of Shares

* * * *

§ 6.21 Issuance of Shares

(a) The powers granted in this section to the board of directors may be reserved to the shareholders by the articles of incorporation.

(b) The board of directors may authorize shares to be issued for consideration consisting of any tangible or intangible property or benefit to the corporation, including cash, promissory notes, services performed, contracts for services to be performed, or other securities of the corporation.

(c) Before the corporation issues shares, the board of directors must determine that the consideration received or to be received for shares to be issued is adequate. That determination by the board of directors is conclusive insofar as the adequacy of consideration for the issuance of shares relates to whether the shares are validly issued, fully paid, and nonassessable.

(d) When the corporation receives the consideration for which the board of directors authorized the issuance of shares, the shares issued therefor are fully paid and nonassessable.

(e) The corporation may place in escrow shares issued for a contract for future services or benefits or a promissory note, or make other arrangements to restrict the transfer of the shares, and may credit distributions in respect of the shares against their purchase price, until the services are performed, the note is paid, or the benefits received. If the services are not performed, the note is not paid, or the benefits are not received, the shares escrowed or restricted and the distributions credited may be cancelled in whole or part.

* * * *

§ 6.27 Restriction on Transfer or Registration of Shares and Other Securities

(a) The articles of incorporation, bylaws, an agreement among shareholders, or an agreement between shareholders and the corporation may impose restrictions on the transfer or registration of transfer of shares of the corporation. A restriction does not affect shares issued before the restriction was adopted unless the holders of the shares are parties to the restriction agreement or voted in favor of the restriction.

(b) A restriction on the transfer or registration of transfer of shares is valid and enforceable against the holder or a transferee of the holder if the restriction is authorized by this section and its existence is noted conspicuously on the front or back of the certificate or is contained in the information statement [sent to the shareholder]. Unless so noted, a restriction is not enforceable against a person without knowledge of the restriction.

(c) A restriction on the transfer or registration of transfer of shares is authorized:

(1) to maintain the corporation's status when it is dependent on the number or identity of its shareholders;

(2) to preserve exemptions under federal or state securities law;

(3) for any other reasonable purpose.

(d) A restriction on the transfer or registration of transfer of shares may:

(1) obligate the shareholder first to offer the corporation or other persons (separately, consecutively, or simultaneously) an opportunity to acquire the restricted shares;

(2) obligate the corporate or other persons (separately, consecutively, or simultaneously) to acquire the restricted shares;

(3) require the corporation, the holders of any class of its shares, or another person to approve the transfer of the restricted shares, if the requirement is not manifestly unreasonable;

(4) prohibit the transfer of the restricted shares to designated persons or classes of persons, if the prohibition is not manifestly unreasonable.

(e) For purposes of this section, "shares" includes a security convertible into or carrying a right to subscribe for or acquire shares.

* * * *

Chapter 7. SHAREHOLDERS

Subchapter A. Meetings

§ 7.01 Annual Meeting

(a) A corporation shall hold annually at a time stated in or fixed in accordance with the bylaws a meeting of shareholders.

(b) Annual shareholders' meetings may be held in or out of this state at the place stated in or fixed in accordance with the bylaws. If no place is stated in or fixed in accordance with the bylaws, annual meetings shall be held at the corporation's principal office.

(c) The failure to hold an annual meeting at the time stated in or fixed in accordance with a corporation's bylaws does not affect the validity of any corporate action.

* * * *

§ 7.05 Notice of Meeting

(a) A corporation shall notify shareholders of the date, time, and place of each annual and special shareholders' meeting no fewer than 10 nor more than 60 days before the meeting date. Unless this Act or the articles of incorporation require otherwise, the corporation is required to give notice only to shareholders entitled to vote at the meeting.

(b) Unless this Act or the articles of incorporation require otherwise, notice of an annual meeting need not include a description of the purpose or purposes for which the meeting is called.

(c) Notice of a special meeting must include a description of the purpose or purposes for which the meeting is called.

(d) If not otherwise fixed * * *, the record date for determining shareholders entitled to notice of and to vote at an annual or special shareholders' meeting is the day before the first notice is delivered to shareholders.

(e) Unless the bylaws require otherwise, if an annual or special shareholders' meeting is adjourned to a different date, time, or place, notice need not be given of the new date, time, or place if the new date, time, or place is announced at the meeting before adjournment. * * *

* * * *

§ 7.07 Record Date

(a) The bylaws may fix or provide the manner of fixing the record date for one or more voting groups in order to determine the shareholders entitled to notice of a shareholders' meeting, to demand a special meeting, to vote, or to take any other action. If the bylaws do not fix or provide for fixing a record date, the board of directors of the corporation may fix a future date as the record date.

(b) A record date fixed under this section may not be more than 70 days before the meeting or action requiring a determination of shareholders.

(c) A determination of shareholders entitled to notice of or to vote at a shareholders' meeting is effective for any adjournment of the meeting unless the board of directors fixes a new record date, which it must do if the meeting is adjourned to a date more than 120 days after the date fixed for the original meeting.

(d) If a court orders a meeting adjourned to a date more than 120 days after the date fixed for the original meeting, it may provide that the original record date continues in effect or it may fix a new record date.

Subchapter B. Voting

§ 7.20 Shareholders' List for Meeting

(a) After fixing a record date for a meeting, a corporation shall prepare an alphabetical list of the names of all its shareholders who are entitled to notice of a shareholders' meeting. The list must be arranged by voting group (and within each voting group by class or series of shares) and show the address of and number of shares held by each shareholder.

(b) The shareholders' list must be available for inspection by any shareholder, beginning two business days after notice of the meeting is given for which the list was prepared and continuing through the meeting, at the corporation's principal office or at a place identified in the meeting notice in the city where the meeting will be held. A shareholder, his agent, or attorney is entitled on written demand to inspect and, subject to the requirements of section 16.02(c), to copy the list, during regular business hours and at his expense, during the period it is available for inspection.

(c) The corporation shall make the shareholders' list available at the meeting, and any shareholder, his agent, or attorney is entitled to inspect the list at any time during the meeting or any adjournment.

(d) If the corporation refuses to allow a shareholder, his agent, or attorney to inspect the shareholders' list before or at the meeting (or copy the list as permitted by subsection (b)), the [name or describe] court of the county where a corporation's principal office (or, if none in this state, its registered office) is located, on application of the shareholder, may summarily order the inspection or copying at the corporation's expense and may postpone the meeting for which the list was prepared until the inspection or copying is complete.

(e) Refusal or failure to prepare or make available the shareholders' list does not affect the validity of action taken at the meeting.

* * * *

§ 7.22 Proxies

(a) A shareholder may vote his shares in person or by proxy.

(b) A shareholder may appoint a proxy to vote or otherwise act for him by signing an appointment form, either personally or by his attorney-in-fact.

(c) An appointment of a proxy is effective when received by the secretary or other officer or agent authorized to tabulate votes. An appointment is valid for 11 months unless a longer period is expressly provided in the appointment form.

* * * *

§ 7.28 Voting for Directors; Cumulative Voting

(a) Unless otherwise provided in the articles of incorporation, directors are elected by a plurality of the votes cast by the shares entitled to vote in the election at a meeting at which a quorum is present.

(b) Shareholders do not have a right to cumulate their votes for directors unless the articles of incorporation so provide.

(c) A statement included in the articles of incorporation that "[all] [a designated voting group of] shareholders are entitled to cumulate their votes for directors" (or words of similar import) means that the shareholders designated are entitled to multiply the number of votes they are entitled to cast by the number of directors for whom they are entitled to vote and cast the product for a single candidate or distribute the product among two or more candidates.

(d) Shares otherwise entitled to vote cumulatively may not be voted cumulatively at a particular meeting unless:

(1) the meeting notice or proxy statement accompanying the notice states conspicuously that cumulative voting is authorized; or

(2) a shareholder who has the right to cumulate his votes gives notice to the corporation not less than 48 hours before the time set for the meeting of his intent to cumulate his votes during the meeting, and if one shareholder gives this notice all other shareholders in the same voting group participating in the election are entitled to cumulate their votes without giving further notice.

* * * *

Subchapter D. Derivative Proceedings

* * * *

§ 7.41 Standing

A shareholder may not commence or maintain a derivative proceeding unless the shareholder:

(1) was a shareholder of the corporation at the time of the act or omission complained of or became a shareholder through transfer by operation of law from one who was a shareholder at that time; and

(2) fairly and adequately represents the interests of the corporation in enforcing the right of the corporation.

§ 7.42 Demand

No shareholder may commence a derivative proceeding until:

(1) a written demand has been made upon the corporation to take suitable action; and

(2) 90 days have expired from the date the demand was made unless the shareholder has earlier been notified that the demand has been rejected by the corporation or unless irreparable injury to the corporation would result by waiting for the expiration of the 90 day period.

* * * *

Chapter 8. DIRECTORS AND OFFICERS

Subchapter A. Board of Directors

* * * *

§ 8.02 Qualifications of Directors

The articles of incorporation or bylaws may prescribe qualifications for directors. A director need not be a resident of this state or a shareholder of the corporation unless the articles of incorporation or bylaws so prescribe.

§ 8.03 Number and Election of Directors

(a) A board of directors must consist of one or more individuals, with the number specified in or fixed in accordance with the articles of incorporation or bylaws.

(b) If a board of directors has power to fix or change the number of directors, the board may increase or decrease by 30 percent or less the number of directors last approved by the shareholders, but only the shareholders may increase or decrease by more than 30 percent the number of directors last approved by the shareholders.

(c) The articles of incorporation or bylaws may establish a variable range for the size of the board of directors by fixing a minimum and maximum number of directors. If a variable range is established, the number of directors may be fixed or changed from time to time, within the minimum and maximum, by the shareholders or the board of directors. After shares are issued, only the shareholders may change the range for the size of the board or change from a fixed to a variable-range size board or vice versa.

(d) Directors are elected at the first annual shareholders' meeting and at each annual meeting thereafter unless their terms are staggered under section 8.06.

* * * *

§ 8.08 Removal of Directors by Shareholders

(a) The shareholders may remove one or more directors with or without cause unless the articles of incorporation provide that directors may be removed only for cause.

(b) If a director is elected by a voting group of shareholders, only the shareholders of that voting group may participate in the vote to remove him.

(c) If cumulative voting is authorized, a director may not be removed if the number of votes sufficient to elect him under cumulative voting is voted against his removal. If cumulative voting is not authorized, a director may be removed only if the number of votes cast to remove him exceeds the number of votes cast not to remove him.

(d) A director may be removed by the shareholders only at a meeting called for the purpose of removing him and the meeting notice must state that the purpose, or one of the purposes, of the meeting is removal of the director.

* * * *

Subchapter B. Meetings and Action of the Board

§ 8.20 Meetings

(a) The board of directors may hold regular or special meetings in or out of this state.

(b) Unless the articles of incorporation or bylaws provide otherwise, the board of directors may permit any or all directors to participate in a regular or special meeting by, or conduct the meeting through the use of, any means of communication by which all directors participating may simultaneously hear each other during the meeting. A director participating in a meeting by this means is deemed to be present in person at the meeting.

* * * *

§ 8.22 Notice of Meeting

(a) Unless the articles of incorporation or bylaws provide otherwise, regular meetings of the board of directors may be held without notice of the date, time, place, or purpose of the meeting.

(b) Unless the articles of incorporation or bylaws provide for a longer or shorter period, special meetings of the board of directors must be preceded by at least two days' notice of the date, time, and place of the meeting. The notice need not describe the purpose of the special meeting unless required by the articles of incorporation or bylaws.

* * * *

§ 8.24 Quorum and Voting

(a) Unless the articles of incorporation or bylaws require a greater number, a quorum of a board of directors consists of:

(1) a majority of the fixed number of directors if the corporation has a fixed board size; or

(2) a majority of the number of directors prescribed, or if no number is prescribed the number in office immediately before the meeting begins, if the corporation has a variable-range size board.

(b) The articles of incorporation or bylaws may authorize a quorum of a board of directors to consist of no fewer than one-third of the fixed or prescribed number of directors determined under subsection (a).

(c) If a quorum is present when a vote is taken, the affirmative vote of a majority of directors present is the act of the board of directors unless the articles of incorporation or bylaws require the vote of a greater number of directors.

(d) A director who is present at a meeting of the board of directors or a committee of the board of directors when corporate action is taken is deemed to have assented to the action taken unless: (1) he objects at the beginning of the meeting (or promptly upon his arrival) to holding it or transacting business at the meeting; (2) his dissent or abstention from the action taken is entered in the minutes of the meeting; or (3) he delivers written notice of his dissent or abstention to the presiding officer of the meeting before its adjournment or to the corporation immediately after adjournment of the meeting. The right of dissent or abstention is not available to a director who votes in favor of the action taken.

* * * *

Subchapter C. Standards of Conduct

§ 8.30 General Standards for Directors

(a) A director shall discharge his duties as a director, including his duties as a member of a committee:

(1) in good faith;

(2) with the care an ordinarily prudent person in a like position would exercise under similar circumstances; and

(3) in a manner he reasonably believes to be in the best interests of the corporation.

(b) In discharging his duties a director is entitled to rely on information, opinions, reports, or statements, including financial statements and other financial data, if prepared or presented by:

(1) one or more officers or employees of the corporation whom the director reasonably believes to be reliable and competent in the matters presented;

(2) legal counsel, public accountants, or other persons as to matters the director reasonably believes are within the person's professional or expert competence; or

(3) a committee of the board of directors of which he is not a member if the director reasonably believes the committee merits confidence.

(c) A director is not acting in good faith if he has knowledge concerning the matter in question that makes reliance otherwise permitted by subsection (b) unwarranted.

(d) A director is not liable for any action taken as a director, or any failure to take any action, if he performed the duties of his office in compliance with this section.

* * * *

Subchapter D. Officers

* * * *

§ 8.41 Duties of Officers

Each officer has the authority and shall perform the duties set forth in the bylaws or, to the extent consistent with the bylaws, the duties prescribed by the board of directors or by direction of an officer authorized by the board of directors to prescribe the duties of other officers.

§ 8.42 Standards of Conduct for Officers

(a) An officer with discretionary authority shall discharge his duties under that authority:

(1) in good faith;

(2) with the care an ordinarily prudent person in a like position would exercise under similar circumstances; and

(3) in a manner he reasonably believes to be in the best interests of the corporation.

(b) In discharging his duties an officer is entitled to rely on information, opinions, reports, or statements, including financial statements and other financial data, if prepared or presented by:

(1) one or more officers or employees of the corporation whom the officer reasonably believes to be reliable and competent in the matters presented; or

(2) legal counsel, public accountants, or other persons as to matters the officer reasonably believes are within the person's professional or expert competence.

(c) An officer is not acting in good faith if he has knowledge concerning the matter in question that makes reliance otherwise permitted by subsection (b) unwarranted.

(d) An officer is not liable for any action taken as an officer, or any failure to take any action, if he performed the duties of his office in compliance with this section.

* * * *

Chapter 11. MERGER AND SHARE EXCHANGE

§ 11.01 Merger

(a) One or more corporations may merge into another corporation if the board of directors of each corporation adopts and its shareholders (if required * * *) approve a plan of merger.

(b) The plan of merger must set forth:

(1) the name of each corporation planning to merge and the name of the surviving corporation into which each other corporation plans to merge;

(2) the terms and conditions of the merger; and

(3) the manner and basis of converting the shares of each corporation into shares, obligations, or other securities of the surviving or any other corporation or into cash or other property in whole or part.

(c) The plan of merger may set forth:

(1) amendments to the articles of incorporation of the surviving corporation; and

(2) other provisions relating to the merger.

* * * *

§ 11.04 Merger of Subsidiary

(a) A parent corporation owning at least 90 percent of the outstanding shares of each class of a subsidiary corporation may merge the subsidiary into itself without approval of the shareholders of the parent or subsidiary.

(b) The board of directors of the parent shall adopt a plan of merger that sets forth:

(1) the names of the parent and subsidiary; and

(2) the manner and basis of converting the shares of the subsidiary into shares, obligations, or other securities of the parent or any other corporation or into cash or other property in whole or part.

(c) The parent shall mail a copy or summary of the plan of merger to each shareholder of the subsidiary who does not waive the mailing requirement in writing.

(d) The parent may not deliver articles of merger to the secretary of state for filing until at least 30 days after the date it mailed a copy of the plan of merger to each shareholder of the subsidiary who did not waive the mailing requirement.

(e) Articles of merger under this section may not contain amendments to the articles of incorporation of the parent corporation (except for amendments enumerated in section 10.02).

* * * *

§ 11.06 Effect of Merger or Share Exchange

(a) When a merger takes effect:

(1) every other corporation party to the merger merges into the surviving corporation and the separate existence of every corporation except the surviving corporation ceases;

(2) the title to all real estate and other property owned by each corporation party to the merger is vested in the surviving corporation without reversion or impairment;

(3) the surviving corporation has all liabilities of each corporation party to the merger;

(4) a proceeding pending against any corporation party to the merger may be continued as if the merger did not occur or the surviving corporation may be substituted in the proceeding for the corporation whose existence ceased;

(5) the articles of incorporation of the surviving corporation are amended to the extent provided in the plan of merger; and

(6) the shares of each corporation party to the merger that are to be converted into shares, obligations, or other securities of the surviving or any other corporation or into cash or other property are converted and the former holders of the shares are entitled only to the rights provided in the articles of merger or to their rights under chapter 13.

(b) When a share exchange takes effect, the shares of each acquired corporation are exchanged as provided in the plan, and the former holders of the shares are entitled only to the exchange rights provided in the articles of share exchange or to their rights under chapter 13.

* * * *

Chapter 13.
DISSENTERS' RIGHTS

Subchapter A. Right to Dissent and Obtain Payment for Shares

* * * *

§ 13.02 Right to Dissent

(a) A shareholder is entitled to dissent from, and obtain payment of the fair value of his shares in the event of, any of the following corporate actions:

(1) consummation of a plan of merger to which the corporation is a party (i) if shareholder approval is required for the merger by [statute] or the articles of incorporation and the shareholder is entitled to vote on the merger or (ii) if the corporation is a subsidiary that is merged with its parent under section 11.04;

(2) consummation of a plan of share exchange to which the corporation is a party as the corporation whose shares will be acquired, if the shareholder is entitled to vote on the plan;

(3) consummation of a sale or exchange of all, or substantially all, of the property of the corporation other than in the usual and regular course of business, if the shareholder is entitled to vote on the sale or exchange, including a sale in dissolution, but not including a sale pursuant to court order or a sale for cash pursuant to a plan by which all or substantially all of the net proceeds of the sale will be distributed to the shareholders within one year after the date of sale;

(4) an amendment of the articles of incorporation that materially and adversely affects rights in respect of a dissenter's shares because it:

(i) alters or abolishes a preferential right of the shares;

(ii) creates, alters, or abolishes a right in respect of redemption, including a provision respecting a sinking fund for the redemption or repurchase, of the shares;

(iii) alters or abolishes a preemptive right of the holder of the shares to acquire shares or other securities;

(iv) excludes or limits the right of the shares to vote on any matter, or to cumulate votes, other than a limitation by dilution through issuance of shares or other securities with similar voting rights; or

(v) reduces the number of shares owned by the shareholder to a fraction of a share if the fractional share so created is to be acquired for cash * * * ; or

(5) any corporate action taken pursuant to a shareholder vote to the extent the articles of incorporation, bylaws, or a resolution of the board of directors provides that voting or nonvoting shareholders are entitled to dissent and obtain payment for their shares.

(b) A shareholder entitled to dissent and obtain payment for his shares under this chapter may not challenge the corporate action creating his entitlement unless the action is unlawful or fraudulent with respect to the shareholder or the corporation.

* * * *

Subchapter B. Procedure for Exercise of Dissenters' Rights

* * * *

§ 13.21 Notice of Intent to Demand Payment

(a) If proposed corporate action creating dissenters' rights under section 13.02 is submitted to a vote at a shareholders' meeting, a shareholder who wishes to assert dissenters' rights (1) must deliver to the corporation before the vote is taken written notice of his intent to demand payment for his shares if the proposed action is effectuated and (2) must not vote his shares in favor of the proposed action.

(b) A shareholder who does not satisfy the requirements of subsection (a) is not entitled to payment for his shares under this chapter.

* * * *

§ 13.25 Payment

(a) * * * [A]s soon as the proposed corporate action is taken, or upon receipt of a payment demand, the corporation shall pay each dissenter * * * the amount the corporation estimates to be the fair value of his shares, plus accrued interest.

* * * *

§ 13.28 Procedure If Shareholder Dissatisfied with Payment or Offer

(a) A dissenter may notify the corporation in writing of his own estimate of the fair value of his shares and amount of interest due, and demand payment of his estimate (less any payment under section 13.25) * * * if:

(1) the dissenter believes that the amount paid under section 13.25 * * * is less than the fair value of his shares or that the interest due is incorrectly calculated;

(2) the corporation fails to make payment under section 13.25 within 60 days after the date set for demanding payment; or

(3) the corporation, having failed to take the proposed action, does not return the deposited certificates or release the transfer restrictions imposed on uncertificated shares within 60 days after the date set for demanding payment.

(b) A dissenter waives his right to demand payment under this section unless he notifies the corporation of his demand in writing under subsection (a) within 30 days after the corporation made or offered payment for his shares.

* * * *

Chapter 14. DISSOLUTION

Subchapter A. Voluntary Dissolution

* * * *

§ 14.02 Dissolution by Board of Directors and Shareholders

(a) A corporation's board of directors may propose dissolution for submission to the shareholders.

(b) For a proposal to dissolve to be adopted:

(1) the board of directors must recommend dissolution to the shareholders unless the board of directors determines that because of conflict of interest or other special circumstances it should make no recommendation and communicates the basis for its determination to the shareholders; and

(2) the shareholders entitled to vote must approve the proposal to dissolve as provided in subsection (e).

(c) The board of directors may condition its submission of the proposal for dissolution on any basis.

(d) The corporation shall notify each shareholder, whether or not entitled to vote, of the proposed shareholders' meeting in accordance with section 7.05. The notice must also state that the purpose, or one of the purposes, of the meeting is to consider dissolving the corporation.

(e) Unless the articles of incorporation or the board of directors (acting pursuant to subsection (c)) require a greater vote or a vote by voting groups, the proposal to dissolve to be adopted must be approved by a majority of all the votes entitled to be cast on that proposal.

* * * *

§ 14.05 Effect of Dissolution

(a) A dissolved corporation continues its corporate existence but may not carry on any business except that appropriate to wind up and liquidate its business and affairs, including:

(1) collecting its assets;

(2) disposing of its properties that will not be distributed in kind to its shareholders;

(3) discharging or making provision for discharging its liabilities;

(4) distributing its remaining property among its shareholders according to their interests; and

(5) doing every other act necessary to wind up and liquidate its business and affairs.

(b) Dissolution of a corporation does not:

(1) transfer title to the corporation's property;

(2) prevent transfer of its shares or securities, although the authorization to dissolve may provide for closing the corporation's share transfer records;

(3) subject its directors or officers to standards of conduct different from those prescribed in chapter 8;

(4) change quorum or voting requirements for its board of directors or shareholders; change provisions for selection, resignation, or removal of its directors or officers or both; or change provisions for amending its bylaws;

(5) prevent commencement of a proceeding by or against the corporation in its corporate name;

(6) abate or suspend a proceeding pending by or against the corporation on the effective date of dissolution; or

(7) terminate the authority of the registered agent of the corporation.

* * * *

Subchapter C. Judicial Dissolution

§ 14.30 Grounds for Judicial Dissolution

The [name or describe court or courts] may dissolve a corporation:

(1) in a proceeding by the attorney general if it is established that:

(i) the corporation obtained its articles of incorporation through fraud; or

(ii) the corporation has continued to exceed or abuse the authority conferred upon it by law;

(2) in a proceeding by a shareholder if it is established that:

(i) the directors are deadlocked in the management of the corporate affairs, the shareholders are unable to break the deadlock, and irreparable injury to the corporation is threatened or being suffered, or the business and affairs of the corporation can no longer be conducted to the advantage of the shareholders generally, because of the deadlock;

(ii) the directors or those in control of the corporation have acted, are acting, or will act in a manner that is illegal, oppressive, or fraudulent;

(iii) the shareholders are deadlocked in voting power and have failed, for a period that includes at least two consecutive annual meeting dates, to elect successors to directors whose terms have expired; or

(iv) the corporate assets are being misapplied or wasted;

(3) in a proceeding by a creditor if it is established that:

(i) the creditor's claim has been reduced to judgment, the execution on the judgment returned unsatisfied, and the corporation is insolvent; or

(ii) the corporation has admitted in writing that the creditor's claim is due and owing and the corporation is insolvent; or

(4) in a proceeding by the corporation to have its voluntary dissolution continued under court supervision.

* * * *

Chapter 16. RECORDS AND REPORTS

Subchapter A. Records

§ 16.01 Corporate Records

(a) A corporation shall keep as permanent records minutes of all meetings of its shareholders and board of directors, a record of all actions taken by the shareholders or board of directors without a meeting, and a record of all actions taken by a committee of the board of directors in place of the board of directors on behalf of the corporation.

(b) A corporation shall maintain appropriate accounting records.

(c) A corporation or its agent shall maintain a record of its shareholders, in a form that permits preparation of a list of the names and addresses of all shareholders, in alphabetical order by class of shares showing the number and class of shares held by each.

(d) A corporation shall maintain its records in written form or in another form capable of conversion into written form within a reasonable time.

(e) A corporation shall keep a copy of the following records at its principal office:

(1) its articles or restated articles of incorporation and all amendments to them currently in effect;

(2) its bylaws or restated bylaws and all amendments to them currently in effect;

(3) resolutions adopted by its board of directors creating one or more classes or series of shares, and fixing their relative rights, preferences, and limitations, if shares issued pursuant to those resolutions are outstanding;

(4) the minutes of all shareholders' meetings, and records of all action taken by shareholders without a meeting, for the past three years;

(5) all written communications to shareholders generally within the past three years, including the financial statements furnished for the past three years * * *;

(6) a list of the names and business addresses of its current directors and officers; and

(7) its most recent annual report delivered to the secretary of state * * *.

§ 16.02 Inspection of Records by Shareholders

(a) Subject to section 16.03(c), a shareholder of a corporation is entitled to inspect and copy, during regular business hours at the corporation's principal office, any of the records of the corporation described in section 16.01(e) if he gives the corporation written notice of his demand at least five business days before the date on which he wishes to inspect and copy.

(b) A shareholder of a corporation is entitled to inspect and copy, during regular business hours at a reasonable location specified by the corporation, any of the following records of the corporation if the shareholder meets the requirements of subsection (c) and gives the corporation written notice of his demand at least five business days before the date on which he wishes to inspect and copy:

(1) excerpts from minutes of any meeting of the board of directors, records of any action of a committee of the board of directors while acting in place of the board of directors on behalf of the corporation, minutes of any meeting of the shareholders, and records of action taken by the shareholders or board of directors without a meeting, to the extent not subject to inspection under section 16.02(a);

(2) accounting records of the corporation; and

(3) the record of shareholders.

(c) A shareholder may inspect and copy the records identified in subsection (b) only if:

(1) his demand is made in good faith and for a proper purpose;

(2) he describes with reasonable particularity his purpose and the records he desires to inspect; and

(3) the records are directly connected with his purpose.

(d) The right of inspection granted by this section may not be abolished or limited by a corporation's articles of incorporation or bylaws.

(e) This section does not affect:

(1) the right of a shareholder to inspect records under section 7.20 or, if the shareholder is in litigation with the corporation, to the same extent as any other litigant;

(2) the power of a court, independently of this Act, to compel the production of corporate records for examination.

(f) For purposes of this section, "shareholder" includes a beneficial owner whose shares are held in a voting trust or by a nominee on his behalf.

APPENDIX H

The Sarbanes-Oxley Act of 2002 (Excerpts and Explanatory Comments)

Note: The author's explanatory comments appear in italics following the excerpt from each section.

SECTION 302

Corporate responsibility for financial reports[1]

(a) Regulations required

The Commission shall, by rule, require, for each company filing periodic reports under section 13(a) or 15(d) of the Securities Exchange Act of 1934 (15 U.S.C. 78m, 78o(d)), that the principal executive officer or officers and the principal financial officer or officers, or persons performing similar functions, certify in each annual or quarterly report filed or submitted under either such section of such Act that—

(1) the signing officer has reviewed the report;

(2) based on the officer's knowledge, the report does not contain any untrue statement of a material fact or omit to state a material fact necessary in order to make the statements made, in light of the circumstances under which such statements were made, not misleading;

(3) based on such officer's knowledge, the financial statements, and other financial information included in the report, fairly present in all material respects the financial condition and results of operations of the issuer as of, and for, the periods presented in the report;

(4) the signing officers—

(A) are responsible for establishing and maintaining internal controls;

(B) have designed such internal controls to ensure that material information relating to the issuer and its consolidated subsidiaries is made known to such officers by others within those entities, particularly during the period in which the periodic reports are being prepared;

(C) have evaluated the effectiveness of the issuer's internal controls as of a date within 90 days prior to the report; and

(D) have presented in the report their conclusions about the effectiveness of their internal controls based on their evaluation as of that date;

(5) the signing officers have disclosed to the issuer's auditors and the audit committee of the board of directors (or persons fulfilling the equivalent function)—

(A) all significant deficiencies in the design or operation of internal controls which could adversely affect the issuer's ability to record, process, summarize, and report financial data and have identified for the issuer's auditors any material weaknesses in internal controls; and

(B) any fraud, whether or not material, that involves management or other employees who have a significant role in the issuer's internal controls; and

(6) the signing officers have indicated in the report whether or not there were significant changes in internal controls or in other factors that could significantly affect internal controls subsequent to the date of their evaluation, including any corrective actions with regard to significant deficiencies and material weaknesses.

(b) Foreign reincorporations have no effect

Nothing in this section shall be interpreted or applied in any way to allow any issuer to lessen the legal force of the statement required under this section, by an issuer having reincorporated or having engaged in any other transaction that resulted in the transfer of the corporate domicile or offices of the issuer from inside the United States to outside of the United States.

(c) Deadline

The rules required by subsection (a) of this section shall be effective not later than 30 days after July 30, 2002.

EXPLANATORY COMMENTS: *Section 302 requires the chief executive officer (CEO) and chief financial officer (CFO) of each public company to certify that they have reviewed the company's quarterly and annual reports to be filed with the Securities and Exchange Commission (SEC). The CEO and CFO must certify that, based on their knowledge, the reports do not contain any untrue statement of a material fact or any half-truth that would make the report*

1. This section of the Sarbanes-Oxley Act is codified at 15 U.S.C. Section 7241.

misleading, and that the information contained in the reports fairly presents the company's financial condition.

In addition, this section also requires the CEO and CFO to certify that they have created and designed an internal control system for their company and have recently evaluated that system to ensure that it is effectively providing them with relevant and accurate financial information. If the signing officers have found any significant deficiencies or weaknesses in the company's system or have discovered any evidence of fraud, they must have reported the situation, and any corrective actions they have taken, to the auditors and the audit committee.

SECTION 306

Insider trades during pension fund blackout periods[2]

(a) Prohibition of insider trading during pension fund blackout periods

(1) In general

Except to the extent otherwise provided by rule of the Commission pursuant to paragraph (3), it shall be unlawful for any director or executive officer of an issuer of any equity security (other than an exempted security), directly or indirectly, to purchase, sell, or otherwise acquire or transfer any equity security of the issuer (other than an exempted security) during any blackout period with respect to such equity security if such director or officer acquires such equity security in connection with his or her service or employment as a director or executive officer.

(2) Remedy

(A) In general

Any profit realized by a director or executive officer referred to in paragraph (1) from any purchase, sale, or other acquisition or transfer in violation of this subsection shall inure to and be recoverable by the issuer, irrespective of any intention on the part of such director or executive officer in entering into the transaction.

(B) Actions to recover profits

An action to recover profits in accordance with this subsection may be instituted at law or in equity in any court of competent jurisdiction by the issuer, or by the owner of any security of the issuer in the name and in behalf of the issuer if the issuer fails or refuses to bring such action within 60 days after the date of request, or fails diligently to prosecute the action thereafter, except that no such suit shall be brought more than 2 years after the date on which such profit was realized.

(3) Rulemaking authorized

The Commission shall, in consultation with the Secretary of Labor, issue rules to clarify the application of this subsection and to prevent evasion thereof. Such rules shall provide for the application of the requirements of paragraph (1) with respect to entities treated as a single employer with respect to an issuer under section 414(b), (c), (m), or (o) of Title 26 to the extent necessary to clarify the application of such requirements and to prevent evasion thereof. Such rules may also provide for appropriate exceptions from the requirements of this subsection, including exceptions for purchases pursuant to an automatic dividend reinvestment program or purchases or sales made pursuant to an advance election.

(4) Blackout period

For purposes of this subsection, the term "blackout period", with respect to the equity securities of any issuer—

(A) means any period of more than 3 consecutive business days during which the ability of not fewer than 50 percent of the participants or beneficiaries under all individual account plans maintained by the issuer to purchase, sell, or otherwise acquire or transfer an interest in any equity of such issuer held in such an individual account plan is temporarily suspended by the issuer or by a fiduciary of the plan; and

(B) does not include, under regulations which shall be prescribed by the Commission—

(i) a regularly scheduled period in which the participants and beneficiaries may not purchase, sell, or otherwise acquire or transfer an interest in any equity of such issuer, if such period is—

(I) incorporated into the individual account plan; and

(II) timely disclosed to employees before becoming participants under the individual account plan or as a subsequent amendment to the plan; or

(ii) any suspension described in subparagraph (A) that is imposed solely in connection with persons becoming participants or beneficiaries, or ceasing to be participants or beneficiaries, in an individual account plan by reason of a corporate merger, acquisition, divestiture, or similar transaction involving the plan or plan sponsor.

(5) Individual account plan

For purposes of this subsection, the term "individual account plan" has the meaning provided in section 1002(34) of Title 29, except that such term shall not include a one-participant retirement plan (within the meaning of section 1021(i)(8)(B) of Title 29).

(6) Notice to directors, executive officers, and the Commission

2. Codified at 15 U.S.C. Section 7244.

In any case in which a director or executive officer is subject to the requirements of this subsection in connection with a blackout period (as defined in paragraph (4)) with respect to any equity securities, the issuer of such equity securities shall timely notify such director or officer and the Securities and Exchange Commission of such blackout period.

* * * *

EXPLANATORY COMMENTS: *Corporate pension funds typically prohibit employees from trading shares of the corporation during periods when the pension fund is undergoing significant change. Prior to 2002, however, these blackout periods did not affect the corporation's executives, who frequently received shares of the corporate stock as part of their compensation. During the collapse of Enron, for example, its pension plan was scheduled to change administrators at a time when Enron's stock price was falling. Enron's employees therefore could not sell their shares while the price was dropping, but its executives could and did sell their stock, consequently avoiding some of the losses. Section 306 was Congress's solution to the basic unfairness of this situation. This section of the act required the SEC to issue rules that prohibit any director or executive officer from trading during pension fund blackout periods. (The SEC later issued these rules, entitled Regulation Blackout Trading Restriction, or Reg BTR.) Section 306 also provided shareholders with a right to file a shareholder's derivative suit against officers and directors who have profited from trading during these blackout periods (provided that the corporation has failed to bring a suit). The officer or director can be forced to return to the corporation any profits received, regardless of whether the director or officer acted with bad intent.*

SECTION 402

Periodical and other reports[3]

* * * *

(i) Accuracy of financial reports

Each financial report that contains financial statements, and that is required to be prepared in accordance with (or reconciled to) generally accepted accounting principles under this chapter and filed with the Commission shall reflect all material correcting adjustments that have been identified by a registered public accounting firm in accordance with generally accepted accounting principles and the rules and regulations of the Commission.

(j) Off-balance sheet transactions

Not later than 180 days after July 30, 2002, the Commission shall issue final rules providing that each annual and quarterly financial report required to be filed with the Commission shall disclose all material off-balance sheet transactions, arrangements, obligations (including contingent obligations), and other relationships of the issuer with unconsolidated entities or other persons, that may have a material current or future effect on financial condition, changes in financial condition, results of operations, liquidity, capital expenditures, capital resources, or significant components of revenues or expenses.

(k) Prohibition on personal loans to executives

(1) In general

It shall be unlawful for any issuer (as defined in section 7201 of this title), directly or indirectly, including through any subsidiary, to extend or maintain credit, to arrange for the extension of credit, or to renew an extension of credit, in the form of a personal loan to or for any director or executive officer (or equivalent thereof) of that issuer. An extension of credit maintained by the issuer on July 30, 2002, shall not be subject to the provisions of this subsection, provided that there is no material modification to any term of any such extension of credit or any renewal of any such extension of credit on or after July 30, 2002.

(2) Limitation

Paragraph (1) does not preclude any home improvement and manufactured home loans (as that term is defined in section 1464 of Title 12), consumer credit (as defined in section 1602 of this title), or any extension of credit under an open end credit plan (as defined in section 1602 of this title), or a charge card (as defined in section 1637(c)(4)(e) of this title), or any extension of credit by a broker or dealer registered under section 78o of this title to an employee of that broker or dealer to buy, trade, or carry securities, that is permitted under rules or regulations of the Board of Governors of the Federal Reserve System pursuant to section 78g of this title (other than an extension of credit that would be used to purchase the stock of that issuer), that is—

(A) made or provided in the ordinary course of the consumer credit business of such issuer;

(B) of a type that is generally made available by such issuer to the public; and

(C) made by such issuer on market terms, or terms that are no more favorable than those offered by the issuer to the general public for such extensions of credit.

(3) Rule of construction for certain loans

Paragraph (1) does not apply to any loan made or maintained by an insured depository institution (as defined in section 1813 of Title 12), if the loan is subject to the insider lending restrictions of section 375b of Title 12.

(l) Real time issuer disclosures

Each issuer reporting under subsection (a) of this section or section 78o(d) of this title shall disclose to the public on a rapid and current basis such additional information concerning material changes in the financial condition or operations of the issuer, in plain English, which may

3. This section of the Sarbanes-Oxley Act amended some of the provisions of the 1934 Securities Exchange Act and added the paragraphs reproduced here at 15 U.S.C. Section 78m.

include trend and qualitative information and graphic presentations, as the Commission determines, by rule, is necessary or useful for the protection of investors and in the public interest.

EXPLANATORY COMMENTS: *Corporate executives during the Enron era typically received extremely large salaries, significant bonuses, and abundant stock options, even when the companies for which they worked were suffering. Executives were also routinely given personal loans from corporate funds, many of which were never paid back. The average large company during that period loaned almost $1 million a year to top executives, and some companies, including Tyco International and Adelphia Communications Corporation, loaned hundreds of millions of dollars to their executives every year. Section 402 amended the 1934 Securities Exchange Act to prohibit public companies from making personal loans to executive officers and directors. There are a few exceptions to this prohibition, such as home-improvement loans made in the ordinary course of business. Note also that while loans are forbidden, outright gifts are not. A corporation is free to give gifts to its executives, including cash, provided that these gifts are disclosed on its financial reports. The idea is that corporate directors will be deterred from making substantial gifts to their executives by the disclosure requirement—particularly if the corporation's financial condition is questionable—because making such gifts could be perceived as abusing their authority.*

SECTION 403

Directors, officers, and principal stockholders[4]

(a) Disclosures required

(1) Directors, officers, and principal stockholders required to file

Every person who is directly or indirectly the beneficial owner of more than 10 percent of any class of any equity security (other than an exempted security) which is registered pursuant to section 78l of this title, or who is a director or an officer of the issuer of such security, shall file the statements required by this subsection with the Commission (and, if such security is registered on a national securities exchange, also with the exchange).

(2) Time of filing

The statements required by this subsection shall be filed—

(A) at the time of the registration of such security on a national securities exchange or by the effective date of a registration statement filed pursuant to section 78l(g) of this title;

(B) within 10 days after he or she becomes such beneficial owner, director, or officer;

(C) if there has been a change in such ownership, or if such person shall have purchased or sold a security-based swap agreement (as defined in section 206(b) of the Gramm-Leach-Bliley Act (15 U.S.C. 78c note)) involving such equity security, before the end of the second business day following the day on which the subject transaction has been executed, or at such other time as the Commission shall establish, by rule, in any case in which the Commission determines that such 2-day period is not feasible.

(3) Contents of statements

A statement filed—

(A) under subparagraph (A) or (B) of paragraph (2) shall contain a statement of the amount of all equity securities of such issuer of which the filing person is the beneficial owner; and

(B) under subparagraph (C) of such paragraph shall indicate ownership by the filing person at the date of filing, any such changes in such ownership, and such purchases and sales of the security-based swap agreements as have occurred since the most recent such filing under such subparagraph.

(4) Electronic filing and availability

Beginning not later than 1 year after July 30, 2002—

(A) a statement filed under subparagraph (C) of paragraph (2) shall be filed electronically;

(B) the Commission shall provide each such statement on a publicly accessible Internet site not later than the end of the business day following that filing; and

(C) the issuer (if the issuer maintains a corporate website) shall provide that statement on that corporate website, not later than the end of the business day following that filing.

* * * *

EXPLANATORY COMMENTS: *This section dramatically shortens the time period provided in the Securities Exchange Act of 1934 for disclosing transactions by insiders. The prior law stated that most transactions had to be reported within ten days of the beginning of the following month, although certain transactions did not have to be reported until the following fiscal year (within the first forty-five days). Because some of the insider trading that occurred during the Enron fiasco did not have to be disclosed (and was therefore not discovered) until long after the transactions, Congress added this section to reduce the time period for making disclosures. Under Section 403, most transactions by insiders must be electronically filed with the SEC within two business days. Also, any company that maintains a Web site must post these SEC filings on its site by the end of the next business day. Congress enacted this section in the belief that if insiders are required to file reports of their transactions promptly with the SEC, companies will do more to police themselves and prevent insider trading.*

4. This section of the Sarbanes-Oxley Act amended the disclosure provisions of the 1934 Securities Exchange Act, at 15 U.S.C. Section 78p.

SECTION 404

Management assessment of internal controls[5]

(a) Rules required

The Commission shall prescribe rules requiring each annual report required by section 78m(a) or 78o(d) of this title to contain an internal control report, which shall—

(1) state the responsibility of management for establishing and maintaining an adequate internal control structure and procedures for financial reporting; and

(2) contain an assessment, as of the end of the most recent fiscal year of the issuer, of the effectiveness of the internal control structure and procedures of the issuer for financial reporting.

(b) Internal control evaluation and reporting

With respect to the internal control assessment required by subsection (a) of this section, each registered public accounting firm that prepares or issues the audit report for the issuer shall attest to, and report on, the assessment made by the management of the issuer. An attestation made under this subsection shall be made in accordance with standards for attestation engagements issued or adopted by the Board. Any such attestation shall not be the subject of a separate engagement.

EXPLANATORY COMMENTS: *This section was enacted to prevent corporate executives from claiming they were ignorant of significant errors in their companies' financial reports. For instance, several CEOs testified before Congress that they simply had no idea that the corporations' financial statements were off by billions of dollars. Congress therefore passed Section 404, which requires each annual report to contain a description and assessment of the company's internal control structure and financial reporting procedures. The section also requires that an audit be conducted of the internal control assessment, as well as the financial statements contained in the report. This section goes hand in hand with Section 302 (which, as discussed previously, requires various certifications attesting to the accuracy of the information in financial reports).*

Section 404 has been one of the more controversial and expensive provisions in the Sarbanes-Oxley Act because it requires companies to assess their own internal financial controls to make sure that their financial statements are reliable and accurate. A corporation might need to set up a disclosure committee and a coordinator, establish codes of conduct for accounting and financial personnel, create documentation procedures, provide training, and outline the individuals who are responsible for performing each of the procedures. Companies that were already well managed have not experienced substantial difficulty complying with this section. Other companies, however, have spent millions of dollars setting up, documenting, and evaluating their internal financial control systems. Although initially creating the internal financial control system is a one-time-only expense, the costs of maintaining and evaluating it are ongoing. Some corporations that spent considerable sums complying with Section 404 have been able to offset these costs by discovering and correcting inefficiencies or frauds within their systems. Nevertheless, it is unlikely that any corporation will find compliance with this section to be inexpensive.

5. Codified at 15 U.S.C. Section 7262.

SECTION 802 (A)

Destruction, alteration, or falsification of records in Federal investigations and bankruptcy[6]

Whoever knowingly alters, destroys, mutilates, conceals, covers up, falsifies, or makes a false entry in any record, document, or tangible object with the intent to impede, obstruct, or influence the investigation or proper administration of any matter within the jurisdiction of any department or agency of the United States or any case filed under title 11, or in relation to or contemplation of any such matter or case, shall be fined under this title, imprisoned not more than 20 years, or both.

Destruction of corporate audit records[7]

(a)(1) Any accountant who conducts an audit of an issuer of securities to which section 10A(a) of the Securities Exchange Act of 1934 (15 U.S.C. 78j-1(a)) applies, shall maintain all audit or review workpapers for a period of 5 years from the end of the fiscal period in which the audit or review was concluded.

(2) The Securities and Exchange Commission shall promulgate, within 180 days, after adequate notice and an opportunity for comment, such rules and regulations, as are reasonably necessary, relating to the retention of relevant records such as workpapers, documents that form the basis of an audit or review, memoranda, correspondence, communications, other documents, and records (including electronic records) which are created, sent, or received in connection with an audit or review and contain conclusions, opinions, analyses, or financial data relating to such an audit or review, which is conducted by any accountant who conducts an audit of an issuer of securities to which section 10A(a) of the Securities Exchange Act of 1934 (15 U.S.C. 78j-1(a)) applies. The Commission may, from time to time, amend or supplement the rules and regulations that it is required to promulgate under this section, after adequate notice and an opportunity for comment, in order to ensure that such rules and regulations adequately comport with the purposes of this section.

(b) Whoever knowingly and willfully violates subsection (a)(1), or any rule or regulation promulgated by the Securities and Exchange Commission under subsection (a)(2), shall be fined under this title, imprisoned not more than 10 years, or both.

(c) Nothing in this section shall be deemed to diminish or relieve any person of any other duty or obligation

6. Codified at 15 U.S.C. Section 1519.
7. Codified at 15 U.S.C. Section 1520.

imposed by Federal or State law or regulation to maintain, or refrain from destroying, any document.

EXPLANATORY COMMENTS: *Section 802(a) enacted two new statutes that punish those who alter or destroy documents. The first statute is not specifically limited to securities fraud cases. It provides that anyone who alters, destroys, or falsifies records in federal investigations or bankruptcy may be criminally prosecuted and sentenced to a fine or to up to twenty years in prison, or both. The second statute requires auditors of public companies to keep all audit or review working papers for five years but expressly allows the SEC to amend or supplement these requirements as it sees fit. The SEC has, in fact, amended this section by issuing a rule that requires auditors who audit reporting companies to retain working papers for seven years from the conclusion of the review. Section 802(a) further provides that anyone who knowingly and willfully violates this statute is subject to criminal prosecution and can be sentenced to a fine, imprisoned for up to ten years, or both if convicted.*

This portion of the Sarbanes-Oxley Act implicitly recognizes that persons who are under investigation often are tempted to respond by destroying or falsifying documents that might prove their complicity in wrongdoing. The severity of the punishment should provide a strong incentive for these individuals to resist the temptation.

SECTION 804

Time limitations on the commencement of civil actions arising under Acts of Congress[8]

(a) Except as otherwise provided by law, a civil action arising under an Act of Congress enacted after the date of the enactment of this section may not be commenced later than 4 years after the cause of action accrues.

(b) Notwithstanding subsection (a), a private right of action that involves a claim of fraud, deceit, manipulation, or contrivance in contravention of a regulatory requirement concerning the securities laws, as defined in section 3(a)(47) of the Securities Exchange Act of 1934 (15 U.S.C. 78c(a)(47)), may be brought not later than the earlier of—

(1) 2 years after the discovery of the facts constituting the violation; or

(2) 5 years after such violation.

EXPLANATORY COMMENTS: *Prior to the enactment of this section, Section 10(b) of the Securities Exchange Act of 1934 had no express statute of limitations. The courts generally required plaintiffs to have filed suit within one year from the date that they should (using due diligence) have discovered that a fraud had been committed but no later than three years after the fraud occurred. Section 804 extends this period by specifying that plaintiffs must file a lawsuit within two years after they discover (or should have discovered) a fraud but no later than five years after the fraud's occurrence. This provision has prevented the courts from dismissing numerous securities fraud lawsuits.*

SECTION 806

Civil action to protect against retaliation in fraud cases[9]

(a) Whistleblower protection for employees of publicly traded companies.—

No company with a class of securities registered under section 12 of the Securities Exchange Act of 1934 (15 U.S.C. 78l), or that is required to file reports under section 15(d) of the Securities Exchange Act of 1934 (15 U.S.C. 78o(d)), or any officer, employee, contractor, subcontractor, or agent of such company, may discharge, demote, suspend, threaten, harass, or in any other manner discriminate against an employee in the terms and conditions of employment because of any lawful act done by the employee—

(1) to provide information, cause information to be provided, or otherwise assist in an investigation regarding any conduct which the employee reasonably believes constitutes a violation of section 1341, 1343, 1344, or 1348, any rule or regulation of the Securities and Exchange Commission, or any provision of Federal law relating to fraud against shareholders, when the information or assistance is provided to or the investigation is conducted by—

(A) a Federal regulatory or law enforcement agency;

(B) any Member of Congress or any committee of Congress; or

(C) a person with supervisory authority over the employee (or such other person working for the employer who has the authority to investigate, discover, or terminate misconduct); or

(2) to file, cause to be filed, testify, participate in, or otherwise assist in a proceeding filed or about to be filed (with any knowledge of the employer) relating to an alleged violation of section 1341, 1343, 1344, or 1348, any rule or regulation of the Securities and Exchange Commission, or any provision of Federal law relating to fraud against shareholders.

(b) Enforcement action.—

(1) In general.—A person who alleges discharge or other discrimination by any person in violation of subsection (a) may seek relief under subsection (c), by—

(A) filing a complaint with the Secretary of Labor; or

(B) if the Secretary has not issued a final decision within 180 days of the filing of the complaint and there is no showing that such delay is due to the

8. Codified at 28 U.S.C. Section 1658.

9. Codified at 18 U.S.C. Section 1514A.

bad faith of the claimant, bringing an action at law or equity for de novo review in the appropriate district court of the United States, which shall have jurisdiction over such an action without regard to the amount in controversy.

(2) Procedure.—

(A) In general.—An action under paragraph (1)(A) shall be governed under the rules and procedures set forth in section 42121(b) of title 49, United States Code.

(B) Exception.—Notification made under section 42121(b)(1) of title 49, United States Code, shall be made to the person named in the complaint and to the employer.

(C) Burdens of proof.—An action brought under paragraph (1)(B) shall be governed by the legal burdens of proof set forth in section 42121(b) of title 49, United States Code.

(D) Statute of limitations.—An action under paragraph (1) shall be commenced not later than 90 days after the date on which the violation occurs.

(c) Remedies.—

(1) In general.—An employee prevailing in any action under subsection (b)(1) shall be entitled to all relief necessary to make the employee whole.

(2) Compensatory damages.—Relief for any action under paragraph (1) shall include—

(A) reinstatement with the same seniority status that the employee would have had, but for the discrimination;

(B) the amount of back pay, with interest; and

(C) compensation for any special damages sustained as a result of the discrimination, including litigation costs, expert witness fees, and reasonable attorney fees.

(d) Rights retained by employee.—Nothing in this section shall be deemed to diminish the rights, privileges, or remedies of any employee under any Federal or State law, or under any collective bargaining agreement.

EXPLANATORY COMMENTS: *Section 806 is one of several provisions that were included in the Sarbanes-Oxley Act to encourage and protect whistleblowers—that is, employees who report their employer's alleged violations of securities law to the authorities. This section applies to employees, agents, and independent contractors who work for publicly traded companies or testify about such a company during an investigation. It sets up an administrative procedure at the Department of Labor for individuals who claim that their employer retaliated against them (fired or demoted them, for example) for blowing the whistle on the employer's wrongful conduct. It also allows the award of civil damages—including back pay, reinstatement, special damages, attorneys' fees, and court costs—to employees who prove that they suffered retaliation. Since this provision was enacted, whistleblowers have filed numerous complaints with the Department of Labor under this section.*

SECTION 807

Securities fraud[10]

Whoever knowingly executes, or attempts to execute, a scheme or artifice—

(1) to defraud any person in connection with any security of an issuer with a class of securities registered under section 12 of the Securities Exchange Act of 1934 (15 U.S.C. 78l) or that is required to file reports under section 15(d) of the Securities Exchange Act of 1934 (15 U.S.C. 78o(d)); or

(2) to obtain, by means of false or fraudulent pretenses, representations, or promises, any money or property in connection with the purchase or sale of any security of an issuer with a class of securities registered under section 12 of the Securities Exchange Act of 1934 (15 U.S.C. 78l) or that is required to file reports under section 15(d) of the Securities Exchange Act of 1934 (15 U.S.C. 78o(d)); shall be fined under this title, or imprisoned not more than 25 years, or both.

EXPLANATORY COMMENTS: *Section 807 adds a new provision to the federal criminal code that addresses securities fraud. Prior to 2002, federal securities law had already made it a crime—under Section 10(b) of the Securities Exchange Act of 1934 and SEC Rule 10b-5, both of which are discussed in Chapter 41—to intentionally defraud someone in connection with a purchase or sale of securities, but the offense was not listed in the federal criminal code. Also, paragraph 2 of Section 807 goes beyond what is prohibited under securities law by making it a crime to obtain by means of false or fraudulent pretenses any money or property from the purchase or sale of securities. This new provision allows violators to be punished by up to twenty-five years in prison, a fine, or both.*

SECTION 906

Failure of corporate officers to certify financial reports[11]

(a) Certification of periodic financial reports.—Each periodic report containing financial statements filed by an issuer with the Securities Exchange Commission pursuant to section 13(a) or 15(d) of the Securities Exchange Act of 1934 (15 U.S.C. 78m(a) or 78o(d)) shall be accompanied by a written statement by the chief executive officer and chief financial officer (or equivalent thereof) of the issuer.

10. Codified at 18 U.S.C. Section 1348.
11. Codified at 18 U.S.C. Section 1350.

(b) Content.—The statement required under subsection (a) shall certify that the periodic report containing the financial statements fully complies with the requirements of section 13(a) or 15(d) of the Securities Exchange Act of 1934 (15 U.S.C. 78m or 78o(d)) and that information contained in the periodic report fairly presents, in all material respects, the financial condition and results of operations of the issuer.

(c) Criminal penalties.—Whoever—

(1) certifies any statement as set forth in subsections (a) and (b) of this section knowing that the periodic report accompanying the statement does not comport with all the requirements set forth in this section shall be fined not more than $1,000,000 or imprisoned not more than 10 years, or both; or

(2) willfully certifies any statement as set forth in subsections (a) and (b) of this section knowing that the periodic report accompanying the statement does not comport with all the requirements set forth in this section shall be fined not more than $5,000,000, or imprisoned not more than 20 years, or both.

EXPLANATORY COMMENTS: *As previously discussed, under Section 302 a corporation's CEO and CFO are required to certify that they believe the quarterly and annual reports their company files with the SEC are accurate and fairly present the company's financial condition. Section 906 adds "teeth" to these requirements by authorizing criminal penalties for those officers who intentionally certify inaccurate SEC filings. Knowing violations of the requirements are punishable by a fine of up to $1 million, ten years in prison, or both. Willful violators may be fined up to $5 million, sentenced to up to twenty years in prison, or both. Although the difference between a knowing and a willful violation is not entirely clear, the section is obviously intended to remind corporate officers of the serious consequences of certifying inaccurate reports to the SEC.*

APPENDIX I

Sample Answers for End-of-Chapter *Questions with Sample Answer*

1–2A. Question with Sample Answer

At the time of the Nuremberg trials, "crimes against humanity" were new international crimes. The laws criminalized such acts as murder, extermination, enslavement, deportation, and other inhumane acts committed against any civilian population. These international laws derived their legitimacy from "natural law." Natural law, which is the oldest and one of the most significant schools of jurisprudence, holds that governments and legal systems should reflect the moral and ethical ideals that are inherent in human nature. Because natural law is universal and discoverable by reason, its adherents believe that all other law is derived from natural law. Natural law therefore supersedes laws created by humans (national, or "positive," law), and in a conflict between the two, national or positive law loses its legitimacy. The Nuremberg defendants asserted that they had been acting in accordance with German law. The judges dismissed these claims, reasoning that the defendants' acts were commonly regarded as crimes and that the accused must have known that the acts would be considered criminal. The judges clearly believed the tenets of natural law and expected that the defendants, too, should have been able to realize that their acts ran afoul of it. The fact that the "positivist law" of Germany at the time required them to commit these acts is irrelevant. Under natural law theory, the international court was justified in finding the defendants guilty of crimes against humanity.

2–2A. Question with Sample Answer

Trial courts, as explained in the text, are responsible for settling "questions of fact." Often, when parties bring a case to court there is a dispute as to what actually happened. Different witnesses have different versions of what they saw or heard, and there may be only indirect evidence of certain issues in dispute. During the trial, the judge and the jury (if it is a jury trial) listen to the witnesses and view the evidence firsthand. Thus, the trial court is in the best position to assess the credibility (truthfulness) of the witnesses and determine the weight that should be given to various items of evidence. At the end of the trial, the judge and the jury (if it is a jury trial) decide what will be considered facts for the purposes of the case. Trial courts are best suited to this job, as they have the opportunity to observe the witnesses and evidence, and they regularly determine the reliability of certain evidence. Appellate courts, in contrast, see only the written record of the trial court proceedings and cannot evaluate the credibility of witnesses and the persuasiveness of evidence. For these reasons, appellate courts nearly always defer to trial courts' findings of fact. An appellate court can reverse a lower court's findings of fact, however, when so little evidence was presented at trial that no reasonable person could have reached the conclusion that the judge or jury reached.

3–2A. Question with Sample Answer

Because the joint venture in Euphratia would naturally be subject to that country's laws, company lawyers would have to look to the agreements that the joint venture had signed with the national government as well as Euphratia's laws relating to the ownership of natural resources to determine whether they would interfere with the efforts by the two companies to resolve their dispute. All countries have the right to expropriate foreign-owned property as long as they pay adequate compensation to the owners. Because the Federal Arbitration Act accords parties significant discretion in deciding where disputes should be heard and which law should govern, virtually any dispute can be the subject of arbitration. The terms of a voluntary arbitration agreement will normally be enforced by the courts if the agreement does not compel an illegal act or contravene public policy. Assuming that Euphratia's laws did not violate U.S. public policy, the dispute itself should be arbitrable.

4–2A. Question with Sample Answer

This question essentially asks whether good behavior can ever be unethical. The answer to this question depends on which approach to ethical reasoning you are using. Under the outcome-based approach of utilitarianism, it is simply not possible for selfish motives to be unethical if they result in good conduct. A good outcome is moral regardless of the nature of the action itself or the reason for the action. Under a duty-based approach, motive would be more relevant in assessing whether a firm's conduct was ethical. You would need to analyze the firm's conduct in terms of religious truths or to determine whether human beings were being treated with the inherent dignity that they deserve. Although a good motive would not justify a bad act to a religious ethicist, in this situation the actions were good and the motive was questionable (because the firm was simply seeking to increase its profit). Nevertheless, unless one's religion prohibited making a profit, the firm's actions would likely not be considered unethical. Applying Kantian ethics would require you to evaluate the firm's actions in light of what would happen if everyone in society acted that way (categorical imperative). Here, because the conduct was good, it would be positive for society if every firm acted that way. Hence, the profit-seeking motive would be irrelevant in a Kantian analysis. In a debate between motive and conduct, then, conduct is almost always given greater weight in evaluating ethics.

5–2A. Question with Sample Answer

As the text points out, Thomas has a constitutionally protected right to his religion and the free exercise of it. In denying his unemployment benefits, the state violated these rights. Employers are obligated to make reasonable accommodations for their employees' beliefs, right or wrong, that are openly and sincerely held. Thomas's beliefs were openly and sincerely held. By placing him in a department that made military goods, his employer effectively put him in a position of having to choose between his job and his religious principles. This unilateral decision on the part of the employer was the reason Thomas left his job and why the company was required to compensate Thomas for his resulting unemployment.

6–2A. Question with Sample Answer

The court will consider first whether the agency followed the procedures prescribed in the Administrative Procedure Act (APA). Ordinarily, courts will not require agencies to use procedures beyond those of the APA. Courts will, however, compel agencies to follow their own rules. If an agency has adopted a rule granting extra procedures, the agency must provide those extra procedures, at least until the rule is formally rescinded. Ultimately, in this case, the court will most likely rule for the food producers.

7–3A. Question with Sample Answer

As you read in the text, some torts, including assault and battery, provide a basis for criminal prosecution as well as civil liability. This question aptly demonstrates this principle. Double jeopardy is a criminal law concept and does not constitute a defense against a civil lawsuit. The Fifth Amendment prohibition against double jeopardy means that once Armington has been tried and found guilty or not guilty for this assault, he may not be tried for it again. Nevertheless, Jennings may seek damages for his injuries in a civil lawsuit because Armington's prison sentence will do nothing to reimburse him for his medical bills and disability. Armington's guilty verdict has no bearing on the civil lawsuit. The criminal conviction, however, having been proved beyond a reasonable doubt, will likely improve Jennings's chances of recovering damages from Armington in a civil case. As you will recall, in a civil suit the plaintiff merely has to prove his or her case by a preponderance of the evidence. For Jennings, this burden of proof will probably be much easier to meet, given Armington's conviction.

8–2A. Question with Sample Answer

Each system has its advantages and its disadvantages. In a common law system, the courts independently develop the rules governing certain areas of law, such as torts and contracts. This judge-made law exists in addition to the laws passed by a legislature. Judges must follow precedential decisions in their jurisdictions, but courts may modify or even overturn precedents when deemed necessary. Also, if there is no case law to guide a court, the court may create a new rule of law. In a civil law system, the only official source of law is a statutory code. Courts are required to interpret the code and apply the rules to individual cases, but courts may not depart from the code and develop their own laws. In theory, the law code will set forth all the principles needed for the legal system. Common law and civil law systems are not wholly distinct. For example, the United States has a common law system, but crimes are defined by statute as in civil law systems. Civil law systems may allow considerable room for judges to develop law: law codes cannot be so precise as to address every contested issue, so the judiciary must interpret the codes. There are also significant differences among common law countries. The judges of different common law nations have produced differing common law principles. The roles of judges and lawyers under the different systems should be taken into account. Among other factors that should be considered in establishing a business law system and in deciding what regulations to impose are the goals that the system and its regulations are intended to achieve and the expectations of those to whom both will apply, including foreign and domestic investors.

9–2A. Question with Sample Answer

According to the question, Janine was apparently unconscious or otherwise unable to agree to a contract for the nursing services she received while she was in the hospital. As you read in the chapter, however, sometimes the law will create a fictional contract in order to prevent one party from unjustly receiving a benefit at the expense of another. This is known as a quasi contract and provides a basis for Nursing Services to recover the value of the services it provided while Janine was in the hospital. As for the at-home services that were provided to Janine, because Janine was aware that those services were being provided for her, Nursing Services can recover for those services under an implied-in-fact contract. Under this type of contract, the conduct of the parties creates and defines the terms. Janine's acceptance of the services constitutes her agreement to form a contract, and she will probably be required to pay Nursing Services in full.

10–2A. Question with Sample Answer

A novation exists when a new, valid contract expressly or impliedly discharges a prior contract by the substitution of a party. Accord and satisfaction exists when the parties agree that the original obligation can be discharged by a substituted performance. In this case, Fred's agreement with Iba to pay off Junior's debt for $1,100 (as compared to the $1,000 owed) is definitely a valid contract. The terms of the contract substitute Fred as the debtor for Junior, and Junior is definitely discharged from further liability. This agreement is a novation.

11–2A. Question with Sample Answer

Anne has entered into an enforceable contract to subscribe to *E-Commerce Weekly*. In this problem, the offer to deliver, via e-mail, the newsletter was presented by the offeror with a statement of how to accept—by clicking on the "SUBSCRIBE" button. Consideration was in the promise to deliver the newsletter and in the price that the subscriber agreed to pay. The offeree had an opportunity to read the terms of the subscription agreement before making the contract. Whether she actually read those terms does not matter.

12–2A. Question with Sample Answer

To answer this question, you must first decide if there is a legal theory under which Harley may be able to recover. You may recall from your reading the intentional tort of "wrongful interference with a contractual relationship." To recover damages under this theory, Harley would need to show that he and Martha had a valid contract, that Lothar knew of this contractual relationship between Martha and Harley, and that Lothar intentionally convinced Martha to break her contract with Harley. Even though Lothar hoped that his advertisments would persuade Martha to break her contract with Harley, the question states that Martha's decision to change bakers was based solely on the advertising and not on anything else that Lothar did. Lothar's advertisements did not constitute a tort. Note, though, that while Harley cannot collect from Lothar for Martha's actions, he does have a cause of action against Martha for her breach of their contract.

13–3A. Question with Sample Answer

If Colt can prove that all due care was exercised in the manufacture of the pistol, Colt cannot be held in an action based on negligence. Under the theory of strict liability in tort, however, Colt can be held liable regardless of the degree of care exercised. The doctrine of strict liability states that a merchant-seller who sells a defective product that is unreasonably dangerous is liable for injuries caused by that product (even if all possible care in preparation and sale is exercised), provided that the product has not been substantially changed after the time of sale. Therefore, if Wayne can prove the pistol is defective, unreasonably dangerous, and caused him injury, Colt as a merchant is strictly liable, because there is no evidence that the pistol has been altered since the date of its manufacture.

14–2A. Question with Sample Answer

(a) Ursula will not be held liable for copyright infringement in this case because her photocopying pages for use in scholarly research falls squarely under the "fair use" exception to the Copyright Act.

(b) While Ursula's actions are improper, they could constitute trademark infringement, not copyright infringement. Copyrights are granted for literary and artistic productions; trademarks are distinctive marks created and used by manufacturers to differentiate their goods from those of their competitors. Trademark infringement occurs when a mark is copied to a substantial degree, intentionally or unintentionally.

(c) As with the answer to (a) above, Ursula's actions fall within the "fair use" doctrine of copyright law. Her use of the recorded television shows for teaching is the exact type of use the exception is designed to cover.

15–2A. Question with Sample Answer

A trustee is given avoidance powers by the Bankruptcy Code. One situation in which the trustee can avoid transfers of property or payments by a debtor to a creditor is when such transfer constitutes a *preference*. A preference is a transfer of property or payment that favors one creditor over another. For a preference to exist, the debtor must be insolvent and must have made payment for a preexisting debt within ninety days of the filing of the petition in bankruptcy. The Code provides that the debtor is *presumed* to be insolvent during this ninety-day period. If the payment is made to an insider (and in this case payment was made to a close relative), the preference period is extended to one year, but the presumption of insolvency still applies only to the ninety-day period. In this case, the trustee has an excellent chance of having both payments declared preferences. The payment to Cool Springs was within ninety days of the filing of the petition, and it is doubtful that Cool Springs could overcome the presumption that Peaslee was insolvent at the time the payment was made. The $5,000 payment was made to an insider, Peaslee's father, and any payment made to an insider within one year of the petition of bankruptcy is a preference—as long as the debtor was insolvent at the time of payment. The facts indicate that Peaslee probably was insolvent at the time he paid his father. If he was not, the payment is not a preference, and the trustee's avoidance of the transfer would be improper.

16–2A. Question with Sample Answer

The court would likely conclude that National Foods was responsible for the acts of harassment by the manager at the franchised restaurant, on the ground that the employees were the agents of National Foods. An agency relationship can be implied from the circumstances and conduct of the parties. The important question is the degree of control that a franchisor has over its franchisees. Whether it exercises that control is beside the point. Here, National Foods retained considerable control over the new hires and the franchisee's policies, as well as the right to terminate the franchise for violations. That its supervisors routinely approved the policies would not undercut National Foods' liability.

17–3A. Question with Sample Answer

(a) A limited partner's interest is assignable. In fact, assignment allows the assignee to become a substituted limited partner with the consent of the remaining partners. The assignment, however, does not dissolve the limited partnership.

(b) Bankruptcy of the limited partnership itself causes dissolution, but bankruptcy of one of the limited partners does not dissolve the partnership unless it causes the bankruptcy of the firm.

(c) The retirement, death, or insanity of a general partner dissolves the partnership unless the business can be continued by the remaining general partners. Because Dorinda was the only general partner, her death dissolves the limited partnership.

18–2A. Question with Sample Answer

Directors are personally answerable to the corporation and the shareholders for breach of their duty to exercise reasonable care in conducting the affairs of the corporation. Reasonable care is defined as being the degree of care that a reasonably prudent person would use in the conduct of personal business affairs. When directors delegate the running of the corporate affairs to officers, the directors are expected to use reasonable care in the selection and supervision of such officers. Failure to do so will make the directors liable for negligence or mismanagement. A director who dissents to an action by the board is not personally liable for losses resulting from that action. Unless the dissent is entered into the board meeting minutes, however, the director is presumed to have assented. Therefore, the first issue in the case of AstroStar, Inc., is whether the board members failed to use reasonable care in the selection of the president. If so, and particularly if the board failed to provide a reasonable amount of supervision (and openly embezzled funds indicate that failure), the directors will be personally liable. This liability will include Eckhart unless she can prove that she dissented and that she tried to reasonably supervise the new president. Considering the facts in this case, it is questionable that Eckhart could prove this.

19–2A. Question with Sample Answer

On creation of an agency, the agent owes certain fiduciary duties to the principal. Two such duties are the duty of loyalty and the duty to inform or notify. The duty of loyalty is a fundamental concept of the fiduciary relationship. The agent must act solely for the benefit of the principal, not in the agent's own interest or in the interest of another person. One of the principles invoked by this duty is that an agent employed to sell cannot become a purchaser without the principal's consent. When the agent is a partner, contracting to sell to another partner is equivalent to selling to oneself and is therefore a breach of the agent's duty. In addition, the agent has a duty to disclose to the principal any facts pertinent to the subject matter of the agency. Failure to disclose to Peter the knowledge of the shopping mall and the increased market value of the property also was a breach of Alice's fiduciary duties. When an agent breaches fiduciary duties owed to the principal by becoming a recipient of a contract, the contract is voidable at the election of the principal. Neither Carl nor Alice can hold Peter to the contract, and Alice's breach of fiduciary duties also allows Peter to terminate the agency relationship.

20–2A. Question with Sample Answer

The Occupational Health and Safety Act (OSHA) requires employers to provide safe working conditions for employees. The act prohibits employers from discharging or discriminating against any employee who refuses to work when the employee believes in good faith that he or she will risk death or great bodily harm by undertaking the employment activity. Denton and Carlo had sufficient reason to believe that the maintenance job required of them by their employer involved great risk, and therefore, under OSHA, their discharge was wrongful. Denton and Carlo can turn to the Occupational Safety and Health Administration, which is part of the Department of Labor, for assistance.

21–2A. Question with Sample Answer

An employer can legally impose an educational requirement if the requirement is directly related to, and necessary for, performance of the job. In this situation, the employer is requiring a high school diploma as a condition of employment for its cleaning crew. A high school diploma is not related to, or necessary for, the competent performance of a job on a cleaning crew. Chinawa obviously comes under Title VII of the 1964 Civil Rights Act, as amended. Therefore, if someone were to challenge Chinawa's practices, a court would be likely to consider the disparate impact that the educational requirement had on Chinawa's hiring of minorities. Chinawa's educational requirement resulted in its hiring an all-white cleaning crew in an area in which 75 percent of the pool of qualified applicants were minorities. Therefore, Chinawa's educational requirement would likely be considered unintentional (disparate-impact) discrimination against minorities.

22–3A. Question with Sample Answer

The NLRB has consistently been suspicious of companies that grant added benefits during election campaigns. These benefits will be considered as an unfair labor practice that biases elections, unless the employer can demonstrate that the benefits were unrelated to the unionization and would have been granted anyway.

23–3A. Question with Sample Answer

Yes. A regulation of the Federal Trade Commission (FTC) under Section 5 of the Federal Trade Commission Act makes it a violation for door-to-door sellers to fail to give consumers three days to cancel any sale. In addition, a number of state statutes require this three-day "cooling off" period to protect consumers from unscrupulous door-to-door sellers. Because the Gonchars sought to rescind the contract within the three-day period, Renowned Books was obligated to agree to cancel the contract. Its failure to allow rescission was in violation of the FTC regulation and of most state statutes.

24–2A. Question with Sample Answer

Fruitade has violated a number of federal environmental laws if such actions are being taken without a permit. First, because the dumping is in a navigable waterway, the River and Harbor Act of 1886, as amended, has been violated. Second, the Clean Water Act of 1972, as amended, has been violated. This act is designed to make the waters safe for swimming, to protect fish and wildlife, and to eliminate discharge of pollutants into the water. Both the crushed glass and the acid violate this act. Third, the Toxic Substances Control Act of 1976 was passed to regulate chemicals that are known to be toxic and could have an effect on human health and the environment. The acid in the cleaning fluid or compound could come under this act.

25–3A. Question with Sample Answer

Because all land-use regulations necessarily limit the ways in which property may be used, a regulation by itself will not generally be considered a compensable taking. Compensation will be required only if the regulation itself is found to be overly burdensome and thus subject to the requirement that just compensation be paid. Rezoning the land from industrial use to commercial use—despite the expected reduction in its market value—would probably not be considered a compensable taking because it would not prevent the owner from using the land for any reasonable income-producing or private purpose.

26–3A. Question with Sample Answer

Super-Tech's unilateral action is a violation of the Sherman Act, Section 2. Super-Tech already controls a substantial portion of the market for computers and thus has a monopoly position in this business field. Super-Tech's action is a misuse of its monopoly power in the marketplace. Any person who shall monopolize or attempt to monopolize any part of trade or commerce may be in violation of the Sherman Act. Therefore, Alcan can file a private action seeking treble damages, costs, and reasonable attorneys' fees, and the Department of Justice can institute criminal and civil proceedings.

27–3A. Question with Sample Answer

(a) Trujillo's pricing limitations are clearly an attempt at resale price maintenance and vertical price fixing which here are violations of the Sherman Act. The reasons given by the courts for holding these agreements to be illegal are that the limitations (1) tend to provide the same economic rewards to all retailers, regardless of skill, experience, and the like; (2) restrict innovation and deter a retailer from trying out new competitive techniques; and (3) may be so restrictive in the future as to fix a uniform price.

(b) Generally, whenever two or more competitors make any agreement to fix prices, it is considered a per se violation of the Sherman Act, Section 1. This is called horizontal price fixing, and generally the court will find any agreement to fix prices among competitors to be illegal. This can result in a criminal conviction. Whether this agreement will be a violation of the Sherman Act with possible criminal conviction will depend on the intent of the parties. Simply "an effect on prices, without more, will not support a criminal conviction under the Sherman Act." If this is truly a patriotic gesture and an aid to assist the unemployed, this intent could be determinative.

(c) Foam Beer's recommended or suggested prices to its distributors is not a violation of the Sherman Act, Section 1. There is no agreement, express or implied, that a distributor must resell the beer at those prices to continue to do business with Foam. All facts indicate that the price suggestions are merely a benchmark based on past attempts of distributors to make a reasonable profit. No price restrictions are imposed by Foam.

28–2A. Question with Sample Answer

No. Under federal securities law, a stock split is exempt from registration requirements. This is because no *sale* of stock is involved. The existing shares are merely being split, and no consideration is received by the corporation for the additional shares created.

Glossary

A

Abandonment In landlord-tenant law, a tenant's departure from leased premises completely, with no intention of returning before the end of the lease term.

Abus de droit A doctrine developed in the French courts. The doctrine modified employment at will and protected workers exercising their rights from wrongful discharge and other employer abuses.

Acceptance In contract law, the offeree's notification to the offeror that the offeree agrees to be bound by the terms of the offeror's proposal. Although historically the terms of acceptance had to be the mirror image of the terms of the offer, the Uniform Commercial Code provides that even modified terms of the offer in a definite expression of acceptance constitute a contract.

Accredited investors In the context of securities offerings, "sophisticated" investors, such as banks, insurance companies, investment companies, the issuer's executive officers and directors, and persons whose income or net worth exceeds certain limits.

Acquittal A certification or declaration following a trial that the individual accused of a crime is innocent, or free from guilt, and is thus absolved of the charges.

Act of state doctrine A doctrine that provides that the judicial branch of one country will not examine the validity of public acts committed by a recognized foreign government within its own territory.

Actionable Capable of serving as the basis of a lawsuit.

Actual authority Authority of an agent that is express or implied.

Actual malice A condition that exists when a person makes a statement with either knowledge of its falsity or a reckless disregard for the truth. In a defamation suit, a statement made about a public figure normally must be made with actual malice for liability to be incurred.

Actus reus (pronounced *ak*-tus *ray*-uhs) A guilty (prohibited) act. The commission of a prohibited act is one of the two essential elements required for criminal liability, the other element being the intent to commit a crime.

Adequate protection doctrine In bankruptcy law, a doctrine that protects secured creditors from losing their security as a result of an automatic stay on legal proceedings by creditors against the debtor once the debtor petitions for bankruptcy relief. In certain circumstances, the bankruptcy court may provide adequate protection by requiring the debtor or trustee to pay the creditor or provide additional guaranties to protect the creditor against the losses suffered by the creditor as a result of the stay.

Adhesion contract A "standard-form" contract, such as that between a large retailer and a consumer, in which the stronger party dictates the terms.

Adjudicate To render a judicial decision. In the administrative process, the proceeding in which an administrative law judge hears and decides on issues that arise when an administrative agency charges a person or a firm with violating a law or regulation enforced by the agency.

Adjudication The process of adjudicating. *See* Adjudicate

Administrative agency A federal or state government agency established to perform a specific function. Administrative agencies are authorized by legislative acts to make and enforce rules to administer and enforce the acts.

Administrative law The body of law created by administrative agencies (in the form of rules, regulations, orders, and decisions) in order to carry out their duties and responsibilities.

Administrative law judge (ALJ) One who presides over an administrative agency hearing and who has the power to administer oaths, take testimony, rule on questions of evidence, and make determinations of fact.

Adverse possession The acquisition of title to real property by occupying it openly, without the consent of the owner, for a period of time specified by a state statute. The occupation must be actual, open, notorious, exclusive, and in opposition to all others, including the owner.

Affidavit A written or printed voluntary statement of facts, confirmed by the oath or affirmation of the party making it and made before a person having the authority to administer the oath or affirmation.

Affirmative action Job-hiring policies that give special consideration to members of protected classes in an effort to overcome present effects of past discrimination.

Affirmative defense A response to a plaintiff's claim that does not deny the plaintiff's facts but attacks the plaintiff's legal right to bring an action. An example is the running of the statute of limitations.

After-acquired property Property of the debtor that is acquired after the execution of a security agreement.

Age of majority The age at which an individual is considered legally capable of conducting himself or herself responsibly. A person of this age is entitled to the full rights of citizenship, including the right to vote in elections. In contract law, one who is no longer an infant and can no longer disaffirm a contract.

Agency A relationship between two parties in which one party (the agent) agrees to represent or act for the other (the principal).

Agent A person who agrees to represent or act for another, called the principal.

Agreement A meeting of two or more minds in regard to the terms of a contract; usually broken down into two events—an offer by one party to form a contract, and an acceptance of the offer by the person to whom the offer is made.

Alien corporation A designation in the United States for a corporation formed in another country but doing business in the United States.
Allegation A statement, claim, or assertion.
Allege To state, recite, assert, or charge.
Alternative dispute resolution (ADR) The resolution of disputes in ways other than those involved in the traditional judicial process. Negotiation, mediation, and arbitration are forms of ADR.
Analogy In logical reasoning, an assumption that if two things are similar in some respects, they will be similar in other respects also. Often used in legal reasoning to infer the appropriate application of legal principles in a case being decided by referring to previous cases involving different facts but considered to come within the policy underlying the rule.
Answer Procedurally, a defendant's response to the plaintiff's complaint.
Anticipatory repudiation An assertion or action by a party indicating that he or she will not perform an obligation that the party is contractually obligated to perform at a future time.
Antitrust law The body of federal and state laws and statutes protecting trade and commerce from unlawful restraints, price discrimination, price fixing, and monopolies. The principal federal antitrust statues are the Sherman Act of 1890, the Clayton Act of 1914, and the Federal Trade Commission Act of 1914.
Apparent authority Authority that is only apparent, not real. In agency law, a person may be deemed to have had the power to act as an agent for another party if the other party's manifestations to a third party led the third party to believe that an agency existed when, in fact, it did not.
Appeal Resort to a superior court, such as an appellate court, to review the decision of an inferior court, such as a trial court or an administrative agency.
Appellant The party who takes an appeal from one court to another.
Appellate jurisdiction Courts having appellate jurisdiction act as reviewing courts, or appellate courts. Generally, cases can be brought before appellate courts only on appeal from an order or a judgment of a trial court or other lower court.
Appellee The party against whom an appeal is taken—that is, the party who opposes setting aside or reversing the judgment.
Appropriate bargaining unit A designation based on job duties, skill levels, etc., of the proper entity that should be covered by collective bargaining agreement.
Appropriation In tort law, the use by one person of another person's name, likeness, or other identifying characteristic without permission and for the benefit of the user.
Arbitrary and capricious test The court reviewing an informal administrative agency action applies this test to determine whether or not that action was in clear error. The court gives wide discretion to the expertise of the agency and decides if the agency had sufficient factual information on which to base its action. If no clear error was made, then the agency's action stands.
Arbitration The settling of a dispute by submitting it to a disinterested third party (other than a court), who renders a decision. The decision may or may not be legally binding.
Arbitration clause A clause in a contract that provides that, in the event of a dispute, the parties will submit the dispute to arbitration rather than litigate the dispute in court.
Arbitrator A disinterested party who, by prior agreement of the parties submitting their dispute to arbitration, has the power to resolve the dispute and (generally) bind the parties.
Arraignment A procedure in which an accused person is brought before the court to plead to the criminal charge in the indictment or information. The charge is read to the person, and he or she is asked to enter a plea—such as "guilty" or "not guilty."
Arson The malicious burning of another's dwelling. Some statutes have expanded this to include any real property regardless of ownership and the destruction of property by other means—for example, by explosion.
Articles of incorporation The document filed with the appropriate governmental agency, usually the secretary of state, when a business is incorporated; state statutes usually prescribe what kind of information must be contained in the articles of incorporation.
Articles of organization The document filed with a designated state official by which a limited liability company is formed.
Articles of partnership A written agreement that sets forth each partner's rights and obligations with respect to the partnership.
Assault Any word or action intended to make another person fearful of immediate physical harm; a reasonably believable threat.
Assignment The act of transferring to another all or part of one's rights arising under a contract.
Assumption of risk A defense against negligence that can be used when the plaintiff is aware of a danger and voluntarily assumes the risk of injury from that danger.
Attempt to monopolize Any actions by a firm to eliminate competition and gain monopoly power.
Authorization card A card signed by an employee that gives a union permission to act on his or her behalf in negotiations with management. Unions typically use authorization cards as evidence of employee support during union organization.
Automatic stay In bankruptcy proceedings, the suspension of virtually all litigation and other action by creditors against the debtor or the debtor's property; the stay is effective the moment the debtor files a petition in bankruptcy.
Award In the context of litigation, the amount of money awarded to a plaintiff in a civil lawsuit as damages. In the context of arbitration, the arbitrator's decision.

Bailment A situation in which the personal property of one person (a bailor) is entrusted to another (a bailee), who is obligated to return the bailed property to the bailor or dispose of it as directed.
Bailor One who entrusts goods to a bailee.
Bait-and-switch advertising Advertising a product at a very attractive price (the "bait") and then informing the consumer, once he or she is in the store, that the advertised product is either not available or is of poor quality; the customer is then urged to purchase ("switched" to) a more expensive item.
Bankruptcy court A federal court of limited jurisdiction that handles only bankruptcy proceedings. Bankruptcy proceedings are governed by federal bankruptcy law.
Battery The unprivileged, intentional touching of another.
Beyond a reasonable doubt The standard used to determine the guilt or innocence of a person criminally charged. To be guilty of a crime, one must be proved guilty "beyond and to the exclusion of every reasonable doubt." A reasonable doubt is one that would cause a prudent person to hesitate before acting in matters important to him or her.
Bilateral contract A type of contract that arises when a promise is given in exchange for a return promise.
Bill of Rights The first ten amendments to the U.S. Constitution.
Binding authority Any source of law that a court must follow when deciding a case. Binding authorities include constitutions, statutes, and regulations that govern the issue being decided, as well as court decisions that are controlling precedents within the jurisdiction.

Blue sky laws State laws that regulate the offer and sale of securities.
Bona fide Good faith. A bona fide obligation is one made in good faith—that is, sincerely and honestly.
Bona fide occupational qualification (BFOQ) Identifiable characteristics reasonably necessary to the normal operation of a particular business. These characteristics can include gender, national origin, and religion, but not race.
Boycott A concerted refusal to do business with a particular person or entity in order to obtain concessions or to express displeasure with certain acts or practices of that person or business. *See also* Secondary boycott
Breach To violate a law, by an act or an omission, or to break a legal obligation that one owes to another person or to society.
Breach of contract The failure, without legal excuse, of a promisor to perform the obligations of a contract.
Brief A formal legal document submitted by the attorney for the appellant—or the appellee (in answer to the appellant's brief)—to an appellate court when a case is appealed. The appellant's brief outlines the facts and issues of the case, the judge's rulings or jury's findings that should be reversed or modified, the applicable law, and the arguments on the client's behalf.
Browse-wrap terms Terms and conditions of use that are presented to an Internet user at the time certain products, such as software, are being downloaded but that need not be agreed to (by clicking "I agree," for example) before being able to install or use the product.
Bulk zoning Zoning regulations that restrict the amount of structural coverage on a particular parcel of land.
Bureaucracy A large organization that is structured hierarchically to carry out specific functions.
Burglary The unlawful entry into a building with the intent to commit a felony. (Some state statutes expand this to include the intent to commit any crime.)
Business ethics Ethics in a business context; a consensus of what constitutes right or wrong behavior in the world of business and the application of moral principles to situations that arise in a business setting.
Business invitees Those people, such as customers or clients, who are invited onto business premises by the owner of those premises for business purposes.
Business judgment rule A rule that immunizes corporate management from liability for actions that result in corporate losses or damages if the actions are undertaken in good faith and are within both the power of the corporation and the authority of management to make.
Business necessity A defense to allegations of employment discrimination in which the employer demonstrates that an employment practice that discriminates against members of a protected class is related to job performance.
Business tort The wrongful interference with the business rights of another.
Buyer in the ordinary course of business A buyer who, in good faith and without knowledge that the sale to him or her is in violation of the ownership rights or security interest of a third party in the goods, purchases goods in the ordinary course of business from a person in the business of selling goods of that kind.
Buyout price The amount payable to a partner on his or her dissociation from a partnership, based on the amount distributable to that partner if the firm were wound up on that date, and offset by any damages for wrongful dissociation.
Buy-sell agreement In the context of partnerships, an express agreement made at the time of partnership formation for one or more of the partners to buy out the other or others should the situation warrant—and thus provide for the smooth dissolution of the partnership.
Bylaws A set of governing rules adopted by a corporation or other association.

C

Case law The rules of law announced in court decisions. Case law includes the aggregate of reported cases that interpret judicial precedents, statutes, regulations, and constitutional provisions.
Case on point A previous case involving factual circumstances and issues that are similar to the case before the court.
Categorical imperative A concept developed by the philosopher Immanuel Kant as an ethical guideline for behavior. In deciding whether an action is right or wrong, or desirable or undesirable, a person should evaluate the action in terms of what would happen if everybody else in the same situation, or category, acted the same way.
Causation in fact An act or omission without ("but for") which an event would not have occurred.
Cease-and-desist order An administrative or judicial order prohibiting a person or business firm from conducting activities that an agency or court has deemed illegal.
Certificate of limited partnership The basic document filed with a designated state official by which a limited partnership is formed.
Certification mark A mark used by one or more persons, other than the owner, to certify the region, materials, mode of manufacture, quality, or accuracy of the owner's goods or services. When used by members of a cooperative, association, or other organization, such a mark is referred to as a collective mark. Examples of certification marks include the "Good Housekeeping Seal of Approval" and "UL Tested."
Chancellor An adviser to the king at the time of the early king's courts of England. Individuals petitioned the king for relief when they could not obtain an adequate remedy in a court of law, and these petitions were decided by the chancellor.
Charging order In partnership law, an order granted by a court to a judgment creditor that entitles the creditor to attach profits or assets of a partner on dissolution of the partnership.
Checks and balances The national government is composed of three separate branches: the executive, the legislative, and the judicial branches. Each branch of the government exercises a check on the actions of the others.
Citation A reference to a publication in which a legal authority—such as a statute or a court decision—or other source can be found.
Civil law The branch of law dealing with the definition and enforcement of all private or public rights, as opposed to criminal matters.
Civil law system A system of law derived from that of the Roman Empire and based on a code rather than case law; the predominant system of law in the nations of continental Europe and the nations that were once their colonies. In the United States, Louisiana is the only state that has a civil law system.
Click-on agreement An agreement that arises when a buyer, engaging in a transaction on a computer, indicates his or her assent to be bound by the terms of an offer by clicking on a button that says, for example, "I agree"; sometimes referred to as a *click-on license* or a *click-wrap agreement.*
Close corporation A corporation whose shareholders are limited to a small group of persons, often including only family members. The rights of shareholders of a close corporation usually are restricted regarding the transfer of shares to others.
Closed shop A firm that requires union membership by its workers as a condition of employment. The closed shop was made illegal by the Labor-Management Relations Act of 1947.

Closing The final step in the sale of real estate—also called *settlement* or *closing escrow*. The escrow agent coordinates the closing with the recording of deeds, the obtaining of title insurance, and other concurrent closing activities. A number of costs must be paid, in cash, at the time of closing, and they can range from several hundred to several thousand dollars, depending on the amount of the mortgage loan and other conditions of the sale.

Closing argument An argument made after the plaintiff and defendant have rested their cases. Closing arguments are made prior to the jury charges.

Collective bargaining The process by which labor and management negotiate the terms and conditions of employment, including working hours and workplace conditions.

Collective mark A mark used by members of a cooperative, association, or other organization to certify the region, materials, mode of manufacture, quality, or accuracy of the specific goods or services. Examples of collective marks include the labor union marks found on tags of certain products and the credits of movies, which indicate the various associations and organizations that participated in the making of the movies.

Comity A deference by which one nation gives effect to the laws and judicial decrees of another nation. This recognition is based primarily on respect.

Commerce clause The provision in Article I, Section 8, of the U.S. Constitution that gives Congress the power to regulate interstate commerce.

Commercial impracticability A doctrine under which a seller may be excused from performing a contract when (1) a contingency occurs, (2) the contingency's occurrence makes performance impracticable, and (3) the nonoccurrence of the contingency was a basic assumption on which the contract was made. Despite the fact that UCC 2–615 expressly frees only sellers under this doctrine, courts have not distinguished between buyers and sellers in applying it.

Commingle To mix together. To put funds or goods together into one mass so that the funds or goods are so mixed that they no longer have separate identities. In corporate law, if personal and corporate interests are commingled to the extent that the corporation has no separate identity, a court may "pierce the corporate veil" and expose the shareholders to personal liability.

Common law That body of law developed from custom or judicial decisions in English and U.S. courts, not attributable to a legislature.

Common situs picketing The illegal picketing of an entire construction site by workers who are involved in a labor dispute with a particular subcontractor.

Community property A form of concurrent ownership of property in which each spouse technically owns an undivided one-half interest in property acquired during the marriage. This form of joint ownership occurs in only nine states and Puerto Rico.

Comparative law The study and comparison of legal systems and laws across nations.

Comparative negligence A theory in tort law under which the liability for injuries resulting from negligent acts is shared by all parties who were negligent (including the injured party), on the basis of each person's proportionate negligence.

Compensatory damages A monetary award equivalent to the actual value of injuries or damages sustained by the aggrieved party.

Complaint The pleading made by a plaintiff alleging wrongdoing on the part of the defendant; the document that, when filed with a court, initiates a lawsuit.

Computer crime Any wrongful act that is directed against computers and computer parties, or wrongful use or abuse of computers or software.

Concentrated industry An industry in which a large percentage of market sales is controlled by either a single firm or a small number of firms.

Concerted action Action by employees, such as a strike or picketing, with the purpose of furthering their bargaining demands or other mutual interests.

Conciliation A form of alternative dispute resolution in which the parties reach an agreement themselves with the help of a neutral third party, called a conciliator, who facilitates the negotiations.

Concurrent jurisdiction Jurisdiction that exists when two different courts have the power to hear a case. For example, some cases can be heard in either a federal or a state court.

Concurrent ownership Joint ownership.

Condemnation The process of taking private property for public use through the government's power of eminent domain.

Condition A qualification, provision, or clause in a contractual agreement, the occurrence of which creates, suspends, or terminates the obligations of the contracting parties.

Confession of judgment The act of a debtor in permitting a judgment to be entered against him or her by a creditor, for an agreed sum, without the institution of legal proceedings.

Confiscation A government's taking of privately owned business or personal property without a proper public purpose or an award of just compensation.

Conforming goods Goods that conform to contract specifications.

Conglomerate merger A merger between firms that do not compete with each other because they are in different markets (as opposed to horizontal and vertical mergers).

Consent Voluntary agreement to a proposition or an act of another. A concurrence of wills.

Consequential damages Special damages that compensate for a loss that is not direct or immediate (for example, lost profits). The special damages must have been reasonably foreseeable at the time the breach or injury occurred in order for the plaintiff to collect them.

Consideration Generally, the value given in return for a promise. The consideration, which must be present to make the contract legally binding, must be something of legally sufficient value and bargained for and must result in a detriment to the promisee or a benefit to the promisor.

Consignment A transaction in which an owner of goods (the consignor) delivers the goods to another (the consignee) for the consignee to sell. The consignee pays the consignor for the goods when they are sold by the consignee.

Constitutional law Law that is based on the U.S. Constitution and the constitutions of the various states.

Constructive delivery An act equivalent to the actual, physical delivery of property that cannot be physically delivered because of difficulty or impossibility; for example, the transfer of a key to a safe constructively delivers the contents of the safe.

Constructive discharge A termination of employment brought about by making an employee's working conditions so intolerable that the employee reasonably feels compelled to leave.

Constructive eviction A form of eviction that occurs when a landlord fails to perform adequately any of the undertakings (such as providing heat in the winter) required by the lease, thereby making the tenant's further use and enjoyment of the property exceedingly difficult or impossible.

Consumer-debtor An individual whose debts are primarily consumer debts (debts for purchases made primarily for personal or household use).

Consumer goods Goods that are primarily for personal or household use.

Consumer law The body of statutes, agency rules, and judicial decisions protecting consumers of goods and services from dangerous manufacturing techniques, mislabeling, unfair credit practices, deceptive advertising, and so on. Consumer laws provide remedies and protections that are not ordinarily available to merchants or to businesses.

Contract An agreement that can be enforced in court; formed by two or more parties, each of whom agrees to perform or to refrain from performing some act now or in the future.

Contractual capacity The threshold mental capacity required by the law for a party who enters into a contract to be bound by that contract.

Contributory negligence A theory in tort law under which a complaining party's own negligence contributed to or caused his or her injuries. Contributory negligence is an absolute bar to recovery in a minority of jurisdictions.

Conversion The wrongful taking, using, or retaining possession of personal property that belongs to another.

Conveyance The transfer of a title to land from one person to another by deed; a document (such as a deed) by which an interest in land is transferred from one person to another.

Co-ownership Joint ownership.

Copyright The exclusive right of authors to publish, print, or sell an intellectual production for a statutory period of time. A copyright has the same monopolistic nature as a patent or trademark, but it differs in that it applies exclusively to works of art, literature, and other works of authorship, including computer programs.

Corporate governance The system by which corporations are directed and controlled and which governs the relationship of the corporation to its shareholders. The corporate governance structure specifies the distribution of rights and responsibilities among different groups within the corporation and spells out the rules and procedures for making corporate decisions.

Corporate social responsibility The concept that corporations can and should act ethically and be accountable to society for their actions.

Corporation A legal entity formed in compliance with statutory requirements. The entity is distinct from its shareholders-owners.

Cost-benefit analysis A decision-making technique that involves weighing the costs of a given action against the benefits of the action.

Co-surety A joint surety. One who assumes liability jointly with another surety for the payment of an obligation.

Counteradvertising New advertising that is undertaken pursuant to a Federal Trade Commission order for the purpose of correcting earlier false claims that were made about a product.

Counterclaim A claim made by a defendant in a civil lawsuit that in effect sues the plaintiff.

Counteroffer An offeree's response to an offer in which the offeree rejects the original offer and at the same time makes a new offer.

Court of equity A court that decides controversies and administers justice according to the rules, principles, and precedents of equity.

Court of law A court in which the only remedies that could be granted were things of value, such as money damages. In the early English king's courts, courts of law were distinct from courts of equity.

Covenant not to compete A contractual promise to refrain from competing with another party for a certain period of time (not excessive in duration) and within a reasonable geographic area. Although covenants not to compete restrain trade, they are commonly found in partnership agreements, business sale agreements, and employment contracts. If they are ancillary to such agreements, covenants not to compete will normally be enforced by the courts unless the time period or geographic area is deemed unreasonable.

Covenant of quiet enjoyment A promise by a grantor (or landlord) that the grantee (or tenant) will not be evicted or disturbed by the grantor or a person having a lien or superior title.

Covenant running with the land An executory promise made between a grantor and a grantee to which they and subsequent owners of the land are bound.

Cover Under the Uniform Commercial Code, a remedy of the buyer or lessee that allows the buyer or lessee, on the seller's or lessor's breach, to purchase the goods from another seller or lessor and substitute them for the goods due under the contract. If the cost of cover exceeds the cost of the contract goods, the breaching seller or lessor will be liable to the buyer or lessee for the difference. In obtaining cover, the buyer or lessee must act in good faith and without unreasonable delay.

Cram-down provision A provision of the Bankruptcy Code that allows a court to confirm a debtor's Chapter 11 reorganization plan even though only one class of creditors has accepted it. To exercise the court's right under this provision, the court must demonstrate that the plan does not discriminate unfairly against any creditors and is fair and equitable.

Crashworthiness doctrine A doctrine that imposes liability for defects in the design or construction of motor vehicles that increase the extent of injuries to passengers if an accident occurs. The doctrine holds even when the defects do not actually cause the accident.

Creditor A person to whom a debt is owed by another person (the debtor).

Crime A wrong against society proclaimed in a statute and, if committed, punishable by society through fines and/or imprisonment—and, in some cases, death.

Criminal law Law that defines and governs actions that constitute crimes. Generally, criminal law has to do with wrongful actions committed against society for which society demands redress.

Cross-examination The questioning of an opposing witness during a trial.

Cure Under the Uniform Commercial Code, the right of a party who tenders nonconforming performance to correct his or her performance within the contract period.

Cyber crime A crime that occurs online, in the virtual community of the Internet, as opposed to the physical world.

Cyber mark A trademark in cyberspace.

Cyber tort A tort committed in cyberspace.

Cyberlaw An informal term used to refer to all laws governing electronic communications and transactions, particularly those conducted via the Internet.

Cybersquatting The act of registering a domain name that is the same as, or confusingly similar to, the trademark of another and then offering to sell that domain name back to the trademark owner.

Cyberterrorist A hacker whose purpose is to exploit a target computer for a serious impact, such as the corruption of a program to sabotage a business.

D

Damages The monetary amount sought as a remedy for a breach of contract or for a tortious act.

De novo Anew; afresh; a second time. In a hearing *de novo,* an appellate court hears the case as a court of original jurisdiction—that is, as if the case had not previously been tried and a decision rendered.

Debtor in possession (DIP) In Chapter 11 bankruptcy proceedings, a debtor who is allowed to continue in possession of the estate in property (the business) and to continue business operations.

Deceptive advertising Advertising that misleads consumers, either by making unjustified claims concerning a product's performance or by omitting a material fact concerning the product's composition or performance.

Deed A document by which title to property (usually real property) is passed.

Defalcation The misuse of funds.

Defamation Any published or publicly spoken false statement that causes injury to another's good name, reputation, or character.

Default The failure to observe a promise or discharge an obligation. The term is commonly used to mean the failure to pay a debt when it is due.

Default judgment A judgment entered by a court against a defendant who has failed to appear in court to answer or defend against the plaintiff's claim.

Defendant One against whom a lawsuit is brought; the accused person in a criminal proceeding.

Defense That which a defendant offers and alleges in an action or suit as a reason why the plaintiff should not recover or establish what he or she seeks.

Delegation The transfer of a contractual duty to a third party. The party delegating the duty (the delegator) to the third party (the delegatee) is still obliged to perform on the contract should the delegatee fail to perform.

Delegation doctrine A doctrine based on Article I, Section 8, of the U.S. Constitution, which has been construed to allow Congress to delegate some of its power to make and implement laws to administrative agencies. The delegation is considered to be proper as long as Congress sets standards outlining the scope of the agency's authority.

Deposition The testimony of a party to a lawsuit or a witness taken under oath before a trial.

Destination contract A contract for the sale of goods in which the seller is required or authorized to ship the goods by carrier and deliver them at a particular destination. The seller assumes liability for any losses or damage to the goods until they are tendered at the destination specified in the contract.

Dilution With respect to trademarks, a doctrine under which distinctive or famous trademarks are protected from certain unauthorized uses of the marks regardless of a showing of competition or a likelihood of confusion. Congress created a federal cause of action for dilution in 1995 with the passage of the Federal Trademark Dilution Act.

Direct examination The examination of a witness by the attorney who calls the witness to the stand to testify on behalf of the attorney's client.

Discharge The termination of an obligation. (1) In contract law, discharge occurs when the parties have fully performed their contractual obligations or when events, conduct of the parties, or operation of the law releases the parties from performance. (2) In bankruptcy proceedings, the extinction of the debtor's dischargeable debts.

Disclosed principal A principal whose identity is known to a third party at the time the agent makes a contract with the third party.

Discovery A phase in the litigation process during which the opposing parties may obtain information from each other and from third parties prior to trial.

Disparagement of property An economically injurious falsehood made about another's product or property. A general term for torts that are more specifically referred to as *slander of quality* or *slander of title.*

Disparate-impact discrimination A form of employment discrimination that results from certain employer practices or procedures that, although not discriminatory on their face, have a discriminatory effect.

Disparate-treatment discrimination A form of employment discrimination that results when an employer intentionally discriminates against employees who are members of protected classes.

Dissociation Occurs when a partner ceases to be associated in the carrying on of the partnership business. The severance of the relationship between a partner and a partnership.

Dissolution The formal disbanding of a partnership or a corporation. It can take place by (1) acts of the partners or, in a corporation, of the shareholders and board of directors; (2) the death of a partner; (3) the expiration of a time period stated in a partnership agreement or a certificate of incorporation; or (4) judicial decree.

Distributed network A network that can be used by persons located (distributed) around the country or the globe to share computer files.

Distribution agreement A contract between a seller and a distributor of the seller's products setting out the terms and conditions of the distributorship.

Diversity of citizenship Under Article III, Section 2, of the Constitution, a basis for federal court jurisdiction over a lawsuit between (1) citizens of different states, (2) a foreign country and citizens of a state or of different states, or (3) citizens of a state and citizens or subjects of a foreign country. The amount in controversy must be more than $75,000 before a federal court can take jurisdiction in such cases.

Divestiture The act of selling one or more of a company's parts, such as a subsidiary or plant; often mandated by the courts in merger or monopolization cases.

Dividend A distribution to corporate shareholders of corporate profits or income, disbursed in proportion to the number of shares held.

Domain name The series of letters and symbols used to identify site operators on the Internet; Internet "addresses."

Domestic corporation In a given state, a corporation that does business in, and is organized under the law of, that state.

Double jeopardy A situation occurring when a person is tried twice for the same criminal offense; prohibited by the Fifth Amendment to the Constitution.

Dram shop act A state statute that imposes liability on the owners of bars and taverns, as well as those who serve alcoholic drinks to the public, for injuries resulting from accidents caused by intoxicated persons when the sellers or servers of alcoholic drinks contributed to the intoxication.

Due process clause The provisions of the Fifth and Fourteenth Amendments to the Constitution that guarantee that no person shall be deprived of life, liberty, or property without due process of law. Similar clauses are found in most state constitutions.

Dumping The selling of goods in a foreign country at a price below the price charged for the same goods in the domestic market.

Duress Unlawful pressure brought to bear on a person, causing the person to perform an act that he or she would not otherwise perform.

Duty of care The duty of all persons, as established by tort law, to exercise a reasonable amount of care in their dealings with others. Failure to exercise due care, which is normally determined by the "reasonable person standard," constitutes the tort of negligence.

E

E-agent A computer program, electronic, or other automated means used to perform specific tasks without review by an individual.

Early neutral case evaluation A form of alternative dispute resolution in which a neutral third party evaluates the strengths and weakness of the disputing parties' positions; the evaluator's opinion forms the basis for negotiating a settlement.
Easement A nonpossessory right to use another's property in a manner established by either express or implied agreement.
E-commerce Business transacted in cyberspace.
E-contract A contract that is entered into in cyberspace and is evidenced only by electronic impulses (such as those that make up a computer's memory), rather than, for example, a typewritten form.
E-evidence A type of evidence that consists of computer-generated or electronically recorded information, including e-mail, voice mail, spreadsheets, word processing documents, and other data.
Eight-day cooling-off period A provision of the Taft-Hartley Act that allows federal courts to issue injunctions against strikes that might create a national emergency.
Embezzlement The fraudulent appropriation of money or other property by a person to whom the money or property has been entrusted.
Eminent domain The power of a government to take land for public use from private citizens for just compensation.
Employee committee A committee created by an employer and composed of representatives of management and nonunion employees to act together to improve workplace conditions.
Employment at will A common law doctrine under which either party may terminate an employment relationship at any time for any reason, unless a contract specifies otherwise.
Employment discrimination Treating employees or job applicants unequally on the basis of race, color, national origin, religion, gender, age, or disability; prohibited by federal statutes.
Enabling legislation A statute enacted by Congress that authorizes the creation of an administrative agency and specifies the name, composition, purpose, and powers of the agency being created.
Encryption The process by which a message (plaintext) is transformed into something (ciphertext) that the sender and receiver intend third parties not to understand.
Entrapment In criminal law, a defense in which the defendant claims that he or she was induced by a public official—usually an undercover agent or police officer—to commit a crime that he or she would otherwise not have committed.
Entrepreneur One who initiates and assumes the financial risks of a new enterprise and who undertakes to provide or control its management.
Environmental impact statement (EIS) A statement required by the National Environmental Policy Act for any major federal action that will significantly affect the quality of the environment. The statement must analyze the action's impact on the environment and explore alternative actions that might be taken.
Environmental law The body of statutory, regulatory, and common law relating to the protection of the environment.
Equal dignity rule In most states, a rule stating that express authority given to an agent must be in writing if the contract to be made on behalf of the principal is required to be in writing.
Equal protection clause The provision in the Fourteenth Amendment to the Constitution that guarantees that no state will "deny to any person within its jurisdiction the equal protection of the laws." This clause mandates that state governments treat similarly situated individuals in a similar manner.
Equitable maxims General propositions or principles of law that have to do with fairness (equity).
Escrow account An account that is generally held in the name of the depositor and escrow agent; the funds in the account are paid to a third person only on fulfillment of the escrow condition.
E-signature As defined by the Uniform Electronic Transactions Act, "an electronic sound, symbol, or process attached to or logically associated with a record and executed or adopted by a person with the intent to sign the record."
Establishment clause The provision in the First Amendment to the U.S. Constitution that prohibits Congress from creating any law "respecting an establishment of religion."
Ethics Moral principles and values applied to social behavior.
Eviction A landlord's act of depriving a tenant of possession of the leased premises.
Exclusionary rule In criminal procedure, a rule under which any evidence that is obtained in violation of the accused's constitutional rights guaranteed by the Fourth, Fifth, and Sixth Amendments, as well as any evidence derived from illegally obtained evidence, will not be admissible in court.
Exclusive-dealing contract An agreement under which a seller forbids a buyer to purchase products from the seller's competitors.
Exclusive distributorship A distributorship in which the seller and the distributor of the seller's products agree that the distributor has the exclusive right to distribute the seller's products in a certain geographic area.
Exclusive jurisdiction Jurisdiction that exists when a case can be heard only in a particular court or type of court, such as a federal court or a state court.
Executive agency An administrative agency within the executive branch of government. At the federal level, executive agencies are those within the cabinet departments.
Executory contract A contract that has not as yet been fully performed.
Export To sell products to buyers located in other countries.
Express authority Authority expressly given by one party to another. In agency law, an agent has express authority to act for a principal if both parties agree, orally or in writing, that an agency relationship exists in which the agent had the power (authority) to act in the place of, and on behalf of, the principal.
Express contract A contract in which the terms of the agreement are fully and explicitly stated in words, oral or written.
Express warranty A seller's or lessor's oral or written promise, ancillary to an underlying sales or lease agreement, as to the quality, description, or performance of the goods being sold or leased.
Expropriation The seizure by a government of privately owned business or personal property for a proper public purpose and with just compensation.

F

Facilitation A form of alternative dispute resolution in which the parties reach an agreement themselves with the help of a neutral third party, called a *facilitator,* who facilitates the negotiations.
Family limited liability partnership (FLLP) A limited liability partnership (LLP) in which the majority of the partners are persons related to each other, essentially as spouses, parents, grandparents, siblings, cousins, nephews, or nieces. A person acting in a fiduciary capacity for persons so related could also be a partner. All of the partners must be natural persons or persons acting in a fiduciary capacity for the benefit of natural persons.
Featherbedding A requirement that more workers be employed to do a particular job than are actually needed.
Federal form of government A system of government in which the states form a union and the sovereign power is divided between a central government and the member states.
Federal question A question that pertains to the U.S. Constitution, acts of Congress, or treaties. A federal question provides a basis for federal jurisdiction.

Federal Rules of Civil Procedure (FRCP) The rules controlling procedural matters in civil trials brought before the federal district courts.

Fee simple absolute An ownership interest in land in which the owner has the greatest possible aggregation of rights, privileges, and power. Ownership in fee simple absolute is limited absolutely to a person and his or her heirs.

Felony A crime—such as arson, murder, rape, or robbery—that carries the most severe sanctions, usually ranging from one year in a state or federal prison to the forfeiture of one's life.

Fiduciary As a noun, a person having a duty created by his or her undertaking to act primarily for another's benefit in matters connected with the undertaking. As an adjective, a relationship founded on trust and confidence.

Fiduciary duty The duty, imposed on a fiduciary by virtue of his or her position, to act primarily for another's benefit.

Filtering software A computer program that includes a pattern through which data are passed. When designed to block access to certain Web sites, the pattern blocks the retrieval of a site whose URL or key words are on a list within the program.

Final order The final decision of an administrative agency on an issue. If no appeal is taken, or if the case is not reviewed or considered anew by the agency commission, the administrative law judge's initial order becomes the final order of the agency.

Firm offer An offer (by a merchant) that is irrevocable without consideration for a period of time (not longer than three months). A firm offer by a merchant must be in writing and must be signed by the offeror.

Fixed-term tenancy A type of tenancy under which property is leased for a specified period of time, such as a month, a year, or a period of years; also called a *tenancy for years*.

Fixture A thing that was once personal property but that has become attached to real property in such a way that it takes on the characteristics of real property and becomes part of that real property.

Forbearance The act of refraining from an action that one has a legal right to undertake.

Foreign corporation In a given state, a corporation that does business in the state without being incorporated therein.

Forgery The fraudulent making or altering of any writing in a way that changes the legal rights and liabilities of another.

Forum-selection clause A provision in a contract designating the court, jurisdiction, or tribunal that will decide any disputes arising under the contract.

Franchise Any arrangement in which the owner of a trademark, trade name, or copyright licenses another to use that trademark, trade name, or copyright, under specified conditions or limitations, in the selling of goods and services.

Franchisee One receiving a license to use another's (the franchisor's) trademark, trade name, or copyright in the sale of goods and services.

Franchisor One licensing another (the franchisee) to use his or her trademark, trade name, or copyright in the sale of goods or services.

Fraudulent misrepresentation (fraud) Any misrepresentation, either by misstatement or omission of a material fact, knowingly made with the intention of deceiving another and on which a reasonable person would and does rely to his or her detriment.

Free exercise clause The provision in the First Amendment to the U.S. Constitution that prohibits Congress from making any law "prohibiting the free exercise" of religion.

Free-writing prospectus A free-writing prospectus is any type of written, electronic, or graphic offer that describes the issuing corporation or its securities and includes a legend indicating that the investor may obtain the prospectus at the SEC's Web site.

Frustration of purpose A court-created doctrine under which a party to a contract will be relieved of his or her duty to perform when the objective purpose for performance no longer exists (due to reasons beyond that party's control).

Full faith and credit clause A clause in Article IV, Section 1, of the Constitution that provides that "Full Faith and Credit shall be given in each State to the public Acts, Records, and Judicial Proceedings of every othere States." The clause ensures that rights established under deeds, wills, contracts, and the like in one state will be honored by the other states and that any judicial decision with respect to such property rights will be honored and enforced in all states.

G

Garnishment A legal process used by a creditor to collect a debt by seizing property of the debtor (such as wages) that is being held by a third party (such as the debtor's employer).

General partner In a limited partnership, a partner who assumes responsibility for the management of the partnership and liability for all partnership debts.

General plan A comprehensive document that local jurisdictions are often required by state law to devise and implement as a precursor to specific land-use regulations.

Genuineness of assent Knowing and voluntary assent to the terms of a contract. If a contract is formed as a result of a mistake, misrepresentation, undue influence, or duress, genuineness of assent is lacking, and the contract will be voidable.

Good faith purchaser A purchaser who buys without notice of any circumstance that would put a person of ordinary prudence on inquiry as to whether the seller has valid title to the goods being sold.

Good Samaritan statute A state statute that provides that persons who rescue or provide emergency services to others in peril—unless they do so recklessly, thus causing further harm—cannot be sued for negligence.

Grand jury A group of citizens called to decide, after hearing the state's evidence, whether a reasonable basis (probable cause) exists for believing that a crime has been committed and whether a trial ought to be held.

Grant deed A deed that simply recites words of consideration and conveyance. Under statute, a grant deed may impliedly warrant that at least the grantor has not conveyed the property's title to someone else.

Group boycott The refusal to deal with a particular person or firm by a group of competitors; prohibited by the Sherman Act.

H

Hacker A person who uses one computer to break into another. Professional computer programmers refer to such persons as "crackers."

Hirfindahl-Hirschman Index (HHI) An index of market power used to calculate whether a merger of two businesses will result in sufficient monopoly power to violate antitrust laws.

Historical school A school of legal thought that emphasizes the evolutionary process of law and that looks to the past to discover what the principles of contemporary law should be.

Holding company A company whose business activity is holding shares in another company.

Homestead exemption A law permitting a debtor to retain the family home, either in its entirety or up to a specified dollar amount, free from the claims of unsecured creditors or trustees in bankruptcy.

Horizontal market division A market division that occurs when competitors agree to divide up the market for their products or services among themselves, either geographically or by functional class of customers (such as retailers or wholesalers). Such market division constitutes a *per se* violation of the Sherman Act.

Horizontal merger A merger between two firms that are competing in the same market.

Horizontal restraint Any agreement that in some way restrains competition between rival firms competing in the same market.

Hot-cargo agreement An agreement in which employers voluntarily agree with unions not to handle, use, or deal in nonunion-produced goods of other employers; a type of secondary boycott explicitly prohibited by the Labor-Management Reporting and Disclosure Act of 1959.

I

I-9 verification All employers must verify the employment eligibility and identity of any worker hired in the U.S. To comply with the law, employers must complete an I-9 Employment Eligibility Verification Form for all new hires within three business days.

I-551 Alien Registration Receipt Commonly referred to as a "green card," the I-551 Alien Registration Receipt is proof that a foreign-born individual is lawfully admitted for permanent residence in the United States. Persons seeking employment can prove to prospective employers that they are legally within the U.S. by showing this receipt.

Identification In a sale of goods, the express designation of the goods provided for in the contract.

Identity theft The act of stealing another's identifying information—such as a name, date of birth, or Social Security number—and using that information to access the victim's financial resources.

Implied authority Authority that is created not by an explicit oral or written agreement but by implication. In agency law, implied authority (of the agent) can be conferred by custom, inferred from the position the agent occupies, or implied by virtue of being reasonably necessary to carry out express authority.

Implied-in-fact contract A contract formed in whole or in part from the conduct of the parties (as opposed to an express contract).

Implied warranty A warranty that the law derives by implication or inference from the nature of the transaction or the relative situation or circumstances of the parties.

Implied warranty of fitness for a particular purpose A warranty that goods sold or leased are fit for a particular purpose. The warranty arises when any seller or lessor knows the particular purpose for which a buyer or lessee will use the goods and knows that the buyer or lessee is relying on the skill and judgment of the seller or lessor to select suitable goods.

Implied warranty of habitability An implied promise by a landlord that rented residential premises are fit for human habitation—that is, in a condition that is safe and suitable for people to live in.

Implied warranty of merchantability A warranty that goods being sold or leased are reasonably fit for the general purpose for which they are sold or leased, are properly packaged and labeled, and are of proper quality. The warranty automatically arises in every sale or lease of goods made by a merchant who deals in goods of the kind sold or leased.

Impossibility of performance A doctrine under which a party to a contract is relieved of his or her duty to perform when performance becomes impossible or totally impracticable (through no fault of either party).

***In personam* jurisdiction** Court jurisdiction over the "person" involved in a legal action; personal jurisdiction.

***In rem* jurisdiction** Court jurisdiction over a defendant's property.

Incidental beneficiary A third party who incidentally benefits from a contract but whose benefit was not the reason the contract was formed; an incidental beneficiary has no rights in a contract and cannot sue to have the contract enforced.

Independent contractor One who works for, and receives payment from, an employer but whose working conditions and methods are not controlled by the employer. An independent contractor is not an employee but may be an agent.

Independent regulatory agency An administrative agency that is not considered part of the government's executive branch and is not subject to the authority of the president. Independent agency officials cannot be removed without cause.

Indictment (pronounced in-*dyte*-ment) A charge by a grand jury that a named person has committed a crime.

Informal contract A contract that does not require a specified form or formality in order to be valid.

Information A formal accusation or complaint (without an indictment) issued in certain types of actions (usually criminal actions involving lesser crimes) by a law officer, such as a magistrate.

Information return A tax return submitted by a partnership that only reports the income earned by the business. The partnership as an entity does not pay taxes on the income received by the partnership. A partner's profit from the partnership (whether distributed or not) is taxed as individual income to the individual partner.

Initial order In the context of administrative law, an agency's disposition in a matter other than a rulemaking. An administrative law judge's initial order becomes final unless it is appealed.

Insider A corporate director or officer, or other employee or agent, with access to confidential information and a duty not to disclose that information in violation of insider-trading laws.

Insider trading The purchase or sale of securities on the basis of "inside information" (information that has not been made available to the public) in violation of a duty owed to the company whose stock is being traded.

Insurable interest An interest either in a person's life or well-being or in property that is sufficiently substantial that insuring against injury to (or the death of) the person or against damage to the property does not amount to a mere wagering (betting) contract.

Intangible property Property that is incapable of being apprehended by the senses (such as by sight or touch); intellectual property is an example of intangible property.

Intellectual property Property resulting from intellectual, creative processes. Patents, trademarks, and copyrights are examples of intellectual property.

Intended beneficiary A third party for whose benefit a contract is formed; an intended beneficiary can sue the promisor if such a contract is breached.

Intentional tort A wrongful act knowingly committed.

International law The law that governs relations among nations. International customs and treaties are generally considered to be two of the most important sources of international law.

International organization In international law, a term that generally refers to an organization composed mainly of nations and usually established by treaty. The United States is a member of more than one hundred multilateral and bilateral organizations, including at least twenty through the United Nations.

Interpretive rule An administrative agency rule that is simply a statement or opinion issued by the agency explaining how it interprets and intends to apply the statutes it enforces. Such rules are not automatically binding on private individuals or organizations.

Investment company A company that acts on behalf of many smaller shareholder-owners by buying a large portfolio of securities and professionally managing that portfolio.
Investment contract In securities law, a transaction in which a person invests in a common enterprise reasonably expecting profits that are derived primarily from the efforts of others.
Irrevocable offer An offer that cannot be revoked or recalled by the offeror without liability. A merchant's firm offer is an example of an irrevocable offer.

J

Joint and several liability In partnership law, a doctrine under which a plaintiff may sue, and collect a judgment from, one or more of the partners separately (severally, or individually) or all of the partners together (jointly). This is true even if one of the partners sued did not participate in, ratify, or know about whatever it was that gave rise to the cause of action.
Joint liability Shared liability. In partnership law, partners incur joint liability for partnership obligations and debts. For example, if a third party sues a partner on a partnership debt, the partner has the right to insist that the other partners be sued with him or her.
Joint tenancy The joint ownership of property by two or more co-owners in which each co-owner owns an undivided portion of the property. On the death of one of the joint tenants, his or her interest automatically passes to the surviving joint tenants.
Joint venture A joint undertaking of a specific commercial enterprise by an association of persons. A joint venture is normally not a legal entity and is treated like a partnership for federal income tax purposes.
Judgment The final order or decision resulting from a legal action.
Judicial review The process by which courts decide on the constitutionality of legislative enactments and actions of the executive branch.
Jurisdiction The authority of a court to hear and decide a specific action.
Jurisprudence The science or philosophy of law.
Justiciable (pronounced jus-*tish*-a-bul) **controversy** A controversy that is not hypothetical or academic but real and substantial; a requirement that must be satisfied before a court will hear a case.

L

Laches The equitable doctrine that bars a party's right to legal action if the party has neglected for an unreasonable length of time to act on his or her rights.
Land-use control The control over the ownership and uses of real property by authorized public agencies.
Larceny The wrongful taking and carrying away of another person's personal property with the intent to permanently deprive the owner of the property. Some states classify larceny as either grand or petit, depending on the property's value.
Law A body of enforceable rules governing relationships among individuals and between individuals and their society.
Lease In real property law, a contract by which the owner of real property (the landlord, or lessor) grants to a person (the tenant, or lessee) an exclusive right to use and possess the property, usually for a specified period of time, in return for rent or some other form of payment.
Lease agreement In regard to the lease of goods, an agreement in which one person (the lessor) agrees to transfer the right to the possession and use of property to another person (the lessee) in exchange for rental payments.
Leasehold estate An estate in realty held by a tenant under a lease. In every leasehold estate, the tenant has a qualified right to possess and/or use the land.
Legal realism A school of legal thought that was popular in the 1920s and 1930s and that challenged many existing jurisprudential assumptions, particularly the assumption that subjective elements play no part in judicial reasoning. Legal realists generally advocated a less abstract and more realistic approach to the law, an approach that would take into account customary practices and the circumstances in which transactions take place. The school left a lasting imprint on American jurisprudence.
Legal reasoning The process of reasoning by which a judge harmonizes his or her decision with the judicial decisions of previous cases.
Legislative rule An administrative agency rule that carries the same weight as a congressionally enacted statute.
Lessee A person who acquires the right to the possession and use of another's property in exchange for rental payments.
Lessor A person who sells the right to the possession and use of property to another in exchange for rental payments.
Liability Any actual or potential legal obligation, duty, debt, or responsibility.
Libel Defamation in writing or other form (such as in a videotape) having the quality of permanence.
License A revocable right or privilege of a person to come on another person's land.
Licensee One who receives a license to use, or enter onto, another's property.
Lien (pronounced *leen*) An encumbrance on a property to satisfy a debt or protect a claim for payment of a debt.
Lien creditor One whose claim is secured by a lien on particular property, as distinguished from a general creditor, who has no such security.
Life estate An interest in land that exists only for the duration of the life of some person, usually the holder of the estate.
Limited jurisdiction Exists when a court's subject-matter jurisdiction is limited. Bankruptcy courts and probate courts are examples of courts with limited jurisdiction.
Limited liability Exists when the liability of the owners of a business is limited to the amount of their investments in the firm.
Limited liability company (LLC) A hybrid form of business enterprise that offers the limited liability of the corporation but the tax advantages of a partnership.
Limited liability limited partnership (LLLP) A type of limited partnership. The difference between a limited partnership and an LLLP is that the liability of the general partner in an LLLP is the same as the liability of the limited partner—that is, the liability of all partners is limited to the amount of their investments in the firm.
Limited liability partnership (LLP) A form of partnership that allows professionals to enjoy the tax benefits of a partnership while limiting their personal liability for the malpractice of other partners.
Limited partner In a limited partnership, a partner who contributes capital to the partnership but has no right to participate in the management and operation of the business. The limited partner assumes no liability for partnership debts beyond the capital contributed.
Limited partnership A partnership consisting of one or more general partners (who manage the business and are liable to the full extent of their personal assets for debts of the partnership) and one or more limited partners (who contribute only assets and are liable only to the extent of their contributions).
Liquidated damages An amount, stipulated in the contract, that the parties to a contract believe to be a reasonable estimation of the damages that will occur in the event of a breach.

Liquidated debt A debt that is due and certain in amount.
Liquidation (1) In regard to bankruptcy, the sale of all of the nonexempt assets of a debtor and the distribution of the proceeds to the debtor's creditors. Chapter 7 of the Bankruptcy Code provides for liquidation bankruptcy proceedings. (2) In regard to corporations, the process by which corporate assets are converted into cash and distributed among creditors and shareholders according to specific rules of preference.
Lockout The closing of a plant to employees by an employer to gain leverage in collective bargaining negotiations.
Long arm statute A state statute that permits a state to obtain personal jurisdiction over nonresident defendants. A defendant must have "minimum contacts" with that state for the statute to apply.

M

Mailbox rule A rule providing that an acceptance of an offer becomes effective on dispatch (on being placed in a mailbox), if mail is, expressly or impliedly, an authorized means of communication of acceptance to the offeror.
Malpractice Professional misconduct or the failure to exercise the requisite degree of skill as a professional. Negligence—the failure to exercise due care—on the part of a professional, such as a physician or an attorney, is commonly referred to as malpractice.
Mark *See* Trademark
Market concentration A situation that exists when a small number of firms share the market for a particular good or service. For example, if the four largest grocery stores in Chicago accounted for 80 percent of all retail food sales, the market clearly would be concentrated in those four firms.
Market power The power of a firm to control the market price of its product. A monopoly has the greatest degree of market power.
Market-share liability A method of sharing liability among several firms that manufactured or marketed a particular product that may have caused a plaintiff's injury. This form of liability sharing is used when the true source of the product is unidentifiable. Each firm's liability is proportionate to its respective share of the relevant market for the product. Market-share liability applies only if the injuring product is fungible, the true manufacturer is unidentifiable, and the unknown character of the manufacturer is not the plaintiff's fault.
Market-share test The primary measure of monopoly power. A firm's market share is the percentage of a market that the firm controls.
Marketable title Title to real estate that is reasonably free from encumbrances, defects in the chain of title, and other events that affect title, such as adverse possession.
Mediation A method of settling disputes outside of court by using the services of a neutral third party, called a mediator. The mediator acts as a communicating agent between the parties and suggests ways in which the parties can resolve their dispute.
Mediator A person who attempts to reconcile the differences between two or more parties.
Member The term used to designate a person who has an ownership interest in a limited liability company.
Mens rea (pronounced *mehns ray*-uh) Mental state, or intent. A wrongful mental state is as necessary as a wrongful act to establish criminal liability. What constitutes a mental state varies according to the wrongful action. Thus, for murder, the *mens rea* is the intent to take a life; for theft, the *mens rea* must involve both the knowledge that the property belongs to another and the intent to deprive the owner of it.
Merchant A person who is engaged in the purchase and sale of goods. Under the Uniform Commercial Code, a person who deals in goods of the kind involved in the sales contract; for further definitions, see UCC 2–104.
Merger A contractual and statutory process in which one corporation (the surviving corporation) acquires all of the assets and liabilities of another corporation (the merged corporation). The shareholders of the merged corporation receive either payment for their shares or shares in the surviving corporation.
Meta tags Words inserted into a Web site's key-words field to increase the site's appearance in search engine results.
Metes and bounds Metes and bounds is a system of measuring boundary lines by the distance between two points, often using physical features of the local geography, such as roads, intersections, rivers, or bridges. The legal descriptions of real property contained in deeds often are phrased in terms of metes and bounds.
Minimum-contacts requirement The requirement that before a state court can exercise jurisdiction over a foreign corporation, the foreign corporation must have sufficient contacts with the state. A foreign corporation that has its home office in the state or that has manufacturing plants in the state meets this requirement.
Minimum wage The lowest wage, either by government regulation or union contract, that an employer may pay an hourly worker.
Mini-trial A private proceeding in which each party to a dispute argues its position before the other side, and vice versa. A neutral third party may be present and act as an adviser if the parties fail to reach an agreement.
Mirror image rule A common law rule that requires, for a valid contractual agreement, that the terms of the offeree's acceptance adhere exactly to the terms of the offeror's offer.
Misdemeanor A lesser crime than a felony, punishable by a fine or imprisonment for up to one year in other than a state or federal penitentiary.
Mitigation of damages A rule requiring a plaintiff to have done whatever was reasonable to minimize the damages caused by the defendant.
Money laundering Falsely reporting income that has been obtained through criminal activity as income obtained through a legitimate business enterprise—in effect, "laundering" the "dirty money."
Monopolization The possession of monopoly power in the relevant market and the willful acquisition or maintenance of the power, as distinguished from growth or development as a consequence of a superior product, business acumen, or historic accident.
Monopoly A term generally used to describe a market in which there is a single seller or a limited number of sellers.
Monopoly power The ability of a monopoly to dictate what takes place in a given market.
Moral minimum The minimum degree of ethical behavior expected of a business firm, which is usually defined as compliance with the law.
Mortgage A written instrument giving a creditor (the mortgagee) an interest in (a lien on) the debtor's (mortgagor's) property as security for a debt.
Mortgage bond A bond that pledges specific property. If the corporation defaults on the bond, the bondholder can take the property.
Mortgagee Under a mortgage agreement, the creditor who takes a security interest in the debtor's property.
Mortgagor Under a mortgage agreement, the debtor who gives the creditor a security interest in the debtor's property in return for a mortgage loan.

Motion A procedural request or application presented by an attorney to the court on behalf of a client.
Motion for a directed verdict In a jury trial, a motion for the judge to take the decision out of the hands of the jury and direct a verdict for the moving party on the ground that the other party has not produced sufficient evidence to support his or her claim; referred to as a motion for judgment as a matter of law in the federal courts.
Motion for a new trial A motion asserting that the trial was so fundamentally flawed (because of error, newly discovered evidence, prejudice, or other reason) that a new trial is necessary to prevent a miscarriage of justice.
Motion for judgment *n.o.v.* A motion requesting the court to grant judgment in favor of the party making the motion on the ground that the jury verdict against him or her was unreasonable and erroneous.
Motion for judgment on the pleadings A motion by either party to a lawsuit at the close of the pleadings requesting the court to decide the issue solely on the pleadings without proceeding to trial. The motion will be granted only if no facts are in dispute.
Motion for summary judgment A motion requesting the court to enter a judgment without proceeding to trial. The motion can be based on evidence outside the pleadings and will be granted only if no facts are in dispute.
Motion to dismiss A pleading in which a defendant asserts that the plaintiff's claim fails to state a cause of action (that is, has no basis in law) or that there are other grounds on which a suit should be dismissed.
Multiple product order An order issued by the Federal Trade Commission to a firm that has engaged in deceptive advertising by which the firm is required to cease and desist from false advertising not only in regard to the product that was the subject of the action but also in regard to all the firm's other products.
Mutual assent The element of agreement in the formation of a contract. The manifestation of contract parties' mutual assent to the same bargain is required to establish a contract.
Mutual fund A specific type of investment company that continually buys or sells to investors shares of ownership in a portfolio.
Mutual rescission An agreement between the parties to cancel their contract, releasing the parties from further obligations under the contract. The object of the agreement is to restore the parties to the positions they would have occupied had no contract ever been formed. *See also* Rescission

N

National law Law that pertains to a particular nation (as opposed to international law).
Natural law The belief that government and the legal system should reflect universal moral and ethical principles that are inherent in human nature. The natural law school is the oldest and one of the most significant schools of legal thought.
Necessaries Necessities required for life, such as food, shelter, clothing, and medical attention; may include whatever is believed to be necessary to maintain a person's standard of living or financial and social status.
Negligence The failure to exercise the standard of care that a reasonable person would exercise in similar circumstances.
Negligence *per se* An act (or failure to act) in violation of a statutory requirement.
Negotiation In regard to dispute settlement, a process in which parties attempt to settle their dispute without going to court, with or without attorneys to represent them.
***Noerr-Pennington* doctrine** A series of cases that permits competitors to lobby for changes in the law to gain greater protection from competition.
Nominal damages A small monetary award (often one dollar) granted to a plaintiff when no actual damage was suffered.
Nonconforming goods Goods that do not conform to contract specifications.
Nonpossessory interest Interests in land, such as a right of way, that do not include any right to possess the land, but only confer the right to use the real property of another for a specified purpose. Nonpossessory interests include easements, profits, and licenses.
Normal trade relations (NTR) status A status granted through an international treaty by which each member nation must treat other members at least as well as it treats the country that receives its most favorable treatment. This status was formerly known as most-favored-nation status.
No-strike clause Provision in a collective bargaining agreement that states the employees will not strike for any reason and labor disputes will be resolved by arbitration.
Notary public A public official authorized to attest to the authenticity of signatures.
Notice-and-comment rulemaking An administrative rulemaking procedure that involves the publication of a notice of a proposed rulemaking in the *Federal Register*, a comment period for interested parties to express their views on the proposed rule, and the publication of the agency's final rule in the *Federal Register*.
Novation The substitution, by agreement, of a new contract for an old one, with the rights under the old one being terminated. Typically, there is a substitution of a new person who is responsible for the contract and the removal of an original party's rights and duties under the contract.
Nuisance A common law doctrine under which persons may be held liable for using their property in a manner that unreasonably interferes with others' rights to use or enjoy their own property.

O

Objective theory of contracts A theory under which the intent to form a contract will be judged by outward, objective facts (what the party said when entering into the contract, how the party acted or appeared, and the circumstances surrounding the transaction) as interpreted by a reasonable person, rather than by the party's own secret, subjective intentions.
Offer A promise or commitment to perform or refrain from performing some specified act in the future.
Online dispute resolution (ODR) The resolution of disputes with the assistance of organizations that offer dispute-resolution services via the Internet.
Operating agreement In a limited liability company, an agreement in which the members set forth the details of how the business will be managed and operated.
Opinion A statement by the court expressing the reasons for its decision in a case.
Order for relief A court's grant of assistance to a complainant. In bankruptcy proceedings, the order relieves the debtor of the immediate obligation to pay the debts listed in the bankruptcy petition.
Ordinance A law passed by a local governing unit, such as a municipality or a county.
Output contract An agreement in which a seller agrees to sell and a buyer agrees to buy all or up to a stated amount of what the seller produces.

P

Parent-subsidiary merger A merger of companies in which one company (the parent corporation) owns most of the stock of the other (the subsidiary corporation). A parent-subsidiary merger (short-form merger) can use a simplified procedure when the parent corporation owns at least 90 percent of the outstanding shares of each class of stock of the subsidiary corporation.

Partially disclosed principal A principal whose identity is unknown by a third person, but the third person knows that the agent is or may be acting for a principal at the time the agent and the third person form a contract.

Partner A co-owner of a partnership.

Partnership An agreement by two or more persons to carry on, as co-owners, a business for profit.

Partnership by estoppel A judicially created partnership that may, at the court's discretion, be imposed for purposes of fairness. The court can prevent those who present themselves as partners (but who are not) from escaping liability if a third person relies on an alleged partnership in good faith and is harmed as a result.

Past consideration An act done before the contract is made, which ordinarily, by itself, cannot be consideration for a later promise to pay for the act.

Patent A government grant that gives an inventor the exclusive right or privilege to make, use, or sell his or her invention for a limited time period. The word *patent* usually refers to some invention and designates either the instrument by which patent rights are evidenced or the patent itself.

Peer-to-peer (P2P) networking The sharing of resources (such as files, hard drives, and processing styles) among multiple computers without necessarily requiring a central network server.

Penalty A sum inserted into a contract, not as a measure of compensation for its breach but rather as punishment for a default. The agreement as to the amount will not be enforced, and recovery will be limited to actual damages.

Per curiam By the whole court; a court opinion written by the court as a whole instead of being authored by a judge or justice.

Per se A Latin term meaning "in itself" or "by itself."

***Per se* violation** A type of anticompetitive agreement—such as a horizontal price-fixing agreement—that is considered to be so injurious to the public that there is no need to determine whether it actually injures market competition; rather, it is in itself (*per se*) a violation of the Sherman Act.

Perfect tender rule A common law rule under which a seller was required to deliver to the buyer goods that conformed perfectly to the requirements stipulated in the sales contract. A tender of nonconforming goods would automatically constitute a breach of contract. Under the Uniform Commercial Code, the rule has been greatly modified.

Performance In contract law, the fulfillment of one's duties arising under a contract with another; the normal way of discharging one's contractual obligations.

Periodic tenancy A lease interest in land for an indefinite period involving payment of rent at fixed intervals, such as week to week, month to month, or year to year.

Personal jurisdiction *See In personam* jurisdiction

Personal property Property that is movable; any property that is not real property.

Petition in bankruptcy The document that is filed with a bankruptcy court to initiate bankruptcy proceedings. The official forms required for a petition in bankruptcy must be completed accurately, sworn to under oath, and signed by the debtor.

Petitioner In equity practice, a party that initiates a lawsuit.

Petty offense In criminal law, the least serious kind of criminal offense, such as a traffic or building-code violation.

Pierce the corporate veil To disregard the corporate entity, which limits the liability of shareholders, and hold the shareholders personally liable for a corporate obligation.

Plaintiff One who initiates a lawsuit.

Plea In criminal law, a defendant's allegation, in response to the charges brought against him or her, of guilt or innocence.

Plea bargaining The process by which a criminal defendant and the prosecutor in a criminal case work out a mutually satisfactory disposition of the case, subject to court approval; usually involves the defendant's pleading guilty to a lesser offense in return for a lighter sentence.

Pleadings Statements made by the plaintiff and the defendant in a lawsuit that detail the facts, charges, and defenses involved in the litigation; the complaint and answer are part of the pleadings.

Police powers Powers possessed by states as part of their inherent sovereignty. These powers may be exercised to protect or promote the public order, health, safety, morals, and general welfare.

Positive law The body of conventional, or written, law of a particular society at a particular point in time.

Positivist school A school of legal thought whose adherents believe that there can be no higher law than a nation's positive law—the body of conventional, or written, law of a particular society at a particular time.

Potentially responsible party (PRP) A potentially liable party under the Comprehensive Environmental Response, Compensation and Liability Act (CERCLA). Any person who generated hazardous waste, transported the hazardous waste, owned or operated a waste site at the time of disposal, or currently owns or operates a site may be responsible for some or all of the clean-up costs involved in removing the hazardous chemicals.

Power of attorney A written document, which is usually notarized, authorizing another to act as one's agent; can be special (permitting the agent to do specified acts only) or general (permitting the agent to transact all business for the principal).

Precedent A court decision that furnishes an example or authority for deciding subsequent cases involving identical or similar facts.

Predatory pricing The pricing of a product below cost with the intent to drive competitors out of the market.

Preemption A doctrine under which certain federal laws preempt, or take precedence over, conflicting state or local laws.

Preference In bankruptcy proceedings, property transfers or payments made by the debtor that favor (give preference to) one creditor over others. The bankruptcy trustee is allowed to recover payments made both voluntarily and involuntarily to one creditor in preference over another.

Preferred creditor In the context of bankruptcy, a creditor who has received a preferential transfer from a debtor.

Pretrial motion A written or oral application to a court for a ruling or order, made before trial.

Price discrimination Setting prices in such a way that two competing buyers pay two different prices for an identical product or service.

Price fixing Fixing—by means of an anticompetitive agreement between competitors—the prices of products or services.

Price-fixing agreement An agreement between competitors in which the competitors agree to fix the prices of products or services at a certain level; prohibited by the Sherman Act.

***Prima facie* case** A case in which the plaintiff has produced sufficient evidence of his or her conclusion that the case can go to to a jury; a case in which the evidence compels the plaintiff's conclusion if the defendant produces no evidence to disprove it.

Principal In agency law, a person who agrees to have another, called the agent, act on his or her behalf.

Principle of rights The principle that human beings have certain fundamental rights (to life, freedom, and the pursuit of happiness, for example). Those who adhere to this "rights theory" believe that a key factor in determining whether a business decision is ethical is how that decision affects the rights of others. These others include the firm's owners, its employees, the consumers of its products or services, its suppliers, the community in which it does business, and society as a whole.

Privilege In tort law, the ability to act contrary to another person's right without that person's having legal redress for such acts. Privilege may be raised as a defense to defamation.

Privileges and immunities clause Special rights and exceptions provided by law. Article IV, Section 2, of the Constitution requires states not to discriminate against one another's citizens. A resident of one state cannot be treated as an alien when in another state; he or she may not be denied such privileges and immunities as legal protection, access to courts, travel rights, or property rights.

Privity of contract The relationship that exists between the promisor and the promisee of a contract.

Probable cause Reasonable grounds to believe the existence of facts warranting certain actions, such as the search or arrest of a person.

Probate court A state court of limited jurisdiction that conducts proceedings relating to the settlement of a deceased person's estate.

Procedural law Rules that define the manner in which the rights and duties of individuals may be enforced.

Product liability The legal liability of manufacturers, sellers, and lessors of goods to consumers, users, and bystanders for injuries or damages that are caused by the goods.

Product misuse A defense against product liability that may be raised when the plaintiff used a product in a manner not intended by the manufacturer. If the misuse is reasonably foreseeable, the seller will not escape liability unless measures were taken to guard against the harm that could result from the misuse.

Profit In real property law, the right to enter onto and remove things from the property of another (for example, the right to enter onto a person's land and remove sand and gravel therefrom).

Promise A declaration that something either will or will not happen in the future.

Promissory estoppel A doctrine that applies when a promisor makes a clear and definite promise on which the promisee justifiably relies; such a promise is binding if justice will be better served by the enforcement of the promise.

Prospectus A document required by federal or state securities laws that describes the financial operations of the corporation, thus allowing investors to make informed decisions.

Protected class A class of persons with identifiable characteristics who historically have been victimized by discriminatory treatment for certain purposes. Depending on the context, these characteristics include age, color, gender, national origin, race, and religion.

Proximate cause Legal cause; exists when the connection between an act and an injury is strong enough to justify imposing liability.

Proxy In corporation law, a written agreement between a stockholder and another under which the stockholder authorizes the other to vote the stockholder's shares in a certain manner.

Proxy fight A conflict between an individual, group, or firm attempting to take control of a corporation and the corporation's management for the votes of the shareholders.

Public figures Individuals who are thrust into the public limelight. Public figures include government officials and politicians, movie stars, well-known businesspersons, and generally anybody who becomes known to the public because of his or her position or activities.

Public policy A government policy based on widely held societal values and (usually) expressed or implied in laws or regulations.

Puffery A salesperson's often-exaggerated claims concerning the quality of property offered for sale. Such claims involve opinions rather than facts and are not considered to be legally binding promises or warranties.

Punitive damages Monetary damages that may be awarded to a plaintiff to punish the defendant and deter future similar conduct.

Q

Quasi contract A fictional contract imposed on parties by a court in the interests of fairness and justice; usually, quasi contracts are imposed to avoid the unjust enrichment of one party at the expense of another.

Question of fact In a lawsuit, an issue involving a factual dispute that can only be decided by a judge (or, in a jury trial, a jury).

Question of law In a lawsuit, an issue involving the application or interpretation of a law; therefore, the judge, and not the jury, decides the issue.

Quitclaim deed A deed intended to pass any title, interest, or claim that the grantor may have in the property but not warranting that such title is valid. A quitclaim deed offers the least amount of protection against defects in the title.

Quorum The number of members of a decision-making body that must be present before business may be transacted.

Quota An assigned import limit on goods.

R

Ratification The act of accepting and giving legal force to an obligation that previously was not enforceable.

Reaffirmation agreement An agreement between a debtor and a creditor in which the debtor reaffirms, or promises to pay, a debt dischargeable in bankruptcy. To be enforceable, the agreement must be made prior to the discharge of the debt by the bankruptcy court.

Real property Land and everything attached to it, such as foliage and buildings.

Reasonable person standard The standard of behavior expected of a hypothetical "reasonable person." The standard against which negligence is measured and that must be observed to avoid liability for negligence.

Recording statutes Statutes that allow deeds, mortgages, and other real property transactions to be recorded so as to provide notice to future purchasers or creditors of an existing claim on the property.

Red herring prospectus A preliminary prospectus that can be distributed to potential investors after the registration statement (for a securities offering) has been filed with the Securities and Exchange Commission. The name derives from the red legend printed across the prospectus stating that the registration has been filed but has not become effective.

Reformation A court-ordered correction of a written contract so that it reflects the true intentions of the parties.

Regulation Z A set of rules promulgated by the Federal Reserve Board to implement the provisions of the Truth-in-Lending Act.
Rejection In contract law, an offeree's express or implied manifestation not to accept an offer. In the law governing contracts for the sale of goods, a buyer's manifest refusal to accept goods on the ground that they do not conform to contract specifications.
Relevant evidence Evidence tending to make a fact at issue in the case more or less probable than it would be without the evidence. Only relevant evidence is admissible in court.
Remanded Sent back. If an appellate court disagrees with a lower court's judgment, the case may be remanded to the lower court for further proceedings in which the lower court's decision should be consistent with the appellate court's opinion on the matter.
Remedy The relief given to an innocent party to enforce a right or compensate for the violation of a right.
Remedy at law A remedy available in a court of law. Money damages are awarded as a remedy at law.
Remedy in equity A remedy allowed by courts in situations where remedies at law are not appropriate. Remedies in equity are based on settled rules of fairness, justice, and honesty, and include injunction, specific performance, rescission and restitution, and reformation.
Reporter A publication in which court cases are published, or reported.
Requirements contract An agreement in which a buyer agrees to purchase and the seller agrees to sell all or up to a stated amount of what the buyer needs or requires.
Res ipsa loquitur (pronounced *rehs ehp*-suh *low*-quuh-duhr) A doctrine under which negligence may be inferred simply because an event occurred, if it is the type of event that would not occur in the absence of negligence. Literally, the term means "the facts speak for themselves."
Resale price maintenance agreement An agreement between a manufacturer and a retailer in which the manufacturer specifies the minimum retail price of its products.
Rescind (pronounced reh-*sihnd*) To cancel. *See also* Rescission
Rescission (pronounced reh-*sih*-zhen) A remedy whereby a contract is canceled and the parties are returned to the positions they occupied before the contract was made; may be effected through the mutual consent of the parties, by their conduct, or by court decree.
Respondeat superior (pronounced ree-*spahn*-dee-uht soo-*peer*-ee-your) In Latin, "Let the master respond." A doctrine under which a principal or an employer is held liable for the wrongful acts committed by agents or employees while acting within the course and scope of their agency or employment.
Respondent In equity practice, the party who answers a bill or other proceeding.
Restitution An equitable remedy under which a person is restored to his or her original position prior to loss or injury, or placed in the position he or she would have been in had the breach not occurred.
Restraint of trade Any contract or combination that tends to eliminate or reduce competition, effect a monopoly, artificially maintain prices, or otherwise hamper the course of trade and commerce as it would be carried on if left to the control of natural economic forces.
Restrictive covenant A private restriction on the use of land that is binding on the party that purchases the property originally as well as on subsequent purchasers. If its benefit or obligation passes with the land's ownership, it is said to "run with the land."
Retained earnings The portion of a corporation's profits that has not been paid out as dividends to shareholders.
Revocation In contract law, the withdrawal of an offer by an offeror. Unless an offer is irrevocable, it can be revoked at any time prior to acceptance without liability.
Right-to-work law A state law providing that employees are not to be required to join a union as a condition of obtaining or retaining employment.
Robbery The act of forcefully and unlawfully taking personal property of any value from another; force or intimidation is usually necessary for an act of theft to be considered a robbery.
Rule of four A rule of the United States Supreme Court under which the Court will not issue a writ of *certiorari* unless at least four justices approve of the decision to issue the writ.
Rule of reason A test by which a court balances the positive effects (such as economic efficiency) of an agreement against its potentially anticompetitive effects. In antitrust litigation, many practices are analyzed under the rule of reason.
Rulemaking The process undertaken by an administrative agency when formally adopting a new regulation or amending an old one. Rulemaking involves notifying the public of a proposed rule or change and receiving and considering the public's comments.
Rules of evidence Rules governing the admissibility of evidence in trial courts.

S corporation A close business corporation that has met certain requirements as set out by the Internal Revenue Code and thus qualifies for special income tax treatment. Essentially, an S corporation is taxed the same as a partnership, but its owners enjoy the privilege of limited liability.
Sale The passing of title from the seller to the buyer for a price.
Sale on approval A type of conditional sale in which the buyer may take the goods on a trial basis. The sale becomes absolute only when the buyer approves of (or is satisfied with) the goods being sold.
Sale or return A type of conditional sale in which title and possession pass from the seller to the buyer; however, the buyer retains the option to return the goods during a specified period even though the goods conform to the contract.
Sales contract A contract for the sale of goods under which the ownership of goods is transferred from a seller to a buyer for a price.
Scienter (pronounced *sy-en*-ter) Knowledge by the misrepresenting party that material facts have been falsely represented or omitted with an intent to deceive.
Search warrant An order granted by a public authority, such as a judge, that authorizes law enforcement personnel to search particular premises or property.
Seasonably Within a specified time period, or, if no period is specified, within a reasonable time.
SEC Rule 10b-5 A rule of the Securities and Exchange Commission that makes it unlawful, in connection with the purchase or sale of any security, to make any untrue statement of a material fact or to omit a material fact if such omission causes the statement to be misleading.
Secondary boycott A union's refusal to work for, purchase from, or handle the products of a secondary employer, with whom the union has no dispute, for the purpose of forcing that employer to stop doing business with the primary employer, with whom the union has a labor dispute.
Securities Generally, corporate stocks and bonds. A security may also be a note, debenture, stock warrant, or any document given as evidence of an ownership interest in a corporation or as a promise of repayment by a corporation.

Self-defense The legally recognized privilege to protect one's self or property against injury by another. The privilege of self-defense protects only acts that are reasonably necessary to protect one's self or property.

Seniority system In regard to employment relationships, a system in which those who have worked longest for the company are first in line for promotions, salary increases, and other benefits; they are also the last to be laid off if the workforce must be reduced.

Service mark A mark used in the sale or the advertising of services, such as to distinguish the services of one person from the services of others. Titles, character names, and other distinctive features of radio and television programs may be registered as service marks.

Service of process The delivery of the complaint and summons to a defendant.

Severance pay A payment by an employer to an employee that exceeds the employee's wages due on termination.

Settlor One creating a trust.

Sexual harassment In the employment context, the granting of job promotions or other benefits in return for sexual favors or language or conduct that is so sexually offensive that it creates a hostile working environment.

Shareholder One who purchases shares of a corporation's stock, thus acquiring an equity interest in the corporation.

Sheriff's deed The deed given to the purchaser of property at a sheriff's sale as part of the foreclosure process against the owner of the property.

Shipment contract A contract for the sale of goods in which the seller is required or authorized to ship the goods by carrier. The buyer assumes liability for any losses or damage to the goods after they are delivered to the carrier.

Slander Defamation in oral form.

Slander of quality (trade libel) The publication of false information about another's product, alleging that it is not what its seller claims.

Slander of title The publication of a statement that denies or casts doubt on another's legal ownership of any property, causing financial loss to that property's owner.

Small claims courts Special courts in which parties may litigate small claims (usually, claims involving $5,000 or less). Attorneys are not required in small claims courts, and in many states attorneys are not allowed to represent the parties.

Sociological school A school of legal thought that views the law as a tool for promoting justice in society.

Sole proprietorship The simplest form of business, in which the owner is the business; the owner reports business income on his or her personal income tax return and is legally responsible for all debts and obligations incurred by the business.

Sovereign immunity A doctrine that immunizes foreign nations from the jurisdiction of U.S. courts when certain conditions are satisfied.

Spam Bulk, unsolicited ("junk") e-mail.

Special warranty deed A deed in which the grantor only covenants to warrant and defend the title against claims and demands of the grantor and all persons claiming by, through, and under the grantor.

Specific performance An equitable remedy requiring exactly the performance that was specified in a contract; usually granted only when money damages would be an inadequate remedy and the subject matter of the contract is unique (for example, real property).

Standing to sue The requirement that an individual must have a sufficient stake in a controversy before he or she can bring a lawsuit. The plaintiff must demonstrate that he or she either has been injured or threatened with injury.

Stare decisis (pronounced *ster*-ay dih-*si*-ses) A common law doctrine under which judges are obligated to follow the precedents established in prior decisions.

Statute of Frauds A state statute under which certain types of contracts must be in writing to be enforceable.

Statute of limitations A federal or state statute setting the maximum time period during which a certain action can be brought or certain rights enforced.

Statute of repose Basically, a statute of limitations that is not dependent on the happening of a cause of action. Statutes of repose generally begin to run at an earlier date and run for a longer period of time than statutes of limitations.

Statutory law The body of law enacted by legislative bodies (as opposed to constitutional law, administrative law, or case law).

Stock An equity (ownership) interest in a corporation, measured in units of shares.

Strict liability Liability regardless of fault. In tort law, strict liability may be imposed on defendants in cases involving abnormally dangerous activities, dangerous animals, or defective products.

Strike An extreme action undertaken by unionized workers when collective bargaining fails; the workers leave their jobs, refuse to work, and (typically) picket the employer's workplace.

Sublease A lease executed by the lessee of real estate to a third person, conveying the same interest that the lessee enjoys but for a shorter term than that held by the lessee.

Submission An agreement by two or more parties to refer any disputes they may have under their contract to a disinterested third party, such as an arbitrator, who has the power to render a binding decision.

Substantial performance Performance that does not vary greatly from the performance promised in a contract; the performance must create substantially the same benefits as those promised in the contract.

Substantive due process A requirement that focuses on the content, or substance, of legislation. If a law or other governmental action limits a fundamental right, such as the right to travel or to vote, it will be held to violate substantive due process unless it promotes a compelling or overriding state interest.

Substantive law Law that defines the rights and duties of individuals with respect to each other, as opposed to procedural law, which defines the manner in which these rights and duties may be enforced.

Summary jury trial (SJT) A method of settling disputes in which a trial is held, but the jury's verdict is not binding. The verdict acts only as a guide to both sides in reaching an agreement during the mandatory negotiations that immediately follow the summary jury trial.

Supremacy clause The provision in Article VI of the Constitution that provides that the Constitution, laws, and treaties of the United States are "the supreme Law of the Land." Under this clause, state and local laws that directly conflict with federal law will be rendered invalid.

Syllogism A form of deductive reasoning consisting of a major premise, a minor premise, and a conclusion.

Symbolic speech Nonverbal conduct that expresses opinions or thoughts about a subject. Symbolic speech is protected under the First Amendment's guarantee of freedom of speech.

T

Taking The taking of private property by the government for public use. Under the Fifth Amendment to the Constitution, the government may not take private property for public use without "just compensation."

Tangible employment action A significant change in employment status, such as firing or failing to promote an employee; reassigning the employee to a position with significantly different responsibilities; or effecting a significant change in employment benefits.

Tangible property Property that has physical existence and can be distinguished by the senses of touch, sight, and so on. A car is tangible property; a patent right is intangible property.

Tariff A tax on imported goods.

Tenancy at sufferance A type of tenancy under which one who, after rightfully being in possession of leased premises, continues (wrongfully) to occupy the property after the lease has been terminated. The tenant has no rights to possess the property and occupies it only because the person entitled to evict the tenant has not done so.

Tenancy at will A type of tenancy under which either party can terminate the tenancy without notice; usually arises when a tenant who has been under a tenancy for years retains possession, with the landlord's consent, after the tenancy for years has terminated.

Tenancy by the entirety The joint ownership of property by a husband and wife. Neither party can transfer his or her interest in the property without the consent of the other.

Tenancy in common Co-ownership of property in which each party owns an undivided interest that passes to his or her heirs at death.

Tender An unconditional offer to perform an obligation by a person who is ready, willing, and able to do so.

Tender of delivery Under the Uniform Commercial Code, a seller's or lessor's act of placing conforming goods at the disposal of the buyer or lessee and giving the buyer or lessee whatever notification is reasonably necessary to enable the buyer or lessee to take delivery.

Tender offer An offer to purchase made by one company directly to the shareholders of another (target) company; often referred to as a "takeover bid."

Third party beneficiary One for whose benefit a promise is made in a contract but who is not a party to the contract.

Tippee A person who receives inside information.

Title insurance Insurance commonly purchased by a purchaser of real property to protect against loss in the event that the title to the property is not free from liens or superior ownership claims.

Tombstone ad An advertisement, historically in a format resembling a tombstone, of a securities offering. The ad informs potential investors of where and how they may obtain a prospectus.

Tort A civil wrong not arising from a breach of contract. A breach of a legal duty that proximately causes harm or injury to another.

Tortfeasor One who commits a tort.

Toxic tort Failure to use or to clean up properly toxic chemicals that cause harm to a person or society.

Trade dress The image and overall appearance of a product—for example, the distinctive decor, menu, layout, and style of service of a particular restaurant. Basically, trade dress is subject to the same protection as trademarks.

Trade libel The publication of false information about another's product, alleging it is not what its seller claims; also referred to as *slander of quality.*

Trade name A term that is used to indicate part or all of a business's name and that is directly related to the business's reputation and goodwill. Trade names are protected under the common law (and under trademark law, if the name is the same as the firm's trademarked property).

Trade secret Information or a process that gives a business an advantage over competitors who do not know the information or process.

Trademark A distinctive mark, motto, device, or implement that a manufacturer stamps, prints, or otherwise affixes to the goods it produces so that they may be identified on the market and their origins made known. Once a trademark is established (under the common law or through registration), the owner is entitled to its exclusive use.

Treaty An agreement formed between two or more independent nations.

Treble damages Damages consisting of single damages determined by a jury and tripled in amount in certain cases as required by statute.

Trespass to land The entry onto, above, or below the surface of land owned by another without the owner's permission or legal authorization.

Trespass to personal property The unlawful taking or harming of another's personal property; interference with another's right to the exclusive possession of his or her personal property.

Trust An arrangement in which title to property is held by one person (a trustee) for the benefit of another (a beneficiary).

Trustee One who holds title to property for the use or benefit of another (the beneficiary).

Tying arrangement An agreement between a buyer and a seller in which the buyer of a specific product or service becomes obligated to purchase additional products or services from the seller.

U

Use zoning Zoning classifications within a particular municipality that may be distinguished based upon the uses to which the land is to be put.

U.S. trustee A government official who performs certain administrative tasks that a bankruptcy judge would otherwise have to perform.

Ultra vires (pronounced *uhl*-trah *vye*-reez) A Latin term meaning "beyond the powers"; in corporate law, acts of a corporation that are beyond its express and implied powers to undertake.

Unconscionable (pronounced un-*kon*-shun-uh-bul) **contract or clause** A contract or clause that is void on the basis of public policy because one party, as a result of his or her disproportionate bargaining power, is forced to accept terms that are unfairly burdensome and that unfairly benefit the dominating party. *See also* Procedural unconscionability; Substantive unconscionability

Undisclosed principal A principal whose identity is unknown by a third person, and the third person has no knowledge that the agent is acting for a principal at the time the agent and the third person form a contract.

Unenforceable contract A valid contract rendered unenforceable by some statute or law.

Uniform law A model law created by the National Conference of Commissioners on Uniform State Laws and/or the American Law Institute for the states to consider adopting. If the state adopts the law, it becomes statutory law in that state. Each state has the option of adopting or rejecting all or part of a uniform law.

Unilateral contract A contract that results when an offer can only be accepted by the offeree's performance.

Union shop A place of employment in which all workers, once employed, must become union members within a specified period of time as a condition of their continued employment.

Unreasonably dangerous product In product liability, a product that is defective to the point of threatening a consumer's health and safety. A product will be considered unreasonably dangerous if it is dangerous beyond the expectation of the ordinary consumer or if a less dangerous alternative was

economically feasible for the manufacturer, but the manufacturer failed to produce it.
Utilitarianism An approach to ethical reasoning in which ethically correct behavior is not related to any absolute ethical or moral values but to an evaluation of the consequences of a given action on those who will be affected by it. In utilitarian reasoning, a "good" decision is one that results in the greatest good for the greatest number of people affected by the decision.

V

Valid contract A contract that results when elements necessary for contract formation (agreement, consideration, legal purpose, and contractual capacity) are present.
Validation notice An initial notice to a debtor from a collection agency informing the debtor that he or she has thirty days to challenge the debt and request verification.
Vendee One who purchases property from another, called the vendor.
Vertical merger The acquisition by a company at one stage of production of a company at a higher or lower stage of production (such as a company merging with one of its suppliers or retailers).
Vertical restraint Any restraint on trade created by agreements between firms at different levels in the manufacturing and distribution process.
Vertically integrated firm A firm that carries out two or more functional phases—for example, manufacture, distribution, retailing—of a product.
Vesting The creation of an absolute or unconditional right or power.
Vicarious liability Legal responsibility placed on one person for the acts of another.
Void contract A contract having no legal force or binding effect.
Voidable contract A contract that may be legally avoided (canceled, or annulled) at the option of one of the parties.

W

Waiver An intentional, knowing relinquishment of a legal right.
Warehouser One in the business of operating a warehouse.
Warranty A promise that certain facts are truly as they are represented to be.
Warranty deed A deed in which the grantor guarantees to the grantee that the grantor has title to the property conveyed in the deed, that there are no encumbrances on the property other than what the grantor has represented, and that the grantee will enjoy quiet possession of the property; a deed that provides the greatest amount of protection for the grantee.
Warranty disclaimer A seller's or lessor's negation or qualification of a warranty.
Warranty of fitness *See* Implied warranty of fitness for a particular purpose
Warranty of merchantability *See* Implied warranty of merchantability
Warranty of title An implied warranty made by a seller that the seller has good and valid title to the goods sold and that the transfer of the title is rightful.
Waste The abuse or destructive use of real property by one who is in rightful possession of the property but who does not have title to it. Waste does not include ordinary depreciation due to age and normal use.
Watered stock Shares of stock issued by a corporation for which the corporation receives, as payment, less than the stated value of the shares.
Whistleblowing An employee's disclosure to government, the press, or upper-management authorities that the employer is engaged in unsafe or illegal activities.
White-collar crime Nonviolent crime committed by individuals or corporations to obtain a personal or business advantage.
Wildcat strike A strike that is not authorized by the union that ordinarily represents the striking employees.
Willful Intentional.
Winding up The second of two stages involved in the termination of a partnership or corporation. Once the firm is dissolved, it continues to exist legally until the process of winding up all business affairs (collecting and distributing the firm's assets) is complete.
Workers' compensation laws State statutes establishing an administrative procedure for compensating workers' injuries that arise out of—or in the course of—their employment, regardless of fault.
Workout An out-of-court agreement between a debtor and his or her creditors in which the parties work out a payment plan or schedule under which the debtor's debts can be discharged.
Writ of *certiorari* (pronounced sur-shee-uh-*rah*-ree) A writ from a higher court asking the lower court for the record of a case.
Wrongful discharge An employer's termination of an employee's employment in violation of an employment contract or laws that protect employees.

Z

Zoning The division of a city by legislative regulation into districts and the application in each district of regulations having to do with structural and architectural designs of buildings and prescribing the use to which buildings within designated districts may be put.
Zoning variance The granting of permission by a municipality or other public board to a landowner to use his or her property in a way that does not strictly conform with the zoning regulations so as to avoid causing the landowner undue hardship.

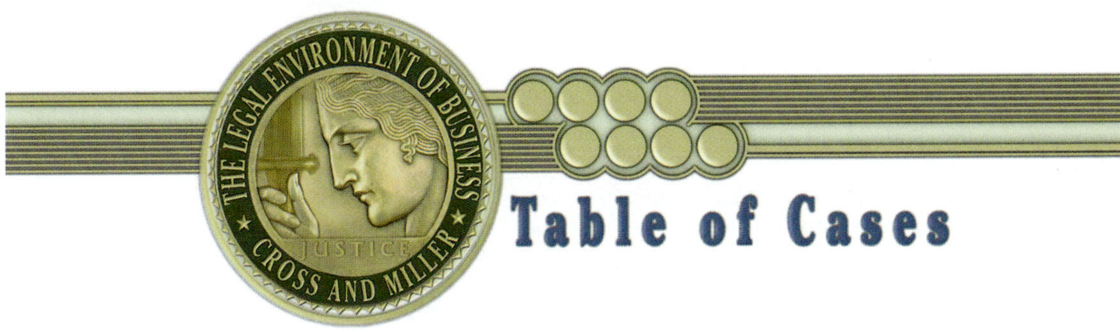

Table of Cases

C

D

E

H

I

J

K

L

M

N

O

P

Q

R

S

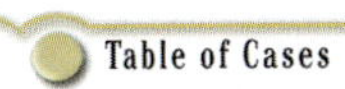

THE LEGAL ENVIRONMENT OF BUSINESS
JUSTICE
CROSS AND MILLER

Index

E

F

J

M

N

O

P

T

U